Dictionary of Literary Biography • Volume Fifty-nine

American Literary Critics and Scholars, 1800-1850

Dictionary of Literary Biography

1: *The American Renaissance in New England,* edited by Joel Myerson (1978)

2: *American Novelists Since World War II,* edited by Jeffrey Helterman and Richard Layman (1978)

3: *Antebellum Writers in New York and the South,* edited by Joel Myerson (1979)

4: *American Writers in Paris, 1920-1939,* edited by Karen Lane Rood (1980)

5: *American Poets Since World War II,* 2 parts, edited by Donald J. Greiner (1980)

6: *American Novelists Since World War II,* Second Series, edited by James E. Kibler, Jr. (1980)

7: *Twentieth-Century American Dramatists,* 2 parts, edited by John MacNicholas (1981)

8: *Twentieth-Century American Science-Fiction Writers,* 2 parts, edited by David Cowart and Thomas L. Wymer (1981)

9: *American Novelists, 1910-1945,* 3 parts, edited by James J. Martine (1981)

10: *Modern British Dramatists, 1900-1945,* 2 parts, edited by Stanley Weintraub (1982)

11: *American Humorists, 1800-1950,* 2 parts, edited by Stanley Trachtenberg (1982)

12: *American Realists and Naturalists,* edited by Donald Pizer and Earl N. Harbert (1982)

13: *British Dramatists Since World War II,* 2 parts, edited by Stanley Weintraub (1982)

14: *British Novelists Since 1960,* 2 parts, edited by Jay L. Halio (1983)

15: *British Novelists, 1930-1959,* 2 parts, edited by Bernard Oldsey (1983)

16: *The Beats: Literary Bohemians in Postwar America,* 2 parts, edited by Ann Charters (1983)

17: *Twentieth-Century American Historians,* edited by Clyde N. Wilson (1983)

18: *Victorian Novelists After 1885,* edited by Ira B. Nadel and William E. Fredeman (1983)

19: *British Poets, 1880-1914,* edited by Donald E. Stanford (1983)

20: *British Poets, 1914-1945,* edited by Donald E. Stanford (1983)

21: *Victorian Novelists Before 1885,* edited by Ira B. Nadel and William E. Fredeman (1983)

22: *American Writers for Children, 1900-1960,* edited by John Cech (1983)

23: *American Newspaper Journalists, 1873-1900,* edited by Perry J. Ashley (1983)

24: *American Colonial Writers, 1606-1734,* edited by Emory Elliott (1984)

25: *American Newspaper Journalists, 1901-1925,* edited by Perry J. Ashley (1984)

26: *American Screenwriters,* edited by Robert E. Morsberger, Stephen O. Lesser, and Randall Clark (1984)

27: *Poets of Great Britain and Ireland, 1945-1960,* edited by Vincent B. Sherry, Jr. (1984)

28: *Twentieth-Century American-Jewish Fiction Writers,* edited by Daniel Walden (1984)

29: *American Newspaper Journalists, 1926-1950,* edited by Perry J. Ashley (1984)

30: *American Historians, 1607-1865,* edited by Clyde N. Wilson (1984)

31: *American Colonial Writers, 1735-1781,* edited by Emory Elliott (1984)

32: *Victorian Poets Before 1850,* edited by William E. Fredeman and Ira B. Nadel (1984)

33: *Afro-American Fiction Writers After 1955,* edited by Thadious M. Davis and Trudier Harris (1984)

34: *British Novelists, 1890-1929: Traditionalists,* edited by Thomas F. Staley (1985)

35: *Victorian Poets After 1850,* edited by William E. Fredeman and Ira B. Nadel (1985)

36: *British Novelists, 1890-1929: Modernists,* edited by Thomas F. Staley (1985)

37: *American Writers of the Early Republic,* edited by Emory Elliott (1985)

38: *Afro-American Writers After 1955: Dramatists and Prose Writers,* edited by Thadious M. Davis and Trudier Harris (1985)

39: *British Novelists, 1660-1800,* 2 parts, edited by Martin C. Battestin (1985)

40: *Poets of Great Britain and Ireland Since 1960,* 2 parts, edited by Vincent B. Sherry, Jr. (1985)

41: *Afro-American Poets Since 1955,* edited by Trudier Harris and Thadious M. Davis (1985)

42: *American Writers for Children Before 1900,* edited by Glenn E. Estes (1985)

43: *American Newspaper Journalists, 1690-1872,* edited by Perry J. Ashley (1986)

44: *American Screenwriters,* Second Series, edited by Randall Clark, Robert E. Morsberger, and Stephen O. Lesser (1986)

45: *American Poets, 1880-1945,* First Series, edited by Peter Quartermain (1986)

46: *American Literary Publishing Houses, 1900-1980: Trade and Paperback,* edited by Peter Dzwonkoski (1986)

47: *American Historians, 1866-1912,* edited by Clyde N. Wilson (1986)

48: *American Poets, 1880-1945,* Second Series, edited by Peter Quartermain (1986)

49: *American Literary Publishing Houses, 1638-1899,* 2 parts, edited by Peter Dzwonkoski (1986)

50: *Afro-American Writers Before the Harlem Renaissance,* edited by Trudier Harris (1986)

51: *Afro-American Writers from the Harlem Renaissance to 1940,* edited by Trudier Harris (1987)

52: *American Writers for Children Since 1960: Fiction,* edited by Glenn E. Estes (1986)

53: *Canadian Writers Since 1960,* First Series, edited by W. H. New (1986)

54: *American Poets, 1880-1945,* Third Series, 2 parts, edited by Peter Quartermain (1987)

55: *Victorian Prose Writers Before 1867,* edited by William B. Thesing (1987)

56: *German Fiction Writers, 1914-1945,* edited by James Hardin (1987)

57: *Victorian Prose Writers After 1867,* edited by William B. Thesing (1987)

58: *Jacobean and Caroline Dramatists,* edited by Fredson Bowers (1987)

59: *American Literary Critics and Scholars, 1800-1850,* edited by John W. Rathbun and Monica M. Grecu (1987)

Documentary Series

1: *Sherwood Anderson, Willa Cather, John Dos Passos, Theodore Dreiser, F. Scott Fitzgerald, Ernest Hemingway, Sinclair Lewis,* edited by Margaret A. Van Antwerp (1982)

2: *James Gould Cozzens, James T. Farrell, William Faulkner, John O'Hara, John Steinbeck, Thomas Wolfe, Richard Wright,* edited by Margaret A. Van Antwerp (1982)

3: *Saul Bellow, Jack Kerouac, Norman Mailer, Vladimir Nabokov, John Updike, Kurt Vonnegut,* edited by Mary Bruccoli (1983)

4: *Tennessee Williams,* edited by Margaret A. Van Antwerp and Sally Johns (1984)

Yearbooks

1980, edited by Karen L. Rood, Jean W. Ross, and Richard Ziegfeld (1981)

1981, edited by Karen L. Rood, Jean W. Ross, and Richard Ziegfeld (1982)

1982, edited by Richard Ziegfeld; associate editors: Jean W. Ross and Lynne C. Zeigler (1983)

1983, edited by Mary Bruccoli and Jean W. Ross; associate editor: Richard Ziegfeld (1984)

1984, edited by Jean W. Ross (1985)

1985, edited by Jean W. Ross (1986)

1986, edited by J. M. Brook (1987)

Concise Series

The New Consciousness, 1941-1968 (1987)

Dictionary of Literary Biography • Volume Fifty-nine

American Literary Critics and Scholars, 1800-1850

6892

Edited by
John W. Rathbun
California State University, Los Angeles
and
Monica M. Grecu
University of Nevada at Reno

A Bruccoli Clark Layman Book
Gale Research Company • Book Tower • Detroit, Michigan 48226

Matthew J. Bruccoli and Richard Layman, *Editorial Directors*
C. E. Frazer Clark, Jr., *Managing Editor*

Manufactured by Edwards Brothers, Inc.
Ann Arbor, Michigan
Printed in the United States of America

Library of Congress Cataloging-in-Publication Data

American literary critics and scholars, 1800-1850.

(Dictionary of literary biography; v. 59)
"A Bruccoli Clark Layman book."
Includes index.
1. Criticism—United States—History—19th century. 2. Criticism—United States—Bio-bibliography. 3. Critics—United States—Biography—Dictionaries. 4. Literary historians—United States—Biography—Dictionaries. 5. American literature—19th century—History and criticism. I. Rathbun, John Wilbert, 1924- . II. Grecu, Monica M. III. Series.
PS74.A44 1987 801'.95'0973 87-11828
ISBN 0-8103-1737-0

For Cornelia Grecu-Arghir

Contents

Plan of the Series

. . . Almost the most prodigious asset of a country, and perhaps its most precious possession, is its native literary product–when that product is fine and noble and enduring.

Mark Twain*

The advisory board, the editors, and the publisher of the *Dictionary of Literary Biography* are joined in endorsing Mark Twain's declaration. The literature of a nation provides an inexhaustible resource of permanent worth. It is our expectation that this endeavor will make literature and its creators better understood and more accessible to students and the literate public, while satisfying the standards of teachers and scholars.

To meet these requirements, *literary biography* has been construed in terms of the author's achievement. The most important thing about a writer is his writing. Accordingly, the entries in *DLB* are career biographies, tracing the development of the author's canon and the evolution of his reputation.

The publication plan for *DLB* resulted from two years of preparation. The project was proposed to Bruccoli Clark by Frederick G. Ruffner, president of the Gale Research Company, in November 1975. After specimen entries were prepared and typeset, an advisory board was formed to refine the entry format and develop the series rationale. In meetings held during 1976, the publisher, series editors, and advisory board approved the scheme for a comprehensive biographical dictionary of persons who contributed to North American literature. Editorial work on the first volume began in January 1977, and it was published in 1978.

In order to make *DLB* more than a reference tool and to compile volumes that individually have claim to status as literary history, it was decided to organize volumes by topic or period or genre. Each of these freestanding volumes provides a biographical-bibliographical guide and overview for a particular area of literature. We are convinced that this organization—as opposed to a single alphabet method—constitutes a valuable innovation in the presentation of reference material. The volume plan necessarily requires many decisions for the placement and treatment of authors who might properly be included in two or three volumes. In some instances a major figure will be included in separate volumes, but with different entries emphasizing the aspect of his career appropriate to each volume. Ernest Hemingway, for example, is represented in *American Writers in Paris, 1920-1939* by an entry focusing on his expatriate apprenticeship; he is also in *American Novelists, 1910-1945* with an entry surveying his entire career. Each volume includes a cumulative index of subject authors and articles. The final *DLB* volume will be a comprehensive index to the entire series.

With volume ten in 1982 it was decided to enlarge the scope of *DLB*. By the end of 1986 twenty-one volumes treating British literature had been published, and volumes for Commonwealth and Modern European literature were in progress. The series has been further augmented by the *DLB Yearbooks* (since 1981) which update published entries and add new entries to keep the *DLB* current with contemporary activity. There have also been occasional *DLB Documentary Series* volumes which provide biographical and critical background source materials for figures whose work is judged to have particular interest for students. One of these companion volumes is entirely devoted to Tennessee Williams.

The purpose of *DLB* is not only to provide reliable information in a convenient format but also to place the figures in the larger perspective of literary history and to offer appraisals of their accomplishments by qualified scholars.

We define literature as the *intellectual commerce of a nation:* not merely as belles lettres but as that ample and complex process by which ideas are generated, shaped, and transmitted. *DLB* entries are not limited to "creative writers" but extend to other figures who in this time and in this way influenced the mind of a people. Thus the series encompasses historians, journalists, publishers, and screenwriters. By this means readers of *DLB* may be aided to perceive literature not as cult scripture in the keeping of cultural high priests but as at the center of a nation's life.

DLB includes the major writers appropriate to each volume and those standing in the ranks immediately behind them. Scholarly and critical coun-

*From an unpublished section of Mark Twain's autobiography, copyright © by the Mark Twain Company.

sel has been sought in deciding which minor figures to include and how full their entries should be. Wherever possible, useful references are made to figures who do not warrant separate entries.

Each *DLB* volume has a volume editor responsible for planning the volume, selecting the figures for inclusion, and assigning the entries. Volume editors are also responsible for preparing, where appropriate, appendices surveying the major periodicals and literary and intellectual movements for their volumes, as well as lists of further readings. Work on the series as a whole is coordinated at the Bruccoli Clark Layman editorial center in Columbia, South Carolina, where the editorial staff is responsible for the accuracy of the published volumes.

One feature that distinguishes *DLB* is the illustration policy—its concern with the iconography of literature. Just as an author is influenced by his surroundings, so is the reader's understanding of the author enhanced by a knowledge of his environment. Therefore *DLB* volumes include not only drawings, paintings, and photographs of authors, often depicting them at various stages in their careers, but also illustrations of their families and places where they lived. Title pages are regularly reproduced in facsimile along with dust jackets for modern authors. The dust jackets are a special feature of *DLB* because they often document better than anything else the way in which an author's work was launched in its own time. Specimens of the writers' manuscripts are included when feasible.

A supplement to *DLB*—tentatively titled *A Guide, Chronology, and Glossary for American Literature*—will outline the history of literature in North America and trace the influences that shaped it. This volume will provide a framework for the study of American literature by means of chronological tables, literary affiliation charts, glossarial entries, and concise surveys of the major movements. It has been planned to stand on its own as a vade mecum, providing a ready-reference guide to the study of American literature as well as a companion to the *DLB* volumes for American literature.

Samuel Johnson rightly decreed that "The chief glory of every people arises from its authors." The purpose of the *Dictionary of Literary Biography* is to compile literary history in the surest way available to us—by accurate and comprehensive treatment of the lives and work of those who contributed to it.

The *DLB* Advisory Board

Foreword

This volume of the *Dictionary of Literary Biography* is the first of three designed to survey comprehensively the contributions of nineteenth-century American literary critics and scholars to letters in the United States. These three volumes will cover the periods 1800 to 1850, 1851 to 1880, and 1881 to 1900.

The period 1800 to 1850, the focus of this volume, is of interest on a number of counts. The nation having gained political independence in a very near past, much attention was given by critics and scholars to whether and in what ways America could expect a literature of its own. Following the War of 1812 a huge number of weeklies, monthlies, and quarterlies were established. These publications collectively provided critics and scholars with forums for the expression of a variety of views on the nature of literature and its relevance to society. Colleges also multiplied, and their faculties increasingly became involved in expanding curricula in order to stay abreast of contemporary concerns, at home and abroad. Finally, these fifty years were witness to the work of two separate generations of critics and scholars, and a survey of their work demonstrates how each generation established and promoted its view of a distinctive literary canon expressive of that generation's values.

The period is really too early in the republic's history for prominent critics and schools of criticism to have emerged. Of the critics represented in this volume, only Ralph Waldo Emerson and Edgar Allan Poe warrant master entries–entries which sift through their critical principles in detail and which clarify the continuing relevance of the two to criticism in our own day. Another seven critics, because of their influence, the integrity of their criticism, or their relative productivity, have been awarded space double that for most entries in order to reflect what is most characteristic in their work. These critics are Orestes Brownson, Edward Tyrrell Channing, Margaret Fuller, William Alfred Jones, Henry Wadsworth Longfellow, William Gilmore Simms, and Gulian Verplanck. The remaining thirty-four critics, less important in the intrinsic value of their publications, are accorded space sufficient to describe their critical attitudes and goals and their relations to the critical scenes of the time.

A number of insights emerge when the information contained in these entries is used to understand the critical climate of the time. Almost all critics, for example, subordinated literature to the purposes of the larger social community. Poe is virtually alone in refusing to dwell on social concerns, although in his practical criticism there are many instances in which he attacks literary works on grounds extraneous to a consideration of literature in and of itself. And while critics endorsed the idea that societal values should prevail, they of course sharply differed in defining just what those values were.

Still, this remarkable unanimity of thinking on general theory is arresting. It fostered a view that literature should endorse and promote national social interests and purposes. Critics as diverse as William Gilmore Simms and Edward Everett thought that literature was a tool for honing society's values and advancing its objectives. Literature was important precisely because it explained and illustrated the principles that informed and animated the society, they argued. In its mission, then, literature should be a consensus-builder. This view goes far in explaining why critics dwelt so on truth rather than aesthetic qualities as the final end of literature. It explains, too, the bewilderment and almost palpable shock critics experienced when they first faced Emerson's early work. He seemed so *outside* the perceptual frame by which they habitually viewed literature that they were unable to cope with his tone of alienation. On a lesser note, the pragmatic view accounts for much of the asperity with which literary works were used in the interests of political, religious, and social groups as each vied for supremacy of its views.

The entries in this volume also document the relative distribution of critics in America and their intellectual backgrounds. Most critics were concentrated in New England and the Middle Atlantic states. With only one-fifth of the nation's population living in the South, the number of southern critics was small, and those in the West numbered even fewer. Almost all critics were college graduates, many of whom went on to obtain degrees in divinity or read in the law. This fact is not accidental. Ministers and lawyers enjoyed enough leisure that they could cultivate an avocational interest in literature. Ministerial training obviously can account for much of the moral earnestness of criticism, especially in the years prior to 1830 and especially in New England. Prior to 1830 a sizable number of critics subscribed to the view that criticism should appraise and judge literary works according to standards found in eighteenth-century criticism and books of rhetoric. After 1830 an increasing sense of professionalism–as marked by higher status and a more self-conscious, sophisticated approach to literature–can be detected in literary criticism, even as sectarian and party spirit intensified rather than declined. While New England writers continued to exert a strong force on the critical scene, New York rapidly expanded as a lively center of intellectual and publishing activity.

The literary canon shifted concomitantly. Classical studies and Shakespeare worship continued, but they increasingly became subjects for the academy due to new recensions of texts and increasing awareness of English and continental scholarship. The impact on the popular mind of such writers as Sir Walter Scott and Lord Byron–the former usually commended and the latter usually reviled in the American press–helped to dampen interest in eighteenth-century English writers and enhance the stock of nineteenth-century romantic writers both native and foreign. The shift was not without its attendant controversies. When such major romantic figures as Samuel Taylor Coleridge and Johann Wolfgang von Goethe had difficulty winning acceptance, the cool reserve accorded George Sand or even William Wordsworth is understandable. The rise of romantic writers can also be ascribed to a new spirit of latitudinarianism that noticeably began to take hold in the 1830s. The displacement of taste which resulted led to the elaboration of new critical criteria for examining literary works. These criteria encouraged a more tolerant ear for new voices, as evidenced in the reception of the folkloric studies of Therese Robinson and others, the popularity of Longfellow's translations from the Scandinavian and Italian, or the rise to critical esteem of a whole new group of American writers, among them Emerson, Nathaniel Hawthorne, and Herman Melville.

Generally speaking, except for the nationalistic spirit that had taken hold, the years 1800 to 1850 were a time for cautious advance in critical theory. Critics were hesitant to depart from the precedents and literary conventions by which readers' expectations were steered and, in a sense, delimited. They valued clearheadedness and native good judgment, for clarity increased the accessibility of literary works and thereby widened their appeal. While not wholly averse to romance fiction and the lyric, critics disapproved of the subjectivity these forms seemed to invite, preferring their romance a little more realistic and their lyric more in line with the traditional ode.

By midcentury these views were giving way as younger critics sought to defend a new kind of literature that had begun to appear. Among knowledgeable readers there was a sharper sense that writers could pick their audiences and so did not have to strive to be universally appealing. Precedent and tradition were held of less account than creative imagination and originality. A new stress on lyrical and psychological subjectivity implicitly acknowledged that *soul* and not *head* was the common bond that united human beings as a species. The means to plumb the rich lode of the soul was sympathy, an intuitive faculty capable of comprehending the most intimate feelings of others. Thus, harmony and accord were realized on a level below consciousness. Uniformity of response and thought was discounted in favor of all that was diverse, irregular, and various. This dethronement of intellect was a further stage in the persistent erosion of confidence in human reason from the seventeenth century on. But to many intellectuals of the time it was hailed as a liberating move against fossil customs that deadened human response and deprived life of its native vitality.

Finally, the entries in this volume reveal the increasing role of academics in furthering scholarship, as they brought a more informed critical approach to literature and provided a more cordial response to controversial writers. This aspect of antebellum criticism needs closer study. In general the spirit of historicism that had earlier swept Europe found fertile ground in the United States as well. To intellectuals of the time it was an exhilarating, liberating influence in its stress on intelligible change, the primacy of sequence in cultural development, the need to sympathetically understand new developments rather than rush to judgment. Chairs were established and curricula were broadened for the study of national languages and literatures. Knowledge was institutionalized in order to extend its boundaries systematically. Scholars were recruited as contributors to the newly established reviews and journals. As a matter of policy, in a sense designating themselves the custodians of the culture, the colleges took upon themselves responsibility for collecting the works of a wide range of writers and literatures in order to further literary study.

In hindsight the changes in the literary scene that occurred between 1800 and 1850 seem part of a surge not to be withstood. Many of the participants in those changes, however, found it difficult to rise above the hubbub. Political differences, as John Stafford and Guy R. Woodall suggest in their entries on Jones and Robert Walsh, often made for an acerbic tone when critics were addressing the works of rival camps. Radical Transcendentalists were often attacked, and as often responded in kind. Southern critics became more and more estranged from northern intellectual centers, as in the case of Simms. Upholders of the Scottish Realist philosophy, people intellectually committed to common sense, were suspicious of the possible subversive implications of continental idealism, which they thought too visionary.

As the country drifted to civil war, it was obvious that no one party, sect, or literary credo would achieve and exercise hegemony over others, which meant that the longed-for democratic consensus would never be realized. By 1830 the culture was far too complex to any longer anticipate a closed, harmonious system of social organization which literature would serve as handmaid. Urbanization, the nationalization of the economy, the dominance of middle-class views, the emergence of the federal government as an instrument for change, including reform: these actions and others besides all suggest confused, perplexing strains in the society so deep as to be almost ineradicable. Literature, and by extension literary criticism, seemed less a factor for achieving social consensus than a mirror of the deep fractures social diversity seemed to foster.

—John W. Rathbun and Monica M. Grecu

Acknowledgments

This book was produced by Bruccoli Clark Layman, Inc. Karen L. Rood is senior editor for the *Dictionary of Literary Biography* series. Ellen Rosenberg Kovner was the in-house editor.

Copyediting supervisor is Patricia Coate. Production coordinator is Kimberly Casey. Typesetting supervisor is Laura Ingram. Lucia Tarbox is editorial assistant. The production staff includes Rowena Betts, David R. Bowdler, Mary S. Dye, Charles Egleston, Gabrielle Elliott, Sarah A. Estes, Kathleen M. Flanagan, Joyce Fowler, Karen Fritz, Cynthia Hallman, Judith K. Ingle, Judith E. McCray, Warren McInnis, Sheri Neal, Janet Phelps, Joan Price, Joycelyn R. Smith, Debra Straw, and Elizabeth York. Jean W. Ross is permissions editor. Joseph Caldwell, photography editor, and Joseph Matthew Bruccoli did photographic copy work for the volume.

Walter W. Ross and Rhonda Marshall did the library research with the assistance of the staff at the Thomas Cooper Library of the University of South Carolina: Lynn Barron, Daniel Boice, Connie Crider, Kathy Eckman, Michael Freeman, Gary Geer, David L. Haggard, Jens Holley, Marcia Martin, Dana Rabon, Jean Rhyne, Jan Squire, Ellen Tillett, and Virginia Weathers.

Special thanks are due to Joel Myerson for his help in providing illustrations.

Dictionary of Literary Biography • Volume Fifty-nine

American Literary Critics and Scholars, 1800-1850

Dictionary of Literary Biography

George Allen

(17 December 1808-28 May 1876)

John W. Rathbun
California State University, Los Angeles

SELECTED BOOKS: *The Life of Philidor, Musician and Chess-Player* (Philadelphia: P. Miller & Son, 1858); expanded by Tassilo von Heydebrand und der Lasa (Philadelphia: E. H. Butler, 1863);

The Question of Shakespeare's Religion. The State of the Question and a Study of the Manuscript Note of Richard Davies "He Dyed a Papist" (Philadelphia: American Catholic Historical Society, 1922).

OTHER: *Remains of William S. Graham . . . With a Memoir,* edited by Allen (Philadelphia: J. W. Moore, 1849).

PERIODICAL PUBLICATIONS: "The Study of Works of Genius, &c," anonymous, *New-York Review,* 1 (March 1837): 161-178;

"Reproductive Criticism," anonymous, *New-York Review,* 2 (January 1838): 49-75.

George Allen's critical theory is of interest on two counts. He sought to reconcile romantic art with the religious sense of Christianity, and he sought to develop a "scientific" theory of literary criticism that could be practically turned to the analysis of literary works. On both counts he was influenced by Samuel Taylor Coleridge and was as well indebted to German theorists like Johann Gottfried von Herder. The particular cast he gave his views can be ascribed to the philosopher James Marsh, under whom he studied at the University of Vermont and for whom he felt unquestioning admiration and loyalty. Viewing Christianity as essentially a spiritual impulse marked by deep feeling and inward exaltation, Allen contended that Coleridgean philosophy was a better buttress to Christianity than the basically nonspiritual philosophies of Francis Bacon and John Locke. Through Coleridge, the Christian spirit could be renewed in terms of the inner self, intuition, and the infinite, thereby escaping externalism and undue bibliolatry. Coleridge performed a like service for romantic art. The same quickening force thus vitalized spiritual faith and the new literature. This reconciliation of the religious and artistic senses meant that the truths expressed by poets corresponded on the deepest levels to the truths accepted by their Christian audiences. As a writer in the *Boston Quarterly Review* put it, "when the God within moves, the oracle will give forth his responses."

Allen's attempt to develop a theoretical and practical model of literary criticism is along lines which anticipate the later work of Benedetto Croce and Joel Spingarn. He called his form of critical expressionism "reproductive" criticism, as did the more important and influential critic, Edwin Percy Whipple. The objective was to reify such abstract Coleridgean terms as reason, imagination, understanding, and fancy and to then develop a critical procedure within which these terms could be continually evoked. The linkage forged between the religious devotional impulse and the impulse to beauty provided the touchstone for estimating the relative power of literary works. At the same time, the linkage enabled the critic to lodge literary works in a larger spiritual context. The distinctive contribution of Allen, however, is in the way he refused to classify or group works according to genre, type, or theme. Individual works were independent in existence and function. Having a solid base in the actual, such works could be analyzed as they existed in themselves, in all their fresh distinctive features. The individual work, so to speak, was a law to itself. It thus made more sense to follow out all that was most precious in the work. Allen argued

George Allen

for these views in several trenchant articles. Unfortunately he failed to follow up on his insights in further articles, and so he occupies an interesting but very modest position in the history of nineteenth-century criticism.

Allen was born at Milton, Vermont, the son of Heman and Sarah Prentiss Allen. After a public school education, in 1823 he entered the University of Vermont. There he studied under such well-known figures as Noah Porter and James Marsh, the latter particularly influencing him, but on the whole he tended to discount the quality of instruction at the university and claimed that his own efforts were more important than his classroom experiences. Allen graduated in 1827 and the next year began teaching there in languages. He left the university in 1830 in order to study the law and was admitted to the bar in 1831. The law seems to have held little interest for him, however, though he did work in his father's firm after the latter was elected to Congress. The year he was admitted to the bar, he married Mary Hancock Withington, a grandniece of John Hancock. The couple had two sons, both of whom became accomplished musicians, and two daughters.

During these years Allen had become increasingly interested in religion and in 1832 began the study of Hebrew and theology while teaching classical languages and literature at Vermont Episcopal Institute. Preaching and teaching, however, proved a substantial drain on his energy, and so he accepted a position as rector of St. Luke's Church in St. Albans, Vermont. By all accounts the three years that he spent there were especially happy ones for Allen as he experienced a "reawakening of a literary spirit."

Partly to increase his income, but also because he enjoyed teaching, Allen, in 1837, accepted an appointment as professor of languages at Delaware College. Somewhere along the way he met Caleb Sprague Henry, who had shifted from a Congregational to an Episcopal ministry in 1835 and who, two years later, established together with Francis L. Hawks the *New-York Review*. The first issue was published in March 1837 and included Allen's article on "The Study of Works of Genius." Allen also likely met Joseph Green Cogswell about the same time, for Cogswell taught at the University of the City of New York (presently New York University). His friend Henry assumed a similar position there in 1838, and Cogswell succeeded Henry as editor of the *New-York Review* in 1840.

"The Study of Works of Genius," ostensibly a review of William G. Goddard's address to the Phi Beta Kappa Society of Rhode Island, takes for its task the resolution of issues that Allen thought divided religion and literature. He is at some pains to rebut two points of view: the religious belief that literature is "merely a seductive and profitless amusement"; and the tendency of religion to accept literature, when it accepts it at all, only when it is "useful," that is, when literature is overtly moral or pious. To Allen, the religious sense is not something which is inherently strong in human beings. It needs to be cultivated. The dreariest kinds of religious expression and the easiest are those of the "lower" faculties: the intoning of moral platitudes and the droning of ceremonial forms lacking substance. The religious sense is properly exercised by the "higher" faculties, by which Allen meant the Coleridgean intuitive reason, though he uses such words as *moral* and *spirit* as synonyms. On this higher level, religious expression becomes a matter of individual initiative as the person strives to make sense of the world and of his own self. Reflection aids in this task, and the result is a self-reliant, inner-directed human being who independently has defined a body of virtues by which he resolves to live. Once these virtues become integral to a human being, religion becomes simply "the mind placed under the influence of the Spirit of God."

In this process of religious cultivation Allen believed that literature can play a significant role. He meant, of course, the "best" literature, the kind that takes the facts and judgments of experience, penetrates to their significance within the whole, and expresses its discoveries with an exciting power that moves us by its beauty. The idea of beauty has its seat in the mind alongside ideas of truth and right. All are innate, and they are intimately connected. This interconnectedness allows genius to subserve religion in cultivating the religious sense, for "genius is simply the exertion of a part of the same higher powers to produce the Creations of art."

Allen ascribes to genius six attributes by which it cultivates the soul and thus strengthens the religious sense. Imagination generates revelatory acts which open us to the invisible world, while taste discloses the harmony existent in creation. A "peculiarly profound insight into our moral natures" strengthens the Christian's "introspective eye," so that "true moral feeling" comes to rest in an equation established between the good and the beautiful. Finally, the perceptions of genius result in a "placid, cheerful, equable temper" that checks any tendency to skepticism. Thus true genius does more than furnish amusement. Its works are profoundly deep. And normally they are not to be penetrated upon a first reading. They require a type of creative reading which itself must be learned. The manner in which one should read provided Allen the subject for his next article.

In "Reproductive Criticism" Allen opposes both neoclassical critical theory as overly preoccupied with outward forms and associationist theory as more absorbed in the principles of art than in its actual productions. Both approaches dwelt on the "purely intellectual" examination of works of art to the neglect of their moral dimensions. If reading itself is to be a creative act, it is necessary to sympathetically bring the mind into

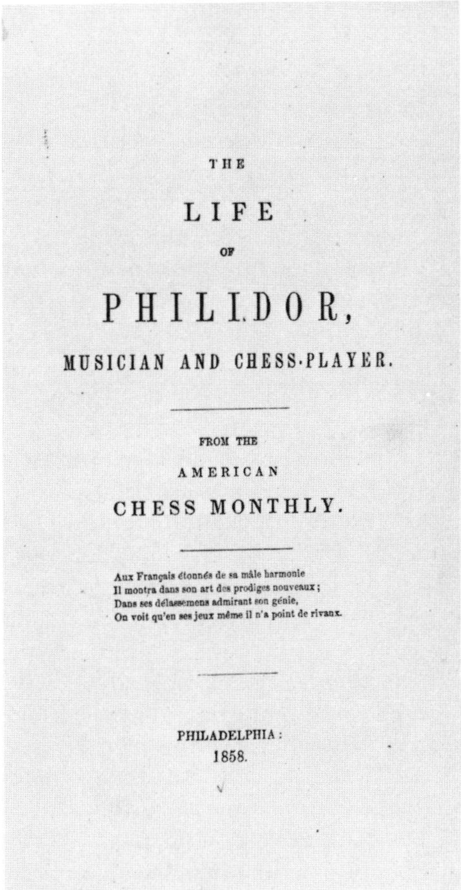
THE

LIFE

OF

PHILIDOR,

MUSICIAN AND CHESS-PLAYER.

FROM THE

AMERICAN

CHESS MONTHLY.

Aux Français étonnés de sa mâle harmonie
Il montra dans son art des prodiges nouveaux;
Dans ses délassemens admirant son génie,
On voit qu'en ses jeux même il n'a point de rivanx.

PHILADELPHIA:
1858.

Title page for Allen's biography of French composer François André Philidor (courtesy of the Library Company of Philadelphia)

contact with the mind of the individual writer. The reader must take the writer's "point of view, and adopt, for the time, his habits of thought and feeling." This tactic guards against bias or prejudice. It guards, too, against any relaxation into momentary unproved impressions which can abort inquiry into the organic harmony of a literary work. In support of this sympathetic immersion of the reader in the literary text Allen cites Herder's views as interpreted by James Marsh. Through force of imagination the reader seeks to apprehend the thoughts and feelings of the writer, no matter how strange the writer's language, habits, and modes of thought might strike him.

This concentration on the work in order to follow out the psychological "productive process" is an attractive first step. The means by which we might trace out the process, however, are not really limned in. Basically Allen calls for a sympathetic understanding so intimate that the feelings, thoughts, and motives of the writer are readily comprehended by the readers as the readers immerse themselves in the work. But there is a procedural gap between the initial critical steps and the readers' final position. Allen fails to specify exactly how the readers are to approximate and thereby understand the creative strategies of the writer. Instead empathy (that is, intuitively intimate comprehension) is made the touchstone of critical perception. As a result the procedure itself appears recondite simply because so much is entrusted to the reader's own good sensibilities.

Allen provides an insight into just how quickly initial interest in Coleridge evolved into sophisticated use of his various principles in forging a new critical approach to literature. This is a phenomenon of the 1830s, and Allen was a part of it. Many Americans, both conservative and liberal, were anxious to invigorate both religion and literature through a renewed sense of devotion, and it was this aspect of Coleridge's writing to which they were attracted. They excitedly responded to such statements of Coleridge as the following (in *The Friend,* 1809-1810), in which he observes that criticism comes naturally "to a mind which has become accustomed to contemplate not things only, or for their own sake alone, but likewise and chiefly the relations of things, either their relations to each other, or to the observer, or to the state and apprehension of the hearers. To enumerate and analyze these relations, with the conditions under which alone they are discoverable, is to teach the science of method." Those Americans influenced by Coleridge seem almost obsessively concerned with organic interconnectedness as a principle to be evoked in scholarly study, no matter the field. Often their tone is heady with a sense of something excitingly "new," as it is in Allen, C. S. Henry, J. F. Clarke, Henry Reed, and many others.

One other article marks Allen's tenure at Delaware College. This was a vigorous defense of James Marsh directed at John McVickar's religious attack on Marsh in his 1839 edition of Coleridge's *Aids to Reflection.* In 1845 Allen was called to the University of Pennsylvania as professor of Greek and Latin (in 1864 becoming professor of Greek exclusively), and there he remained for the rest of his teaching career. It was a time for quiet scholarly reading and teaching, though he did stir himself to oppose unsuccessfully an administrative proposal to shift from a college to a university focus. His conversion to Roman Catholicism in 1847 caused an initial flurry, but most friends and colleagues reconciled themselves to it, and it did not seriously affect his teaching position. For a time he even served as papal counsel for Pope Pius IX. Sometime before 1854 he wrote an essay, unpublished at his death, entitled "The Question about Shakespeare's Religion, the State of the Question and a Study of the Manuscript Note of Richard Davies, 'He Dyed [*sic*] a Papist,' " which Allen may have read before the Philadelphia Shakspere Society, of which he was a member. The essay was published by the American Catholic Historical Society in 1922.

The years at Pennsylvania were tranquil ones during which he indulged himself in his various interests. He had a passion for chess and ultimately amassed one of the largest collections on the subject. Upon his death it was purchased by the Library Company of Philadelphia. He also published a biography of the musician and chess player Philidor in 1858. Another edition in 1863 included Tassilo von Heydebrand und der Lasa's essay on Philidor as chess author and chess player. Among other interests were music and military science. He wrote a number of articles on the latter for his friend and colleague Henry Coppée, who was editor of the *United States Service Magazine.* Esteemed for intelligence and learning and sweetness of spirit, upon his death in Worcester, Massachusetts, he was mourned by all who knew him: "The exercises at the University were suspended from the date of his death until after the funeral, the Faculties of Arts and of the Towne Scientific School wore a badge of mourning for thirty days and the chair which he had occupied in Chapel was draped until the end of the first term of the following year."

Reference:

Joshua Chamberlain, ed., *University of Pennsylvania,* 1 (1901): 326.

Papers:

The archives of the University of Pennsylvania contain many of Allen's letters, manuscripts, and lecture materials.

George Bancroft

(3 October 1800-17 January 1891)

John W. Rathbun
California State University, Los Angeles

See also the Bancroft entries in *DLB 1, The American Renaissance in New England* and *DLB 30, American Historians, 1607-1865.*

SELECTED BOOKS: *Poems* (Cambridge, Mass.: Hilliard & Metcalf, 1823);

Prospectus of a School to be Established at Round Hill, Northampton, Massachusetts, by Bancroft and Joseph Green Cogswell (Cambridge, Mass.: Hilliard & Metcalf, 1823);

History of the United States from the Discovery of the American Continent to the Present Time, 10 volumes, 1834-1875: volumes 1 and 2 (Boston: Charles Bowen/London: R. J. Kennett, 1834, 1837); volumes 3-8, 10 (Boston: Little, Brown, 1840-1860, 1874); volume 9 (Boston: Little, Brown/London: Sampson Low, 1866); revised as *History of the United States of America from the Discovery of the Continent,* 6 volumes (Boston: Little, Brown, 1876; London: Macmillan, 1876); revised again as *History of the United States of America* (New York: Appleton, 1883-1885);

Literary and Historical Miscellanies (New York: Harper, 1855);

History of the Formation of the Constitution of the United States of America, 2 volumes (New York: Appleton, 1882);

Martin Van Buren to the End of His Public Career (New York: Harper, 1889).

OTHER: *Greek Grammar, Principally Abridged from That of Buttman, for the Use of Schools,* edited by Bancroft (Boston: Cummings, Hilliard, 1824);

Arnold H. L. Heeren, *Reflections on the Politics of Ancient Greece,* translated by Bancroft (Boston: Cummings, Hilliard, 1824);

The Latin Reader. From the Fifth German Edition. By Frederic Jacobs, edited, with a preface, by Bancroft (Northampton, Mass.: Printed by T. W. Shepard, 1825);

Heeren, *History of the States of Antiquity,* translated and edited, with a preface, by Bancroft (Northampton, Mass.: S. Butler/New York: G. & C. Carvill, 1828);

Heeren, *History of the Political System of Europe . . . ,* 2 volumes, translated by Bancroft: volume 1 (Northampton, Mass.: S. Butler/New York: G. & C. Carvill, 1828); volume 2 (Northampton, Mass.: S. Butler/Boston: Richardson & Lord/New York: G. & C. Carvill, 1829);

"Morality of Poetry," in *The American Commonplace Book of Prose,* edited by George Cheever (Boston: S. G. Goodrich, 1828);

Memoirs of General Andrew Jackson . . . to Which Is Added the Eulogy of Hon. Geo. Bancroft, Delivered at Washington . . . , compiled by A Citizen of Western New York (Auburn, N.Y.: J. C. Derby/Cincinnati: H. W. Derby, 1845);

"History of the Battle of Lake Erie," "A Day with Lord Byron," "Edward Everett," "Washington's Birthday. A Monument," in Oliver Dyer, *History of the Battle of Lake Erie and Miscellaneous Papers: Life and Writings of George Bancroft* (New York: R. Boner, 1891), pp. 129-264.

PERIODICAL PUBLICATIONS: "Friedrich von Schiller's Gedichte.–Schiller's Minor Poems," *North American Review,* 17 (October 1823): 268-287;

Review of *Greek Grammar,* translated from the German of Philip Buttmann, by Edward Everett, *North American Review,* 18 (January 1824): 99-105;

Review of *The Greek Reader,* by Frederick Jacobs, *North American Review,* 18 (April 1824): 280-284;

Review of *A Course of Study preparatory to the Bar and the Senate . . . ,* by George Watterston, *North American Review,* 19 (July 1824): 125-137;

Review of *ANAΛEKTA 'E HNIKAMMEIZONA . . . ,* by Andreas Dalzel, *North American Review,* 19 (July 1824): 125-137;

Review of Goethe's *Werke,* &c, *North American Review,* 19 (October 1824): 303-325;

Review of *Johann Gottfried von Herder's sümmtliche Werke, North American Review,* 20 (January 1825): 138-147;

Review of *An Oration, pronounced at Cambridge, . . . August 26, 1824,* by Edward Everett; *An Oration, delivered at Plymouth, December 22, 1824,* by Everett; and *An Oration, delivered at Concord, April the nineteenth, 1825,* by Everett, *New-York Review,* 1 (25 October 1825): 333-341;

Review of *The League of the Alps . . . and other Poems,* and *The Forest Sanctuary, and other Poems,* by Felicia Hemans, *North American Review,* 24 (April 1827): 443-463;

Review of *Die Poesie und Beredsamkeil der Deutschen, von Luthers Zeit bis zur Gegenwart,* edited by Franz Horn, *American Quarterly Review,* 2 (September 1827): 171-186;

Review of *sämmtliche Werke,* by C. M. Wieland, and *sämmtliche Werke,* by Gotthold Ephraim Lessing, *American Quarterly Review,* 3 (March 1828): 150-173;

Review of *Geschichte der Deutschen Poesie und Beredsamkeit,* by Friedrich Bouterwek; review of *Andenken an Deutsche Historiker aus den letzten fünfzig Uayreh,* by A. H. L. Heeren; review of *Andenken an Deutsche Historiker aus den letzten fünfzig Uayreh,* by Heeren; review of *Umrisse, &c,* by Franz Horn, *American Quarterly Review,* 4 (September 1828): 157-190;

Review of *Travels in the North of Germany, in the years 1825 and 1826,* by Henry E. Dwight, *American Quarterly Review,* 6 (September 1829): 189-216;

Review of volumes 1 and 2 of *Historic Survey of German Poetry . . . ,* by W. Taylor, *American Quarterly Review,* 7 (June 1830): 436-449;

Review of volume 3 of *Historic Survey of German Poetry . . . ,* by Taylor, *American Quarterly Review,* 10 (September 1831): 194-210;

"William Ellery Channing," *Democratic Review,* 12 (May 1843): 524-526;

"Our Ablest Critic," *Literary World,* 16 (June 1855): 217-218;

"George Bancroft on Washington Irving," *Living Age,* 65 (June 1860): 620-621;

"Whittier . . . , on the occasion of his seventieth birthday . . . ," *Literary World,* 8 (December 1877): 122;

"Holmes's Life of Emerson," *North American Review,* 140 (February 1885): 129-143.

George Bancroft's chief reputation rests in his association with William H. Prescott, John Lothrop Motley, and Francis Parkman as members of the "Literary" or "Middle Historians," known for the grace of their writing and their pioneering scholarship. His contribution to American literary criticism lay in popularizing the principles of German philosophy, letters, historicism, and critical theory. His dedication to and knowledge of German scholarship began with his doctoral study at the University of Göttingen in 1818. In 1820 he successfully defended his dissertation, received his degree, and after the obligatory tour of Europe returned to Cambridge, Massachusetts, in 1822 to briefly serve as a tutor in Greek at Harvard University. His first published article, "Schiller's Minor Poems" (1823), proved to be the beginning of a series of essays spanning

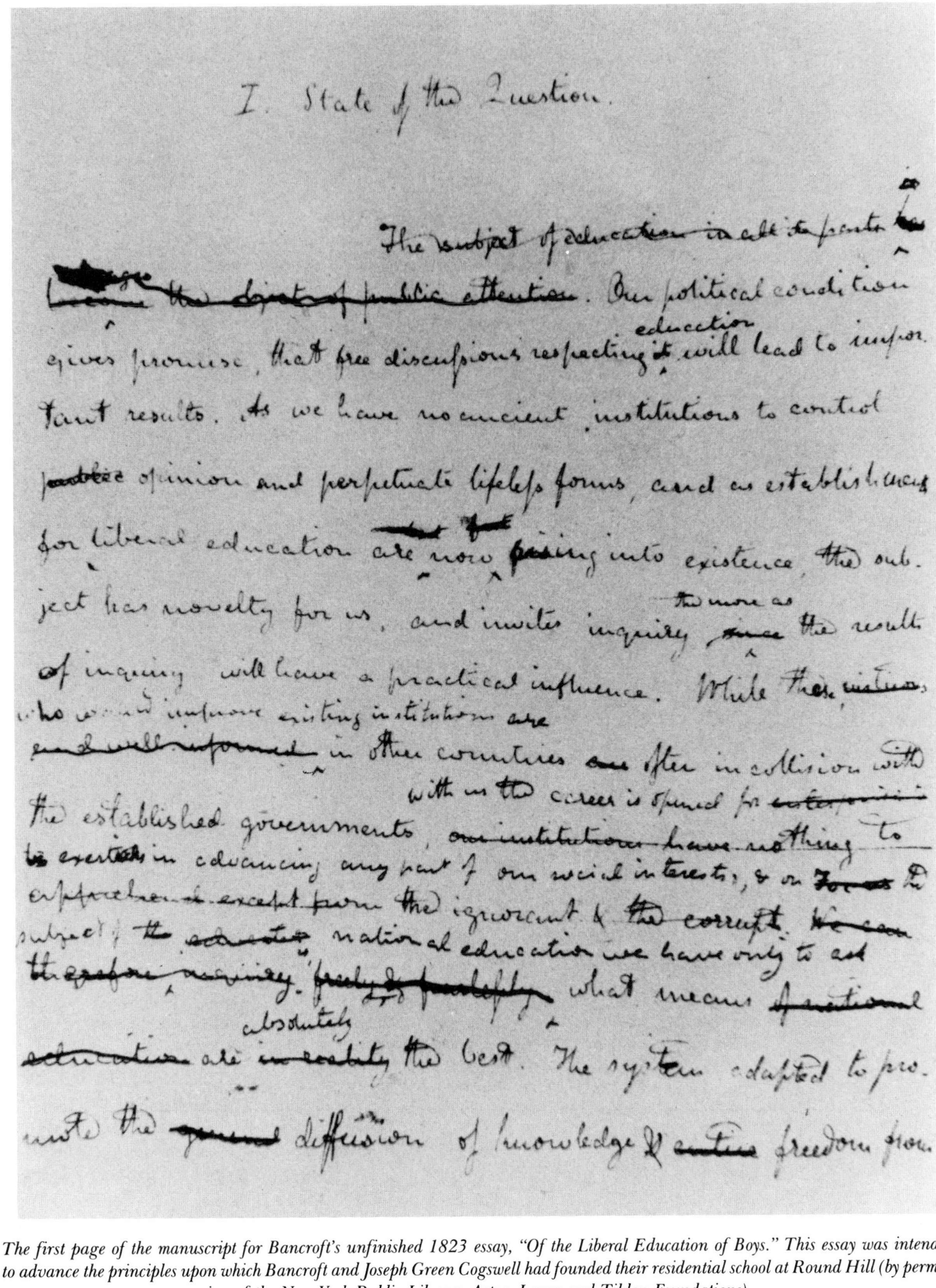

I. State of the Question.

The subject of education in all its parts [illegible] become the object of public attention. Our political condition gives promise, that free discussions respecting education will lead to important results. As we have no ancient institutions to control opinion and perpetuate lifeless forms, and as establishments for liberal education are now springing into existence, the subject has novelty for us, and invites inquiry the more as the results of inquiry will have a practical influence. While those who would improve existing institutions are in other countries often in collision with the established governments, with us the career is opened for [illegible] to in advancing any part of our social interests, & on the subject of national education we have only to ask what means are absolutely the best. The system adapted to promote the diffusion of knowledge & freedom from

The first page of the manuscript for Bancroft's unfinished 1823 essay, "Of the Liberal Education of Boys." This essay was intended to advance the principles upon which Bancroft and Joseph Green Cogswell had founded their residential school at Round Hill (by permission of the New York Public Library, Astor, Lenox and Tilden Foundations).

the period from 1823 to 1831 which promoted the principles of German historical criticism. Within that period he also published a few articles on such subjects as Felicia Dorothea Browne Hemans's *Poems,* but once he entered upon the writing of the *History of the United States from the Discovery of the American Continent* (1834-1875) in the early 1830s his interest in criticism waned. He did publish a few short articles, mainly tributes to old friends such as Washington Irving, John Greenleaf Whittier, and James Russell Lowell. His last lengthy article on literature was an extensive review of Oliver Wendell Holmes, Sr.'s biography *Ralph Waldo Emerson* (1885).

Bancroft's articles on things German lack the drive and intellectual depth of Thomas Carlyle's comparable series, which began to appear in English journals toward the end of the 1820s. On the other hand, they partly antedated Carlyle's series, and they benefited from being published in prestigious periodicals like the *North American Review* and the *American Quarterly Review.* Furthermore, they were sharply focused explications of the ground principles of German criticism. These same principles were later to inform his historical scholarship. The major tenets included a belief in providential universal history, the peculiarly expressive powers of diverse national characters as they forge their cultures, a deterministic concept of organic continuity, and the primacy of the group in the historical process.

Bancroft was born in Worcester, Massachusetts, in 1800, the son of Aaron and Lucretia Chandler Bancroft. The father was the liberal pastor of the Second Congregational Church of Worcester, a position he held until his retirement. He was by all accounts a gentle man with a taste for scholarship (in 1807, for example, he published a *Life of Washington*). Family financial resources were scant, but the father somehow dug up the money to enroll young George in Phillips Academy in Exeter, New Hampshire, in 1811 and in Harvard University in 1813, where the boy studied divinity. Bancroft was a serious student, something of a loner, subject to bouts of anxiety and lack of confidence for which he compensated by burying himself in books. President of Harvard John Thornton Kirkland befriended him and, following Bancroft's graduation in 1817, was instrumental in encouraging the lad to follow in the footsteps of Edward Everett and George Ticknor and study in Germany.

The historian Arnold H. L. Heeren (whose

Photograph of Bancroft's second wife, Elizabeth Davis Bliss Bancroft, probably taken at Mathew Brady's National Gallery in New York, circa 1849

works Bancroft would later translate) was a major influence in Bancroft's development, but more generally it is the complex of German studies rather than any single individual to which he was indebted. Thus Heeren represents ethnography, Friedrich Bouterwek literary history, Karl Friedrich Eichorn intellectual and biblical history, Johann Blumenbach anthropology, Johann Christoph Friedrich von Schiller and Goethe literature. Ambivalent about pursuing the ministry, Bancroft, upon his return to the United States, inquired into possible occupations but was unable to decide upon one. He aspired to a position at Harvard but was unsuccessful, partly because the influential Andrews Norton had begun to suspect Bancroft's emotional stability. He published a volume of Byronesque *Poems* in 1823, but both silence attendant upon the event and his own critical consciousness told him that a literary career

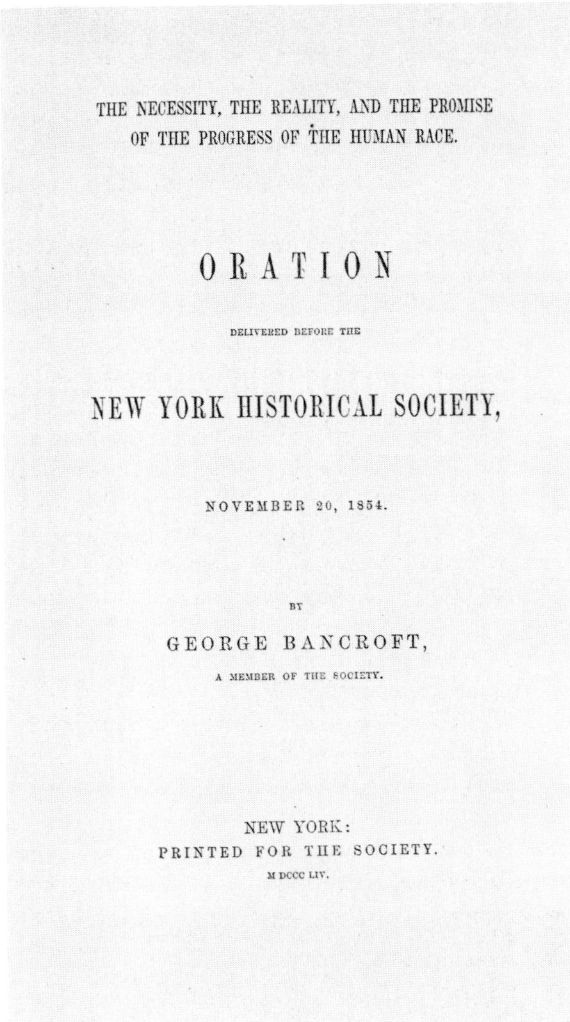
THE NECESSITY, THE REALITY, AND THE PROMISE
OF THE PROGRESS OF THE HUMAN RACE.

ORATION

DELIVERED BEFORE THE

NEW YORK HISTORICAL SOCIETY,

NOVEMBER 20, 1854.

BY

GEORGE BANCROFT,

A MEMBER OF THE SOCIETY.

NEW YORK:
PRINTED FOR THE SOCIETY.
M DCCC LIV.

Title page for the address Bancroft delivered at Niblo's Garden in New York City on the New-York Historical Society's fiftieth anniversary

was not in the works.

That same year he published his article on Schiller, probably through the good graces of Edward Everett, in the *North American Review*. It reveals his main touchstones of pious morality, sturdy confidence in human nature, reverence for the "domestic affections," harmony, and expressiveness. It also reveals an unfortunate tendency to overquote in the interests of padding out, though in the case of German literature it can be defended as a means for acquainting readers with particular literary texts. Recurrent adjectives as they troop along through the essay are tip-offs to Bancroft's attitudes: chaste, delicate, virtuous, gentle, cheerful, liberal, and the like. He indulges in declamatory endings, as in this tribute to the feminine: "He [Schiller] gained also what to the poet is more desirable than private ease; he gained that which is the best inspiration of the bard, and the best reward of bravery,–that which made Hector valiant, and the Lacedemonians temperate,–that which best encourages eloquence and excites to mental labour,–the Praise of Woman."

Frustrated in his hopes of a Harvard appointment, Bancroft joined with Joseph Cogswell to found the Round Hill School in Northampton, modeled on the German gymnasium. He stayed with the school until 1831. Within that time he published a number of articles, entered politics as a liberal, and in 1827 married Sarah Dwight, who came from a conservative, wealthy family. Sarah died in childbirth in 1837, and the following year he married Elizabeth Davis Bliss. Three articles in 1824 deal with Greek grammar and the value of a classical education and are basically spin-offs of his German education and tutoring in Greek at Harvard. Another article of 1824 is a substantial study of Goethe.

Like many American intellectuals, Bancroft thought Goethe "too dirty, too bestial in his conception"–until he met him. Then he melted, just as later he melted in meeting Byron. Bancroft's *North American Review* article on Goethe is temperate, perceptive in its evaluation of him, and it reflects a good grasp of the principles of historical criticism.

Bancroft's strategy is to recognize the transcendent genius of Goethe while viewing him in the context of German culture. Arguing that the "literature of a great nation must be approached with respect," he warns against a critical parochialism which fails to take into account climate, situation, and national character as these affect the sentiments and modes of thought of other nations. "The literature of each nation is national, and the true critic must endeavor to regard it from the same point of view with the nation, on which it was designed to produce an effect." In these terms, Bancroft sees Goethe as the "most national" of poets, representative of his country's aspirations, sensitive to its values. Bancroft then traces the link between Goethe the public figure and Goethe the private man. The royal court, Weimar intellectuals, and travel to Switzerland and Italy are made to account for the discipline of Goethe's mind, the cultivation of his taste and cosmopolitanism, and the accuracy of his aesthetic perceptions and judgment. The relative obscurity of his writings is attributed to the fact that they are "original, national, and unlike the foreign models." Bancroft expresses "surprise and disgust" at Goethe's indulgence in "earthly passions," but he claims that there is a sort of "practical morality" in Goethe which positively affects his personal life, literary activity, and search for truth.

Three months later Bancroft appeared again in the *North American Review* with an article on Herder. It is slighter than the one on Goethe, but Herder was more congenial to Bancroft's mind. Eight years later Herder would be the focus of controversy in a debate between conservative Unitarians and the newly emerging Transcendentalists. Bancroft's article scarcely made a ripple, even though he took the occasion to make a ringing declaration for intellectual freedom. Acknowledging Herder's centrality to the rise of biblical criticism in Germany, Bancroft praises the intellectual range and humanity of Herder and his clarity and steadiness and even forgives Herder his skepticism of the divine inspiration of the Hebrew prophets. The fact is, Bancroft wrote, "religion does not suffer from freedom of inquiry, that by the conditions of our being, the elevating feelings and faith, which connect man with his Maker, appear under the most various forms, and are modified by the different circumstances of times and countries, by national character, and the diversity in the intellectual habits of all reasoning men." He ends with a real tribute to the German intellectual: "The influence of Herder on his age was wide, and entirely beneficial to the best interests of our race. . . ."

Bancroft's next several efforts were slight. A review of an oration by Edward Everett overpraised a superficial work. Hemans's *The League of the Alps* elicited a curious effort in which Bancroft had some good things to say about the differences between poetical and moral justice, reality and probability, prudishness and the affectations to be found in landscape poetry. Bancroft was on the side of mind. When, however, he turned to Hemans herself, he lapsed into stereotypical ideas of what it means to be a female: that is, domesticity, maternal duty, speaking from the heart of the natural and true. He did inadvertently make one just characterization of her poetry. He called it "tranquilizing."

Between 1827 and 1831 Bancroft published a series of six articles on German literature in the *American Quarterly Review*. Collectively they extol the principles of critical historicism. There is some justice to the remark of Lilian Handlin that the series represents work-ups of old class notes

George Bancroft in his Washington study

and occasional jottings, for the general impression is of a hurried overview of German literature. Yet this last was exactly Bancroft's intent: to promote the cause of German literature by tracing its history.

What is interesting in the series is Bancroft's formulation of critical theory. The 1830s would be witness to a virtual explosion of interest in historicism, but to propound such a view in the 1820s was to be in the vanguard of a movement. The principles are clearly stated. To exercise freedom of mind and to triumph over critical narrowness, one has to cultivate an "enlightened curiosity" attentive to national peculiarities. Nations are not simply political units but rather complexes of interrelated institutions that collectively form distinct cultures. Each culture is complete in itself, a "living plant" so to speak, which follows an "indwelling necessity" that directs the nature of change. Within the culture, individuals are but "shadows," whereas the population is "immortal." The merit of individuals, therefore, is directly related to the general character of the society. When faced with differences of customs and forms, it is incumbent upon the critic to practice a "tolerant spirit" as he melts into a foreign culture to sympathetically respond to its arts. Bancroft's tolerance, however, often evaporates when he detects irreligious views and "inappropriate" depictions of women.

With the completion of the series in 1831, Bancroft's work as a critic pretty much came to an end, and as well he terminated his interest in the Round Hill School. Politics and historical scholarship had caught his attention. In 1830 he unsuccessfully ran for the Massachusetts Senate as the nominee of the Workingman's party; in 1834 he lost as the Anti-Mason candidate for the Massachusetts General Court; and in 1836, following his registration as a Democrat, he ran for and lost the vote for a congressional seat. He was instrumental in arranging for the 1844 nomination of Polk for president, and in the same year he lost a race for governor of Massachusetts. Meanwhile his publication in 1834 of the first volume of *History of the United States* had met with commercial and critical success. The tenth and final volume was published in 1875. *Literary and Historical Miscellanies,* a collection of articles published in 1855, was not successful. But his career certainly was, and he came to enjoy a mild affluence. In 1845 he became Secretary of the Navy and for a time Acting Secretary of War. The following year he was in London as United States Minister, serving until 1849, and between 1867 and 1873 he served as United States Minister to Prussia. In 1885 he published a short tribute to James Russell Lowell as a critic and a review of Holmes's *Life of Emerson,* the latter very sympathetic to the radicalism of Emerson's early period and the whole article couched in the context of American intellectual history.

Bancroft was a Germanophile at a time when German intellectuals were widely suspected of religious infidelity, and he lived long enough to see the triumph of German principles of scholarship and the establishment of German models of graduate study in American universities. As one of the pioneers in popularizing critical historicism he helped to establish the nature of academic and critical scholarship in this country.

Letters:

"Martin Van Buren-George Bancroft Correspondence, 1830-1845," *Proceedings of the Massachusetts Historical Society,* 42 (October 1908-June 1909): 381-443;

John Spencer Bassett, ed., "The Correspondence of George Bancroft and Jared Sparks," *Smith College Studies in History,* 2 (January 1917): 67-143.

Biographies:

Mark A. DeWolfe Howe, *The Life and Letters of George Bancroft,* 2 volumes (New York: Scribners, 1908);

Russel B. Nye, *George Bancroft: Brahmin Rebel* (New York: Knopf, 1944);

Nye, *George Bancroft* (New York: Washington Square, 1964).

References:

John Spencer Bassett, *The Middle Group of American Historians* (New York: Macmillan, 1917);

Fred L. Burwick, "The Göttingen Influence on George Bancroft's Idea of Humanity," *Jahrbuch für Amerikastudien,* 11 (1966): 194-212;

George H. Calcott, *History in the United States, 1800-1860* (Baltimore: Johns Hopkins University, 1970);

Robert H. Canary, *George Bancroft* (New York: Twayne, 1974);

N. H. Dawes and F. T. Nichols, "Revaluing Bancroft," *New England Quarterly,* 6 (June 1933): 278-293;

Sydney George Fisher, "Legendary and Myth-

Making Process in Histories of the American Revolution," *Proceedings of the American Philosophical Society,* 51 (April 1912): 53-75;

Lilian Handlin, *George Bancroft: The Intellectual as Democrat* (New York: Harper & Row, 1984);

David Levin, *History as Romantic Art* (Stanford, Cal.: Stanford University Press, 1959);

Orie Long, *Literary Pioneers* (Cambridge, Mass.: Harvard University Press, 1935);

Russel B. Nye, *Society and Culture in America, 1830-1860* (New York: Harper & Row, 1974);

John W. Rathbun, "Early American Historiography: the Case for George Bancroft," *Studia,* 28 (1983): 62-76;

Rathbun, "George Bancroft on Man and History," *Transactions of the Wisconsin Academy of Sciences, Arts, and Letters,* 43 (1954): 51-72;

Watt Stewart, "George Bancroft," in *The Marcus W. Jernegan Essays in American Historiography,* edited by William T. Hutchinson (Chicago: University of Chicago Press, 1937);

David D. Van Tassel, *Recording America's Past: An Interpretation of the Development of Historical Studies in America, 1607-1884* (Chicago: University of Chicago Press, 1960);

Richard C. Vitzhum, *The American Compromise: Theme and Method in the Histories of Bancroft, Parkman, and Adams* (Norman: University of Oklahoma Press, 1974).

Papers:

The major collections of George Bancroft's papers are housed at the Massachusetts Historical Society, the New York Public Library, and the American Antiquarian Society.

Park Benjamin

(14 August 1809-12 September 1864)

Roger George
University of Washington

See also the Benjamin entry in *DLB 3, Antebellum Writers in New York and the South.*

SELECTED BOOKS: *A Poem on the Meditation of Nature, Spoken September 26th, 1832, Before the Association of the Alumni of Washington College* (Hartford: F. J. Huntington, 1832);

The Harbinger: A May-Gift, by Benjamin, Oliver Wendell Holmes, and John D. Sargent (Boston: Carter, Hendee, 1833);

Poetry: A Satire, Pronounced Before the Mercantile Library Association at Its Twenty Second Anniversary (New York: J. Winchester, 1842);

Infatuation: A Poem Spoken Before the Mercantile Library Association of Boston October 9, 1844 (Boston: W. D. Ticknor, 1844);

True Patriotism: An Address Spoken at the Presbyterian Church, Geneva, N.Y., on the Fourth of July, 1851 (Geneva, N.Y.: I. & S. H. Parker, 1851);

Poems of Park Benjamin, edited by Merle M. Hoover (New York: Columbia University Press, 1948).

OTHER: Alexander Dumas, *The Three Guardsmen,* translated by Benjamin (Baltimore: Taylor, Wilde, 1846; revised, New York & Baltimore: William Taylor, 1846).

PERIODICAL PUBLICATIONS: "American Criticism," *New-Yorker,* 7 (6 April 1839);

"Reflections After the Manner of Rochefoucauld," *New-Yorker,* 8 (28 September 1839);

"Valedictory," *New-Yorker,* 8 (17 October 1839);

"Ralph Waldo Emerson," *New World* (29 February 1840);

"James Fenimore Cooper," *New World* (21 March 1840);

"Hints on Criticism," *New World* (28 March 1840);

"Mr. Hoffman's Romance," *New World* (11 July 1840);

"Once More Unto the Breach," *New World* (29 August 1840);

"The Old School House," *New World* (3 April 1841).

Portrait of Park Benjamin by Chester Harding (from Merle M. Hoover, Park Benjamin, *1948)*

Park Benjamin was a poet, lecturer, and literary agent, but he was also one of the magazine and newspaper editors most typical of New York's "Knickerbocker" era. In this capacity he established a reputation as a practical literary critic, occasionally vicious and acid, but often thoughtful and analytical. As an editor, he introduced the American reading public to much of the best writing of his day; as a critic, he judged work with a consistent goal of elevating general literary taste. In the opinion of one biographer he was "the father of cheap literature in the United States."

The second living son, Benjamin was born in 1809 in Demerara, British Guiana, to Park (or Parke) Benjamin, a New England sea captain and plantation owner, and Mary Judith Gall Benjamin, a planter's daughter. By the age of four, a tropical disease had left him with one weakened leg, a disability which was to remain for the rest of his life.

In 1813 he was sent to Norwich, Connecticut, where he was raised by his widowed aunt until his father moved the family to New Haven. Young Benjamin entered Harvard University in 1825 but, due to illness, he left Harvard in his second year, completing college at Washington College in Hartford, where he delivered the English Salutatory Address and oration and read a poem at graduation ceremonies on 6 August 1829. In 1830 Benjamin entered Harvard Law School, transferring to the Yale Law School in 1832 where he earned his law degree.

Although trained as a lawyer, Benjamin chose a literary career. While at Washington College he had become a friend of George D. Prentice, the editor of the *New-England Weekly Review,* and he contributed his poems to the *American Monthly Magazine.* For a brief time he was part owner and editor of a small newspaper, the *Norwich Spectator.* In 1833 he, Oliver Wendell Holmes, and John D. Sargent collaborated to publish a collection of poems, *The Harbinger.* In the same year Benjamin prepared an edition of Thomas Carlyle's *The Life of Friedrich Schiller,* which he published anonymously and without Carlyle's permission. At the end of 1834 Benjamin was asked to join the editorial board of Boston's *New-England Magazine,* and when the other members of the board, Samuel Gridley Howe and John D. Sargent, withdrew, Benjamin, in March 1835, became the sole editor and owner of this magazine.

In December 1835 Benjamin decided to move to New York, which had become the center of the magazine industry, and he merged the *New-England Magazine* with New York's *American Monthly Magazine,* retaining the latter name. This magazine encouraged original contributions by rising American authors including Hawthorne, Holmes, and Edgar Allan Poe, but it was short-lived; the editor's mistake in identifying it as a mouthpiece of the Whig party, as well as the consequences of the depression of 1837, led to the magazine's failure in October 1838.

While he was with the *American Monthly Magazine,* Benjamin had also acted as literary editor of Horace Greeley's *New-Yorker.* When his own paper failed, Benjamin turned over its subscription list to Greeley and resumed his position as editor, in which capacity he was to establish firmly his reputation as a literary critic.

His legal training no doubt influenced his critical style, for Benjamin essentially conducted a trial as each new work came to his attention, commending or condemning it and moving on to the next work. Most of his reviews were short and perfunctory, more like notices than genuine reviews, although they always included a value judgment.

In October 1839 he left Greeley's paper to start, in conjunction with Rev. Rufus Griswold, a new enterprise, the weekly *Brother Jonathan.* Nathaniel Parker Willis, once Benjamin's friend but now a bitter rival, thanks, apparently, to a failed courtship of Benjamin's sister Mary Elizabeth, had, earlier in the same year, launched a paper called the *Corsair* to take advantage of the lack of an international copyright agreement by printing full-length British works before authorized book publishers could obtain and print them. Benjamin and Griswold followed suit in this literary "piracy"; although *Brother Jonathan* printed some original American works, including serial novels by John Neal and some early poems by Walt Whitman, it devoted much space to novels by Dickens and other popular British and Continental authors.

After only six months Benjamin and Griswold abandoned *Brother Jonathan* and joined forces with Greeley's printer, Jonas Winchester, to directly compete with the *New-Yorker.* The new ventures were a daily, the *Evening Signal,* and a weekly, the *New World.*

The *New World,* in particular, was an immediate popular success, and it made Benjamin, for a time at least, one of the most influential editors and critics in the country. The paper was huge–four feet long and eleven columns wide–and its space allowed not only the printing of long excerpts but also of longer and more thorough criticism. In the latter Benjamin now had the opportunity to resist the trend toward the short, impressionistic critiques he deplored. "The public taste," he wrote sarcastically, "requires that no criticism shall exceed thirty lines. . . . To be readable they must be pithy and epigrammatic–relating to yourself rather than to your author. An anecdote, in some cases, is sufficient; it matters little whether it relates to the subject or not." But he saw himself as a molder, rather than a servant, of "the public taste," and he insisted upon his own form of criticism. In the past, he lamented, criticism had been a science, and the critic an expert upon his subject. A review was expected to be "erudite and analytical," and the critic had to "furnish arguments and proofs to sustain his decisions." In this insistence upon rigorous textual analysis he not only allied himself with the older style but also anticipated by a century the advent of New Criticism.

At its best, as in a review of Ralph Waldo Emerson's lectures, Benjamin's criticism was, as he claimed, balanced and relatively objective. Although he confessed that he was not "completely enamored" of Emerson, he conceded that Emerson was a "man of considerable attainment and a certain degree of poetical taste." Emerson lacked, though, "profound originality and completeness." And his lectures had formal problems as well: "The law of association is lost sight of in his discourses. They often are without any apparent connection. Hence most persons carry away a blended and confused notion of the discourse." Nevertheless, he concluded, Emerson had potential: "He has given brilliant examples of what he can do, and we trust he will yield his friends a specimen of his literary abilities, stript of all affectation and ambitious style." From what Emerson lacked one may infer qualities Benjamin the critic valued–simplicity, lack of "affectation" or authorial ego, and formal unity–a direct and easily followed chain of reasoning or development.

His tendency was more to damn than to praise. In part this was a reaction to the "appreciative" criticism practiced by such rival editors as Willis, who "evince an alacrity at puffing that we cannot hope to rival." But, as in the case of his diatribes against James Fenimore Cooper, his critical attacks became excessive to a degree equal to his rivals' worst puffery. Most critics of the period, including Benjamin, concentrated upon the plot as the most important formal element, at least in fiction, followed by such other elements as characterization and dialogue. Benjamin found that Cooper fell short. In a review of *The Pathfinder* he wrote:

> It must ever remain among the inexplicable anomalies of poor human nature that Mr. Cooper should really believe himself capable of writing respectable, natural, sensible and flowing dialogue. He fails wretchedly in his plots–in his characters he is still worse–but patience and good taste deliver us from his dialogue! It is far the worst of the three; and yet the man flatters himself that herein he especially excels.

After examining formal elements, most critics then went on to evaluate a work's "moral tendency," and it was for his lapses in this area that Cooper received Benjamin's sharpest invective. The *New World* of 29 August 1840 devoted its entire, massive, front page to a textual analysis of

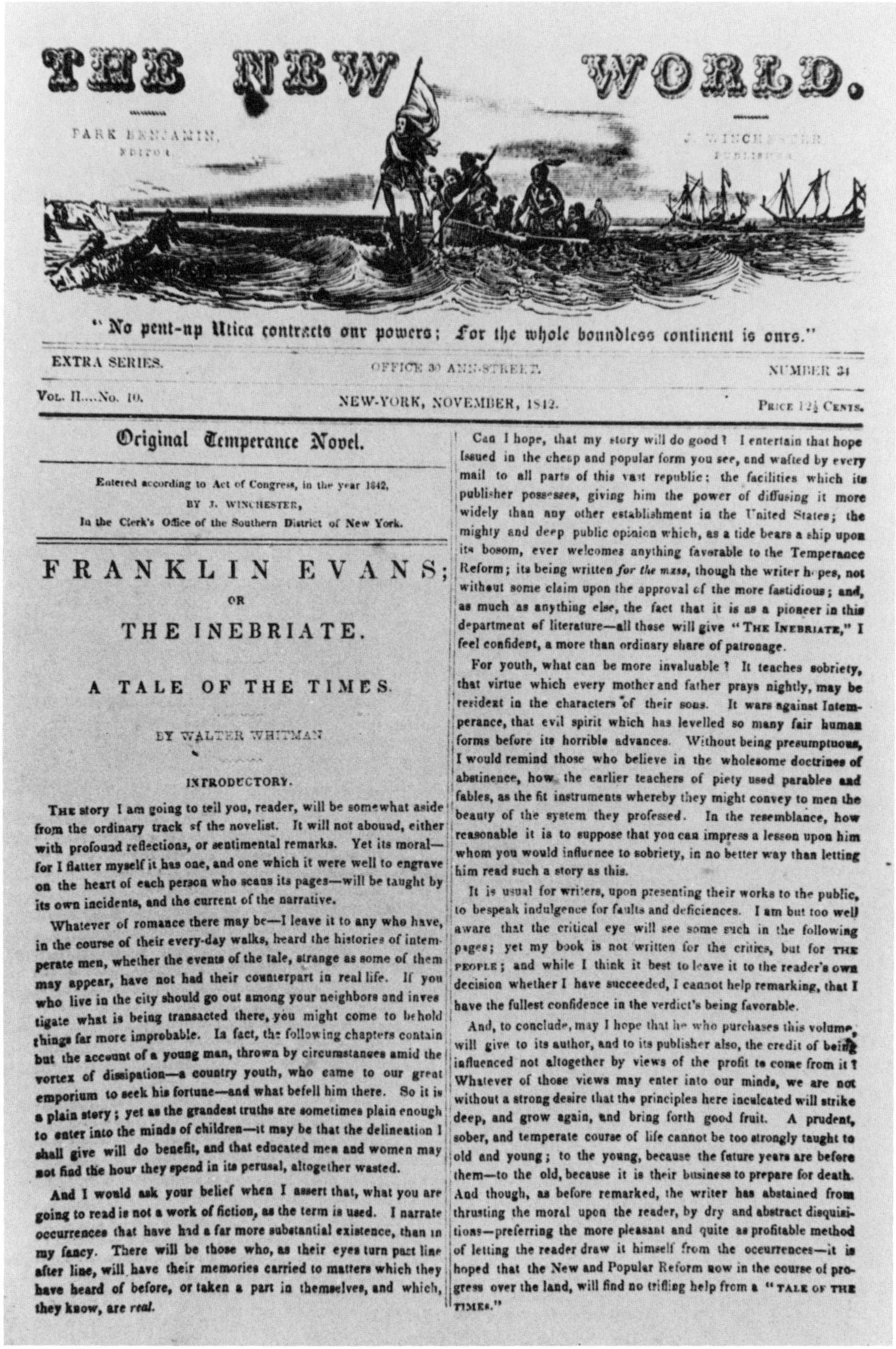

THE NEW WORLD.

PARK BENJAMIN, EDITOR.

"No pent-up Utica contracts our powers; For the whole boundless continent is ours."

EXTRA SERIES. OFFICE 30 ANN-STREET. NUMBER 34

VOL. II....NO. 10. NEW-YORK, NOVEMBER, 1842. PRICE 12½ CENTS.

Original Temperance Novel.

Entered according to Act of Congress, in the year 1842,
BY J. WINCHESTER,
In the Clerk's Office of the Southern District of New York.

FRANKLIN EVANS;
OR
THE INEBRIATE.
A TALE OF THE TIMES.

BY WALTER WHITMAN

INTRODUCTORY.

THE story I am going to tell you, reader, will be somewhat aside from the ordinary track of the novelist. It will not abound, either with profound reflections, or sentimental remarks. Yet its moral—for I flatter myself it has one, and one which it were well to engrave on the heart of each person who scans its pages—will be taught by its own incidents, and the current of the narrative.

Whatever of romance there may be—I leave it to any who have, in the course of their every-day walks, heard the histories of intemperate men, whether the events of the tale, strange as some of them may appear, have not had their counterpart in real life. If you who live in the city should go out among your neighbors and investigate what is being transacted there, you might come to behold things far more improbable. In fact, the following chapters contain but the account of a young man, thrown by circumstances amid the vortex of dissipation—a country youth, who came to our great emporium to seek his fortune—and what befell him there. So it is a plain story; yet as the grandest truths are sometimes plain enough to enter into the minds of children—it may be that the delineation I shall give will do benefit, and that educated men and women may not find the hour they spend in its perusal, altogether wasted.

And I would ask your belief when I assert that, what you are going to read is not a work of fiction, as the term is used. I narrate occurrences that have had a far more substantial existence, than in my fancy. There will be those who, as their eyes turn past line after line, will have their memories carried to matters which they have heard of before, or taken a part in themselves, and which, they know, are *real*.

Can I hope, that my story will do good? I entertain that hope. Issued in the cheap and popular form you see, and wafted by every mail to all parts of this vast republic; the facilities which its publisher possesses, giving him the power of diffusing it more widely than any other establishment in the United States; the mighty and deep public opinion which, as a tide bears a ship upon its bosom, ever welcomes anything favorable to the Temperance Reform; its being written *for the mass*, though the writer hopes, not without some claim upon the approval of the more fastidious; and, as much as anything else, the fact that it is as a pioneer in this department of literature—all these will give "THE INEBRIATE," I feel confident, a more than ordinary share of patronage.

For youth, what can be more invaluable? It teaches sobriety, that virtue which every mother and father prays nightly, may be resident in the characters of their sons. It wars against Intemperance, that evil spirit which has levelled so many fair human forms before its horrible advances. Without being presumptuous, I would remind those who believe in the wholesome doctrines of abstinence, how the earlier teachers of piety used parables and fables, as the fit instruments whereby they might convey to men the beauty of the system they professed. In the resemblance, how reasonable it is to suppose that you can impress a lesson upon him whom you would influence to sobriety, in no better way than letting him read such a story as this.

It is usual for writers, upon presenting their works to the public, to bespeak indulgence for faults and deficiences. I am but too well aware that the critical eye will see some such in the following pages; yet my book is not written for the critics, but for THE PEOPLE; and while I think it best to leave it to the reader's own decision whether I have succeeded, I cannot help remarking, that I have the fullest confidence in the verdict's being favorable.

And, to conclude, may I hope that he who purchases this volume, will give to its author, and to its publisher also, the credit of being influenced not altogether by views of the profit to come from it? Whatever of those views may enter into our minds, we are not without a strong desire that the principles here inculcated will strike deep, and grow again, and bring forth good fruit. A prudent, sober, and temperate course of life cannot be too strongly taught to old and young; to the young, because the future years are before them—to the old, because it is their business to prepare for death. And though, as before remarked, the writer has abstained from thrusting the moral upon the reader, by dry and abstract disquisitions—preferring the more pleasant and quite as profitable method of letting the reader draw it himself from the occurrences—it is hoped that the New and Popular Reform now in the course of progress over the land, will find no trifling help from a "TALE OF THE TIMES."

Front page of the November 1842 supplement to Benjamin's New World, *which consisted of Walt Whitman's first separately published work*

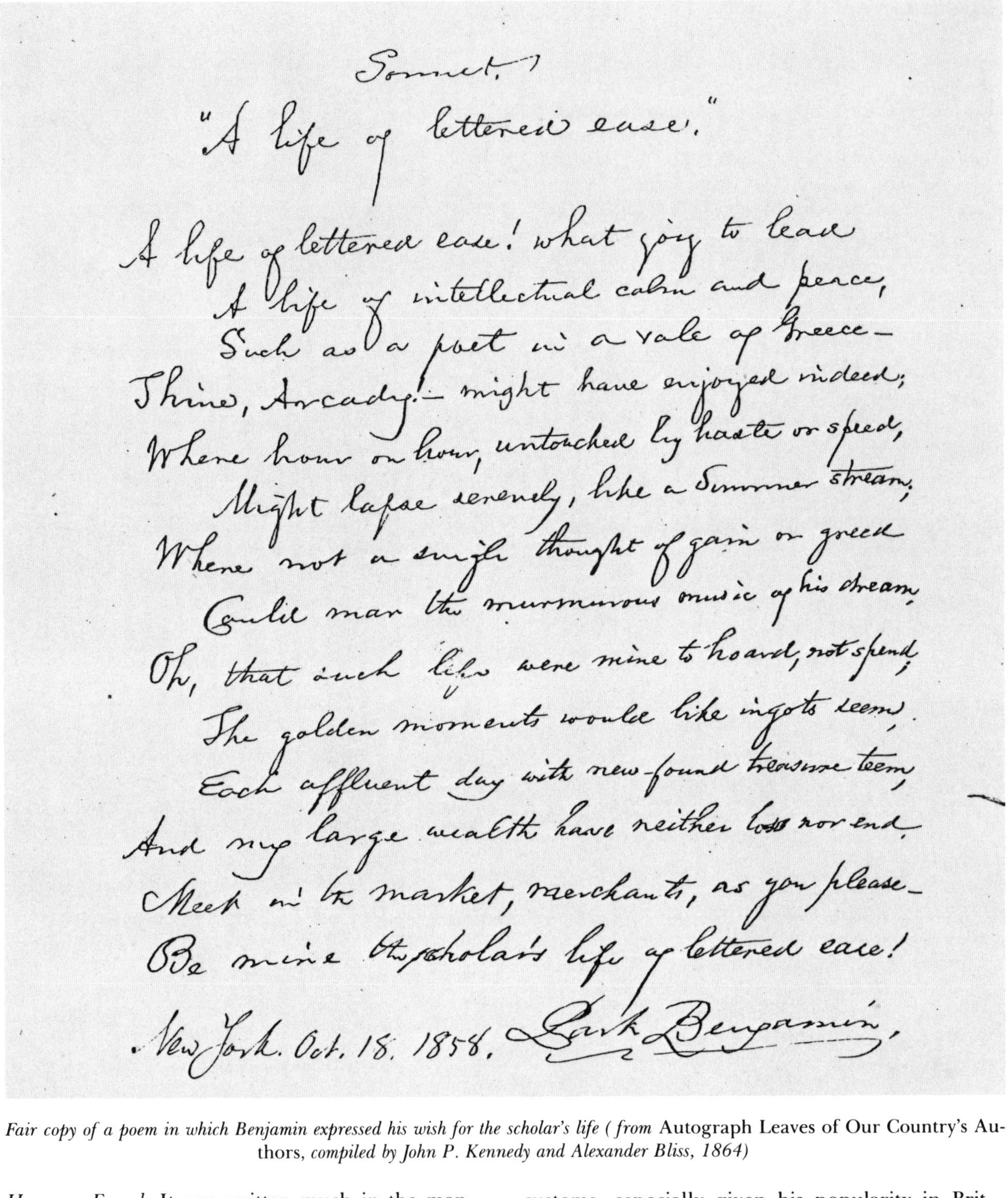

Sonnet.

"A life of lettered ease."

A life of lettered ease! what joy to lead
A life of intellectual calm and peace,
Such as a poet in a vale of Greece—
Thine, Arcady!—might have enjoyed indeed;
Where hour on hour, untouched by haste or speed,
Might lapse serenely, like a Summer stream;
Where not a single thought of gain or greed
Could mar the murmurous music of his dream.
Oh, that such life were mine to hoard, not spend;
The golden moments would like ingots seem;
Each affluent day with new-found treasure teem,
And my large wealth have neither loss nor end.
Meet in the market, merchants, as you please—
Be mine the scholar's life of lettered ease!

New York. Oct. 18. 1858. Park Benjamin.

Fair copy of a poem in which Benjamin expressed his wish for the scholar's life (from Autograph Leaves of Our Country's Authors, *compiled by John P. Kennedy and Alexander Bliss, 1864)*

Home as Found. It was written much in the manner of a court trial. In a separate column Benjamin announced that the analysis would prove that Cooper, "for the paltry purpose of aggrandizing himself in the eyes of Europeans," had "grossly slandered American customs and American people." Cooper's satire of American life and customs, especially given his popularity in Britain, was, Benjamin charged, immoral. Cooper had already filed libel suits against other editors for similar comments, and he quickly proceeded to add Benjamin to the list–no doubt as Benjamin had intended. Cooper asked for $5,000 in damages; the court eventually found in his favor, but only awarded $375.

Such criticism drew publicity and helped build circulation, and Benjamin clearly reveled in it. But it called into question the sincerity of his critical principles. In such cases Benjamin changed his role from judge to prosecutor, and his style from reasoned to histrionic. Before leaving the *New-Yorker,* he had noted that American critical journals were brought into contempt in England because they carried to excess either praise or condemnation. "This style of superlative speaking and writing among critics must be abandoned," he wrote. There must be "moderation, good sense, discrimination; hyperbolical puffing must give way to the calm expressions of judgement. . . ." But calm and moderate criticism clearly was not as popular with the readers as hyperbole.

In order to accommodate even longer works, the *New World* began to publish "extras"–quarto editions which could accommodate full-length books. One such extra in November 1842 printed a novel by Walt Whitman, *Franklin Evans, or The Inebriate,* and the list of other works included such authors as Bulwer-Lytton, Frederick Marryat, Dumas père, Balzac, and Eugène Sue. The extras also included biographies and even scientific and historical works, making a wide variety of literature, often of high quality, available to a mass audience at very little cost. Faced with such competition, book publishers lobbied for protection, and in 1843 the Post Office Department ordered pamphlet postage to be paid on all extras, reducing their price advantage. This move proved to be a swift and effective deathblow to publications like the *New World,* which printed its last issue on 10 May 1845.

With its demise, Benjamin lost his critical and editorial influence. He tried a variety of literary enterprises during the remainder of his life, including editing new papers (even to a brief revival of the *New World*), lecturing, and reading poems on the lyceum circuit, and acting as one of the country's first literary agents, but he never regained his former prominence.

While he was editor with the *New-Yorker,* he wrote: "whatever severity of animadversion I might draw down upon myself and my own compositions, I would, to the last, be rigidly just in my criticisms, swayed neither by power nor favor." His standard, he claimed, was the work itself, not his personal friendship with or animosity toward the author. "I feel no enmities," he went on, "however many may be entertained toward myself."

Park Benjamin, engraving by John C. Buttre

In fact, though, his performance as a critic often fell below this standard. He was opinionated, and as an editor he was acutely aware of his readers' demands for lively, entertaining writing. Thus he was more polemical than objective and as feared as he was respected. Edgar Allan Poe observed that Benjamin owed his influence to his "combined ability, activity, causticity, fearlessness, and independence," but he called into question the nature of that independence: "We can never be sure that he will defend a cause merely because it is the cause of truth–or even because he regards it as such." And, despite Benjamin's protestation that he ignored personal factors in his evaluations, Poe concluded that he was "a warm friend and a bitter, but not implacable, enemy." At his worst, he was partisan and insincere, but at his best, Benjamin directed attention to the text rather than the author's personality or reputation and tried to identify, carefully and analytically, those qualities which comprised good writing. As an editor, he helped introduce important American authors, including Hawthorne and Whitman, to a large reading public, and, to that extent, he shaped the public taste for the best writing available, on both sides of the Atlantic, at the time.

References:

Nina Baym, *Novels, Readers, and Reviewers* (Ithaca: Cornell University Press, 1984);

Merle M. Hoover, *Park Benjamin Poet & Editor* (New York: Columbia University Press, 1948);

Frederic Hudson, *Journalism in the United States From 1690 to 1872* (New York: Harper, 1873);

Frank L. Mott, *American Journalism: A History of Newspapers in the United States through 250 Years, 1690 to 1940* (New York: Macmillan, 1941).

Francis Bowen

(8 September 1811-21 January 1890)

Monica Maria Grecu
University of Nevada at Reno

See also the Bowen entry in *DLB 1, The American Renaissance in New England.*

SELECTED BOOKS: *Critical Essays, on a Few Subjects Connected with the History and Present Condition of Speculative Philosophy* (Boston: Williams, 1842);

Lowell Lectures on the Application of Metaphysical and Ethical Science to Evidences of Religion (Boston: Little, Brown, 1849); revised as *The Principles of Metaphysical and Ethical Science Applied to the Evidences of Logic* (Boston: Hickling, Swan & Brown, 1855);

The Principles of Political Economy Applied to the Condition, the Resources, and the Institutions of the American People (Boston: Little, Brown, 1856);

A Treatise on Logic, or, the Laws of Pure Thought; Comprising Both the Aristotelic and Hamiltonian Analyses of Logical Forms, and Some Chapters of Applied Logic (Cambridge, Mass.: Sever & Francis, 1864);

American Political Economy; Including Strictures on the Management of the Currency and the Finances Since 1861 (New York: Scribners, 1870);

Modern Philosophy from Descartes to Schopenhauer and Hartmann (New York: Scribner, Armstrong, 1877; London: Sampson Low, 1877);

Gleanings From a Literary Life, 1838-1880 (New York: Scribners, 1880);

A Layman's Study of the English Bible Considered in its Literary and Secular Aspect (New York: Scribners, 1885).

OTHER: "Life of Sir William Phips," in *Lives of Sir William Phips, Major-General Israel Putnam, Lucretia Davidson, and David Rittenhouse: The Library of American Biography,* volume 7, edited by Jared Sparks (Boston: Hilliard, Gray/London: Richard James Kennett, 1837), pp. 3-102;

"Life of Baron Steuben," in *Lives of Baron Steuben, Sebastian Cabot, and William Eaton: The Library of American Biography,* volume 9, edited by Sparks (Boston: Hilliard, Gray/London: Richard James Kennett, 1838), pp. 5-88;

"Life of James Otis," in *Lives of James Otis and James Oglethorpe: The Library of American Biography,* volume 2, second series, edited by Sparks (Boston: Little, Brown, 1844), pp. 5-199;

"Life of Benjamin Lincoln, Major-General in the Army of the Revolution," in *Lives of Daniel Boone and Benjamin Lincoln: The Library of American Biography,* volume 23, edited by Sparks (Boston: Little, Brown, 1847), pp. 205-434;

Outlines of Universal History, From the Creation of the World to the Present Time, translated, revised, with a history of the United States, by

Bowen (Boston: Jenks, Hickling & Swan, 1853);

Documents on the Constitutions of England and America from Magna Carta to the Federal Constitution of 1789, compiled and edited, with notes, by Bowen (Cambridge, Mass.: J. Bartlett, 1854);

Alexis de Tocqueville, *Democracy in America,* translated by Henry Reeve, esq., edited and revised, with notes and translation of additions to the Paris edition, by Bowen (Cambridge, Mass.: Sever & Francis, 1862);

The Metaphysics of Sir William Hamilton, collected, arranged, and abridged by Bowen (Cambridge, Mass.: Sever & Francis, 1867).

PERIODICAL PUBLICATIONS: Review of *Gleanings in Europe,* by the author of "The Spy," &c., &c., *North American Review,* 46 (January 1838): 1-19;

Review of *Œuvres,* by George Sand, *North American Review,* 53 (July 1841): 103-139;

Review of *Introduction to the Literature of Europe in the Fifteenth, Sixteenth, and Seventeenth Centuries,* by Henry Hallam, *North American Review,* 56 (January 1843): 44-89;

Review of *Œuvres,* by Alexandre Dumas, *North American Review,* 56 (January 1843): 109-137;

Review of *Romans,* by Paul de Kock, *North American Review,* 56 (April 1843): 271-300;

Review of the *Poets and Poetry of Europe, with Introductions and Biographical Notices,* by Henry Wadsworth Longfellow, *North American Review,* 61 (July 1845): 199-231;

Review of *Poems,* by Ralph Waldo Emerson; *Poems,* by William Ellery Channing; *Schiller's Homage of the Arts, with Miscellaneous Pieces from Rückert, Freilgrath, and other German Poets,* by Charles T. Brooks; *Poems,* by William W. Story; *Poems,* by Thomas Buchanan Read; *The Island Bride, and Other Poems,* by James F. Coleman; *Poems,* by Frances Elizabeth Browne; *Songs of the Sea, with other poems,* by Epes Sargent; *Shells from the Strand of the Sea of Genius,* by Harriet Farley, *North American Review,* 64 (April 1847): 402-434;

Review of *Poems,* second series, by James Russell Lowell, *North American Review,* 66 (April 1848): 458-482;

Review of *Meliboeus-Hipponax. The Bigelow Papers, edited, with an Introduction Notes, Glossary, and Copious Index,* by Homer Wilbur, A.M. . . . , *A Fable for Critics, or a Glance at a Few of our Literary Progenice, from the Tub of Diogenes. By a Wonderful Quiz; Poems,* by Oliver Wendell Holmes, *North American Review,* 68 (January 1849): 183-203;

Review of *Lectures on Subjects Connected with Literature and Life,* by Edwin F. Whipple . . . , *North American Review,* 70 (January 1850): 153-165;

Review of *The Life and Correspondence of Robert Southey . . . , North American Review,* 73 (July 1851): 1-33;

Review of *Life of Lord Jeffrey, with a Selection from His Correspondence,* by Lord Cockburn . . . , *North American Review,* 75 (October 1852): 296-331;

Review of *Notes and Emendations to the Text of Shakespeare's Plays, from Early Manuscript Corrections in a Copy of the Folio 1632 . . . , Manuscript Corrections from a Copy of the Fourth Folio of Shakespear's [sic] Plays,* by John Payne Collier; *The Text of Shakespeare Vindicated from the Interpolations and Corruptions Advocated by John Payne Collier, Esq., in His Notes and Emendations,* by Samuel Weller Singer; *A Few Notes on Shakespeare; with Occasional Remarks on the Emendations of the Manuscript Corrections in Mr. Collier's Copy of the Folio 1632,* by the Rev. Alexander Dyce, *North American Review,* 78 (April 1854): 371-423.

Francis Bowen championed no discernible theory of criticism, nor did he consider himself primarily a literary critic. Yet as editor and critic he made significant contributions to the cause of literary criticism in America. He was editor of the *North American Review* from 1843 to 1853, a period during which the journal prospered. Under Bowen the periodical's layout and typography were improved, the subscription list broadened, and the articles written in much livelier fashion. Since he is reputed to have written over a fourth of the articles he was undoubtedly central to the increased attractiveness of the journal. The subjects to which he addressed himself seem to have been randomly selected. In fact the general scope of his scholarship was so broad that a certain thinness seems to have been unavoidable. Yet so far as his literary criticism is concerned, some constants can be noted. He was suspicious of the propensity in German scholarship for abstract critical theorizing, which he thought nonsensical. The French infatuation with changing literary fads struck him as clearly related to instability in their temperament. Their romantic exaltation of

the poet as superior in insight to others, a notion he thought incongruous in itself, misled them into impressionistic self-indulgence when the proper office of criticism was to inquire into craftsmanship and insightfulness. He prized traditional touchstones in evaluating literature: inventiveness, intelligence, probability, perspicuity, the ability of literature to extend intellectual and spiritual horizons. In Bowen's criticism these touchstones were invoked with genial grace and spots of wit.

Bowen was born in Charlestown, Massachusetts, the son of Dijah and Elizabeth Flint Bowen. He studied at the Mayhew Grammar School, Boston, and after spending several years in a Boston publishing house, he entered the Phillips Exeter Academy. The following year, in 1830, he transferred to Harvard as a sophomore. Three years later he graduated with highest honors. Following two years of teaching mathematics at Exeter, he accepted a Harvard appointment as a tutor in intellectual philosophy and political economy.

In 1839 Bowen resigned his Harvard position in order to spend a year of study and travel in Europe, where he met some of the more important French intellectuals. Returning to Cambridge in 1840, he busied himself publishing an edition of Virgil and a collection of essays on speculative philosophy. Then, as proprietor and editor, he took over the *North American Review* from John Gorham Palfrey and guided it for over ten years before handing the reins to Andrew Preston Peabody. In 1848 he married Arabela Stuart, with whom he had a son and two daughters. The period was immensely productive for Bowen. Between 1843 and 1853 he published eight books on various nonliterary subjects, a large number of articles on political economy and philosophy, and a respectable number of well-considered articles directly related to literature.

The same success did not attend his pursuit of a teaching position. With the support of the teaching faculty he was named to the McLean professorship in history at Harvard but failed to win confirmation by the Board of Overseers. The sticking point was a series of articles in the *North American Review* (published as a book in 1851) which supported the Magyar monarchy over Kossuth. Later, in 1853, when James Walker left the Alford professorship in natural religion, moral philosophy, and civil polity in order to become president of Harvard, Bowen was named to and overwhelmingly approved for the position. He retained the post until his retirement in 1889.

It is hard to characterize Bowen's philosophical position. John W. Rathbun identifies him as a Lockean empiricist, but that is perhaps to circumscribe him too narrowly. He was opposed on general principles to German and French philosophy, especially as found in the work of Immanuel Kant and Victor Cousin. Somewhat loosely he reflects the Common Sense orientation of Scottish philosophy while staying aloof from any one influence. He may owe more to William Hamilton than to any other philosopher. In his work on religion Bowen based his argument for the existence of a Deity on the natural order of the phenomenal world and, generally speaking, sought to harmonize revealed religion with philosophy. In political science he steered a middle course between protectionism and Adam Smith's laissez-faire. And in philosophy he militantly opposed the development theory of Darwin and its philosophical extension by Herbert Spencer.

Bowen's first literary article in the *North American Review* was a review of James Fenimore Cooper's novels. Bowen was twenty-six at the time, but his work already evinces the control, levelheadedness, and capacity for turning a phrase that appear continually in his critical work. Turning first to a consideration of the novel as genre, he specifies its criteria. Basically an imitation of "the normal course of things," its plot must be probable and consistent, not just a string of incidents, and so must have a beginning, middle, and end. Plot reflects the inventiveness of the author in devising circumstances that test the characters. The conflicts with which the characters cope flesh them out in personality and motive and fully individualize them, even as they become representative of human nature.

Judged by these criteria Cooper fails Bowen's test. He has narrative drive, a sense of pace, and observational powers. Lacking tact and delicacy and, moreover, prone to carelessness and negligence, Cooper's work continually suffers by falling into the gap between intent and achievement. The male characters are wooden; the females, worse. Bowen himself is platitudinous on the traits of female "character" (sweet, affectionate, tender), but he is right in complaining that Cooper's women, by so continually getting in the way, become "part of the machinery" that creates the difficulties from which they need rescue. Bowen's assessment of Cooper's strengths and weaknesses is not appreciably different from the modern view.

A series of three essays, one each on George Sand, Alexandre Dumas père, and Paul de Kock, published between 1841 and 1843, articulates Bowen's attitudes toward contemporary French fiction. Outwardly the essays seem unnecessarily moralistic, but Bowen is no simple reactionary, and he is persuasive in documenting his reservations. He finds no convincing reasons why the French should be so *extreme.* How can a people so radically veer from the remote frosty edges of neoclassicism to the equally remote edges of romantic subjectivity? Yet he acknowledges that French social manners palliate negative criticism. Romantic French fiction may be "intentionally gross and corrupting," but it is also thoroughly honest.

Sand particularly fascinates Bowen. She is morbid, gloomy, and passionate, yet so eloquent and vivid that he must reckon with her. Bowen takes a certain pleasure in noting her "perfect earnestness and sincerity," even while he regrets all the gloom and misanthropy. Part of her superiority to the others, and even to Hugo, is due to the fact that she throws everything into the fight against "the law of God and man" and disdains adopting the careless mocking airs of her contemporaries. Bowen is good in characterizing her weakness, which he ascribes to an egoistic emphasis on the sanctity of passion. He argues that Sand implicitly recognizes that passion is selfish and inimical to the rights of others and that she seeks to evade this recognition by clothing passion in the colors of magnanimity, refinement, and exalted virtue. The ruse is given away, however, by the actions of her heroines. They are constantly falling in love before they are asked to, then go "whining about" accusing the men of coldness and indifference to their plight.

Throughout these essays Bowen observes a certain scrupulousness. The works of Sand, Dumas, and Kock should not be recommended to those of "tender age or sex," but they pose no problems to readers of "mature minds and confirmed principles." While perhaps unsuited to English and American taste, the works do warrant periodical notice and discussion, for they have some things to offer. For example, Paul de Kock may be a rogue, but he is merry, pleasant and engaging, observes well, has a sense of humor, and clothes his "coarse" characters with "liveliness and truth." Furthermore, Bowen believes, such works are curiosities as subjects for both warning and study: they tell us something about human excess, and they throw light on the reading public of France–an index and a cause of why the French are as they are.

If Bowen adhered to no particular school of criticism, he had a theory of literature that led him in empirical fashion to embrace certain expectations that could lead to a critical position. Writers enjoyed no "special inspiration," nor were they as a group peculiar in any way. To speak of the *poeta nascitur* was to subscribe to a "lying old proverb." To become a good writer involved a capacity for hard work combined with keen sensibility, strong imagination, temperamental balance, openness and frankness. Unfortunately too many writers tried to substitute trust in a "divine *afflatus*" for the hard work of forging lines. They rushed into print, failed to make a splash, complained of their bad luck, and vaguely suspected conspiracy against them. The result was a glut on the literary market and a trial to the reviewer. Bowen fantasized about reading "The Lay of the

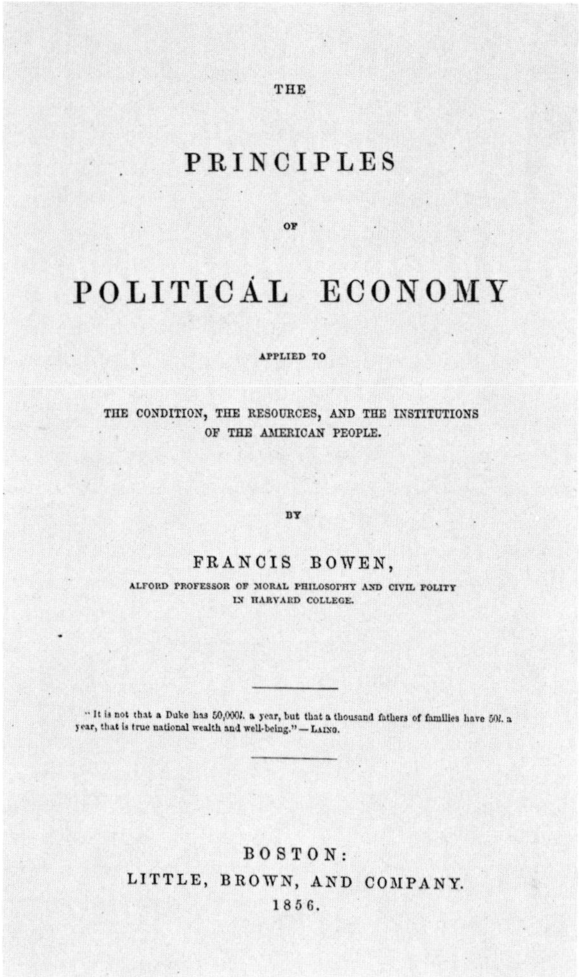

THE

PRINCIPLES

OF

POLITICAL ECONOMY

APPLIED TO

THE CONDITION, THE RESOURCES, AND THE INSTITUTIONS
OF THE AMERICAN PEOPLE.

BY

FRANCIS BOWEN,

ALFORD PROFESSOR OF MORAL PHILOSOPHY AND CIVIL POLITY
IN HARVARD COLLEGE.

"It is not that a Duke has 50,000*l*. a year, but that a thousand fathers of families have 50*l*. a year, that is true national wealth and well-being."—LAING.

BOSTON:
LITTLE, BROWN, AND COMPANY.
1856.

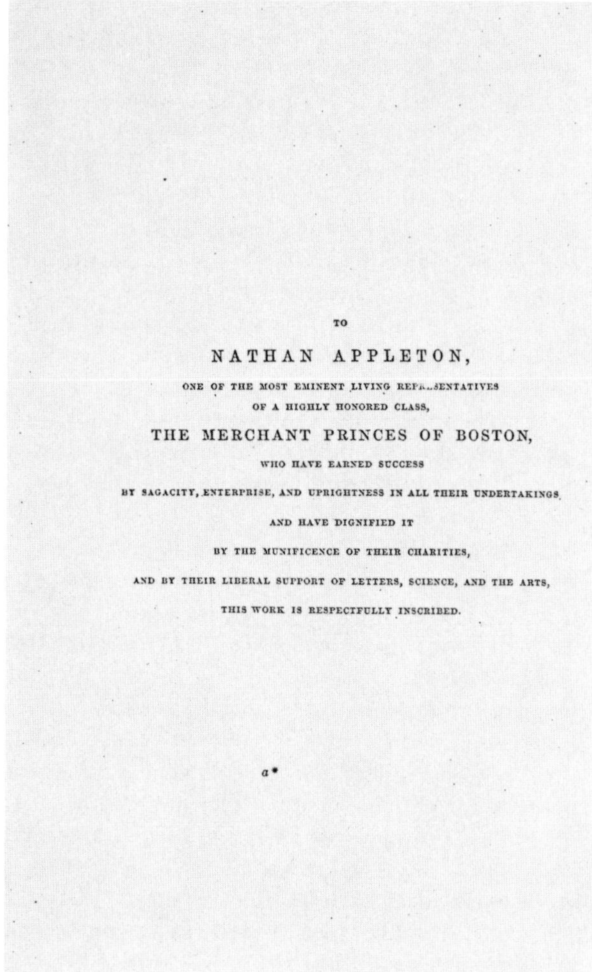

TO

NATHAN APPLETON,

ONE OF THE MOST EMINENT LIVING REPRESENTATIVES
OF A HIGHLY HONORED CLASS,

THE MERCHANT PRINCES OF BOSTON,

WHO HAVE EARNED SUCCESS

BY SAGACITY, ENTERPRISE, AND UPRIGHTNESS IN ALL THEIR UNDERTAKINGS,

AND HAVE DIGNIFIED IT

BY THE MUNIFICENCE OF THEIR CHARITIES,

AND BY THEIR LIBERAL SUPPORT OF LETTERS, SCIENCE, AND THE ARTS,

THIS WORK IS RESPECTFULLY INSCRIBED.

*a**

Title page and dedication page for one of Bowen's studies of American economic life. Nathan Appleton was a pioneer in the textile industry.

Last Minstrel," but he did not expect the day to arrive.

In Bowen's view the good writers seemed to be in the minority, while the critic, a proxy for the public, was beset by aspiring laureates and earnest drudges. Among the laureates Ralph Waldo Emerson and romantics like the poet William Ellery Channing seemed to substitute ingenuity and obscurity for talent and genuine feeling. Emerson's best poetry was lodged in his prose. The poetry was deficient in rhythm, meter, grammar, and common sense, for which Emerson compensated with witty apothegms, occasional sweet felicities of phrasing, and studied "oddities of expression." On the other hand were poets like William Wetmore Story and Frances Elizabeth Browne, who did not so much write poems as studies for poems. Having no glaring faults or conspicuous merits such as could be found in Emerson, the drudges stumbled amiably along to the point where Bowen was moved to quote Dogberry's line: "it is quite tolerable, and not to be endured." When, then, Bowen came across a poet like James Russell Lowell, he was grateful. Sometimes the finish was too elaborate–like painting in enamel–but in general he found diction equal to purpose, a "true" lyric voice, and an imagination that, hopefully, would round into maturity. He also liked Lowell's satirical bent. What with 4 July orators, philanthropists, utopians, abolitionists, and the like, Bowen felt that there was enough at which to laugh. He appreciated the "quaint and monstrous exaggerations" of the tall tale, which he thought exemplified the national wit, as well as the "very quiet and saturnine" wit of the Yankee.

In a purely practical, seemingly self-taught way that stemmed from the strengths of his own character, Bowen observed a group of critical tenets from which he did not swerve. A primary tenet was impartiality, freedom from party spirit. On occasion he became impatient with abolitionist sentiments, and it is clear enough that abolitionism did not elicit his sympathy. But he defended his impatience not on political or moral grounds, but on the ground that strident expressions of such sentiments broke unity of tone and effect. He also prized a cultivated taste unwarped by modern associations or national spirit. So much "aesthetical cant" based on continental theory was being published that Bowen confessed to almost perversely favoring a "subdued, temperate, and unambitious" kind of critical response.

In his own day, Bowen felt, criticism was too flaccid: "we talk what we dare not print." Poets felt they were the only ones who could comment on other poets. Some critics held that criticism should not inquire into the "intrinsic merits" of a literary work, but instead should view the work from the author's point of view, asking what the author was seeking to accomplish. That struck Bowen as plain surrender of the critical task. If accused of a fault, the writer could simply reply that that was what he had intended, and so it was no fault at all but rather a virtue. Neither was Bowen attracted to the German and French positioning of a book in a context of external and internal circumstances that made it *this* way and no other. Too much "pre-conceived" theory was involved.

Bowen sought a ground midway between the despotism of an older judicial criticism and what he considered the limp abandonment of standards of the newer criticism. Judicial pronouncements were no longer appropriate in a day when the rising popular press had taken over distinguishing between what was good and what was bad, and often judicial criticism was too quick to squelch innovation and raw new forms. Bowen rather liked the criticism of William Hazlitt and Edwin Whipple. Both men, whom Bowen found overly fond of "metaphysical" terms when plain English would serve well enough, had styles that were, nonetheless, transparent and smartly exuberant. There was absolutely no affectation in their work, only instinct with clarity and directness of statement, full of common sense. Always direct and on the whole sensible, Bowen's own criticism was strong-minded, practical, and hard-hitting when he wished it to be. He was intolerant of sham and of romantic posturing, even while he was receptive to such romantics as William Wordsworth and John Keats. Open to talent when he saw it, even when it went against the grain of his own convictions, he registered his responses in measured tones that underline his authority in so doing. A moral fastidiousness is often apparent in his criticism, but not to the point of compromising spiritual and aesthetic insights into the works under review.

Following his 1853 appointment as Alford professor, Bowen's interest turned to history, political economy, and world philosophy. The years between 1853 and 1885 were enormously productive ones for him in these fields. Hostile to the rise of Darwinian evolutionary theory, following the publication of the *Origin of Species* (1859), he especially opposed himself to the work of Herbert Spencer and argued his positions both tellingly and with graceful effect. He died 21 January 1890 in Cambridge, Massachusetts.

References:

Daniel Walker Howe, *The Unitarian Consciousness: Harvard Moral Philosophy, 1805-1861* (Cambridge, Mass.: Harvard University Press, 1970);

John W. Rathbun, *American Literary Criticism 1800-1860* (Boston: G. K. Hall, 1979).

Charles Brockden Brown

(17 January 1771-21 February 1810)

John Cleman
California State University, Los Angeles

See also the Brown entry in *DLB 37, American Writers of the Early Republic.*

SELECTED BOOKS: *Alcuin: A Dialogue* (New York: Printed by T. & J. Swords, 1798);

Wieland; or, The Transformation. An American Tale (New York: Printed by T. & J. Swords for H. Caritat, 1798; London: H. Colburn, 1811);

Ormond; or, the Secret Witness (New York: Printed by G. Forman for H. Caritat, 1799; London: William Lane, 1800);

Arthur Mervyn; or, Memoirs of the Year 1793 (Philadelphia: Printed & published by H. Maxwell, 1799); part 2 (New York: Printed & sold by George F. Hopkins, 1800); parts 1 & 2 (London: Lane & Newman, 1803);

Edgar Huntly; or, Memoirs of a Sleep-Walker, 3 volumes (Philadelphia: Printed by H. Maxwell, 1799; London: Lane & Newman, 1803);

Clara Howard; In a Series of Letters (Philadelphia: Printed by H. Maxwell & published by Asbury Dickins, 1801); republished as *Philip Stanley; or, The Enthusiasm of Love,* 2 volumes (London: Printed at the Minerva Press for Lane, Newman, 1807); republished as *Clara Howard; or, The Enthusiasm of Love* (Boston: S. G. Goodrich, 1827);

Jane Talbot, A Novel (Philadelphia: John Conrad/Baltimore: M. & J. Conrad/Washington: Rapin, Conrad, 1801; London: Lane, Newman, 1804);

An Address to the Government of the United States, on the Cession of Louisiana to the French; and on the Late Breach of Treaty by the Spaniards: Including the Translation of a Memorial, on the War of St. Domingo, and Cession of the Mississippi to France. Drawn up by a French Counsellor of State (Philadelphia: John Conrad/Baltimore: M. & J. Conrad/Washington: Rapin, Conrad, 1803);

Monroe's Embassy; or, The Conduct of the Government in Relation to Our Claims to the Navigation of the Mississippi Considered (Philadelphia: Printed by H. Maxwell & published by John Conrad, 1803);

The British Treaty of Commerce and Navigation, Concluded December 31, 1806, attributed to Brown (Philadelphia, 1807); enlarged as *The British Treaty. With an Appendix of State Papers* (London: Printed for John Joseph Stockdale, 1808);

An Address to the Congress of the United States on the Utility and Justice of Restrictions upon Foreign Commerce . . . (Philadelphia: Printed by John Binns & published by C. & A. Conrad, 1809);

Carwin, the Biloquist, and Other American Tales and Pieces (London: Henry Colburn, 1822);

The Rhapsodist and Other Uncollected Writings of Charles Brockden Brown (New York: Scholars' Facsimiles & Reprints, 1943);

Memoirs of Stephen Calvert, edited by Hans Borchers (Frankfurt am Main, Bern & Las Vegas: Lang, 1978).

Collection: *The Novels of Charles Brockden Brown,* 7 volumes (Boston: Published by S. G. Goodrich, 1827).

OTHER: C. F. Volney, *A View of the Soil and Climate of the United States of America: With Supplementary Remarks upon Florida; on the French Colonies on the Mississippi and Ohio, and in Canada; and on the Aboriginal Tribes of America,* translated by Brown (Philadelphia: Printed by T. & G. Palmer & published by John Conrad, 1804);

"A Sketch of the Life and Character of John Blair Linn," in *Valerian, A Narrative Poem,* by John Blair Linn (Philadelphia: Printed by Thomas & George Palmer, 1805), pp. iii-xxiv.

Charles Brockden Brown is best known as America's first professional man of letters, a novelist, publisher, and editor whose morally earnest Gothic tales attracted the attention of Keats and

Shelley abroad and, among others, Poe and Hawthorne at home. His career as a novelist was brief and intense and, by comparison with his American contemporaries, brilliant (four extraordinary and two rather mundane novels published between 1798 and 1801). Between 1799 and his death in 1810 he also published, edited, and was frequently a major contributor to three different magazines. He has been described by David Lee Clark in *Charles Brockden Brown, Pioneer Voice of America* (1952) as "the greatest critic in America before Edgar Allen Poe," but such a high estimate of his importance as a critic is not widely shared. None of his novels was wholly an artistic success, and none of his journals or novels was a commercial success. Nor did he exhibit in any of his prefaces, editorials, articles, or reviews either an original and coherent literary theory or a significantly discerning critical eye. Nevertheless, through his magazines and by the example of his fictional achievements, he championed the cause of a native American literature and began to indicate some of its features. Thus, by precept, example, and anticipation Brown helped prepare for the more luxuriant flowering of American letters that was to come.

Brown was born on 17 January 1771 in Philadelphia, the fifth of six children of staunch Quaker parents. From the faith of his ancestors he may have derived his distaste for war and bloodshed and his interest in listening to the voice within, as well as some of his political ideology. He was, from an early age, an avid reader, melancholy and somewhat solitary, impassioned by ideas, pursuing his interests even at the expense of his own health. Between the ages of eleven and sixteen he received a classical education at the Friends Latin School in Philadelphia but left the school to apprentice as a lawyer, a choice urged by his parents and one that he soon regretted. The issues of classical versus practical education and of his particular career choice were among the central concerns in Brown's life, and they appear as major themes in his fiction. On the one hand, the commercial spirit of the times, his merchant father who had lost a business during the Revolutionary War, and the simplicity and pragmatism of his Quaker faith influenced him to choose a profession in which he could serve the public and be well paid. On the other hand, his own temperament and his bookishness and idealism drove him to the more solitary and unremunerative trade of authorship. In

Portrait by James Sharples, circa January 1798 (by permission of the Worcester Art Museum, Worcester, Massachusetts)

1793, when he was twenty-two, Brown left the law firm, to the great disappointment of his family and friends, and sought to support himself by his pen.

Partly this choice of a literary career resulted from his involvement in the Belles Lettres Club while he was still studying law. The function of the club, whose membership was primarily young professional men, was to improve the members' writing and eloquence, as well as give rise to some literary dueling. The "Rhapsodist," a kind of reformed romanticist's confessions, was written during this period. After he left the law firm, he apparently traveled back and forth between New York, New England, and Philadelphia for about four years, working for a time as a schoolmaster and writing novels that either were never finished, never published, or lost. He moved to New York in 1798, the year of his first two major publications and also the year in which he contracted and nearly died of yellow fever. His closest friend, Elihu Hubbard Smith, did die of the same disease in that year, and the pain of his loss contributed greatly to the melancholy tone of his first four novels.

Tracing a development in Brown's thought and writing career has been a difficult task since the bulk of his fictional achievements–six novels and a dialogue–appeared in the very short time span from 1798 to 1801. All of these works show signs of haste, and some are reworkings of earlier material or of elements from one of his other novels. *Alcuin: A Dialogue* (1798), his first important work to be printed, reflects his interest in the radical political and social ideas of the late eighteenth century, particularly those of William Godwin's *Political Justice* (1793) and Mary Wollstonecraft's *The Rights of Women* (1792). Brown had become acquainted with these ideas from his own reading in his father's library and from conversations in the Belles Lettres Club and then in the Friendly Club in New York. His friend Smith was a radical deist, for example, and talk about equal rights for women, universal benevolence, human perfectibility, and the state as the enemy of progress were regularly part of the discourse between many young intellectuals at that time. *Alcuin,* written in the form of a dialogue between a stuffy schoolmaster and a Philadelphia bluestocking widow, is, for the most part, dull. It is important mainly as a prelude, an articulation of some of the ideas about equal education for women that later shaped the portraits of Clara Wieland, Ascha Fielding, and Constantia Dudley in Brown's major novels. *Alcuin* may also suggest an extreme form of the literary technique he would employ in all of his novels wherein specific ideas are associated with different characters who then engage in a kind of dramatic–and sometimes actual–debate as a way of testing these ideas. Although Brown may not have written fiction to prove specific points, the clash of ideas was central to the way he conceived characters and plotted action.

Brown's four major novels–*Wieland; or, The Transformation. An American Tale* (1798), *Ormond; or, the Secret Witness* (1799), *Arthur Mervyn; or, Memoirs of the Year 1793* (1799, 1800), and *Edgar Huntly; or, Memoirs of a Sleep-Walker* (1799)–have all attracted modern critical attention and have appeared in modern editions. Their appeal for twentieth-century readers has to do, in large part, with Brown's use of Gothic conventions to explore psychological themes. For example, in *Wieland,* the theme is religious fanaticism that leads to madness and murder; in *Ormond* and *Arthur Mervyn* vivid scenes of the plague in Philadelphia create an atmosphere of terror and mystery; and in *Edgar Huntly* wilderness settings and Indian wars become Gothic trappings for another tale of madness and murder, told by a sleepwalker. Brown's fascination for such scenes and themes of terror, buttressed by his image as a sickly and melancholy man, has fostered the idea that he is primarily a romantic writer. Indeed, the interest his fiction held for Shelley and Poe would seem to substantiate that position. Thus, in adapting native materials to the conventions of Gothic romance, Brown demonstrated one of the more important critical positions associated with his fiction, the Americanization of Old World literary modes.

The elements and themes that predominate in Brown's fiction, however, are less Gothic than moral, social, and intellectual. All events that first appear mysterious, supernatural, or irrational in the works are eventually explained scientifically and rationally: the disembodied voices in *Wieland* are the work of Carwin, the ventriloquist; Ormond's extraordinary range of knowledge is due to his artful eavesdropping; and Edgar Huntly's inexplicable adventures result from his sleepwalking. Perhaps the most pervasive theme is the ambiguity of good and evil, and particularly the misguided assumption that benevolent purposes always lead to beneficent ends. Brown's central characters–male and female–are do-gooders whose attempts to help others or to practice some virtue invariably lead to tragedy. Thus at one extreme, Theodore Wieland serves God by killing his wife and children, while more subtly, Constantia Dudley's calm rationalism in coping with Ormond leads to her near-rape and to Ormond's death.

Furthermore, underlying this theme of the ambiguity of virtue is the question of whether or not the senses and the rational intellect can be relied on for a truthful version of the world on which moral action must be based. Since Theodore Wieland's hearing is tricked by Carwin's ventriloquism, since Constantia's sight and rational thinking are duped by Ormond's powers of con-

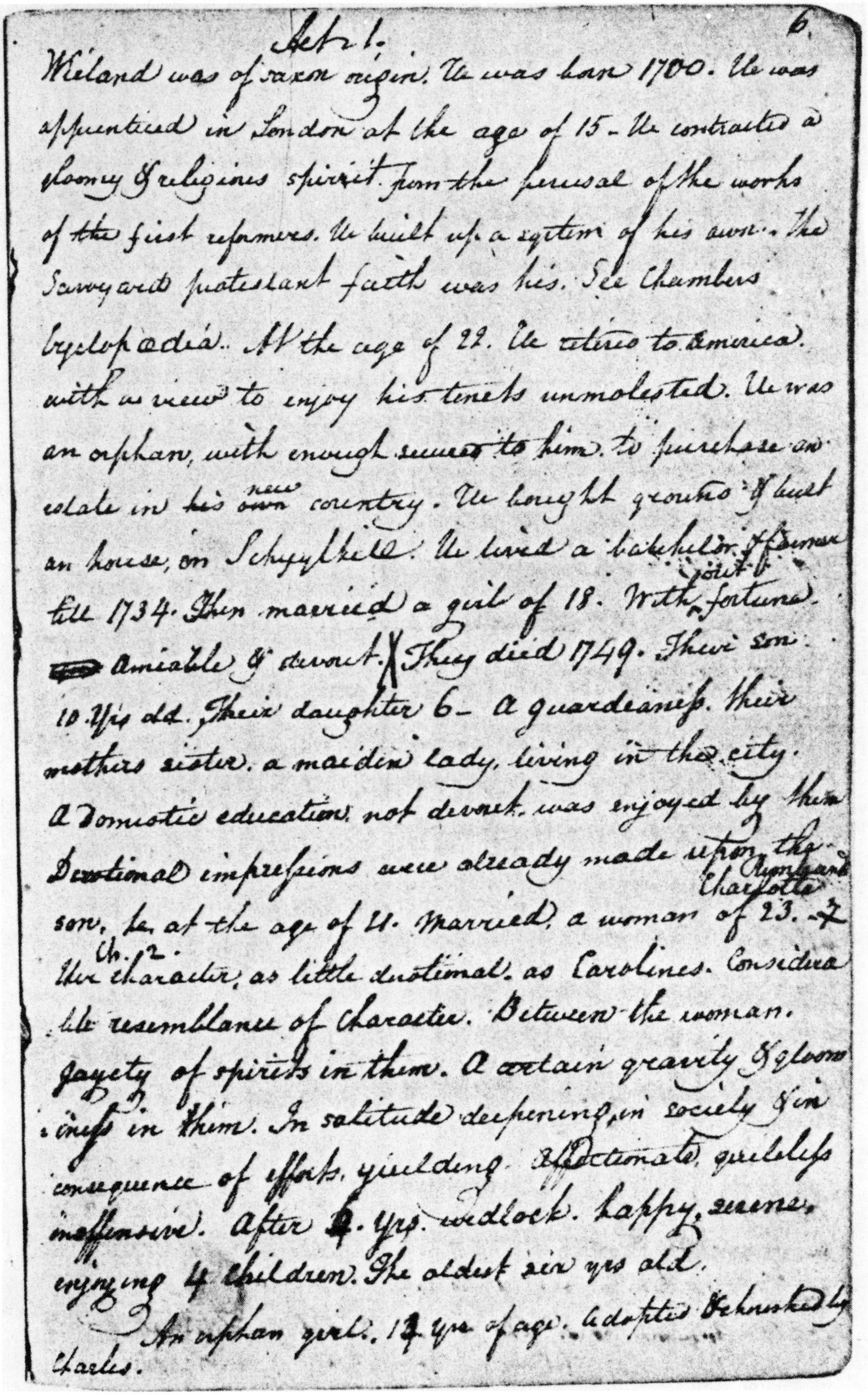
Act 1. 6.
Wieland was of saxon origin. He was born 1700. He was
apprenticed in London at the age of 15. He contracted a
gloomy & religious spirit from the perusal of the works
of the first reformers. He built up a system of his own. the
Savoyard protestant faith was his. See Chambers
Cyclopaedia. At the age of 22. He retired to America
with a view to enjoy his tenets unmolested. He was
an orphan, with enough secured to him to purchase an
estate in his new country. He bought ground & built
an house, on Schuylkill. He lived a batchelor & farmer
till 1734. Then married a girl of 18. With joint fortune.
amiable & devout. They died 1749. Their son
10 yrs old. Their daughter 6. A guardianship. Their
mothers sister. a maiden lady, living in the city.
A domestic education: not devout. was enjoyed by them
Devotional impressions were already made upon the
son. He at the age of 21. married a woman of 23. Charlotte
Her character as little devotional as Carolines. Consider
the resemblance of character. Between the woman.
gayety of spirits in them. A certain gravity & gloom
iness in them. In solitude deepening, in society & in
consequence of efforts. yielding. Affectionate. guileless
inoffensive. After 4. yrs wedlock. happy. seems
enjoying 4 children. The oldest six yrs old.
An orphan girl. 14 yrs of age. adopted & educated by
Charles.

A page from Brown's outline for his 1798 novel, Wieland; or, The Transformation. An American Tale *(Brown Papers, MS 03398; by permission of the Historical Society of Pennsylvania)*

cealment, since Arthur Mervyn is similarly misled by what he sees and hears while he is hidden, and since Edgar Huntly draws false inferences from what he observes of Clithero, Brown would seem to argue against the reliability of the senses and understanding. However much Brown is torn between his fascination with the irrational and his interest in testing the strengths of rationally educated individuals, the key recurring moral point in his fiction seems to be a reaffirmation of basic Christianity: his flawed do-gooders all pointedly lack orthodox Christian training. His last published novel, *Jane Talbot* (1801), even more clearly demonstrates his belief in the value of basic Christian principles against radical idealism. The social-moral philosophy of his fiction, thus, seems to move from an early, brief, and none-too-committed flirtation with rationalism and deism to a fairly conservative reaffirmation of the plain morality of his parents' Quakerism.

As a body of work attracting the attention of such nineteenth-century, American writers as Poe, Cooper, Hawthorne, William Prescott, Richard Henry Dana, and John Neal, Brown's major fiction–in its methods and themes–constitutes his most significant critical, as well as literary, contribution. In form and technique his novels seem rather conventional, showing the obvious influence of the types of fiction popular in his day: sentimental romances like Samuel Richardson's *Clarissa* (1747, 1748), Gothic romances like Ann Radcliffe's *The Mysteries of Udolpho* (1794), and novels of purpose like William Godwin's *Caleb Williams* (1794). Brown's aim, as he put the matter in an advertisement for the unpublished "Skywalk," was to "employ the European models merely for the improvement of his taste, and adapt his fiction to all that is genuine and peculiar in the scene before him" (*The Rhapsodist and Other Uncollected Writings of Charles Brockden Brown*, 1943). However, Brown was no realist; the conventions he used for models supplied him with neither a technique nor a vocabulary for rendering in sharp and abundant detail the American scene he observed. Rather he was a "moral painter" intent upon "inculcating on mankind the lessons of justice and humanity" (Preface to *Arthur Mervyn*, 1799). He did this not by fictively treating ideas in order to illustrate them, but by dramatizing conflicts of ideas–through characterization, sequences of events, and powerfully rendered scenes–in order to test them. The resulting ambiguities in his work, sometimes attributed to his haste and carelessness in writing, are better described as the result of the very uncertainties that existed in the emerging national society, the "culture of contradictions" as Richard Chase described it in his *The American Novel and Its Tradition* (1957). In this ambiguity, as well as in his concerns with epistemology and multiple points of view, with the psychology of terror, with undermining a bland faith in human perfectibility and the capacity of reason and enlightened education to eradicate error, with the melodramatic charm of the powerfully erring individual will–the Promethean villain–Brown launched American literature in the directions that would be pursued by Poe, Hawthorne, Melville, Dickinson, James, and Faulkner.

One of the contradictions Brown felt most acutely was the conflict between the commercial spirit in American life and the artistic sensibility. This concern is the central issue of Stephen Dudley's life which dominates the first half of *Ormond*. Brown's major, "lofty" villains are all linked with art and artifice, with the imagination and duplicity, and this may suggest Brown's own anxiety over his choice of a literary profession, especially since his fiction writing did not provide enough income for him to live on. Consequently, in 1799, during the period of his major fictional output, Brown began publishing the first of his three journals, the *Monthly Magazine and American Review*. He did so in response to the earlier urging of his literary associates in the New York Friendly Club, whose membership had included the dramatist William Dunlap, Brown's poet-physician friend Elihu Hubbard Smith, and Samuel Miller, author of *A Brief Retrospect of the Eighteenth Century* (1803). Brown's dual aim was to promote literature in America and to make money. In this and his subsequent magazines Brown assumed a more direct and obvious role as critic, and his most important contributions were made to the discussion of the problems confronting the growth of literary expression and the profession of writing in America.

The *Monthly Magazine* was short-lived, running from April 1799 to January 1800, and, because articles were customarily unsigned, Brown's actual contributions are difficult to determine with certainty. The periodical printed original and borrowed poetry, fiction, and articles on various subjects, including American science, history, literature, and manners, and one section–"American Review"–was devoted to commentary on recent American publications. Brown's literary opinions, in general, reflect the same mix of romantic interest and neoclassical moralizing apparent in his novels. The novelist must use realistic depictions of life to instruct morally, focusing particularly on individuals of great intellectual and emotional power, because such individuals lead and shape society and their moral natures, therefore, are more powerfully and significantly instructive. His taste in English poetry ran to the neoclassical rather than romantic, although he praised Robert Burns and rarely commented on the American neoclassicists, the Hartford Wits. However, his most frequent and important concern was literary nationalism.

Brown was vigorous in his defense of the prospects for literature to flourish in America, denying that the scarcity of literary accomplishments was the result of lack of intelligence or lack of readers. The problem, as he both saw and experienced, was the lack of remuneration which made the profession of letters nearly impossible, whether as fiction writer, poet, or magazine publisher. The population was too thinly and widely dispersed to make distribution of publications easy, and the absence of copyright laws made it difficult for unknown or unestablished American writers to gain space either in the few magazines that sprang up or on the booksellers' shelves, since the popular European classics could be published without royalties. Yet Brown insisted that American creations not be unduly praised simply because they were American. By being held to high standards of universal taste, the works would better represent American culture to the world. Even more importantly, he urged American writers not to imitate European models slavishly, but to focus attention on American life as the source out of which would come ultimate literary greatness.

Not long after the collapse of the *Monthly Magazine* in December 1800, Brown acquiesced to the urgings of his family, returned to Philadelphia, and entered into partnership with two of his brothers in a mercantile firm. He began a somewhat prolonged courtship of Elizabeth Linn, the daughter of a New York Presbyterian minister, and in November 1804, facing his family's disapproval and excommunication from the Society of Friends, they married. Four children were born to them, and by every account Brown was an involved, devoted family man.

A year before his marriage Brown had embarked on his second editorial venture, the *Literary Magazine and American Register.* He continued both to edit and to participate actively in the mercantile firm until 1806 when the firm dissolved, and he gave up the editorship of the magazine. Ostensibly more of a literary journal than his first publication, the *Literary Magazine* actually offered fewer book reviews, although in his introductory "Address to the Public" he argued that it was through such reviews that "the history of our native literature shall be carefully detailed" (October 1803). In fact, the literary opinions expressed in this magazine show signs of Brown's discouragement over his own failure to support himself by writing. He remained nationalistic but complained more pessimistically about the lack of public support for any writing except newspapers, sermons, and political pamphlets. He was even more critical of the moral dangers in novel reading, and the overall focus of the journal was on such practical subjects as history, politics, science, manners and uplifting morality. This shift away from imaginative writing was illustrated in his other publications after 1801: political pamphlets on the cession of Louisiana (1803), U.S. navigation rights on the Mississippi (1803), and foreign commerce (1809); a translation of Volney's *A View of the Soil and Climate of the United States* (1804); and a biographical sketch of his brother-in-law, John Blair Linn (1805).

His last journal effort, the *American Register, or General Repository of History, Politics, and Science,* focused primarily on recording historical and political facts, although there were also sections devoted to poetry and reviews of literature. He once again bemoaned the scarcity of good American poems, and his nationalism had abated to the point where he emphasized the shared literary culture between England and America. Once again, however, in a "Sketch of American Literature," he provided a detailed account of why the literary profession did not thrive in America, laying the blame not upon the lack of creative genius or interested readers but upon the economics of publication itself. The *American Register* continued publication from 1806 until Brown's death from tuberculosis in 1810.

Brown's most significant critical observation, then, was reflected in his professional activities. He saw the question of a rise of national literature to hinge on the establishment of letters, not as an avocation or as an occasional effort of the affluent, but as a profession. Through his

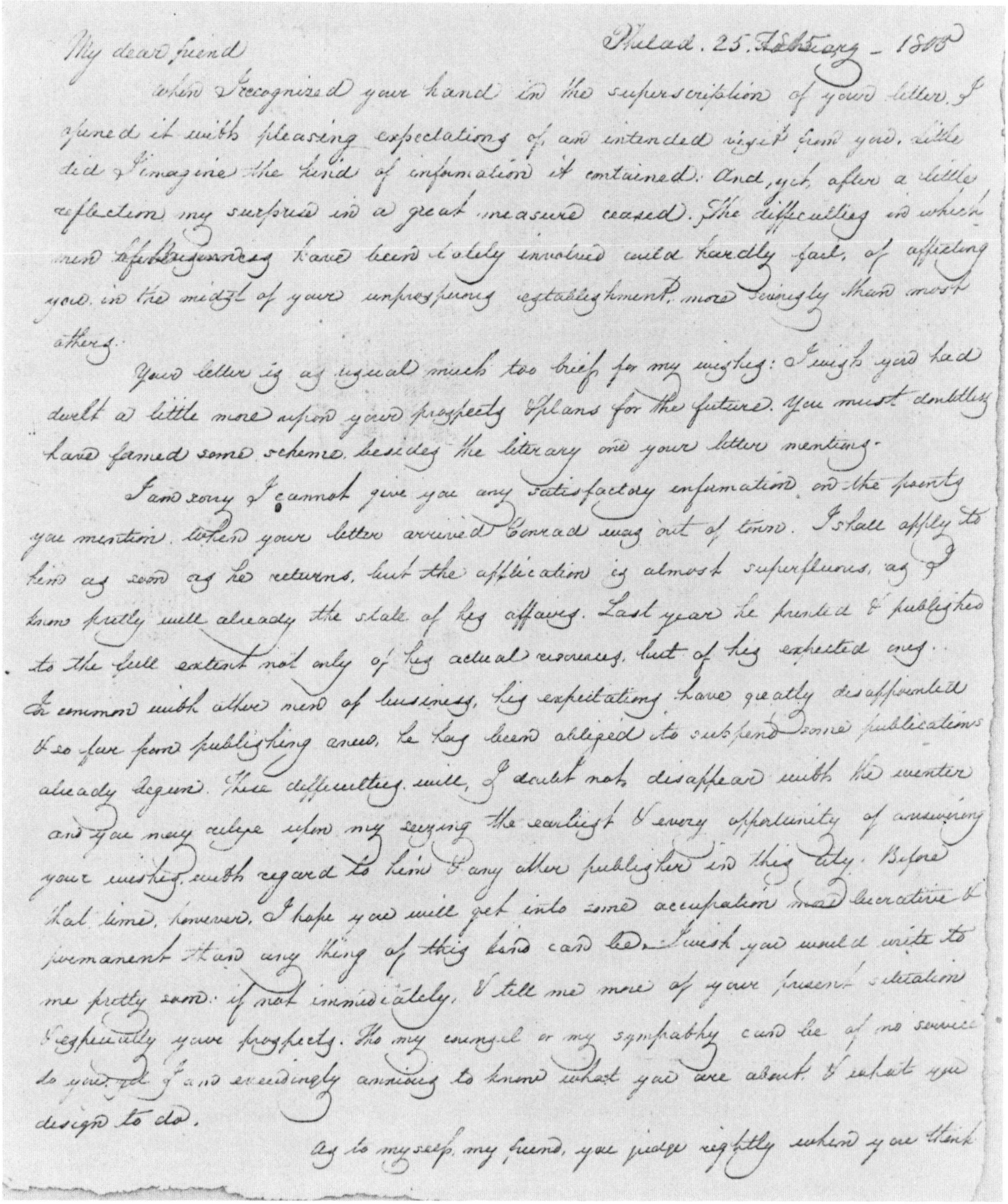

My dear friend Philad. 25 February — 1805

When I recognized your hand in the superscription of your letter, I opened it with pleasing expectations of an intended visit from you. Little did I imagine the kind of information it contained. And, yet, after a little reflection my surprise in a great measure ceased. The difficulties in which men [illegible] have been lately involved could hardly fail, of affecting you, in the midst of your unprosperous establishment, more severely than most others.

Your letter is as usual much too brief for my wishes: I wish you had dwelt a little more upon your prospects & plans for the future. You must doubtless have formed some scheme, besides the literary one your letter mentions.

I am sorry I cannot give you any satisfactory information on the points you mention. When your letter arrived Conrad was out of town. I shall apply to him as soon as he returns, but the application is almost superfluous, as I know pretty well already the state of his affairs. Last year he printed & published to the full extent not only of his actual resources, but of his expected ones. In common with other men of business, his expectations have greatly disappointed & so far from publishing anew, he has been obliged to suspend some publications already begun. These difficulties will, I doubt not, disappear with the winter and you may rely upon my seizing the earliest & every opportunity of answering your wishes, with regard to him & any other publisher in this city. Before that time, however, I hope you will get into some occupation more lucrative & permanent than any thing of this kind can be. I wish you would write to me pretty soon: if not immediately, & tell me more of your present situation & especially your prospects. Tho' my counsel or my sympathy can be of no service to you, yet I am exceedingly anxious to know what you are about, & what you design to do.

As to myself, my friend, you judge rightly when you think

Letter to William Dunlap (by permission of Special Collections, Kent State University Libraries)

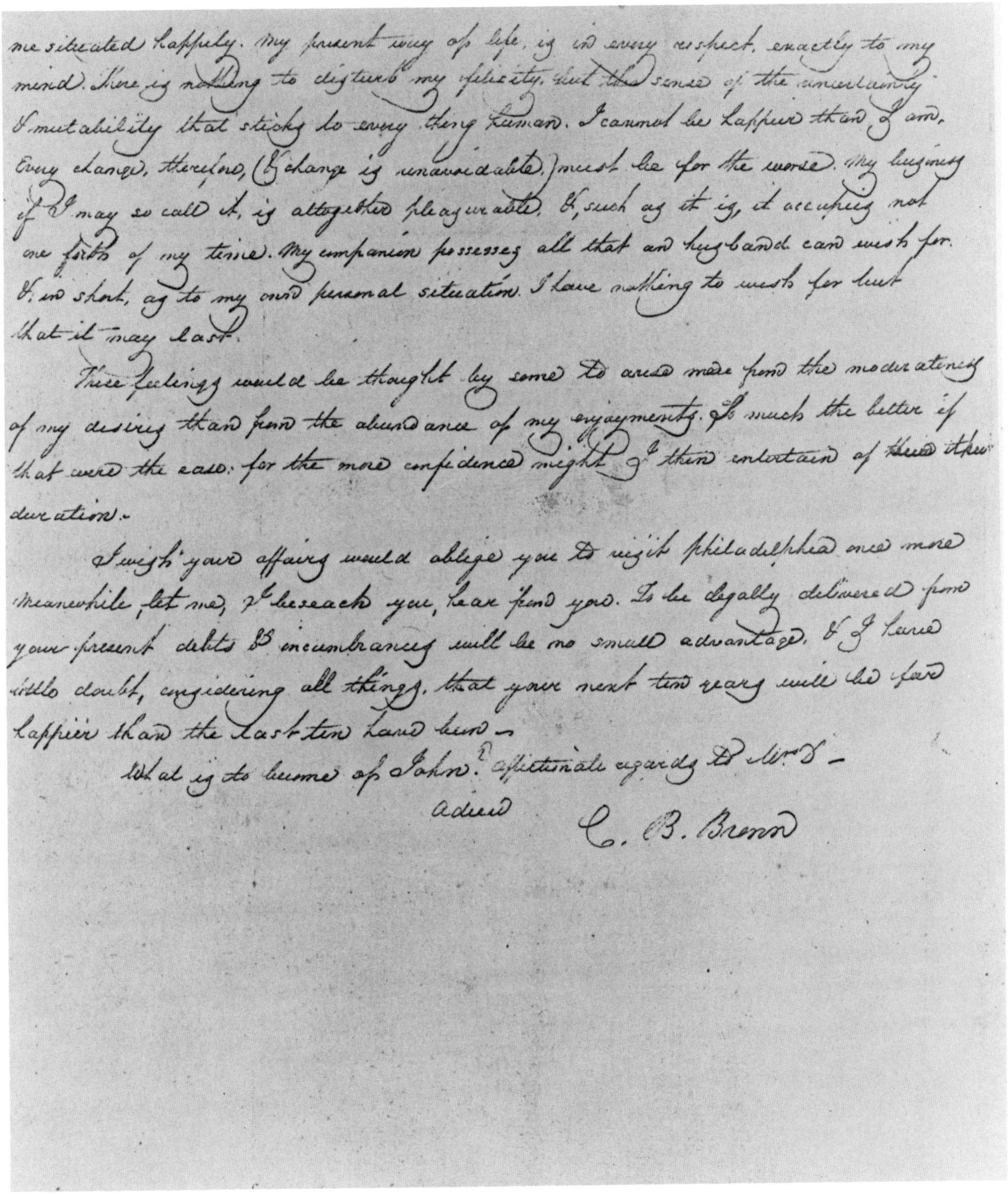

me situated happily. My present way of life, is in every respect, exactly to my mind. There is nothing to disturb my felicity, but the sense of the uncertainty & mutability that sticks to every thing human. I cannot be happier than I am. Every change, therefore, (& change is unavoidable,) must be for the worse. My business if I may so call it, is altogether pleasurable, & such as it is, it occupies not one fifth of my time. My companion possesses all that an husband can wish for. & in short, as to my own personal situation I have nothing to wish for but that it may last.

These feelings would be thought by some to arise more from the moderateness of my desires than from the abundance of my enjoyments. So much the better if that were the case: for the more confidence might I then entertain of ~~these~~ their duration.-

I wish your affairs would oblige you to visit Philadelphia once more. Meanwhile, let me, I beseech you, hear from you. To be legally delivered from your present debts & incumbrances will be no small advantage, & I have little doubt, considering all things, that your next ten years will be far happier than the last ten have been.

What is to become of John? affectionate regards to Mrs D-

adieu C. B. Brown

editorships and through the writing of his own fiction, he worked hard to support, promote, and develop an American literature, but because America in the early 1800s was not yet ready for the professional man of letters, his efforts were not rewarded with immediate results. Modern critical opinion recognizes and tries to account for the weaknesses in his work, but it finds of primary interest the ways he prefigures, both in his theory and especially in his practice of fiction, the tendencies and interests of some of America's most characteristic writers. If he was looked upon as a pioneer by those who came after, it may be because he articulated–and his efforts so well illustrated–the dilemma most American writers in the nineteenth century would feel, the conflict between art and commerce. He remains the prototype of a certain kind of tragic American artist: brilliant, gifted, erratic, naively idealistic, his imaginative gifts at war with a commercial culture, and after an early burst of creative achievement, defeat by society and a premature death.

Bibliographies:

Robert E. Hemenway and Dean H. Keller, "Charles Brockden Brown, America's First Important Novelist: A Check List of Biography and Criticism," *Papers of the Bibliographical Society of America,* 60 (1966): 349-362;

Sydney J. Krause, with assistance of Jane Nieset, "A Census of the Works of Charles Brockden Brown," *Serif,* 3, no. 4 (1966): 27-55;

Paul Witherington, "Charles Brockden Brown: A Bibliographical Essay," *Early American Literature,* 9 (Fall 1974): 164-187;

Charles E. Bennett, "The Charles Brockden Brown Canon," Ph.D dissertation, University of North Carolina at Chapel Hill, 1974;

Bennett, "The Letters of Charles Brockden Brown: An Annotated Census," *Resources for American Literary Study,* 6 (1976): 164-190;

Patricia Parker, *Charles Brockden Brown: A Reference Guide* (Boston: G. K. Hall, 1980);

Charles A. Carpenter, "Selective Bibliography of Writings about Charles Brockden Brown," in *Critical Essays on Charles Brockden Brown,* edited by Bernard Rosenthal (Boston: G. K. Hall, 1981), pp. 224-239.

Biographies:

William Dunlap,, *The Life of Charles Brockden Brown: Together With Selections from the Rarest of His Printed Works, from His Original Letters, and from His Manuscripts Before Unpublished,* 2 volumes (Philadelphia: James P. Parke, 1815);

William Hickling Prescott, "Memoir of Charles Brockden Brown, the American Novelist," in *The Library of American Biography,* edited by Jared Sparks, first series (Boston: Hilliard, Gray, 1834), I: 117-180; republished in Prescott's *Biographical and Critical Miscellanies* (New York: Harper, 1845), pp. 1-56;

Harry R. Warfel, *Charles Brockden Brown, American Gothic Novelist* (Gainesville: University of Florida Press, 1949);

David Lee Clark, *Charles Brockden Brown, Pioneer Voice of America* (Durham: Duke University Press, 1952);

Paul Allen, *The Life of Charles Brockden Brown: A Facsimile Reproduction,* edited by Charles E. Bennett (Delmar, N.Y.: Scholars' Facsimiles and Reprints, 1975); also published as *The Late Charles Brockden Brown,* edited by Robert E. Hemenway and Joseph Katz (Columbia, S.C.: Faust, 1976).

References:

Alan Axelrod, *Charles Brockden Brown: An American Tale* (Austin: University of Texas Press, 1983);

Michael Davitt Bell, " 'The Double-Tongued Deceiver': Sincerity and Duplicity in the Novels of Charles Brockden Brown," *Early American Literature,* 9 (Fall 1974): 143-163;

Warner B. Berthoff, "Adventures of the Young Man: Approach to Charles Brockden Brown," *American Quarterly,* 9 (Winter 1957): 421-434;

Berthoff, " 'A Lesson on Concealment': Brockden Brown's Method in Fiction," *Philological Quarterly,* 37 (January 1958): 45-57;

Richard Chase, *The American Novel and Its Tradition* (New York: Doubleday, 1957);

Alexander Cowie, *The Rise of the American Novel* (New York: American Book, 1948);

Leslie A. Fiedler, *Love and Death in the American Novel* (New York: Criterion Books, 1960);

Norman S. Grabo, *The Coincidental Art of Charles Brockden Brown* (Chapel Hill: University of North Carolina Press, 1981);

William L. Hedges, "Charles Brockden Brown and the Culture of Contradictions," *Early American Literature,* 9 (Fall 1974): 107-142;

R. W. B. Lewis, *The American Adam: Innocence, Tragedy, and Tradition in the Nineteenth Century* (Chicago: University of Chicago Press, 1955);

Ernest Marchand, "The Literary Opinions of Charles Brockden Brown," *Studies in Philology*, 31 (October 1934): 541-566;

Fred Lewis Pattee, *The First Century of American Literature* (New York: Appleton Century, 1935);

Donald A. Ringe, *Charles Brockden Brown* (New York: Twayne, 1966);

Bernard Rosenthal, ed., *Critical Essays on Charles Brockden Brown* (Boston: G. K. Hall, 1981);

Lulu Rumsey Wiley, *Sources and Influences in the Novels of Charles Brockden Brown* (New York: Vantage, 1950);

Larzer Ziff, "A Reading of Wieland," *PMLA*, 77 (March 1962): 51-57.

Papers:

Holdings of Brown manuscript material may be found at the University of Texas at Austin, the University of Virginia, the Historical Society of Pennsylvania in Philadelphia, and Bowdoin College.

Orestes A. Brownson

(16 September 1803-17 April 1876)

Roger Lips

University of Minnesota at Duluth

See also the Brownson entry in *DLB 1, The American Renaissance in New England.*

BOOKS: *An Address, on the Fifty-fifth Anniversary of American Independence Delivered at Ovid, Seneca Co. N.Y. July 4, 1831* (Ithaca: S. S. Chatterton, 1831);

An Address on Intemperance, Delivered in Walpole, N.H. February 26, 1833 (Keene, N.H.: J. & J. Prentiss, 1833);

An Address, Delivered at Dedham, on the Fifty-eighth Anniversary of American Independence, July 4, 1834 (Dedham, Mass.: H. Mann, 1834);

A Sermon Delivered to the Young People of the First Congregational Society in Canton, on Sunday, May 24th, 1835 (Dedham, Mass.: H. Mann, 1835);

New Views of Christianity, Society, and the Church (Boston: James Munroe, 1836);

A Discourse on the Wants of the Times, Delivered in Lyceum Hall, Hanover Street, Boston, Sunday, May 29, 1836 (Boston: James Munroe, 1836);

Babylon is Falling. A Discourse Preached in the Masonic Temple, to the Society for Christian Union and Progress, on Sunday Morning, May 28, 1837 (Boston: I. R. Butts, 1837);

An Address Delivered on Popular Education. Delivered in Winnisimmet Village, on Sunday Evening, July 23, 1837 (Boston: John Putnam, 1837);

An Oration Delivered Before the United Brothers Society of Brown University, at Providence, R.I., September 3, 1839 (Cambridge: Metcalf, Torry & Ballou, 1839);

Brownson's Defence. Defence of the Article on the Laboring Classes (Boston: Benjamin H. Greene, 1840);

Charles Elwood: or the Infidel Converted (Boston: Little, Brown, 1840; London: Chapman Brothers, 1845);

The Labouring Classes, an Article from the Boston Quarterly Review (Boston: Benjamin H. Greene, 1840);

An Oration before the Democracy of Worcester and Vicinity, Delivered at Worcester, Mass., July 4, 1840 (Boston: E. Littlefield/Worcester: M. D. Phillips, 1840);

The Policy to be Pursued Hereafter by the Friends of the Constitution, and of Equal Rights (Boston: Benjamin H. Greene, 1841);

A Review of Mr. Parker's Discourse on the Transient and Permanent in Christianity (Boston: Benjamin H. Greene, 1841);

Oration of Orestes A. Brownson, Delivered at Washing-

ton Hall, July 5th, 1841 (New York: G. Washfington Dixon, 1841);
Constitutional Government (Boston: Benjamin H. Greene, 1842);
The Mediatorial Life of Jesus. A Letter to Rev. William Ellery Channing, D.D. (Boston: Little, Brown, 1842);
An Oration on the Scholar's Mission (Boston: Benjamin H. Greene, 1843);
Social Reform. An Address before the Society of the Mystical Seven in the Wesleyan University, Middletown, Conn. August 7, 1844 (Boston: Waite, Peirce, 1844);
A Review of the Sermon by Dr. Potts, on the Dangers of Jesuit Instruction, Preached at the Second Presbyterian Church, St. Louis, on the 25th September, 1845 (St. Louis: "News-Letter" Publication Office, 1846);
Essays and Reviews Chiefly on Theology, Politics, and Socialism (New York, Boston & Montreal: D. & J. Sadlier, 1852);
An Oration on Liberal Studies, Delivered before the Philomathian Society, of Mount Saint Mary's College, MD., June 29th, 1853 (Baltimore: Hedian & O'Brien, 1853);
The Spirit-Rapper; an Autobiography (Boston: Little, Brown/London: Charles Dolman, 1854);
The Convert: or, Leaves from My Experience (New York: D. & J. Sadlier, 1857; New York: Edward Dunigan, 1857);
The War for the Union. Speech by Dr. O. A. Brownson. How the War Should Be Prosecuted. The Duty of the Government and the Duty of the Citizen (New York: George F. Nesbitt, 1862);
The American Republic: Its Constitution, Tendencies, and Destiny (New York: P. O'Shea, 1865);
Conversations on Liberalism and the Church (New York: D. & J. Sadlier/Boston & Montreal: P. H. Brady, 1870);
An Essay in Refutation of Atheism, edited by Henry F. Brownson (Detroit: Thorndike, Nourse, 1882);
Uncle Jack and His Nephew; or Conversations of an Old Fogy with a Young American, edited by Henry F. Brownson (Detroit: H. F. Brownson, 1888);
The Two Brothers; or Why are You a Protestant?, edited by Henry F. Brownson (Detroit: H. F. Brownson, 1888).

Collections: *The Work of Orestes A. Brownson,* edited by Henry F. Brownson, 20 volumes: volumes 1-19 (Detroit: Thorndike Nourse, 1882-1887); volume 20 (Detroit: Henry F. Brownson, 1887);
Literary, Scientific, and Political Views of Orestes A. Brownson, edited by Henry F. Brownson (New York: Benziger, 1893);
Orestes Brownson: Selected Essays, edited by Russell Kirk (Chicago: Regnery, 1955);
The Brownson Reader, edited by Arvan S. Ryan (New York: P. J. Kenedy, 1955).

Orestes Augustus Brownson, a provincial Vermont man of hardscrabble origins, was welcomed into the tight, aristocratic circle of Boston Unitarian society by eminences such as William Ellery Channing and George Ripley, and he helped to start the Transcendental Club. In 1840 he wrote the best apologia of Transcendentalism against the charge of infidelity by Andrews Norton. His impoverished youth denied him formal schooling, but the self-taught man read and thought so widely that he wrote with hard-hitting authority about economics, religion, politics, philosophy, history, theology, and literature. Boston was replete with exciting intellectuals when he arrived, but his effective preaching, his knowledge of European philosophy, and his forceful style of conversation and journalism combined to make him a significant influence on Protestant intellectuals of Boston until 1844 when he became Catholic. Important enough for a section in *A Fable for Critics . . .* (1864), Brownson is praised by James Russell Lowell for his forceful prose and chided for his "weathercock" changes of opinion. He enjoyed debate and participated vigorously in intellectual groups, but he wielded influence mainly through his *Boston Quarterly Review,* which had roughly one thousand readers. Its admirers included Theodore Parker, Bronson Alcott, George Ripley, and William H. Channing. Perry Miller thought it the best journal of its time and deplored the "inexplicable negligence" with which historians have treated it. Publishing *Boston Quarterly Review* for five years with little help, a weary Brownson merged it with the *Democratic Review* in 1842 and served that important journal for a year as coeditor and contributor of unsigned book reviews and signed articles, some politically controversial.

When he became Catholic, Brownson abruptly lost most of his Protestant readers, but he became the first important Catholic journalist in the U.S. and created a new audience for his ideas by founding *Brownson's Quarterly Review* in Boston in 1844. Not an original thinker,

Brownson wrote methodical, lengthy discussions evaluating well the worth of other people's ideas. The most rigorous philosopher of the Transcendentalists, he always displayed a sternly logical and analytical mind, and he expressed his conclusions bluntly and candidly. His good opinion could be bought only with the coin of intellectual merit. *Boston Quarterly Review* featured the most independent journalistic voice in America, but Brownson compromised his independence during the first ten years of *Brownson's Quarterly Review* when he submitted his issues for prepublication review by Boston's Bishop Fitzpatrick. However, after 1854 he discontinued this practice. Articulating unpopular positions was his lifelong habit, and he made enemies as much by his manner of argument as by his opinions. He was disputatious, forceful, unyielding. Whether speaking or writing, he hoped to teach society by identifying errors of fact or reasoning and by passionately presenting his intellectual values. He never understood that he gained almost no converts because he alienated people.

Brownson reviewed more than five hundred books in his long career, but relatively few volumes of poetry or fiction. He probably discussed whatever publishers sent him, because few of the books he discussed are among the significant literary publications of his time. Before 1844 his literary criticism, strongly reflecting his liberal political views, announced him as America's first sociological critic, and some sentences seem almost Marxist. His literary criticism after his 1844 conversion established Brownson as the best nineteenth-century Catholic critic, an accomplishment made less significant because he often chose to evaluate insignificant novels. His strength as a literary critic was his assessment of the worth of ideas, and his weakness was that he usually failed to provide adequate discussion of the artistic form. Moreover, when he discussed a book's ideas, he usually decided their social and religious utility according to his own biases. His discussions of literature do not remain centered on artistic concerns but often shift to matters deemed more important by Brownson. Once he wrote tellingly: "But we have forgotten the little book before us." While his literary reviews are filled with acute comments about many authors, he provided only short discussions explaining his criteria. No Brownson essay sets out a coherent theory of literary criticism, although, because of his talent for philosophy and his ability to compose long essays rapidly, he could easily have written at length about critical theory. He did not partly because he thought literature's impact was largely emotional, that it seized (or failed to seize) the reader's appreciation in a manner which defies rational analysis. His omission can be further explained by things he wrote about himself: he thought he had read too narrowly to be an expert literary critic; he thought his deficiency of artistic talent made him less competent to judge art; and he preferred to give his best journalistic effort to other subjects, especially philosophy and theology.

Born in 1803 in Stockbridge, Vermont, he grew up on a farm raised by elderly foster parents, Congregationalists, who taught him to read at home using their few books, which included a

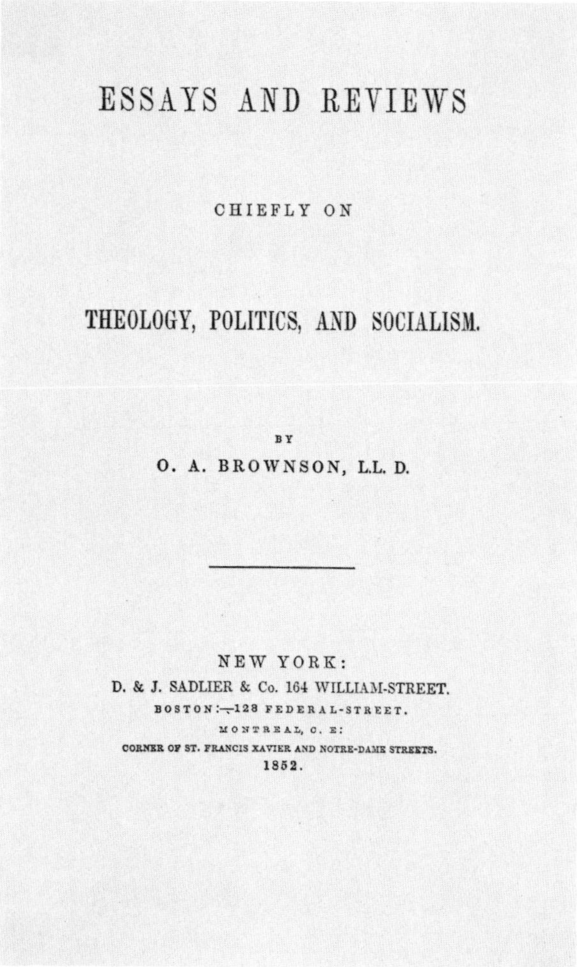
ESSAYS AND REVIEWS

CHIEFLY ON

THEOLOGY, POLITICS, AND SOCIALISM.

BY

O. A. BROWNSON, LL. D.

NEW YORK:
D. & J. SADLIER & Co. 164 WILLIAM-STREET.
BOSTON:—128 FEDERAL-STREET.
MONTREAL, C. E:
CORNER OF ST. FRANCIS XAVIER AND NOTRE-DAME STREETS.
1852.

Title page for a collection of Brownson's essays first published in his Quarterly Review. *In the preface Brownson cautions the reader not to look "for something new, original, or striking" in his work.*

King James Bible and the *History of the Work of Redemption* (1774) by Jonathan Edwards. Brownson quickly read all books in his community and astounded adults with his ability to discuss them. In 1817 his mother decided to move her children to Ballston Spa in upstate New York where Orestes received some months of schooling and where he apprenticed as a printer. In 1822 a religious experience led him to become a Presbyterian, and he decided to earn his living as a teacher. Four years later, after teaching in Michigan and New York, he changed his religion and became a Universalist preacher at Jaffrey, New Hampshire. Soon rejecting Universalism, he became interested in social reform according to the ideas of Robert Dale Owen and Frances Wright, and he worked to advance their ideas in New York State through his efforts for the Workingmen's party. By 1831 he was a nondenominational minister in Ithaca, but he became a fervent admirer of William Ellery Channing's writing. In 1832 he became a Unitarian minister, serving first at Walpole, New Hampshire, and later, in 1834, at Canton, Massachusetts, where Henry Thoreau was a temporary lodger while teaching. Thoreau later described their relationship as "an era in my life–the morning of a new Lebenstag."

Drawn to the intellectual life of Boston, he moved there in 1836 to become Unitarian minister for the Society of Christian Union and Progress. His church services attempted to bring working-class people into Unitarian membership, work he enjoyed partly due to his own impoverished origins and partly because of his enthusiasm for the ideas of Frances Wright and Robert Owen. He quickly gained access to the Boston intelligentsia, his membership sponsored by William Ellery Channing and George Ripley, who admired his published essays and vigorous conversation. Soon his literary skills demanded most of his time. In 1838 he left the ministry, supported financially by a patronage position at the United States Marine Hospital at Chelsea, Massachusetts.

His publishing career began in 1826 when he contributed to the *Gospel Advocate* and became corresponding editor of the *Free Enquirer.* In 1828 he became editor of the *Gospel Advocate* and in 1829 of the *Genesee Republican.* In 1831 he ceased writing for these papers when he became a Unitarian and began publishing the *Philanthropist.* That, too, he soon dropped to write for three Boston magazines (the *Unitarian,* the *Christian Register,* and the *Christian Examiner*) where his contributions soon gained him many admirers. In 1836 he became editor of the *Boston Reformer.* Also that year he published his first book, *New Views of Christianity, Society, and the Church,* a work of intellectual and religious history critical of rational Unitarianism. A few years later he published a fictionalized account of his religious development, *Charles Elwood: or the Infidel Converted* (1840). Edgar Allan Poe said that "few theological treatises . . . can be compared to it."

His greatest achievement during 1838-1842 was the *Boston Quarterly Review,* most of which he wrote. The periodical discussed politics, philosophy, religion, literature, and economics. All his essays reflected Brownson's strong liberal biases, as represented by his remarkable 1840 essay on "The Labouring Classes." A *Boston Quarterly Re-*

view issue usually contained one long review article concerning literature. Authors discussed included John Greenleaf Whittier, Thomas Carlyle, Ralph Waldo Emerson, William Wordsworth, Edward George Bulwer-Lytton, Theodore Parker, and Nathaniel Hawthorne. The amount of literary criticism, as well as the manner, shows that Brownson regarded literary criticism as relatively unimportant. His reviews not only lack adequate critical theory, they lack the rich sufficiency of comparative literary judgments which marks the best critics of an era. Often he uses the book reviewed merely as a springboard from which to launch into discussions of his own ideas. Many reviews include only a few illustrative quotes from the literature being discussed, and many contain only scant analysis of aspects of form of works being evaluated.

One Brownson principle is that literature is good when its ideas seem true. Whittier is praised for his humanitarian concern and for promoting universal freedom in America in an essay published in January 1838. But the essay states that, regarding the structure of Whittier's verse and his skill in the art of verse making, "We have nothing to say." In another essay published in July of the same year, he praises Cooper's *The American Democrat* because he values the book's political ideas. For example, he notes with pleasure that Cooper discusses the danger to American democracy caused by wealthy Americans, aristocratic in their sympathies, who do not support free institutions.

Another principle of his *Boston Quarterly Review* criticism is that the best American literature is anti-aristocratic. He boldly stated in an essay published in April of that year that: "Aristocracy dies in this country the day it loses the aid of our literature." Brownson wanted an American democratic literature contrasting with what he perceived as "aristocratic" English literature "deficient in true reverence for man as man." Brownson goes on in this essay to criticize American authors who are literary vassals of England: "Our literature is tame and servile, wanting in freshness, freedom, and originality." His writing before 1844 reflects his attention to what authors say about various societal classes and what class they favor. He believed that literature in a democracy has no value unless it aims to function as a means of individual and societal growth and reform.

The criticism of the *Boston Quarterly Review* also demanded that literature should be the expression of the artist's community and his time. Discussing Emerson in 1839 Brownson rejected the idea that literature is the product of a few solitary geniuses. He believed the intellectual community should stimulate the masses to "wake up just sentiments, quicken elevated thoughts in them," and one result would be the appearance of worthy artists. Literature is a by-product of the intellectual and social development of society. Brownson scorned writers without social purpose and even those living apart from society.

In this period, as well as later, Brownson evaluated literature by considering the source of its inspiration. Religion and art were inseparable for Brownson. Consistent with his transcendentalism, he insisted that poets receive truth intuitively from God. In an article published in April of that year he says the poet is "seer," guiding others by a divine sentiment "not distinguishable from the religious sentiment." He added a sociological turn to this doctrine in insisting that the masses support poets whose wisdom they approve. Thus he said that because Wordsworth lacked inspiration, a result was "great want of popularity" with the masses.

Another Brownson standard is that a literary work must exhibit an obvious moral tendency without exhibiting explicit didacticism and/or dogmatism. Thus, he criticized writers such as Goethe and Scott for deficiency of morality whereas he praised Bulwer-Lytton for writing fiction with moral purpose. Brownson constantly thought about the potential effect of a book on society. In relation to this principle, before 1844 he always found more to praise in Emerson's writing than to blame, despite many disagreements with his ideas, because he believed that moral purpose undergirded Emerson's writing.

Brownson yearned for original, distinctively American literature, but he was unable to define well the characteristics he expected, except that in 1840 he thought uniquely American writing should portray the struggle between the rich and the poor. One of his most significant *Boston Quarterly Review* discussions of literature, published in January 1840, attacks American literary imitation of and dependency on English models. Nothing was more certain to him than that writers "who create a national literature, must be filled with the spirit of the nation."

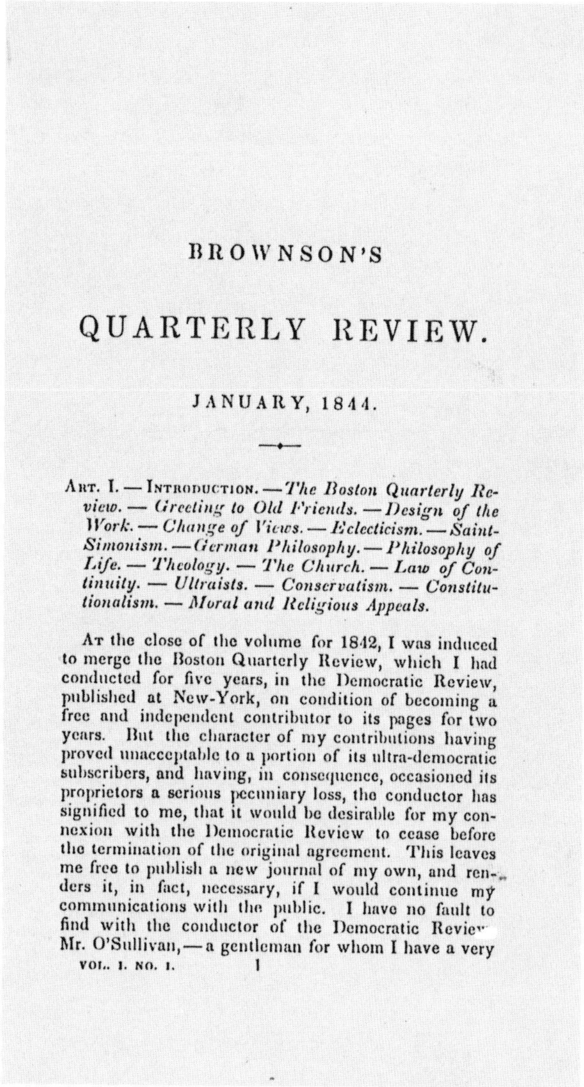

BROWNSON'S

QUARTERLY REVIEW.

JANUARY, 1844.

Art. I. — Introduction. — *The Boston Quarterly Review. — Greeting to Old Friends. — Design of the Work. — Change of Views. — Eclecticism. — Saint-Simonism. — German Philosophy. — Philosophy of Life. — Theology. — The Church. — Law of Continuity. — Ultraists. — Conservatism. — Constitutionalism. — Moral and Religious Appeals.*

At the close of the volume for 1842, I was induced to merge the Boston Quarterly Review, which I had conducted for five years, in the Democratic Review, published at New-York, on condition of becoming a free and independent contributor to its pages for two years. But the character of my contributions having proved unacceptable to a portion of its ultra-democratic subscribers, and having, in consequence, occasioned its proprietors a serious pecuniary loss, the conductor has signified to me, that it would be desirable for my connexion with the Democratic Review to cease before the termination of the original agreement. This leaves me free to publish a new journal of my own, and renders it, in fact, necessary, if I would continue my communications with the public. I have no fault to find with the conductor of the Democratic Review, Mr. O'Sullivan,—a gentleman for whom I have a very

VOL. I. NO. I. 1

First page of the first issue of the periodical that Brownson founded after his ties with the Democratic Review *were severed*

Because he was a skilled philosopher, to the extent that a literary work happened to contain explicit philosophy, his expectations rose. His article on Emerson's *Essays* displays an interesting struggle within Brownson as he tries to praise Emerson as the good man who loves humanity and writes with moral purpose and poetic expression, while at the same time Brownson bluntly disparages the philosophy which "explains nothing, accounts for nothing, solves no intellectual problems, and affords no practical instruction."

One author generously praised in the columns of the *Boston Quarterly Review* is Hawthorne. A short review of *Twice-Told Tales* (1837) says that he is "fitted to stand at the head of American literature"; his stories display moral purpose, tender sympathy and love for all people, vigorous intellect, as well as wit and humor. Moreover, Brownson admired Hawthorne's ability to render the wild and picturesque natural beauty of America. Had it offered more than fulsome praise for someone Brownson regarded as a kindred spirit, this review might have helped to establish his reputation as a critic. Yet he merely praised the book without articulating critical principles or extending his review with analysis of specific passages and formal aspects of the stories. Many a nonliterary subject would draw out of Brownson a careful, thirty-page analysis, but Hawthorne's artistry could not.

After the presidential election of 1840, Brownson began to lose faith in the masses. He became noticeably more conservative in politics and religion and wrote *The Mediatorial Life of Jesus* (1842). His need for religious certainty brought him to Catholicism in 1844, the year he began *Brownson's Quarterly Review.* After his conversion he also published several books: the novel *The Spirit-Rapper* (1854); *The Convert* (1857); and a book on political thought, *The American Republic* (1865).

His literary criticism after 1844 was written mostly for *Brownson's Quarterly Review,* published from 1844 to 1864 and from 1873 to 1875. That he wrote to American Catholics can be seen in his topics and manner of argument. Catholicism changed his literary criticism. He wrote less about the conflict between rich and poor, although he continued to consider the social effect of literature. His essays displayed more interest in the struggle between spiritual forces and secular forces in society. He displayed less respect for each writer's individual, inner, moral voice because he expected literature to express ideas consistent with Catholic theology. His style of argument reflected his study and acceptance of scholastic theology. He realized novels were increasingly influential so he reviewed many, but without much attention to their quality. For example, he reviewed *The Blakes and Flanigans* by J. Sadlier, apparently because it enabled him to discuss the parochial behavior of Irish Catholics with regard to Catholic schools (April 1856). Because of the book's "high moral aim," he called it a "work of genius."

He continued to be modest about his literary criticism, saying, "We have little literary taste or literary culture" (July 1852). In fact he failed to discuss most of the important literature published during the years of *Brownson's Quarterly Review,* including books by Thoreau, Melville, Whitman, Poe. While he reviewed favorably one book by Cooper, he ignored his best novels. He largely ignored most of England's major nineteenth-century authors, except Reade, and depreciated writers such as Dickens and Trollope, blaming them for sentimentalism and sympathetic portrayals of immoral behavior. While his obiter dicta extolled the stylistic merits of English writers such as Chaucer, Spenser, Shakespeare, Milton, Pope, and Dryden, he never explained adequately his reasons. The eccentricity of his judgment is seen in his celebration of Daniel Webster's writing as an ideal mixture of truth and good style. In a lengthy review of Webster's six-volume *Works,* he suggested that Webster was without rival in secular American literature (July 1852).

The Catholic Brownson measured literature by a test of faith and morals. He said, "art simply as art is indifferent to good or evil," becoming one or the other according to its thought. The standard by which to test whether its thought is good is "always and everywhere Christian faith and morals" (January 1849). When he reviewed Emerson's *Poems* and Hawthorne's *The Scarlet Letter,* he praised aspects of these books, but he warned readers against their profane content. Emerson's poems failed to meet his first test of art because "they embody a doctrine essentially false," and some are "hymns to the devil" (April 1847). Similarly he warned that *The Scarlet Letter* may corrupt readers by making immorality seem attractive. Arthur and Hester never repent but instead "hug their illicit love" (October 1850). He defended the novelist's right to show evil behavior, but not the novelist's right to create sympathy for that behavior. He disapproved of realist writers who portrayed human vices and familiarized readers with them (January 1873).

However, he expected moral literature not only to avoid explicit didacticism, but also the mixture of "the sentimental story, and the grave religious discussion." *Brownson's Quarterly Review* essays attack sentimentalism as dangerous to good character because it "subverts the judgment and lays open the heart to every temptation" (January 1847). Brownson thought explicit discussion of religion should be written in nonfiction prose, "the natural language of the understanding." He regarded the novel, along with poetry, as having

Orestes Brownson

as its primary aim to "move and please" (January 1848). In the style and matter of its presentation, art properly aims at sentiments, that is, the emotions. However, he praised the literature of profane love which is implicitly religious without using explicit dogma, such as may be found in European literature in the Middle Ages.

Brownson sometimes wrote diatribes against women such as, "The curse of the age is its femininity" (July 1864). He harshly criticized many women novelists who "produce so large a share of modern popular literature" because he thought they too frequently used sentimentalism, which damages "mind and heart" (July 1875). One such was Lady Georgiana Fullerton, a Catholic, who wrote *Grantley Manor* with "too much sighing, weeping." Elsewhere he criticized Fullerton for being one of the women novelists who "degrade" women in their fictional portrayals by "the recklessness with which they reveal the mysteries of the sex, expose all her little feminine arts and tricks."

Brownson observed with discouragement in essays of *Brownson's Quarterly Review* that an increasing percentage of the literature published in magazines and novels represented the work of an emerging class of professional writers without social, moral, or intellectual purpose. Commercial authors who write for profit to amuse the public seemed to him "one of the greatest pests of modern society."

Twentieth-century admirers of Brownson include eminences such as Arthur Schlesinger, Jr., and Perry Miller. In recent years many scholars have thoroughly reevaluated his accomplishments. Probably his future reputation will depend on his contributions to other subject areas than literary criticism. His criticism, while better than most written for periodicals of his time, seems today woefully inadequate in its treatment of form and too intolerant of ideas with which Brownson disagreed. Too many words of his reviews are used for digressions, egotistic displays of personal opinions, and needless attacks on opposing viewpoints. Another major weakness is the poor selection of books Brownson chose for discussion. Since Brownson himself was explicitly ambivalent about the importance of literature and his own literary criticism, he would not be surprised to find his criticism ranked behind that of Poe, Emerson, and Whitman. Yet the sheer bulk of his criticism, the intellectual seriousness with which he handled every discussion, and the force of his thought make many of his reviews worthwhile reading for specialists in nineteenth-century American literature.

Letters:

Daniel Ramon Barnes, "An Edition of the Early Letters of Orestes Brownson," Ph.D dissertation, University of Kentucky, 1970;

The Brownson-Hecker Correspondence, edited by Joseph F. Gower and Richard M. Leliaert (Notre Dame: University of Notre Dame Press, 1979).

Biographies:

Henry F. Brownson, *Orestes A. Brownson's Early Life, From 1803-1844; Orestes A. Brownson's Middle Life, From 1845-1855; Orestes A. Brownson's Late Life, From 1856-1876,* 3 volumes (Detroit: H. F. Brownson, 1898-1900);

Arthur M. Schlesinger, Jr., *Orestes A. Brownson: A Pilgrim's Progress* (Boston: Little, Brown, 1939);

Theodore Maynard, *Orestes Brownson: Yankee, Radical, Catholic* (New York: Macmillan, 1943);

Thomas R. Ryan, *Orestes A. Brownson: A Definitive Biography* (Huntington, Ind.: Our Sunday Visitor, 1976).

References:

A. R. Caponigri, "Brownson and Emerson: Nature and History," *New England Quarterly,* 18 (September 1945): 368-390;

Octavius Brooks Frothingham, *Transcendentalism in New England* (New York: Putnam's, 1876);

Leonard Gilhooley, *Contradiction and Dilemma: Orestes Brownson and the American Idea* (New York: Fordham University Press, 1972);

Gilhooley, ed., *No Divided Allegiance: Essays in Brownson's Thought* (New York: Fordham University Press, 1980);

Clarence L. Gohdes, *The Periodicals of American Transcendentalism* (Durham: Duke University Press, 1931);

C. Carol Hollis, "The Literary Criticism of Orestes Brownson," Ph.D dissertation, University of Michigan, 1954;

Alexander Kern, "The Rise of Transcendentalism: 1818-1860," in *Transitions in American Literary History,* edited by Harry Hayden Clark (Durham: Duke University Press, 1953), pp. 245-314;

Russell Kirk, *The Conservative Mind From Burke to Santayana* (Chicago: Regnery, 1953);

Americo D. Lapati, *Orestes A. Brownson* (New York: Twayne, 1965);

Virgil Michel, "The Critical Principles of Orestes A. Brownson," Ph.D dissertation, Catholic University of America, 1918;

Perry Miller, *The American Transcendentalists, Their Prose and Poetry* (Garden City: Doubleday, 1957);

Miller, *The Transcendentalists, An Anthology* (Cambridge, Mass.: Harvard University Press, 1960);

Joel Myerson, ed., *The Transcendentalists* (New York: Modern Language Association of America, 1984);

Alvan S. Ryan, "Orestes Brownson: The Critique of Transcendentalism," in *American Classics Reconsidered: A Christian Appraisal,* edited by Harold C. Gardiner (New York: Scribners, 1958), pp. 98-120;

Chester Soleta, "The Literary Criticism of O. A. Brownson," *Review of Politics,* 16 (July 1954): 334-351;

Per Sveino, *Orestes A. Brownson's Road to Catholicism* (New York: Humanities Press, 1970);

René Wellek, "The Minor Transcendentalists and German Philosophy," *New England Quarterly*, 15 (December 1942): 652-680.

Papers:

The major collection of Orestes A. Brownson papers is held by the University of Notre Dame Archives which produced a nineteen-roll microfilm copy of letters by Brownson, drafts of essays and books by Brownson, letters to or about Brownson, and newspaper clippings concerning him. Besides the University of Notre Dame collection, other Brownson manuscripts exist in the Archives of the Paulist Fathers, St. Paul's Church, New York City; Library of Congress; Harvard University Libraries; Birmingham Oratory, Birmingham, England; Pius XII Memorial Library, St. Louis, Missouri.

William Cullen Bryant

(3 November 1794-12 June 1878)

William J. Free
University of Georgia

See also the Bryant entries in *DLB 3, Antebellum Writers in New York and the South* and *DLB 43, American Newspaper Journalists, 1690-1872.*

SELECTED BOOKS: *The Embargo; or, Sketches of the Times; A Satire; by a Youth of Thirteen*, anonymous (Boston: Printed for the purchasers, 1808); second edition, corrected and enlarged, as Bryant (Boston: Printed for the author by E. G. House, 1809);

An Oration, Delivered at Stockbridge. July 4th, 1820 (Stockbridge, Mass.: Printed by Charles Webster, 1820);

Poems (Cambridge: Printed by Hilliard & Metcalf, 1821);

Poems, by William Cullen Bryant, An American (New York: E. Bliss, 1832); edited by Washington Irving (London: J. Andrews, 1832); expanded (Boston: Russell, Odiorne & Metcalf/Philadelphia: Marshall, Clark, 1834);

The Fountain and Other Poems (New York & London: Wiley & Putnam, 1842);

An Address to the People of the United States in Behalf of the American Copyright Club, attributed to Bryant, Francis L. Hawks, and Cornelius Mathews (New York, 1843);

The White-Footed Deer and Other Poems (New York: I. S. Platt, 1844);

A Funeral Oration, Occasioned by the Death of Thomas Cole, Delivered before the National Academy of Design, New-York, May 4, 1848 (New York & Philadelphia: Appleton, 1848);

Letters of a Traveller; or, Notes of Things Seen in Europe and America (New York: Putnam's, 1850);

Reminiscences of the Evening Post: Extracted from the Evening Post of November 15, 1851. With Additions and Corrections by the Writer (New York: William C. Bryant, 1851);

Letters of a Traveller. Second Series (New York: D. Appleton, 1859);

A Discourse on the Life, Character and Genius of Washington Irving, Delivered before the New York Historical Society on the 3d of April, 1860 (New York: Putnam's, 1860);

Thirty Poems (New York: D. Appleton, 1864);

Letters from the East (New York: Putnam's, 1869);

Some Notices of the Life and Writings of Fitz-Greene Halleck, Read Before the New York Historical Society, on the 3d of February, 1869 (New York, 1869);

A Discourse on the Life, Character and Writings of Gulian Crommelin Verplanck, Delivered before the New-York Historical Society, May 17th, 1870 (New York: The Society, 1870);

Orations and Addresses by William Cullen Bryant (New York: Putnam's, 1873);

Thanatopsis. (A Poem.) (New York: D. Appleton, 1874);

Among the Trees, by William Cullen Bryant, Illustrated from Designs by Jervis McEntee, Engraved by Harley (New York: Putnam's, 1874);

Tremaine McDowell, ed., *William Cullen Bryant:*

William Cullen Bryant, circa 1845; from a daguerreotype attributed to Mathew Brady (courtesy of William Cullen Bryant II)

Representative Selections, with Introduction, Bibliography, and Notes (New York & Cincinnati: American Book Company, 1935).

Collections: *Poems,* edited by Bryant, 2 volumes (New York & London: Appleton, 1855);

The Life and Works of William Cullen Bryant, 6 volumes, edited, with a biography, by Parke Godwin (New York: D. Appleton, 1883-1884).

OTHER: *The American Landscape, No. 1,* with contributions by Bryant (New York: E. Bliss, 1830);

Tales of Glauber-Spa, edited, with contributions, by Bryant (New York: Harper, 1832);

The Iliad of Homer. Translated into English Blank Verse, translated by Bryant, 2 volumes (Boston: Fields, Osgood, 1870);

A Library of Poetry and Song: Being Choice Selections from the Best Poets, edited by Bryant (New York: J. B. Ford, 1871);

The Odyssey of Homer, translated by Bryant, 2 volumes (Boston: James R. Osgood, 1871-1872);

Sidney Howard Gay, *A Popular History of the United States, from the First Discovery of the Western Hemisphere by the Northmen, to the End of the First Century of the Union of States,* introduction by Bryant, 4 volumes (New York: Scribner, Armstrong, 1876-1881).

In 1813 William Cullen Bryant, then a law student at Yale University, had a run-in with his tutor, Samuel Howe. Howe had caught Bryant reading William Wordsworth's *Lyrical Ballads* and warned young Cullen not to waste his time. From the standpoint of the history of American poetry the time was not wasted, but Bryant's submission to the authority of the then-popular English romantics caused later generations to dismiss his criticism as derivative, as a mere recasting of his youthful reading. However, Bryant's reading was far more extensive than his detractors knew. In addition to Wordsworth Bryant was familiar with the critical works of John Dryden, Alexander Pope, and Samuel Johnson, Archibald Alison's *Essays on the Nature and Principles of Taste* (1790), Edmund Burke's *A Philosophical Inquiry into the Origin of Our Ideas of the Sublime and Beautiful* (1757), the essays of the Scotch rhetoricians, and a smattering of the Greek and Latin classic theorists.

Bryant was born into a family in which books and literature were an everyday part of life. His father, physician Peter Bryant, wrote verse in both Latin and English and owned a well-stocked library in which Cullen read from his early childhood. His mother, Sarah Snell, a Mayflower descendant, taught Cullen his alphabet at eighteen months and tutored him in Latin throughout his childhood. Peter Bryant served terms in both houses of the Massachusetts legislature, which brought young Cullen into contact with Boston literary society. In 1809 Bryant prepared to enter Williams College by studying extensively with two tutors, Rev. Thomas Snell for Latin and Rev. Moses Hallock for Greek. Disillusioned with Williams, he spent the summer of 1811 reading to prepare for the junior class at Yale. His encounter with Wordsworth was simply part of a long and thorough literary education.

Like most poets-critics, Bryant wrote criticism to lay a theoretical foundation for his own poetry. In 1817 Bryant, a practicing attorney in his mid twenties, established himself as a promising American poet by the publication of an early ver-

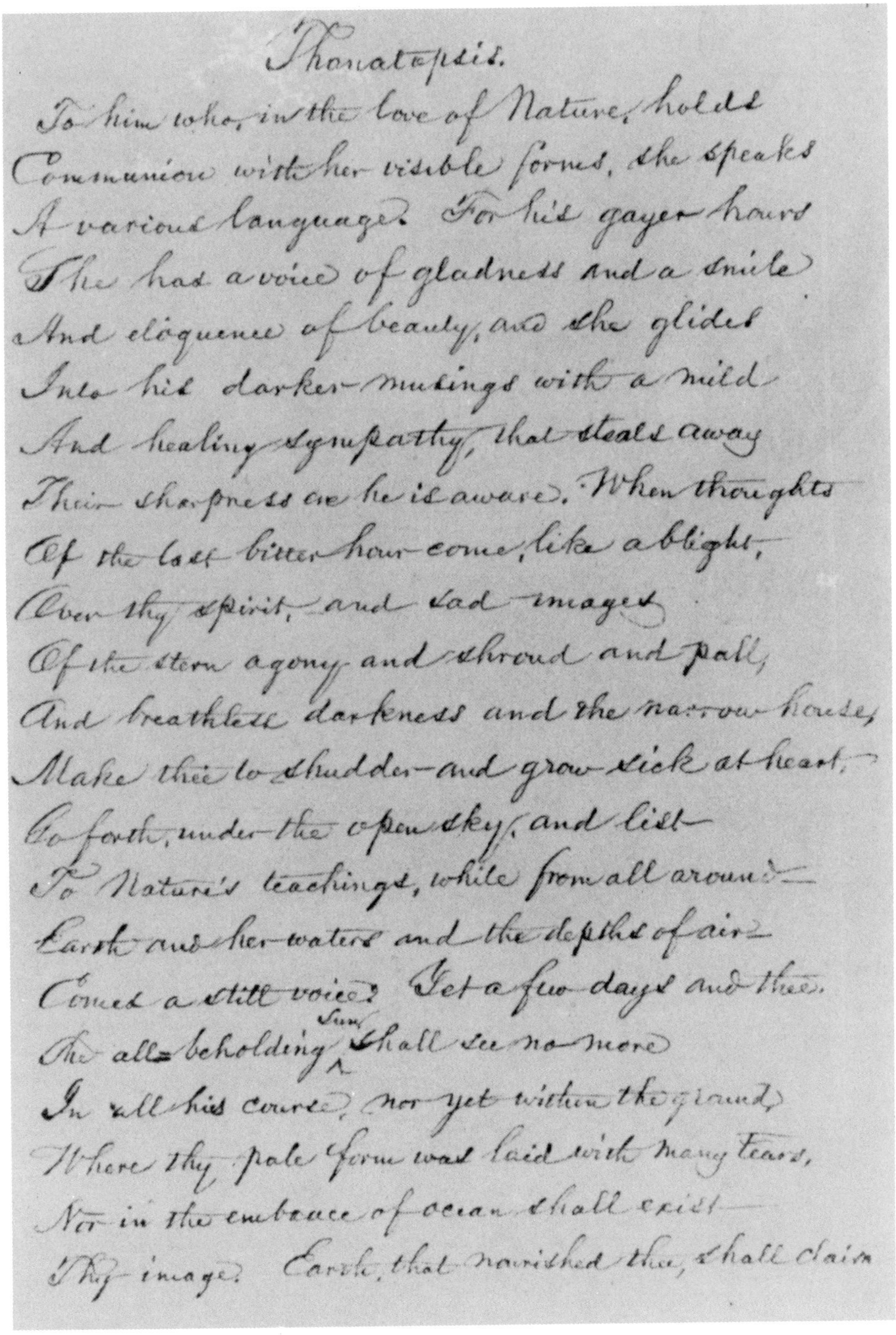
Thanatopsis.

To him who, in the love of Nature, holds
Communion with her visible forms, she speaks
A various language. For his gayer hours
She has a voice of gladness and a smile
And eloquence of beauty, and she glides
Into his darker musings with a mild
And healing sympathy, that steals away
Their sharpness ere he is aware. When thoughts
Of the last bitter hour come, like a blight,
Over thy spirit, and sad images
Of the stern agony and shroud and pall,
And breathless darkness and the narrow house,
Make thee to shudder and grow sick at heart,
Go forth, under the open sky, and list
To Nature's teachings, while from all around—
Earth and her waters and the depths of air—
Comes a still voice. Yet a few days and thee,
The all-beholding sun shall see no more
In all his course; nor yet within the ground,
Where thy pale form was laid with many tears,
Nor in the embrace of ocean shall exist
Thy image. Earth, that nourished thee, shall claim

A fair copy of the first part of Bryant's best-known work. Bryant recalled that he wrote the poem when he was seventeen or eighteen, though it was not published until 1817, when he was twenty-one (Personal [MISC.] Papers of William Cullen Bryant; by permission of the Manuscript Division, the New York Public Library, Astor, Lenox and Tilden Foundations).

sion of "Thanatopsis" and four other poems in the *North American Review*. The success of these poems caused the editor, Willard Phillips, to solicit from Bryant a historical essay evaluating American poetry. The publication of this essay in 1819 initiated Bryant's career as a critic. For all practical purposes, this phase of Bryant's career ended with his delivery of a series of four lectures on poetry at the New York Athenaeum in 1825.

The central problem with which Bryant struggled was the creation of a national literature. Immediately following the Revolution, many American periodicals foolishly demanded the total divorce of American culture from all things English. No culture can immediately dissociate itself from its roots without a profound dislocation. But like most of the writers of his time, Bryant felt compelled to examine the possibility of a uniquely American poetry.

In "Early American Verse," published in the *North American Review* in 1819, Bryant locates a poetic tradition in his immediate predecessors. He focuses chiefly on the Connecticut Wits–Joel Barlow, Timothy Dwight, David Humphreys, and John Trumbull–and on such late-eighteenth-century poets as William Clifton, Philip Freneau, and Robert Treat Paine. Bryant finds them derivative and wanting in three areas which occupied him in the rest of his critical writings: their imaginations were prosaic; their versification was monotonous, and they lacked feeling.

Phillips was sufficiently fond of Bryant's essay to solicit further contributions. In 1819 the *North American Review* published "On Trisyllabic Feet," parts of which Bryant may have written as early as 1811. In this essay Bryant attacks the problem of monotony of versification, thus extending Wordsworth's argument against Augustan "poetic diction" begun in his preface to the *Lyrical Bal-*

Pencil sketch of a cabin on the prairie, drawn by Bryant during his 1832 visit to his brother John in Jacksonville, Illinois (by permission of the William Cullen Bryant Homestead Collection of the Trustees of Reservations, Cummington, Massachusetts)

lads. The enemies are Pope and his imitators, on both sides of the Atlantic, whose success had accustomed the ear to regular iambic couplets as the only medium for verse. Bryant argues that the occasional substitution of trisyllabic feet forms the dominant tradition in English verse.

Bryant's next attempt to come to grips with the problem of literary nationalism came in a review of Catherine Sedgwick's novel *Redwood* in the 1824 *North American Review.* The review is interesting not so much for what it says about Sedgwick's novel as for its attempt to synthesize the conflicting critical demands for universality (a holdover from Samuel Johnson and the Scotch rhetoricians) and for American particularity. The basic passions, Bryant argues, are universal across time and space. But their particular imagistic manifestations are individual and, therefore, national. American literature records how the universals of love, heroism, and the higher values which define the poetic sensibility become manifested in a nation with the characteristics of the United States.

Bryant's other periodical contributions from the period before 1825 are of negligible value, largely because of the ephemeral nature of the works he was reviewing.

In 1825, after several months of negotiation, Bryant moved to New York to become editor of the *New York Review and Atheneum Magazine.* His relationship to the New York Athenaeum, the literary society which copublished the magazine with Henry J. Anderson, owner of the *Atlantic Magazine,* led to Bryant's most significant contribution to critical theory. In April 1825 the Athenaeum engaged Bryant to deliver four lectures on poetry. The lectures not only gave Bryant a welcome introduction into New York literary society, they also provided him the chance to bring his theory of American poetry to a culmination.

In the first lecture, "On the Nature of Poetry," Bryant defines poetry as a "suggestive" rather than mimetic art and distinguishes poetic imagery from that of painting and sculpture. Unlike these arts, which appeal directly to the senses and construct images which bear a strong visual analogy to our perception of reality, poetry employs arbitrary symbols that suggest associations which appeal to the imagination, the emotions, and the understanding (not coincidentally, the three faculties that Bryant had found wanting in early American poetry). The lecture focuses on the two dominant influences of Bryant's thought.

An 1853 photograph of Bryant wearing a Turkish costume that he bought in Damascus during his tour of Europe, Egypt, and the Holy Land the previous year (photograph by Charles D. Fredricks; courtesy of William Cullen Bryant II)

His emphasis on imagination and on the image comes from Wordsworth and the romantic tradition; his insistence on high moral truth, from the Scotch rhetoricians and Archibald Alison.

This contradiction between image and moral concepts seems to trouble Bryant in the second lecture, "On the Value and Use of Poetry." As in the previous lecture, he centers his discussion on imagination, emotion, and understanding as providing poetry its value, but he has trouble finding a logical relationship among his terms. Bryant's trouble involves the value of the passions raised by poetry, for his theory obliges him to exclude cruelty, injustice, and depravity as nonpoetic even though these are common human emotions that have traditionally found a place in poetry.

This distinction forces Bryant into two conspicuous contradictions. In his first essay he had unconditionally condemned American poetry for its lack of emotion; however, his refusal to accept some emotions as poetic forces him to accept the very didacticism he had criticized in others. The second contradiction involves Bryant's attempt to argue, in a long discussion, that impure and, therefore, nonpoetic passions might enter poetry and cause mistaken judgments. Bryant contends that we admire Homer's heroes not because they cut throats but because of the "greatness of mind" with which they do it. So depravity of any sort (which is not poetry) can enter the poem so long as it is done in the proper frame of mind (which is poetry). Anyone in Bryant's audience who had read the *Iliad* might wonder at the high-mindedness with which Achilles drags Hector around the walls of Troy.

Bryant seems to be aware of the logical contradictions in his argument. His rhetoric is tentative, qualified, and less confident, quite unlike the first lecture. He concludes with a long rhetorical peroration by William Ellery Channing which, although it passionately acclaims poetry one of the highest achievements of civilization, bears little reference to the argument of Bryant's lecture. Of the four lectures, the second is clearly the least satisfactory.

In the two concluding lectures Bryant addresses the question of American poetry. In "On Poetry in Its Relation to Our Age and Country," Bryant denies the assertions that America is barren of poetic materials, that the American language is too primitive and impoverished for poetry, and that America is too materialistic and practical a country to cultivate poetry. In "On Originality and Imitation" he asserts that originality, even when motivated by national pride, can often lead to extravagance and that good poetry is built by rivaling the skill of the past.

These lectures conclude Bryant's concern with literary nationalism by placing poetry in a larger, international context in which the poet's community is comprised of other poets whose skill with language becomes the model through which the poet can view the local and immediate

Front cover for the 3 May 1862 issue of Vanity Fair, *with a caricature of Bryant by Albert Bobbett and Edward Hooper*

William Cullen Bryant (top, right) and his brothers, Austin, William, Peter Rush, and Arthur, 1864 (courtesy of William Cullen Bryant II)

nature he finds around him. In these lectures Bryant's thinking joins him with international romanticism.

The remainder of Bryant's writing about literature belongs to the category of occasional journalism rather than literary criticism proper. Bryant continued to write reviews throughout his long career as editor of the *New York Post,* but most of those pieces have never been collected and are accessible chiefly in the collection of the New York Public Library. They are most accurately described as superficial reactions to the books under review rather than as thoughtful critical statements.

A third type of literary comment comes late in Bryant's life, when he, along with Emerson and Longfellow, was revered as one of the grand old men of American letters. These comments occur mostly in the form of introductions to anthologies and commemorative or funeral addresses for many of his famous contemporaries–among them James Fenimore Cooper, Washington Irving, and Fitz-Greene Halleck.It is tempting to dismiss all of Bryant's essays about literature as either warmed-over English romanticism or as journalistic hackwork. However, such an attitude does injustice to the essays which Bryant wrote in his twenties. In this body of work he gave voice for the first time to a thoughtful and informed theory of American poetry and built a bridge between his continental contemporaries and emerging national culture.

Letters:

The Letters of William Cullen Bryant, edited by William Cullen Bryant II and Thomas G. Voss, 4 volumes (New York: Fordham University Press, 1975-1984).

Bibliography:

Henry C. Sturges, *Chronologies of the Life and Writ-*

ings of William Cullen Bryant (New York: Appleton, 1903).

Biographies:

George W. Curtis, *The Life, Character, and Writings of William Cullen Bryant* (New York: Scribners, 1879);

James Grant Wilson, *Bryant and His Friends: Some Reminiscences of Knickerbocker Writers* (New York: Fords, Howard & Halbert, 1886);

John Bigelow, *William Cullen Bryant* (Boston & New York: Houghton Mifflin, 1890);

William A. Bradley, *William Cullen Bryant* (New York: Macmillan, 1905);

Allan Nevins, *The Evening Post: A Century of Journalism* (New York: Boni & Liveright, 1922);

Henry Houston Peckham, *Gotham Yankee* (New York: Vantage Press, 1950);

Curtiss S. Johnson, *Politics and a Belly-Full: The Journalistic Career of William Cullen Bryant* (New York: Vantage Press, 1962);

Charles H. Brown, *William Cullen Bryant* (New York: Scribners, 1971).

References:

William Charvat, *The Origins of American Critical Thought, 1810-1835* (Philadelphia: University of Pennsylvania Press, 1936; London: Oxford University Press, 1936);

Bernard Duffey, "Romantic Coherence and Romantic Incoherence in American Poetry," *Centennial Review*, 7 (Spring 1963, Fall 1964): 219-236;

William J. Free, "William Cullen Bryant on Nationalism, Imitation, and Originality in Poetry," *Studies in Philology*, 66 (July 1969): 672-687;

Tremaine McDowell, *William Cullen Bryant: Representative Selections* (New York: American Book, 1935);

Albert F. McLean, Jr., *William Cullen Bryant* (New York: Twayne, 1964);

John Paul Pritchard, *Literary Wise Men of Gotham: Criticism in New York, 1815-1860* (Baton Rouge: Louisiana State University Press, 1963);

Floyd Stovall, ed., *The Development of American Literary Criticism*, by Harry H. Clark and others (Chapel Hill: University of North Carolina Press, 1955).

Papers:

The major collections of William Cullen Bryant's papers are the Henry W. and Albert A. Berg Collection, New York Public Library; the Bryant Family Papers, Manuscript Division, New York Public Library; the Bryant Family Association Papers, Bureau County Historical Society, Princeton, Illinois; the Bryant-Godwin Collection, Manuscript Division, New York Public Library; the Bryant Miscellaneous Papers, Manuscript Division, New York Public Library; the Flagg Collection, Manuscript Division, New York Public Library; and the Goddard-Roslyn Collection, including financial records of the *Evening Post*, Manuscript Division, New York Public Library.

Edward Tyrrell Channing

(12 December 1790-8 February 1856)

Waldo W. Braden
Louisiana State University

See also the Channing entry in *DLB 1, The American Renaissance in New England.*

BOOK: *Lectures Read to the Seniors in Harvard College*, edited by Richard H. Dana, Jr. (Boston: Ticknor & Fields, 1856).

OTHER: "The Life of William Ellery," in *The Library of American Biography*, volume 6, edited by Jared Sparks (Boston: Gray, 1834).

PERIODICAL PUBLICATIONS: "On Models in Literature," *North American Review*, 3 (July 1816): 202-209;

"The Abuses of Political Discussions," *North American Review*, 4 (January 1817): 193-201;

Review of James Ogilvie's *Philosophical Essays*, *North American Review*, 4 (March 1817): 378-408;

Review of *Memoir of the Early Life of William Cowper, Esq., by Himself*, *North American Review*, 5 (May 1817): 48-55;

Review of Thomas Moore's *Lalla Rookh, An Oriental Romance*, *North American Review*, 6 (November 1817): 1-25;

Review of Walter Scott's *Rob Roy*, *North American Review*, 7 (July 1818): 149-184;

Review of John Neal's *Battle of Niagara, A Poem Without Notes; and Goldau, or the Maniac Harper*, *North American Review*, 8 (December 1818): 142-156;

Review of William Dunlap's *Charles Brockden Brown*, *North American Review*, 9 (June 1819): 58-77;

Review of *The Poetical Works of James Montgomery*, *North American Review*, 9 (September 1819): 276-288;

Review of Robert Southey's *Works of William Cowper, With a Life of the Author*, *North American Review*, 44 (January 1837): 29-55;

Review of James Prior's *The Life of Oliver Goldsmith*, *North American Review*, 45 (July 1837): 91-116;

"Periodical Essays of the Age of Anne," *North American Review*, 46 (April 1838): 341-366;

Review of Robert Phillip's *The Life and Times of Reverend George Whitefield, M.A.*, *North American Review*, 48 (April 1839): 478-500;

Review of *The Works of Lord Chesterfield, Including his Letters to his Son, etc.*, *North American Review*, 50 (April 1840): 404-432;

Review of Richard Henry Dana's *Two Years Before the Mast, A Personal Narrative of Life at Sea*, *North American Review*, 52 (January 1841): 56-75.

In an 1893 article Edward Everett Hale suggested "that Harvard College had trained the only men in America who could write the English language and that its ability to do this began with the year 1819 and ended with the year 1851." That statement referred primarily to the tenure of one man, Edward Tyrrell Channing, who held the Boylston Professorship of Rhetoric and Oratory during those thirty-two years. The accomplishments of the students who came under his influence at Harvard testify to his stature as critic and perhaps as one of the most influential teachers of rhetoric and composition in the nineteenth century. The roll of Channing's students includes essayists, historians, poets, editors, lecturers, philosophers, and politicians, and it reads like a who's who of American letters: Charles Frances Adams, Richard Henry Dana, Jr., Ralph Waldo Emerson, Edward Everett Hale, Thomas Wentworth Higginson, Oliver Wendell Holmes, James Russell Lowell, John L. Motley, Francis Parkman, Wendell Phillips, Andrew Preston Peabody, Charles Sumner, and Henry David Thoreau.

In his *The Flowering of New England* (1936), Van Wyck Brooks concluded "that Channing sowed more of the seeds that make a man of letters . . . than all the other teachers of composition and all the writers of ingenious textbooks that have ever taught a much-taught country."

Edward Tyrrell Channing (courtesy of The Harvard University Portrait Collection)

Born in Newport, Rhode Island, Channing came from a distinguished family. He was the son of a prominent lawyer who served as U.S. district attorney and attorney general of Rhode Island, and the grandson of William Ellery, a signer of the Declaration of Independence. Channing is most often spoken of as the brother of William Ellery Channing (1780-1842), prominent Unitarian minister and abolitionist, whose reputation in his time far overshadowed that of his younger brother. Another brother became a dean of the Harvard Medical School. At the age of thirteen Edward entered Harvard, but he failed to complete a degree because in 1807 he was expelled for participating in a student rebellion. After leaving Harvard he studied law with his eldest brother and was admitted to the Boston bar in 1813. He pursued a legal career only briefly. In 1815 he became associated with a club of young men who promoted and founded the *North American Review,* a literary, critical, and historical journal. Following the editorships of William Tudor (1815-1817) and Jared Sparks (1817), Channing served as editor in 1818-1819. He wrote nine important articles for the *Review* and played such a prominent role in its development that he gained the attention of the Harvard Committee, which invited him to become the third Boylston professor, following John Quincy Adams (who served from 1806 to 1808) and Joseph McKean (who served from 1809 to 1818).

The Boylston professorship, one of the earliest to be endowed at Harvard, became the most distinguished chair of its kind in America. A wealthy Boston merchant, Nicholas Boylston, in 1771 "bequested fifteen hundred pounds law money, as a foundation for a professorship of rhetoric and oratory in Harvard college." In 1804 a college committee prepared "rules, directions and statutes" to guide the appointees. Based largely on John Ward's *System of Oratory* (1759), a two-volume English rhetoric with strong classical overtones, the rules prescribed instruction on all four class levels which would include recitation and the giving of public lectures. The teacher was to discuss the history of oratory, paying attention to the classical canons of invention, disposition, style, and delivery. He was to hear student declamations and orations and supervise public exhibitions. Finally he was "to give particular care" to aid in the application of principles and rules of the art.

Although Adams had served concomitantly as Boylston professor and U.S. senator from Massachusetts, and McKean had been a former minister, better known for his mathematical ability than his rhetorical skills, the appointment of Channing as the third Boylston professor came as a surprise to many who thought that the committee should have chosen "an able practical orator," directly acquainted with public speaking, a knowledge of mankind, and the nature and operation of government. Some remembered that Channing had been expelled from Harvard. One critic argued in the *Columbian Centinel* (22 September 1819) that a professor of rhetoric "should be able to instruct by example, to rouse the genius and excite the emulation of youth by exhibiting before them a model for imitation." Opposition to the appointment had no effect, for the choice of Channing signaled a trend away from oratory and oral discourse and toward written composition and literature. Channing's successor, for example, was his former assistant, Francis James Child, who clearly moved the focus of the chair from oratory to linguistics and literature. He, in turn, was succeeded by grammarian and composition instructor Adam Sherman Hill. The appointees continued to be increasingly literary.

Turning away from the classical orientation of Adams and McKean, Channing felt no compulsion to limit himself to oral discourse or to classical precepts or Ward's interpretations of them. Hinting at his change in focus, Channing "extended" rhetoric beyond the supervision of orators and speeches to include "all communication by language." He said that he was "inclined to consider rhetoric . . . as a body of rules derived from experience and observation extending to all communication by language. . . . It does not ask whether a man is to be a speaker or writer,–a poet, philosopher, or debater; but simply,–is it his wish to be put in the right way of communicating his mind with power to others, by words spoken or written."

He made clear that his purview included poetry as well as "the written book, the novel, the history, the fable and the acted play." He added that he could not "see how a liberal and philosophical rhetoric can overlook any form of composition, any use of language that aims at power over the heart." Indeed he was so comprehensive that he stretched the scope of rhetoric considerably far beyond the limits set by many earlier American and English rhetorical writers or their Roman and Greek predecessors. It is evident that Channing stands as a pivotal American figure in the shift of rhetoric from its ancient concentration on the theory of persuasive speaking, to a concern with written composition.

Among his duties as professor, Channing was "to instruct the students of several classes in the nature, excellence and acquisition of the important art of Rhetorick, in its most extended and comprehensive sense in the theory and practice of writing and speaking." In that connection, Channing directed his students to such textbooks as Hugh Blair's *Lectures on Rhetoric and Belles Lettres* (1783), George Campbell's *Philosophy of Rhetoric* (1776), Levi Hedge's *Elements of Logic* (1816), Robert Lowth's *A Short Introduction to English Grammar* (1762), and Richard Whately's *Elements of Logic* (1826) and *Elements of Rhetoric* (1828).

The classes of freshmen and sophomores were divided according to ability into two or three sections that met two or three times per week. Hale remembers that Channing divided Whately into ten-page "takes" and the students discussed each at length, with the professor carrying "on a running commentary of the text [that] made it more interesting."

Another aspect of Channing's duties was to supervise the speaking exercises in declamation (memorized readings): once a week for freshmen; each fortnight for sophomores; and four times a year for juniors and seniors. In addition he was instructed to attend "the rehearsals previous to Exhibition and Commencement, making remarks on pronunciation, emphasis and gesture, as the performance of those who speak or read suggest[s]." Finding such responsibilities less interesting, Channing concentrated mainly on content and composition, leaving instruction in delivery mainly to assistants. Having become, during his early years at Harvard, painfully aware of the inarticulateness and awkwardness of his students, he was willing to concede the need for training in voice, gesture, and platform manner. In his published lecture on elocution, he endorsed Whately's ideas about putting trust in nature but argued that natural deficiencies, shyness, and unpleasant habits required direct attention. "We are not wrong in thinking the delivery natural whenever it is spontaneous; but it may not be natural in the highest sense," he said. "The want of some native gift, or of discretion and skill may perpetually betray itself to harm or defeat an effort that was full of promise." Consequently Jonathan Barber, the well-known elocutionist, was employed to serve as Channing's assistant from 1829 to 1835. After his departure less well-known assistants assumed these duties, using exercises from Ebenezer Porter's *Analysis of the Principles of Rhetorical Delivery* (1827).

A good part of Channing's teaching involved "Exercises in Composition," recitations, and discussions of such sources as Blair, Campbell, and Whately, correcting and critiquing themes: about eighteen per year for each member of the three upper classes. Former students later commended the professor for his skill in teaching them composition and knowledge of grammar. Hale writes, "We anticipated that exercise with Channing as we should have done an agreeable hour's conversation with any person whom we knew to be our superior. Beside this, we had to write a theme for his examination once a fortnight. . . . He gave out a subject. It was one which supposed some knowledge on our part of matters of literature or of life which very frequently we did not have. . . . For instance, our first theme was The Descriptions of Winter as given by the Poets or Others. . . . But, such as it [the theme] was, we carried it in at three o'clock on alternate Friday afternoons. You sat down in the recitation-room and were called man by man, or boy by boy, in the order in which you came into the room; you therefore heard his criticism on each of your predecessors."

"Channing and Edward Everett," according to the historian Samuel E. Morison, "created the classic New England diction." In one of his published lectures Channing declared, "Our present business is not with pretenders and showmen, but with good writers and with permanent principles. Our warning to the young writer is, never to suppose that there is any genuine vigor and warmth in embellishment. The peril is, false glitter and universal tawdriness." It was perhaps this attitude that Van Wyck Brooks was thinking about when he wrote of Channing's war on "the 'turgid' rhetoric . . . the bane of letters in the days of Boston orators whom every boy adored. [Channing] had a remorseless eye for the highfalutin, the swelling period, the emphatic word, morbid tissue for this ruthless surgeon whose Puritan instincts had been clarified by a sensible classical culture."

Richard H. Dana, Jr., Cornelius Conway Felton, Edward Everett Hale, Thomas Wentworth Higginson, and Andrew Peabody expressed their appreciation for Channing's pure taste and admirable simplicity and for teaching them the craft of writing effective English sentences. Channing expressed his philosophy of style in the dictum that rhetoric "has no more to do with grace and ornament than with clearness and precision."

An important duty of the Boylston professor was to deliver "a course of publick lectures" to the juniors prior to 1833-1834 and in the years following to the seniors. The "Rules, Directions and Statutes" of 1825, probably written by Channing himself, listed "the general subjects" to be covered: (1) the uses, objects, and dangers of criticism; (2) the right selection and use of words; (3) the structure of sentences; (4) the true character of eloquence; (5) the different kinds of eloquence in ancient and modern times; (6) the motives and helps to its cultivation.

Student lecture notes of 1833 indicate that Channing delivered at least twenty-one lectures, some titles of which were similar to what he later published. Included among the total were six lectures on four types of oratory, five on literary criticism, two on types of criticism, one on poetry, one on criticism of poems and novels, and one on an analysis of Scott's novels. Judging by the list, it would appear that Channing did not attempt to discuss all the suggested topics.

The one extant published source of Channing's rhetorical concepts is his sole book, *Lectures Read to the Seniors in Harvard College,* published posthumously in 1856. In his preface Channing explained that the lectures were "written at far distant periods," "sometimes divided according to the prominent topics," not as they were originally conceived, and that they were to be "more justly regarded as essays . . . than orderly treatises." He did not relate how he made his choices, but he emphasized that he had "not attempted a systematic view of rhetoric either in compliance with the statutes of the professorship, or according to any idea of [his] own."

In addition to Dana's biographical notice on Channing and an address, "The Orator and His Times," delivered 8 December 1819 on the occasion of Channing's induction, *Lectures Read to the Seniors in Harvard College* included twelve essays on rhetoric and eight on composition, criticism, and language. The chapters were directed toward the speaker, writer, and reader and were more descriptive and critical than practical or prescriptive. His explanation of the objectives of the formal lecture may well have covered his own intentions in this publication. He wrote that the purpose was not "to furnish a great amount of exact knowledge . . . used like that which we amass in our private studies . . . [but] to hold a sort of conversation . . . in order that they [listeners] may compare their ideas with those of a fellow-inquirer. Generally . . . the effect is to stimulate . . . the thinking and inquiring." Much in the manner of Blair, Channing analyzed how the occasion and audience influenced demonstrative, deliberative, judicial, and sermonic modes, and he discussed the characteristics, aims, atmosphere, peculiar demands, and needed resources of each type. He hoped, of course, to isolate elements that led to eloquence, hence providing standards of judgment, but he left for "private studies" hints concerning practical applications. Curiously during an era sometimes called the Golden Age of American Oratory, Channing did not examine in depth any orators or orations, seldom mentioned any by name, ancient or modern, and did not offer any information about history and trends of public address in general. What he said about the four types was abstract and philosophical but passed over intrinsic qualities. Freed from ancient and traditional theory, Channing, like

Blair, concentrated on language. He gave no attention to ethical or pathetic appeals, to special kinds of analysis, patterns of organization, elements of style, hints about memory and delivery. His chapter on delivery endorsed trust in nature as a guide to effectiveness and analyzed at length what Whately said on the subject, but offered no practical suggestions. He made clear that he disapproved of imitation and the use of models in teaching. "That a student is exposed," he said, "to perils from his constant association with great writers is not disputed. I refer not to the grossest of these perils–such as the temptation to take the thoughts or copy the style of another–nor yet to the subtle enchantment which draws one unconsciously into imitation of his special favorite or the popular idols of the day. . . . Each must do his own work according to his power and natural tendencies."

Of course Channing had studied classical and English rhetoric and critical theory; but in his published essays he made few direct references to any of these, even his favorites Blair and Campbell. According to Dana, Channing drew his metaphysical theories from Thomas Reid, the Scottish common-sense philosopher (1710-1796) who suggested that the principles of rhetoric were "derived from experience and from observation of human nature." There can be little doubt that Channing preferred teaching written composition and literary criticism to developing the speaker. He often grouped the speaker with the writer and recommended writing as a means of clarifying thought, refining analysis, and polishing style for the speaker. In approaching language and style he saw no difference between public speaking and writing.

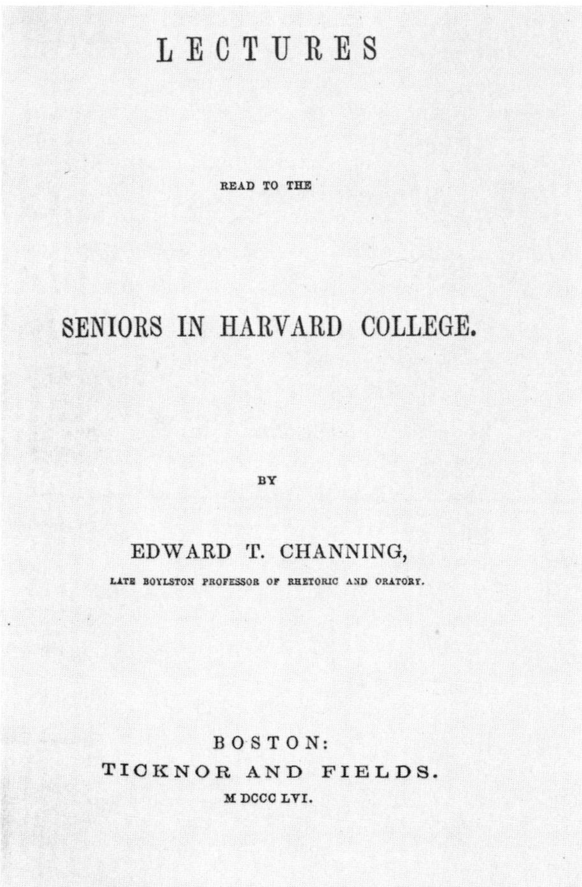
LECTURES

READ TO THE

SENIORS IN HARVARD COLLEGE.

BY

EDWARD T. CHANNING,

LATE BOYLSTON PROFESSOR OF RHETORIC AND ORATORY.

BOSTON:
TICKNOR AND FIELDS.
M DCCC LVI.

Title page for Channing's only published book

In spite of his pronouncement that rhetoric as a comprehensive art had "nothing to do with the different departments of Belles Lettres," he drew a thin line between his concept of rhetoric, literary criticism, and belles lettres. He labored to burn into the consciousness of his students a critical appreciation of "the high exercises of the mind which pass under the general name of taste."

Two of his most lucid essays, "Literary Tribunals" and "Permanent Literary Fame," addressed to writers and students of literature, give attention to the standards that produce "permanent literature" and assure an "author's future place in the judgment and affection of men." Other of his essays are devoted to a writer's preparation, reading, and other habits, the study of language, clarity, and ornamentation. In the lecture "Forms of Criticism" he speaks of how critics can help writers in refining their thinking and polishing their style, suggesting the pedagogical image that his students often attributed to him in his war against tawdriness and turgid style.

In his teaching and published criticism Channing insisted upon the need for the assimilation of familiar surroundings, customs, language, and history, saying that he preferred writing that had "a strangely marked local personal and natural character." The essay "On Models in Literature" encourages writers to free themselves of blind imitation, "excessive fondness" for the "ancient classics," concern about popular preferences, and the opinions of the critics and to place emphasis on independence and sensitivity to what is near at hand. He encourages writers to express their deepest feelings and thoughts.

He published a small number of reviews in two brief periods: nine between 1816 and 1819, and six between 1837 and 1841. His taste is most discernible in three of these pieces. He was highly critical of Thomas Moore's *Lalla Rookh,* calling it "studied and artificial," "more of inanity than sentiment." Clearly he considered Moore's subject matter contrived and an attempt to cater to vulgar preferences. In direct contrast Channing commended Richard Steele's work in the *Tatler Papers* (4 volumes, 1710-1711) and Sir Walter Scott's *Rob Roy* (1818) for naturalness, sensitivity to human emotion and character, and faithful portrayal of detail. He was most impressed with Scott's skill in presenting "man in harmony with the landscape, and at home in the presence of objects that were about him in infancy."

"We leave," said Channing, "the highest criticism in a very few hands." His critical essays on poetry, essays, biography, and history, brief as they were, showed that Channing could penetrate an artist's subtleties and offer informed judgments with lucidity.

Testimony by his former students suggests that Channing's greatest distinction came from his influence upon molding the taste of Harvard students in the classroom and in private conference. He encouraged them to perfect their written style and broaden their literary outlooks, and he introduced them to the best English and American thought. He was "a significant figure," declared William Charvat, "in the literary life of the period." While his published criticism (valuable and sound as it is) was too limited to account for his reputation and his published lectures (while suggestive of his theories of rhetoric) are hardly extensive enough to have had much influence on the rhetorical stream, it is evident that Channing, under the influence of Blair, helped move American rhetorical theory away from the classical influence and from public address toward written composition and criticism.

References:

John Quincy Adams, *Lectures on Rhetoric and Oratory* (New York: Russell & Russell, 1962);

Dorothy I. Anderson, "Edward T. Channing's Definition of Rhetoric," *Speech Monographs,* 14 (1947): 81-92;

Anderson, "Edward T. Channing's Teaching of Rhetoric," *Speech Monographs,* 16 (August 1949): 69-81;

Anderson and Waldo W. Braden, "Critical Introduction to Channing," *Lectures Read to the Seniors in Harvard College* (Carbondale: Southern Illinois University Press, 1968), pp. ix-li;

William Charvat, *The Origins of American Critical Thought 1810-1835* (Philadelphia: University of Pennsylvania Press, 1936);

Warren Guthrie, "The Development of Rhetorical Theory in America: 1635-1850," *Speech Monographs,* 16 (August 1949): 98-113;

John W. Rathbun, *American Literary Criticism, 1800-1860* (Boston: Hall, 1979), pp. 62-79;

Ronald F. Reid, "The Boylston Professorship of Rhetoric and Oratory, 1804-1904: A Case Study in Changing Concepts of Rhetoric and Pedagogy," *Quarterly Journal of Speech,* 45 (October 1959): 239-257;

Reid, "John Ward's Influence in America: Joseph McKean and the Boylston Lectures on Rhetoric and Oratory," *Speech Monographs,* 27 (1960): 340-344;

Karl R. Wallace, ed., *History of Speech Education in America* (New York: Appleton-Century-Crofts, 1954);

Samuel Lee Wolff, "Scholars," in *The Cambridge History of American Literature* (New York: Putnam's, 1921), IV: 471-472.

William Ellery Channing

(7 April 1780-2 October 1842)

Charles Hackenberry
Pennsylvania State University

See also the Channing entry in *DLB 1, The American Renaissance in New England.*

Portrait of William Ellery Channing, attributed to Washington Allston (by permission of the William Ellery Channing Memorial, Inc.)

SELECTED BOOKS: *The Duties of Children. A Sermon Delivered on Lord's Day, April 12, 1807, to the Religious Society in Federal Street, Boston* (Boston: Manning & Loring, 1807; Liverpool: F. B. Wright, 1828);

A Sermon, Delivered at the Ordination of the Rev. John Codman, to the Pastoral Care of the Second Church of Christ in Dorchester, Dec. 7, 1808 (Boston: Joshua Belcher, 1808);

A Sermon Preached in Boston, April 5, 1810, the Day of the Public Fast (Boston: John Eliot, Jr., 1810; Boston: Samuel Avery, 1810);

A Sermon Preached in Boston, July 23, 1812, the Day of the Publick Fast, Appointed by the Executive of the Commonwealth Massachusetts, in Consequence of the Declaration of War Against Great Britain (Boston: Greenough & Stebbins, 1812; Boston: Greenough & Stebbins/ Birmingham, U.K.: C. Wilks, 1812);

A Sermon Preached in Boston, August 20, 1812, the Day of Humiliation and Prayer, Appointed by the President of the United States, in Consequence of the Declaration of War Against Great Britain (Boston: C. Stebbins, 1812);

Elements of Religion and Morality (Boston: John Eliot, 1813);

Two Sermons on Infidelity, Delivered October 24, 1813 (Boston: Cummings & Hilliard/Cambridge, Mass.: Hilliard & Metcalf, 1813);

A Discourse, Delivered in Boston at the Solemn Festival in Commemoration of the Goodness of God in Delivering the Christian World from Military Despotism, June 15, 1814 (Boston: Henry Channing/ Cambridge, Mass.: Hilliard & Metcalf, 1814; London: J & J Hardy, 1815?);

A Sermon, Delivered in Boston, September 18, 1814 (Boston: Henry Channing, 1814);

A Letter to the Rev. Samuel C. Thacher, on the Aspersions Contained in a Late Number of the Panoplist, on the Ministers of Boston and the Vicinity (Boston: Wells & Lilly, 1815);

Observations on the Proposition for Increasing the Means of Theological Education at the University in Cambridge (Cambridge, Mass.: Hilliard & Metcalf, 1815);

Remarks on the Rev. Dr. Worcester's Letter to Mr. Channing, on the "Review of American Unitarianism" in a Late Panoplist (Boston: Wells & Lilly, 1815);

Remarks on the Rev. Dr. Worcester's Second Letter to Mr. Channing, On American Unitarianism (Boston: Wells & Lilly, 1815);

A Sermon, Delivered at the Ordination of the Rev. John Emery Abbot to the Pastoral Care of the North Church of Christ in Salem, April 20,

1815 (Salem: Thomas C. Cushing, 1815);

A Sermon on War: Delivered before the Convention of Congregational Ministers of Massachusetts, May 30, 1816 (Boston: Wells & Lilly, 1816);

An Examination of Passages of Scripture Supposed to Prove the Deity of Jesus Christ (Boston: Bowles, 1819; Liverpool: F. B. Wright, 1828);

A Letter to Professor Stuart, in Answer to his Letters to Rev. William E. Channing, and in Vindication of a Large and Respectible Body of the New England and Other Clergy, From the Unfounded Aspersions Cast on Them, in Said Letters, by Channing, anonymous (Boston: Sylvester T. Goss, 1819);

Objections to Unitarian Christianity Considered (Boston: [Christian Register office], 1819; London: R. Hunter, 1831?; Smallfield, 1831);

A Sermon Delivered at the Ordination of the Rev. Jared Sparks, to the Pastoral Care of the First Independent Church in Baltimore, May 5, 1819 (Baltimore: Benjamin Edes, 1819; Newcastle: J. Marshall, 1820);

Note for the Second Baltimore Edition, of the Rev. Mr. Channing's Sermon, Delivered at the Ordination of the Rev. Jared Sparks. Together With a Table of Errata, in the Baltimore and Boston Editions of That Publication (Boston: Hews & Gross, 1819);

Religion A Social Principle. A Sermon, Delivered in the Church in Federal Street, Boston, December 10, 1820 (Boston: Russell & Gardner, 1820);

Memoir of John Gallison, Esq. (Boston: Wells & Lilly, 1821); republished as *Christian Biography. A Memoir of John Gallison, Esq. of Boston in New England, Counsellor at Law, Who Died Dec. 24, 1820, Aged 32 Years* (Bristol, U.K.: William Browne, 1828);

A Discourse on the Evidences of Revealed Religion, Delivered Before the University in Cambridge, at the Dudleian Lecture, March 14, 1821 (Boston: Cummings & Hilliard, 1821; Bristol, U.K.: Parsons & Brown, 1822);

A Sermon, Delivered at the Ordination of the Rev. Ezra Stiles Gannett, as Colleague Pastor of the Church of Christ, in Federal Street, Boston, June 30, 1824 (Boston: Christian Register Office, 1824); republished as *Christianity Adapted to Every Age and Condition of Mankind* (Liverpool: F. B. Wright, 1824);

Discourse Delivered at the Dedication of Divinity Hall, Cambridge, 1826 (Boston: Carter & Hendee, 1826);

Remarks on the Character and Writings of John Milton; Occasioned by the Publication of his Lately Discovered "Treatise on Christian Doctrine" (Boston: Isaac R. Butts, 1826; London: Edward Rainford, 1826);

A Discourse, Preached at the Dedication of the Second Congregational Unitarian Church, New-York, December 7, 1826 (New York: Second Congregational Unitarian Church, 1826); republished as *The Superior Tendency of Unitarianism to Form an Elevated Religious Character* (Liverpool: F. B. Wright, 1827);

Remarks on the Character of Napoleon Bonaparte, Occasioned by the Publication of Scott's Life of Napoleon (Boston: Bowles & Dearborn, 1827; Boston: Bowles & Dearborn/Liverpool: W. Wales, 1828); republished as *Analysis of the Character of Napoleon Bonaparte, Suggested by the Publication of Scott's Life of Napoleon* (London: Edward Rainford, 1828);

A Continuation of Remarks on the Character of Napoleon Bonaparte, Occasioned by Publication of Scott's Life of Napoleon (Boston: Bowles & Dearborn, 1828); republished as *Thoughts on Power and Greatness, Political, Intellectual, and Moral; in Continuation of an Analysis of the Character of Napoleon Bonaparte* (London: Edward Rainford, 1828);

A Discourse Delivered at the Installation of the Rev. Mellish Irving Motte, as Pastor of the South Congregational Society, in Boston, May 21, 1828 (Boston: Bowles & Dearborn, 1828; London: R. Hunter, 1828); republished as *The Great Design of Christianity. A Discourse, Delivered at the Installation of the Rev. Mellish Irving Motte, as Pastor of the South Congregational Society, in Boston, May 21st, 1828* (Liverpool: F. B. Wright, 1828);

A Discourse Delivered at the Ordination of the Rev. Frederick A. Farley, as Pastor of the Westminster Congregational Society in Providence, Rhode Island, September 10, 1828 (Boston: Bowles & Dearborn, 1828; London: Edward Rainford, 1829); republished as *Man the Image of his Maker. A Discourse Delivered at The Ordination of the Rev. Frederick A. Farley, as Pastor of the Westminster Congregational Society, in Providence, Rhode Island, September 10, 1828* (Liverpool: F. B. Wright, 1829);

Sermons and Tracts, Including the Analysis of the Character of Napoleon Bonaparte and Remarks on the Writings of John Milton (London: R. Hunter, 1828);

Remarks on the Character and Writings of Fenelon

(London: Edward Rainford, 1829); republished as *An Essay, on the Character and Writings of Fenelon* (Liverpool: F. B. Wright, 1829);

Discourse, Reviews and Miscellanies (Boston: Carter & Hendee, 1830); republished in 2 volumes (London: John Mardon, 1834; London: O. Rich, 1834);

The Importance and Means of a National Literature (London: Edward Rainford, 1830);

Remarks on the Disposition Which now Prevails to Form Associations, and to Accomplish all Objects by Organized Masses (London: Edward Rainford, 1830);

A Sermon, Preached at the Annual Election, May 26, 1830, Before His Excellency Levi Lincoln, Governor, His Honor Thomas L. Winthrop, Lieutenant Governor, the Honorable Council, and the Legislature of Massachusetts (Boston: Carter & Hendee, 1830; London: British & Foreign Unitarian Association, 1830);

The System of Exclusion and Denunciation Considered (London: R. Hunter, 1831?);

Discourses (Boston: Charles Bowen, 1832; London: R. J. Kennett, 1833);

Remarks on the Associations Formed by the Working Classes of America, Designed to Relieve the Distresses of Mechanics and Their Families, to Promote Inventions and Improvements in the Mechanic Art, by Granting Premiums and Assisting Young Mechanics by Loans of Money (London: John Mardon, 1833);

Political Writings of W. E. Channing, D. D., of Boston (Edinburgh: W. Tait, 1835);

The Future Life. A Sermon Preached on Easter Sunday, 1834, in the Federal Street Church, Boston (Boston: James Munroe, 1835; London: John Mardon, 1836);

A Sermon on War, Delivered January 25, 1835 (Boston: Homer & Palmer, 1835); republished as *On War. A Discourse* (London: R. Hunter/J. Mardon/Manchester: T. Forrest, 1835);

The Ministry for the Poor. A Discourse Delivered Before the Benevolent Fraternity of Churches in Boston, on their First Anniversary, April 9, 1835 (Boston: Russell, Odiorne & Metcalf, 1835; London: Richard James Kennett, 1835);

Slavery (Boston: James Munroe, 1835; London: Rowland Hunter, 1836; Edinburgh: Thomas Clark, 1836);

Dr. Channing's Letter, on Catholicism, &C (Louisville: Morton & Smith, 1836; Liverpool: Willmer & Smith, 1837; Glasgow: J. Hedderwick & Son, 1837);

Letter of William E. Channing to James G. Birney (Boston: James Munroe, 1836); republished as *Letter of Dr. William E. Channing to James G. Birney* (Cincinnati: A. Pugh, 1836);

A Discourse Delivered at the Dedication of the Unitarian Congregational Church in Newport, Rhode Island, July 27, 1836 (Boston: S. N. Dickinson, 1836; London: Richard Kinder, 1837);

An Address on Temperance (Boston: Weeks, Jordan, 1837; London: John Green, 1837; Glasgow: J. Hedderwick & Son, 1837);

Character of Napoleon, and Other Essays, Literary and Philosophical, 2 volumes (London: Charles Tilt/Edinburgh: J. Menzies/Philadelphia: T. Wardle, 1837);

Essays, Literary & Political (Glasgow: James Hedderwick & Son/London: Simpkin, Marshall/Edinburgh: Oliver & Boyd, 1837);

A Letter to the Abolitionists (Boston: Isaac Knapp, 1837);

A Letter to the Hon. Henry Clay, on the Annexation of

Drawing of Channing during his years at Harvard

Texas to the United States (Boston: James Munroe, 1837; Glasgow: James Hedderwick & Son/London: Simpkin, Marshall/Edinburgh: Oliver & Boyd, 1837); republished as *Thoughts on the Evils of a Spirit of Conquest, and on Slavery. A Letter on the Annexation of Texas to the United States* (London: John Green, 1837);

Remarks on Creeds, Intolerance, and Exclusion (Boston: James Munroe, 1837); republished as *Letter on Creeds, &C* (Liverpool: Willmer & Smith, 1837);

The Sunday School. A Discourse Pronounced Before the Sunday School Society (Boston: James Munroe, 1837; London: R. J. Kennett, 1837);

A Tribute to the Memory of the Rev. Noah Worcester, D.D. (Boston: James Munroe, 1837; Boston: J. Dowe, 1837); republished as *A Discourse Delivered in Boston, November 12, 1837. Being a Tribute to the Memory of the Reverend Noah Worcester, D.D.* (London: John Green, 1838);

The Evidences of Christianity (Glasgow: J. Hedderwick & Son, 1838);

Self-Culture. An Address Introductory to the Franklin Lectures, Delivered at Boston, September, 1838 (London: William Strange/Joseph Noble, 1838?);

The Worship of the Father, A Service of Gratitude and Joy (Boston: James Munroe, 1838);

Lecture on War (Boston: Dutton & Wentworth, 1839; London: John Green, 1839);

Remarks on the Slavery Question, in a Letter to Jonathan Phillips, Esq. (Boston: James Munroe, 1839; London: John Green/Bristol: Philp & Evans, 1839; London: Wiley & Putnam/Charles Fox, 1839);

A Discourse Occasioned by the Death of the Rev. Dr. Follen (Boston: James Munroe, 1840); republished as *Christian Views of Human Suffering* (Boston: James Munroe, 1840);

Emancipation (Boston: E. P. Peabody, 1840; London: C. Fox, 1841);

Lectures on the Elevation of the Labouring Portion of the Community (Boston: William D. Ticknor, 1840; Bristol: Philp & Evans/London: J. Greene, 1840; Manchester: Abel Heywood, 1840);

The Power of Unitarian Christianity to Produce an Enlightened and Fervent Piety (Boston: James Munroe, 1840);

Letter of the Rev. William E. Channing to the Standing Committee of the Proprietors of the Meeting-House in Federal Street, in the Town of Boston, Read at the Annual Meeting, May 6, 1840; and the Reply of the Proprietors Thereto (Boston: Joseph Dowe, 1840);

The Church. A Discourse, Delivered in the First Congregational Unitarian Church of Philadelphia, Sunday, May 30th, 1841 (Philadelphia: J. Crissy, 1841; London: John Green, 1841; Glasgow: James Hedderwick & Son/Edinburgh: Oliver & Boyd/London: Simpkin, Marshall, 1841);

A Discourse on the Life and Character of the Rev. Joseph Tuckerman, D.D. Delivered at the Warren Street Chapel, on Sunday Evening, Jan. 31, 1841(Boston: William Crosby, 1841); republished as *The Obligation of a City to Care For and Watch Over the Moral Health of Its Members; With Remarks on the Life & Character of the Rev. Dr. Tuckerman, Founder of the Ministry at Large. A Discourse, Delivered at the Warren-Street Chapel, Boston, Jan. 31, 1841* (Glasgow: James Hedderwick & Son/Edinburgh: Oliver & Boyd/London: Simpkin, Marshall, 1841);

An Address, Delivered Before the Mercantile Library Company, of Philadelphia, May 11, 1841 (Philadelphia: J. Crissy, 1841); republished as *The Present Age: An Address Delivered Before the Mercantile Library Company of Philadelphia, May 11, 1841* (Glasgow: James Hedderwick/Edinburgh: Oliver & Boyd/London: Simpkin, Marshall, 1841; Manchester: Abel Heywood, 1841);

An Address Delivered at Lenox, on the First of August, 1842, the Anniversary of Emancipation, in the British West Indies (Lenox: J. G. Stanly, 1842); republished as *Dr. Channing's Last Address, Delivered at Lenox, on the First of August, 1842, the Anniversary of Emancipation in the British West Indies* (Boston: Oliver Johnson, 1842; London: John Green, 1842); republished as *Address on Occasion of the Anniversary of the Emancipation of the Slaves in the British West India Islands* (Glasgow: J. Hedderwick & Son, 1842);

The Duty of the Free States, or Remarks Suggested by the Case of the Creole, 2 parts (Boston: William Crosby, 1842; Glasgow: James Hedderwick & Son/Edinburgh: Oliver & Boyd/ London: Simpkin, Marshall, 1842);

A Discourse on the Church (Boston: James Munroe, 1843);

Memoir of William Ellery Channing, with Extracts from His Correspondence and Manuscripts, 3 volumes, edited by William Henry Channing (Boston: W. Crosby & H. P. Nichols/ London: J. Chapman, 1848);

The Perfect Life. In Twelve Discourses, edited by William Henry Channing (Boston: Roberts Brothers, 1873; London: Williams & Norgate, 1873);

Dr. Channing's Note-Book Passages from the Unpublished Manuscripts of William Ellery Channing, edited by Grace Ellery Channing (Boston & New York: Houghton Mifflin, 1887);

Remarks on Some Texts of Scripture, Frequently Alleged in Defence of the Supreme Deity of our Lord Jesus Christ (Belfast: Unitarian Society for the Diffusion of Christian Knowledge, n.d.);

On National Literature (Boston: Directors of the Old South Work, 1903).

Collection: *The Works of William E. Channing, D.D.* (Boston: American Unitarian Association, 1875).

Though he wrote only a few works that dealt expressly with literature, William Ellery Channing influenced American letters profoundly. Widely known as the father of Unitarianism, he articulated the principles, often spiritual in nature, upon which much of the important literature of the early nineteenth century would be founded. The ideas of Ralph Waldo Emerson, Margaret Fuller, Amos Bronson Alcott, and several other lesser-known members of the Transcendental movement all bear the stamp of his thinking; their works embodied his vision of a national literature that spoke to the condition of men and women in America. Even the political ideas of Thoreau, as original as they seem to almost all readers, have roots in Channing's conceptions. Contemporary accounts speak of the melodious quality of Channing's voice when he spoke before an audience, of the charm of his oratorical performances, and Emerson noted that he was "made for the Public; he was the most unprofitable private companion."

Channing's father, William, graduated from Princeton in 1769 and shortly thereafter began to practice law. Channing's mother, Lucy Ellery, was the daughter of William Ellery, who graduated from Harvard in 1747 and was one of the signers of the Declaration of Independence. Because of his mother's ill health, Channing entered school at a very early age. His family referred to him affectionately as the "Little Minister" because he frequently assembled them with his playmates so that he could deliver sermons. By the time he entered Harvard, possibly before, Channing knew he wanted to enter the ministry. As a student, he was patient and diligent. He especially enjoyed history and literary studies and became known at Harvard for the power of his written compositions. Within a year of his graduation in 1798 he moved to Virginia in order to accept a position as tutor, a post which left its influence on almost all of his writings. At Richmond, in addition to his tutorial responsibilities, Channing pursued his professional studies and grew even more firm in his dedication to his calling. To his mother he wrote: "I am resolved to prosecute divinity . . . I cannot do more good to mankind than by teaching them also to lay up treasures where neither moth nor rust can corrupt them."

The Old Federal Street Meetinghouse, site of Channing's ordination

Robert E. Spiller has suggested that William

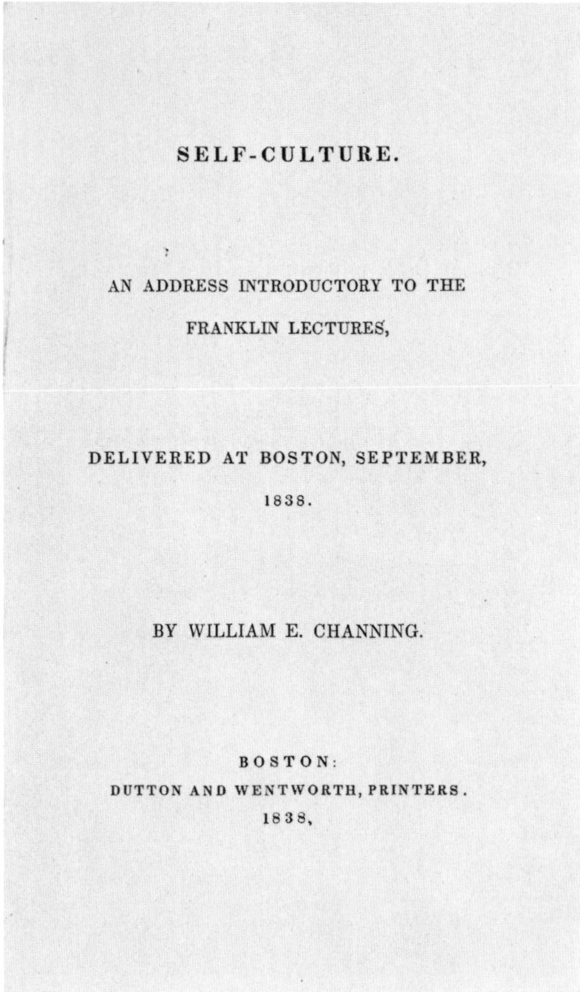
SELF-CULTURE.

AN ADDRESS INTRODUCTORY TO THE

FRANKLIN LECTURES,

DELIVERED AT BOSTON, SEPTEMBER,

1838.

BY WILLIAM E. CHANNING.

BOSTON:

DUTTON AND WENTWORTH, PRINTERS.

1838.

Title page for the address in which Channing advocated education for the working class (collection of Joel Myerson)

Ellery Channing's position in American literary history has been underestimated. Perhaps the chief reason his work has been neglected came about because Channing wrote didactic, wide-ranging essays, a popular form in his day, but one that modern readers find unfocused and lacking in support. Channing's bold, instructive assertions do little to mask their denominational underpinnings and biases, even though the creed they spring from is liberal and eclectic; the objective viewpoint that marks much of modern criticism, even when it is only a rhetorical stance, is rarely found in his essays.

He returned to Boston in 1802, accepting the position of Regent at Harvard. The following year he was elected minister of the Federal Street Church, a pastorate which he held for the rest of his life, even through ill health and the altercation that surrounded the major religious dispute of the period, the Unitarian controversy. Most of Channing's surviving works deal with the spiritual and doctrinal matters connected to that controversy; his writings about literature, as influential as they were, form only a small part of his canon. But even so, his religious works reveal a scholar's broad reading, an interest in textual analysis, and a thorough understanding of classical philosophy as well as that of his own day.

Channing's most important critical statement is undoubtedly his "Remarks on National Literature" delivered to the American Philosophical Society at the University of Pennsylvania in 1823 and printed in the *Christian Examiner* in 1830. It received its first separate publication in 1903 as *On National Literature.* The oration is structured in the typical sermon form of the age with a definition of terms beginning the inquiry. Channing interpreted the work's chief term, *national literature,* as "an expression of superior mind in writing," rather than as the existence (or lack, as he also asserted) of a recognizably significant body of critically important works. In the main Channing found little of value in the American works written up to his day, for they had failed to perform the chief function of literature as he saw it, the creation of superior minds in its readers. By taking this viewpoint, Channing identified himself with a concern of late-eighteenth-century criticism that had persisted and later found currency among nineteenth-century critical thinkers such as Thomas Carlyle and Ralph Waldo Emerson. As purpose for the piece, Channing meant "to correct what we deem a disproportioned attention to physical good." Sounding much the same note that Thoreau would later trumpet in *Walden; or Life in the Woods* (1854), Channing suggests that "institutions have value only by the impulse which they give to the mind," and his essay is offered as a corrective to the false values that inhibit the creation of a true national literature. His didactic critical aims are nowhere more apparent than in this essay.

Two men whom Channing names in the essay as possible "eminent writers" are Jonathan Edwards and Benjamin Franklin, the first of

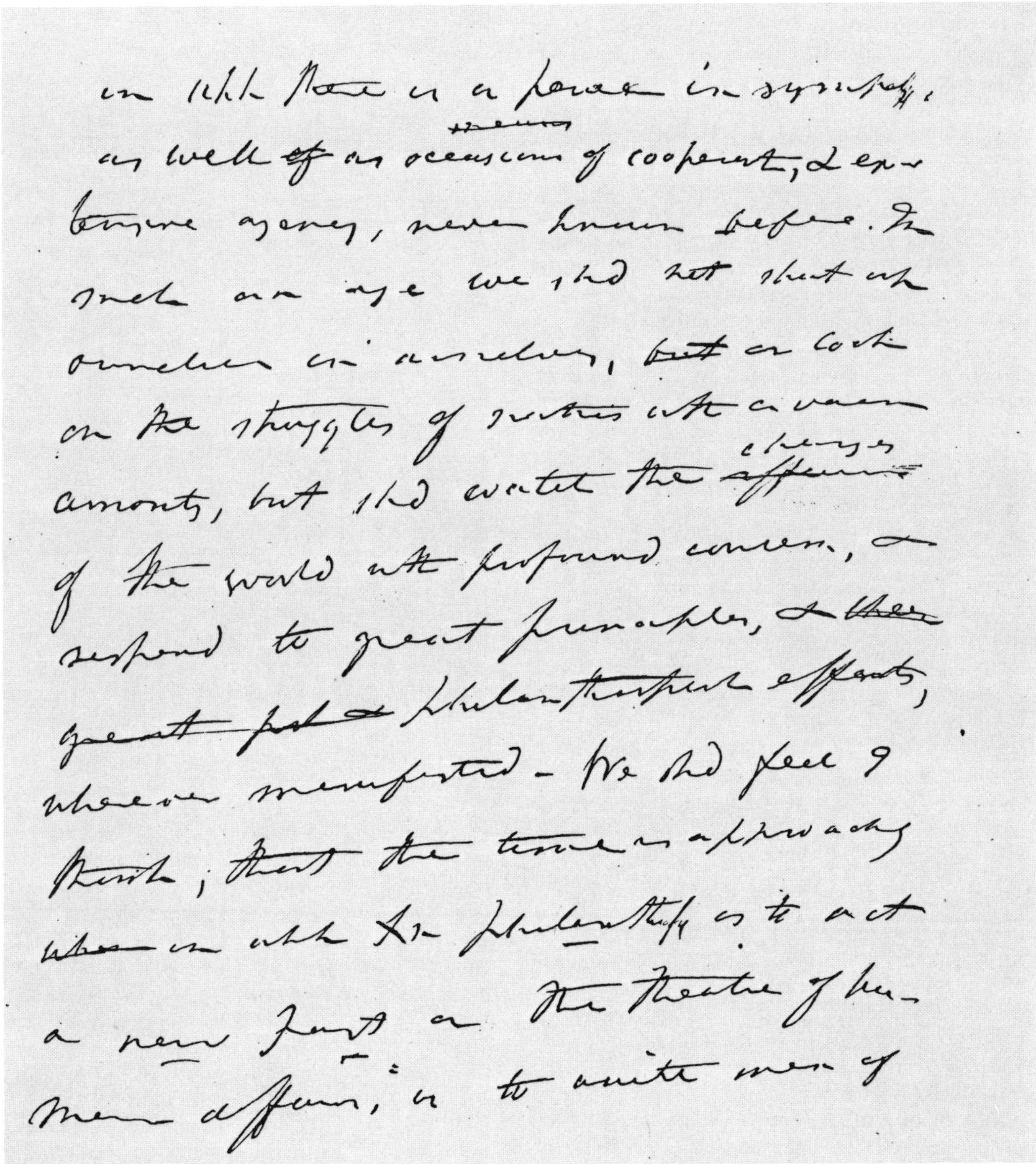

Page from the manuscript for a discourse Channing delivered in Boston in June 1831, after he returned from a trip to St. Croix and Havana (from Autograph Leaves of Our Country's Authors, *compiled by Alexander Bliss and John P. Kennedy, 1864)*

whom he dismisses because of his "vassalage to a false theology." Channing finds that "his work on the Will throws . . . no light on human nature, and, notwithstanding the nobleness of the subject, gives no great or elevated thoughts; but, as a specimen of logical acuteness and controversial power, it certainly ranks in the very highest class of metaphysical writings." This passage is typical of Channing's style of analysis; he judges the content of a work according to his own position before he evaluates its merits as a piece on its own. Channing is kinder to Franklin but his comments suggest that what he liked most about his fellow Bostonian was his international reputation, which gave at least some credence to the idea that America was capable of producing thinkers.

While Channing's conception was, like Emerson's, on the grand scale, valuing whatever tended to further intellectual and spiritual life, he was nevertheless in touch with the prevailing currents of thought of his countrymen, who believed that if an elegant literature were necessary for an enriched life, then it would be more practical to import it from Britain than to produce it at home. Much of Channing's energy in *On National Literature* is focused upon refuting this idea. Unwilling to forego the "spring and life" that great thinkers impart to their country, Channing is equally unwilling to have American minds dominated by foreign ideas, especially British ideas, a condition that would lead Americans to become "intellectually tame and enslaved." If Americans must read another literature, he recommends Continental writers over English authors and invites American writers to share their broader views, a suggestion that the Transcendentalists followed closely.

Channing praises his society for its progress in practical matters, but he feels that a too careful attention to "the necessaries and comforts of life" distracts man from his higher purpose, the elevation of his mind, though Channing is quick to concede that useful knowledge must be "our first and chief care." Only at our peril, he maintains, can practicality become our only concern: "Happily, human nature is too stubborn to yield to this narrow utility." Channing urges native writers to create a national literature in which men and women of genius will deal with matters of truth and virtue. He calls for a literary Declaration of Independence to complete the severance that had been formalized in government half a century earlier. Though he finds little to praise in what had already been written, he ends the essay on a positive note. "We hope for our country the happiness and glory of a pure, deep, rich, beautiful, and ennobling literature." Of all Channing's works that deal with the topic, his *On National Literature* is the only one that is read by more than a handful of literary scholars and historians. His most important statements on the matter are to be found in this work.

Channing's review of the works of Fenelon, a French priest and writer of the age of Louis XIV, gave him more of an occasion to expound upon his own literary and religious ideas than it did an opportunity to say very much at all about the book he was reviewing, a characteristic shared by many other long "reviews" published at the time. In general Channing performs a "very gratifying duty, in introducing and recommending to our readers" Fenelon's book. Chan-

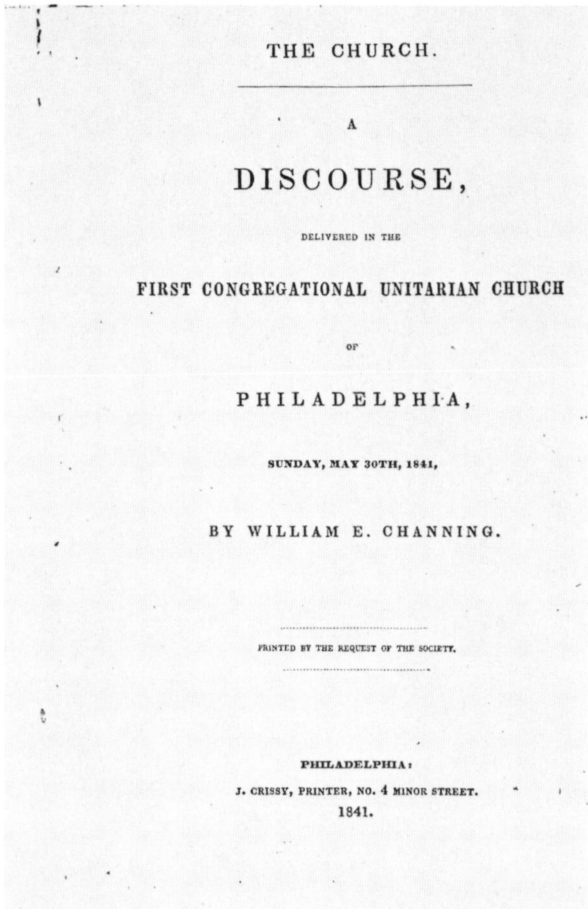
THE CHURCH.

A

DISCOURSE,

DELIVERED IN THE

FIRST CONGREGATIONAL UNITARIAN CHURCH

OF

PHILADELPHIA,

SUNDAY, MAY 30TH, 1841,

BY WILLIAM E. CHANNING.

PRINTED BY THE REQUEST OF THE SOCIETY.

PHILADELPHIA:

J. CRISSY, PRINTER, NO. 4 MINOR STREET.

1841.

Title page for Channing's sermon proclaiming his membership in "the universal church" from which no one could be excommunicated "but by himself, by the death of goodness in his own breast"

ning felt it necessary to defend his recommendation of a work by a Catholic priest, and his broad religious toleration, judged by the standards of his day, served him well in this regard. In this essay his statements are not entirely without wit: "If we wished to impoverish a man's intellect, we could devise few means more effectual than to confine him to what is called a course of theological reading."

Channing felt all literature needed a religious underpinning, but not the religious creed of any one faith. He was aware that this view would be unpopular with both his readers and with many writers of the early nineteenth century, and he erected a substantial fortress to defend this idea as the centerpiece of his essay. Channing lamented the fact that literary works were often produced by "minds which have not in some measure been quickened by the spirit of religion." Genius, he felt, would not endure if it did not gain contact with the "Universal Mind." It is very easy to misread Channing's intent if his broad concept of faith, so much like Emerson's, is overlooked or misunderstood. Only writers whose minds have been ennobled by their contact with the infinite, he felt, were capable of dealing with subjects noble enough for literature; even the baser emotions could be portrayed profitably by those of enlarged vision, and Channing cites Shakespeare as proof of this assertion.

Channing's conception of the relationship between the spiritualized mind and the production of literature, which had been a major theme of "Remarks on National Literature," are enlarged upon and further defined in his *Remarks on the Character and Writings of Fenelon* (1829). This essay's importance rests upon its delineation of what Channing means by the terms *spiritual* and *religion.* Again Channing uses a loose, discursive style. Most important, the essay reveals the heady brew the Transcendentalists were drinking in with their monthly readings and it highlights the boldness that allowed them to be as unconventional and controversial in their thinking as Channing was in his.

When William Ellery Channing came to write his review of a Milton work that was newly published, he was quite aware of the significance of his undertaking. In *Remarks on the Character and Writings of John Milton; Occasioned by the Publication of his Lately Discovered "Treatise on Christian Doctrine"* (1826), he articulated his realization that the work was "an important event in literary history," and he used the occasion to point out Milton's "unconfined mind" and great learning, precisely the kind of model he would appropriate for American writers. Though Milton's work under review is prose, Channing speaks first and at length about his poetry and presents what later became the roots of the broader conception of the meaning of the poet embraced by Transcendental writers. Channing sees in poetry "the same aim with Christianity; that is, to spiritualize our nature." Milton was for Channing a religious hero, one whose conception of Christ closely matched his own. When Channing does address the subject of Milton's prose, he finds both energy and richness to be the hallmarks of his style. Milton's party spirit, coarse invective, and asperity were not overlooked by Channing, however, and he feels that such characteristics weaken the writing. Echoing his own advice in *On National Literature* and delineating Milton's greatest ability, Channing notes that "the great and decisive test of genius is, that it calls forth *power* in the souls of others. It not merely gives knowledge, but breathes energy." This praise is Channing's highest.

Often overlooked in assessments of Channing's literary theory and practice are his introductory comments written for the 1841-1843 edition of his *Works.* Here Channing summarizes both his religious and literary thinking. Coming down even harder on Edwards than he had in *On National Literature,* he asserts that "if Edwards's work on the will could really answer its end . . . it would be one of the most pernicious books ever issued from our press." Fenelon, too, "whose quietism . . . we must look on as a disease," receives harsher treatment than he does in the earlier review devoted to his collected works. Here, too, is the culmination of Channing's main theme, the greatness of human nature, and he applies it to matters religious, political, and literary with characteristic energy and certainty. His remark at the end of this essay serves well to place Channing's works in a good historical perspective: "Books which are to pass away, may yet render much service, by their fitness to the intellectual struggles and moral aspirations of the times in which they are written."

Channing had great influence in his own day on literary trends, writers, and the works they produced. His love of truth and liberty, together with his philosophy that placed the soul of man directly at the center of all concerns, casts its long shadow over the works of American Transcendental writers and those such as Emily Dickinson, Walt Whitman, and Robert Frost, who later benefited from this rich tradition.

Letters:

Correspondence of William Ellery Channing, D.D., and Lucy Aiken, From 1826 to 1842, edited by Anna Letitia Le Breton (Boston: Roberts Brothers, 1874; London: Williams & Norgate, 1874).

Biography:

Arthur W. Brown, *Always Young for Liberty: A Biography of William Ellery Channing* (Syracuse, N.Y.: Syracuse University Press, 1956).

References:

Sydney Ahlstrom, "The Interpretation of Channing," *New England Quarterly,* 30 (March 1957): 99-105;

Van Wyck Brooks, *The Flowering of New England 1815-1865* (New York: Dutton, 1936);

Andrew Delbanco, *William Ellery Channing: An Essay on the Liberal Spirit in America* (Cambridge: Harvard University Press, 1981);

L. D. Geller, *Between Concord and Plymouth* (Concord: Thoreau Foundation, 1973);

Robert Leet Patterson, *The Philosophy of William Ellery Channing* (New York: Bookman Associates, 1952).

William Henry Channing

(25 May 1810-23 December 1884)

Robert D. Habich
Ball State University

See also the Channing entry in *DLB 1, The American Renaissance in New England.*

SELECTED BOOKS: *Correspondence and Remarks Relative to a Recent Attempt to Exclude Unitarians from Young Men's Bible Society* (Cincinnati, 1841);

The Gospel of To-day. A Discourse Delivered at the Ordination of T. W. Higginson, as Minister of the First Religious Society in Newburyport, Mass., Sept. 15, 1847. By William Henry Channing. Together with the Charge, Right Hand of Fellowship, and Address to the People (Boston: W. Crosby & H. P. Nichols/Newburyport, Mass.: A. A. Call, 1847);

The Christian Church and Social Reform. A Discourse Delivered Before the Religious Union of Associationists (Boston: W. Crosby & H. P. Nichols, 1848);

Lessons from the Life of Theodore Parker; A Discourse Delivered in Hope Street Church, Liverpool, on Sunday Evening, June 10, 1860 (London: E. T. Whitfield, 1860);

The Civil War in America; or, The Slaveholders' Conspiracy (Liverpool: W. Vaughn/London: G. Vickers, 1861?).

OTHER: Théodore Simon Jouffroy, *Introduction to Ethics, Including a Critical Survey of Moral Systems,* translated by Channing (Boston: Hilliard, Gray, 1841);

Memoir of William Ellery Channing, with Extracts from His Correspondence and Manuscripts, edited by Channing, 3 volumes (Boston: W. Crosby & H. P. Nichols/London: J. Chapman, 1848);

The Memoir and Writings of James Handasyd Perkins, edited by Channing (Cincinnati: Trueman & Spofford/Boston: W. Crosby & H. P. Nichols, 1851);

Memoirs of Margaret Fuller Ossoli, edited by Channing, Ralph Waldo Emerson, and James Freeman Clarke, 2 volumes (Boston: Phillips, Sampson, 1852);

William Ellery Channing, *The Perfect Life. In Twelve Discourses,* edited by Channing (Boston: Roberts Brothers, 1873).

PERIODICAL PUBLICATIONS: "Coleridge," *Western Messenger,* 7 (August 1839): 258-264;

Review of *Mosses from an Old Manse* by Nathaniel Hawthorne, *Harbinger,* 3 (27 June 1846): 43-44.

Translator, literary critic, magazine editor, and biographer, William Henry Channing is numbered (in Ralph Waldo Emerson's phrase) among the "young men with knives in their brains" who constituted the first generation of New England Transcendentalists. He was born into a stable, prominent family–his uncle Dr. William Ellery Channing was arguably the most influential Unitarian minister of his day–yet his intellectual and spiritual wanderlust began early. He attended Harvard College, graduating with the famous class of 1829, and went on to Harvard's Divinity School. At Cambridge he became imbued with German romanticism, filtered through the writings of Samuel Taylor Coleridge and Thomas Carlyle; like others of the Transcendental circle, he read prodigiously and widely, in philosophy and world religions as well as in belles lettres. His eclectic education, combined with an apparently constitutional inability to stay put, made him a wide-ranging critic of literature and culture whose work suffered from lack of depth. Both his criticism and his literary scholarship were often turned toward spiritual things, as he attempted to show in the figures he treated the evidences of "transfigured humanity."

Following his graduation from Harvard's Divinity School in 1833, Channing preached independently in New York, toured Europe, and in 1838 accepted the pulpit at the Unitarian church in Cincinnati. In nearby Louisville, Kentucky, his classmate and friend James Freeman Clarke had been editing the *Western Messenger,* a religious and literary monthly whose independence had allied it with the New England Transcendentalists; Channing became the *Western Messenger*'s editor in 1839. Under Channing the magazine turned increasingly to social criticism, and as a result the amount of literary commentary shrank. When the magazine folded in 1841, he returned to Massachusetts, then to New York, where from 1843 to 1844 he edited a Fourierist journal, the *Present.* In 1849 he attempted another magazine, the *Spirit of the Age,* which lasted less than a year. A reformer at heart, he was a frequent visitor at the Brook Farm community and at other communitarian experiments. In 1854 he left for England, there serving radical Unitarian societies for the remainder of his life, though he visited the United States frequently.

William Henry Channing (courtesy of the Unitarian Universalist Association Archives, Boston, Massachusetts)

Channing's literary criticism appears primarily in magazines, where it is overshadowed by his social and religious writings. As a critic of literature, though, Channing was quite unwilling to separate his artistic and religious sensibilities. For him, as for many others of the time, art was a window into the soul of the artist, and for Channing the Transcendental ideal of the poet–as seer, conduit for divine truth, and healer of the spiritually sick–was strong. His appraisal of Coleridge for the *Western Messenger* in 1839 is a prime example.

Passing over the "wild melody" of Coleridge's poetry and the "incongruities and disproportionativeness" of his theology, Channing confines his criticism to Coleridge the man, in an attempt to moderate some of the adverse reaction to the poet's late conservatism. How, Channing asks, can we account for Coleridge's "mental and moral incongruities"? Channing decides that the poet was at war with his better instincts. Too soon turned to scholarship, Coleridge's "head gathered faster than his heart," and his "self-consciousness" as a writer prevented him from realizing his full promise as a poet: "We know not how to explain the fewness of his complete productions, when compared with his evidently fertile creative power, except by saying, that he could not refrain from pulling up his plants to see how much the roots grew and were fed." Finally, according to Channing, this introspection led to egotism, frustrating the poet's thought and limiting his poetic gifts. "He was meant for a poet and became a metaphysician; for a religious reformer, but was changed to a bigoted son of the church." Still, Channing decides, Coleridge must be classed among the truly remarkable writers of his day, one whose works continue to "exert a salutary influence." It is hard to imagine more equivocal praise than Channing's opinion of Coleridge's writings, which "by the habits of reflection they are fitted to train up, neutralize the effects of whatever errors they may instil [*sic*]." Yet Channing's amateurish attempt at psychological biography is at least a notably balanced piece compared to the carping criticism that marked so many of the periodical reviews of the day.

A more successful attempt at literary criticism is Channing's review of Nathaniel Hawthorne's *Mosses from an Old Manse* for the *Harbinger* in 1846. Like Coleridge, Hawthorne was not early appreciated; Channing was one of the first American critics to recognize what Herman Melville would later call Hawthorne's "great power of blackness." Channing cites the pervading sadness in Hawthorne's fiction, the "subterranean Hell" that seethes within his characters, and contrasts it to the "serene brightness" of other contemporary fictions which casts an artificial glow upon human affairs. No optimist, Hawthorne is not "morbid or extravagant" either; his "gift of *insight* which can penetrate appearance, and detect realities beneath shams" leads finally to a vision of hope. Turning to individual pieces, Channing praises the sketch of the manse ("Lamb, or Irving never gave us anything . . . so beautiful") but recoils from some of the tales, "too horrible perhaps for publication any where." Though later critics may wonder whether, as he maintains, Hawthorne's tales reveal a trust in "an all providing God," Channing was well in advance of most readers, recognizing in Hawthorne a writer "baptized in the deep waters of *Tragedy*."

While he was still in Cincinnati, Channing began translating Théodore Simon Jouffroy's *Introduction to Ethics, Including a Critical Survey of Moral Systems.* The translation was published in 1841, part of George Ripley's series, *Specimens of Foreign Standard Literature.* It was journeyman work, sandwiched among his many duties as a minister and editor and valuable simply because it made Jouffroy available in English. Channing's brief interpretive introduction is marred by the same caution that marked his evaluation of Coleridge; in place of analysis, Channing merely states that Jouffroy's "love of truth and liberality" atone for the errors in his lectures.

The death of his beloved uncle Dr. William Ellery Channing in 1842 presented another opportunity to sketch a worthy, and only partially understood, figure in literary and religious history. Channing probably began work on the memoir soon after his uncle's death, but he found the task more taxing than he had anticipated. In part, it was difficult for him to distance himself from his subject; in part, too, he was, as always, struggling with an overload of responsibilities, each competing for his attention.

With the advantage of access to manuscript and family material, he originally planned a full biography of his uncle in his times; but the mass of material apparently overwhelmed him. What appeared instead, the *Memoir of William Ellery Channing, with Extracts from His Correspondence and Manuscripts* (1848), was a compendium of "extracts from private papers, sermons, and letters, with such remarks only interwoven as seemed needed for purposes of illustration." Channing claimed that his preference of "silence to partiality" redeemed the book, made it a more objective record of his uncle's views and less a reflection of the biographer's own. Of course the very act of selection makes any biography interpretive, and the portrait that emerges of the famous Unitarian divine is one of a sublimely compassionate and intellectual spirit with very little mooring in the real world. Even the most basic facts of his adult life–the names of some of his children, for instance–are omitted. And the subject's role in such key events as the Transcendental controversy of the 1830s is smoothed over or ignored. The elder Channing's letters are severely excerpted, frequently undated or grouped by "theme," and his sermons are apparently intermingled with passages from his private writings. The virtue of this monumental collection of material lies in the act of collecting itself; much of Dr. William Ellery Channing's papers were, and still are, unavailable in print. His widow spoke for many readers when she called the memoir a "perfectly true and just" portrait of her husband. Yet there is equal truth in the review in the London *Spectator:* "The idea was not bad . . . but the execution is too minute, and will seem tedious to all except disciples of Channing."

The year following the publication of the memoir, another of William Henry's relatives died–this one less famous, more troubled than the revered uncle. James Handasyd Perkins, Channing's cousin and a co-editor with him on the *Western Messenger,* had remained in Cincinnati after the magazine failed, devoting himself to civic reforms, education, and his ministry-at-large to the poor. Like Channing, Perkins found himself overworked and overextended; but he enjoyed none of the emotional resiliency that enabled his cousin to shrug off defeat and turn to other projects. In December 1849, suffering from depression, Perkins boarded a river ferry, carefully placed his cloak and personal papers aside, and stepped off the deck into the icy waters of the Ohio. Perkins's suicide stunned even those who knew his emotional turmoil, and of all his friends, Channing was best fitted, intellectually and by experience, to undertake the delicate task of writing his biography. Yet the press of other duties and the understandable reluctance to probe too deeply into the psyche of his troubled friend weighed heavily on Channing.

As with the life of Dr. William Ellery Channing, *The Memoir and Writings of James Handasyd Perkins* (1851) turned out to be less than the author had originally intended: a "faithful portrait for the home circle," Channing admitted in his preface, "an off-hand outline of his genius and growth as I observed them, filled up with extracts from his writings, and memorials supplied by others." In fact Channing's self-deprecating

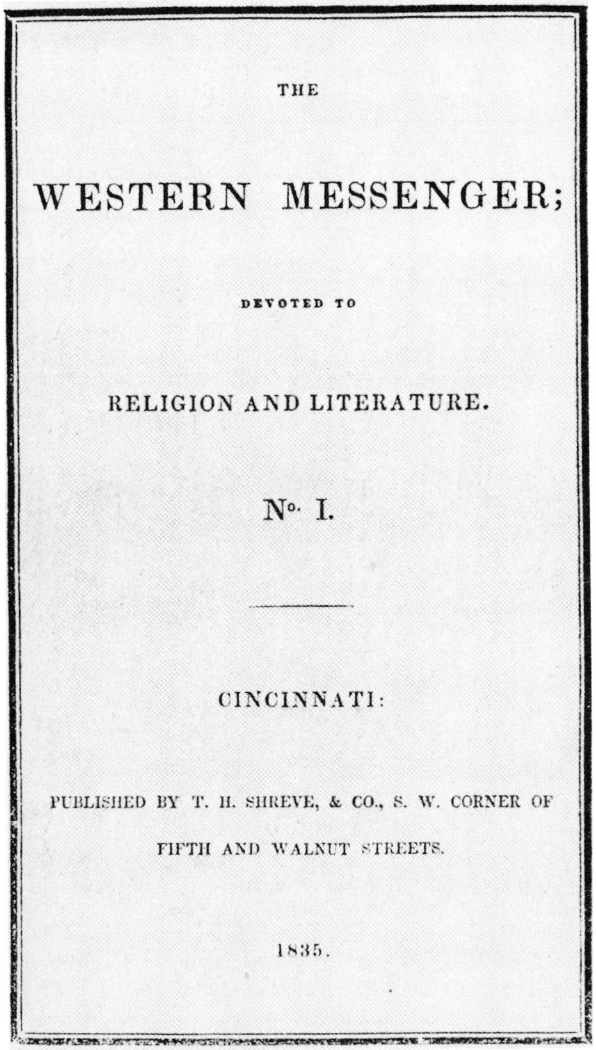

THE

WESTERN MESSENGER;

DEVOTED TO

RELIGION AND LITERATURE.

No. I.

CINCINNATI:

PUBLISHED BY T. H. SHREVE, & CO., S. W. CORNER OF FIFTH AND WALNUT STREETS.

1835.

Front wrapper for the first issue of the periodical Channing edited through 1839

evaluation of his work (he listed himself as "editor," not really "author") is less than accurate. Perkins's life is sketched with greater fullness, and in greater detail, than Dr. William Ellery Channing's. Indeed it is the only published source of information about his many activities in the West; the extracts supplement, rather than replace, the biographer's discussion of Perkins's ideas and conflicts; the dates, sometimes inaccurate, are at least more frequent than in Channing's first attempt at biography. Clearly, Channing had matured as a biographer, more concerned now with grounding opinion in facts. Not even Channing, however, could confront Perkins's suicide directly. Subject to moods and passions that were "in many respects extravagant,"

James Handasyd Perkins, whose writings were edited by Channing (courtesy of the Massachusetts Historical Society)

Perkins seems genuinely an enigma to his cousin: "the true LIFE of Mr. Perkins was a guarded centre," Channing admits, "to which friends, children, wife even, seldom penetrated." In more accomplished hands, Perkins's impassioned death may have called forth better interpretation than this. Channing wisely stayed clear of speculation and, at the same time, avoided the temptation to gloss over what seemed to him a terrible act of conscience. Despite real and tragic flaws, Channing concludes, Perkins succeeded to a great degree in mastering his passions. This balanced evaluation, along with the extensive collection of Perkins's otherwise unavailable writings, makes the memoir a valuable, if not wholly complete, biography of a complex, compelling figure.

Channing's work on the memoirs of his uncle and Perkins prepared him for his most important book, *Memoirs of Margaret Fuller Ossoli* (1852), which he co-edited with Ralph Waldo Emerson and James Freeman Clarke. The lives of Fuller and Channing had intersected often over the years: she was his uncle's unpaid secretary for a time; she contributed essays to the *Western Messenger;* and she and Channing shared a circle of New England friends, an abiding interest in literature and social reform, and a mercurial temperament. In the 1840s they were together in New York City, she as a reviewer for Horace Greeley's *New-York Tribune,* he as an independent minister and social activist. When Fuller died in July 1850, in a shipwreck off the coast of Long Island, Channing and other friends almost immediately began collecting letters and other material to memorialize the life of the much misunderstood critic, feminist, and reformer.

Channing wrote and edited the second volume of the memoirs, covering roughly the last decade of Fuller's life, and he may well have overseen the entire book. A highly interpretive portrait of a compelling life, the two volumes collect Fuller's letters, journals, and published writings as evidence of her thought and range of opinions. The first of many studies of Fuller, it remains the most influential. The editors, all close friends of their subject, combined their own reminiscences with Fuller's accounts of herself. As interpretive biography, it makes fascinating reading; according to standards of modern scholarship, however, it is a "mess," as one of Fuller's later editors puts it. Documents have been excised; letters are misdated, undated, and rewritten; names are changed or omitted. The surviving manuscripts used in Channing's section are heavily cancelled in thick purple ink.

Exactly why the *Memoirs of Margaret Fuller Ossoli,* and particularly Channing's part of it, turned out to be such an expurgated version of the truth has as much to do with cultural history as with scholarly principles. As a recent critic has argued convincingly, "where Fuller's individuality seemed to threaten deep-seated cultural, social, and political norms of femininity, the editors tempered or obscured it." Close examination of the surviving materials indicates a conscious attempt to sanitize Fuller's sexuality and intellectual boldness, "to *make over* the moral image" and in doing so to protect her reputation. For Channing in particular, charged with relating the most tumultuous years of Fuller's life, the task of presenting sensitive events like her disputed marriage to an Italian nobleman was particularly delicate. With some justification, Emerson worried whether Channing might have been "too much her friend" to portray Fuller objectively. Some three decades later, in a letter to another biographer of

Fuller, Channing insisted that his version of her was "juster, deeper, purer, truer, loftier, than has ever been given elsewhere."

That Channing believed his scholarship "pure" despite his intentional tampering with the evidence says volumes about his conception of his role as scholar. Convinced as a minister that the deep and "lofty" are true, he put truth to the service of loftiness, creating in his portraits of Dr. William Ellery Channing, Perkins, and Fuller versions of their spiritual reality while ignoring or submerging those facts that were incongruent, base, or accidental. Channing's literary criticism, slim in volume and biographical in its focus, is on the whole deservedly forgotten. But his achievements as an editor and biographer remain of value, despite their flaws. As an on-site observer of important figures in nineteenth-century New England, William Henry Channing joins other "memorializers" such as Thomas Wentworth Higginson and Octavius Brooks Frothingham, Channing's own biographer, who wrote that Channing's "biographical works deserve a place with the prominent contributions of that department."

Biography:

Octavius Brooks Frothingham, *Memoir of William Henry Channing* (Boston & New York: Houghton, Mifflin, 1886).

References:

Bell Gale Chevigny, "The Long Arm of Censorship: Myth-Making in Margaret Fuller's Time and Our Own," *Signs: Journal of Women in Culture and Society*, 2 (Winter 1976): 450-460;

Sterling F. Delano, *"The Harbinger" and New England Transcendentalism: A Portrait of Associationism in America* (Rutherford, N.J.: Fairleigh Dickinson University Press, 1984);

Robert D. Habich, "The 'Spiral Ascending Path' of William Henry Channing: An Autobiographical Letter," *ESQ: A Journal of the American Renaissance*, 30 (First Quarter 1984): 22-26;

Habich, *Transcendentalism and the "Western Messenger": A History of the Magazine and Its Contributors, 1835-1841* (Rutherford, N.J.: Fairleigh Dickinson University Press, 1985);

Robert N. Hudspeth, ed., *The Letters of Margaret Fuller*, volume 1 (Ithaca: Cornell University Press, 1983);

Elizabeth R. McKinsey, "William Henry Channing," in *The Transcendentalists: A Review of Research and Criticism*, edited by Joel Myerson (New York: Modern Language Association, 1984), pp. 108-111;

David M. Robinson, "The Political Odyssey of William Henry Channing," *American Quarterly*, 34 (Summer 1982): 165-184;

Walter Samuel Swisher, "William Henry Channing: A Neglected Figure in the History of Unitarianism," *Proceedings of the Unitarian Historical Society*, 6 (1939): 1-12.

Papers:

The best collections of Channing's correspondence are those at the Houghton Library, Harvard University; the Massachusetts Historical Society; the Boston Public Library; and the Henry E. Huntington Library.

George Barrell Cheever

(17 April 1807-1 October 1890)

Guy R. Woodall
Tennessee Technological University

SELECTED BOOKS: *Studies in Poetry. Embracing Notices of Lives and Writings of the Best Poets in the English Language, a Copious Selection of Elegant Extracts, a Short Analysis of Hebrew Poetry, and Translations from the Sacred Poets: Designed to Illustrate the Principles of Rhetoric, and Teach Their Application to Poetry* (Boston: Carter & Hendee, 1830);

Some of the Principles according to which this World is Managed, Contrasted with the Government of God, and the Principles Exhibited for Man's Guidance in the Bible. Delivered on the Fourth of July (Boston, 1833);

A Defence in Abatement of Judgment for an Alleged Libel in the Story Entitled "Inquire at Amos Giles' Distillery." Addressed to the Hon. Chief Justice Shaw, at the Session of the Supreme Judicial Court of Massachusetts held in Salem, Dec. 4, 1835 (New York: Leavitt, Lord, 1836);

God's Hand in America (New York: M. W. Dodd/ London: Wiley & Putnam, 1841);

Punishment by Death: Its Authority and Expediency (Boston: M. W. Dodd, 1842);

Capital Punishment. The Argument of Rev. George B. Cheever, in Reply to J. L. O'Sullivan, Esq., in the Broadway Tabernacle, on the Evenings of January 27th, and February 3d & 17th. (New York: Saxton & Miles/Boston: Saxton & Peirce, 1843);

Characteristics of the Christian Philosopher: A Discourse Commemorative of the Virtues and Attainments of Rev. James Marsh, D.D. (New York: Wiley & Putnam, 1843);

The Elements of National Greatness. An Address Before the New England Society of the City of New York, December 22, 1842 (New York: J. S. Taylor, 1843);

Lectures on the Pilgrim's Progress and on the Life and Times of John Bunyan (New York: Wiley & Putnam, 1844; Glasgow & London: W. Collins, 1846);

Sophisms of the Apostolical Despotism (New York, 1844);

The True History of Deacon Giles' Distillery. Reported for the Benefit of Posterity (New York, 1844);

Wanderings of a Pilgrim in the Shadow of Mount Blanc (New York: Wiley & Putnam, 1845; London: Wiley & Putnam, 1845);

A Defence of Capital Punishment . . . and An Essay on the Ground and Reason of Punishment, with Special Reference to the Penalty of Death, by Cheever and Taylor Lewis, Esq. (New York: Wiley & Putnam, 1846);

The Pilgrim in the Shadow of the Jungfrau Alp (New York: Wiley & Putnam, 1846);

The Hill Difficulty, and Some Experiences of Life in the Plains of Ease. With Other Miscellanies (New York: John Wiley, 1849);

The Powers of the World to Come: and the Church's Stewardship, as Invested With Them (New York: Carter, 1853);

Right of the Bible in our Public Schools (New York: Carter, 1854);

Lectures on the Life, Genius, and Insanity of Cowper (New York: Robert Carter & Brothers, 1856);

God Against Slavery: and the Freedom and Duty of the Pulpit to Rebuke it, as a Sin Against God (New York: J. H. Ladd, 1857);

The Commission from God, of the Missionary Enterprise, Against the Sin of Slavery; and the Responsibility on the Church and Ministry for its Fulfilment [sic]. *An Address Delivered in Tremont Temple, Boston, Thursday May 27th, 1858* (Boston: J. P. Jewett/Cleveland: H. P. B. Jewett, 1858);

The Fire and Hammer of God's Word Against the Sin of Slavery. Speech of George B. Cheever, D.D., at the Anniversary of the American Abolition Society (New York: American Abolition Society, 1858);

. . . The Sin of Slavery, the Guilt of the Church, and the Duty of the Ministry. An Address Delivered Before the Abolition Society at New York, on Anniversary Week, 1858 (Boston: J. P. Jewett/Cleve-

land: H. P. B. Jewett, 1858);

The Curse of God Against Political Atheism: With Some of the Lessons of Harper's Ferry. A Discourse Delivered in the Church of the Puritans, New York, on Sabbath Evening, Nov. 6, 1859 (Boston: Walker, Wise, 1859);

The Guilt of Slavery and the Crime of Slaveholding Demonstrated from the Hebrew and Greek Scriptures (Boston: J. P. Jewett, 1860);

God's Way of Crushing the Rebellion (New York, 1861);

Rights of the Coloured Race to Citizenship and Representation; and the Guilt and Consequences of Legislation Against Them (New York: Frances & Loutrel, printers, 1864);

Protest Against the Robbery of the Colored Race by the Proposed Amendment of the Constitution (New York: R. J. Johnston, printer, 1866);

Faith, Doubt, and Evidence: God's Vouchers for His Written Word (New York: A. D. F. Randolph, 1881);

God's Timepiece for Man's Eternity. Its Purpose of Love and Mercy; its Plenary Infallible Inspiration; and its Personal Experiment of Forgiveness and Eternal Life in Christ (London: Hodder & Stoughton/New York: A. C. Armstrong, 1883).

OTHER: *The American Common-place Book of Prose,* edited by Cheever (Boston: Samuel G. Goodrich, 1828); republished as *The Prose Writers of America* (New York: Leavitt, 1851);

The American Common-place Book of Poetry, with Occasional Notes, edited by Cheever (Boston: Carter, Hendee & Babcock/Baltimore: C. Carter, 1831); republished as *The Poets of America* (Hartford, Conn.: S. Andrus, 1847);

[Mourt's Relation.] Journal of the Pilgrims at Plymouth in New England, in 1620: Reprinted from the Original Volume. With Historical and Local Illustrations of Providences, Principles, and Persons, edited by Cheever (New York: John Wiley, 1848; Glasgow & London: W. Collins, 1849).

PERIODICAL PUBLICATIONS: Review of *Lectures on the Sacred Poetry of the Hebrews,* by Robert Lowth, *North American Review,* 31 (October 1830): 337-379;

"Study of Greek Literature," *American Quarterly Register,* 4 (May 1832): 273-290; 4 (August 1832): 33-46; 5 (February 1833): 218-236;

"Southey's *Life of Bunyan,*" *North American Review,* 36 (April 1833): 449-471;

"A Review of Andrews Norton's A Statement of Reasons for not Believing the Doctrines of the Trinitarians Concerning the Nature of God and the Person of Christ," *Quarterly Christian Spectator,* 5 (September 1833): 421-447;

"An Examination of Coleridge's *The Friend:* A Series of Essays to Aid in the Formation of Fixed Principles in Politics, Morals and Religion: with Literary Amusements Interspersed," *North American Review,* 40 (April 1835): 299-351.

George Barrell Cheever–clergyman, reformer, editor, and critic–was born in Hallowell, Maine, to Nathaniel and Charlotte Barrell Cheever on 17 April 1807. His strong conservative political and religious tendencies were formed early in life chiefly by his mother, a zealous Federalist and Congregationalist. It is interesting to speculate what turn his life would have taken if his father, a Jeffersonian-Republican and Unitarian who died when Cheever was twelve, had lived to liberalize him. Cheever rose to national prominence as a Congregational clergyman and antislavery and temperance reformer. He won respect as a literary and journal editor, and author of about sixty books and pamphlets on diverse subjects. He published at least twenty-five articles on literary and religious subjects in such established journals as the *Arena,* the *American Quarterly Register,* the *Biblical Repository, Bibliotheca Sacra,* the *New Monthly* magazine, the *North American Review,* and the *United States Literary Register.*

Cheever's early formal education took place at the Hallowell Academy and then at Bowdoin College, from which he graduated with Phi Beta Kappa honors in 1825 in the distinguished class that included Nathaniel Hawthorne, Henry W. Longfellow, Franklin Pierce, and Calvin Stowe. He formed no friendship in college with any of these future greats, although he later was a great admirer of Longfellow's poetry. After Bowdoin, his mother directed him in November 1825 to the Andover Theological School at Newton, Massachusetts, a stronghold of Congregational orthodoxy. At Andover he wrestled with his conscience about accepting the austere Puritan doctrines and becoming a minister, and twice dropped out of school before graduating in 1830. After graduation, however, he was ordained and thereafter de-

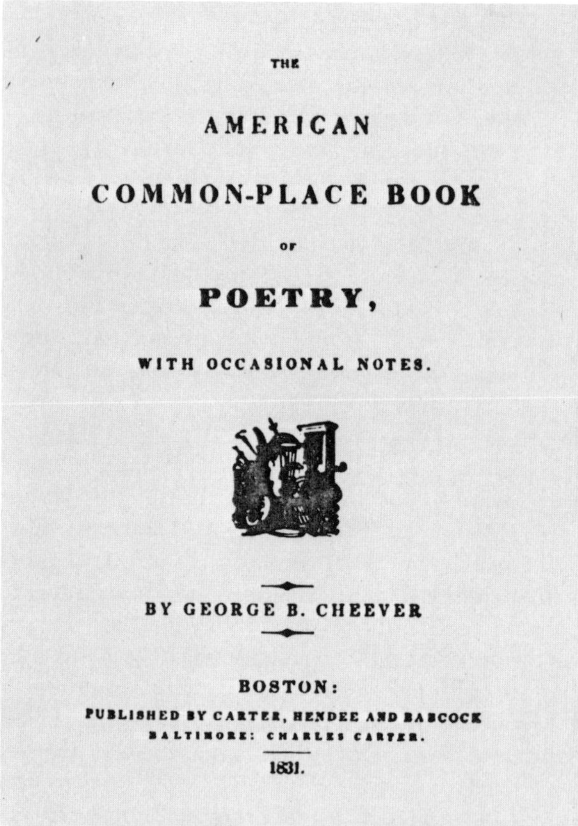
THE

AMERICAN

COMMON-PLACE BOOK

OF

POETRY,

WITH OCCASIONAL NOTES.

BY GEORGE B. CHEEVER

BOSTON:

PUBLISHED BY CARTER, HENDEE AND BABCOCK

BALTIMORE: CHARLES CARTER.

1831.

Title page for one of Cheever's popular anthologies

voted his life to propagating the old New England theology. Though religious studies occupied most of his time in college, literature was his second love. At the Vaughan Library in Hallowell, and at Bowdoin and Andover, he read widely and deeply in literature, science, history, and philosophy. From Andover he wrote his mother to explain his inordinate expenditure on secular books: "These are, some of them, Seminary Books, and the others were such beauties, and ones I had so long coveted, and withal so cheap! that I could not resist the temptation of buying them nor have I ever for a moment regretted it. . . . They have been the solace of my downcast, and the amusement of my leisure hours; and in such society as that of Goldsmith and Johnson, and Shakespeare, and Addison, and Milton, and Cowper and a host of such other literary worthies, it would be a pity if I could not make some improvement."

At Andover, in August 1827, he began his literary career by editing an anthology of American prose. Choosing selections from nearly seventy American authors, he published *The American Common-place Book of Prose* in 1828. Its success was aided by his choice of Samuel G. Goodrich of Boston as a publisher. He was encouraged in this project by the spirit of nationalism prevalent in the age calling for more American productions. In his preface he expressed the wish that his volume would "not be found inferior in excellence or interest to any of those compilations which have hitherto embraced only the *morceaux delicieuse* of English genius." To the nationalistic purpose he added a didactic intention: "There is a period, too, in education, in which an enlightened instructor will not omit a candid comparison of our native literature with the contemporary productions of English writers,–not for the sake of indulging national prejudice of any kind, but of enlarging the intelligence and disciplining the taste, of the rising minds, which, in their subsequent advancement, are to influence the literary estimation of their country." Among the prose writers included were Fisher Ames, John Q. Adams, George Bancroft, James Fenimore Cooper, Joseph Dennie, Washington Irving, Thomas Jefferson, Catherine Sedgwick, Daniel Webster, Nathaniel P. Willis, and William Wirt.

At Andover, Cheever enhanced his reputation by writing several substantial reviews, a few of which were: "Review of Moses Stuart's *Hebrew Grammar and Hebrew Chrestomathy*" in *Spirit of the Puritans* (May 1829); "Junius Unmasqued or Lord Sackville Proved to be Junius" in the *North American Review* (October 1829); Robert Lowth's *Lectures on the Sacred Poetry of the Hebrews* in the *North American Review* (October 1830); and "Milman's History of the Jews" in *Spirit of the Pilgrims* (October 1830). Encouraged by the success of his earlier edition of prose selections and by favorable comments on his reviews, Cheever undertook editing a volume of poetry.The volume was registered on 3 December 1829 under the title *Studies in Poetry. Embracing Notices of Lives and Writings of the Best Poets in the English Language . . . Designed to Illustrate the Principles of Rhetoric and Teach Their Application to Poetry.* In his Preface Cheever announced that the highest aim of the book was "to present the pupil with what may be called a book of practical poetical rhetoric; a volume which shall refine and regulate the taste and prepare the youthful mind to judge for itself, and to relish with discrimination, whatever is beautiful in the whole compass of English poetry." In this, as in all of his literary selections and judgments, Cheever applied a moral criterion, noting that wherever he could find poetry that combined the religious and poetic spirit he had included it. Of Chaucer, Cheever said that "his moral tendency is generally sensual and degraded"; of Shakespeare, he wrote: "His works therefore are to be studied with great caution and with much judgment in the selection. In their entire form they should never be put into the hands of children; but it gives pleasure to be able to state that the pupil may be referred with safety to 'Bowdler's Family Shakespeare',–an edition which is truly beautiful, while it excludes everything injurious in its tendency." Likewise, in his essays on Dryden, Pope, Young, Gray, and Burns, he applied the aesthetics of morality.

In *Studies in Poetry* he chose selections from fifty English poets, beginning with Chaucer; a dozen American poets, beginning with William Cullen Bryant; and six Hebrew writers. Most of the biographical and critical matter in the prefatory essays was derived from John Aiken, Thomas Campbell, Samuel Johnson, and Thomas James Mathias, though there is a fair amount of original commentary. He was in agreement with most critics of his time in his harsh judgment of Byron:

> Very little of Byron's poetry can be read without a most destructive influence upon the moral sensibilities. Humiliating was the waste and degradation of his genius, and melancholy is the power, which his poetry has exerted upon multitudes of minds. Some of his volumes are more pernicious in their moral tendency than any other books that were ever written. His complete works ought never to be purchased, and we feel proud not to be acquainted with them except by extracts, and beauties;– of these there will always be sufficient to satisfy the curiosity, exhibit the character of his genius, and give the imagination all of the delight which it can innocently receive from the perusal of any portion of his writing.

Cheever placed Coleridge and Wordsworth at the head of all modern poets. He appreciated Coleridge's sublimity, tenderness, fidelity to nature, and Christian philosophical views and was drawn to Wordsworth by his ability to describe and elevate the small in nature to sublimity, and to enlighten the understanding and meliorate the affections. Coleridge he felt to be the superior poet because his genius was "more wild and energetic" than that of Wordsworth and had "more fancy and invention." Of the American poets included in the collection, Bryant was most praised. Cheever commended his simple and graceful imagery, fresh and accurate descriptions of nature, and moral influence. He posted "Thanatopsis" as the best of Bryant's poems and ranked it with the most "elevated productions" of Wordsworth. *Studies in Poetry* was well reviewed in the journals, and several reprintings attest its popularity.

Cheever's next editorial venture was his *American Common-place Book of Poetry* (1831), a collection of about 400 poems from eighty American authors. He based his selections upon American authorship, religious sentiment, and potential salutary effect upon the reader. In the preface he says: "All the pieces in this volume are of the purest moral character; and, considering its limits, and the comparative scantiness of American poetry, a good number of them contain, in an uncommon degree, the religious and poetic spirit united. The importance of having books of this nature sweet and chaste in their moral influence, as well as refined in their intellectual and poetical character, is not enough appreciated. None can tell how much good a volume like this may accomplish, if an editor keeps such a purpose in view." Time has not vindicated some of Cheever's critical judgments in this volume. For example, he erred in ranking Robert H. Dana at the head of all American poets. He praised Bryant's superior elegance of language and polished beauty in his compositions, but he found more commendable qualities in Dana who, he said, "has attempted and proved successful in a higher and more difficult range of poetry; he exhibits loftier powers, and his compositions agitate the soul in deeper emotion. His language, without being so beautiful and finished, is yet more vivid, concise, and alive and informed with meaning. His descriptions of natural objects may not pass before the mind with sweet harmony, but they often present in a single line, a whole picture before the imagination, with a vividness and power of compression which are astonishing."

Next to the poetry of Dana and Bryant he esteemed highest the poetry of Longfellow: "It possesses what has been a rare quality in the American poets–simplicity of expression without any attempt to startle the reader or produce an effect by far-sought epithets. There is much sweetness in his imagery and language; and sometimes he is hardly excelled by anyone for the quiet accuracy exhibited in his pictures of natural objects. His poetry . . . some of it . . . will be remembered with that of Dana and Bryant." In some of John Pierpont's patriotic poetry, he also appreciated the sublimity and the "uncommon grandeur of expression." The poets represented with the most selections were Bryant with twenty-three; Dana, seventeen; Fitzgreen Halleck, eight; James A. Hillhouse, eleven; Longfellow, seven; W. O. B. Peabody, eight; James Gates Percival, fifteen; Pierpont, sixteen; Lydia Sigourney, thirteen; John Greenleaf Whittier, six; Carlos Wilcox, fourteen; and Nathaniel P. Willis, thirteen. Despite a strong bias against Unitarians, he included quite a few in his collection–Bryant, Longfellow, Peabody, Pierpont, Sigourney, and even an antagonist, Andrews Norton–as well as anonymous selections from the leading Unitarian organ, the *Christian Examiner. The American Common-place Book of Poetry* was well reviewed and underwent several editions.

With *The American Common-place Book of Poetry* Cheever ceased editing collections of poetry, but he continued his critical activities with several reviews that drew attention: "Study of Greek Literature" in the *American Quarterly Register* (May and August 1832 and February 1833), which was a strong plea for Greek to be studied in modern times; and "Southey's *Life of Bunyan*" in the *North American Review* (1833), in which he advanced Dr. Henry More, Milton, Shakespeare, Bacon, and Bunyan as the greatest writers of the seventeenth century but cited Bunyan as the most original writer and the best moral influence. His writing this review led to the preparation of a popular series of lectures on the great Puritan author which were eventually published as *Lectures on the Pilgrim's Progress and on the Life and Times of John Bunyan* (1844). In his review of Bunyan, Cheever–citing as evidence Blair, Cowper, and Herbert–took issue with Samuel Johnson's position that devotional and inspirational poetry was inferior because it did not allow for novelty and invention in sentiment. Another prominent review of this period was his critique of Coleridge's *The Friend* in the *North American Review* (April 1835). He was effusive on Coleridge's greatness: "We regard him with feelings of veneration and love, which we have paid to few other names in literature." He praised the excellence of Coleridge's monumental intellect, unaffected greatness, nobility of character, devotion to principles (particularly moral principles), spiritual rather than sensual

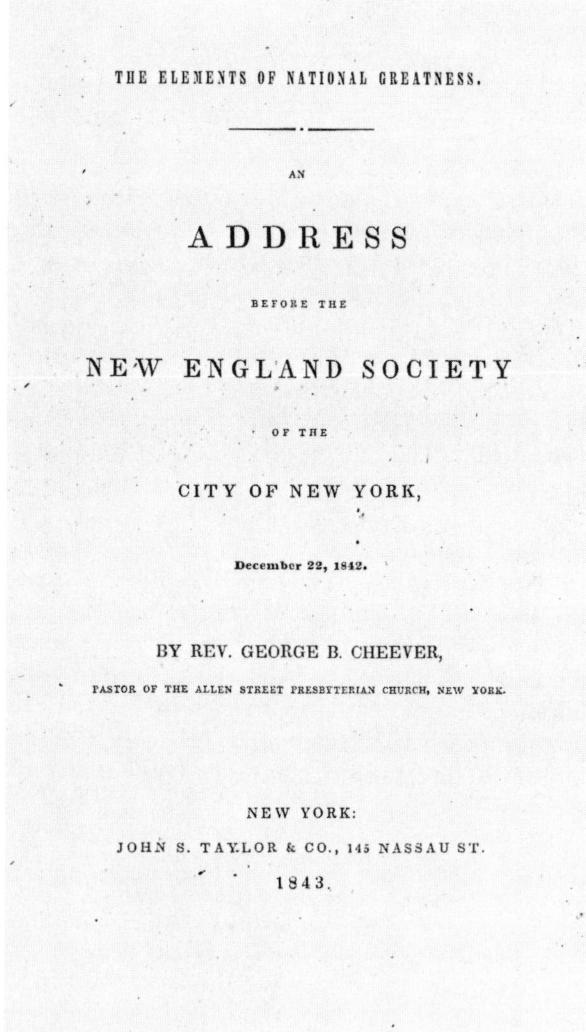
THE ELEMENTS OF NATIONAL GREATNESS.

AN

ADDRESS

BEFORE THE

NEW ENGLAND SOCIETY

OF THE

CITY OF NEW YORK,

December 22, 1842.

BY REV. GEORGE B. CHEEVER,

PASTOR OF THE ALLEN STREET PRESBYTERIAN CHURCH, NEW YORK.

NEW YORK:

JOHN S. TAYLOR & CO., 145 NASSAU ST.

1843.

Title page for Cheever's exegesis of the requirements of a modern nation

quality, and joining of both Platonic and Christian philosophy. He remained an admirer of Coleridge, but in later times felt that the American Transcendentalists had misapplied his philosophy.

Cheever had begun his Christian ministry, which occupied most of his career, in 1830 by supplying Congregational pulpits in Newburyport and Boston and assisting the famed evangelist Charles G. Finney. On 13 February 1833 he was ordained as pastor of the Howard Street Congregational Church in Salem, Massachusetts, where he served until 4 January 1838. A fiery Puritan, he denounced the Unitarian William Ellery Channing and his "infidel" followers and debated with the *Christian Examiner.* One notable attack upon the Unitarians was voiced in his fourth of July address, *Some of the Principles according to which this*

World is Managed, Contrasted with the Government of God . . . (1833), prompted by an anti-Trinitarian piece that had been written by Andrews Norton, editor of the *Examiner.* In Salem he continued with vigor a crusade for temperance reform which he had begun in 1832 when he published "The Temperance Reformation" in the *American Quarterly Observer.* In 1835 Cheever precipitated a long and bitter controversy when he combined his attack upon the Unitarians and his antitemperance foes. In a "dream story" in the *Salem Landmark* on 31 January 1835, he poked fun at a respectable Unitarian deacon, John Stone, who distilled liquor and allegedly sold Bibles in the same establishment. He then published the newspaper essay as a pamphlet entitled *Inquire at Amos Giles' Distillery* (1835). As a result of his satirical attack, he was horsewhipped in the streets by ruffians who worked in the distillery, had to pay a $1,000 fine for libeling deacon Stone, and was put into jail for thirty days. He won a token settlement against Stone's employees who horsewhipped him; but his greatest reward was that the affair made him a hero among temperance crusaders and the orthodox Congregationalists. His *Inquire at Amos Giles' Distillery* advanced the temperance cause considerably. The reform-minded Cheever embraced the antislavery cause as early as 1831 as an independent abolitionist; but he did not enter the slavery controversy with great enthusiasm until after the Compromise of 1850 and did not ally himself with the national abolition organization for several years afterwards.

In November 1836 Cheever went abroad to rest from his labors; but as he traveled through the British Isles and on the Continent, he continued to preach with zeal messages of Congregationalism, temperance, and antislavery. On this vacation he also devoted himself to an intense study of Catholicism, Protestantism, and Mohammedanism. Back in New York City on 25 May 1839, he was called immediately to become pastor of the Allen Street Presbyterian Church. From the time of his settlement until he severed his connection with this church in 1844, he crusaded for capital punishment and against what he felt to be the errors of the Catholics, High Church Episcopalians, Transcendentalists, liquor interests, desecrators of the Christian sabbath, and slaveholders. He wrote several books and pamphlets on reforms that he espoused, three of which were: *The Religion of Experience and that of Imitation* (1843), one

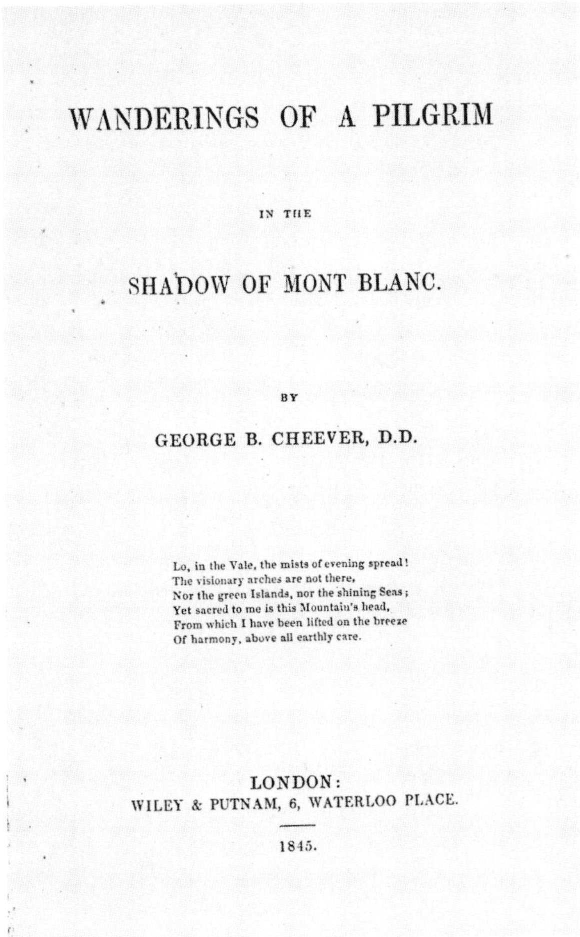
WANDERINGS OF A PILGRIM

IN THE

SHADOW OF MONT BLANC.

BY

GEORGE B. CHEEVER, D.D.

Lo, in the Vale, the mists of evening spread!
The visionary arches are not there,
Nor the green Islands, nor the shining Seas;
Yet sacred to me is this Mountain's head,
From which I have been lifted on the breeze
Of harmony, above all earthly care.

LONDON:
WILEY & PUTNAM, 6, WATERLOO PLACE.

1845.

Title page for the London edition of one of Cheever's accounts of his experiences in Switzerland

of several savage attacks upon Episcopalianism and Catholicism; *Lectures on the Pilgrim's Progress* (1844), containing his ideas on religion and reform based upon a popular series of lectures that he had delivered; and *A Defence of Capital Punishment* (1846), an argument for capital punishment based upon the Scriptures. Another work of significance that he wrote while he was at Allen Street was *Characteristics of the Christian Philosopher: A Discourse Commemorative of the Virtues and Attainments of Rev. James Marsh, D.D.* (1843). In this published discourse Cheever praised James Marsh, former president and professor of philosophy at the University of Vermont, as a Christian philosopher and condemned the present-day Transcendentalists, with whom some had associated Marsh. Cheever explained Marsh's sympathy for a spiritual philosophy as well as his antipathy to an altogether sensuous philosophy. He asserted that Marsh was always a Christian philosopher who rooted his philosophy in the Holy Scriptures and opposed the beliefs of the Boston Transcendentalists in a depersonalized God, Pantheism, Deism, and Oriental mysticism. Cheever personally believed that the Transcendentalists were reverting to infidelity.

Fatigue from a rigorous schedule of preaching, lecturing, and writing forced Cheever again to go to Europe in search of health in May 1844; while he was abroad the University of New York awarded him the honorary D.D.; upon returning in November 1844, he assumed the editorship of the New York *Evangelist,* the leading Presbyterian journal. As editor of the *Evangelist* for two years, he opposed the annexation of Texas as a slave territory and advocated a peaceful settlement of the Oregon dispute. Appealing always to Scriptural authority, he denounced with regularity "papal usurpation," polygamy, drunkenness, slavery, Puseyism, and the "Continental sabbath." He recorded an account of his experiences in the Swiss Alps in his *Wanderings of a Pilgrim in the Shadow of Mount Blanc* in 1845. On 21 November 1845 Cheever married Elizabeth Hoppin Wetmore of New York City.

A stormy phase of Cheever's life began when he accepted a call to become pastor of the Church of the Puritans in New York City in 1846. In this wealthy center of Congregationalism, he continued his barrage of preachments against the "Continental sabbath" (especially against such violations as Sunday train service), liquor, Catholicism, and slavery. With the passing of time, his intransigent reform views caused contention among his parishioners. He hated slavery but found it difficult to join forces with William Lloyd Garrison (whom he considered an infidel) and women crusaders. He castigated Chief Justice Taney for the Dred Scott decision, accused the American Tract Society and American Board of Foreign Missionaries of abetting slavery, proclaimed John Brown a "true patriot," and preached "the irrepressible conflict." Between 1857 and 1861 there were constant quarrels between the pro-Cheever and anti-Cheever factions in the Church of the Puritans, with the wealthiest members usually opposing Cheever's uncompromising positions. When Cheever could not raise enough financial support in 1860-1861 from his church to support his fight against slavery, he toured England to raise $50,000. His "begging mission" further divided the members of his congregation. As a fundraiser he was not successful,

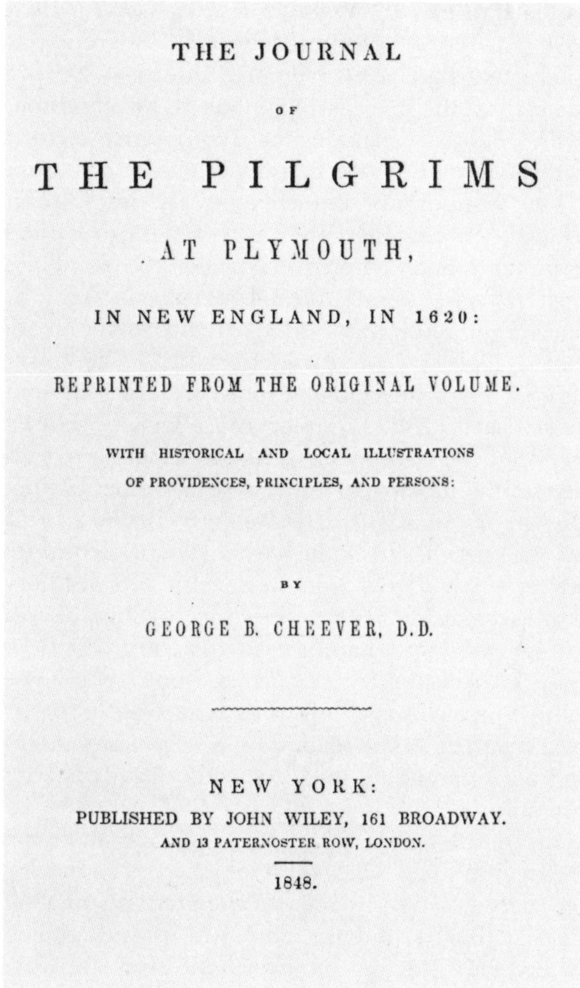
THE JOURNAL

OF

THE PILGRIMS

AT PLYMOUTH,

IN NEW ENGLAND, IN 1620:

REPRINTED FROM THE ORIGINAL VOLUME.

WITH HISTORICAL AND LOCAL ILLUSTRATIONS
OF PROVIDENCES, PRINCIPLES, AND PERSONS:

BY

GEORGE B. CHEEVER, D.D.

NEW YORK:
PUBLISHED BY JOHN WILEY, 161 BROADWAY.
AND 13 PATERNOSTER ROW, LONDON.

1848.

Title page for Cheever's edition of Mourt's Relation, *an account of the first pilgrims' experiences*

but he gained fame in England as a leading American abolitionist. Back at home, he became a strident critic of Lincoln for his slowness in emancipating the slaves and for his pacific policies. Throughout the Civil War and the Reconstruction he was an unrelenting critic of Lincoln and Johnson for every kind word and magnanimous gesture toward the South.

During his pastorate at the Church of the Puritans, Cheever wrote several books on religion and reform, touching upon a wide range of issues, including *The Pilgrim Fathers: or the Journal of the Pilgrims of Plymouth* (1849); *The Voices of Nature to Her Foster Child, the Soul of Man* (1853); *Right of the Bible in our Public Schools* (1854); *God Against Slavery* (1857); *The Fire and Hammer of God's Word Against the Sin of Slavery* (1858); and *The Guilt of Slavery and the Crime of Slaveholding*

Demonstrated from the Hebrew and Greek Scriptures (1860), the latter two works being classic arguments against the position that the Scriptures sanction slavery. During this period Cheever's one notable work on a literary figure was *Lectures on the Life, Genius, and Insanity of Cowper* (1856), but the book dealt primarily with Cowper's religious rather than his literary life.

Beset by internal strife, the Church of the Puritans began to decline shortly after the Civil War and finally dissolved in the summer of 1871. Cheever continued to preach for the congregation until its dissolution, and afterward he moved to Englewood, New Jersey, where he lived until he died on 1 October 1890. At Englewood he gradually closed out his pulpit activities but continued his vigorous defense of religious fundamentalism with his pen. In two books written in his last years, he attacked the errors of modernism in religion and the new science and Catholicism: *Faith, Doubt, and Evidence: God's Vouchers for His Written Word* (1881); and *God's Timepiece for Man's Eternity* (1883).

Throughout his career Cheever was a controversialist of questionable success. His crusade against the Unitarians achieved nothing of significance; likewise, his fulminations against the Catholics produced no positive results. His denunciations of slavery were commendable but often weakened by his refusal to cooperate with viable abolitionist movements. In his stands for capital punishment and temperance he found many sympathetic followers. He was an uncompromising moralist who viewed all national problems through the eyes of a Puritan, jaundiced by the laws of the Old Testament. As a literary editor and critic he did not change the course of American literature and did not affect any authors significantly, but he raised the aesthetic and national consciousness of the American reading public by making more accessible to them selections of representative and often good literature in his *American Common-place Book of Prose, American Common-place Book of Poetry,* and *Studies in Poetry* and by writing several worthwhile literary reviews in widely circulated periodicals.

References:

Henry T. Cheever, *Memorabilia of George B. Cheever, D.D.: Late Pastor of the Church of the Puritans Union Square, New York, and of his Wife, Elizabeth Wetmore Cheever in Verse and in Prose* (New York: Wiley, 1890);

William Herries, *Sketch of the Life of Rev. George B. Cheever, D.[D.]* (New York, 1861);

Robert M. York, *George B. Cheever, Religious and Social Reformer: 1807-1809,* in University of Maine Studies, second series, no. 69 (Orono: University of Maine Press, 1955).

Papers:

Cheever's correspondence, as well as various manuscripts, can be found in about a dozen libraries and depositories, but the largest collections of materials are located at the American Antiquarian Society, Worcester, Massachusetts; the Boston Public Library; and the Houghton Library at Harvard University.

James Freeman Clarke

(4 April 1810-8 June 1888)

Leonard N. Neufeldt
Purdue University

See also the Clarke entry in *DLB 1, The American Renaissance in New England.*

SELECTED BOOKS: *False Witness Answered* (Boston: Leonard C. Bowles, 1835);

The Unitarian Reform (Boston: James Munroe, 1839);

The Church of the Disciples in Boston. A Sermon on the Principles and Methods of the Church of the Disciples. Delivered Sunday Morning and Evening, Dec. 7, 1845 (Boston: Benjamin H. Greene, 1846);

Slavery in Its Relation to God. A Review of Rev. Dr. Lord's Thanksgiving Sermon, in Favor of Domestic Slavery, Entitled the Higher Law, in Its Application to the Fugitive Slave Bill. By a Minister of the Gospel, in Massachusetts (Buffalo: A. M. Clapp, 1851);

The Christian Doctrine of Forgiveness of Sin; An Essay (Boston: Crosby & Nichols/New York: C. S. Francis, 1852);

Eleven Weeks in Europe; and What May Be Seen in That Time (Boston: Ticknor, Reed & Fields, 1852);

The Rendition of Anthony Burns. Its Causes and Consequences. A Discourse on Christian Politics, Delivered in Williams Hall, Boston, on Whitsunday, June 4, 1854 (Boston: Crosby, Nichols, 1854);

Causes and Consequences of the Affair at Harper's Ferry. A Sermon Preached in the Indiana Place Chapel, on Sunday Morning, Nov. 6, 1859 (Boston: Walker, Wise, 1859);

Theodore Parker and his Theology: A Discourse Delivered in the Music Hall, Boston, Sunday, Sept. 25, 1859 (Boston: Walker, Wise, 1859);

Secession, Concession, or Self-Possession: Which? (Boston: Walker, Wise, 1861);

Discourse on the Aspects of War, Delivered in the Indiana-Place Chapel, Boston, on Fast Day, April 2, 1863 (Boston: Walker, Wise, 1863);

Natural and Artificial Methods in Education. Lectures Delivered Before the American Institute of Instruction, at Concord, N.H., August 27, 1863 (Boston: Ticknor & Fields, 1864);

Courtesy of the Unitarian Universalist Association Archives, Boston

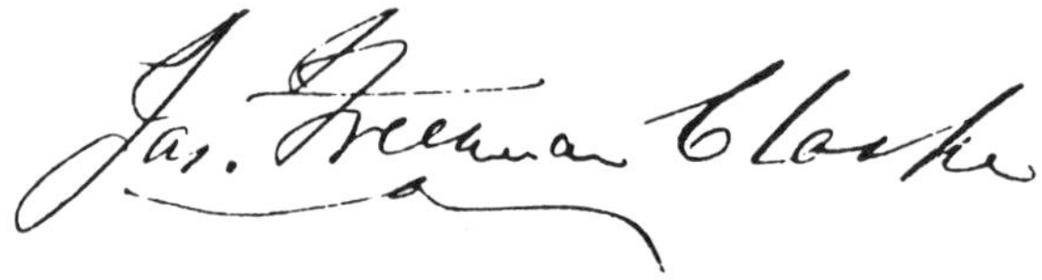

Orthodoxy: Its Truths and Errors (Boston: American Unitarian Association/Walker, Fuller/New York: James Miller, 1866);

Ten Great Religions: An Essay in Comparative Theology (Boston: James R. Osgood, 1871);

Common-Sense in Religion: A Series of Essays (Boston: James R. Osgood, 1874);

Essentials and Non-Essentials in Religion. Six Lectures Delivered in the Music Hall, Boston (Boston: American Unitarian Association, 1877);

How to Find the Stars with Indications of the Most Interesting Objects in the Starry Heavens, and an Account of the Astronomical Lantern and Its Use (Boston: Lockwood, Brooks, 1878);

Memorial and Biographical Sketches (Boston: Houghton, Osgood, 1878);

Self-Culture: Physical, Intellectual, Moral, and Spiritual. A Course of Lectures (Boston: James R. Osgood, 1880);

Events and Epochs in Religious History: Being the Substance of a Course of Twelve Lectures Delivered in the Lowell Institute, Boston, in 1880 (Boston: James R. Osgood, 1881);

The Legend of Thomas Didymus the Jewish Sceptic (Boston: Lee & Shepard/New York: Charles T. Dillingham, 1881);

Anti-Slavery Days, A Sketch of the Struggle Which Ended in the Abolition of Slavery in the United States (New York: J. W. Lovell, 1883);

Ten Great Religions. Part II. A Comparison of All Religions (Boston & New York: Houghton, Mifflin, 1883);

Manual of Unitarian Belief (Boston: Unitarian Sunday-School Society, 1884; revised, Boston: Beacon, 1924);

Agnosticism vs. Positivism: An Essay (Boston: Geo. H. Ellis, 1886);

The Mutual Obligations of Science and Religion (Boston: George H. Ellis, 1887);

Temperance Efforts and Temperance Methods (Boston: George H. Ellis, 1887);

Woman Suffrage: Reasons For and Against (Boston: George H. Ellis, 1888);

The Lord's Prayer. Being the Last Eight Discourses of the Rev. James Freeman Clarke, D.D. (London: Christian Life Office, 1888; Boston: American Unitarian Association, 1891);

James Freeman Clarke Autobiography, Diary and Correspondence, edited by Edward Everett Hale (Boston & New York: Houghton, Mifflin, 1891);

Nineteenth Century Questions (Boston & New York: Houghton, Mifflin, 1897; London: Gay & Bird, 1898);

Hymns and Poems (Boston: Geo. H. Ellis, 1908);

The Transfiguration of Life (Boston: American Unitarian Association, 1909).

OTHER: *Theodore; or, the Skeptic's Conversion. History of the Culture of a Protestant Clergyman, Translated from the German of De Wette,* 2 volumes, translated by Clarke (Boston: Hilliard, Gray, 1841);

Memoirs of Margaret Fuller Ossoli, edited by Clarke with Ralph Waldo Emerson and William Henry Channing (2 volumes, Boston: Phillips, Sampson, 1852; 3 volumes, London: Bentley, 1852);

"Address [on Shakespeare]," in *New England Genealogical Society. Tercentenary Celebration of the Birth of Shakespeare* (Boston, 1864), pp. 11-52;

Exotics: Attempts to Domesticate Them, translated by Clarke, with Lillian Rebecca Clarke (Boston: James R. Osgood, 1875);

"The Anti-Slavery Movement in Boston," in *The Memorial History of Boston,* volume 3, edited by J. Windsor (Boston, 1881), pp. 369-400.

PERIODICAL PUBLICATIONS: "Thomas Carlyle–the German Scholar," *Western Messenger,* 4 (February 1838): 417-423;

"R. W. Emerson and the New School," by Clarke and C. P. Cranch, *Western Messenger,* 6 (November 1838): 37-47;

"Margaret Fuller," *Christian Register,* 62 (1 November 1883): 698;

"Hawthorne and Margaret Fuller," *Independent,* 37 (1 January 1885): 1.

James Freeman Clarke, born in Hanover, New Hampshire, and educated at the Latin School of Boston, Harvard College, and Harvard Divinity School, was a liberal Unitarian minister who, as editor of the *Western Messenger* in Louisville, Kentucky, from 1836 to 1839 and as pastor of the Church of the Disciples in Boston from 1841 until his death (except for a three-year hiatus), established a reputation as editor, translator of German literature, Transcendentalist fellow-traveler, minor poet, literary scholar, eloquent preacher, social reformer, prolific theological writer, and leading figure in the New England and national Unitarian movement of his time. From 1866 to 1885 he served virtually without interruption as member of the Board of Overseers of Harvard College. From 1867 to 1871 and in 1876 he taught courses in comparative religion at Harvard Divinity School. His role as radical thinker, litterateur, and churchman contrasts with that of his friends Orestes Brownson, William Henry Channing, Christopher Cranch, John S. Dwight, and Ralph Waldo Emerson, all of whom resigned from the Unitarian pulpit. He is also distinguished from them by his perdurable optimism in historical progress, science and technology, and the prospects of American culture. Eventually he received more income than any of these colleagues except, perhaps, Emerson, through his pastoral salary, publications, lectures, and shrewd investments in stocks, improved and unimproved land (including Brook Farm after its collapse), apartment dwellings, and loan financing.

"I am not of an anxious temperament . . . and it has never disturbed me when I have been censured," Clarke wrote in his old age. Much earlier he had observed that although some wise and good people oppose reform, if they study the issue thoroughly they will eventually support the reformer. Add to these reflections his admission that "I love work, and especially brain work" and one is well on the way to accounting not only for Clarke's championing of abolitionism, woman suffrage, temperance, introduction of income tax, educational reform, slum improvements, prison reorganization, abolition of capital punishment, and better conditions for the working class, but also his strong friendship with Margaret Fuller, admiration of Emerson, spirited defense of Theodore Parker, introduction of German writers to America, interest in Charles Darwin, pioneering work in comparative religions, and his considerable political and diplomatic skills within Unitarianism.

Although Clarke's literary criticism spanning the period from the 1830s to the 1880s reveals no major shifts, his principal critical articles and theoretical arguments belong to the decades after the 1860s. In this period he also accomplished his work in comparative religions and produced a gargantuan corpus of practical and repetitious writings for American Unitarianism. During the 1850s, when he rebuilt his Church of the Disciples congregation and began to make his mark in Unitarianism, his literary criticism was slight in comparison to his earlier and later years, and it repeated his sentiments of the 1830s and 1840s, when he was thoroughly taken with literary and theological developments in Europe and with New England Transcendentalism.

Clarke's watercolor of the First Unitarian Church of Louisville, circa 1835 (courtesy of the Filson Club, Louisville, Kentucky)

In the year that he accepted his first pastorate Clarke confided in his journal, "I wish to write a great deal . . . and to read little, and that principally German. . . . I think . . . of writing a drama." As it turned out, he developed the habit of reading and writing a great deal. He also devoted much time to German literature and to his own literary writing. No drama came to be, but he composed hundreds of poems (the Houghton Library of Harvard alone holds over 500 pages of autographed poetry manuscripts, many of them never published). His verse appeared in numerous journals, newspapers, four anthologies, and in pamphlet format. In his extensive reading of British and German writers, he was most engaged by literary works, and poetry, in particular, stimulated him to produce more written commentary than did any other genre. Five of the thirteen names on his list of "My Teachers" are poets, and William Wordsworth, Samuel Taylor Coleridge, and Goethe rank near the top. Also revealing are his stipulations for the *Saturday Evening Gazette* of Boston, which published about 475 of his sermons in his later years: he did not allow any liquor advertisements on his pages; he preferred to have poetry above his column; and he insisted on selecting each poem. "He approached all subjects from the poetical side," F. H. Hedge is reported to have said about Clarke.

With characteristic imperiousness and breathless honesty the young Clarke expressed to Fuller his "sentiment of contempt" for third-rate poets, a conviction and pose that probably lay behind his observation a year later that he had been writing poetry "not with a view to publish, but to ease my feelings by expression." As the poetry accumulated in his commonplace books, however, he began to reconsider both his published and unpublished verse; as late as age sixty-five he considered publishing "a small volume of my own poems," if his forthcoming volume of translations of poetry would be well received. He never did launch a volume of his own verse.

Despite Clarke's apparent interest in the fusion of traditional poetic modes and conventions with vigorous new experimentation in Germany and Britain, his own verse from early to late years is conventional and frequently sentimental, and his assessment of American contemporaries is consistent with his practice. Walt Whitman is ignored, but in 1867 James Russell Lowell is described as "one of our best poets," and John Greenleaf Whittier is "our other great American poet."

Self-portrait by Clarke, from his journal for 1839-1840 (by permission of the Houghton Library, Harvard University)

In "The Evolution of a Great Poem" (first published in *Independent* in May 1884), Clarke's discussion of Thomas Gray's "Elegy" helps to clarify his regard for Lowell, Whittier, and, for that matter, William Cullen Bryant, Henry Wadsworth Longfellow, and T. B. Aldrich. In their best work they are poets of both imagination and discipline, revealed in "perfect finish" and expert diction. Gray's painstaking revisions of his poem mark it as carefully crafted, elegantly finished, tonally harmonious art rather than a work of inspiration. Spenser's and Shakespeare's extraordinary "inspiration" produced "high art," whereas in Wordsworth (second rank), "inspiration is at its maximum, and art at its minimum" and in Gray and John Keats (third rank), "art is at its maximum" and inspiration is lacking. Although Clarke appears to invoke the argument in the middle chapters of Coleridge's *Biographia Literaria* (1817), Clarke's appeal to cultivated taste and his formula for great art (more than usual imagination and more than usual control) suggest a strong neoclassical bent as well.

This double inclination in his critical practice was compatible with another of his traits, a New England Unitarian version of moral-aestheticism that required the truly beautiful to be morally attractive. In this regard Clarke's translations and advocacy of Goethe indicate more than an interest in German literature. *Hermann und Dorothea* and *Wilhelm Meisters Lehrjahre* were Clarke's favorite long works, the former because of its elegantly simple poetry and the latter for its ethical "look at the inside of life." His principle of selection in translating Goethe favors the more intellectual and less radical over the morally controversial writer, a principle that one discerns in Clarke's translation work in general. As translator he preferred Goethe over Schiller, whom he also admired, because Goethe "requires less enthusiasm and more study." The early Tennyson struck Clarke as exquisite but somewhat trivial. And Julian Hawthorne's profile of Margaret Fuller, in which the suspicions of the father are raised to hostility by the son, was objectionable because Julian Hawthorne's mean-spirited attitude prevented him from recognizing her intellectual, moral, and imaginative energies.

Not surprisingly Clarke's manuscript lecture "Realism & Idealism in Art" (written in the late 1860s or 1870s) acknowledges the importance of both "Naturalism" and "Idealism" but endorses "Realism" as the true equator between the two extremes. In "Realism . . . the idea gives unity to the facts, and the life of nature vitalizes all with its variety." The great artist adds "something of himself" (inventiveness, power of unifying, personal attitudes, attitudes of his age, and a long history of art, in short, "Idealism") to nature, yet is always thoroughly instructed by nature (quoted with the permission of the Andover-Harvard Library). The commodious generalizations of this lecture indicate that in Clarke's mind salient principles of Joshua Reynolds, Gotthold Lessing, Goethe, Coleridge, and Emerson were reconciled.

A different polarity is central to "Lyric and Dramatic Elements in Literature and Art" (completed in the 1870s after Clarke purchased his first typewriter and published posthumously in *Nineteenth Century Questions*, 1897). This essay proposes that all literature falls into two categories. In the lyric the personality and sensibility of the writer are strongly present in every line and stanza; in the dramatic the writer's personality is extinguished and the formal poetic aspects of the work and its ideas are in the foreground. Petrarch, Milton, Schiller, and Lowell are examples

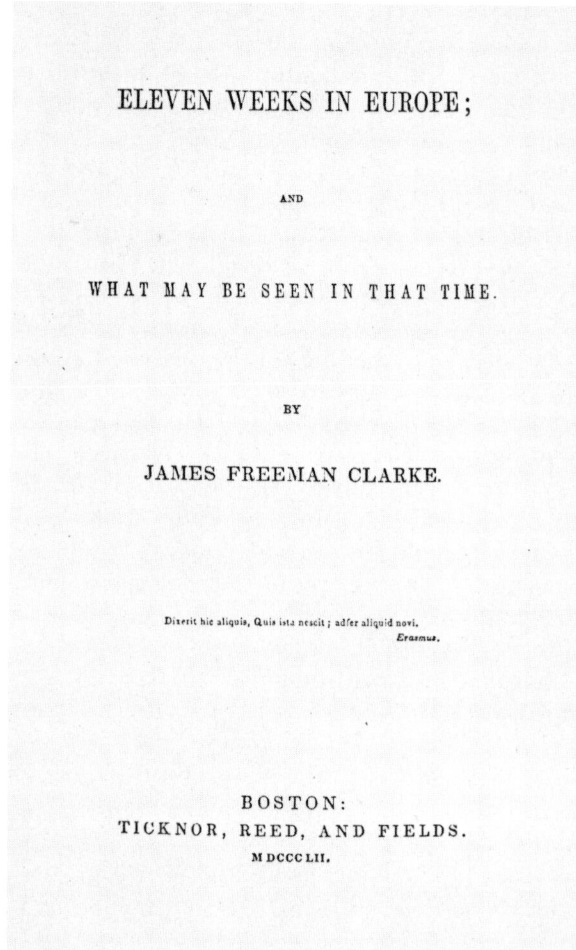

ELEVEN WEEKS IN EUROPE;

AND

WHAT MAY BE SEEN IN THAT TIME.

BY

JAMES FREEMAN CLARKE.

Dixerit hic aliquis, Quis ista nescit; adfer aliquid novi.
Erasmus.

BOSTON:
TICKNOR, REED, AND FIELDS.
MDCCCLII.

Title page for the collection of travel sketches that Clarke culled from his journals and letters

of lyric writers distinguished, respectively, from their dramatic counterparts Dante, Shakespeare, Goethe, and Longfellow. Both kinds of poets have demonstrated excellent philosophical minds, Clarke notes in an essay on Francis Bacon, but no philosopher has been a great poet.

Clarke's standard in "The Evolution of a Great Poem" is applicable to other genres as well, and "Lyric and Dramatic Elements" includes several writers of prose fiction in its grouping of artists. His efforts at original prose, which produced a novel, *The Legend of Thomas Didymus the Jewish Sceptic* (1881), a preliminary draft of what appears to be the first chapter of another novel, and a preliminary or intermediate draft of a short story, suggest that his own practice in prose fiction (and later poetry) should be identified with his definition of dramatic writers. His novel focuses on the protagonist, Jesus, prior to, during, and following his crucifixion, and on the changing perceptions of the narrator, Thomas. In Clarke's words, the novel presents "a remarkable man" who left an eternal imprint on history. In the company of other great souls, Jesus is the first among equals: Theodore Parker, for instance, is characterized elsewhere as Elijah and Thomas Carlyle as John the Baptist.

More germane to a sorting out and organizing of Clarke's views on prose fiction are his numerous comments on his reading and his manuscript lectures "The Older English Novelists" and "The Later English Novelists," written in the late 1870s. On the whole, especially in his later years, he recommended a via media between mere description of nature and of society on the one hand and abstract idea on the other. Moreover, he preferred fiction that follows a protagonist's progress, a view of fiction essentially identical with Emerson's. *Robinson Crusoe* (1719), *Rasselas* (1759), *The Vicar of Wakefield* (1766), *Joseph Andrews* (1742), Walter Scott's Waverly novels, and *Uncle Tom's Cabin* (1852) were among Clarke's favorites. His ambitious translation of Wilhelm De Wette's *Theodor* had less to do with its being a novel than with its religious nature, its cornucopia of opinions on philosophy, theology, ethics, morality, and politics, the presence of a number of poems by De Wette and others in the work, and above all, the fact that *Theodor* follows the development of a man's mind, personality, and character, a schema similar to that of *Thomas Didymus*. The strong imprint of Goethe's *Wilhelm Meister* on Clarke had much to do with its principle of moral and philosophical investigation and the protagonist's development.

With few exceptions, scholars have identified Clarke's work in German literature as his major contribution to American letters. His interest in things German was awakened during his divinity studies, when he and Margaret Fuller tried to teach each other German. Her rapid progress fascinated rather than intimidated him. Reading and translating Goethe soon became their chief project, and his preoccupation with Goethe started his life anew. As editor of the *Western Messenger* in the 1830s he recommended and commented in journalistic flourishes on a "fair circle of gifted minds," including Immanuel Kant, Johann Fichte, Goethe, Friedrich Schiller, Jean Paul Richter, Novalis, and Ludwig Tieck. No doubt many of Clarke's readers knew little more about German literature and Goethe than he had

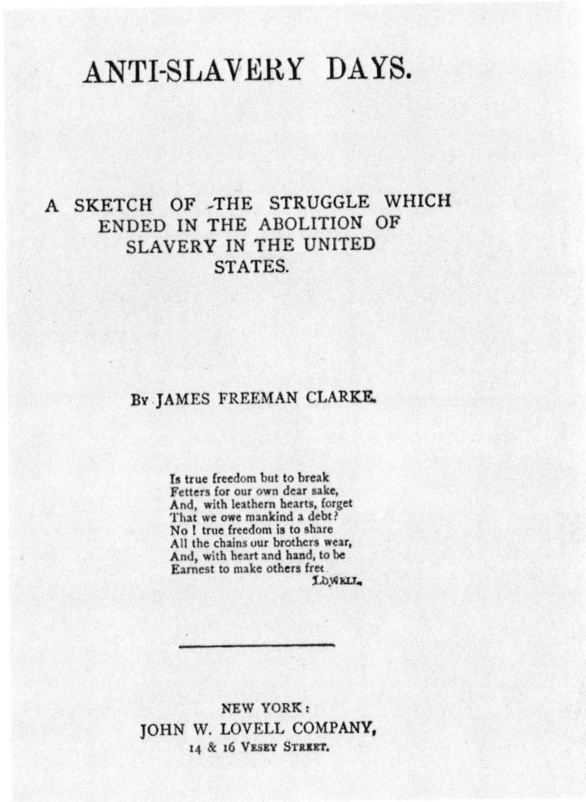

ANTI-SLAVERY DAYS.

A SKETCH OF THE STRUGGLE WHICH ENDED IN THE ABOLITION OF SLAVERY IN THE UNITED STATES.

BY JAMES FREEMAN CLARKE.

Is true freedom but to break
Fetters for our own dear sake,
And, with leathern hearts, forget
That we owe mankind a debt?
No! true freedom is to share
All the chains our brothers wear,
And, with heart and hand, to be
Earnest to make others free.
LOWELL.

NEW YORK:
JOHN W. LOVELL COMPANY,
14 & 16 VESEY STREET.

Title page for Clarke's detailed account of the abolition of American slavery

exposed them to in his commentaries and translations.

The quality of his published translations was usually high. In 1839 he contributed to John S. Dwight's edition of *Select Minor Poems, Translated from the German of Goethe and Schiller* and quite possibly drafted the favorable anonymous review in the *Messenger*. Two years later his impressive book *Theodore; or, the Skeptics Conversion . . . Translated from the German of De Wette* (1841) was published in two volumes after having appeared serially. Also important is *Exotics: Attempts to Domesticate Them* (1875), in which he collected a number of his poetry translations from Latin, French, Persian, but mostly from German. His principle of selection for the volume was influenced by at least five considerations: the response of critics to previous publications of his translations; the recommendations of his family; his own assessments; his decision to limit the volume to translations of short and relatively simple lyrical poems; and his definition of the translator's faithfulness to the original in his brief manuscript lecture on "Versified Translations of Lyrical Poetry" (a sepa-

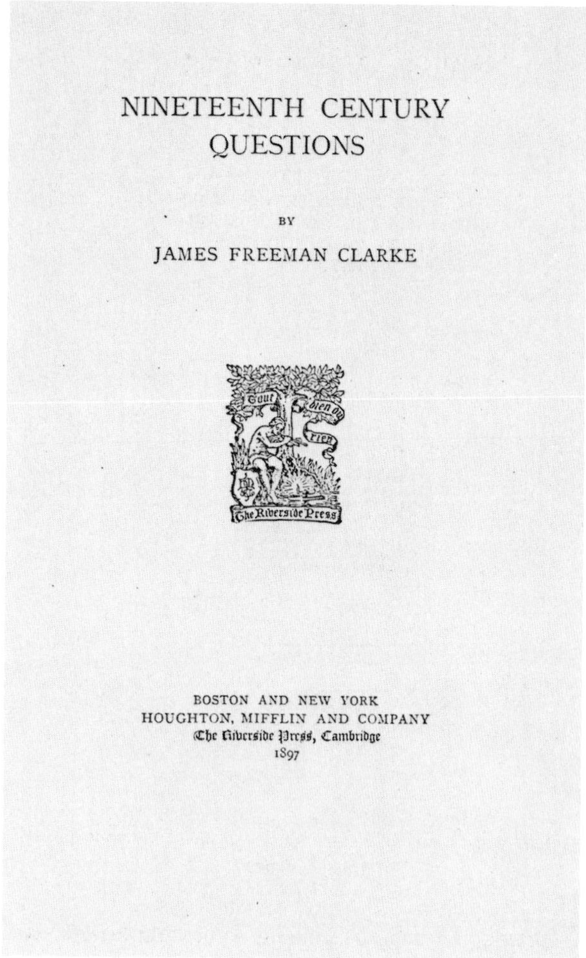
NINETEENTH CENTURY
QUESTIONS

BY

JAMES FREEMAN CLARKE

BOSTON AND NEW YORK
HOUGHTON, MIFFLIN AND COMPANY
The Riverside Press, Cambridge
1897

Title page for Clarke's collection of his biographical, historical, philosophical, religious, and literary essays

rate section of his unpublished "Lecture on Poetry" manuscript, written in the 1870s, at the Andover-Harvard Theological Library). In a balancing act that recalls his opposing forces of "Idealism" and "Naturalism," he suggested that translations should reconcile what the translator brings to the poem and the literalness of the original. Being faithful means faithfulness to the thought, tone, and effect of the original.

In his later years he stressed the importance of translation work and the quality of his translations. When Epes Sargent requested poems for his *Harper's Cyclopaedia of British and American Poetry* (1880), Clarke sent him a copy of *Exotics* and permission to choose at will ("my poetic translations are better than my original verses"). Clarke's "Versified Translations" includes the notable pronouncement that if translators "tell us in their Preface, 'it was the amusement of an idle hour' . . . I shut the book." No doubt Clarke's efforts at raising German, French, Italian, and Spanish at Harvard to the same rank as the classics was a natural extension of his work with foreign languages and literature and his high view of the work of the translator.

Clarke was preeminently a translator in a larger sense of that term, for he regarded his vocation as one of translating to readers and hearers both the conflict of truth with error, as he put it in one of his lectures, and the different kinds of truth with their various scripts, claims, and personal and cultural value. These two kinds of translation, both evident in his sermons and lectures, are best represented in his work as reformer and, as this essay has explained, as literary author, critic, and theorist.

Letters:

The Letters of James Freeman Clarke to Margaret Fuller, edited by John Wesley Thomas (Hamburg: Cram, de Gruyter, 1957).

Biography:

Arthur S. Bolster, Jr., *James Freeman Clarke: Disciple to Advancing Truth* (Boston: Beacon, 1954).

References:

Charles E. Blackburn, "James Freeman Clarke: An Interpretation of the Western Years (1833-1840)," Ph.D dissertation, Yale University, 1952;

Derek K. Colville, "James Freeman Clarke: A Practical Transcendentalist and his Writings," Ph.D dissertation, Washington University, 1953;

Judith A. Green, "Religion, Life, and Literature in the *Western Messenger,*" Ph.D dissertation, University of Wisconsin, 1981;

Robert D. Habich, "The History and Achievement of the *Western Messenger,*" Ph.D dissertation, Pennsylvania State University, 1982;

Elizabeth McKinsey, *The Western Experiment: New England Transcendentalism in the Ohio Valley* (Cambridge: Harvard University Press, 1973);

Joel Myerson, *The New England Transcendentalists and the "Dial": A History of the Magazine and its Contributors* (Rutherford: Fairleigh Dickinson University Press, 1980), pp. 19-76, 127-133;

Leonard N. Neufeldt. "James Freeman Clarke:

Notes Toward a Comprehensive Bibliography," *Studies in the American Renaissance: 1982,* edited by Myerson (Boston: G. K. Hall, 1982), pp. 209-226;

John Wesley Thomas, *James Freeman Clarke: Apostle of German Culture to America* (Boston: Luce, 1949).

Papers:

The major collections of Clarke manuscripts are located at the Houghton Library of Harvard University, the Massachusetts Historical Society, and the Andover-Harvard Theological Library.

Philip Pendleton Cooke

(26 October 1816-20 January 1850)

Donald R. Noble
University of Alabama

See also the Cooke entry in *DLB 3, Antebellum Writers in New York and the South.*

BOOK: *Froissart Ballads, and Other Poems* (Philadelphia: Carey & Hart, 1847).

PERIODICAL PUBLICATIONS:

NONFICTION

"English Poetry," *Southern Literary Messenger,* 1 (April 1835): 397-401; 1 (June 1835): 557-565; 2 (January 1836): 101-106;

"Leaves From My Scrap Book," *Southern Literary Messenger,* 2 (April 1836): 314-316;

"Leaf from My Scrap Book," *Southern Literary Messenger,* 2 (May 1836): 372;

"Old Books and New Authors," *Southern Literary Messenger,* 12 (April 1846): 199-203;

"Dante," *Southern Literary Messenger,* 12 (September 1846): 545-554;

"Living Novelists," *Southern Literary Messenger,* 13 (June 1847): 367-373; 13 (September 1847): 529-536; 13 (December 1847): 745-752;

"Edgar A. Poe," *Southern Literary Messenger,* 14 (January 1848): 34-38;

"The Feudal Armies of France and England," *Southern Literary Messenger,* 14 (June 1848): 362-365.

FICTION

John Carper, the Hunter of Lost River, Southern Literary Messenger, 14 (February 1848): 90-94; 14 (March 1848): 167-175; 14 (April 1848): 222-228;

The Two Country Houses, Southern Literary Messenger, 14 (May 1848): 307-318; 14 (June 1848): 349-356; 14 (July 1848): 436-450;

The Gregories of Hackwood, Southern Literary Messenger, 14 (September 1848): 537-543; 14 (October 1848): 612-622;

"Captain Guy; or, The Unpardonable Sin," *Illustrated Monthly Courier,* 1 (2 October 1848);

"Joseph Jenkins' Researches into Antiquity: Erisicthon," *Southern Literary Messenger,* 14 (December 1848): 721-726;

The Crime of Andrew Blair, Southern Literary Messenger, 15 (January 1849): 46-54; 15 (February 1849): 101-108; 15 (March 1849): 148-154;

The Chevalier Merlin, Southern Literary Messenger, 15 (June 1849): 326-335; 15 (July 1849): 417-426; 15 (August 1849): 473-481; 15 (September 1849): 569-576; 15 (November 1849): 641-650; 15 (December 1849): 727-734; 16 (January 1850): 42-50;

"A Morning with Cagliostro. From Notes of a Conversation with Mr. Joseph Jenkins," *Southern Literary Messenger,* 16 (December 1850): 743-752;

"The Turkey-hunter in the Closet," *Southern Literary Messenger,* 17 (October-November 1851): 659-662.

POETRY

"Autumn," as E. B. C., *Knickerbocker,* 2 (November 1833): 368;

"The Creation of the Antelope," "A Song of the

Seasons," as E. D., *Southern Literary Messenger,* 1 (January 1835): 216, 232;

"Young Rosalie Lee," as L. L., *Southern Literary Messenger,* 1 (March 1835): 332;

"The Last Indian," *Southern Literary Messenger,* 1 (April 1835): 402-403;

"Lady Leonore and Her Lover," as L. L., *Southern Literary Messenger,* 2 (January 1836): 109-110;

"Sonnet–To Mary," "On Dreaming That I Heard a Lady Engaged in Prayer," as L. L., *Southern Literary Messenger,* 4 (August 1838): 488, 542;

"Earl March and his Daughter," *Burton's Gentleman's Magazine* (February 1840): 92;

"Florence Vane," *Burton's Gentleman's Magazine* (March 1840): 108;

"Life in the Autumn Woods," *Southern Literary Messenger,* 9 (December 1843): 729-730;

"The Mountains," *Broadway Journal,* 2 (20 December 1845);

"Emily. Proem to the 'Froissart Ballads,'" *Graham's Magazine,* 28 (January 1846): 30-32.

Commentators on the life and work of Philip Pendleton Cooke have often found it useful to compare him with John Keats. An enormously promising young lyric poet and a handsome, intelligent man, Cooke died before he could accomplish more than a small portion of what was expected of him. Raised in the Shenandoah Valley, Cooke was an accomplished, avid outdoorsman. His love of nature, combined with his interest in the writing of his own time and the medieval romances which so absorbed him, make him one of the early southern romantics.

Cooke was the quintessential Virginian. His father, John Rogers Cooke, born in Bermuda in 1788, immigrated to Martinsburg, Virginia, in Berkeley County about 1810, practiced law, and in 1813 married Maria Pendleton. John Cooke's own family was one of considerable reknown; his two brothers were John Esten, a figure in both medicine and in the ministry, and Philip St. George, who later served as a brigadier general in the Union Army and was the author of a number of works of military strategy and history. Maria Pendleton was the aunt of the novelist and United States congressman John Pendleton Kennedy, his brother the outdoorsman and novelist Philip Pendleton Kennedy (*The Blackwater Chronicles*), and the writer/artist David Hunter Strother, better known by his nom de plume, Porte Crayon.

Martinsburg was, in the 1820s and 1830s, a small country town. There was an academy Cooke may have attended, but without doubt hunting, fishing, and the outdoors in general were his education, his passion, and the inspiration for much of his verse. In 1828 the Cookes moved to Winchester, a more sophisticated town, and after attending the Winchester Academy for two years, Philip entered Princeton University in 1831 at the age of fifteen.

As an undergraduate Cooke studied classical and modern languages, including French, German, and Italian, and the masterworks of English literature: Spenser, Shakespeare, and Chaucer. He also published several poems in the *Knickerbocker Magazine.* At Princeton, Cooke would have been better described as a high-spirited rather than serious scholar. He graduated eighteenth in a class of thirty-four. One of the few mentions of Cooke in the Princeton records refers to his suspension from the college, along with another student, on 17 July 1834, "for a mutual personal assault upon each other." Cooke graduated with a B.A. degree on 13 August 1834 and returned to Winchester to study law, as his father had insisted, and meanwhile write verse and resume his avocation as a hunter.

Things had changed somewhat at home. His family had moved into Glengary, the home his mother had inherited, and Cooke joined them there. Besides his parents there were his two older sisters, Mary Pendleton and Sarah Dandridge, and his much younger brother, John Esten, who was to achieve considerable fame as a novelist of Virginia and of the Civil War in particular. (Cooke had eight siblings who died in infancy or youth and another brother, Edward St. George, who died as a young man in 1858.) Cooke's father, a financially reckless man, had cosigned loans for friends, was himself a spendthrift, and was in deep trouble in the panic of 1837. The situation worsened when Glengary, which he had planned to sell, burned in 1839, and the senior Cooke was forced to move his family first to Charlestown and then to Richmond where he struggled unsuccessfully to achieve some financial security. Maria Pendleton Cooke died in 1849 and John R. Cooke less than five years later in 1854.

In the meantime Philip had taken on responsibilities of his own. Of his long infatuation with his cousin Mary Evelina Dandridge, whom he had known since childhood, Cooke fashioned one of his most enduring lyrics, "Florence Vane." This poem, one of many composed during this period when he was supposed to be studying law, was a great success, but the courtship was not. On 1 May 1837 Cooke married Willianne Corbin Taylor Burwell, descended from the Burwells

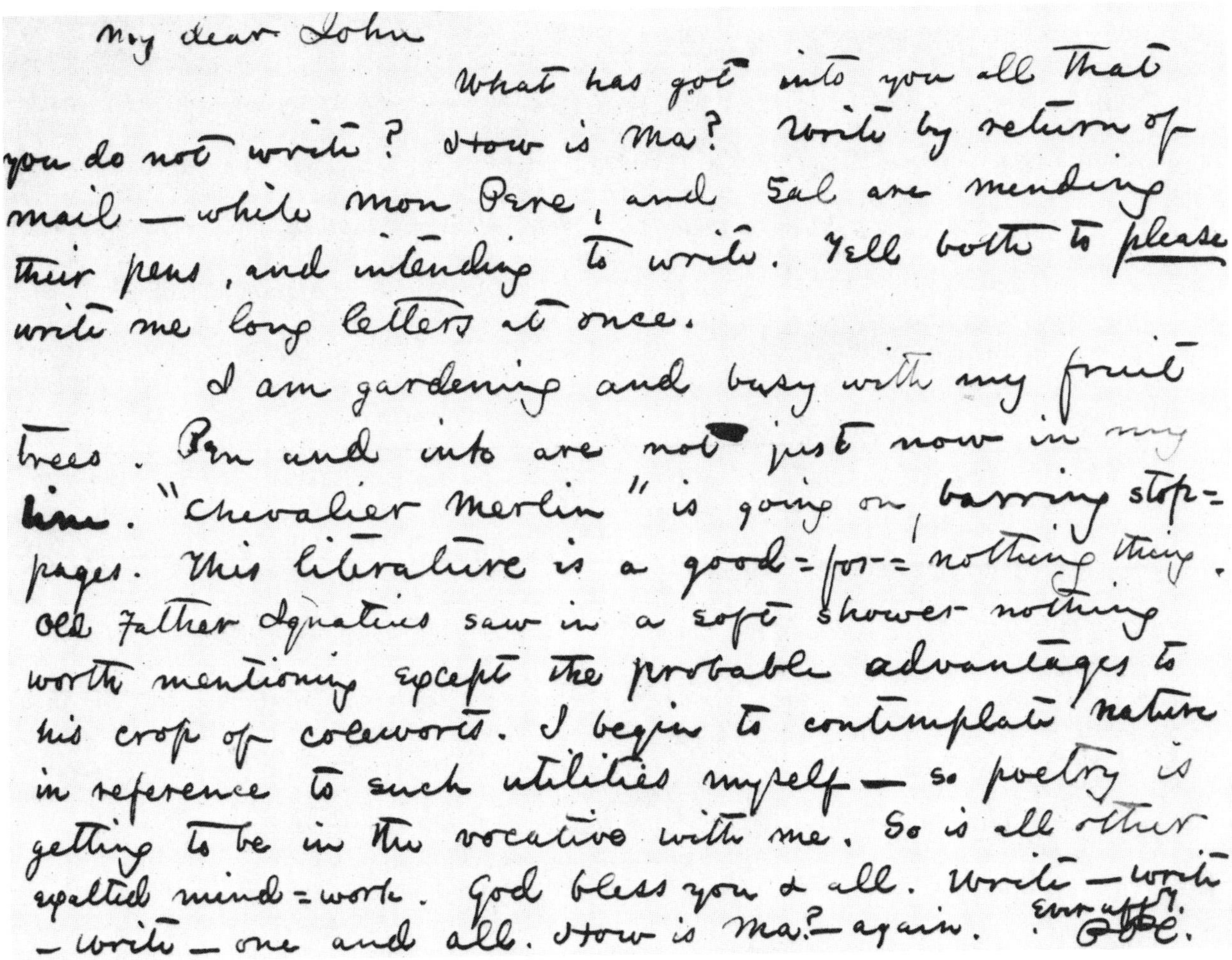

My dear John

What has got into you all that you do not write? How is Ma? Write by return of mail — while mon Pere, and Sal are mending their pens, and intending to write. Tell both to please write me long letters at once.

I am gardening and busy with my fruit trees. Pen and ink are not just now in my line. "Chevalier Merlin" is going on, barring stop-pages. This literature is a good-for-nothing thing. Old Father Ignatius saw in a soft shower nothing worth mentioning except the probable advantages to his crop of coleworts. I begin to contemplate nature in reference to such utilities myself — so poetry is getting to be in the vocative with me. So is all other exalted mind-work. God bless you & all. Write — write — write — one and all. How is Ma? — again. Evr affly. PPC.

Letter to John Esten Cooke written while Philip Pendleton Cooke was a student at Princeton (by permission of the Philip P. Cooke Collection [#7548], Clifton Waller Barrett Library, University of Virginia Library)

and Carters of Corotoman. They lived at Glengary until it burned and then moved to Martinsburg proper.

Cooke wrote very little between 1837 and 1840. He was beset with money troubles, earning only a modest income as a lawyer. In fact, he was constantly borrowing small sums from his father, who could ill afford to send them. Cooke was also involved in an unsuccessful coal-mining venture and was so discouraged that in 1840 he traveled to Palmyra, Missouri, to look it over as a possible site for a new home. Palmyra was a staunchly Whig town, and Cooke thought he might be able to make a career there as a lawyer and Whig politician. He decided against this move, however, and returned to Martinsburg. There he lived modestly but happily with his growing family. Cooke had five children altogether: Elizabeth Lewis, born 22 July 1838; Maria Pendleton, born 15 April 1840; Nancy Burwell, born 27 April 1843; Nathaniel Burwell, born 24 April 1845; and Alethea Collins, born 23 January 1848, just two years before Cooke's death.

A turning point in Cooke's spirits and in his career seems to have pivoted on a letter received from Edgar Allan Poe in 1839, the first of several in their long association. From 1835 to 1838 Poe, as an editor of the *Southern Literary Messenger*, had published no fewer than nine of Cooke's poems. These pieces included "Young Rosalie Lee," which has the musical qualities one would expect Poe to admire, and "The Last Indian" and "A Song of the Seasons," poems which illustrate Cooke's fondness for the history and nature of his native Shenandoah Valley, as do indeed a number of his other youthful efforts. Since then, Poe had moved and was serving as coeditor of *Burton's Gentleman's Magazine* in Philadelphia. Poe had been exceedingly generous in his praise of Cooke's contributions to the *Messenger* and in an 1839 letter solicited more from him. Cooke expressed his thanks and answered Poe's questions regarding his opinion of "Ligeia," saying that he admired the story greatly, suggesting that the scene in which Ligeia takes over the body of Lady Rowena is a little abrupt, and assuring Poe that he not only "took" his "idea throughout" but also understood that Poe was attempting to reproduce not reality, but the dream state. "You *write* as I sometimes *dream* on a heavy supper (not heavy enough for nightmare)." He closed his reply with the self-deprecating: "I am very impertinent."

Poe obviously did not think Cooke impertinent, and he replied at once that he valued Cooke's opinion highly, that in fact he had been praised concerning "The Fall of the House of Usher" by none other than Washington Irving, but "I regarded his best word as but dust in the balance when weighted with those discriminating opinions of your own, which teach me that you feel and perceive." Poe assured Cooke these sentiments were "from the bottom of [his] heart." In response Cooke wrote a long letter expressing his opinion on a number of Poe stories, pronouncing "Usher" especially excellent in the prolonged ending after the death of Madeleine. He said he admired "William Wilson" greatly but did not entirely comprehend it. He praised Poe's choice of title for his first volume of stories–*Tales of the Grotesque and Arabesque* (1839)–and included two poems for publication, "Earl March and his Daughter" and "Florence Vane." They appeared in the February and March numbers of 1840.

Cooke's remarks in his letter to Poe were among his earliest critical reflections. He had published to this date only an essay, "English Poetry," in the *Messenger* in three parts in 1835-1836; a three-page essay, "Leaves From My Scrap Book," in April 1836; and the one-page "Leaf From My Scrap Book" in May 1836. In the April number of the *Messenger* (1846) and in June, September, and December 1847 he published his two major critical pieces: "Old Books and New Authors" and "Living Novelists."

In "Old Books and New Authors" Cooke addresses the problems of influence, imitation, and especially the accusations of servile imitation leveled at the American poet. Cooke asserts that every poet is "in spite of himself, an imitator," and modern American poets in particular seem vulnerable to this charge because they are considered derivative, literary offshoots of the mother country. (That Cooke was still concerned about matters like this in 1847, after the New England writers had, in the main, stopped worrying about it, may be attributable to his isolation in western Virginia, far from any literary center. Ralph Waldo Emerson's "The American Scholar" had, after all, first been printed in 1837.)

Imitation is inevitable, according to Cooke, especially among the moderns. The poet becomes "in spite of himself, an imitator." "I wish to call the reader's attention fully and particularly to this certain consequence of a derivative literature: because it furnishes a defense of much

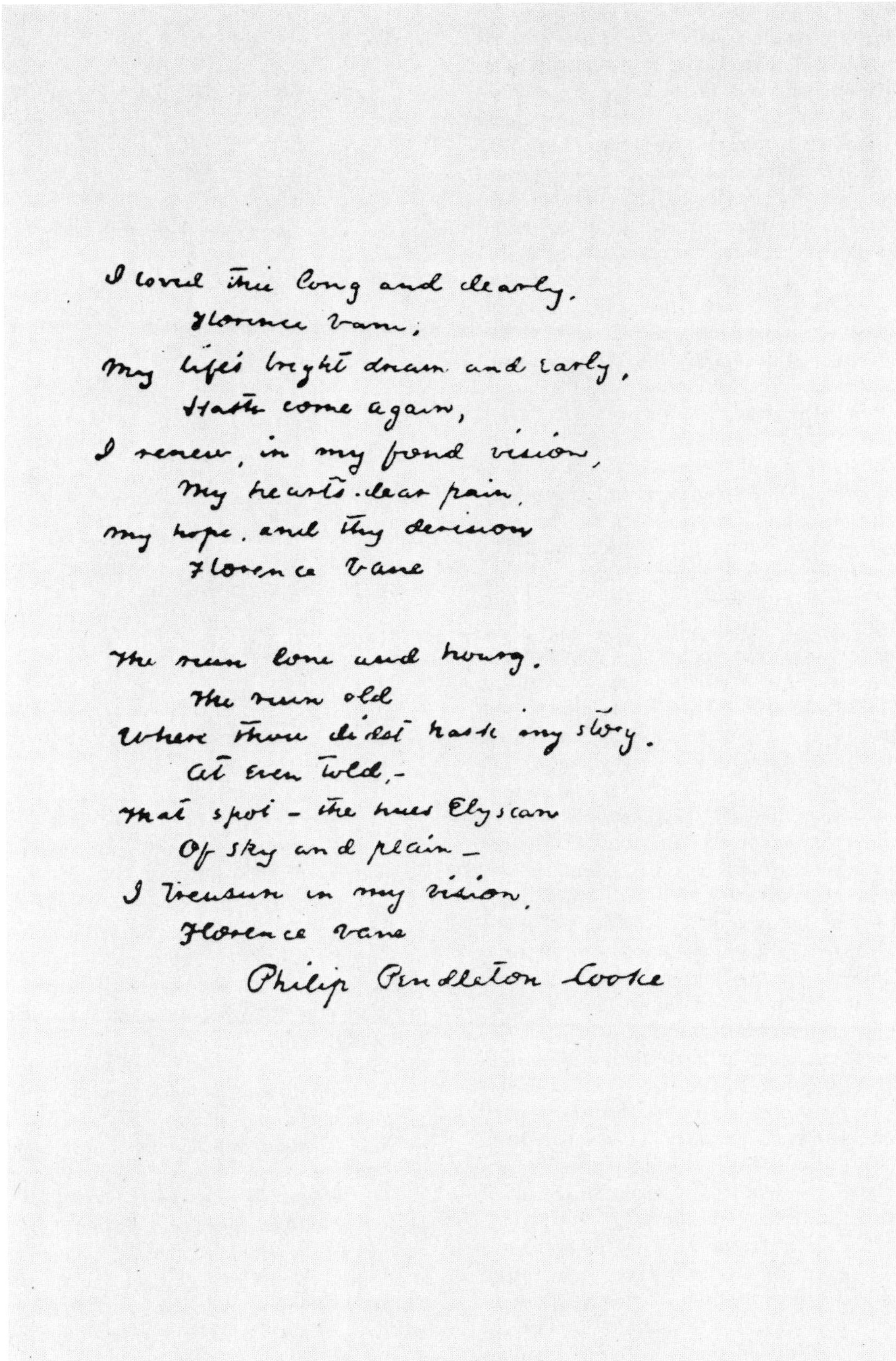

I loved thee long and dearly,
Florence Vane;
My life's bright dream and early,
Hath come again,
I renew, in my fond vision,
My heart's dear pain,
My hope, and thy derision
Florence Vane

The ruin lone and hoary.
The ruin old
Where thou didst hark my story.
At even told,-
That spot - the hues Elysian
Of sky and plain -
I treasure in my vision,
Florence Vane
Philip Pendleton Cooke

Fair copy of the first two stanzas of "Florence Vane," written by Cooke in 1839 (from the Illustrated Library of Favorite Songs, *1873)*

of our American poetry, which the critics have censured as wanting in originality." In an orderly and persuasive defense Cooke says that the poetry of the past may very properly be the inspiration for poetry; that subject matter, verse measures, stanza structures, rhythms, even characters' names will inevitably have been used before; and even language and phraseology may not be original, although sometimes the usage will be unconscious, accidental. Cooke goes on to show that great poets of the past have been imitators and borrowers–Chaucer from Boccaccio, Spenser from Tasso, Byron from Goethe, and Shakespeare from a wide variety of sources. Unlike many of the New England critics who had called for a more "American" literature, Cooke urges the cross-influence of poetry. He is antichauvinistic and says that when we force poets to be patriotic "voila Barlow's *Columbiad*!" Cooke concludes the essay by suggesting that imitation by writers of fiction is much less understandable, since they have so much more freedom of form and expression, and he demonstrates the outright plagiarism of Benjamin Disraeli in a section of *Vivian Grey* (1826) by juxtaposing it to the passage from which it was taken in Sir Thomas Browne's *Religio Medici* (1642). He adds, "the worst feature in the plagiarism is the concealing care visible in the changes made by the pilferer."

In "Living Novelists," Cooke's much longer, three-part piece, he says, "We propose to give our opinions upon some of the most prominent of the numerous living writers of fiction." In section one he takes up the case of Edward Bulwer-Lytton, whom he accuses of writing essentially melodrama, whatever he may have been attempting. He has no use for Bulwer-Lytton's dialogue. In a section reminiscent of Mark Twain's criticism of James Fenimore Cooper, Cooke says, "of natural dialogue, such as living men and women talk, there is next to nothing." Of Bulwer-Lytton's plays he says, they "are dramas, but by no means necessarily dramatic." Bulwer-Lytton's style as a novelist is "False, bad. It is painfully ornate, ambitious (a fatal fault of style), full of musical circumlocution . . . often slovenly."

In the second section of the essay Cooke heaps praise on Alexandre Dumas père, especially his dialogue and depth of characterization. His mind, Cooke says, is a fountain, not a cistern; it flows perpetual and fresh. Although Dumas has set up something of a fiction factory, Cooke excuses it, for Cooke was himself especially sensitive to the need for an author to keep his name ever before the public lest it be forgotten. G. P. R. James is a man of personal virtue, Cooke assures us. "[H]e has never written a sentence unbecoming a Christian gentleman," but Cooke assesses him a writer of very little talent. "We do not remember to have met with a particle of wit or humor in the whole range of his writings." Although Cooke finds he is not a bad storyteller, he thinks that James is otherwise talentless.

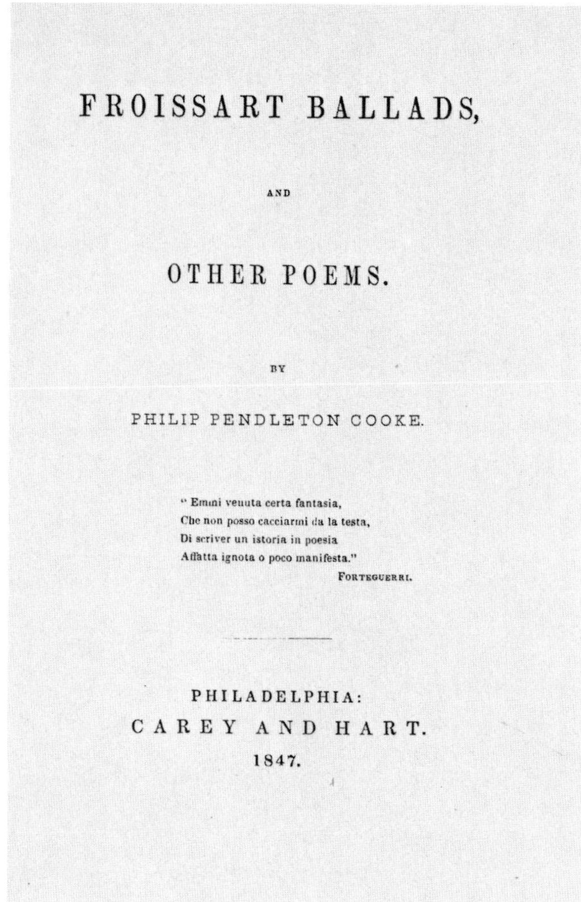
FROISSART BALLADS,

AND

OTHER POEMS.

BY

PHILIP PENDLETON COOKE.

" Emmi venuta certa fantasia,
Che non posso cacciarmi da la testa,
Di scriver un istoria in poesia
Affatta ignota o poco manifesta."

FORTEGUERRI.

PHILADELPHIA:
CAREY AND HART.
1847.

Title page for Cooke's only book

In his third section Cooke takes up the work of Disraeli and Cooper, with high praise for both writers. "The younger D'Israeli," he writes, "is one of the most gifted and accomplished minds in the world." He has a "perfect mastery of the English language." He has imagination and "universal knowledge"; apparently Cooke is willing to overlook the plagiarism in *Vivian Grey*, for he prophesies that the readers of the future will never allow that book to die.

Finally Cooke comes to some discussion of American fiction writers. Although he mentions his kinsman J. P. Kennedy, James Kirke Paulding, and William Gilmore Simms, all of these figures fall far below the writer Cooke believes to be the one and only American master of fiction: James Fenimore Cooper, "the very head of our American novelists." "Natty Bumpo is a triumph of creative genius," Cooke declares, and Cooper's style is downright "poetical." Apparently Cooke was keeping up with Cooper's public troubles, for he advises him to leave off lawsuits and pay less attention to his negative social critics. For Cooke, *The Deerslayer* (1841) is Cooper's best book, *The Bravo* (1831) a dull book, and *The Last of the Mohicans* (1826) "most absorbing in interest of all . . . yet very meanly written."

It is remarkable that Cooke, harried as he was by financial cares and far from the northeastern literary centers, would have kept up as thoroughly as he did with the publication of American fiction. It is also lamentable that such a keen critic of fiction did not live to see *The Scarlet Letter* which would be coming out in 1850 or *Moby-Dick* in the year following. After "Living Novelists" Cooke wrote only two more nonfiction works, "Edgar A. Poe," an appreciation, in January 1848, and an essay, "The Feudal Armies of France and England," in June 1848. Cooke had nothing but praise for the works of his old supporter Poe: "The fires of a great poet are seething under those analytic and narrative powers *in which no living writer equals him.*"

Through the 1840s Cooke published nine fictions, some of them novella length, in the *Messenger*, hoping to find fame and fortune in prose fiction as Cooper had found it; yet, like so many other romancers of the time, Cooke earned neither. *The Crime of Andrew Blair,* published in installments in the first half of 1849, and *The Chevalier Merlin,* published from June 1849 through January 1850, were his best efforts, but neither of these melodramatic, quasi-medieval tales made the splash he was hoping for.

Although Cooke had a discerning critical mind and some energy as a fiction writer, the bulk of his reputation rests on poetry he published in the 1840s. Rufus W. Griswold, the anthologizer and popularizer of American literature in the nineteenth century, had heard of Cooke, probably through Poe, and published several of Cooke's poems and a biographical sketch in his *The Poets and Poetry of America* (1846). In 1847 *Froissart Ballads, and Other Poems,* Cooke's only book, was published. This volume of his poetry, only three poems of which were actually modeled after Froissart, received good reviews but did not sell. His financial need at the time was so great that his disappointment at receiving no royalties is almost surely what drove him to prose fiction. Although Cooke showed some talent for humor and satire and could present scenes of bloodshed and violence with sensational effect, fiction was not his strength. Cooke was meant to be a poet of love and the outdoors and would have made a reputation as a critic of taste. None of this was to be, however, for Cooke, who had been acknowledged in his youth to be the finest hunter in all the Shenandoah Valley, contracted pneumonia and died after wading into the icy Shenandoah River to retrieve a wounded bird. At his death he had published only thirty-eight poems, nine works of fiction, and eight essays. There are extant a couple dozen letters and some few other unsigned items that may be his. Cooke had a wonderful talent which, had he lived to develop it, might have made him a major figure in the early years of our literature.

References:

John D. Allen, *Philip Pendleton Cooke* (Chapel Hill: University of North Carolina Press, 1942);

Allen, ed., *Philip Pendleton Cooke: Poet, Critic, Novelist* (Johnson City: East Tennessee State University, 1969);

John Esten Cooke, "Recollections of Philip Pendleton Cooke," *Southern Literary Messenger,* 26 (June 1858): 419-432;

Rufus W. Griswold, "Philip Pendleton Cooke," *International Magazine,* 4 (October 1851): 300-303;

Jay B. Hubbell, *The South in American Literature, 1607-1900* (Durham: Duke University Press, 1954), pp. 502-511;

David K. Jackson, *The Contributors and Contributions to The Southern Literary Messenger (1834-1864)* (Charlottesville, Va.: Historical Publishing, 1936);

Jackson, "Philip Pendleton Cooke: Virginia Gentleman, Lawyer, Hunter and Poet," in *American Studies in Honor of William Kenneth Boyd,* edited by Jackson (Durham: Duke University Press, 1940), pp. 282-326;

Edd Winfield Parks, ed., *Southern Poets* (New York: American Book, 1936), pp. 83-88;

W. H. Whiting, Jr., "Philip Pendleton Cooke," *Hampton-Sydney* (April 1928): 9-14.

Joseph Dennie

(30 August 1768-7 January 1812)

Guy R. Woodall
Tennessee Technological University

See also the Dennie entries in *DLB 37, American Writers of the Early Republic* and *DLB 43, American Newspaper Journalists, 1690-1872.*

SELECTED BOOKS: *The Lay Preacher, or Short Sermons for Idle Readers* (Walpole, N.H.: Printed & sold by David Carlisle, Jr., 1796);

A Collection of Essays, on a Variety of Subjects, in Prose and Verse (Newark, N.J.: Printed by John Woods, 1797);

The Lay Preacher, edited by John E. Hall (Philadelphia: Printed by J. Maxwell & published by Harrison Hall, 1817).

Collection: *The Lay Preacher,* edited by Milton Ellis (New York: Scholars' Facsimiles & Reprints, 1943).

OTHER: *The Spirit of the Farmers' Museum, and Lay Preacher's Gazette. Being a Judicious Selection of the Fugitive and Valuable Productions, Which Have Occasionally Appeared in That Paper, since the Commencement of Its Establishment,* edited, with contributions, by Dennie (Walpole, N.H.: Printed for Thomas & Thomas by D. & T. Carlisle, 1801);

The Plays of William Shakespeare . . . with the Corrections and Illustrations of Various Commentators, volume 2, edited by Dennie (Philadelphia: C. & A. Conrad/Baltimore: Conrad, Lucas, 1805); volume 1, probably edited wholly or in part by Dennie (Philadelphia: C. & A. Conrad/Baltimore: Conrad, Lucas, 1809);

Thomas Moore, Esq., *Epistles, Odes and Other Poems,* edited, with notes, by Dennie (Philadelphia: John Watts, 1806);

Robert Hutchinson Rose, *Sketches in Verse,* edited by Dennie (Philadelphia: Printed for C. & A. Conrad by Smith & Maxwell, 1810).

PERIODICAL PUBLICATIONS: On Cooper's *Macbeth,* in "Theatrical Review. No. VII," *Port Folio,* 1 (14 February 1801): 50-51;

On Franklin's lack of originality, in "An Author's Evenings," *Port Folio,* 1 (14 February 1801): 53-54;

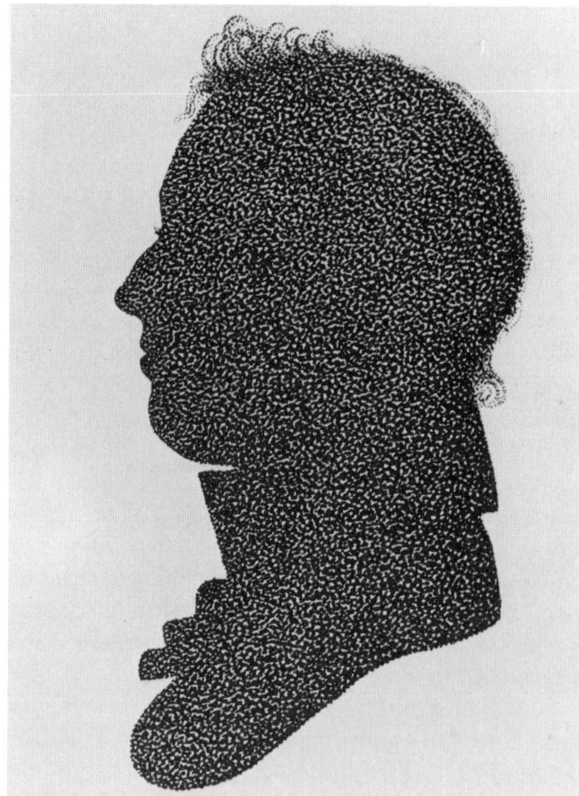

Silhouette of Joseph Dennie

Review of *Joan of Arc,* by Robert Southey, in "An Author's Evenings," *Port Folio,* 1 (29 August 1801): 274;

On novels, in "An Author's Evenings," *Port Folio,* 2 (8 May 1802): 138-139;

"Biography. The Life of the Right Hon. William Windham," *Port Folio,* 2 (15 May 1802): 149-151;

Review of *American Dictionary,* by Noah Webster, in "An Author's Evenings," *Port Folio,* 2 (28 August 1802): 268;

On Gray, Wharton, Wordsworth, and others, in "An Author's Evenings," *Port Folio,* 3 (2 July

1803): 209-210;

On Mrs. Radcliffe's romances, in "The Lay Preacher," *Port Folio,* 3 (9 July 1803): 217; (15 July 1803): 226; (23 July 1803): 233;

On Rousseau, in "Miscellaneous Paragraphs," *Port Folio,* 3 (10 September 1803): 295;

On Webster's *American Dictionary,* in "Miscellany," *Port Folio,* new series 1 (25 January 1806): 38-40;

On the classics, in "To Readers and Correspondents," *Port Folio,* second series 9 (8 August 1807): 94-96;

"Polite Literature," *Port Folio,* third series 6 (22 October 1808): 264-266.

Joseph Dennie–editor, literary critic, and essayist–was a pioneer litterateur in America in the Federalist period. As a professional man of letters, he was preceded only by Charles Brockden Brown. He was the first American editor to attempt a department of literary criticism in a periodical; in criticism, his was the most insistent voice for classical propriety and taste in letters. He was the first American to conduct a domestic literary magazine which enjoyed a widespread national circulation and patronage. Often called the "American Addison," he was the country's foremost serial essayist after Benjamin Franklin and was the precursor of such other writers in this genre as Washington Irving and William Wirt. He was overpraised by Timothy Dwight as "the Father of Belles-Lettres" in America, but few critics, if any, stimulated more interest than he in polite literature in the formative years of the new republic.

Dennie was born in Boston on 30 August 1768, the only child of Joseph and Mary Dennie. His father was a prosperous and reputable import merchant. In expectation of the siege of Boston, Joseph Dennie, Sr., moved his family in late April 1775 from Boston to nearby Lexington, where they remained during his life. The Dennies, like most people of property in that area, were Loyalists during the Revolution and afterward Federalists in the young republic. The parents instilled in their son an aristocratic attitude that made him contemptuous of his lower bred townspeople and countrymen. Dennie's later classical conservatism in literary taste was a correlation of the aristocratic and Federal sentiment implanted in him by his family. In Lexington Dennie was educated in a dame school and in a grammar school. He later attended, for a brief time, a school of commerce in Boston; but a great part of his education came privately in his father's extensive library, where he very early became acquainted with the classics, which were always so precious to him. In 1787 he entered the sophomore class at Harvard College, where he excelled in the classics and wrote poetry "after the manner of Horace." He was popular with his classmates, being considered brilliant, witty, eloquent, and fiercely independent in spirit. For insulting one of his tutors, he was reprimanded by the president, downgraded in class, and suspended for six months of private tutoring. On 8 July 1790 he was allowed to return to Harvard and restored to his class after being forced to make a public apology in chapel. He graduated with the class of 1790, but he never forgave his alma mater for humiliating him.

In late 1790 Dennie moved to rural Charlestown, New Hampshire, to read law with Benjamin West. Once admitted to the bar, he practiced law rather indifferently. He supplemented his meager salary by serving for a time as a lay reader in local Episcopal churches, but he was never happy in the legal or clerical professions. He was dissatisfied with the law because the rural jurists poked fun at his eloquent, literate pleadings in court. He was equally restive under the restrictive ministry due to his fondness for wine, cards, and tobacco. At Charlestown Dennie began to contribute essays to local newspapers and to attract a coterie of young men interested in literature. Among these was Royall Tyler, destined for fame as a poet and playwright. Dennie used the pseudonym of "Colon," and Tyler "Spondee"; and between 1794 and 1807 they collaborated in the *Hanover Eagle, Boston Federal Orrey, Walpole Farmer's Museum,* the *Philadelphia Gazette of the United States,* and *Port Folio* in essays entitled "From the Shop of Messrs. Colon and Spondee." In Charlestown also Dennie began to write for the newspapers sprightly serial essays that he called "The Farrago." His literary fame spread as "The Farrago" was reprinted in the *Boston Centinel* and other large city newspapers. Encouraged by the success of these pieces, Dennie, while visiting in Boston in early 1795, decided to publish a weekly literary journal. William Spotswood, a Boston bookseller, joined him in the enterprise to furnish the type; Dennie was to provide a weekly Farrago.

On 19 May 1795 they issued the first number of the *Tablet: A Miscellaneous Paper Devoted to*

Belles Lettres, modeled after Addison and Steele's *Spectator* and *Tatler* and Johnson's *Rambler* and *Idler.* Like Addison's essays, the Farrago pieces have a persona, but, unlike Addison's serials, they do not have a great amount of philosophical speculation, morality, and criticism. Usually placed on the first page, "The Farrago" was the periodical's featured piece; the fourth page was devoted mainly to original and selected verse, epigrams, and anecdotes; and the intervening pages were filled with the departments of criticism, literary intelligence, biography, and miscellany. Among the notable contributors that Dennie enlisted were Tyler, who wrote some original poetry, and John Sylvester John Gardiner, who wrote most of the criticism. Gardiner, with Dennie's approval, established the critical authorities in the *Tablet* by favorably naming Samuel Johnson, Hugh Blair, John Dennis, the two Whartons, and Owen Ruffhead. Gardiner said he would follow the analytical method of Ruffhead, "as we cannot be too particular in the exemplification of general rules on subjects little understood in this country"; and he begged that an indulgent public would not discourage "the first attempt at critical disquisition in America." The small amount and common quality of the criticism had nothing to do with its demise when the *Tablet* was discontinued with its thirteenth number on 11 August 1795. Dennie blamed the dullness and stinginess of Bostonians for its death, but one of his peevish Farrago essays directed at Harvard might have cost him local support.

Disappointed but undaunted by the death of the *Tablet,* Dennie moved the following year to Walpole, New Hampshire, where he undertook the editorship of the *New Hampshire Journal; or, the Farmer's Weekly Museum,* a newspaper owned jointly by David Carlisle and Isaiah Thomas. Assuming the persona of a lay preacher Dennie inserted each week a serial essay. His choice of format was influenced by his earlier experiences as a lay minister and by his reading of Laurence Sterne's *The Sermons of Mr. Yorick.* The persona in "The Lay Preacher," a little like Dennie, is a bachelor; he once hated women but does not now, is addicted to tobacco, has a cordial regard for the clergy, and is a Federalist in politics. Forming each essay as a short "sermon," complete with Bible text or a motto, Dennie censured nearly every aspect of American society–education, dress, manners, literature, and politics. There is only one substantial piece of literary criticism in "The Lay Preacher": an essay on Ann Radcliffe and the Gothic novel. Dennie preferred the sentimental and picaresque novels of Laurence Sterne, Samuel Richardson, Henry Fielding, and Fanny Burney to Radcliffe's. Like the English essays from the time of Addison, Dennie's "sermons" were moral, witty, and classical in flavor.

Copied in newspapers in most of the major cities, and collected and published in book form for the first time as *The Lay Preacher, or Short Sermons for Idle Readers* (1796), "The Lay Preacher" enhanced Dennie's reputation greatly. As editor of the *Farmer's Museum,* Dennie secured the help of several able contributors: Jeremiah Mason, Samuel Hunt, Samuel Mason, John Curtis Chamberlain, Roger Vose, and Elihu Hubbard Smith. Also, Tyler, writing as "Spondee," contributed original poetry and joined Dennie, who wrote as "Colon," in a new series of pieces "From the Shop of Messrs. Colon and Spondee." Thomas Green Fessenden wrote political lampoons as "Spunky." The writers contributed essays and poetry, extracts from English authors, biographies of contemporary authors and public figures, such as Joel Barlow, Timothy Dwight, John Adams, and Oliver Wolcott. The *Farmer's Museum* reached the peak of its popularity in 1797 with 2,000 subscribers and thereafter began to decline, probably because of Dennie's dilatory work habits. Replaced as editor in June 1798, he continued to supply his lay sermons and miscellaneous essays for a while.

In financial straits because of losing this editorship and tiring of literary and social stultification among the New Hampshire rustics, Dennie sought employment elsewhere. His reputation as a partisan Federalist writer secured for him a comfortable position as the private and confidential secretary to Timothy Pickering, the U.S. secretary of state, in Philadelphia. He continued to send essays to the *Farmer's Museum,* but he became a major contributor to John Ward Fenno's *Philadelphia Gazette of the United States,* a leading Federalist organ. He continued to write as the lay preacher, calling his new serial the "Lay Preacher of Pennsylvania." He once again revived "From the Shop of Messrs. Colon and Spondee," and he enlivened the dull *Gazette* with his sharp attacks upon the Jeffersonians and their newspaper supporters.

In the *Gazette* he began increasingly to discuss foreign and domestic literature. He scorned most American authors, but noticed Charles

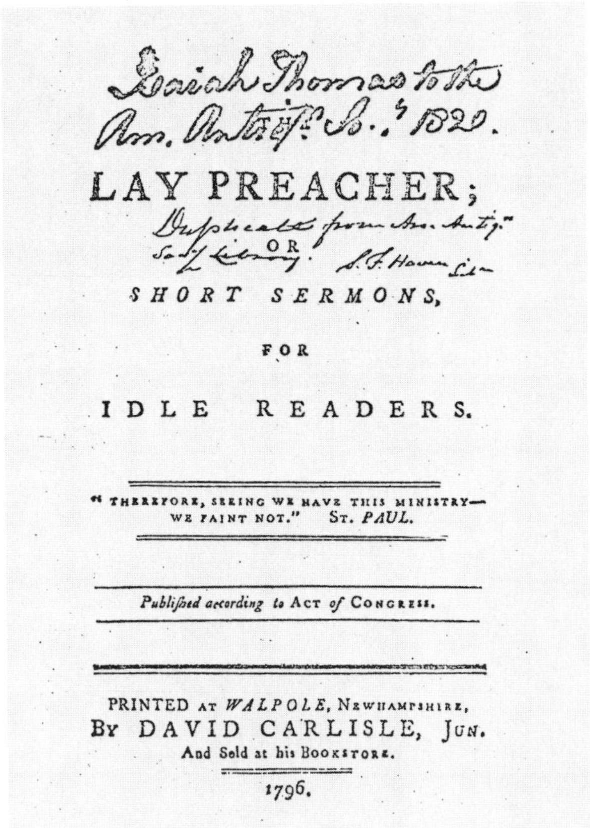
LAY PREACHER;
OR
SHORT SERMONS,
FOR
IDLE READERS.

"THEREFORE, SEEING WE HAVE THIS MINISTRY—WE FAINT NOT." St. PAUL.

Publiſhed according to Act of Congress.

PRINTED AT WALPOLE, NEWHAMPSHIRE,
BY DAVID CARLISLE, JUN.
And Sold at his Bookstore.
1796.

Title page for the copy of the collection of Dennie's popular essays that printer Isaiah Thomas gave to the American Antiquarian Society. It was later given or sold to Evert A. Duyckinck, editor of the Cyclopaedia of American Literature *(by permission of the New York Public Library, Astor, Lenox and Tilden Foundations).*

Brockden Brown and Royall Tyler favorably. In reviewing Brown's *Edgar Huntly* (1799), he warned against the excesses of German romanticism; but he found Tyler's *Algerine Captive* (1797) altogether worthy of praise. Some thought Dennie's criticism against the perversions of the English language in America was too severe and sarcastic, but Dennie, in defense, explained his position as a critic in the *Gazette* on 29 April 1800:

> Criticism is useful, and shall speak, though her voice "grate and harsh thunder" to the ears of the *true patriots,* bombastic editors, fustian orators, college boys and *id genus omne.* Reproach and ridicule are intended to reform. America has indulged this rant too much. It is time it should be ridiculed and reasoned away. We *must choose this day whom we will serve.* We have "The Moses and the Prophets" of language. We have Dean *Swift,* Dr. *Robertson,* and Sir William *Jones.* We have too the miserable remnants of Cromwell's Puritanism, the Babylonish dialect of the "forefathers at Plymouth," the red lattice phrases of acquitted felons, and the "hissing hot" speeches from many a *town* meeting. Of these deformities let us be ashamed, and strive to emulate a diction pure, simple, expressive and English.

Dennie lost his position as Pickering's secretary in 1800, but he continued as literary editor of the *Gazette.*

In the *Gazette,* on 16 October 1800, he announced his plans to launch another literary magazine: "In a few days, Mr. *ASBURY DICKINS,* bookseller of this city, will publish a *PROSPECTUS* of a new weekly Paper, to be conducted on an extensive and liberal plan, combining in the manner of the *TATLER,* Politics with Essays and disquisitions on topics scientific, moral, humorous, and literary. It will appear every Saturday under the title of the *PORT FOLIO.*" In December a prospectus for the journal was published in which Dennie introduced himself as a "humble historian of the hour" who had formerly edited a "*Farmer's* Museum [*sic*]" and a "*Lay Preacher's* Gazette [*sic*]." But, as he explained, he intended to change his pen name in the new journal to "OLDSCHOOL": "Fond of this title, indicative of his moral, political, and literary creed, he proposes publishing every Saturday, on super-royal quarto sheets,"

> A new weekly paper,
>
> to be called
>
> *THE PORT FOLIO*
>
> *By Oliver Oldschool, Esq.*

Dennie summed up in a sentence what he wanted to accomplish in the *Port Folio*: "To relieve the dryness of news, and the severity of political argument, with wholesome morals and gay miscellany–to insert interesting articles of biography, criticism, and poetry, and merriment, and 'bind the rod of the moralist with the roses of the muse.' " The first number was issued on 3 January 1801 with a poem by Dennie and the two departments "An Author's Evenings" and "Literary Intelligence." The first and subsequent numbers contained many of the same columns that Dennie had used in his previous journals: "Amusement," "Biography," "Law Intelligence," "Original Poetry," "Selected Poetry," and "Miscellany." In the last column some of his old and, occasionally, some new "Farrago" and "Lay Preacher" essays appeared from time to time. In the *Port Folio* Dennie continued his old themes: the curse of democracy, provincialism of America, efficacy of moral sentiment, requirement of proper dress and manners, and need for classical correctness and utility in letters. A lover of the classics, Dennie often printed essays on and translations of the ancients, such as Anacreon, Horace, Juvenal, Ovid, Livy, Plautus, Seneca, Terence, Virgil, and Xenephon.

Dennie wrote few lengthy critical essays, choosing to comment upon authors and their works in the various serial departments of the *Port Folio*. Some of his most amusing and strident literary commentary was in his "To Readers and Correspondents": "Flouricourt is a coxcomb writer, and his essay is overwhelmed with cant expressions"; " 'Lines on a Lady Bathing' are inadmissible. The subject is dangerous and indelicate, and it is prudent to suffer this 'Lady' to remain in that *flannel,* with which the bard has invested her"; and " 'The Ode to the Moon' surpasses in stupidity whatever of crude or imperfect we have ever had the misfortune to read."

Dennie often praised British poetry in the *Port Folio*. Surprisingly, in light of his general contempt for the Romantic impulse, he was one of the first to welcome William Wordsworth and Samuel Taylor Coleridge's *Lyrical Ballads* (1798) to America as a collection "remarkable for originality, simplicity, and nature"; and when the second edition appeared, he said that it contained "more genuine poetry than is to be found, except in the volumes of *Shakespeare* and *Chatterton*." Though nearly always finding some fault with them, Dennie praised for correctness in style, pure diction, and appropriate subject matter British writers George Crabbe, Robert Southey, Sir Walter Scott, William Gifford, Charlotte Smith, and W. L. Bowles. Some British and Continental writers who did not fare too well were Rousseau, "an eloquent lunatic" and "splendid scoundrel"; Thomas Paine, "a creeping thing" and "drunken atheist"; William Godwin, "a lunatic"; Joseph Priestley, a "trickster"; and Ann Radcliffe, "an imitator of German romanticism." Some highly acceptable contemporary British poets who contributed original poetry to the *Port Folio* were Thomas Campbell, Leigh Hunt, and Thomas Moore. After visiting America, Moore repaid Dennie's affections by noting one of his poems: "Mr. Dennie has succeeded in diffusing through his cultivated little circle that love of good literature and sound politics which he so zealously feels himself, and which is so rarely the characteristic of his countrymen."

Dennie was generally harsh in his treatment of everything distinctively American, but he had a special animus for American writers who corrupted the English language. In "An Author's Evenings," he sarcastically offered to help Noah Webster publish his *American Dictionary*:

> The papers have announced that a certain critic of Mr. Gibbon, and a grammarian who had the hardihood to oppose Bishop Lowth, and fairly kick the *subjunctive mood* down stairs, is about to publish a Dictionary of the *American vulgar* tongue. We deem it, therefore, our duty as good patriots, and as fond lovers of provincial idioms, and colloquial meanness, and, in short, of everything hostile to English sense, and English stile, to furnish this great lexicographer with all the barbarous words we can procure.

Not all Americans, however, were derided in the *Port Folio*. Among the native poets generally appreciated were Timothy Dwight, Samuel Ewing, Thomas Green Fessenden, Philip Freneau, John Blair Linn, Robert Treat Paine, John Howard Payne, John Trumbull, and Royall Tyler. While never liking the democratic politics of Freneau, Dennie justly said of his poetry that "by the impartial, it will be, at length, considered as entitled to no ordinary place in a judicious estimate of American genius." Native prose fictionists were not often noticed in the *Port Folio,* but those a little praised were Charles Brockden Brown, Washington Irving, and James K. Paulding.

The *Port Folio* was successful from the beginning, and between 1802 and 1805 had a larger subscription list than any other American magazine. Much of Dennie's success with his magazine can be attributed to the Tuesday Club, which he established. It was a convivial group of literary lawyers, doctors, academicians, and clerics who supported him and contributed essays and poetry gratis. A few of the contributors in the Tuesday Club were Nicholas Biddle, Horace Binney, Thomas Cadwallader, Nathaniel Chapman,

THE PORT FOLIO.

BY OLIVER OLDSCHOOL, ESQ.

"VARIOUS, THAT THE MIND
OF DESULTORY MAN, STUDIOUS OF CHANGE,
AND PLEAS'D WITH NOVELTY, MAY BE INDULGED."
COWPER.

VOL. I.] PHILADELPHIA, SATURDAY, JANUARY 3d, 1801. [No. 1.

TRAVELS.

FOR THE PORT FOLIO.

[The subsequent letter is the commencement of a series, which will be regularly published in this paper. It is unnecessary to dwell upon the general excellence of the following tour. It will be obvious to every intelligent reader that it has been made by no vulgar traveller, but by a man of genius and observation, who, in happy union, combines the power of selecting the most interesting and picturesque objects, and of describing them gracefully.]

JOURNAL OF A TOUR THROUGH SILESIA.

LETTER I.

Frankfort, on the Oder, 20th July, 1800.

As I have bespoken your company, upon our journey into Silesia, I begin this letter at our first resting station from Berlin. Hitherto, we have indeed seen little more than the usual Brandenburg sands, and perhaps you will find our tour as tiresome, as we have found it ourselves. I cannot promise you an amusing journey, though I hope it will prove so to us. My letters to you, on this tour, will be in the form, and serve as the substitute of a journal. They will, of course, be fragments, written at different times and places; nay, perhaps in different humours. Therefore, make up your account, to receive patiently all my tediousness.

On Thursday, the 17th inst. we left Berlin, just after three in the morning, and arrived here at about nine the same evening. The distance is ten German miles and a quarter; which you know is a very long day's journey in this country. In the course of a few years, it will be an easy journey of eight hours; for the present king, who has the very laudable ambition of improving the roads through his dominions, is now making a turnpike road, like that to Potsdam, the whole way hither; as yet, not more than one German mile of it is finished, and the rest of the way, is like that, which on every side surrounds the *Tadmor* of modern times. As we approach within a few miles of Frankfort the country becomes somewhat hilly, and of course more variegated and pleasant than round Berlin; but we could perceive little difference in the downy softness of the ground beneath us, or in the *needles* of the pines within our view. Part of the country is cultivated, as much as it is susceptible of cultivation, and here and there we could see scattered spires of wheat, rye, barley, and oats shoot from the sands, like the hairs upon a head almost bald. We came through few villages, and those few had a miserable appearance. A meagre composition of mud and thatch composed the cottages, in which a ragged and pallid race of beggars reside; yet we must not be unjust, and confess, that we passed by one nobleman's seat, which had the appearance of a handsome and comfortable house.

We arrived here just in time to see the last dregs of an annual *fair*, such as you have often seen in the towns of Holland, and as you know are customary in those of Germany. But we hear great complaints against the minister Struensee, for having ruined the value of the *fair*, by prohibiting the sale of foreign woollen manufactures, which have heretofore been the most essential articles of sale at this fair. This prohibition is for the sake of encouraging the manufactures of this country, a principle, which the government pursue on all possible occasions. They are no converts to the opinions of Adam Smith and the French economists, concerning the balance of trade, and always catch with delight at any thing which can prevent money from *going out of the country*. Of this disposition we have seen a notable instance in the attempts lately made here for producing sugar from beets, of which I believe you heard something while you were here, and about which much has been said and done since then. At one time we were assured beyond all question, that one mile square of beets would furnish sugar for the whole Prussian dominions. The question was submitted to a committee of the Academy of Sciences, who, after long examination and deliberation, reported, that in truth, sugar, and even brandy, could be produced from beets, and in process of time might be raised in great quantities; but that, for the present, it would be expedient to continue the use of sugars and brandies, such as had been in use hitherto. Since this report, we have heard little or nothing of beet sugar.

This is an old town, pleasantly situated, and containing about twelve thousand inhabitants, of which a quarter part are Jews. It is therefore distinguished by those peculiarities, which mark all European towns where a large proportion of Israelites reside, and to express which, I suppose, resort must be had to the Hebrew language. The English at least is inadequate to it; for the word *filth* conveys an idea of spotless purity, in comparison to the Jewish nastiness. The garrison of the town consists of one regiment. There is here likewise an university; and by the introduction of a letter from Berlin, we have become acquainted with two of the professors. The number of students is less than two hundred; and of them, one hundred and fifty are students of law; ten or fifteen of divinity; and not more than two or three of medicine. The library, the museum, and the botanical garden, the professors tell me, are all so miserable, that they are ashamed to show them.

The banks of the Oder, on one side, are bordered with small hills, upon which at small distances, are little summer-houses with vineyards, at which, during summer, many inhabitants of the town reside. On the other side, the land is flat, and the river is restrained from overflowing only by a large dyke, which has been built since the year 1785. At that time the river broke down the smaller dyke, which had, until then, existed, and overflowed the country to a considerable extent. Prince Leopold of Brunswick, a brother of the present reigning duke, was then colonel of the regiment in garrison here, and lost his life in attempting to save some of the people, whom the inundation was carrying away. You have probably seen prints of this melancholy accident, and there is an account of it in the last editions of Moore's *Travels*. (I mean his first work.) There is a small monument erected in honour of the prince, upon the spot where his body was found. It was done by the free-masons of this place, of which society he was a member. But there is nothing remarkable in it. There is likewise in the burying ground a little monument, or rather tomb-stone, to *Kleist*, one of the most celebrated German poets, whom his countrymen call their Thomson. He was an officer in the service of Frederick the second, and was killed at the battle of Cunersdorf, a village distant only a couple miles from this place.

Just at the gate of the town, there is a spring of mineral water, at which a bathing house has been built, with accommodations for lodgers. This bath has been considerably frequented for some years past, and the physicians of the town say, that the waters are as good as those of Freyenwalde. I am willing to believe them as good as those of Toeplitz; for my faith in mineral waters in general, was not much edified by the success of our tour there last summer.

22d July. Still at Frankfort. We had left Berlin without being fully aware of the precise nature of the journey we had undertaken; and had not thought of taking with us furs, and winter-cloathing for a tour in the dog-days. But one of the professors, whose acquaintance we have made here, had formerly gone the same journey; and from his representations, we have been induced to send back to Berlin for thick cloathing, and this circumstance has prolonged our stay here a couple of days more than we at first intended. Yesterday we took a ride of three or four miles, to the country seat of a Mr. Schoening, the *land-rath* of the *circle*. The functions of his office are to collect the territorial taxes within a certain district called a *circle*, which is a subdivision of the province. You know the importance and extent of this title of *rath* or *councillor*, in the constitutions of the German states. It is a general name, designating every officer in all the subordinate parts of the administration; and sometimes a mere honorary title, which Frederic the second, by way of joke, once granted to a man, *upon condition* that he should never presume to give any *counsel*. For the principle upon which the name is founded is, that the person holding the title gives the king occasionally counsel, and the first part of it usually designates the particular department in which he gives it.

Mr. Schoening and his lady received us with great kindness and hospitality. From the neighbourhood of their house, and on our return, we had the pleasure of agreeable prospects of the

First page of the first issue of Dennie's weekly journal

Charles Jared, Joseph Hopkinson, William Meredith, Richard Rush, and Robert Walsh. The *Port Folio* began to decline after 1806, mainly because of prolonged spells of illness of the editor. One of Dennie's early biographers, John E. Hall, indicates, however, that the decline might have been a result of Dennie's becoming careless and easygoing, and relying too much on his friends for contributions. Dennie gave up the ownership in 1809 but remained as editor through a long period of declining health until his death on 7 January 1812. He was interred in the burying ground of St. Peter's Church, Philadelphia. John Quincy Adams wrote a lengthy inscription for his burial monument, a part of which reads: "As author of the Lay Preacher/And the first editor of the Port Folio,/He contributed to chasten the morals, and to refine/the taste of the nation."

Dennie's place as a harbinger in American periodical literature has been assured by his establishing the *Port Folio* as America's first successful literary magazine. It lasted an unprecedented twenty-six years. A follower of the ancient and modern classical writers, he added nothing new as a literary critic. No claim, moreover, can be made for his greatly influencing any one major American writer, but he exerted a salutary influence by creating an interest in belles lettres in the new republic. A writer in the *Port Folio* in February 1812 capsulated Dennie's literary goal: "The great purpose of all his exertions, the uniform pursuit of his life, was to disseminate among his countrymen a taste for elegant literature, to give to education and to letters their proper elevation in the public esteem, and reclaiming the youth of America from the low career of sordid interests, to fix steadily their ambition on objects of a more exalted character." Dennie's essays well illustrate his sharp wit, pungent humor, love of all branches of literature, and commitment to elevating native literature to the best English and classical taste.

Letters:

The Letters of Joseph Dennie, 1768-1812, edited by Laura Green Pedder (Orono, Maine: Printed at the University Press, 1936).

Biography:

Harold Milton Ellis, *Joseph Dennie and His Circle: A Study in American Literature from 1792-1812* (Austin: University of Texas, 1915).

References:

Joseph Tinker Buckingham, *Specimens of Newspaper Literature,* volume 2 (Boston: Little, Brown, 1850), pp. 174-202;

William Warland Clapp, *Joseph Dennie: Editor of "The Port Folio," and Author of "The Lay Preacher"* (Cambridge, Mass.: John Wilson/ University Press, 1880);

T. P. Govan, "The Death of Joseph Dennie: A Memoir by Nicholas Biddle," *Pennsylvania Magazine of History and Biography,* 75 (January 1951): 36-46;

Bruce Granger, *American Serial Essays from Franklin to Irving* (Knoxville: University of Tennessee Press, 1978), pp. 145-163;

John E. Hall, *The Philadelphia Souvenir; A Collection of Fugitive Pieces from the Philadelphia Press* (Philadelphia: Harrison Hall, 1826), pp. 70-94;

Lewis Leary, "Joseph Dennie on Benjamin Franklin: A Note on Early American Literary Criticism," *Pennsylvania Magazine of History and Biography,* 72 (July 1948): 240-246;

Leary, *Soundings: Some Early American Writers* (Athens: University of Georgia Press, 1975), pp. 253-270;

Annie Russell Marble, *Heralds of American Literature* (Chicago: University of Chicago Press, 1907), pp. 193-231;

John T. Queenan, "The *Port Folio*: A Study of the History and Significance of an Early American Magazine," Ph.D. dissertation, University of Pennsylvania, 1955;

Randolph C. Randall, "Joseph Dennie's Literary Attitudes in the *Port Folio,* 1801-1812," in *Essays Mostly on Periodical Publishing in America,* edited by James Woodress (Durham, N.C.: Duke University Press, 1973), pp. 57-91.

Papers:

Joseph Dennie's papers are held by Harvard University. Correspondence can also be found at the Massachusetts Historical Society, New Hampshire Historical Society, and Historical Society of Pennsylvania.

William Dunlap

(19 February 1766-28 September 1839)

Robert D. Harvey
University of Nevada at Reno

See also the Dunlap entries in *DLB 30, American Historians, 1607-1865* and *DLB 37, American Writers of the Early Republic.*

SELECTED BOOKS: *The Father; or American Shandy-ism. A Comedy, as Performed at the New-York Theatre, by the Old American Company. Written in the Year 1788 . . . ,* anonymous (New York: Printed by Hodge, Allen & Campbell, 1789); revised as *The Father of an Only Child,* in *The Dramatic Works of William Dunlap . . . ,* volume 1 (Philadelphia: Printed by T. & G. Palmer, 1806);

Darby's Return. A Comic Sketch. As Performed at the New-York Theatre, November 24, 1789 . . . (New York: Printed & sold by Hodge, Allen & Campbell and sold by Berry & Rogers, 1789);

The Archers or Mountaineers of Switzerland: An Opera, in Three Acts, As Performed by the Old American Company, in New-York; To Which is Subjoined a Brief Historical Account of Switzerland, from the Dissolution of the Roman Empire, to the Final Establishment of the Helvetic Confederacy, by the Battle of Sempach (New York: Printed by T. & J. Swords, 1796);

Tell Truth and Shame the Devil: A Comedy, in Two Acts, As Performed by the Old American Company, New-York, January, 1797, adapted from *Jérôme Pointu,* by A. L. B. Robineau (New York: Printed by T. & J. Swords, 1797);

André; A Tragedy, in Five Acts: As Performed by the Old American Company, New-York, March 30, 1798. To which are added authentic documents respecting Major André; Consisting of letters to Miss Seward, the Cow Chace, Proceedings of the court martial, &c. . . . (New York: Printed by T. & J. Swords, 1798; London: D. Ogilvy & Son, 1799);

The Wild-Goose Chace: A Play, in Four Acts With Songs . . . , adapted from Der Wildfang, by Augustus von Kotzebue (New York: Printed & sold by G. F. Hopkins and sold by T. & J. Swords, Gaine & Ten-Eyck, John Black, Alex Somerville . . . , 1800);

The Virgin of the Sun: A Play, in Five Acts . . . , adapted from *Die Sonnenjungfrau,* by von Kotzebue (New York: Printed & sold by G. F. Hopkins and sold by T. & J. Swords, Gaine & Ten-Eyck, John Black, Alex Somerville . . . , 1800);

Pizarro in Peru; Or, the Death of Rolla. A Play, in Five Acts . . . , adapted from Die Spanier in Peru, by von Kotzebue (New York: Printed & sold by G. F. Hopkins and sold by T. & J. Swords, Gaine & Ten-Eyck, John Black, Alex Somerville . . . , 1800);

Abaellino, the Great Bandit. Translated from the German and Adapted to the New-York Theatre . . . , translated and adapted from the dramatic version of *Abällino der Grosse Bandit,* by Johann Heinrich Daniel Zschokke (New York: Printed by L. Nichols & published by D. Longworth, 1802);

The Glory Of Columbia: Her Yeomanry. A Play in Five Acts. The songs, duets, and chorusses, intended for the celebration of the fourth of July at the New-York Theatre (songs, duets, and choruses only, New York: Printed and published by D. Longworth, 1803; published in full, New York: Published by David Longworth, 1817);

Ribbemont; or, The Feudal Baron, A Tragedy in Five Acts. As Performed at the New-York Theatre . . . (New York: Printed & published by D. Longworth, 1803);

The Voice of Nature, a Drama in Three Acts . . . , translated and adapted from *Le Jugement de Salomon,* by L. C. Caigniez (New York: Printed by L. Nichols & published by David Longworth, 1803);

The Wife of Two Husbands. A Drama, in Five Acts. As Performed at the New-York Theatre. Interspersed with Songs, Choruses, Music and Dances . . . , adapted from *La Femme à Deux Maris,* by Guilbert de Pixerécourt (New York: Printed & published by D. Longworth, 1804);

The Dramatic Works of William Dunlap, volume 1 (Philadelphia: Printed by T. & J. Palmer, 1806); volumes 2 and 3 (New York: Published by D. Longworth, 1816);

Fontainville Abbey, A Tragedy (New York: Published by David Longworth, 1807);

Fraternal Discord: A Drama, in Five Acts . . . , adapted from *Die Versöhnung,* by von Kotzebue (New York: Published by D. Longworth, 1809);

The Italian Father: A Comedy in Five Acts, By William Dunlap, esq. As performed at the New-York Theatre (New York: Published by D. Longworth, 1810);

Yankee Chronology; Or, Huzza For the Constitution! A Musical Interlude in One Act. To which are added the patriotic songs of The Freedom of the Seas, and Yankee Tars . . . (New York: Published by D. Longworth, 1812);

Memoirs of the Life of George Frederick Cooke, Esquire, Late of the Theatre Royal, Covent Garden. By William Dunlap, esq. Composed principally from journals and other authentic documents, left by Mr. Cooke; and the personal knowledge of the writer, 2 volumes (New York: Published by D. Longworth, 1813); revised as *The Life of George Fred. Cooke . . .* (London: Published by Henry Colburn, 1813);

Lovers Vows; a Play, in Five Acts . . . , adapted from *Das Kind der Liebe,* by von Kotzebue (New York: Published by David Longworth, 1814);

The Good Neighbor; an Interlude. In One Act. Altered from a Scene of Iffland's . . . (New York: Published by David Longworth, 1814);

Peter the Great; or, the Russian Mother: A Play, In Five Acts . . . , adapted from *Die Strelizen,* by J. M. Babo (New York: Published by David Longworth, 1814);

The Life of the Most Noble Arthur, Marquis and Earl of Wellington . . . the First Part by Francis L. Clarke. The Second Part, from the Attack on the Castle of Burgos to the Taking of Bordeaux, by William Dunlap (New York: Printed & published by Van Winkle & Wiley, 1814);

A Narrative of the Events Which Followed Bonaparte's Campaign in Russia To the Period of His Dethronement . . . (Hartford: Published by George Sheldon & Co., 1814);

The Life of Charles Brockden Brown: Together with Selections from the Rarest of His Printed Works, From His Original Letters, and from His Manuscripts before Unpublished, 2 volumes (Philadelphia: Published by James P. Parke, 1815); republished as *Memoirs of Charles Brockden Brown, The American Novelist. Author of Wieland, Ormond, Arthur Mervyn, etc. With selections from his original letters, and miscellaneous writings* (London: H. Colburn & Co., 1822);

A Trip to Niagara; Or, Travellers in America. A Farce, In Three Acts. Written for the Bowery Theatre, New-York . . . (New York: Printed & published by E. B. Clayton, 1830);

Address to the Students of the National Academy of Design, at the Delivery of the Premiums, Monday, the 18th of April, 1831 . . . (New York: Printed by Clayton & Van Norden, 1831);

A History of the American Theatre . . . (New York: Printed & published by J. & J. Harper, 1832; 2 volumes, London: R. Bentley, 1832);

History of the Rise and Progress of the Arts of Design in the United States . . . , 2 volumes (New York: Printed by G. P. Scott & Co., 1834);

Thirty Years Ago; or The Memoirs of a Water Drinker . . . (New York: Published by Bancroft & Holley, 1836);

A History of New York, for Schools . . . , 2 volumes (New York: Collins, Keese & Co., 1837);

History of the New Netherlands, Province of New York, and State of New York, to the Adoption of the Federal Constitution . . . , 2 volumes (New York: Printed for the author by Carter & Thorp, 1839, 1840);

Diary of William Dunlap (1766-1839) The Memoirs of a Dramatist, Theatrical Manager, Painter, Critic, Novelist, and Historian . . . , 3 volumes (New York: Printed for the New-York Historical Society, 1930);

False Shame and Thirty Years: Two Plays, edited by Oral Sumner Coad (Princeton: Princeton University Press, 1940).

OTHER: "Gilbert Charles Stuart" and "Charles Brockden Brown," in volumes 1 and 3, *National Portrait Gallery of Americans* . . . (New York, Philadelphia & London: Herring & Longacre, 1834, 1836).

PERIODICAL PUBLICATIONS: "Remarks on the Love of Country," *New York Magazine,* new series 2 (November 1797): 582-584;

"Biographical Sketch of the Late Gilbert Stuart," *Knickerbocker,* 1 (April 1833): 195-223;

"Memoir of Thomas Abthorpe Cooper," *New York Mirror,* 11 (2 November 1833): 225-252.

William Dunlap's energetic though financially fruitless career as a painter, playwright, theater manager, biographer, and historian in the early decades of the American Republic won him recognition as "The Father of the American Theater" and "the American Vasari." Without genius as a painter or dramatist, he strove within his limits to define and achieve professional ideals for the arts and the stage in his still-provincial country. His exhaustive efforts–more antiquarian

The Artist Showing a Picture from *Hamlet* to His Parents, *painting by William Dunlap, circa 1788 (by permission of the New-York Historical Society)*

than theoretically critical–to record the experiences of his countrymen in his *A History of the American Theatre* (1832) and his *History of the Rise and Progress of the Arts of Design in the United States* (1834), together with what has survived of his diary, published as *Diary of William Dunlap ...* (1930), provide basic materials upon which modern understanding of the period depends.

For forty years Dunlap kept his eye clearly focused on the rise and progress of the arts in the new republic. Reared in a Tory bourgeois family, Dunlap chose a life of struggle to clarify to his countrymen the importance of the arts in a democratic society. His father had been a slaveholder; at his death Dunlap freed the estate's slaves and worked in the early abolition movement. A freethinking Deist and admirer of William Godwin, he despised religious bigotry (a brother-in-law was the Federalist puritan Timothy Dwight) and stood for the American notions of freedom and equality as a lifelong Democrat. He deplored Jacobin violence in the French Revolution but celebrated the revolution's openness to a better future than the ancien régime could offer. Both as painter and playwright, he came to understand the importance of educating audiences in the marketplace of the arts. He rejected the class implications of the English patronage system and advocated a national subsidy for the theater as well as private wealth supporting artistic activities in a free society. As he notes in his diary, he saw in his provincial republic the opportunity not of "the bringing down of the few but the exaltation of the many."

Dunlap's father, Samuel, was an Irish soldier with the British army at the fall of Quebec in 1762. He later sold his commission, married, and took up shopkeeping in Perth Amboy, New Jersey, where he met and married Margaret Sargent. William, their only child, was born in 1766. The family was loyalist during the Revolutionary War, and they moved to New York to be near British headquarters. Dunlap later remembered colorful redcoat parades and wagons loaded with British dead and wounded. He discovered that war was real, however, not romantic, a lesson painfully reinforced when the twelve-year-old William lost an eye in boyhood playing war. With independence won by the colonialists, Samuel Dunlap prospered by importing china and sent William to London for three years of study, from 1784 to 1787. Already, despite the loss of his eye, William was trying his hand at portrait painting; a

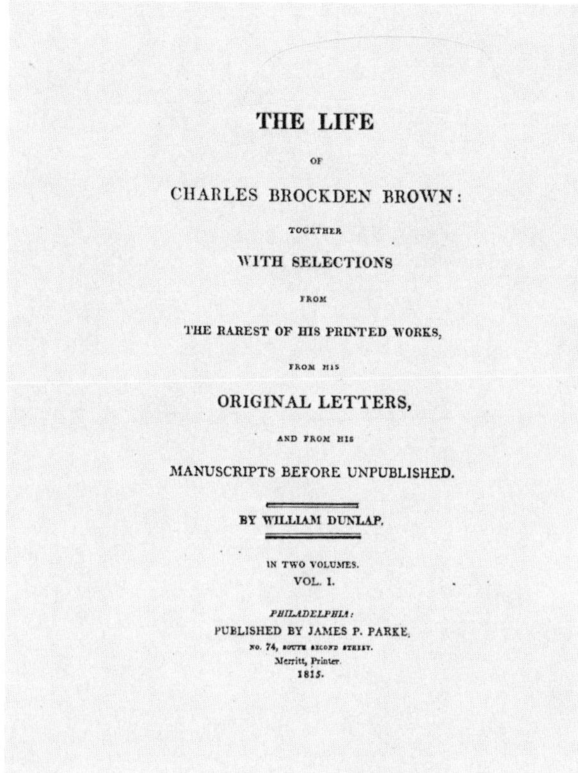
THE LIFE
OF
CHARLES BROCKDEN BROWN:
TOGETHER
WITH SELECTIONS
FROM
THE RAREST OF HIS PRINTED WORKS,
FROM HIS
ORIGINAL LETTERS,
AND FROM HIS
MANUSCRIPTS BEFORE UNPUBLISHED.

BY WILLIAM DUNLAP.

IN TWO VOLUMES.
VOL. I.

PHILADELPHIA:
PUBLISHED BY JAMES P. PARKE,
NO. 74, SOUTH SECOND STREET.
Merritt, Printer.
1815.

Title page for the first volume of Dunlap's biography of his old friend, who had died in 1810

very early sitter was Gen. George Washington. In London, though the young American did visit Benjamin West, he avoided the course of study at the Royal Academy, preferring tavern conviviality and the attractions of the theater. Suddenly called home by his concerned father, William married, gave up drink, and submitted to working in the family business; but he found friends in the nascent New York theater, for which he began to write plays.

At age thirty Dunlap made a fateful decision: using his legacy from Samuel Dunlap, he bought half-interest in a New York theater company (which became the Park Street Theatre) and became its manager. Box office realities and ferocious infighting among the actors used up his father's modest fortune, and he was forced to declare bankruptcy in 1805. By that time he had written many of his some thirty original plays and another thirty or so translations and adaptations of continental works, mainly from the German (for example, the popular August von Kotzebue) and the French. His works included sentimental comedies and farces, such as *The Father; or American Shandy-ism ...* (1789); gothic terror plays, *Fontainville Abbey* (produced in 1795) and *Ribbemont; or, The Feudal Baron, A Tragedy in Five Acts* . . . (produced in 1796); and blank verse tragedies, *Leicester* (produced in 1794 under the title *The Fatal Deception; or, the Progress of Guilt . . .)* and the popular *André; A Tragedy, in Five Acts* . . . (produced in 1798). None of this work is important as drama, though much of it displays competence. Its importance, along with Dunlap's troubles as a theater manager, is in that wealth of actual experience with actors, writers, and audiences in the early American theater which is reflected later in *A History of the American Theatre.*

Bankrupt, Dunlap became an itinerant portrait painter and miniaturist, looking for commissions from Montreal to South Carolina. It was sustenance and a sense of social actuality rather than profit he gained. For a while, from 1806 to 1811, he worked on salary as assistant manager for the Park Street theater he had once owned; his life of George Frederick Cooke, the distinguished but dissolute British comic actor, resulted from this period and was published in 1813. The book appreciated Cooke's comic genius while it lamented his immoral and self-destructive propensities. The distinction this memoir insists upon between the aesthetic and the moral in art is characteristic of Dunlap's later histories.

While acting as a paymaster to the New York militia during the War of 1812, Dunlap assembled a hodgepodge critical life of his friend Charles Brockden Brown, preserving source materials but providing no clear assessment of Brown's novels. He then turned again to painting, and four large historical canvases on the life of Christ, in imitation of Benjamin West, made some money on tour of rural areas in the 1820s. In 1826 he helped found the new National Academy of Design, where he became an unpaid professor and worked on his *History of the Rise and Progress of the Arts of Design.* Dunlap's life, crowded with many loyal friends and a few well-hated enemies, was marked by repeated failure and hand-to-mouth working conditions; but he never seems to have been reduced to despair or bitterness. In ill health during the 1830s, he nevertheless completed his two important histories, wrote a long temperance-tract novel, *Thirty Years Ago; or The Memoirs of a Water Drinker* (1836), and worked on *A History of New York, for Schools* (1837), written in dialogue form, and *History of the New Netherlands, Province of New York, and State of New York* (1839, 1840), featuring Peter Stuyvesant and George Washington as American heroes.

Dunlap's 1823 painting of a scene from C. P. Clinch's dramatic version of James Fenimore Cooper's novel The Spy *(by permission of the New York State Historical Association, Cooperstown)*

Aware of the necessity to look to Europe for genius in literature and the arts, Dunlap sought to provide his New York audience with continental plays, and he believed that Reynolds and Benjamin West surpassed native American talent. But he felt the American republic had great potential: "The American returning from Europe who does not feel the glow of patriotism at the recollections of the free institutions of his country, the unparalleled diffusion of enjoyment among the *people,* and the improvement of every kind of flowing from the establishment of Democracy–is a wretch to pity or abhor."

The *History of the Rise and Progress of the Arts of Design in the United States* provides a chronological series of biographical notices about 287 artists working in America, whether native or foreign-born. The lives vary in length from one line to sixty-nine pages. Dunlap defends his anecdotal, even gossipy biographical sketches as "more amusing, and not less instructive." An example of his humor appears in his treatment of one Gilbert Fox, who "was a pretty young man, had a sweet voice, and an irresistible lisp, and taught 'love's dream' to one of his pupils, who became Mrs. Fox. Contrary to all rational calculation the boarding school proprietors would no longer trust the Fox among their flocks now that he was caught, and he had to seek some other mode of gaining a living for himself and family."

Without sentimentality, Dunlap's histories strive for accuracy, with a moral conviction about

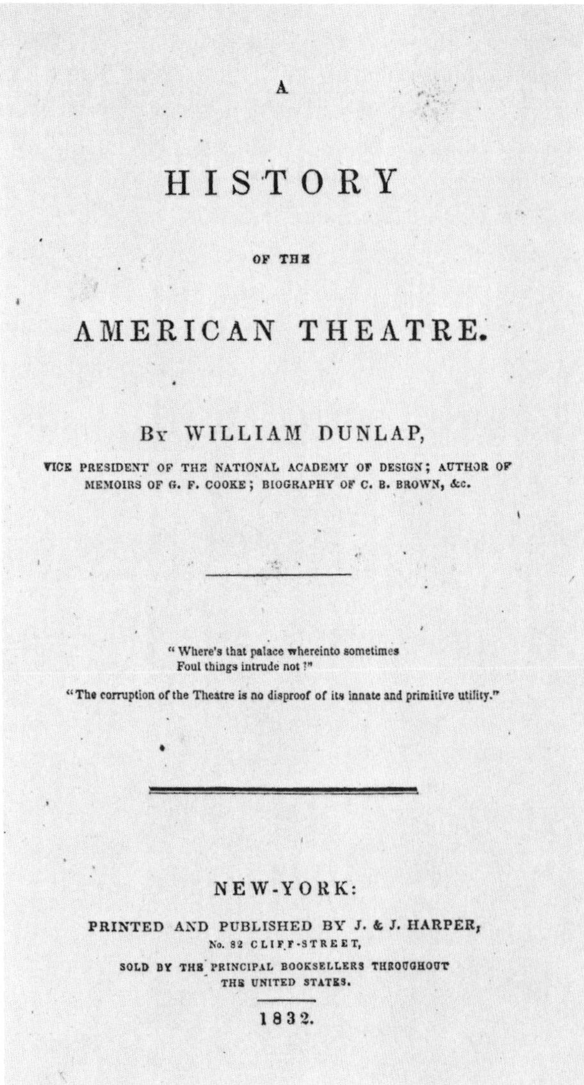
A

HISTORY

OF THE

AMERICAN THEATRE.

BY WILLIAM DUNLAP,

VICE PRESIDENT OF THE NATIONAL ACADEMY OF DESIGN; AUTHOR OF MEMOIRS OF G. F. COOKE; BIOGRAPHY OF C. B. BROWN, &c.

" Where's that palace whereinto sometimes
Foul things intrude not !"

"The corruption of the Theatre is no disproof of its innate and primitive utility."

NEW-YORK:

PRINTED AND PUBLISHED BY J. & J. HARPER,
No. 82 CLIFF-STREET,

SOLD BY THE PRINCIPAL BOOKSELLERS THROUGHOUT THE UNITED STATES.

1832.

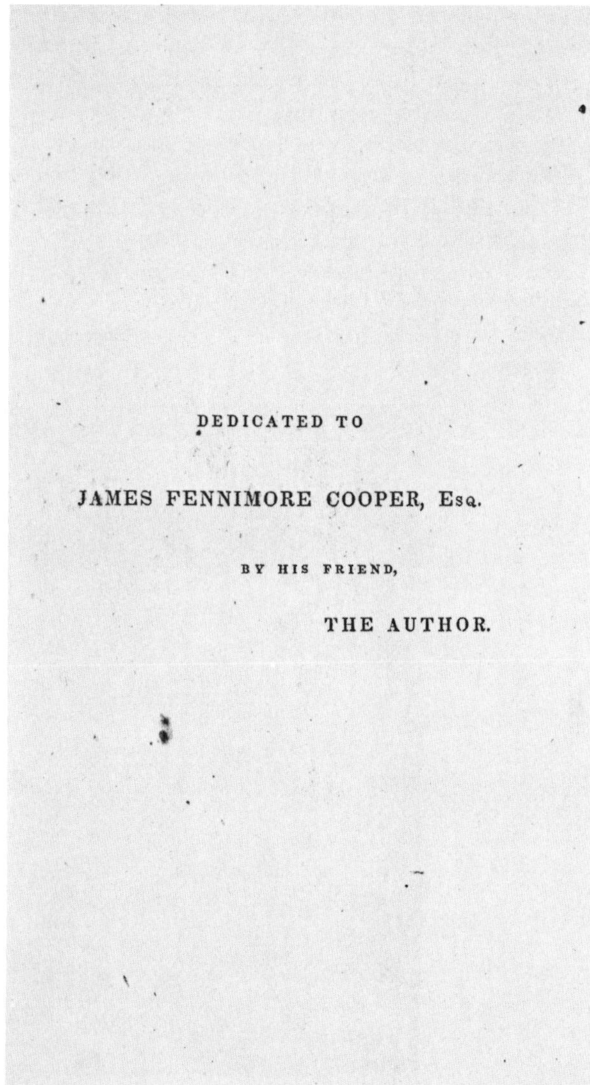
DEDICATED TO

JAMES FENNIMORE COOPER, Esq.

BY HIS FRIEND,

THE AUTHOR.

Title page and dedication page for the work in which Dunlap advocated a state-supported theater

the role of the artist in society: "Truth is the object of this book," he states in the *History of the Rise and Progress of the Arts of Design . . .*, "and good or evil shall be recorded of dead or living, as Truth shall dictate." If an individual is a writer, he says, "we have a desire to know if his conduct squares with the lessons he teaches; if an artist, we wish to know how art has affected his character, and whether the contemplation of the sublime productions of human genius has raised and purified mind, or the contrary. The good artist who is not a good man, is a traitor to the arts, and an enemy to society." Dunlap knew the distinction between the moral and aesthetic; an artist may be gifted without being good, but following Horace, he insists on the moral purpose of the arts in society: *docere* as well as *placere*. In a country still emerging from a narrow puritanism he defended the theater against the old charge of immorality by insisting on drama's moral function in society. He felt the historian owes his audience the truth of life as well as art: "If a man is worth the world's attention, let the world know the truth of him, and as far as possible the true cause of his actions." Hence as biographer Dunlap can reveal the actor Cooke's sins while celebrating his comic genius, and he allows for John Trumbull's artistic successes while denouncing his personal arrogance.

Dunlap's scholarly work has no philosophical depth. It is permeated with his strong and simple moral personality. His efforts to establish an accurate record of character and incident in the visual and theatrical arts from 1790 to 1830 provide an engaging and irreplaceable body of source materials. The strength of his historical work emerges from his practical experience in the craft of the arts he knew firsthand, and from his hard-won knowledge of the social audience to which these arts must appeal or fail.

Bibliography:

Oscar Wegelin, *A Bibliographical Checklist of Plays and Miscellaneous Writings of William Dunlap* (New York: Charles F. Heartman, 1916).

Biographies:

Oscar Wegelin, *William Dunlap and His Writings* (New York: Privately printed, 1904);

Oral S. Coad, *William Dunlap* (New York: Dunlap Society, 1917);

Edward Southern Hipp, *Drama's Father in America, William Dunlap* (Newark, 1934);

William Carroll McGinnis, *William Dunlap* (Perth Amboy, N.J.: City of Perth Amboy, 1956);

Robert H. Canady, *William Dunlap* (New York: Twayne, 1970).

References:

Mary Rives Bowman, "Dunlap and the 'Theatrical Register' of the *New York Magazine*," *Studies in Philology*, 24 (July 1927): 413-425;

Van Wyck Brooks, *The World of Washington Irving* (New York: Dutton, 1944), pp. 119-137;

Charles M. Getchell, "The Mind and Art of William Dunlap (1766-1839)," Ph.D. dissertation, University of Wisconsin, 1946;

David Grimsted, *Melodrama Unveiled: American Theater and Culture, 1800-1850* (Chicago: University of Chicago, 1968);

Fred Moramarco, "The Early Dramatic Criticism of William Dunlap," *American Literature*, 40 (March 1968): 9-14;

G. C. D. Odell, *Annals of the New York Stage*, 15 volumes (New York: Columbia University Press, 1929-1949);

Phillips Academy, *William Dunlap: Painter and Critic* (Andover, Mass.: Addison Gallery of American Art, 1939);

James H. Pickering, "*Satanstoe:* Cooper's Debt to William Dunlap," *American Literature*, 38 (January 1967): 468-477;

Arthur Hobson Quinn, *A History of American Drama. From the Beginning to the Civil War* (New York: Harper, 1923), pp. 73-112;

T. S. Woolsey, "American Vasari," *Yale Review*, 3 (July 1914): 778-789.

Papers:

Manuscripts relating to William Dunlap's work can be found at the Boston Public Library, the Historical Society of Pennsylvania, the Massachusetts Historical Society, the New York State Library, the University of Virginia Library, and the New York Public Library's theater collection.

Ralph Waldo Emerson

Robert D. Richardson, Jr.
University of Colorado

See also the Emerson entry in *DLB 1, The American Renaissance in New England.*

BIRTH: Boston, Massachusetts, 25 May 1803, to William and Ruth Haskins Emerson.

EDUCATION: A.B., Harvard College, 1821; Theological School at Cambridge (Harvard Divinity School), 1825-1829.

MARRIAGES: 30 September 1829 to Ellen Tucker (deceased). 14 September 1835 to Lydia Jackson; children: Waldo, Ellen, Edith, Edward.

DEATH: Concord, Massachusetts, 27 April 1882.

Ralph Waldo Emerson, 1848

SELECTED BOOKS: *Letter from the Rev. R. W. Emerson, to the Second Church and Society* (Boston: Printed by I. R. Butts, 1832);

Nature (Boston: Munroe, 1836); republished as *Nature Essays* (London & Edinburgh: T. N. Foulis, 1910);

An Oration, Delivered Before the Phi Beta Kappa Society, at Cambridge, August 31, 1837 (Boston: Munroe, 1837); republished as *Man Thinking* (London: Mudie, 1844);

An Address Delivered Before the Senior Class in Divinity College, Cambridge Sunday Evening, 15 July 1838 (Boston: Munroe, 1838; London: Green, 1903);

An Oration, Delivered Before the Literary Societies of Dartmouth College, July 24, 1838 (Boston: Little, Brown, 1838);

Essays [First Series] (Boston: Munroe, 1841; London: Fraser, 1841; expanded, Boston: Munroe, 1847);

Nature; An Essay, and Lectures on the Times (London: Clarke, 1844);

Orations, Lectures, and Addresses (London: Clarke, 1844);

Essays: Second Series (Boston: Munroe, 1844; London: Chapman, 1844);

An Address Delivered in the Courthouse in Concord, Massachusetts, on 1st August, 1844, on the Anniversary of the Emancipation of the Negroes in the British West Indies (Boston: Munroe, 1844); republished as *The Emancipation of the Negroes in the British West Indies. An Address Delivered at Concord, Massachusetts, on 1st August, 1844* (London: Chapman, 1844);

Poems (London: Chapman Brothers, 1847; Boston: Munroe, 1847); enlarged and revised as *Selected Poems* (Boston: Osgood, 1876); enlarged again and revised as *Poems* (Boston & New York: Houghton Mifflin, 1884 [volume 9, Riverside Edition]; London: Routledge, 1884; revised, Boston & New York: Houghton Mifflin, 1904 [volume 9, Centenary Edition]);

Nature; Addresses, and Lectures (Boston & Cambridge: Munroe, 1849); republished as *Miscellanies; Embracing Nature, Addresses, and Lec-*

tures (Boston: Phillips, Sampson, 1856); republished as *Miscellanies* (London: Macmillan, 1884);

Representative Men: Seven Lectures (Boston: Phillips, Sampson, 1850; London: John Chapman, 1850);

English Traits (Boston: Phillips, Sampson, 1856; London: Routledge, 1856);

The Conduct of Life (Boston: Ticknor & Fields, 1860; London: Smith, Elder, 1860);

May-Day and Other Pieces (Boston: Ticknor & Fields, 1867; London: Routledge, 1867);

Society and Solitude. Twelve Chapters (Boston: Fields, Osgood, 1870; London: Sampson Low, Son & Marston, 1870);

Letters and Social Aims (Boston: Osgood, 1876; London: Chatto & Windus, 1876);

Miscellanies (Boston: Houghton Mifflin, 1884 [volume 11, Riverside Edition]; London: Routledge, 1884);

Lectures and Biographical Sketches (Boston & New York: Houghton Mifflin, 1884; London: Routledge, 1884);

Natural History of Intellect and Other Papers (Boston & New York: Houghton Mifflin, 1893 [volume 12, Riverside Edition]; London: Routledge, 1894);

Two Unpublished Essays: The Character of Socrates; The Present State of Ethical Philosophy (Boston & New York: Lamson, Wolffe, 1896);

The Journals of Ralph Waldo Emerson, 10 volumes, edited by Edward Waldo Emerson and Waldo Emerson Forbes (Boston & New York: Houghton Mifflin, 1909-1914);

Uncollected Writings: Essays, Addresses, Poems, Reviews and Letters (New York: Lamb, 1912);

Young Emerson Speaks: Unpublished Discourses on Many Subjects, edited by Arthur Cushman McGiffert, Jr. (Boston: Houghton Mifflin, 1938);

The Early Lectures of Ralph Waldo Emerson, volume 1, edited by Stephen E. Whicher and Robert E. Spiller (Cambridge, Mass.: Harvard University Press, 1959); volume 2, edited by Whicher, Spiller, and Wallace E. Williams (Cambridge, Mass.: Harvard University Press, 1964); volume 3, edited by Spiller and Williams (Cambridge, Mass.: Harvard University Press, 1972);

The Journals and Miscellaneous Notebooks of Ralph Waldo Emerson, 16 volumes, edited by William H. Gilman, et al. (Cambridge, Mass.: Harvard University Press, 1960-1983).

Collections: *Emerson's Complete Works,* 12 volumes, edited by J. E. Cabot (Boston & New York: Houghton Mifflin, 1883-1893 [Riverside Edition]; London: Routledge, 1883-1894);

Complete Works of Ralph Waldo Emerson, 12 volumes (Boston & New York: Houghton Mifflin, 1903-1904 [Centenary Edition]);

The Collected Works of Ralph Waldo Emerson, 3 volumes to date (Cambridge, Mass.: Harvard University Press, 1971-).

OTHER: *Memoirs of Margaret Fuller Ossoli,* 2 volumes, written and edited by Emerson, William Henry Channing, and James Freeman Clarke (Boston: Phillips, Sampson, 1852); 3 volumes (London: Bentley, 1852);

Parnassus, edited by Emerson (Boston: Osgood, 1875).

Ralph Waldo Emerson was not a practicing literary critic in the sense that Edgar Allan Poe and William Dean Howells were, and he was not a theorist as Immanuel Kant, Friedrich Wilhelm Joseph von Schelling or Friedrich Ernst Schleiermacher were. Yet he was for America what Samuel Taylor Coleridge was for England, the major spokesman for a new conception of literature. From his early essays on English literature and his important first book, *Nature* (1836), to his greatest single literary essay, "The Poet" (1844), to his late essays on "Poetry and Imagination" and "Persian Poetry" in 1875, Emerson developed and championed a concept of literature as literary activity. The essence of that activity is a symbolizing process. Both reader and writer are involved in acts of literary expression which are representative or symbolic. Emerson's position is an extreme one, and in *A History of Modern Criticism* (1965) René Wellek has said that "the very extremity with which he held his views makes him the outstanding representative of romantic symbolism in the English-speaking world." Emerson's romantic symbolism, biographical and ethical in intent, poetic in expression, is an attitude that still stirs debate and still can have a liberating and encouraging effect on the modern reader. Emerson always cared more for the present than the past, more for his reader than for the text in hand or the author in question. Poets, he said, are "liberating gods"; and Emerson at his best is also a liberator. "Meek young men grow up in libraries, believing it their duty to accept the views, which Cicero, which Locke, which Bacon have given, forgetful that Cicero, Locke, and Bacon were only young men in libraries, when they wrote those books."

Emerson is the chief figure in the American literary movement called Transcendentalism, which was also a philosophical and religious movement. Transcendentalism is complex, drawing upon Platonic, Christian, Stoic, and Hindu thought, but its most immediate affinity is with German Idealism as worked out from Kant to Schelling. Indeed Emerson himself said in a lecture called "The Transcendentalist," delivered in December 1841, "What is popularly called Transcendentalism among us, is Idealism." He then described it: "As thinkers, mankind have ever divided into two sects, Materialists and Idealists; the first class founding on experience, the second on consciousness; the first class beginning to think from the data of the senses, the second class perceive that the senses are not final, and say, the senses gives us representations of things, but what are the things themselves, they cannot tell. The materialist insists on facts, on history, on the force of circumstances, and the animal wants of man; the idealist on the power of Thought and of Will, on inspiration, on miracle, on individual culture." Materialist criticism focuses on facts, on literary history, on the life and mind of the author and his or her intention, and on the text itself. Emerson's ethical and idealist criticism concentrates almost entirely upon the reader and his or her response to a text. Emerson is mainly concerned not with the fact of literary history but with the *uses* of literature, with its effects on the reader, and its power or lack of power to move us.

Emersonian Idealism was extremely influential in the middle third of the nineteenth century, though it was eventually supplanted by realism and naturalism and the rise of the realist movement. But the reader-centered nature of Emerson's critical stance was important to such thinkers and writers as Friedrich Nietzsche, Marcel Proust, and Virginia Woolf and is now of interest again to postformalist and poststructuralist critics who are newly concerned with the reader's relation to the text.

Emerson's father, William Emerson, the Unitarian minister at Boston's First Church from 1799 until his death in 1811, was an active, popular preacher and a staunch Federalist of very limited means but descended from a long line of Concord, Massachusetts, ministers. Emerson was eight when his father died. His mother, Ruth Haskins Emerson, a quiet, devout, and undemonstrative woman, lived till 1853, long enough to see her fourth child's fame. Emerson had seven siblings. Three died in infancy or childhood. Of those who lived to maturity, Edward died young, at twenty-nine, in 1834 as did Charles at twenty-eight in 1836, while Robert Bulkeley, who lived to age fifty-two, dying in 1859, was feeble-minded. Besides Ralph, only William lived a full and reasonably long life, dying at sixty-seven in 1868.

Emerson went to Boston Public Latin School when he was nine, and to Harvard College when he was fourteen. After college, he tried teaching, then attended divinity school at Harvard. In 1829 he was ordained minister of Boston's Second Church. That same year he married Ellen Tucker. It was very much a love match, and Emerson was deeply shaken by her death only a year and a half later on 8 February 1831. At the same time, he was becoming increasingly reluctant to remain as minister to his church. In October 1832 he resigned, the immediate reason being that he felt he could no longer officiate at a ceremony (communion) that had become meaningless to him. With his wife dead and his career broken off, Emerson now sold his house and furniture and set out for Europe. He spent nine months abroad, almost six of them in Italy, working from Sicily to Naples to Rome, Florence, Venice, then on to Switzerland and Paris. In Paris, at the Jardin des Plantes, he experienced the full power and appeal of the new botanical and zoological sciences, and he now turned decisively from theology to science, vowing to become a naturalist. Going on to England and Scotland, he met Samuel Taylor Coleridge, William Wordsworth, and, particularly, Thomas Carlyle, who became a lifelong friend and correspondent.

Returning home in October 1833, Emerson immediately embraced a new career, that of public lecturer. One month after disembarking, he was invited by the Boston Natural History Society to deliver the first of his four lectures on science. That winter he lectured in Concord and Bedford on his Italian trip, and, beginning in January 1835, at Boston's Masonic Temple, he delivered his first open public lecture series, six lectures on "Biography." The fourth lecture in the series, that on Milton, was his first important statement about literature. The Milton lecture was published, posthumously, in *Natural History of Intellect*

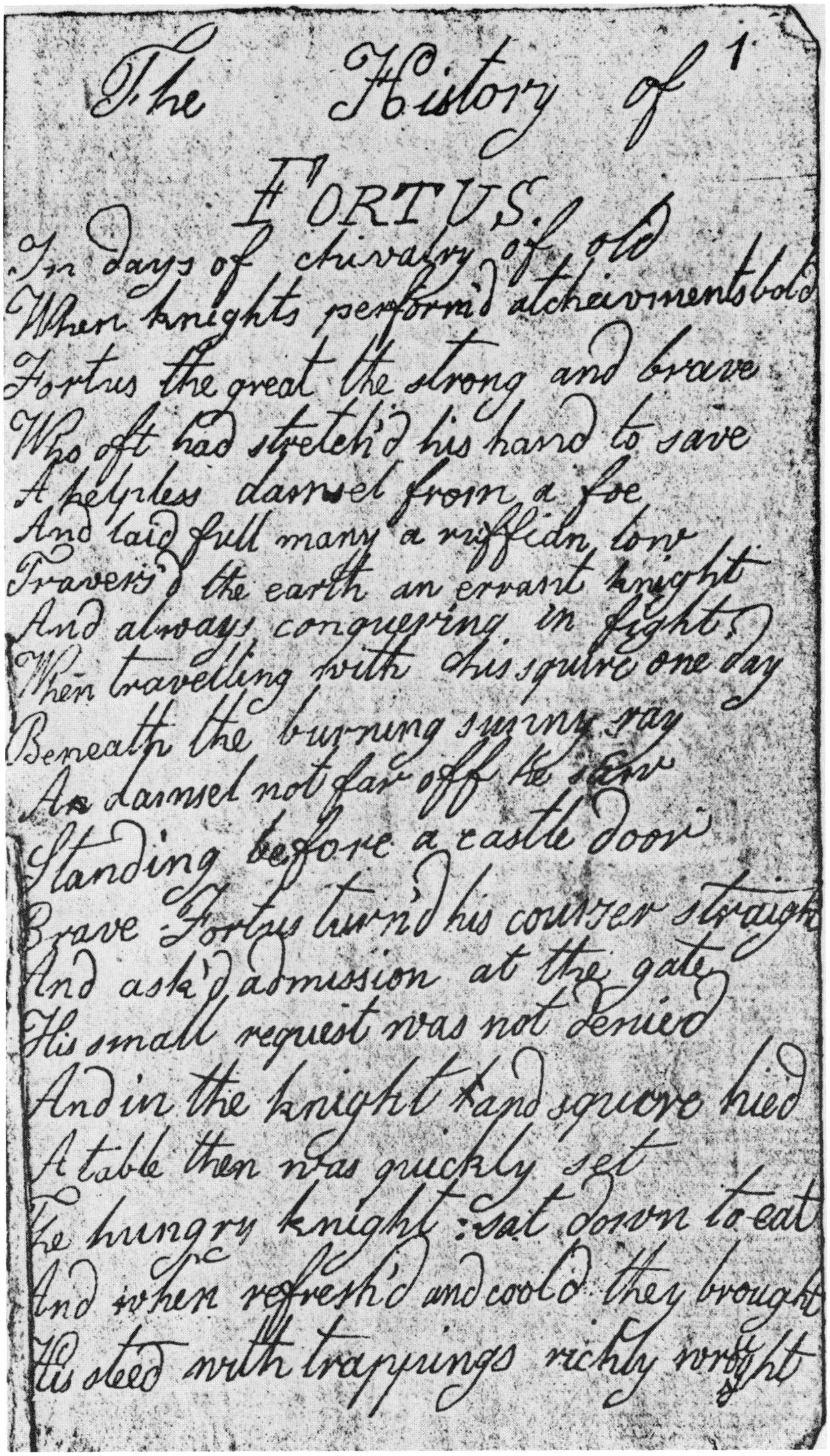

The History of 1
FORTUS.
In days of chivalry of old
When knights perform'd atcheivments bold
Fortus the great the strong and brave
Who oft had stretch'd his hand to save
A helpless damsel from a foe
And laid full many a ruffian low
Travers'd the earth an errant knight
And always conquering in fight:
When travelling with his squire one day
Beneath the burning sunny ray
A damsel not far off he saw
Standing before a castle door
Brave Fortus turn'd his courser straight
And ask'd admission at the gate
His small request was not denied
And in the knight and squire hied
A table then was quickly set
The hungry knight sat down to eat
And when refresh'd and coold they brought
His steed with trappings richly wrought

Page from the manuscript for "Fortus A Poem," written by Emerson when he was ten years old (from Records of a Lifelong Friendship, 1807-1882, Ralph Waldo Emerson and William Henry Furness, *1910)*

(1893), but the other five lectures in the "Biography" series of 1835, like the ten lectures he gave on "English Literature" later that same year, the twelve lectures on "The Philosophy of History" in 1836-1837, and the ten on "Human Culture" of 1837-1838, were only published beginning in 1959 as *The Early Lectures of Ralph Waldo Emerson.* Many of the ideas and phrases were incorporated by Emerson in subsequent lectures and books, which is why he did not publish them. But the early lectures show vividly the development of Emerson's characteristic views about literature.

Also in 1835, Emerson moved to Concord and, in September, married Lydia Jackson of Plymouth whom he came to call Lidian (and, sometimes, Asia) and who he tried to get to call him something besides Mr. E. He once told his cousin Sarah Ripley that those "who had baptised the child Lydia had been ill-advised, for her name was Lidian." In 1836 the so-called Transcendental Club met for the first time, bringing together with Emerson, George Putnam, George Ripley, and Frederic Hedge. The group expanded in

Ellen Louisa Tucker, Emerson's first wife (from the 1909 edition of Emerson's journals)

just a week and a half to include Orestes Brownson, James Freeman Clarke, Convers Francis, and Bronson Alcott. It again expanded to include Theodore Parker, Margaret Fuller, Elizabeth Peabody, and Henry Thoreau. Eighteen thirty-six also saw the publication of Emerson's first book and the birth of his first child, Waldo.

Emerson spent the rest of his life centered in Concord, with another trip to England in 1847-1848, one to California in 1871, and a final trip to Egypt in 1872. Each winter he would travel through New England and the East Coast, and as far west as there were cities on his annual lecture tour, for which he was his own booking agent, advertiser, and arranger. The rest of the year he spent in Concord, which soon became one of the intellectual centers of the country, a sort of American Weimar. The group around Emerson, usually called the Transcendentalists, were defined in one way by Emerson's 1838 Divinity School address, which offended orthodox Unitarians by locating religious authority in the religious nature of human beings, rather than in the Bible or the person of Christ. The *Dial,* a new magazine founded by the group and edited first by Margaret Fuller, showed the group's interest in the literature of Idealism. In religion, in philosophy, and in literature, the group around Emerson was liberal, learned, forward-looking and reform-minded. The Emersonian "movement" (it was Emerson who said there are always two parties in society, the Establishment and the Movement) or "the newness" was eventually overshadowed by the Civil War, the coming of industrialism, and the rise of realism. But in the late 1830s, 1840s, and into the 1850s, Emerson was at the center of much that was new, exciting, and vital in American cultural life.

His contributions to literary criticism begin with the lecture called "Milton," given first in February 1835. Many of what would become Emerson's characteristic emphases are already evident in the Milton lecture. What Emerson really values in Milton is not his high critical reputation but his power to inspire, which is, Emerson says, greater than that of any other writer. "We think no man can be named, whose mind still acts on the cultivated intellect of England and America with an energy comparable to that of Milton." "Power," "energy," "inspiration": these are the qualities Emerson looks for in a work of literature or in an author. Indeed Emerson is always more interested in the author than the text, and

The Emerson house in Concord, Massachusetts

he quotes with approval Milton's comment that "he who would aspire to write well hereafter in laudable things, ought himself to be a true poem; that is, a composition and pattern of the best and honorablest things." Emerson would say later that the reader ought to think of himself as the text and books as the commentary.

Milton's great subject, says Emerson, is not so much the fall of man as liberty. The English poet advocated civil, ecclesiastical, literary, and domestic liberty. He opposed slavery, denied predestination, argued for freedom of the press, and favored the principle of divorce. Milton's writings are valuable not as literary artifacts, Emerson argues, but as pathways to the man. Emerson insists on linking the person and the writing. Milton's poems, like his prose, reflect the "opinions, the feelings, even the incidents of the poet's life." In general Emerson rates Milton's prose at least as high as his poetry, and he boldly redefines Milton's prose *as* poetry in an important critical statement. "Of his prose in general, not the style alone, but the argument also, is poetic; according to Lord Bacon's definition of poetry, following that of Aristotle, 'Poetry, not finding the actual world exactly conformed to its idea of good and fair, seeks to accommodate the shows of things to the desires of the mind, and to create an ideal world better than the world of experience.' "

In August 1835 Emerson delivered a lecture to the sixth annual meeting of the American Institute of Instruction in Boston "On the Best Mode of Inspiring a Correct Taste in English Literature." In strong contrast to the starchy, neoclassical title, the surviving pages of this talk, published in *The Early Lectures of Ralph Waldo Emerson* (volume one, 1959), emphasize the idea that a reader must approach a text with sympathy, empathy, openness, and a willingness to try out the author's point of view. It is, he says, a major principle "that a truth or a book of truths can be received only by the same spirit that gave it forth." This notion is very different from learning a few rules or current ideas and then judging works of literature by whether they conform to those rules and ideas. Emerson also makes a distinction between types of reading and warns us "reading must not be passive." An active reader is one who engages fully with the text. "As we say translations are rare because to be a good translator needs all the talents of an original author so to be a good reader needs the high qualities of a good writer." Above all the reader is to remember that books and poems are not ends in themselves. They convey truths or wisdom, they stand for and convey to us things that exist in nature. "I should aim to show him [the young reader] that the poem was a transcript of Nature as much as a mariner's chart is of the coast."

In the introductory lecture for his 1835 series, "English Literature," Emerson offers a very broad definition of literature as "the books that are written. It is the recorded thinking of man." Later he excludes "records of facts," but even so it is evident that he meant the term literature to take in far more than just poems, plays, and novels. More important, in this lecture Emerson describes all language as "a naming of invisible and spiritual things from visible things," and he here first gives his famous two-part definition of language. First, words are emblematic of things; "supercilious" means literally "the raising of an eyebrow." Second, things are emblematic; "Light and Darkness are not in words but in fact our best expression for knowledge and ignorance." Since both words and things are emblematic, it follows for Emerson that "good writing and brilliant discourse are perpetual allegories." He concludes that "the aim and effort of literature in the largest sense [is] nothing less than to *give voice to the whole of spiritual nature* as events and ages unfold it, to record in words the whole life of the world."

In the next lecture, on "Permanent Traits of the English National Genius," Emerson draws heavily on Sharon Turner's *History of the Anglo Saxons* (1799-1805) and emphasizes the impact of Anglo-Saxon life and culture on modern England and the English. Emerson was never willing, as this lecture demonstrates, to separate literature from the general culture that produced it. In the next lecture, "The Age of Fable," Emerson contrasts Greek fable with Gothic fable, the former having produced classical myth, the latter medieval romance. Emerson also praises English literature for its instinct for what is common. "The poems of Chaucer, Shakspear [*sic*], Jonson, Herrick, Herbert, Raleigh betray a continual instinctive endeavor to recover themselves from every sally of imagination by touching the earth and earthly and common things." Emerson devotes an entire lecture to Chaucer, whom he values for being able to turn everything in his world to literary account, so that his work stands not only for him but for his era. Chaucer's numerous borrowings prompted Emerson to articulate a concept of literary tradition that was very modern. "The truth is all works of literature are Janus faced and look to the future and to the past. Shakspear [*sic*], Pope, and Dryden borrow from Chaucer and shine by his borrowed light. Chaucer reflects Boccaccio and Colonna and the Troubadours: Boccaccio and Colonna elder Greek and Roman authors, and these in their turn others if only history would enable us to trace them. There never was an original writer. Each is a link in an endless chain."

The two central lectures are devoted to Shakespeare, whose works, Emerson says, represent the whole range of human mind. Shakespeare possessed, to a greater degree than any other writer, the power of imagination, what Emerson defines as "the use which the Reason makes of the material world, for purposes of expression." Put another way, this means "Shakspear [*sic*] possesses the power of subordinating nature for the purpose of expression beyond all poets." Emerson also cites with approval Milton's definition of poetry as "thoughts that voluntary move harmonious numbers" to describe how "the sense of [his] verse determines its tune."

Emerson wrote several lectures on other great English authors. He devotes an entire lecture to Francis Bacon, whom he admired for his efforts "to expound the method by which a true History of Nature should be formed." Bacon's

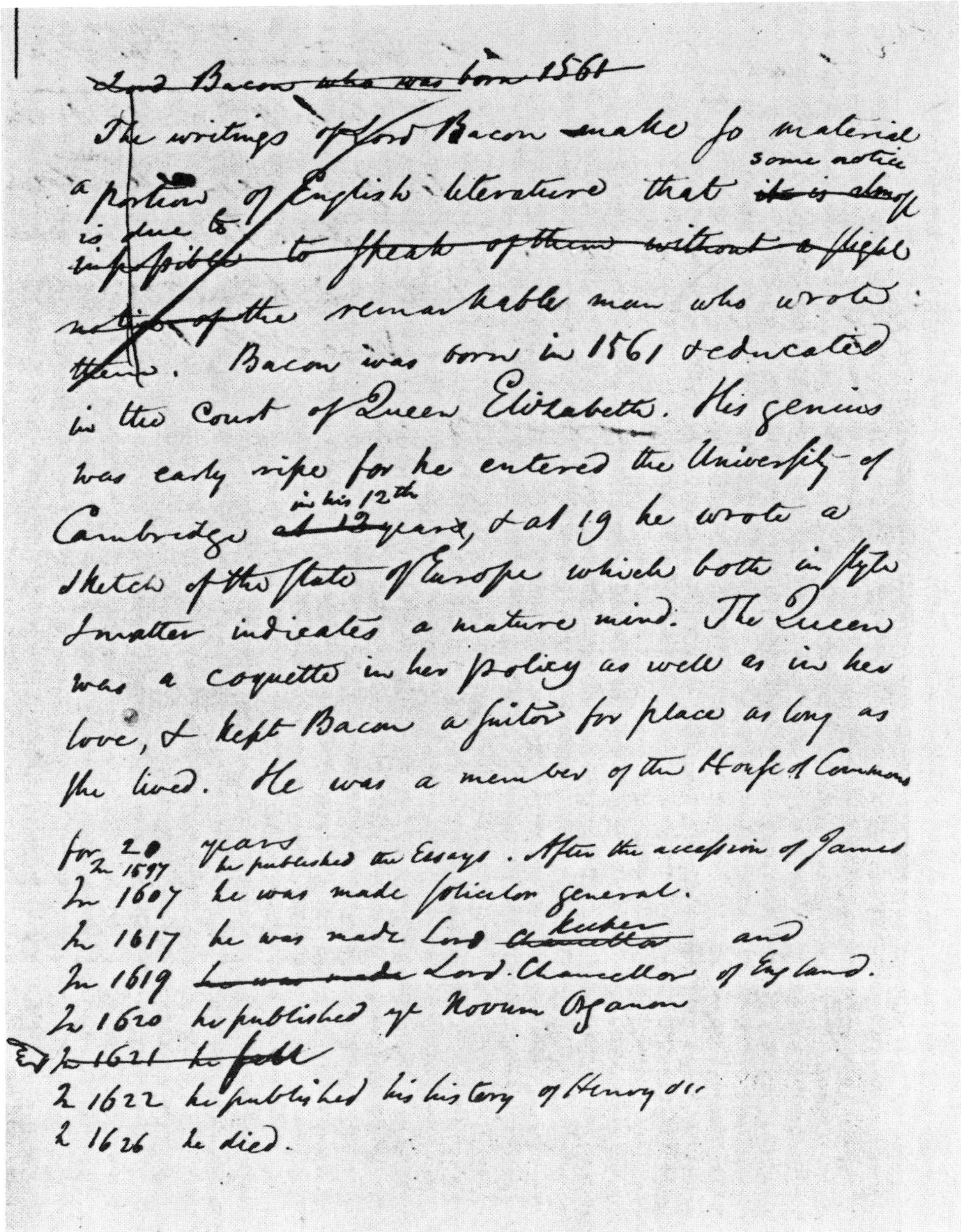

~~Lord Bacon who was born 1561~~

The writings of Lord Bacon ~~make~~ so material a portion of English literature that ~~it is almost impossible to speak of them without a slight notice of~~ some notice is due to the remarkable man who wrote them. Bacon was born in 1561 & educated in the Court of Queen Elizabeth. His genius was early ripe for he entered the University of Cambridge ~~at 13 years~~ in his 12th year, & at 19 he wrote a sketch of the state of Europe which both in style & matter indicates a mature mind. The Queen was a coquette in her policy as well as in her love, & kept Bacon a suitor for place as long as she lived. He was a member of the House of Commons for 20 years. In 1597 he published the Essays. After the accession of James

In 1607 he was made Solicitor general.

In 1617 he was made Lord ~~Chancellor~~ Keeper and

In 1619 ~~he was made~~ Lord Chancellor of England.

In 1620 he published ye Novum Organon

~~In 1621 he fell~~

In 1622 he published his history of Henry VII

In 1626 he died.

Page from the manuscript for Emerson's lecture on Sir Francis Bacon, delivered on 24 December 1835 (by permission of the Houghton Library, Harvard University)

achievement gave him, said Emerson, "a new courage and confidence in the powers of man at the sight of so great works done under such great disadvantages by one scholar." Bacon's great aim, like Emerson's, was to "make man's mind a match for the nature of things," and Bacon believed, as did Emerson, that we only "command Nature by obeying her." Another lecture was devoted to Ben Jonson, Robert Herrick, George Herbert, and Sir Henry Wotton. Noting Jonson's learned and intellectual style as a complement to its era, Emerson observes that "his writings presuppose a great intellectual activity in the audience." Herrick's superb command of language moved Emerson both to admire the poet and to articulate his distrust of language considered as an end in itself. He insisted that words stand for things and that things are what matter. "Rem tene, verba sequntur" [Hold fast to things, words will follow], Cato had observed. Emerson now noted "a proposition set down in words is not therefore affirmed. It must affirm itself or no propriety and no vehemence of language will give it evidence."

Another lecture in the "English Literature" series is called "Ethical Writers." The subject seems puzzling at first, but it is important for a full understanding of Emerson's conception of literature. There is a whole class of writers whose primary function is not entertainment, he says, "who help us by addressing not our taste but our human wants, who treat of the permanent nature of man." Such writers include, among the classics, Plato, Plutarch, Cicero, Marcus Aurelius. In English, the list includes Bacon, Thomas Hooker, Jeremy Taylor, Sir Thomas Browne, John Bunyan, and Samuel Johnson. Emerson also includes poets and playwrights in his list, but his emphasis is clearly on a kind of writing which is not fiction, poetry, or drama but primarily wisdom literature or moral literature, everything that we now place under the heading of nonfiction prose. It is a category that includes much of the best–and most helpful–writing ever done, a category in which Emerson himself now holds a high place.

Emerson's idealism is always mentioned in critical discussions of his thought. The equally important ethical aspect of his work is less often insisted upon. But Emerson's characteristically practical idealism cannot be fully appreciated until one recognizes that he evaluated all literature, all philosophy, all religion, by a simple ethical test: how does it help me to live a better life. Matthew Arnold has defined the moral element in literature as that which teaches us how to live. All of Emerson's idealist conceptions also meet this moral test, and those books which have served successfully over time as practical guides to conduct are the books Emerson values most highly. Samuel Johnson maintained in the "Preface to Shakespeare" that "nothing can please many and please long but just representations of general nature." Emerson used a similar criterion. The best ethical writers, he says, are those who write about "certain feelings and faculties in us which are alike in all men and which no progress of arts and no variety of institutions can alter," those writers, in short, who hold fast to "the general nature of man."

Emerson closed his English literature lecture series with a final talk on "Modern Aspects of Letters," in which he discussed Lord Byron, Sir Walter Scott, Dugald Stewart, James McIntosh, and Coleridge. Of these his favorite is Coleridge, whom he praises particularly as a critic. Emerson rates Coleridge's *Biographia Literaria* (1817) "the best body of criticism in the English language," and it may be added that Emerson as a literary critic is closer to Coleridge and owes more to him than to any other single source. Emerson singles out as especially important, in addition to the *Biographia Literaria,* Coleridge's *The Friend* (1809), especially the third volume, and his *Church and State* (1830). *Aids to Reflexion* (1825), "though a useful book I suppose, is the least valuable." Of particular value to Emerson are Coleridge's "distinction between Reason and Understanding; the distinction of an Idea and a Conception; between Genius and Talent; between Fancy and Imagination: of the nature and end of Poetry: of the Idea of a State." Emerson closes his lecture with an argument that beauty and truth "always face each other and each tends to become the other." He insists that everyone has it in him or her to both create and respond to literature, because literature is based on nature and "all nature, nothing less, is totally given to each new being."

The last of the English literature lectures was given in January 1836. In September *Nature* appeared. It is a major statement, a book which, like Lucretius's *De Rerum Natura,* aims at nothing less than an account of "How Things Are," an intense effort to synthesize a first philosophy. *Nature* shows the warming and shaping influence of Plutarch, Bacon, Coleridge, Plotinus (via Thomas

Emerson with two of his children, Edward and Edith (from the 1909 edition of Emerson's journals)

Taylor), Swedenborg (via Sampson Reed), and Kant (via Carlyle, who was also a major influence by himself). Many of the observations, especially on language, from the English literature lectures found their way, often verbatim and at length, into *Nature*. In some important respects then, key parts of *Nature* came directly out of Emerson's study of English literature.

The main purpose of *Nature* is to recover for the present generation the direct and immediate relationship with the world that our ancestors had. "Why should not we also enjoy an original relation to the universe?," Emerson asks, with emphasis on the word "also." He goes on to inquire, "Why should not we have a poetry and philosophy of insight and not of tradition, and a religion by revelation to us, and not the history of theirs?" He had already discussed the poetry of tradition in his English lecture series. *Nature* is an inquiry into the conditions necessary for a modern literature of insight.

Emerson chose a line of inquiry that had been used before, by the Stoics, among others. In order to find answers to the question of how one should live, one should turn not to God, not to the state, not to society or to history for a starting point, but to nature. Man is part of nature, but by virtue of consciousness, he is also, and at the same time, apart from nature. Consciousness is subject: nature or world is object. They are separate, but as the German philosopher Schelling insisted, consciousness or spirit is subjective nature, nature is objective spirit. The opening chapters of *Nature* describe the different things nature furnishes to consciousness. Passing quickly through "Commodity," in which nature is shown to be useful to human beings in all sorts of material ways, Emerson comes, in chapter three, to "Beauty," in which he argues that our aesthetics are derived from nature. "Primary forms" such as the sky, the mountain, the tree, the animal "give us a delight *in and for themselves.*" Nature is a sea of beautiful forms and the standard of beauty, our conception of beauty in the largest sense, is, says Emerson, "the entire circuit of natural forms,–the totality of nature." Cooperating with nature and complementing it as the source of beauty is the human eye, which is, says Emerson, "the best of artists." Emerson's approach to aesthetics is intensely visual, and this visual quality is so closely tied to his emphasis on subjectivity and his affirmation of the importance of individual vision that a recent writer, Kenneth Burke, equates Emerson's "I" with "eye" and "aye." Typically, too, Emerson is careful to explain that beauty is not simply a matter of beautiful pictures or pleasing landscapes. A higher though similar beauty marks noble human actions. From beautiful pictures we advance to consider beautiful (that is, virtuous) actions. Here, too, nature is the norm. "Every natural action is graceful."

In addition to providing us with beauty, nature also provides us with language, which Emerson treats in chapter four. In a famous–and difficult–opening statement he summarizes his position.

> "Nature is the vehicle of thought, and in a simple, double, and threefold degree."
>
> 1. Words are signs of natural facts.
> 2. Particular natural facts are symbols of particular spiritual facts.
> 3. Nature is the symbol of spirit.

The first point is a theory of language which makes the distinction which the modern linguist Ferdinand de Saussure was to make famous, in his *Cours de Linguistique Général* (1922), that words are not things, but "signs" standing for things. Words are signifiers, things are what are signified. The important distinction is between signifier and signified. Emerson claims that even those words which "express a mood or intellectual fact" will be found, when traced back far enough, to have a root in some material or physical appearance. Thus, he says, "*right* originally means *straight*; *wrong* means *twisted*," and so on. This argument is, of course, an etymological not a semiotic one. But Emerson is not a positivist and could not rest with a flat distinction between words as signs or symbols of material objects, and material objects themselves, for this view leads inevitably to the view that the material or physical world is more "real" than words, which are only signs. Emerson here becomes hard to follow, claiming in point two that "it is not words only that are emblematic, it is things which are emblematic. Every natural fact is a symbol of some spiritual fact." (Insofar as Emerson means "idea" or "concept" when he uses the term "spiritual fact," this is close to a semiotic argument.)

Point two is a theory of symbolism, not just linguistic symbolism, but natural symbolism. He illustrates by saying, "An enraged man is a lion. . . . A lamb is innocence." Emerson believed, following Swedenborg especially, that everything in nature had its correlative in mind, that nature is the externalization of the soul. If modern readers cannot follow Emerson this far, they can at least recognize that Emerson's second point is a useful description of how the writer uses not only language but nature itself as symbols. In reading Herman Melville, for example, we are aware first that the words Moby-Dick stand for a large albino sperm whale and second that the whale itself stands for certain qualities, whether divine, demonic, or natural. Writers use natural objects and events to suggest, mirror, or symbolize inner, mental events.

In the third point, Emerson goes beyond his theories that we use words as signs of things (point 1) and that we find symbolic meanings in things as well as words (point 2) to ask: "Have mountains, and waves, and skies, no significance but what we consciously give them, when we employ them as emblems of our thoughts?" Emerson wants to say more than this. It is not just we humans who treat the world as emblematic; the world, says Emerson, *is* emblematic. "Parts of speech are metaphors because the whole of nature is a metaphor of the human mind." The visible world is, he says in a celebrated metaphor, "the dial plate of the invisible" world. This is the full, Transcendental, Schellingian belief that nature and the human mind are in all things related, that mind is the subjective equivalent of the world, world the objective version of mind. Phrased without German symmetry, this notion is a way of affirming, as the Stoics long ago affirmed, that human beings and nature are both creatures of one set of laws. More recently, Alfred North Whitehead has spoken of the same concept in referring to "the full scientific mentality, which instinctively holds that all things great and small are conceivable as exemplifications of general principles which reign throughout the natural order."

Emerson's insistence on the close links between nature and language has important practical implications. Because our verbal language is based on nature, it will follow that after a period of time, language will come to seem separate from nature. The strong, natural, material roots of words will be forgotten, and lesser writers will go on imitating and repeating words they do not really understand. "Hundreds of writers may be found in every long-civilized nation," says Emerson, "who for a short time believe, and make others believe, that they see and utter truths, who do not of themselves clothe one thought in its natural garment, but who feed unconsciously upon the language created by the primary writers of the country, those, namely, who hold primarily on nature." So the function of the genius, of the true poet, is to reform such language, to "pierce this rotten diction and fasten words again to visible things." The poet is he who can reconnect the word supercilious with the raised eyebrow, who can make us see again, but freshly, that the word "consider" means study the stars [*con sidere*]. "The moment our discourse rises above the ground line of familiar facts, and is inflamed with passion or exalted by thought, it clothes itself in images." Thus Emerson's conception of language as based in nature leads him to outline the task of the poet as the renewal of language, the reattachment of language to nature, of words to things. So, too, the idea that nature is itself a language (an idea that haunts the modern mind from at least Linnaeus and the early eighteenth century on) leads to the view that it is the writer's job to decipher what nature has to say, the view that informs all nature writers from Thoreau to John McPhee.

Nature is Emerson's testament to his belief that ideas, forms, and laws (what Emerson sums up as spirit) are more important than physical, phenomenal, material things (what Emerson calls nature). Both exist, of course, but spirit or mind exists prior to nature, and the natural world is, for Emerson, a product of spirit. In the chapter on "Idealism," Emerson concludes: "It is the uniform effect of culture on the human mind, not to shake our faith in the stability of particular phenomena, as of heat, water, azote [nitrogen]; but to lead us to regard nature as a phenomenon, not a substance; to attribute necessary existence to spirit; to esteem nature as an accident and an effect," not as the final reality.

From December 1836 to March 1837 Emerson gave his first series of independent lectures, the first that is, that he designed himself and gave under his own auspices. It was called the Philosophy of History, and it was a very important series for Emerson, since out of it evolved the great essays on "History" and "Self Reliance" that he would publish in his first volume of *Essays* in 1841. There is also a lecture on "Literature" in the Philosophy of History series, given in January 1837. The general theme of the series is stated in the introductory lecture: "We arrive early at the great discovery that there is one Mind common to all individual men; that what is individual is less than what is universal; that those properties by which you are man are more radical than those by which you are Adam or John; than the individual, nothing is less; than the universal, nothing is greater; that error, vice, and disease have their seat in the superficial or individual nature; that the common nature is whole." Literature, then, is the written record of this mind, and in one important sense literature is always showing us only ourselves. This lecture contains Emerson's most extreme–and least fruitful–statement of his idealist conception of literature. He contrasts art with literature, explaining that while "Art delights in carrying a thought into action, Literature is the conversion of action into thought." In other words, "Literature idealizes action." In an abstract sense this may be so, but Emerson is generally at his best when he sees literature moving us toward action, not away from it. In another place this lecture has a very valuable comment on how literature is able to reach into our unconscious. "Whoever separates for us a truth from our unconscious reason, and makes it an object of consciousness, . . . must of course be to us a great man." And there is also a rather uncharacteristic recognition of what Gustav Flaubert would call *le mot juste*. "The laws of composition are as strict as those of sculpture and architecture. There is always one line that ought to be chosen, one proportion that should be kept, and every other line or proportion is wrong. . . . So, in writing, there is always a right word, and every other than that is wrong."

At the end of August, as part of the commencement ceremonies for the Harvard class that included Henry Thoreau, Emerson delivered to the Phi Beta Kappa Society an address on the American scholar. Often hailed in Oliver Wendell Holmes's phrase as our "intellectual declaration of independence," *An Oration, Delivered Before the Phi Beta Kappa Society, at Cambridge, August 31, 1837* did indeed suggest that "our day of dependence, our long apprenticeship to the learning of other lands, draws to a close." He insisted that "we have listened too long to the courtly muses of Europe." But the address is not primarily, or even strongly, nationalistic. Emerson calls for the self-reliance of the individual, of whatever nationality. "The American Scholar," as the Phi Beta Kappa oration is popularly known, is one of Emerson's most successful, most effective literary statements. It sparkles with good writing, and it leans strongly on common sense and on the ethical and practical aspects of literary activity. He defines "scholar" broadly to include everyone we would class as student or intellectual, but Emerson goes further, trying to identify that aspect of any and all persons which engages in thought. The scholar is "Man Thinking" (as the address was retitled in 1844), which he sharply distinguishes from the specialist, the "mere thinker," who is no longer a whole person.

Books of course are an important part of "The American Scholar," and Emerson gives a description of what he calls "the theory of books." "The scholar of the first age received into him the world around; brooded thereon; gave it the new arrangement of his own mind, and uttered it again. It came into him–life; it went out from him–truth." But once the book is written, says Emerson, there "arises a grave mischief. The sacredness which attaches to the act of creation,–the act of thought,–is instantly transferred to the record." The book is now regarded as perfect, untouchable, unimprovable, and what might have been a guide becomes a tyrant, leading the young people in libraries to read and admire the books of others when they would be better off writing their own. By overvaluing the finished book and underrating the act of book writing, we become mere bookworms, a book-learned class who value books as such. "Hence, the restorers of readings, the emendators, the bibliomaniacs of all degrees." "The American Scholar" makes a major protest against what Walter Jackson Bate has called the burden of the past and what Harold Bloom has called the anxiety of influence. Books "are for nothing but to inspire," Emerson declares. "I had better never see a book than to be warped by its attraction clean out of my own orbit, and made a satellite instead of a system." Books must not be overestimated. They can too easily intimidate us and make us forget that "the one thing in the world of value, is, the active soul." Another way to keep the great work of past writers in proper perspective is to read actively and not passively. "There is then creative reading, as well as creative writing." The most valuable part of the text may be what the reader brings to it. "When the mind is braced by labor and invention, the page of whatever book we read becomes luminous with manifold allusion." Emerson is set against any suggestion that we should worship the great books of the past. We can learn from them, of course, but "the man has never lived that can feed us ever." The human spirit, fluid and restless and charged with heat and energy, will always be breaking out with new experiences, and Emerson draws on personal observation from his Italian trip of 1833 to make a bold metaphor of the human mind as "one central fire which flaming now out of the lips of Etna, lightens the capes of Sicily; and now out of the throat of Vesuvius, illuminates the towers and vineyards of Naples."

The essay makes one more important literary point. Emerson takes it as a welcome sign of the times that "instead of the sublime and beautiful, the near, the low, the common" was being explored and made into poetry. "I embrace the common," he says. "I explore and sit at the feet of the familiar, the low. . . . the meal in the firkin, the milk in the pan." Like Wordsworth's call for a language of common men, this recognition of Emerson's went further than his own practice could usually follow. But Emerson's endorsement of common language had a powerful effect on the rising generation of young American writers, first on Thoreau and Walt Whitman, then on Emily Dickinson and others.

On 15 July 1838 Emerson delivered what has come to be known as the "Divinity School Ad-

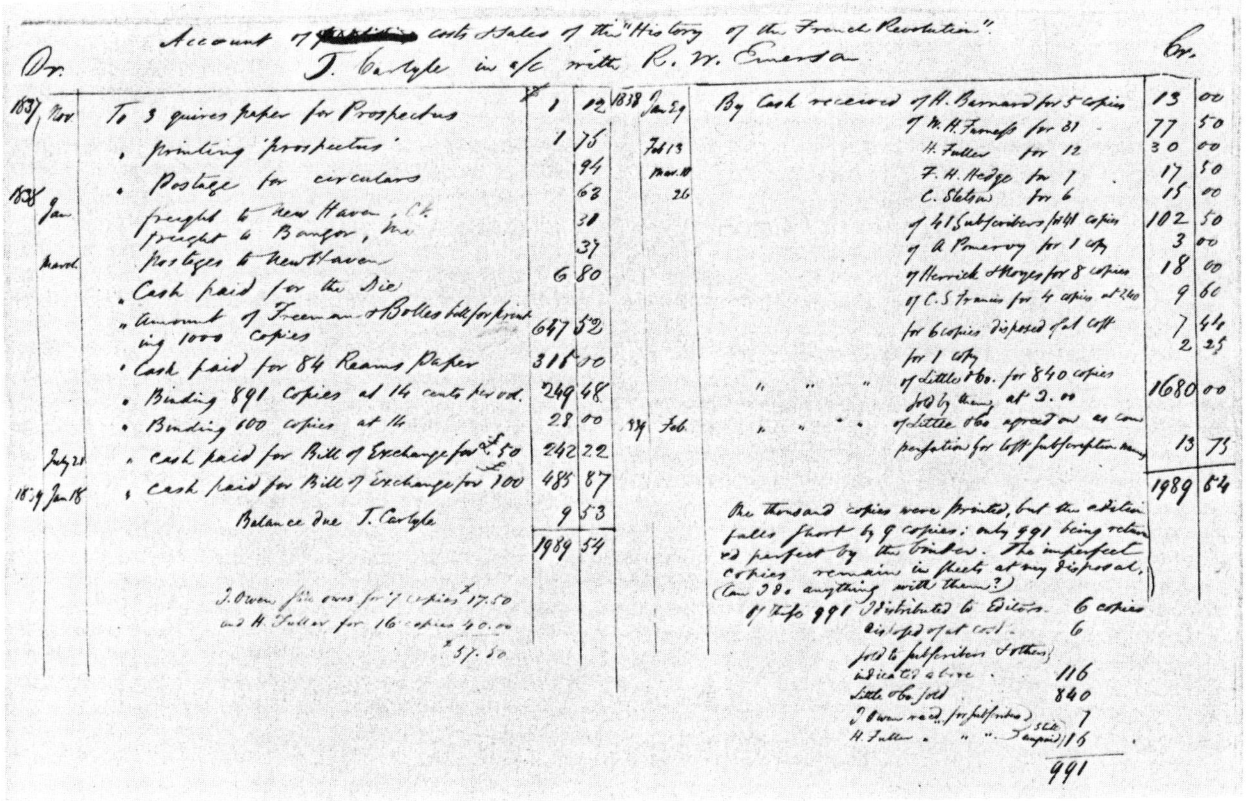

Emerson sent this account of his activities as Thomas Carlyle's unofficial American agent to Carlyle on 25 April 1839 (by permission of the Ralph Waldo Emerson Memorial Association and of the Houghton Library)

dress" before the senior class of the Harvard Divinity School and their guests. In this important speech, which critic Joel Porte says Emerson was born to deliver, Emerson flung down a major challenge to Orthodox and even Unitarian Christianity. Emerson argues that the concept of the divinity of Jesus and the absolute authority of the Bible are obstacles to true religious feeling. This is not to say Emerson did not value the Bible. He did, and very highly; and this very address has been described as taking its form, that of the jeremiad, from a book of the Old Testament. What Emerson wished to do was to warn of the consequences of revering *any* one text as the sole fountain of truth. To hold up the *text* of the Bible as infallible was to divert attention from the *creation* of the text. "The idioms of his [Jehovah's] language, and the figures of his rhetoric, have usurped the place of his truth; and churches are not built on his principles, but on his tropes." Furthermore, if the ancient Hebrew and Greek writings known as the Old and New Testaments respectively are regarded as the sole legitimate revelations, then we in the present age are contenting ourselves with this history of revelations to an earlier generation, and we are denying the possibility of a religion by revelation to us. "Men have come to speak of the revelation as somewhat long ago given and done, as if God were dead." In order to affirm the possibility of a living religion for the present, one must be careful not to get caught in a system that believes no prophet since Jesus has anything to say and no text since the Bible has religious validity.

Emerson contends that religion is a vital principle, as alive today as at any time in the past. It therefore follows that we can and should have our own prophets and our own gospels. This point is a religious one, of course, but it is also literary, since it is essentially a question of how to interpret a text, in this case the Bible. (It is also true for Emerson, as for Whitman, that the function of the prophet is very close to the function of the poet.) Emerson evolved a consistent position in clear contrast to such later theorists as D. H. Lawrence and the New Critics. Emerson's argument is that we should trust the teller, not the tale. Emerson is an antiformalist in literary (as in reli-

An 1862 photograph of Emerson published in the 1883 edition of his works

gious) matters. In more modern terms, his argument is that we should not privilege the text, *any* text, above either the author or the reader. Emerson's interest in the author is not so much a critical position as an interest in the process of creativity.

A week after the epoch-making address to the Divinity School, Emerson gave another address, called "Literary Ethics," at Dartmouth, which, as Porte has noted, is undeservedly neglected. As the Cambridge address called for "a religion by revelation to us," so the Dartmouth address calls for a literature adequate to America. So far, says Emerson, "this country has not fulfilled what seemed the reasonable expectation of mankind." In painting, sculpture, poetry, and fiction, American authors had evolved only "a certain grace without grandeur," in work that was "itself not new but derivative."

In December 1839 Emerson gave two lectures on literature as part of a series called "The Present Age," much of the material of which went into a paper called "Thoughts on Modern Literature," published in the *Dial* in October 1840 and reprinted in *Natural History of Intellect* (1893). Here Emerson lists, in order of importance, three classes of literature. "The highest class of books are those which express the moral element; the next, works of imagination; and the next, works of science." Though he calls Shakespeare "the first literary genius of the world, the highest in whom the moral is not the predominating element," he insists that Shakespeare's work "leans on the Bible: his poetry supposes it." By contrast, "the Prophets do not imply the existence of Shakespeare or Homer." Shakespeare is secondary, the prophets of the Bible are primary. These views compensate and balance those in the Divinity School address. Indeed "Thoughts on Modern Literature" seems to have been intended by Emerson as a sort of corrective of some of his early views and various misinterpretations of them. One of the best things in "Thoughts on Modern Literature" is a long and very specific treatment of the problem of subjectivity. Defending the subjectivism of the age, Emerson is at great pains to distinguish true subjectivism (the right of each single soul, each subject "I" to "sit in judgment on history and literature, and to summon all facts and parties before its tribunal") from narrow-minded insistence on one's own personality or mere "intellectual selfishness." "A man may say *I*, and never refer to himself as an individual," says Emerson in a phrase that prefigures his concept of the representative poet.

Emerson is of most interest as a theorist of literary activity. Of practical criticism of specific texts or reviewing of new books he did relatively little. His most active period of practical criticism covers the years 1840 to 1844, when he was very much involved with the *Dial,* a quarterly magazine designed specifically by Emerson and his friends to champion the new views, including Transcendentalism. The new journal said in its manifesto that it was interested in making new demands on literature, and it complained that the rigors of current convention in religion and education was "turning us to stone." But even as the new journal was launched, Emerson showed himself well aware of the limits of the enterprise, and of language itself. "There is somewhat in all life untranslatable into language. . . . " He continues, "Every thought has a certain imprisoning as well as uplifting quality, and, in proportion to its energy on the will, refuses to become an object of intellectual contemplation. Thus what is great usually slips through our fingers."

Some things did not slip through his fingers. Emerson could be a brilliant and pungent critic on occasion. In a letter to Margaret Fuller on 17 March 1840, he told her he had been reading "one of Lord Brougham's superficial indigent disorderly unbuttoned penny-a-page books called 'Times of George III,'" thereby describing a kind of book of which too many are published in every age. Emerson wrote for the *Dial* notices of Richard Henry Dana's *Two Years Before the Mast* (1840), which he liked, saying "it will serve to hasten the day of reckoning between society and the sailor." He praised the poetry in Jones Very's *Essays and Poems* (1839), "as sincere a litany as the Hebrew songs of David or Isaiah, and only less than they, because indebted to the Hebrew muse for their tone and genius." In a review of Tennyson, he commented, "So large a proportion of even the good poetry of our time is either over-ethical or over-passionate, and the stock poetry is so deeply tainted with a sentimental egotism that this, whose chief merit lay in its melody and picturesque power, was most refreshing." Emerson was also an early admirer of the poetry of Henry Thoreau and Ellery Channing. He was Carlyle's American agent, so to speak, and through Emerson's effort Carlyle's *Sartor Resartus* (1835) was published in book form in Boston before an English publisher could be found for it. When Walt Whitman sent Emerson a copy of the first edition of *Leaves of Grass* (1855), Emerson wrote back an excited letter, calling the poems "the most extraordinary piece of wit and wisdom that America has yet contributed." He recognized the "great power" in the work and praised it for having "the best merits, namely, of fortifying and encouraging."

Indeed, Emerson's practical criticism, like his numerous and repeated offers of help to young writers, was more often encouragement than judgment, meant to be fortifying not critical. Not for nothing did Matthew Arnold rank

Lydia Emerson in later years (courtesy of the Concord Free Public Library)

Emerson with Marcus Aurelius as "the friend and aider of those who would live in the spirit." In October 1844 Emerson published his *Essays: Second Series*, in which the lead essay, "The Poet," was his best and most influential piece of literary criticism. It opens with a sweeping critique of those critics and "umpires of taste" whose "knowledge of the fine arts is some study of rules and particulars, or some limited judgment of color or form, which is exercised for amusement or for show." We have lost, Emerson says, "the perception of the instant dependence of form upon soul." He goes on to say flatly, "there is no doctrine of forms in our philosophy." "The Poet" is

Emerson's response to this challenge. It is his "doctrine of forms."

To begin with, Emerson asserts that "the poet is representative," standing "among partial men for the complete man," apprising us "not of his wealth, but of the commonwealth." Instead of treating the poet as a superior kind of person, placed by his talent above the ordinary run of human beings, Emerson here lays down the cornerstone of a modern democratic aesthetic. The poet is a greater person than the ordinary, but his very greatness is his representative nature. The poet realizes and actualizes the humanity we all share and *can* realize in ourselves. This concept of the representative poet would form the major theme of Emerson's 1850 book, *Representative Men,* and it is an important concept for the early Whitman.

Emerson's second main point is "the poet is the sayer, the namer." That is to say Emerson here rejects the idea that the poet is primarily a maker, a craftsman, or wordsmith. Formalist critics from Jonson to Poe had emphasized the craft of writing, seeing the poet as a maker. For Emerson, the poet is a seer and a sayer, a person inspired, a transmitter of the poetry that inheres in nature and in us. He is not just a maker of verses. Emerson's poet is the inspired, divine, prophet-bard who has access to truth and whose function is to declare it, as Barbara Packer shows in *Emerson's Fall* (1982). From this notion it follows that poems are not "machines made out of words," or "verbal constructs." By contrast, for Emerson, "poetry was all written before time was." The poet's job is to establish contact with the primal, natural world, "where the air is music," and try to write down in words what has always existed in nature. When Robert Frost writes that "Nature's first green is gold," he is giving words to something that has been going on for eons, namely the first appearance of light greenish gold when the leaves first begin to break out of the bud in spring.

Emerson's poet is much more than a technician of meter, a person of "poetic talents." Emerson's poet "announces that which no man foretold. He is the true and only doctor; he knows and tells." Picking up the Miltonic definition of poetry he had endorsed earlier, Emerson says, in a famous phrase, "for it is not metres but a metre-making argument, that makes a poem." The essence of the poem lies not in the words but behind the words, in "a thought so passionate and alive, that, like the spirit of a plant or an animal, it has an architecture of its own, and adorns nature with a new thing."

Emerson is here talking about the concept of "organic form" as opposed to "mechanic form." The distinction was clearly made by Coleridge. "The form is mechanic, when on any given material we impress a pre-determined form, not necessarily arising out of the proportions of the material–as when to a mass of wet clay we give whatever shape we wish it to retain when hardened." Thus, for most modern poets, to use a sonnet form is to use mechanic form. "The organic form, on the other hand, is innate; it shapes as it developes, itself from within, and the fullness of its development is one and the same with the perfection of its outward form." Emerson's own essays grew organically, and both Thoreau's *Walden* and Whitman's *Leaves of Grass* can be seen as examples of the organic form here described. In Emerson's doctrine of forms, the form should follow from the nature of the evolving material. In Emerson's terminology, form depends on soul.

Nature had claimed that education, reflection, and self-cultivation lead us to invert "the vulgar views of nature, and brings the mind to call . . . that real, which it use[d] to call visionary." Now Emerson pushes one step further, poetry is "the science of the real," which is to say that it is not concerned so much with the material or the phenomenal as it is with underlying laws. Emerson had made this stand clear in earlier essays, but in "The Poet" he discusses more fully the poet's use of language. The poet must not only use words, but he must be able to use things–nature–as a language. "Nature offers all her creatures to him as a picture language," Emerson says. "Things admit of being used as symbols, because nature is a symbol, in the whole and in every part." If the student asks what nature is symbolic of, the answer is, symbolic of the human spirit. "The universe is the externalization of the soul." This idea, too, had been said by Emerson before, though not with such epigrammatic authority. What really happens in poetic practice is suggested by Emerson when he says, "the world being thus put under the mind for verb and noun, the poet is he who can articulate it." What the poet realizes is that not only words and things, but "we are symbols, and inhabit symbols."

There is more in the essay on the origin of words. "The etymologist finds the deadest word to have been once a brilliant picture," Emerson says, in a passage that was noted by Richard Trench, the English author who first suggested the idea of the *Oxford English Dictionary*. "Language is fossil poetry," Emerson explains, saying that "Language is made up of images, or tropes, which now, in their secondary use, have long ceased to remind us of their poetic origin." Coleridge had linked genius to organic form, saying genius was the mind's "power of acting creatively under laws of its own origination." Emerson now links genius with the revival and renewal of language. "Genius is the activity which repairs the decays of things," he says, and the epigrammatic force of his own language pushes back against entropy itself.

"The Poet" also suggests the true function of the critic. "And herein is the legitimation of criticism, in the mind's faith, that the poems are a corrupt version of some text in nature, with which they ought to be made to tally." Emerson, however, is still more interested in the function of the poet than in the text, and he goes on now to explain that so many poets flirt with intoxication because they are really trying to tap into a realm of experience larger than that offered by their own private lives. Whether we think of it as the world-soul, or collective consciousness, or the oversoul, the poet must transcend his own limited and personal experience in order to participate in the broader experience of the common human spirit. In an important–and difficult–passage, Emerson says, "it is a secret which every intellectual man quickly learns, that beyond the energy of his possessed and conscious intellect, he is capable of a new energy (as of an intellect doubled on itself), by abandonment to the nature of things; that, besides his privacy of power as an individual man, there is a great public power, on which he can draw. . . ."

It is finally the imagination, not wine, which intoxicates the true poet, and the same quality works in us, too. "The use of symbols has a certain power of emancipation and exhilaration for all men. . . . This is the effect on us of tropes, fables, oracles and all poetic forms." Consider, for example, the sense of delight with which we are momentarily freed of the tyranny of English numbers by the child's book which tells us, if we are tired of counting to ten in the same old way, to try a new way, such as "ounce, dice, trice, quartz, quince, sago, serpent, oxygen, nitrogen, denim." Of such language, Emerson says, "We seem to be touched by a wand, which makes us dance and run about happily like children." He concludes, in a phrase that sums up the essay, "poets are thus liberating gods." Themselves free, they set us free–free, for example, to take only what we want from the books we read. "I think nothing is of any value in books, excepting the transcendental and extraordinary." Thus Emerson cheerfully and knowingly dismisses all but the very best of even his own writing.

An 1876 photograph of Edward Emerson, his son Charles Lowell Emerson, and his father, Ralph Waldo Emerson (courtesy of the Concord Free Public Library)

The true poet will be "the translator of nature into thought" and will not get lost in unintelligible private symbolism, in "the mistake of an accidental and individual symbol for an universal one." Nearing the end of the essay, Emerson notes that he looks "in vain for the poet whom I describe. . . . We have yet had no genius in America, with tyrannous eye, which knew the value of our incomparable materials, and saw, in the barbarism and materialism of the times, another carnival of the same gods whose picture he so much admires in Homer." It is a passage which seems to predict the advent of Walt Whitman. Emerson continues, "yet America is a poem in our eyes, its ample geography dazzles the imagination, and it will not wait long for metres." Eleven years later, Whitman's *Leaves of Grass* appeared as if in answer.

There is only one paragraph about America and American poetry in "The Poet." Emerson specifically says he is "not wise enough for a national criticism," and he ends the essay as he began, with a consideration not of the American poet but of the modern poet. The essay closes with a repetition of the idea that it is the *process* of poetry, not the resulting text, that constitutes the live essence of poetry, and he puts it in yet another of his triumphant aphorisms. "Art is the path of the creator to his work." True poetry is not the finished product, but the process of uttering or writing it.

Representative Men (1850), a book made up of lectures first given in 1845 on Plato, Swedenborg, Montaigne, Shakespeare, Napoleon, and Goethe, is the fullest account of Emerson's biographical approach to literature. This subject is not new with him. It goes back at least to his early lecture on Milton, but it now has a new emphasis. Just as he had once claimed that there is properly no history, only biography, so *Representative Men* comes close to saying there is properly no literature, there are only literary persons. "There must be a man behind the book," he says of Goethe. "It makes a great difference to the force of any sentence whether there be a man behind it or no." Emerson's representative figures are his Plutarchan heroes. The book is a pantheon of heroes, chosen not from among warriors (except for Napoleon), but from among thinkers and writers, who are of use to us because they represent or symbolize qualities that lie in us, too. They are essays in symbolic literary biography. Assuming that language is representative, that is, symbolic, Emerson says that "Behmen and Swedenborg saw that things were representative." Then, moving, not toward circular idealism, but toward biography, he states: "Men also are representative: first of things, and secondly, of ideas." Emerson identifies in each of his figures some permanent quality of the human mind. He is also a prestructuralist in that he believes that the world people make and inhabit is determined partly or even largely by the structure of the human mind. "Our colossal theologies of Judaism, Christism, Buddhism, Mahometism are the necessary and structural action of the human mind." It follows from this that our reading is a process of recognizing our own thoughts, or capabilities for thought and imagination, in the work and lives of others. Emerson sums this up concisely. "The possibility of interpretation lies in the identity of the observer with the observed." The democratic aesthetic also follows from this. "As to what we call the masses, and common men,– there are no common men. All men are at last of a size; and true art is only possible on the conviction that every talent has its apotheosis somewhere."

Emerson calls Plato's work the bible of educated people, claiming that it is "impossible to think, on certain levels, except through him." Swedenborg saw, and stands for, the interconnectedness of human beings and nature. Shakespeare and Goethe exemplify and stand for the power to express, to convert life into life-giving words. Emerson ends each essay with a review of the shortcomings of the subject. Plato is too literary, not enough the prophet. Swedenborg is overwhelmed by a private and rigid symbolism his reader cannot fully share. The effect of these negative conclusions is to prevent the reader from idolizing or enthroning Plato, Swedenborg, or any other great person. The great ones are of interest to us only because each has something to teach us, and it is the present reader, the student, and not the great writer or teacher whom Emerson really cares about. Each great representative figure "must be related to us, and our life receive from him some promise of explanation." So the praise of Goethe, whom Emerson seems to have admired above all writers, is for such things as the creation of Mephistopheles in *Faust* (1808-1832). In order to make the devil real, Goethe the "stripped him of mythologic gear, of horns, cloven foot, harpoon tail, brimstone and blue-fire, and instead of looking in books and pictures, looked for him in his own mind, in every shade of coldness, selfishness, and unbelief that, in crowd or in solitude, darkens over the human thought." Thus Goethe reimagines Mephistopheles: "He shall be real; he shall be modern; he shall be European; he shall dress like a gentleman." The result, says Emerson, is that Goethe "flung into literature, in his Mephistopheles, the first organic figure that has been added for some ages, and which will remain as long as the Prometheus."

Emerson's final word is reserved for Goethe not Faust, the creator not the creation, and what he says of Goethe is true of Emerson himself. "Goethe teaches courage, and the equivalence of all times. . . . We too must write Bibles, to unite again the heavens and the earthly world. The secret of genius is to suffer no fiction to exist for us; to realize all that we know; in the high refinement of modern life, in art, in sciences, in books, in men, to exact good faith, reality and a purpose; and first, last, midst and without end, to honor every truth by use." Thus, Emerson, like most critics who get their bearings from Plato, has little to say about fiction, about the novel. Fiction he regarded as unreal, but poetry was for him, "the science of the real." In his later writings, while he would comment on novels and romances occasionally, he continued to deepen and widen his conception of poetry.

He also continued to be alert to the social and political contexts of literature. In a speech about Robert Burns in 1859, published in *Miscellanies* (1884), he noted shrewdly that Burns, "the poet of the middle class, represents in the mind of men to-day that great uprising of the middle class against the armed and privileged minorities, that uprising which worked politically in the American and French Revolutions, and which, not in governments so much as in education and social order, has changed the face of the world." In 1870 he included an essay called "Books" in a volume titled *Society and Solitude*. The essay contains Emerson's reading list, his recommendations about the best books to read. Coming during the same period as Matthew Arnold's concept of "touchstones," it is an interesting prefiguration of the premise that underlies modern general education, namely that there is a body of knowledge that all educated people should share. For the Greeks, for instance, he lists Homer, Herodotus, Aeschylus, Plato, and Plutarch, then goes on to give some background reading in ancient history and art. It is an eminently practical essay, as well as a useful indication of Emerson's own broad taste.

In 1871, in a short speech on Sir Walter Scott, Emerson linked Scott to his times, noting how Scott, "apprehended in advance the immense enlargement of the reading public . . . which his books and Byron's inaugurated." In 1875 Emerson published an anthology of poetry, called *Parnassus*, which is remarkable both for its inclusions and its exclusions. The volume is heavily weighted toward English poetry. In addition to the expected poets, Shakespeare, Milton, Wordsworth, Keats, there are substantial selections from such poets as Blake and Clough. Among American poets, there is no Poe, no Whitman, and no Emerson, but interesting selections from–among many others–Thoreau, James Freeman Clarke, Frederic H. Hedge, Bret Harte, and Lucy Larcom. Emerson's range is shown in his inclusion of selections from the Greek Simonides to the Hindu Calidasa.

Emerson had been an admirer of ancient Persian poetry since the mid 1840s, though he only published his essay on Persian poetry in the 1876 volume *Letters and Social Aims*. Quoting freely from Firdousi, Saadi, Hafiz, Omar Chiam (Khayyám), and others, Emerson expressed his admiration and helped create an audience for the special qualities of Persian verse. Emerson delightedly describes the open avidity with which the ancient Persians approached poetry. "The excitement [the poems] produced exceeds that of the grape." He admired Hafiz's "intellectual liberty" and his unorthodox, unhypocritical stance. "He tells his mistress, that not the dervis, or the monk, but the lover, has in his heart the spirit which makes the ascetic and the saint." Emerson admires "the erotic and bacchanalian songs" of Hafiz, and he especially prizes the way "Hafiz praises wine, roses, maidens, boys, birds, mornings and music, to give vent to his immense hilarity and sympathy with every form of beauty and joy." In this interest in the great Persian poets, we glimpse the Dionysian side of Emerson, the side that appealed so deeply, for example, to the young Nietzsche. It is an important side, without which we run the risk of missing the real Emerson.

The longest essay in *Letters and Social Aims* is "Poetry and Imagination." It is a fully developed piece, longer in fact than the 1836 book, *Nature*, and important as the last major restatement and reaffirmation of Emerson's conception of the literary process as one of symbolizing. "A good symbol is the best argument," he writes and explains why. "The value of a trope is that the hearer is one; and indeed Nature itself is a vast trope, and all particular natures are tropes. . . . All thinking is analogising, and 'tis the use of life to learn metonomy." If we are symbols and nature is symbol, then what is the reality behind or sustaining the symbols? Emerson's reply is "process." "The endless passing of one element into new forms, the incessant metamorphosis, explains the rank which the imagination holds in our catalogue of mental powers. The imagination is the reader of these [symbolic] forms. The poet accounts all productions and changes of Nature as the nouns of language, uses them representatively." The result is that "every new object so seen gives a shock of agreeable surprise." "Poetry," Emerson concludes, "is the only verity. . . . As a power, it is the perception of the symbolic character of things, and the treating them as representative," and he quotes William Blake to the same end.

Emerson's critical theory did not really change after *Nature* and "The Poet," but it did become more practical, more carefully thought out, and better focused. Emerson began as an American idealist or transcendentalist, and as that position enlarged and deepened with time, Emerson came to be seen not only as a great modern representative of the Platonic, idealist tradition but a major romantic symbolist. His work can also be seen as an early prefiguring, in some ways, of modern movements toward symbolism, structuralism, and reader-centered criticism. The central aspect of his still-vital influence, however, is his insistence that literature means literary activity.

Letters:

A Correspondence Between John Sterling and Ralph Waldo Emerson, edited by Edward Waldo Emerson (Boston & New York: Houghton Mifflin, 1897);

Letters from Ralph Waldo Emerson to a Friend, 1838-1853 [Samuel Gray Ward], edited by Charles Eliot Norton (Boston & New York: Houghton Mifflin, 1899; London: Watt, 1899);

Correspondence between Ralph Waldo Emerson and Herman Grimm, edited by Frederick William Holls (Boston & New York: Houghton Mifflin, 1903);

Records of a Lifelong Friendship, 1807-1882: Ralph Waldo Emerson and William Henry Furness, edited by Horace Howard Furness (Boston & New York: Houghton Mifflin, 1910);

Emerson-Clough Letters, edited by Howard F. Lowry and Ralph Leslie Rusk (Cleveland: Rowfant Club, 1934);

The Letters of Ralph Waldo Emerson, edited by Ralph L. Rusk, 6 volumes (New York: Columbia University Press, 1939);

One First Love: The Letters of Ellen Louisa Tucker to Ralph Waldo Emerson, edited by Edith W. Gregg (Cambridge: Harvard University Press, 1962);

The Correspondence of Emerson and Carlyle, edited by Joseph Slater (New York & London: Columbia University Press, 1964).

Bibliographies:

Frederick Ives Carpenter, *Emerson Handbook* (New York: Hendricks House, 1953);

Jackson R. Bryer and Robert A. Rees, *A Checklist of Emerson Criticism 1951-1961* (Hartford, Conn.: Transcendental Books, 1964);

Floyd Stovall, "Ralph Waldo Emerson," in *Eight American Authors,* edited by James Woodress, revised edition (New York: Norton, 1971), pp. 37-83;

Joel Myerson, *Ralph Waldo Emerson: A Descriptive Bibliography* (Pittsburgh: University of Pittsburgh Press, 1982);

Robert E. Burkholder and Myerson, "Ralph Waldo Emerson," in *The Transcendentalists,* edited by Myerson (New York: Modern Language Association, 1984), pp. 135-167;

Burkholder and Myerson, *Emerson: An Annotated Secondary Bibliography* (Pittsburgh: University of Pittsburgh Press, 1985).

Biographies:

Moncure Daniel Conway, *Emerson at Home and Abroad* (Boston: Osgood, 1882);

James Eliot Cabot, *A Memoir of Ralph Waldo Emerson,* 2 volumes (Boston & New York: Houghton Mifflin, 1889);

Denton J. Snider, *A Biography of Ralph Waldo Emerson* (Saint Louis: William Harvey Miner, 1921);

Townsend Scudder, *The Lonely Wayfaring Man: Emerson and Some Englishmen* (New York: Oxford University Press, 1936);

Ralph L. Rusk, *The Life of Ralph Waldo Emerson* (New York: Scribners, 1949);

Henry F. Pommer, *Emerson's First Marriage* (Carbondale: Southern Illinois University Press, 1967);

Joel Porte, *Representative Man: Ralph Waldo Emerson in his Times* (New York: Oxford University Press, 1979);

Gay Wilson Allen, *Waldo Emerson* (New York: Viking, 1981);

John McAleer, *Ralph Waldo Emerson: Days of Encounter* (Boston: Little, Brown, 1984).

References:

Sacvan Bercovitch, *The Puritan Origins of the Ameri-*

can Self (New Haven: Yale University Press, 1975);
Jonathan Bishop, *Emerson on the Soul* (Cambridge: Harvard University Press, 1964);
Harold Bloom, "Emerson and Whitman: The American Sublime," in *Poetry and Repression* (New Haven: Yale University Press, 1976);
Bloom, "The Self-Reliance of American Optimism," and "The Native Strain, American Orphism" in *Figures of Capable Imagination* (New York: Seabury Press, 1976);
Lawrence Buell, *Literary Transcendentalism* (Ithaca: Cornell University Press, 1973);
Robert E. Burkholder and Joel Myerson, eds., *Critical Essays on Ralph Waldo Emerson* (Boston: G. K. Hall, 1983);
William Charvat, *Emerson's American Lecture Engagements. A Chronological List* (New York: New York Public Library, 1961);
Eric Cheyfitz, *The Trans-Parent: Sexual Politics in the Language of Emerson* (Baltimore: Johns Hopkins University Press, 1981);
Julie K. Ellison, *Emerson's Romantic Style* (Princeton: Princeton University Press, 1984);
Charles Feidelson, Jr., *Symbolism and American Literature* (Chicago: University of Chicago Press, 1961);
Oscar W. Firkins, *Ralph Waldo Emerson* (Boston: Houghton Mifflin, 1915);
Walter Harding, *Emerson's Library* (Charlottesville: University Press of Virginia, 1967);
Vivian Hopkins, *Spires of Form: A Study of Emerson's Aesthetic Theory* (Cambridge: Harvard University Press, 1951);
Gertrude Reif Hughes, *Emerson's Demanding Optimism* (Baton Rouge: Louisiana State University Press, 1984);
Lewis Leary, *Ralph Waldo Emerson* (Boston: G. K. Hall, 1980);
David Levin, ed., *Emerson: Prophecy, Metamorphosis and Influence* (New York: Columbia University Press, 1975);
Jerome Loving, *Emerson, Whitman, and the American Muse* (Chapel Hill: University of North Carolina Press, 1982);
F. O. Matthiessen, *American Renaissance: Art and Expression in the Age of Emerson and Whitman* (New York: Oxford University Press, 1941);
Leonard Neufeldt, *The House of Emerson* (Lincoln: University of Nebraska Press, 1982);
Barbara Packer, *Emerson's Fall* (New York: Continuum, 1982);
Sherman Paul, *Emerson's Angle of Vision* (Cambridge: Harvard University Press, 1952);
Joel Porte, *Emerson and Thoreau: Transcendentalists in Conflict* (Middletown, Conn.: Wesleyan University Press, 1966);
Porte, ed., *Emerson: Prospect and Retrospect* (Cambridge: Harvard University Press, 1982);
Eric Porter, *Emerson and Literary Change* (Cambridge: Harvard University Press, 1978);
John W. Rathbun, *American Literary Criticism: 1800-1860* (Boston: G. K. Hall, 1979);
David Robinson, *Apostle of Culture: Emerson as Preacher and Lecturer* (Philadelphia: University of Pennsylvania Press, 1982);
F. B. Sanborn, *The Genius and Character of Emerson* (Boston: Osgood, 1885);
Taylor Stoehr, *Nay-Saying in Concord: Emerson, Alcott, Thoreau* (Hamden, Conn.: Archon Books, 1979);
Edward Wagenknecht, *Ralph Waldo Emerson: Portrait of a Balanced Soul* (New York: Oxford University Press, 1974);
Hyatt Waggoner, *Emerson as Poet* (Princeton: Princeton University Press, 1975);
René Wellek, "Ralph Waldo Emerson," in *A History of Modern Criticism 1750-1950,* volume 3 (New Haven: Yale University Press, 1965), pp. 163-176;
Stephen E. Whicher, *Freedom and Fate: An Inner Life of Ralph Waldo Emerson* (Philadelphia: University of Pennsylvania Press, 1953);
R. A. Yoder, *Emerson and the Orphic Poet in America* (Berkeley: University of California Press, 1978).

Papers:

The main collection of Emerson papers is the Ralph Waldo Emerson Memorial Association collection in the Houghton Library at Harvard University.

Alexander Hill Everett

(19 March 1790-29 June 1847)

Christina Zwarg
Harvard University

SELECTED BOOKS: *An Address, Delivered Before the Massachusetts Charitable Fire Society; at Their Annual Meeting, May 28, 1813* (Boston: Charles Callender, 1813);

Remarks on the Governor's Speech. By an American (Boston: Patriot Office, 1814);

Eighteen Hundred and Twenty: a Poem (London: Miller, 1821);

Europe: or, A General Survey of the Present Situation of the Principle Powers; with Conjectures on Their Future Prospects. By a Citizen of the United States (Boston: Cummings, Hilliard & O. Everett, 1822; London: Longman, Hurst, Rees, Orme & Brown, 1822);

New Ideas on Population: with Remarks on the Theories of Malthus and Godwin (Boston: Everett, 1823; London: Miller, 1823);

Speech of Mr. Everett on the Proposition to Amend the Constitution of the United States, Delivered in the House of Representatives, March 9, 1826 (Washington: Gales & Seaton, 1826);

America: or, A General Survey of the Political Situation of the Several Powers of the Western Continent, with Conjectures on Their Future Prospects. By a Citizen of the United States (Philadelphia: H. C. Carey & I. Lea, 1827; London: J. Murray, 1828);

An Address to the Phi Beta Kappa Society of Bowdoin College, on the Present State of Polite Learning in England and America, Delivered at Brunswick, Me., September 3, 1834 (Boston: C. Bowen, 1834);

Remarks of Mr. Everett on the French Question (Boston, 1835);

An Address Delivered at Charlestown, Mass., on the 17th of June, 1836, at the Request of the Young Men, without Distinction of Party, in Commemoration of the Battle of Bunker Hill (Boston: Beals & Green, 1836);

An Address Delivered at Salem, on the Eighth of January, 1836, at the Request of the Democratic Young Men of That Place, in Commemoration of the Victory of New Orleans (Boston: Beals & Greene, 1836);

A Defense of the Character and Principles of Mr. Jefferson; Being an Address Delivered at Weymouth, Mass., at the Request of the Anti-Masonic and Democratic Citizens of That Place, on the 4th of July, 1836 (Boston: Beals & Greene, 1836);

An Address to the Philermenian Society of Brown University, on the Moral Character of the Literature of the Last and Present Century. Delivered at Providence, R.I., Sept. 4, 1837 (Providence: Knowles, Vose, 1837);

An Address to the Literary Societies of Dartmouth College, on the Character and Influence of German Literature. Delivered at Hanover, N.H., July 24, 1839 (Boston: H. L. Devereux, 1839);

Poems (Boston: J. Munroe, 1845);

Critical and Miscellaneous Essays. To Which are Added A Few Poems (Boston: James Munroe, 1845);

Critical and Miscellaneous Essays, second series (Boston: James Munroe, 1846);

Cuba; the Everett Letters on Cuba (Boston: G. H. Ellis, 1897);

Prose Pieces and Correspondence, edited by Elizabeth Evans (St. Paul, Minn.: John Colet, 1975).

OTHER: "Life of Joseph Warren," in *Lives of Robert Fulton, Joseph Warren, Henry Hudson and Father Marquette,* in *Library of American Biography,* edited by Jared Sparks, first series, volume 10 (Boston: Hilliard, Gray, 1839; London: R. J. Kennett, 1839), pp. 103-193;

Johannes von Müller, *The History of the World from the Earliest Period to the Year of Our Lord 1783, with Particular Reference to the Affairs of Europe and Her Colonies,* volumes 1-2, translated and edited by Everett (Boston: Marsh, Capen, Lyon & Webb, 1840);

"Life of Patrick Henry," *Lives of Robert Cavelier de la Salle and Patrick Henry,* in *Library of American Biography,* edited by Jared Sparks, second series, volume 11 (Boston: Little, Brown, 1844), pp. 209-390.

PERIODICAL PUBLICATIONS: "Corinna, or Italy by Madame de Stael Holstein," *Monthly Anthology and Boston Review,* 5 (June 1808): 336-339;

"Modern Chivalry," *Monthly Anthology and Boston Review,* 5 (September 1808): 498-508;

Review of *Cours de littérature dramatique: ou Recueil, par ordre de matières, des feuilletons de Geoffroy, North American Review,* 10 (April 1820): 291-316;

Review of *Memoires Historiques sur la vie de M. Suard, et sur le 18me Siècle,* by Dominique Joseph Garat, *North American Review,* 12 (April 1821): 246-268;

Review of *Oeuvres inedites de Madame la Baronne de Stael, Publiées par son fils,* 3 volumes, *North American Review,* 14 (January 1822): 101-128;

Review of *Friedrich von Schiller's Leben,* by Henry Doering, *North American Review,* 16 (April 1823): 397-425;

Review of *Lord Byron's Poems, North American Review,* 20 (January 1825): 1-47;

Review of *American Literature. An Article in the 99th Number of the Edinburgh Review, North American Review,* 31 (July 1830): 26-66;

"American Poets," review of George B. Cheever's *The American Common-Place Book of Poetry, North American Review,* 33 (October 1831): 297-324;

"Irving's Alhambra," *North American Review,* 35 (October 1832): 265-282;

"Swallow Barn," *North American Review,* 36 (April 1833): 519-544;

Review of *Tableau Historique de la Littérature Francaise,* by M. J. de Chénier, and *Historia de la Literatura Española escrita en aleman,* by Friedrich Bouterwek, *North American Review,* 38 (January 1834): 158-177;

"Men and Manners in America," *North American Review,* 38 (January 1834): 210-270;

"Thomas Carlyle," review of *Sartor Resartus, North American Review,* 41 (October 1835): 454-482;

"Mrs. [Lydia] Sigourney," *Democratic Review,* 11 (September 1842): 246-249;

"Contemporary Spanish Poetry," *Democratic Review,* 14 (April 1844): 395-408;

"The Texas Question," *Democratic Review,* 15 (September 1844): 250-270.

Throughout his career Alexander Everett combined the roles of diplomat and man of letters with considerable success. Born in Boston, Massachusetts, to Reverend Oliver and Lucy Hill Everett, a brother of Edward Everett, Alexander entered Harvard College at the age of twelve and a half. After graduating first in his class in 1806, he became a teacher at Phillips Exeter Academy, while he apprenticed in the law office of John Quincy Adams. In 1809 he traveled to Russia as personal secretary to Adams, who had been appointed United States minister. He next served at The Hague in the Netherlands from 1815 to 1823, first as secretary to the American Legation and then as chargé d'affaires. When Adams became president in 1825, he appointed Everett minister to Spain, a post which Everett held for four years. The election of Andrew Jackson put an end to this job, but upon his return to America Everett immediately took controlling interest of the *North American Review.* His brother Edward had already served as editor of the *North American Review* from 1820 to 1824. Alexander Everett maintained editorial control of the journal from 1830 to 1835 and continued to contrib-

Portrait on ivory of Alexander Hill Everett, painted by Washington Blanchard, circa 1830-1835, while Everett was a member of the Massachusetts legislature (by permission of the New-York Historical Society)

ute after he gave up the journal for financial reasons. In part because of his diplomatic experience and in part because of his tenure with the journal, Everett entered into a series of important friendships with Henry Wadsworth Longfellow, Washington Irving, Lydia Sigourney, George Prescott, and George Ticknor.

Everett's influence over the periodical upset author Ralph Waldo Emerson. Everett and Emerson were worlds apart in their appreciation of literary works. Yet their separation was perhaps less a function of uneven critical skills than of different critical goals. Born thirteen years before Emerson, Everett concerned himself with the shifting balance of power emerging from the American Revolution. Because of the era in which he was born and the early diplomatic career into which he was thrust, Everett tended to view the literary environment in highly politicized terms. He felt the need to proclaim a literary break from England even as he was ambivalent about it. Emerson had the same concern, yet in some substantial way could take the "revolution" for granted, in part because of the critical defense of American literature mounted by critics like Everett in the *North American Review.*

In many ways Everett's diplomatic career set the tone for his literary concerns. Everett's early experience abroad developed in him a desire to define the gathering force of American democracy as a world power. This intention explains why his criticism often had about it a curious blend of speculation, bravado, and uncertainty disguised under the control of a cool brio and careful wit. He began publishing articles early in his life, writing on an array of topics in the *Boston Review,* the *Democratic Review,* and the *North American Review.*

Everett's command of foreign languages served him in good stead. An early review of French drama (1820) predictably centered on the great Corneille, Racine, and Molière gave some attention to Voltaire and dismissed the French drama after him (Voltaire) as of "little interest." Everett reacted negatively to a history of French literature in the eighteenth century largely because the author, Dominique Garat, organized his book badly and executed his task in even worse fashion. Hostile to the French Materialists such as Baron Holbach, Everett was temperamentally more in tune with a writer like Montesquieu, whose clarity and grace he found especially appealing. A long review of posthumous works by Madame de Stäel (1822) testifies to Everett's familiarity with both German scholarship and de Stäel's career, and while he finds her deficient in literary inventiveness and philosophical depth, he is prone to accept her as an "extraordinary writer" whose "power & elegance" assured her a reputation in posterity. Everett's first major publication emerged from his experiences in Russia and the Netherlands. Entitled *Europe: or, A General Survey of the Present Situation of the Principle Powers* (1822), the work introduces itself as a "general sketch of the present political situation in Europe," summarizing the various European powers after the fall of Napoleon. The work is interesting less as a summary than as a guide to Everett's developing desire to define and identify the historical forces responsible for the "event" of America. Because of his search for scientific terms to describe these forces, Everett's text makes a useful if skewed preface for the view of Europe that would later be developed by Henry Adams in his famous *Education of Henry Adams* (1907). Certainly Everett's early sense of the European political scene passed through the perceptual filter of John Quincy Adams. In *Europe: or, A General Survey* he characterizes his epoch as the "age of revolution" and attempts through his description of the various European "powers" to show how the "collision of interests" between nations was the "necessary result of the operation of general principles." Throughout the text Everett endeavors to show how establishing peace and prosperity in the Old World would depend upon the federation of separate nations–something like the federation of American states–but only if it could avoid the tyranny of a federated country like Germany or Russia. The success of the confederation in Russia, in fact, emerges in Everett's argument as the great example and peril for the European continent in much the same way that Russia would later figure as the glacier of inertia in *The Education of Henry Adams.*

In an odd way Everett's next book, *New Ideas on Population: with Remarks on the Theories of Malthus and Godwin* (1823), tends to elaborate the "general principles" he thought were functional in *Europe: or, A General Survey.* The topic is not the balance of powers in a direct sense, but the burgeoning power of America. In *Europe: or, A General Survey,* Everett espoused the idea that the "whole body of society is interested in the progress of civilization" and by this he meant the "progress of industry, wealth and knowledge." In *New*

Ideas on Population he sets out to refute the theories of T. R. Malthus and William Godwin as inoperative in the case of the United States. Against the Malthusian theory that the "increase in population" is "the real and only source of all the evil we suffer," Everett summons up the rhetoric of industrial progress and then cites the example of the United States as a fulfillment of that rhetoric. By Everett's reckoning, an increase in population inevitably generates a "division of labor which produces in its turn the invention of new machines, etc." An increase in population, according to Everett, tends to push a culture away from the inefficient modes of hunting, fishing, and herding and into the effective mode of agriculture. He believes this stage "is followed immediately and necessarily by the introduction of commerce and manufactures." Everett supports his agro-industrial theory by espousing the exponential powers of science and technology and exposing what he believes to be Malthus's naiveté concerning those powers. Everett's exploration of the rhetoric of progress is less interesting and palatable for its refutation of the population theory than for the complex political position it forced him to defend. If his initial dismissal of Godwin in the same argument shows an uneasiness with the utopian rhetoric pervading the "era of revolutions," Everett nevertheless hopes to improve the condition of man in society. Malthus uses his argument on population, as Everett notes, to argue that "attempts to increase the happiness of man by the improvement of existing political institutions are hopeless and visionary," and Everett seizes the opportunity to argue that political institutions are neither mischievous (as Godwin would argue) nor indifferent (as Malthus would argue) but "extremely valuable."

This conflict between a rather over-confident rhetoric of progress and a more sensitive commitment to the difficulties and obligations accruing from its pursuit became still more evident in his next book: *America: or, A General Survey of the Political Situation of the Several Powers of the Western Continent, with Conjectures on Their Future Prospects* (1827). Everett openly discusses the leading political role waiting for the United States. He is careful to keep his argument clear of what he considers the "visionary" and nonsensical utopian strain that often saturated arguments about America's "mission" in the world. In so doing, however, he reveals the conservative core that constrains his vision and separates him from writers

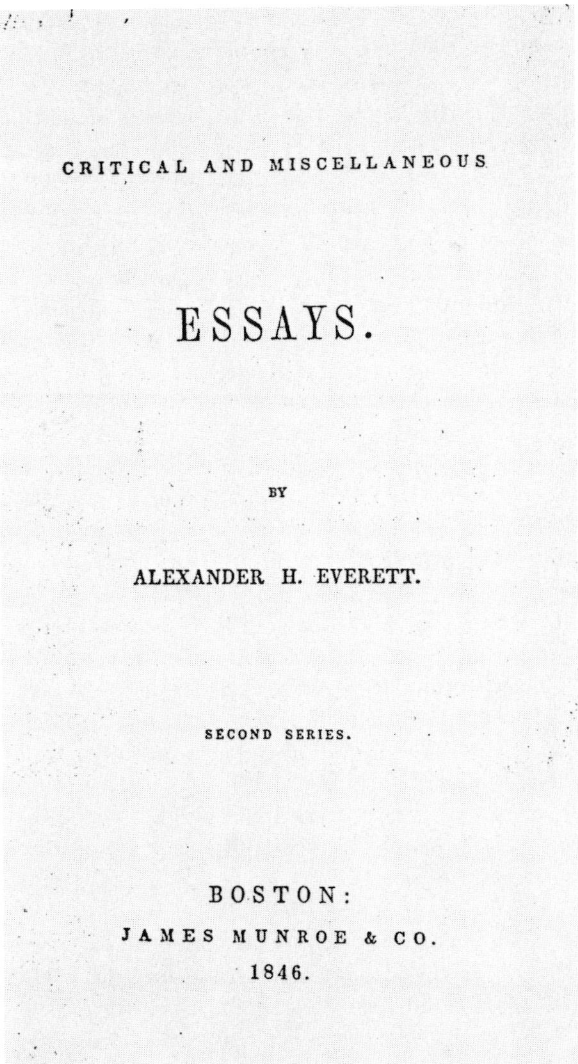
CRITICAL AND MISCELLANEOUS

ESSAYS.

BY

ALEXANDER H. EVERETT.

SECOND SERIES.

BOSTON:
JAMES MUNROE & CO.
1846.

Title page for Everett's last published collection of articles, most of which had been previously published in North American Review. *The essays demonstrate Everett's wide range of artistic and philosophical interests.*

like Emerson. Unlike Emerson Everett found little virtue in the experimental reform movements of his day. Everett could not imagine, for example, that political equality between men and women was a viable possibility. Yet it would be a mistake to say that Everett was inflexible and naive relative to the potential abuses of conservatism. As in his attack on Malthus, there are moments in *America: or, A General Survey* when he develops a sensitive and serious argument against just such abuse; when he addresses the slavery question, for example, Everett observes that the proslavery arguments about the "essential degradation" of the black race are not only self-serving but ahistorical. "Nations and races, like individuals, have their day," according to Everett, and he is quick to point out how a knowledge of African history might show that "the blacks had a long and glorious one."

Indeed it can be said that Everett's career as editor and critic is modeled on this complex political disposition. Everett operated on the premise that sharp criticism, like good government, could provide the New World with a valuable literary heritage, but only if the criticism could be fair and not tyrannical, in the manner of some English periodicals. He early defended American literature against the harsh and undeserved attacks of critics in the *Edinburgh Review* (1830) by defending the literary merit of the political and social writing of men like Adams, Thomas Jefferson, and Benjamin Franklin. More amused than annoyed with the English tone of criticism, and on the whole fairly content with American literary achievements to date, Everett was not inclined to reply in kind. He was obviously fond of the English contribution to literature–an 1825 article on Lord Byron is a model in the accuracy of its critical assessment, while his 1835 review of *Sartor Resartus* accurately attributes it to Thomas Carlyle and concludes by saying that the English writer is destined "to occupy a large space in the literary world."

Everett's interest in the political events at the turn of the century no doubt influenced his decision to write two short biographies on Joseph Warren and Patrick Henry for Jared Sparks's *Library of American Biography*. In a way necessity was the source of a keen critical tendency developed by Everett; his defense of the political foundations of the American literary scene helped him to perceive the literary "value" of letters and political essays from other countries as well. Understanding the literary virtues of a writer like Franklin aided his appreciation and defense of the letters of Madame de Sévigné ("we hardly know any French literary work of the last century for which we would exchange her letters") and the bulk of Rousseau's work, whose political theory he nevertheless disdained ("the spirit of his political writing is excellent; but their scientific value is not perhaps so great as it has sometimes been considered"). This same critical skill helped him to enter into the debate about the authorship of *Gil Blas*, defending the theory that it was written by a Spaniard through a rather close reading of the text. These and other essays were gathered together and published in two volumes of *Critical and Miscellaneous Essays* in 1845 and 1846.

Throughout his career, Everett encouraged American authors to broaden their sights beyond the narrow but significant influence of Anglo-Saxon culture. In an intriguing correspondence with Lydia Sigourney, for example, he not only applauds her decision to write about Pocahontas but urges Sigourney to research the culture of the North American Indian. During the course of his career Everett began to develop a nearly anthropological interest in the forces of cultural interplay at work in the development of the United States, and he grew to believe that a national literary tradition depended upon an acceptance and exploration of those forces. Thus, for example, when Washington Irving expressed the desire to write about Christopher Columbus, Everett told Irving that he could only do so if he studied Spanish sources. Without doubt Everett's sensitivity to the sources of literary power in America enabled him to understand other cultures better than many Americans of his day. Everett went to Canton when he was appointed United States commissioner to China under the Polk Administration. Suffering from poor health, he died shortly after his arrival in 1847 but not before he completed an admirable defense of the Chinese way of life, "The Condition of China," part of a larger defense of his position toward the Malthusian theory of population.

References:

John Adams, "Letters of John Quincy Adams to A. H. Everett, 1817-37," *American Historical Review,* 11 (October 1905): 88-117; 11 (January 1906): 332-354;

Anonymous, "Political Portraits with Pen and Pencil," *Democratic Review,* 10 (May 1842): 460-478;

Claude G. Bowers, *The Spanish Adventures of Washington Irving* (Boston: Houghton Mifflin, 1940);

Harry Hayden Clark, "Literary Criticism in the *North American Review,* 1815-1835," *Transactions of the Wisconsin Academy of Sciences, Arts and Letters,* 32 (1940): 299-350;

Elizabeth Evans, "Alexander Hill Everett: Man of Letters," Ph.D. dissertation, University of North Carolina at Chapel Hill, 1970;

Evans, "The Everett-Longfellow Correspondence," *American Transcendental Quarterly,* part 1 (Winter 1972): 2-15;

Evans, "The Friendship of Alexander Hill Everett and Hugh Swinton Legare," *Mississippi Quarterly,* 28 (1975): 497-504;

Evans, "Mrs. Sigourney's Friend and Mentor," *Connecticut Historical Society Bulletin,* 36 (July 1971): 77-91;

Fred Somkin, "The Writings of Alexander Hill Everett (1790-1847), A Partial Checklist," *Bulletin of Bibliography,* 23 (January-April 1963): 238-239;

Joseph J. Spengler, "Alexander Hill Everett, Early American Opponent of Malthus," *New England Quarterly,* 9 (1936): 97-118.

Papers:

The Massachusetts Historical Society houses the primary collection of unpublished material, including the Alexander Hill Everett Papers and the Everett-Peabody Collection. Letters are collected in various libraries throughout the country including the Library of Congress in Washington, the New-York Historical Society, the Butler Library at Columbia, the Baker Memorial Library at Dartmouth, the Historical Society of Pennsylvania, the Houghton Library at Harvard, the Connecticut Historical Society in Hartford, and the Beinecke Library at Yale.

Edward Everett

(11 April 1794-15 January 1865)

Monica Maria Grecu
University of Nevada at Reno

See also the Everett entry in *DLB 1, The American Renaissance in New England.*

SELECTED BOOKS: *American Poets* (Cambridge: Hilliard & Metcalf, 1812);

A Defence of Christianity, Against the Work of George B. English, A.M., Entitled The Grounds of Christianity Examined, By Comparing the New Testament with the Old (Boston: Cummings & Hilliard, 1814; Cambridge: Hilliard & Metcalf, 1814);

Books, Rare, Curious, Elegant, and Valuable, in the Department of the Classicks, Civil Law, History, Criticism, Belles Lettres and Theology, for Sale at Auction, in Boston, 20 December, 1815 (Boston: J. Eliot, 1815);

A Letter to John Lowell, Esq. in Reply to a Publication Entitled Remarks on a Pamphlet, Printed by the Professors and Tutors of Harvard University, Touching Their Right to the Exclusive Government of that Seminary (Boston: O. Everett, 1824);

An Oration Pronounced at Cambridge Before the Society of Phi Beta Kappa (Boston: Oliver Everett, 1824);

Orations (Boston: Cummings, Hilliard, 1825-1830);

An Address Delivered at Charlestown, August 1, 1826, in Commemoration of John Adams and Thomas Jefferson (Boston: W. L. Lewis, 1826);

The Claims of Citizens of the United States of America on the Government of Naples, Holland, and France (Cambridge: Hilliard & Metcalf, 1826);

Eulogy on Lafayette, Delivered in Faneuil Hall, at the Request of the Young Men of Boston, September 6, 1834 (Boston: N. Hale/Allen & Ticknor, 1834);

An Address Delivered before the Literary Societies of Amherst College (Boston: Russell, Shattuck & Williams, 1835);

Orations and Speeches on Various Occasions (Boston: American Stationers' Company, 1836); revised, 4 volumes (Boston: Little, Brown, 1850-1868);

A Discourse on the Importance to Practical Men of Scientific Knowledge, and on the Encouragements to Its Pursuit (Edinburgh: T. Clark, 1837);

Importance of Practical Education and Useful Knowledge (Boston: Marsh, Capen, Lyon & Webb,

1840; New York: Harper & Brothers, 1840);

Address at the Inauguration of the Hon. Edward Everett, LL.D., as President of the University at Cambridge, Thursday, April 30, 1846 (Boston: Little, Brown, 1846);

A Eulogy on the Life and Character of John Quincy Adams, Delivered at the Request of the Legislature of Massachusetts, in Faneuil Hall, April 15, 1848 (Boston: Dutton & Wentworth, 1848);

The Mount Vernon Papers (New York: New York Ledger, 1858-1859);

Daniel Webster, an Oration, By the Hon. Edward Everett, on the Occasion of the Dedication of the Statue of Mr. Webster, in Boston, September 17th, 1859 (New York: H. H. Lloyd, 1859);

Address Delivered at the Consecration of the National Cemetery at Gettysburg, 19th November, 1863 (Boston: Little, Brown, 1864);

Address in Commemoration of the Life and Services of Charles Francis Adams Delivered in the Stone Temple at Quincy, 4 July, 1887 (Cambridge: J. Wilson, 1887);

Cuba; the Everett Letters on Cuba (Boston: G. H. Ellis, 1897).

OTHER: "Life of John Stark," in *Library of American Biography,* volume 1, edited by Jared Sparks (Boston: Hilliard, Gray, 1834; London: R. J. Kennett, 1834), pp. 3-116;

Biographical memoir, in *The Works of Daniel Webster,* volume 1, edited by Everett (Boston: Little, Brown, 1851);

Address, in *A Discourse on the Life, Character and Genius of Washington Irving,* edited by William C. Bryant (New York: New York Historical Society, 1860), pp. 107-113;

"The Life of George Washington," in *Encyclopaedia Britannica* (New York: Sheldon, 1860; Boston: Gould & Lincoln, 1860);

Introductory Address, in *The Rebellion Record; A Diary of American Events,* edited by Frank Moore (New York: Putnam's, 1861-1863; New York: D. Van Nostrand, 1864-1868);

"Biographical Memoir of the Public Life of Daniel Webster," in *The Writings and Speeches of Daniel Webster,* volume 1 (Boston: Little, Brown, 1903), pp. 1-175;

"Daniel Webster," in *Makers of American History* (New York: University Society, 1904).

PERIODICAL PUBLICATIONS: Review of *Christian Gottlob Heyne–Biographisch dargestellt,* by Arn. Herm. Lud. Helren, *North American Review,* 2 (January 1816): 201-217;

Engraving by H. Wright Smith, after a portrait by M. Wight (Paul Revere Frothingham, Edward Everett, Orator and Statesman, *1925)*

Extract of a letter to the editor from a friend in Germany [on Baron Munchhausen], *North American Review,* 3 (July 1816): 214-215;

Review of *Aus meinen Leben–Dichtung–und Wahrheit,* by Goethe, *North American Review,* 4 (January 1817): 217-262;

Review of *Notizia sul celebre Canova, e sulle sue opere,* in the *Giornale Enciclopedico* of Naples; and *Opera di scultura edi plastica di Antonio Canova,* by Isabella Albrizzi, *North American Review,* 10 (April 1820): 372-386;

Review of *Ueber die Epochen der bildenden-Kunst unter den Griechen,* by Friederich Thiersch, *North American Review,* 12 (January 1821): 178-198;

Review of *An Anniversary Discourse delivered before the New York Historical Society, December, 1820,* by Henry Wheaton, *North American Review,* 13 (July 1821): 154-168;

Review of *Marino Faliero, Doge of Venice. A tragedy in five acts,* by Lord Byron, *North American Re-*

view, 13 (July 1821): 227-246;

Review of *Poems,* by James E. Percival, *North American Review,* 14 (January 1822): 1-15;

Review of *The Comedies of Aristophanes,* volume 1, by T. Mitchell, *North American Review,* 14 (April 1822): 273-296;

Review of *Julia Sévéra, ou l'An quatre cent quatre vingt douze,* by J. C. L. Simonde de Sismondi, 3 volumes, *North American Review,* 15 (July 1822): 163-177;

Review of *Bracebridge Hall, or the Humorists, a Medley,* by Geoffrey Crayon, Gent., 2 volumes, *North American Review,* 15 (July 1822): 204-224;

Review of *The Life of Francis Bacon, Lord Chancellor of England,* by David Mallet, *North American Review,* 16 (April 1823): 300-337;

Review of *The Works of Maria Edgeworth,* 6 volumes, *North American Review,* 17 (October 1823): 383-389;

Review of *Orpheus Poetarum Graeorum Antiquissimus,* by Georgio Henrico Bode, *North American Review,* 21 (October 1825): 388-397;

Review of *Russian Tales; from the French of Count Xavier de Maistre . . . ,* translated by M. de Wallenstein, *North American Review,* 24 (January 1827): 188-193;

Review of *Select Specimens of the Theatre of the Hindus; No. I, The Mrichchakati, or the Toy Cart; a Drama. No. II, Vikrama and Urvasi, or the Hero and the Nymph; a Drama,* 8 volumes, translated by Horace Hayman Wilson, *North American Review,* 26 (January 1828): 111-126;

Review of *The Crayon Miscellany,* by Washington Irving, *North American Review,* 41 (July 1835): 1-28.

Edward Everett was central to the development of American criticism at a critical turning point in its history. Judicial criticism was waning; rhetorical criticism was still strong in the universities, but otherwise beginning to lose its hold; romantic criticism was just beginning its ascendancy. Everett positioned himself to advance the "new" criticism through both editorial policy and personal contributions. Possessed of cautious common sense and a basically conciliatory temperament, within five years of its founding he became the fourth editor of the *North American Review* (founder William Tudor, Jared Sparks, and Edward Tyrrell Channing preceded him). In the four years during which he edited the journal, Everett was instrumental in making it a respected voice for New England intellectualism, and he himself had contributed to that voice by publishing 110 articles in the earlier years of his career.

Everett was born in Dorchester, Massachusetts, in 1794, the fourth son of the Reverend Oliver and Lucy Hill Everett. Alexander Hill Everett was an older brother. Edward distinguished himself as a student, graduating with highest honors from Harvard College in 1811 as the youngest in his class, and earning his M.A. in divinity from the same institution in 1814. That same year, at age nineteen, he was appointed pastor of the Unitarian church on Brattle Square, Boston, where he distinguished himself for his eloquence. The following year he was appointed to a chair in Greek literature at his alma mater.

To prepare himself for his professorial duties, Everett enrolled in the University of Göttingen, Germany, in 1815, earning his Ph.D. two years later. One of the first of a long line of New Englanders who would pursue graduate study there, his cosmopolitan poise and scholarly habits easily won him the high regard and friendship of his European mentors and acquaintances. Following two years spent in the almost obliga-

Charlotte Gray Everett, portrait by Gambardella (Paul Revere Frothingham, Edward Everett: Orator and Statesman, *1925)*

tory European tour, Everett returned to the United States to take up his professorship in the fall of 1819, and in January 1820 he assumed the editorship of the *North American Review.* Two years later he married Charlotte Gray Brooks, and the two began a family.

It has been charged that under the editorship of Edward Everett, and later of his brother Alexander, the journal became less attentive to the contemporary literary scene and more heavy-handed in the types of articles it published, to the point of simply being dull. However, much literature being produced in the period was third-rate or worse and did not warrant reviewing; the Everetts were averse to incubating literature as though it were some hothouse plant, and they genuinely aspired to foster a higher intellectualism among the journal's readers. Certainly under their guidance the intellectual tone of the journal was deepened. More attention was paid to the international scene, even while the general focus of the journal remained on matters American. Furthermore, a concerted effort seems to have been made to recruit high-caliber women and men to write the articles, and what was lost in raciness was redeemed in depth and breadth.

The general bent of Everett's criticism is scholarly. It was almost his habit to review the scholarship on a subject before turning to the subject itself. A strong characteristic of his work, which grew out of his desire to broaden the scope of readers' awareness of the unfamiliar, is his use of extended quotation. Consequently his critical articles often appear to be excessively padded though he defended the practice as providing readers with a sense of the tone and style of the book under review. Another characteristic of his criticism is his attention to cultural matters, rather than the increasingly popular idea of national character, as the context most suitable for positioning a subject. In this respect he may be seen as superior in insight to his contemporaries.

The preponderance of Everett's journalism lies outside the area of literature. Yet between 1816 and 1830 he published a considerable number of literary articles. After that time the vicissitudes following upon twin careers as politician and orator left little time for literary pursuits. His earliest literary criticism naturally draws upon his experiences in Germany. An article on Christian Heyne sensibly pays tribute to his taste, judgment, and learning, then dwells favorably on

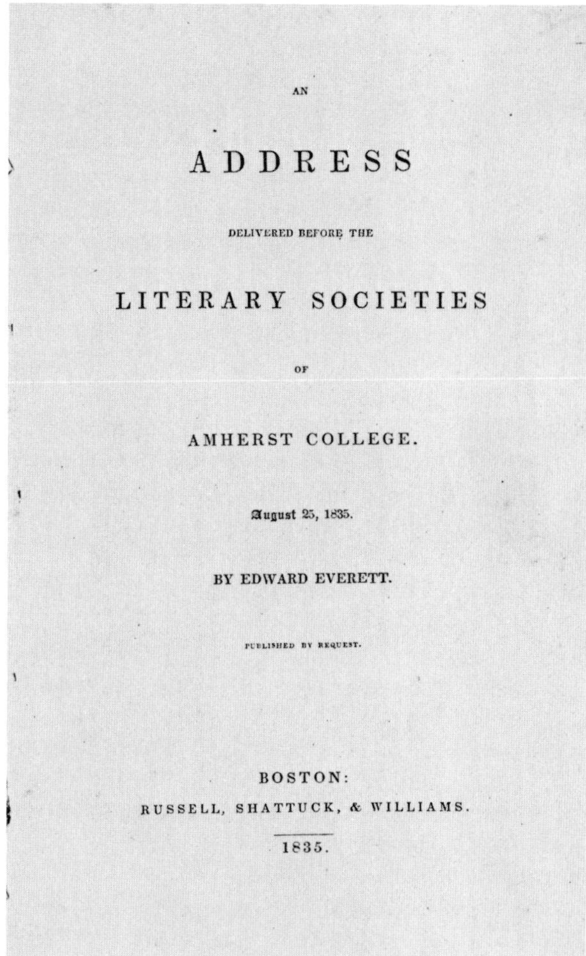

AN

ADDRESS

DELIVERED BEFORE THE

LITERARY SOCIETIES

OF

AMHERST COLLEGE.

August 25, 1835.

BY EDWARD EVERETT.

PUBLISHED BY REQUEST.

BOSTON:

RUSSELL, SHATTUCK, & WILLIAMS.

1835.

Title page for an address published in the year that Everett was elected to his first term as governor of Massachusetts (collection of Joel Myerson)

his editions of Tibullus, Virgil, Pindar, and Homer.

Of more consequence is a review of Goethe's *Dichtung und Wahrheit* (1811, 1812, 1814, 1833). Everett was unsure just how the title should be glossed (what role exactly can *Dichtung* or fiction play in autobiography?), but then correctly saw that the title has something to do with "the mystery of the man." Generally following Goethe's own principles of literary criticism–sympathetic analysis, establishing the subject in age and nation, searching out the "inward traits" of the subject–Everett viewed Goethe as dramatically illustrating a psychological contest between an individual spirit of inwardness, free will, pleasure, and personal desire on the one hand and the despotism of invariable physical and societal laws on the other. Everett's own taste is revealed in an aside in which he dissents from Goethe's praise of Oliver Goldsmith's *The Vicar of Wakefield* (1766). To Everett the novel suffers from too-faithful an adherence to the "natural" at the expense of "elevation," and he illustrates his point by arguing that if something like Maria Edgeworth's "cheerful philosophy" had been grafted onto the good-natured but "disheartening" irony the novel would have been better. He is on firmer ground in citing *Werther* (1774) as "that wonderful book," the elegance of which has been lost in an execrable English translation.

Everett's critical views reflect German models, but are free of the doctrinaire historicism that characterizes the criticism of a writer like George Bancroft. He was impatient with analyzers of national character, however, upon whose work Americans had been "surfeited" for years. But he was interested in how social manners influenced creative writers. The interest was dictated by his belief that literature was integral to all cultures. As a social institution it unavoidably caught up and mirrored the age and milieu, the comprehension of which was necessary in clarifying artistic achievement. To this view he grafted several other criteria: the universality of literature (Goethe's *Weltliteratur*) and Goethe's dictum that the critic should identify what the writer was trying to do and then concentrate on whether the writer succeeded.

These views were sharpened by Everett's levelheadedness and his basically tolerant personality. In addition he generally held that there were rules of art. He left them undefined, but his critical articles provide clues to his mode of reading. He valued probability as well as close observation, a unifying tone, substantive matter, solid characterization, fluency, and perhaps even eloquence in the rhetorical sense of the word. For example, in reviewing Lord Byron's *Marino Faliero* (1820), he found the play "neither very natural nor highly dramatic." Part of the problem lay in the way that Byron seemed to deliberately roughen his lines. Everett admitted that Alexander Pope's lines were too regular, the placement of the caesura being too predictable for impassioned poetry; but he equally quarreled with what seemed eccentric, random placements of junctures in Byron's lines. It is obvious that Everett expected a certain grace or propriety in poetry, and he does support his criticism by quoting lines that really *are* bad, including this one: "As well had there been time to have got together."

Everett's nationalism is in the same moderate key. During his tenure as editor of the *North American Review,* he made it the "first duty" of the journal to encourage the science and literature of the young country. But such a duty was not indiscriminately observed. In reviewing James Gates Percival's poetry, he wrote that "no kindness can be more treacherous than the encouragement given to ordinary verses called poetry." Faced with "pretty good poetry," the "conscientious, patriotic, and good natured" critic should simply leave well enough alone. On quite another note, Everett saw no reason for American writers to suffer a sense of inferiority before older, more established literatures. It annoyed him that Washington Irving should have chosen to mask his self-consciousness by addressing himself to English manners in *Bracebridge Hall* (1822). Irving's disclaimer of provincialism in his preface undercut his seriousness of purpose, Everett felt, while his style became "less original and nervous" as he sought a more "correct" diction and idiom.

His 1823 review of a new six-volume edition of Maria Edgeworth's novel is typical of his critical approach. After establishing the provenance, time, and cultural context of her work, he sees her as inferior to Scott in art and intelligence but possessed of real talents: invention, social observation, wit and sense, imaginative vivacity, and tender feelings. The disadvantages she experienced in her life, he asserts, explain her failure to match her promise. Her origins were in a bleak part of Ireland; she had to defer to a father who was her intellectual inferior; the society in which she lived was indifferent to female development, indeed thought women intellectually inferior to men. Prizing individuality in women less than in men, the society imposed a suffocating series of social expectations on women who threatened to break the mold. Everett is clearly on Edgeworth's side in these matters, even to subtly criticizing his American male contemporaries for refusing to allow women the franchise or to inherit real estate.

By 1830 Everett's literary criticism had pretty much run its course. In 1825 he had been elected a representative to Congress, and politics increasingly preoccupied him. Following a ten-year stint in the Congress, he was elected governor of Massachusetts in 1835 and served four terms until 1839. While traveling in Europe in 1840, he was appointed Minister Plenipotentiary to the court of St. James, a position he occupied

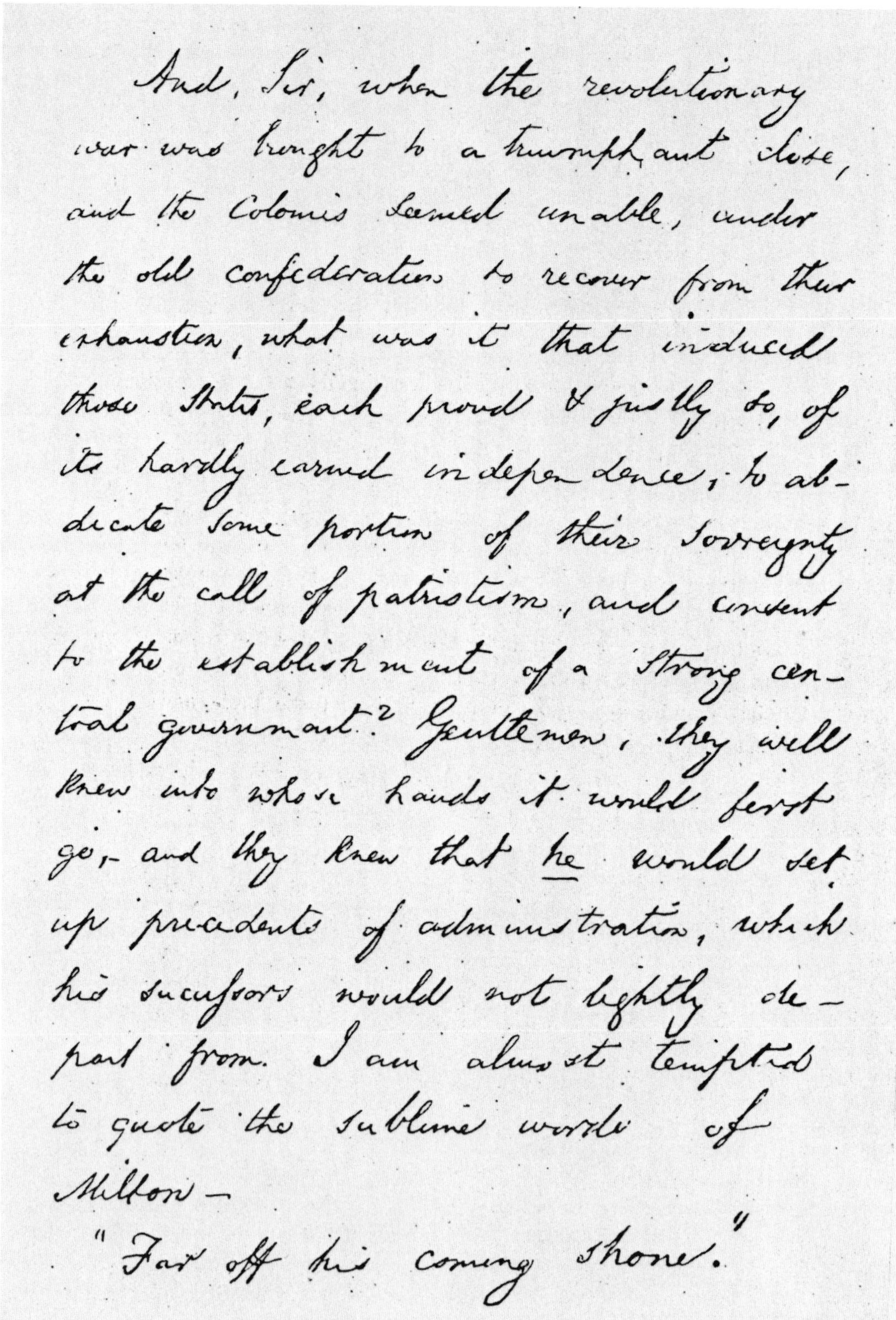
And, Sir, when the revolutionary
war was brought to a triumphant close,
and the Colonies seemed unable, under
the old confederation to recover from their
exhaustion, what was it that induced
those States, each proud & justly so, of
its hardly earned independence, to ab-
dicate some portion of their sovereignty
at the call of patriotism, and consent
to the establishment of a strong central government? Gentlemen, they well
knew into whose hands it would first
go,– and they knew that he would set
up precedents of administration, which
his successors would not lightly depart from. I am almost tempted
to quote the sublime words of
Milton–
"Far off his coming shone."

Page from the manuscript for an oration delivered at Niblo's Garden on 22 February 1852 to honor Washington's birthday (from Homes of American Authors, *1853)*

until his recall in 1845; meanwhile he garnered honorary degrees from Oxford, Dublin, and Cambridge universities. By then his reputation as a sagacious intellectual and brilliant speaker was firmly established. In 1846 he was named to the presidency of Harvard College and headed the institution until 1849. Following very brief service as secretary of state and senator from Massachusetts, and with no great enthusiasm, he ran for vice-president on the Constitutional Union ticket in 1860. At the outbreak of civil war he became a fervent supporter of the Union cause and, at considerable expense to his health, he tirelessly spoke throughout the North on behalf of the war effort. In 1863 he gave the main oration at the dedication of the National Cemetery at Gettysburg, which was followed by Abraham Lincoln's address. The next day he wrote the president: "I should be glad if I could flatter myself that I came as near the central idea of the occasion in two hours as you did in two minutes." Lincoln's response was equally generous.

After canvassing his literary criticism, the reader has the sense that Everett is of a reflective, deliberative intelligence that is well informed and balanced in its views. While his tastes were obviously set by classical literature, he is not prescriptive, nor is he given to ponderous judgments. His tactic is to present his subject in so fair and compelling a manner that the reader sees the particular judgment as virtually inevitable. He is open to what is meritorious in a work and is generally guided by the material under review. A perceptive but cautious reader, he is alert to "moral implications," yet tolerant of what others termed "licentious."

References:

William Charvat, *The Origins of American Critical Thought, 1810-1835* (Philadelphia: University of Pennsylvania Press, 1936);

William K. Christian, "The Mind of Edward Everett," Ph.D. dissertation, Michigan State University, 1953;

Harry Hayden Clark, "Literary Criticism in the *North American Review*, 1815-1835," *Transactions of the Wisconsin Academy of Sciences, Arts and Letters*, 34 (1940): 299-350;

Clark, ed., *Transitions in American Literary History* (Durham: Duke University Press, 1953);

Richard Arthur Firda, "German Philosophy of History and Literature in *The North American Review*, 1815-1860," *Journal of the History of Ideas*, 32 (January-March 1971): 133-142;

Paul Revere Frothingham, *Edward Everett: Orator and Statesman* (Boston & New York: Houghton Mifflin, 1925);

Emma Jaeck, *Madame de Staël and the Spread of German Literature* (New York: Oxford University Press, 1915);

Orie William Long, *Literary Pioneers; Early American Explorers of European Culture* (Cambridge: Harvard University Press, 1935);

Svend Petersen, *The Gettysburg Address: the Story of Two Orations* (New York: Ungar, 1963);

Henry Pochmann, *German Culture in America; Philosophical and Literary Influences, 1600-1900* (Madison: University of Wisconsin Press, 1957);

John Paul Pritchard, *Criticism in America; An Account of the Development of Critical Techniques from the Early Period of the Republic to the Middle Years of the Twentieth Century* (Norman: University of Oklahoma Press, 1956);

John W. Rathbun, *American Literary Criticism, 1800-1860* (Boston: G. K. Hall, 1979);

Allen Walker Read, "Edward Everett's Attitude towards American English," *New England Quarterly*, 12 (1939): 112-129;

Floyd Stovall, ed., *The Development of American Literary Criticism* (Chapel Hill: University of North Carolina Press, 1955).

Papers:

The Everett papers are held by the Massachusetts Historical Society.

Sarah Margaret Fuller, Marchesa D'Ossoli

(23 May 1810-19 July 1850)

Sharon K. George
Texas A&I University

See also the Fuller entry in *DLB 1, The American Renaissance in New England.*

BOOKS: *Summer on the Lakes, in 1843* (Boston: Little, Brown/New York: C. S. Francis, 1844); enlarged as *Summer on the Lakes, with Autobiography . . . and Memoir,* by Ralph Waldo Emerson, et al. (London: Ward & Lock, 1861);

Woman in the Nineteenth Century (New York: Greeley & McElrath, 1845; London: Clarke, 1845); enlarged as *Woman in the Nineteenth Century, and Kindred Papers Relating to the Sphere, Condition, and Duties of Woman,* edited by Arthur B. Fuller (Boston: Jewett/Cleveland: Jewett, Proctor & Worthington/New York: Sheldon, Lamport, 1855);

Papers on Literature and Art, 2 volumes (New York: Wiley & Putnam, 1846; London: Wiley & Putnam, 1846); enlarged as *Art, Literature, and Drama,* edited by Arthur B. Fuller (Boston: Brown, Taggard & Chase/New York: Sheldon/Philadelphia: Lippincott/London: Sampson Low, 1860);

Memoirs of Margaret Fuller Ossoli, edited, with contributions, by Ralph Waldo Emerson, James Freeman Clarke, and William Henry Channing (2 volumes, Boston: Phillips, Sampson, 1852; 3 volumes, London: Bentley, 1852);

At Home and Abroad, or Things and Thoughts in America and Europe, edited by Arthur B. Fuller (Boston: Crosby, Nichols/London: Sampson Low, 1856);

Life Without and Life Within; or, Reviews, Narratives, Essays, and Poems, edited by Arthur B. Fuller (Boston: Brown, Taggard & Chase/New York: Sheldon/Philadelphia: J. B. Lippincott/London: Sampson Low, 1860);

Margaret and Her Friends, or Ten Conversations with Margaret Fuller upon the Mythology of the Greeks and its Expression in Art, reported by Caroline W. Healey (Boston: Roberts Brothers, 1895).

Margaret Fuller, engraving by Henry Bryan Hall, Jr. (courtesy of the National Portrait Gallery, Washington, D.C.)

Collections: *The Writings of Margaret Fuller,* edited by Mason Wade (New York: Viking, 1941);

Margaret Fuller: American Romantic. A Selection from her Writings and Correspondence, edited by Perry Miller (Garden City: Anchor/Doubleday, 1963);

The Woman and the Myth: Margaret Fuller's Life and Writings, edited by Bell Gale Chevigny (Old Westbury, N.Y.: Feminist Press, 1976);

Margaret Fuller: Essays on American Life and Letters, edited by Joel Myerson (New Haven, Conn.:

College & University Press, 1978).

OTHER: Johann Eckermann, *Conversations with Goethe in the Last Years of His Life,* translated by Fuller (Boston: Hilliard, Gray, 1839);
Günderode, translated by Fuller (Boston: E. P. Peabody, 1842).

PERIODICAL PUBLICATIONS: "A Short Essay on Critics," *Dial,* 1 (July 1840): 5-11;
"The Atheneum Exhibition of Painting and Sculpture," *Dial,* 1 (October 1840): 260-263;
"Menzel's View of Goethe," *Dial,* 1 (January 1841): 340-347;
"A Dialogue: Poet. Critic," *Dial,* 1 (April 1841): 494-496;
"Goethe," *Dial,* 2 (July 1841): 1-41;
"To Contributors," *Dial,* 2 (July 1841): 136;
"Lives of the Great Composers, Haydn, Mozart, Handel, Bach, Beethoven," *Dial,* 2 (October 1841): 148-203;
"Festus," *Dial,* 2 (October 1841): 231-261;
"Bettine Brentano and Her Friend Günderode," *Dial,* 2 (January 1842): 313-357;
"Entertainments of the Past Winter," *Dial,* 2 (July 1842): 46-72;
"Romaic and Rhine Ballads," *Dial,* 3 (October 1842): 137-180;
"The Great Lawsuit. Man *versus* Men. Woman *versus* Women," *Dial,* 4 (July 1843): 1-47;
"Dialogue," *Dial,* 4 (April 1844): 458-469;
"Emerson's Essays," *New-York Daily Tribune,* 7 December 1844, p. 1;
"Monument to Goethe," *New-York Daily Tribune,* 16 December 1844, p. 1;
"Miss Barrett's Poems," *New-York Daily Tribune,* 4 January 1845, p. 1;
Review of *The Waif: A Collection of Poems,* edited by Henry Wadsworth Longfellow, *New-York Daily Tribune,* 16 January 1845, p. 1;
Review of *Conversations on Some of the Old Poets,* by James Russell Lowell, *New-York Daily Tribune,* 21 January 1845, p. 1;
"Edgar A. Poe," *New-York Daily Tribune,* 24 January 1845, p. 1;
Review of *Scenes in My Native Land,* by L. H. Sigourney, *New-York Daily Tribune,* 28 January 1845, p. 1;
"French Novelists of the Day: Balzac . . . George Sand . . . Eugene Sue," *New-York Daily Tribune,* 1 February 1845, p. 1;
"English Writers Little Known Here: Milnes . . . Landor . . . Julius Hare," *New-York Daily Tribune,* 4 March 1845, p. 1; 28 March 1845, p. 1;
"Library of Choice Reading," *New-York Daily Tribune,* 4 April 1845, p. 1;
"Hazlitt's *Table-Talk,*" *New-York Daily Tribune,* 30 April 1845, p. 1;
"Mrs. Child's Letters," *New-York Daily Tribune,* 10 May 1845, p. 1;
Review of *Essays on Art,* by Goethe, translated by S. G. Ward, *New-York Daily Tribune,* 29 May 1845, p. 1;
Review of *Philothea,* by L. M. Child, *New-York Daily Tribune,* 5 June 1845, p. 1;
Review of *Margaret: A Tale of the Real and Ideal,* by Sylvester Judd, *New-York Daily Tribune,* 1 September 1845, p. 1;
Review of *The Wigwam and the Cabin,* by William Gilmore Simms, *New-York Daily Tribune,* 11 October 1845, p. 1;
Review of *The Raven and Other Poems,* by Edgar Allan Poe, *New-York Daily Tribune,* 26 November 1845, p. 1;
Review of *Poems,* by Henry Wadsworth Longfellow, *New-York Daily Tribune,* 10 December 1845, p. 1;
"Farewell," *New-York Daily Tribune,* 1 August 1846, p. 2.

Called by herself "the American Corinne," in analogy with Madame de Staël's feminist heroine and later referred to as the "Margaret-ghost" by Henry James because of the haunting fascination she held for the nineteenth century, Margaret Fuller has continued to fascinate twentieth-century readers as well. Although she was best known during her own time for her stimulating conversation and is remembered during ours for her association with the Transcendentalists, Fuller is much more important than these views suggest. A perceptive literary critic, she was as well a capable reporter and a social and political realist. Beginning her public career as the first editor of the *Dial,* the periodical founded and published by the Transcendentalists, Fuller went on to work for Horace Greeley's *New-York Daily Tribune,* becoming the first woman journalist for a major American newspaper and the first American foreign correspondent. Always writing hastily and carelessly because she was always pressured by time and the need for money, she produced a bulky, uneven body of work. Despite her rather clumsy and sometimes pretentious writing style, Fuller's achievements in literary criticism are impressive. She worked out and applied in the pages of the *Dial* a theory of literary criticism which combined the strengths of two traditions, the Scottish common sense philosophy and romanticism; and she produced enough solid literary criticism for the *Daily Tribune* to establish herself, along with Edgar Allan Poe, as one of the two legitimate literary critics in nineteenth-century America. Fuller was also a competent social critic. She published the first full-length American woman's rights manifesto, *Woman in the Nineteenth Century* (1845); her columns of social commentary for the *Daily Tribune* established her reputation as a pioneer in American public education and American social criticism; and her perceptive, intelligent reports of the Italian revolution contributed to the growth of political and social understanding in the United States.

The daughter of Margarett [*sic*] Crane and Timothy Fuller, Sarah Margaret Fuller was born on 23 May 1810 in Cambridgeport, Massachusetts. Disappointed by the birth of a daughter, her father set out to educate her exactly as he would have educated a son. At the age of six, when most children are just entering school, Fuller could read fluently in both Latin and En-

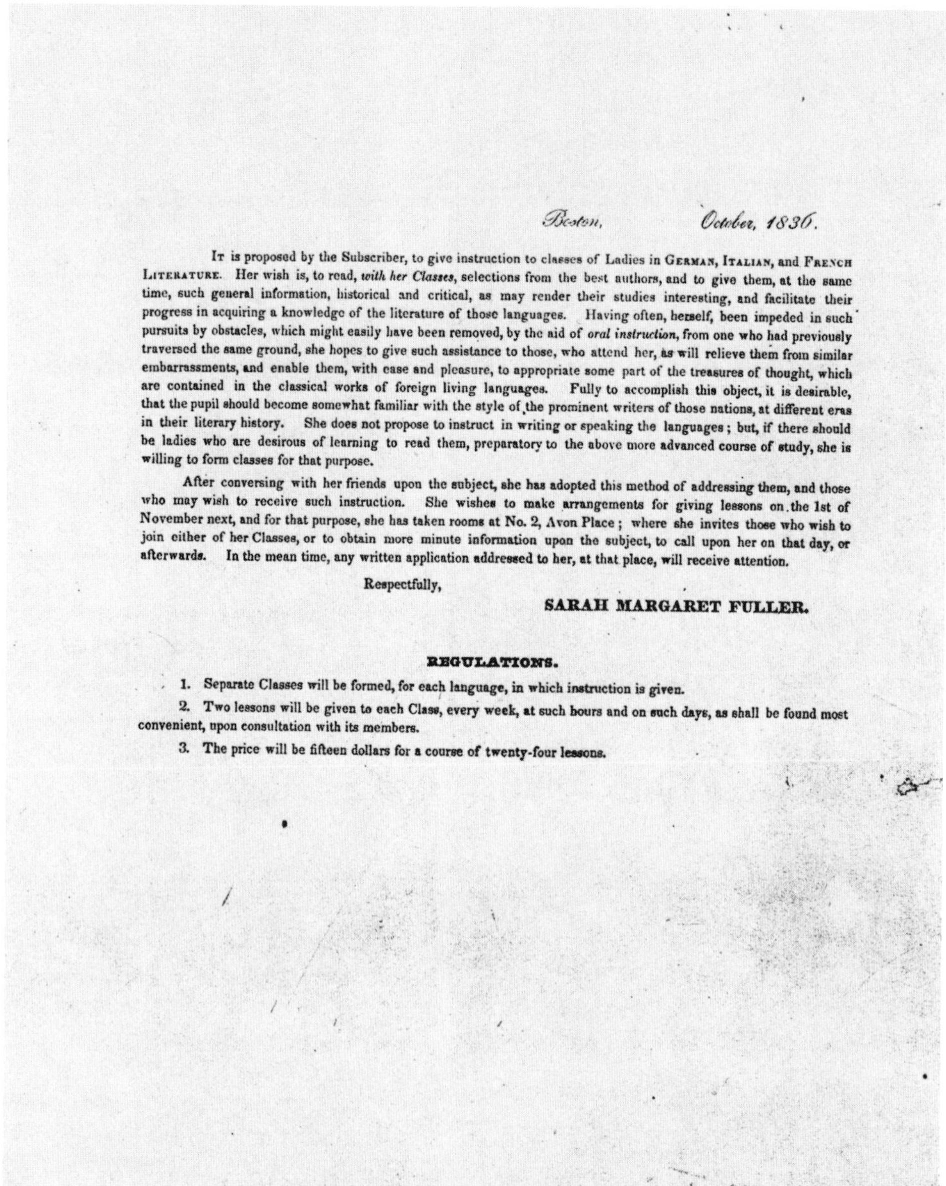

Boston, October, 1836.

It is proposed by the Subscriber, to give instruction to classes of Ladies in German, Italian, and French Literature. Her wish is, to read, *with her Classes*, selections from the best authors, and to give them, at the same time, such general information, historical and critical, as may render their studies interesting, and facilitate their progress in acquiring a knowledge of the literature of those languages. Having often, herself, been impeded in such pursuits by obstacles, which might easily have been removed, by the aid of *oral instruction*, from one who had previously traversed the same ground, she hopes to give such assistance to those, who attend her, as will relieve them from similar embarrassments, and enable them, with ease and pleasure, to appropriate some part of the treasures of thought, which are contained in the classical works of foreign living languages. Fully to accomplish this object, it is desirable, that the pupil should become somewhat familiar with the style of the prominent writers of those nations, at different eras in their literary history. She does not propose to instruct in writing or speaking the languages; but, if there should be ladies who are desirous of learning to read them, preparatory to the above more advanced course of study, she is willing to form classes for that purpose.

After conversing with her friends upon the subject, she has adopted this method of addressing them, and those who may wish to receive such instruction. She wishes to make arrangements for giving lessons on the 1st of November next, and for that purpose, she has taken rooms at No. 2, Avon Place; where she invites those who wish to join either of her Classes, or to obtain more minute information upon the subject, to call upon her on that day, or afterwards. In the mean time, any written application addressed to her, at that place, will receive attention.

Respectfully,

SARAH MARGARET FULLER.

REGULATIONS.

1. Separate Classes will be formed, for each language, in which instruction is given.
2. Two lessons will be given to each Class, every week, at such hours and on such days, as shall be found most convenient, upon consultation with its members.
3. The price will be fifteen dollars for a course of twenty-four lessons.

Margaret Fuller's prospectus for her language and literature classes offered to women in the Boston area

glish; at the age of eight she was reading such works as *Romeo and Juliet;* and during her childhood and her adolescence she read such authors as Henry Fielding and Tobias Smollett, Molière and Cervantes. Under Timothy Fuller's instruction and guidance, Margaret Fuller's intellectual abilities flourished, and by the time of her father's death, when she was twenty-five, she was able to enter nineteenth-century American intellectual life armed with an extensive knowledge of several languages, mathematics, the Bible, English literature, and the works of Thomas Jefferson. Her literary tastes included the Germans, particularly Goethe, and other Continental writers such as Madame de Staël and George Sand. She had no difficulty conversing comfortably with the young Harvard students whom she met at her home in Cambridge, among them James Freeman Clarke and William Henry Channing. So confident was she of her knowledge and of her own intellectual powers, Fuller later asserted to Ralph Waldo Emerson, "I now know all the people worth knowing in America, and I have met no intellect comparable to my own." Although this statement smacks of what Emerson called Fuller's "rather mountainous ME," it was, as Perry Miller has pointed out, probably true.

When her father died in 1835, Fuller became financially and emotionally responsible for her family, a sizeable task since her mother had been totally dependent upon her father and since Fuller was the oldest of six children. In 1836 she took a teaching job in Bronson Alcott's Temple School, where she stayed for several months before moving to Providence, where she taught in Hiram Fuller's (no relation) Greene Street School. Two years later she gave up teaching altogether and moved to Jamaica Plain. While she was living there, she published her translation of Johann Eckermann's *Conversations with Goethe in the Last Years of His Life* (1839) and began her Boston "Conversations." These weekly discussions, attended by the society women of Boston and Cambridge, were so successful that they continued for six years, until 1844. Firmly establishing Fuller's reputation as an intellectual analyst and public speaker, the conversations, which included such figures as Sophia and Elizabeth Peabody, Caroline Healy Dall, Lydia Maria Child, Lydia Emerson, and Elizabeth Bancroft, examined a variety of topics ranging from mythology to fine arts to ethics.

During the period from 1836, when she first met Ralph Waldo Emerson, through 1842, when she left the *Dial,* Fuller was deeply involved with Transcendentalism. In 1837 she joined the Transcendental Club, a group of intellectuals who met informally to discuss philosophical and literary issues, and in 1840 she assumed the editorship of the new Transcendentalist journal, the *Dial.* During her tenure on the *Dial* she was usually responsible not only for editing each volume but also for producing much of the copy. For instance, unable to get as many acceptable submissions as she needed, Fuller herself once wrote 85 of the 136 pages of one issue alone. After two years of sustaining the journal almost singlehandedly, Fuller resigned as editor, but she did continue to submit articles until the *Dial* ceased publication in 1844. During this period also, she was a frequent and welcome visitor at Brook Farm, the associationist experiment begun by George Ripley in 1841. Although she did not believe that the experiment could succeed, Fuller declared that she believed it "an experiment worth trying"–a judgment which could have summed up her experience with Transcendentalism in general.

Her ambivalence toward the Brook Farmers and Transcendentalism was characteristic too of her relationship with Ralph Waldo Emerson. Soon after their initial meeting, she became a frequent guest at the Emerson household, establishing a friendship with Emerson which was to last until Fuller's death. While she apparently felt close enough to Emerson to express affection for his young son Waldo and shared her friend's grief when Waldo died, Fuller was never completely comfortable with Emerson's thinking or his presence. When she had stayed with the Emersons in Concord, she and Emerson were sometimes so uneasy in each other's presence that they could only communicate by notes, which they sent back and forth with young Waldo. In her career as *Dial* editor and later as a columnist for Greeley, Fuller voiced reserved but firm criticisms of Emerson's thinking and his writing.

The nature and variety of the subjects of Fuller's writing during her involvement with the *Dial* reveal both her eclectic tastes and her desire to contribute to the intellectual growth of America. Fuller produced essays and reviews which concerned editorial policy, literature, music, painting, and sculpture. Her statements of editorial policy promised to print all submissions which seemed worthy of attention, even if they were aesthetically flawed. In many more articles–"Goethe," "Menzel's View of Goethe," "Bettine Brentano and Her Friend Günderode," and "Romaic and Rhine Ballads," for instance–she sought to acquaint Americans with those Europeans whose work and thought seemed consistent with American values. Her two general reviews, "Entertainments of the Past Winter" and "A Record of Impressions," reported upon fine arts events in the United States and encouraged Americans to patronize their own artists. In general Fuller's *Dial* work was both far-ranging and ambitious; it was largely impressionistic and theoretical and was intended primarily to spark interest and thought in others.

In her literary criticism, however, Fuller did formulate and apply a consistent theory of literary criticism. Such articles as "A Short Essay on Critics" (1840), which appeared in the very first volume of the *Dial* and "Festus" (1841) constituted her attempt to merge the best points of European common sense philosophy and romantic thought into a critical theory which was both representative of American democratic principles and appropriate for her American audience. "A Short Essay on Critics" argued, like the Scots, that the critic should assert his authority as a guardian of public taste and tolerate no less than the excellent. Like the romantics, she asserted, the critic was a man like any other man except that he was more sensitive than most and was therefore obligated to share his insights with those less sensitive than he. Her examination of Philip James Bailey's *Festus; A Poem* (1839) defined these two critical impulses, showed how they must be combined to produce a proper American criticism and illustrated what she meant when she referred to criticism that was "judicial," "appreciative," or "comprehensive." In this dialogue between two thinkers, Aglauron, like the Scots, feels obligated to render a judicious, objective but somewhat negative evaluation of *Festus*, a moralist version of the Faust legend which underwent radical rewritings during the course of Bailey's career. Laurie, however, like the romantics,

The rural house in Groton, Massachusetts, where Timothy Fuller moved his family in 1832. Margaret Fuller experienced Groton life as banishment from intellectual society.

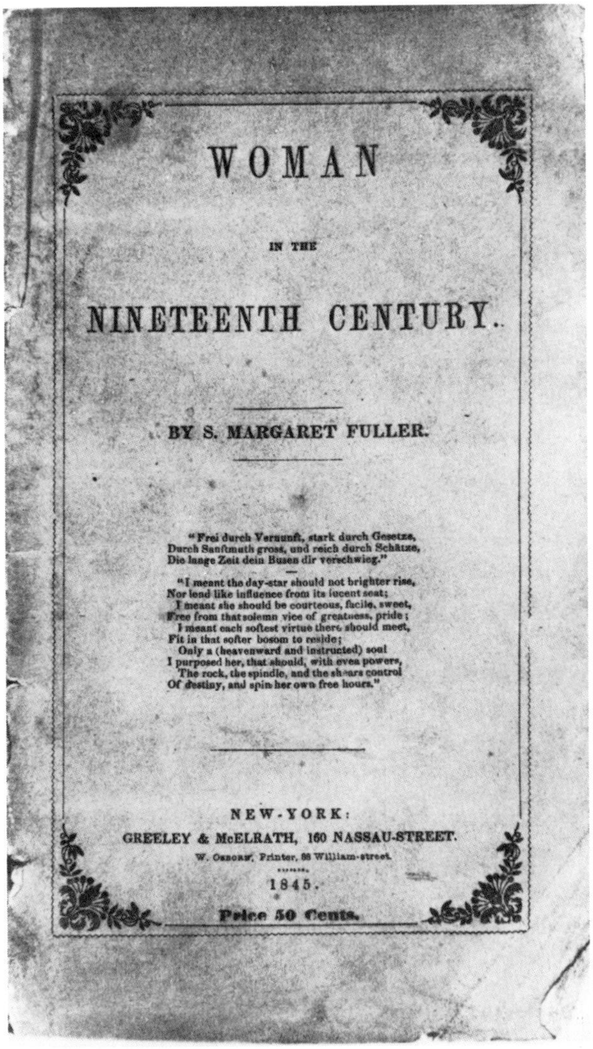

WOMAN
IN THE
NINETEENTH CENTURY.
BY S. MARGARET FULLER.
NEW-YORK:
GREELEY & McELRATH, 160 NASSAU-STREET.
1845.
Price 50 Cents.

Front wrapper for the first printing of Fuller's sociological study advocating women's rights

feels that he must acknowledge the uniqueness of the work and the author's vision. The use of the dialogue form and the thoughtful consensus reached by Aglauron and Laurie demonstrate Fuller's concern with democratic principles. Their admission that their individual approaches have been too narrow and that their combined readings produce a better understanding of the work constitutes what Fuller termed "comprehensive" criticism, a criticism which attempted, by demanding excellence, to cultivate taste in a people more concerned with material than with intellectual matters and, by tolerating sincere but flawed works, to foster native writers and an indigenous literature.

The consistency with which Fuller applied the principles of her critical theory is demonstrated by her practical criticism in the *Dial* and in her correspondence. With a writer of genius such as Goethe, Fuller was the comprehensive critic. Acknowledging his superior artistry and applauding especially his portrayal of women, she nevertheless charged the German writer with settling for too little, with being content to create art and failing to strive for "revelation." With less talented but sincere and worthwhile writers, like Henry Taylor, who wrote *Philip van Artevelde; A Dramatic Romance* (1834), and Bailey, Fuller was a warmly appreciative critic. Admitting that both authors were limited in their abilities, she praised highly the strengths of their works: the creation of Philip van Artevelde, a heroic, worthy figure, and the sincerity and authenticity of vision in *Festus*. With writers she judged deficient, Fuller was sometimes–although not often–an exactingly judicious critic. Finding little to praise in Thoreau's verses, Fuller faulted the poet for his pretentious tone and noted his inability to use metaphor. Similarly her criticism of *Strafford,* an unsuccessful Robert Browning drama produced in 1837, was pointed and exact. In her January 1844 *Dial* article, "The Modern Drama," she objected to Browning's failure to construct rounded, believable characters. Through such practical criticism Fuller demonstrated in the pages of the *Dial* the principles that formed her critical theory.

The years 1843 and 1844 were transitional ones for Margaret Fuller. Accompanied by Sarah Clarke and escorted alternately by Sarah's brothers, James Freeman and William Clarke, Fuller and the Clarkes traveled through the frontier communities of New York, Ohio, Illinois, and Wisconsin. Observing the routine and quality of the life of frontier settlers, Fuller for the first time in her career devoted her attention primarily to realities rather than to ideas and literature. Although she was repelled by the materialism and coarseness of midwestern settlers and although her approach was essentially literary, she tried to understand life on the frontier and to anticipate the type of society which would eventually establish itself on the plains. In particular she shared with the Romantics two prominent concerns: the plight of the Indian and the relationship between man and nature. Returning to New England, Fuller wrote *Summer on the Lakes, in 1843* (1844) and expanded her woman's rights essay, "The Great Lawsuit. Man *versus* Men. Woman *versus* Women," which had appeared in the July 1843

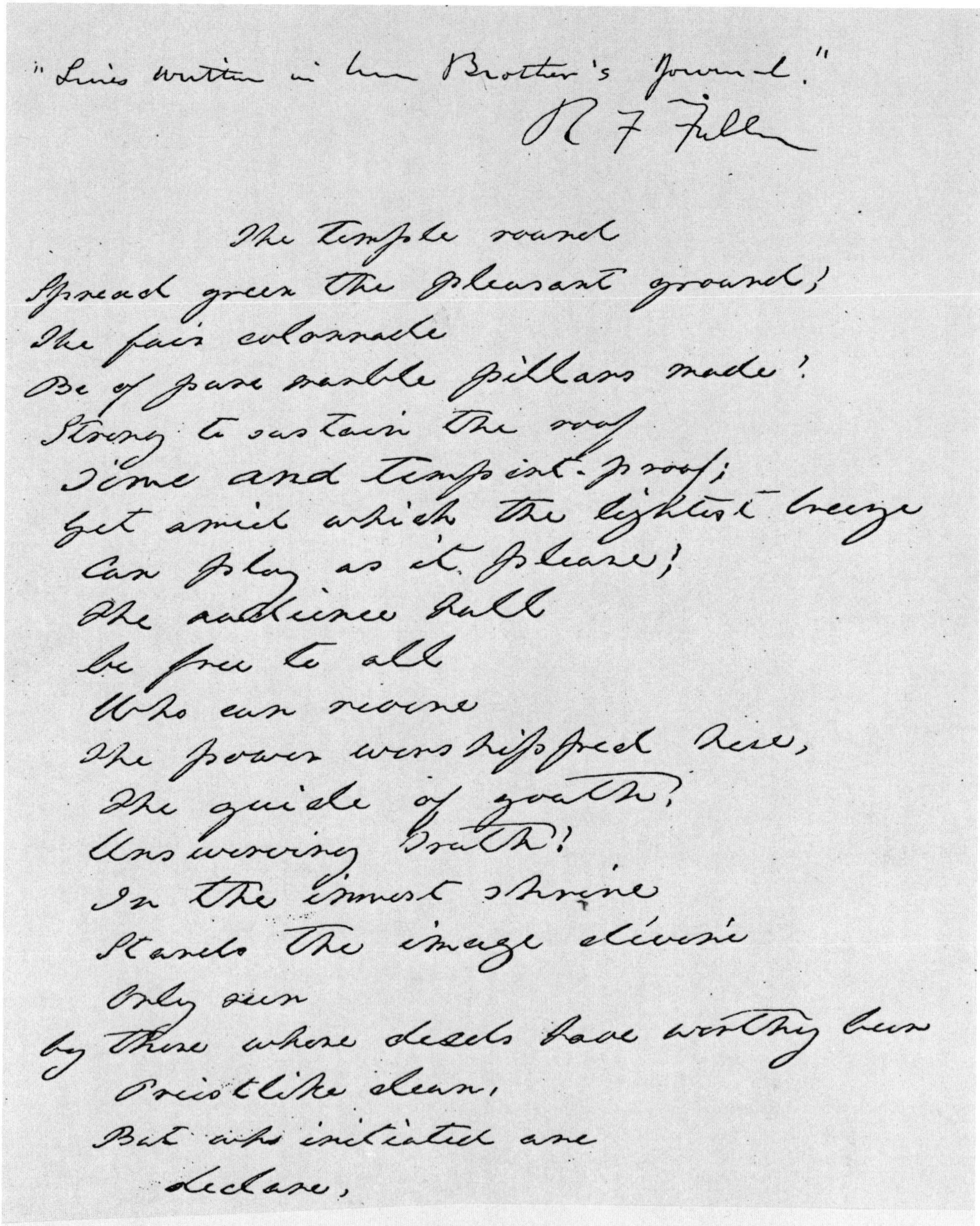
"Lines written in her Brother's Journal."

R F Fuller

The temple round
Spread green the pleasant ground;
The fair colonnade
Be of pure marble pillars made;
Strong to sustain the roof
Time and tempest-proof;
Yet amid which the lightest breeze
Can play as it please;
The audience hall
Be free to all
Who can revere
The power worshipped here,
The guide of youth,
Unswerving truth;
In the inmost shrine
Stands the image divine
Only seen
By those whose deeds have worthy been
Priestlike clean,
But who initiated are
Declare,

Pages Fuller wrote in her brother Robert's journal (from Autograph Leaves of Our Country's Authors, *compiled by Alexander Bliss and J. P. Kennedy, 1864)*

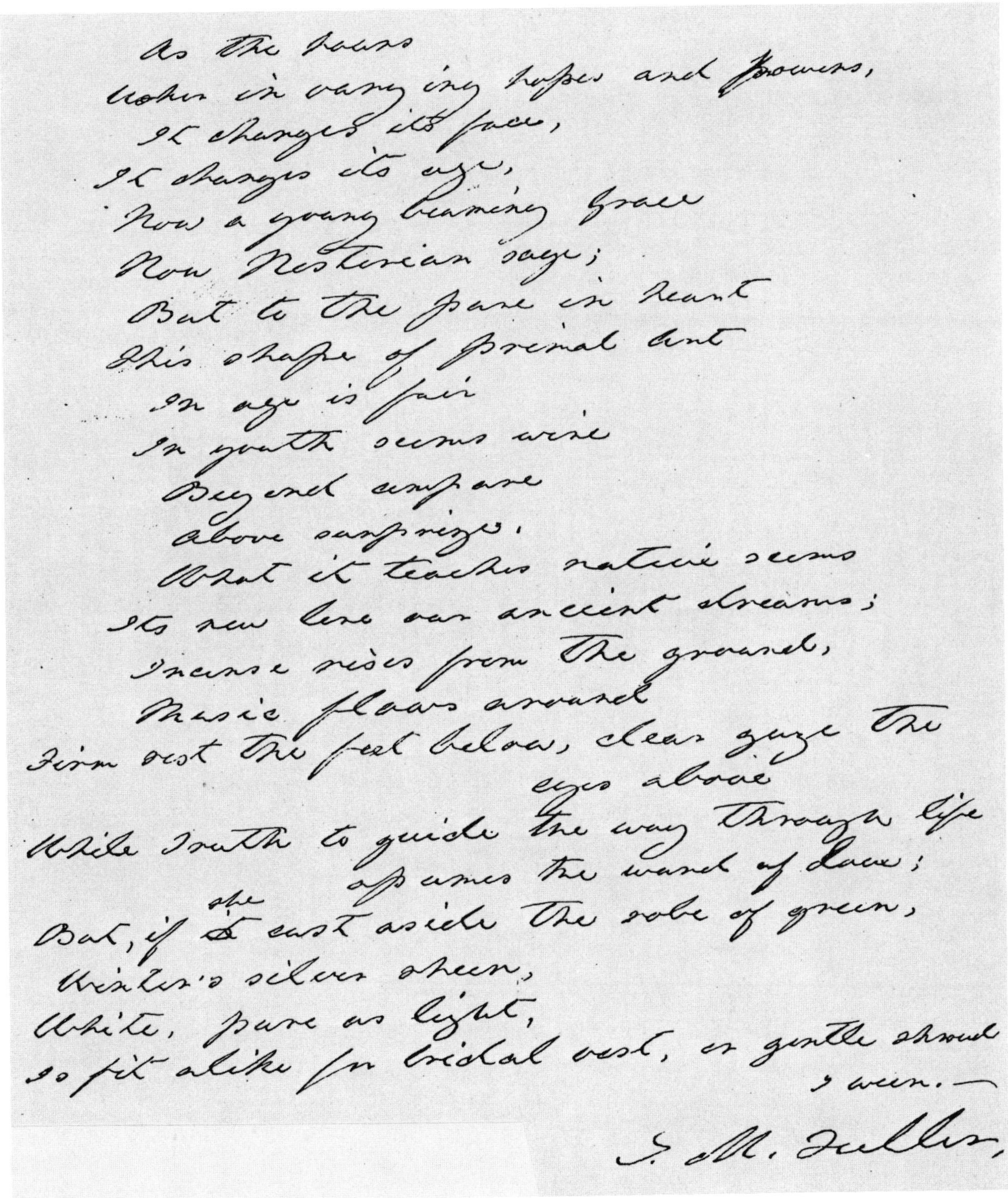
As the hours
Ushers in varying hopes and powers,
It changes its face,
It changes its age,
Now a young beaming grace
Now Nestorian sage;
But to the pure in heart
This shape of primal art
In age is fair
In youth seems wise
Beyond compare
Above surprize.
What it teaches native seems
Its new lore our ancient dreams;
Incense rises from the ground,
Music floats around
Firm rest the feet below, clear gaze the eyes above
While Truth to guide the way through life assumes the wand of Love;
But, if she cast aside the robe of green,
Winter's silver sheen,
White, pure as light,
So fit alike for bridal vest, or gentle shroud I ween.—
S. M. Fuller,

issue of the *Dial,* into a book, *Woman in the Nineteenth Century* (1845).

Although *Summer on the Lakes* and *Woman in the Nineteenth Century* emphasize contemporary issues, they also provide evidence of Fuller's continued reliance upon literary forms and literary concepts. Her vivid and powerful discussion of Niagara in *Summer on the Lakes* marked her attempt to comprehend the relationship between nature and society, a typical romantic theme, and revealed her romantic bias toward nature. In this descriptive section Fuller voiced her concern that human society might impinge upon the majesty of the falls and diminish their impact upon the observer by somehow taming them. In addition Fuller's depiction of Niagara as simultaneously beautiful and terrifying demonstrated another of her romantic interests, the fascination with the sublime. Finally, throughout the rest of the book, Fuller drew upon another literary convention associated with the romantics: the pastoral ideal. In her commentary and in her descriptions of communities which she judged favorably, she stressed the importance of civilization in tempering the wildness of the land.

Woman in the Nineteenth Century was as literary as *Summer on the Lakes,* despite the fact that in it Fuller was attempting to address a very real social problem. Although the book version dealt more specifically with the social disadvantages experienced by women than "The Great Lawsuit. Man *versus* Men. Woman *versus* Women," *Woman in the Nineteenth Century* relied heavily upon the lives of women in fiction rather than upon the actual experiences of real people. In fact Fuller's treatment of fictional women produced a kind of literary criticism. Through her commentary about these characters, she designated the works which she considered the most valuable, and she identified the figures which provided positive role models for real women. Alluding often to figures of Greek mythology, she mentioned Cassandra and Macaria in particular. In Cassandra, who possessed the gift of prophesy but who was herself destined never to be believed, and in Macaria, the daughter of Hercules who sacrificed her life for the good of her country, Fuller found symbols for both the tragedy of women's constricted roles in society and the heroic potential of individual women. Goethe's outstanding female models, she believed, warranted the highest praise. In particular she praised the moral purity and heroism of Margaret in *Faust* (a character who obtained eternal salvation by resisting the power of evil), and she also applauded the qualities of several of the female characters in *Wilhelm Meister's Apprenticeship* and *Wandering Years*–the wisdom and generosity of Natalia, the practicality of Theresa, and the intellect and purity of Makaria. Finally, *Woman in the Nineteenth Century* recommended the works of such female authors as George Sand, Maria Edgeworth, and Mrs. Anna Brownell Jameson–writers who, she felt, had produced insightful books of high moral quality and who therefore demonstrated female potential and provided feminine guidance to their readers. *Woman in the Nineteenth Century* thus used fiction to help order reality.

Impressed by the high caliber of thinking and writing apparent in *Summer on the Lakes* and *Woman in the Nineteenth Century,* Horace Greeley offered Fuller a job as literary critic and social commentator on his *New-York Daily Tribune.* Fuller accepted the position against the advice and wishes of many of her friends, including Emerson. Her move from New England to New York City in 1844 was both the culmination of her summer in the Midwest and the beginning of a new and final phase in her career. Leaving New England and Transcendentalism behind her, Fuller assumed a new life-style in New York City. There, separated from her family, she became truly independent for the first time. With most of her friends left behind in New England, she was free to cultivate new ones, and the responsibilities of her new job forced her to become more engaged with the real world and less concerned with books and theories. Removed from the scrutiny of New England and Emerson, Fuller exercised greater personal freedom; she became romantically involved with James Nathan, and she spent several hundred dollars of her frugal savings to help a Polish writer, Harry Harring, publish his novel. Instead of examining women's lives in mythology and fiction, Fuller began observing the everyday lives of the ordinary, real women around her throughout the city, including the activities of the women inmates of Sing Sing Prison. Instead of speculating about the lot of the poor and the insane, she visited poorhouses and asylums. In short, Fuller's removal from New England to New York was a turning point in her life, resulting from and reinforcing her concern with social reform.

Despite the new focus of Fuller's intellectual life and the social criticism it inspired, she also wrote some of her best literary criticism for the *Daily Tribune*. Essentially, her literary articles of this period fall into two categories: those based upon the critical theory enunciated earlier in the *Dial* and those which conformed to the more general, educational discussions of literature contained in *Summer on the Lakes* and *Woman in the Nineteenth Century*.

In articles about such writers as Elizabeth Barrett Browning, Eugène Sue, and Emerson, Fuller engaged in balanced "comprehensive criticism" which pointed out both qualities and defects. "Miss Barrett's Poems" (1845) praised Barrett Browning's majesty and her poetic vision but noted also her lack of economy and the stiffness of her verse. "French Novelists of the Day" (1845) acknowledged Eugène Sue's commitment to truth but faulted him for allowing his virtuous characters to do evil for the sake of good. Her article "Emerson's Essays" (1844) applauded Emerson's exalted vision and idealism but also criticized his emotional detachment from real life. Her two articles reviewing Longfellow, *The Waif* (1845) and *Poems* (1845), paralleled her earlier treatment of Thoreau in their pointed and concrete analyses. She analyzed at length Longfellow's mixed metaphors, and she deplored his lack of spontaneity and originality.

Writing general commentaries about literature–in the reviews of the *Prose Works of Milton* (October 1845) and the *Poetical Works of Percy Bysshe Shelley* (December 1845), and in "Browning's Poems" (April 1846)–Fuller cited various European authors for their contributions to intellectual history and social development. In Milton, Shelley, Browning, and others, she discovered attitudes and beliefs which she deemed especially important to young America: appreciation of liberty and justice; belief in individualism and democratic principles; and enlightened views on women. These general reviews were motivated primarily by Fuller's interest in public education, for in them she stressed the value of works under discussion as touchstones which would familiarize her audience with sound writing and teach them to judge for themselves.

As she had done in the *Dial*, she also frequently reviewed the work of lesser writers–Caroline Kirkland's novel *Western Clearings* (1845); Lydia H. Sigourney's *Scenes in My Native Land* (1845); Henry R. Schoolcraft's novel *Onéota* (1845); Frederick Douglass's autobiographical *Narrative of the Life of Frederick Douglass* (1845);

Thomas Hicks's portrait of Fuller during the siege of Rome (by permission of the Houghton Library, Harvard University)

and Sylvester Judd's novel *Margaret: A Tale of the Real and Ideal* (1845). In noticing such works as these, Fuller tried simultaneously to encourage American writers and to cultivate in her audience tolerance for the attempts of sincere but merely talented writers.

In August 1846, acknowledging that her twenty months in New York had enriched her far more than twenty years in any other part of the United States could have, Fuller embarked upon a European tour with her Quaker friends, Marcus and Rebecca Spring. In Great Britain Fuller met such prominent writers as Thomas de Quincey, Thomas Carlyle, and William Wordsworth, but she was more interested in political figures like Guiseppe Mazzini, the Italian patriot. In England and in France, she attempted to meet Elizabeth Barrett Browning and to review Rousseau's manuscripts, respectively, but she expended even more energy visiting the industrial districts of various cities. Moved deeply by the poverty of the working classes and by the misery of the women in particular, Fuller became increasingly politically involved, and more sympathetic with radical reform. In Paris she met George Sand, a writer who had always fascinated her. But now she spoke primarily of Sand's life, not her work. The transition complete, from Italy she wrote to Emerson that life itself, rather than art, now preoccupied her.

Italy afforded Fuller a mileau for action, not thought. Deciding soon after she arrived there to stay on by herself instead of to continue the tour with the Springs, she took a young Italian, Giovanni Angelo Ossoli, as her lover. They may have married in December 1847; in 1848 she bore a son, Angelino. At the same time Fuller committed herself wholeheartedly to the Italian revolution, a struggle for self-rule and for independence from foreign powers like Austria and France. In addition to reporting the political developments as directly and straightforwardly as she could, Fuller also began a history of the revolution. Through the dispatches she mailed to the *New-York Daily Tribune,* she attempted to arouse American sympathy for the Italian people. She also contributed to the revolution more directly and more tangibly. When Rome came under siege from French forces, Fuller became "Regolatrice" of the Hospital of the Fate Bene Fratelli and spent days and nights comforting the wounded and dying; after the fall of Rome, she obtained American passports for Mazzini, who had earlier returned home to become one of the Triumvirate which ruled Rome, as well as for some other leaders in the rebellion.

With the fall of Rome, all Fuller's own hopes collapsed. Because of Ossoli's service with the Civic Guard, she and Ossoli had to leave first Rome and eventually Italy itself. Their voyage to America validated Fuller's forebodings and doubts about returning: first, the captain of the ship died of smallpox; then Angelino caught the disease and almost died; finally, the ship was caught in a storm off the New York coast and ran aground at Fire Island. Although some of the crew and passengers were saved, Fuller, Ossoli, and Angelino all perished, and Fuller's manuscript of the history of the Italian revolution was lost.

Despite her deep commitment to social criticism and social reform, Fuller remained a literary critic until her death. Thinking in terms of classical tragedy, just before her death Fuller noted: "My life proceeds as regularly as the fates of a Greek tragedy." Perhaps because of the dramatic quality of Fuller's life, scholars have traditionally

Marchese Giovanni Angelo Ossoli (by permission of the Houghton Library, Harvard University)

been most concerned with biography, a fact attested to by the numerous essays and full-length histories about her life. Recently, however, increased critical interest in Fuller has produced both new editions of her writing and more thoughtful critical assessment of that work.

Letters:

Love-Letters of Margaret Fuller, 1845-1846, introduction by Julia Ward Howe (New York: D. Appleton, 1903; London: T. Fisher Unwin, 1903);

Letters of Margaret Fuller, edited by Robert N. Hudspeth, 4 volumes to date (Ithaca: Cornell University Press, 1983-1987).

Bibliographies:

Joel Myerson, *Margaret Fuller: An Annotated Secondary Bibliography* (New York: Burt Franklin, 1977);

Myerson, *Margaret Fuller: A Descriptive Bibliography* (Pittsburgh: University of Pittsburgh Press, 1978).

Biographies:

Thomas Wentworth Higginson, *Margaret Fuller Ossoli,* American Men of Letters Series (Boston: Houghton Mifflin, 1884);

Joseph Jay Deiss, *The Roman Years of Margaret Fuller* (New York: Crowell, 1969);

Paula Blanchard, *Margaret Fuller: From Transcendentalism to Revolution* (New York: Delacorte/ Seymour Lawrence, 1978).

References:

Margaret Vanderhaar Allen, *The Achievement of Margaret Fuller* (University Park: Pennsylvania State University Press, 1979);

Arthur W. Brown, *Margaret Fuller* (New York: Twayne, 1964);

Caroline Healey Dall, *Margaret and Her Friends* (Boston: Roberts Brothers, 1895);

Karl Knortz, *Brook Farm and Margaret Fuller* (New York: Druck von Hermann Bartsch, 1886);

Joel Myerson, *Critical Essays on Margaret Fuller* (Boston: G. K. Hall, 1980);

Arthur B. Schultz, "Margaret Fuller–Transcendentalist Interpreter of American Literature," *Monatshefte fur Deutschen Unterrecht,* 34 (April 1942): 169-182.

Papers:

Extensive collections of Margaret Fuller's papers are held by the Houghton Library of Harvard University and the Boston Public Library.

Rufus Wilmot Griswold

(13 February 1815-27 August 1857)

Richard J. Calhoun
Clemson University

See also the Griswold entry in *DLB 3, Antebellum Writers in New York and the South.*

SELECTED BOOKS: *The Republican Court or American Society in the Days of Washington* (New York & London: D. Appleton, 1855; revised, New York & London: D. Appleton, 1859);

Washington, A Biography, by Griswold, completed by Benson J. Lossing, 45 parts (New York: Virtue, Emmins, 1856-1860).

OTHER: *The Biographical Annual: Containing Memoirs of Eminent Persons, Recently Deceased,* edited by Griswold (New York: Linen & Fennell, 1841);

Gems from American Female Poets, edited by Griswold (Philadelphia: Hooker, 1842);

The Poets and Poetry of America, with an Historical Introduction, edited by Griswold (Philadelphia: Carey & Hart, 1842; London: Wiley & Putnam, 1842; revised, Philadelphia: Carey & Hart, 1847; revised again, Philadelphia: Carey & Hart, 1850; revised again, Philadelphia: Parry & McMillan, 1855);

Readings in American Poetry, edited by Griswold (New York: Riker, 1843);

"Curiosities of American Literature," in *Curiosities of Literature, and the Literary Character Illustrated,* by Isaac Disraeli (New York: D. Appleton, 1844), pp. 1-63;

Gems from the American Poets, edited by Griswold (Philadelphia: Hooker, 1844);

The Poets and Poetry of England, in the Nineteenth Century, edited by Griswold (Philadelphia: Carey & Hart, 1845);

Poems by Felicia Hemans, edited by Griswold (Philadelphia: Sorin & Ball, 1845);

Prose Works of John Milton, 2 volumes, edited, with a biographical introduction, by Griswold (Philadelphia: Hooker, 1845; London: Wiley & Putnam, 1847);

Scenes in the Life of the Saviour, edited by Griswold (Philadelphia: Lindsay & Blakiston, 1846);

The Prose Writers of America, edited by Griswold (Philadelphia: Carey & Hart, 1847; London: Bentley, 1847);

Washington and the Generals of the American Revolution, 2 volumes, written and edited by Griswold, William Gilmore Simms, E. D. Ingraham, et al. (Philadelphia: Carey & Hart, 1847);

The Sacred Poets of England and America, for Three Centuries, edited by Griswold (New York: D. Appleton, 1849);

The Female Poets of America, edited by Griswold (Philadelphia: Carey & Hart, 1849);

The Works of the Late Edgar Allan Poe, edited by Griswold, 4 volumes: volumes 1-2, *The Works of the Late Edgar Allan Poe: With Notices of His Life and Genius,* edited, with contributions, by Griswold, Nathaniel Parker Willis, and James Russell Lowell (New York: J. S. Redfield, 1850); volume 3, *The Literati: Some Honest Opinions About Autorial Merits and Demerits, with Occasional Words of Personality. Together with Marginalia, Suggestions, and Essays. By Edgar A. Poe . . . with a Sketch of the Author,* edited, with contributions, by Griswold (New York: J. S. Redfield, 1850); volume 4, *The Works of Edgar Allan Poe with a Memoir,* edited, with contributions, by Griswold, Willis, and Lowell (New York: J. S. Redfield, 1856);

"Love Supreme. A Fragment from an Unpublished Story," in *The Knickerbocker Gallery: A Testimonial to the Editor of The Knickerbocker Magazine from Its Contributors* (New York: Samuel Hueston, 1855).

Engraving, based on a portrait by J. B. Read, published in the June 1845 issue of Graham's Magazine

Since Rufus Wilmot Griswold is known chiefly as the infamous literary executor of Edgar Allan Poe and as an anthologist of some good and much bad poetry, his critical views are of interest only to the literary historian. In his own day, he was a prominent figure as an arbiter of literary taste and in a position to affect writers' reputations. Anthologies such as his influential *The Poets and Poetry of America* (1842) were important to aspiring American writers as a means of reaching public attention and of challenging the recognition given English writers. The editors could seldom indulge in critical discrimination, for they were often nationalists interested in promoting a native American literature, and almost anything at hand was made to serve that interest. Criteria for determining what was truly American were broadly construed. In Griswold's judgment the national literature reflected American landscape and democratic sentiments, and was the product, he said, of "an incidental consequence of energetic and well directed action for the moral and spiritual liberation and elevation of man."

Beyond these vague sentiments, it is obvious that Griswold was a political and religious conservative whose tastes prompted him to discount many of his contemporaries. James Russell Lowell was dismissed as a "dreamer" who strove "in vain to make his readers partners in his dreamy, spiritual fancies." Ralph Waldo Emerson might have "a poeticised mind," but his "metrical productions were not very numerous." He found the earlier William Cullen Bryant the kind of poet one should admire and, so, the kind of poet one should publicize. "His works are not only American in their subjects and their imagery but in their spirit and sympathy with mankind."

Griswold's personal life was not an easy one. With fourteen children to care for, the father, a farmer and sometime-tanner, was hard-pressed financially. His mother, Deborah Wass, was a pious woman who encouraged her son to read. Griswold had little formal education. His attendance at Rensselaer School in Troy, New York, ended abruptly in 1830 when he was expelled because of a prank. His subsequent education was informal, as he served a series of apprenticeships to editors of newspapers.

Griswold went to work for his brother, but problems in this relationship soon developed, and he departed for New York City, where he came under the tutelage of George C. Foster, a writer of local color sketches set, for the most part, in New York. Foster undertook the education of his apprentice by lending him copies of his own favorites, mostly romantic poets, and through discussing philosophy and literature with him. In spite of his mentor's preferences for the Romantics, Griswold developed a strong admiration for the older neoclassical writers. When he and Foster split–Griswold preferred more regular habits than his friend was ever able to live by–Griswold supported himself as an itinerant printer in Syracuse. In 1835 he began publishing a paper of his own, the *Porcupine,* in reality more gossip sheet than newspaper. This first effort failed quickly and he moved to Fredonia, New York, to edit the *Western Democratic and Literary Inquirer.* His penchant for controversy–this time, he was involved in a local religious dispute–caused him to be fired after only three weeks. He returned to New York in spring 1835, determined to achieve literary status by seeking out the friendship of influential editors like Horace Greeley. In 1837 he was married, advantageously, to Caroline Searles, after which he affected the most popular demeanor of the day, a Byronic appearance. With the support of his new friend Horace Greeley, Griswold began plans to found a literary magazine, choosing a title that would seem all inclusive by promising something for everyone, the *American Anthology.*

Griswold had chosen the right decade for a magazine, but the wrong year for its financial survival. The Panic of 1837 struck just before his first issue was to appear. It seemed to Griswold that his efforts to become a man of letters were star-crossed. He prepared for an alternative career by studying theology and obtaining a license as a Baptist minister. Some critics have used this aspect of Griswold's career as evidence of his inability to appreciate Poe's darker vision. However, journalism was always his primary interest, and once more he used his friendship with Greeley to get a temporary job in 1838 with the *Vergennes Vermonter.* He shortly left this position because he was unhappy being away from New York, where literary events were taking place and where he thought he might achieve fame.

Portrait of Griswold's first wife, Caroline Searles, probably by Charles Elliot, circa 1840 (from Joy Bayless, Rufus Wilmot Griswold, *1943)*

Returned to New York, Griswold once again found a literary editor who could help him, Park Benjamin. They coedited two papers, *Brother Jonathan* and *Evening Tatler.* Again there was controversy, a quarrel with the publisher that led to resignations, and the two editors joined a daily, the *Evening Signal,* and a weekly, the *New York World.* Arguments followed, and Griswold was forced off both papers. Fortunately the friendly Greeley again came to the rescue of his young protégé, granting Griswold an assistantship until the end of 1840 on his own publication, the *New-Yorker.* When his term expired Griswold moved to Philadelphia, and there his fortunes began to change. While working on the *Philadelphia Daily Standard* he announced plans for *The Poets and Poetry of America.*

Griswold had observed the successes of the nationalistic and liberal Young America group clustered about the Duyckinck brothers and publishing mainly in the *Democratic Review* and the *Literary World.* He decided that the time was ripe for an anthology announcing the arrival of American literature. To his delight nearly all the nation's poets and critics began to court his favor. Although the failure of his newspaper delayed his plans more than a year, and his anthology was not published until 18 April 1842, he had attracted the attention he had always wanted. His reputation was made; the book received three printings during the first year, and revised editions appeared in 1847, 1850, and 1855. In all, the book was destined to pass through twenty editions. The major poets of the day were all there–Emerson, Poe, William Cullen Bryant, Henry Wadsworth Longfellow, James Russell Lowell, and Oliver Wendell Holmes–but many minor poets received more substantial representation. Those poets with influence in New York, where Griswold hoped to get established, received the most substantial representation of all.

In his preface Griswold specifically stated that his chief criterion was inclusiveness and that he had not exercised critical discrimination in determining the book's contents. There is consequently considerable skewing in terms of which poet gets what space. His friend Charles Fenno Hoffman is handsomely represented. While Griswold's selections from Emerson include some of his best poems–"Each and All" and "The Rhodora"–those from Longfellow, whom he admired for "feeling, a rich imagination, and a cultivated taste," included some of his most sentimental–"Rainy Day" and "The Village Blacksmith." Edgar Allan Poe had to talk his way into being included. For all his nationalist sentiment, Griswold did not earn the encomiums of *Democratic Review* and *Literary World* reviewers, who observed that he really did not know what a nationalist literature really implied. Moreover, he clearly failed to comprehend how regionalism made its contribution to the national literature. Poems of William Gilmore Simms, the leading advocate of regionalism, were included, but then Simms was dismissed as "too local."

Griswold's success as anthologist was followed by his best effort as editor. He joined *Graham's Magazine* in May 1842 and quickly se-

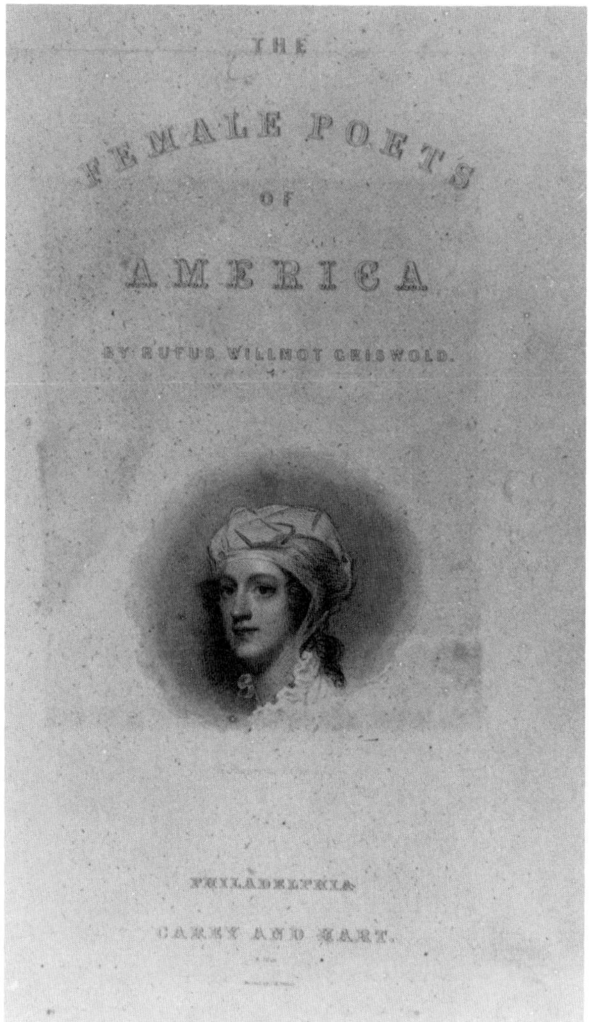

Title page for Griswold's 1849 anthology, which contains the works of ninety-three poets, most of whom were alive when the book was published

cured as contributors Bryant, Holmes, Longfellow, and Nathaniel Hawthorne. At the height of this public success, personal tragedy struck. In November 1842 his wife died, with her infant son, during childbirth. Griswold's behavior was as bizarre and melodramatic as one of Poe's bereaved narrators; he visited her vault in agony to cut off locks of her hair. He turned to work to ease his pain and published *Gems from American Female Poets* (1842). Basically hackwork, the introduction is filled with pious statements about the morality of the American woman and her delicate sensibility, but he shows little understanding of what it might have meant to be a woman poet in nineteenth-century America.

Griswold turned to cashing in on the sentimentality of his day with volumes like *The Poetry of Flowers* (1844) and *The Poetry of the Sentiments* (1845). He also entered the lucrative field of religious gift books with *The Christian's Annual* (1846) and *The Illustrated Book of Christian Ballads and Other Poems* (1844). These endeavors contributed little to his reputation as a critic; even his friends began to complain about his obvious lack of standards as he continued to grind out anthology after anthology. Only one volume added anything positive to his reputation: *The Poets and Poetry of England, in the Nineteenth Century* (1845). Here, as in his similar volume of American poetry, Griswold offered no important discoveries of his own. He cautiously depended on the consensus of critical taste in his day. The book warranted harsh criticism, but his carefully cultivated friendships with such critics as E. P. Whipple helped to moderate critical reaction. Another event also served to mute criticism. An 1845 reviewer in the English periodical *Foreign Quarterly Review* used Griswold's own selections in *The Poets and Poetry of America* as evidence of the poor quality of American literature. To Griswold's fellow editors, this seemed less an attack on him than on the national literary genius, and they rallied to his defense.

He was less fortunate in averting disaster in his private life. In August 1845 he married Charlotte Myers of Charleston, South Carolina, but the marriage ended in separation that same year. He returned to Philadelphia and buried himself in work. A two-volume study of *Washington and the Generals of the American Revolution*, anonymously published in 1847, was written and edited by Griswold, William Gilmore Simms, E. D. Ingraham, and others. He worked out a new formula for self-promotion by using his own anthologies for editorial puffery on the high standing of American literature. An attempt was begun to identify more accurately the important American writers; Hawthorne and Poe were praised for their tales and Emerson for his essays. A showcase for female literature, *The Female Poets of America* (1849), was even by journeymen standards a poor effort.

At this point there began the series of incidents relating to Poe that have affected Griswold scholarship ever since. The two authors had had a falling out when in 1842 Griswold had succeeded Poe at *Graham's Magazine*. Charges were made by one against the other until Poe sought and gained a reconciliation in 1845. The reconciliation lasted about a year, when again there was a falling out. Upon Poe's death, Griswold published an obituary notice, in the 9 October 1849 *New York Tribune*, signed "Ludwig," which criticized Poe's character. At one point Griswold said that Poe was ambitious to succeed so that "he might have the right to despise a world which galled his self-conceit." The notice caused considerable controversy. A number of critics came to Poe's defense, including George R. Graham, owner of *Graham's Magazine*, who deplored the obituary as "ill-judged and misplaced calumny."

Rufus Wilmot Griswold at about age forty, portrait by Kellogg (from Joy Bayless, Rufus Wilmot Griswold, *1943)*

It was against this background that Maria Clemm, Poe's mother-in-law, asked Griswold to edit Poe's works, though apparently not to act as Poe's biographer. The first two volumes of *The Works of the Late Edgar Allan Poe: With Notices of His Life and Genius* (1850) were edited by Griswold and contained remembrances of Poe by Griswold, James Russell Lowell, and Nathaniel Parker Willis. In the third volume of *The Works*, subtitled *The Literati: Some Honest Opinions About Autorial Merits and Demerits, with Occasional Words of Personality. Together with Marginalia, Suggestions, and Essays* (1850), Griswold included his "Memoir of the Author." In this thirty-four page essay, while finding a good deal to praise in Poe's literary works, Griswold attacked and condemned Poe's personal life. His views seem to have been accepted at the time, but opposition began to slowly mount when Graham published a defense of Poe in 1854.

Why Griswold attacked Poe has been variously explained. Clearly it was his intention to rewrite the history of their relationship, even forging documents to make himself look better than he was and Poe, worse. It is possible, as some have suggested, that he resented Poe's apparent squandering of the advantages he enjoyed in his early life, a point he makes in his introductions to Poe in his anthologies. He may simply have resented the fact that Poe had been reared in wealthy circumstances, while he himself had had to struggle throughout his life. Editing the works of the dead poet, he may have taken some satisfaction in melodramatizing Poe's decline while contemplating his own success. The fourth volume of *The Works* was published in 1856, and Griswold's memoir of him was prominently announced in the subtitle.

Griswold, following these unhappy events, continued to edit far too many books and too many magazines. He also sought by every means at his command to persuade his long-estranged wife, Charlotte, to agree to a divorce; he even kidnapped his daughter, Caroline, and held her until Charlotte agreed to free him. The divorce was granted on 18 December 1852, and shortly thereafter he married Harriet McCrillis. Not long after this marriage, Griswold's tubercular condition, diagnosed several years earlier, worsened. He enlarged his *Readings in American Poetry,* and in 1855 published it as *The Knickerbocker Gallery;* the book represented his tribute to the New York writers, especially Lewis Gaylord Clark, who had been his truest friends. *The Republican Court or American Society in the Days of Washington* (1855) drew on over two thousand private letters in his possession to constitute a social history of Washington's presidency. Said by Samuel Osgood to stand "among our important historical monuments," the book still makes for enjoyable reading.

The work that was to displace Griswold as the leading champion and authority of American literature, *The Cyclopedia of American Literature;* was published by the Duyckinck brothers in 1856. The day it was published he gave it a savage review in the *New York Herald.* On 27 August 1857 Griswold died. He left behind a number of unfinished works, including a biography of Washington which was completed by Benson J. Lossing and which was published between 1856 and 1860.

Following Griswold's death, his reputation steadily declined. In the twentieth century his name once again began to appear, mostly in reference to the critical rehabilitation of Poe. Critical opinion does not entirely relegate him to playing his version of Salieri to Poe's Mozart, yet he is known more for his treatment of Poe than for the anthologies he published, the role he aspired to play as man of letters, and the reputation he felt he had earned as a publicist of American literature.

Letters:

Passages from the Correspondence and Other Papers of Rufus W. Griswold, edited by William H. Griswold (Cambridge: W. M. Griswold, 1898).

References:

Joy Bayless, *Rufus Wilmot Griswold, Poe's Literary Executor* (Nashville: Vanderbilt University Press, 1943);

Jacob Neu, "Rufus Wilmot Griswold," *University of Texas Studies in English,* no. 5 (1925).

Papers:

The Griswold papers are housed in the Boston Public Library. Some materials may be found among the J. T. Fields Papers at the Henry E. Huntington Library.

Frederic Henry Hedge

(12 December 1805-21 August 1890)

Guy R. Woodall
Tennessee Technological University

See also the Hedge entry in *DLB 1, The American Renaissance in New England.*

SELECTED BOOKS: *A Sermon Preached Before the Ancient and Honorable Artillery Company, on Their CXCVIth Anniversary, June 2, 1834* (Boston: J. H. Eastburn, 1834);

An Introductory Lecture Delivered at the Opening of the Bangor Lyceum, Nov. 15th, 1836 (Bangor: Nourse & Smith and Duren & Thatcher, 1836);

A Discourse on the Death of William Henry Harrison, Ninth President of the United States. Delivered Before the Independent Congregational Society, on the Day of the National Fast, May 14, 1841 (Bangor: Samuel S. Smith, 1841);

A Sermon on the Character and Ministry of the Late Rev. William Ellery Channing, D.D. Preached in the Independent Congregational Church, Bangor, at the Annual Thanksgiving, November 17th, 1842 (Bangor: Samuel S. Smith, 1842);

Conservatism and Reform. An Oration Pronounced Before the Pecunian Society, Bowdoin College, September 5, 1843 (Boston: Little, Brown, 1843);

Christianity Confined to No Sect. A Sermon Preached at the Dedication of the Church, Presented to the Town of Stetson, by the Hon. Amasa Stetson of Dorchester, Mass. February 22, 1844 (Bangor: Samuel S. Smith, 1844);

Gospel Invitations (Boston: Crosby, Nichols, 1846);

An Address Delivered Before the Graduating Class of the Divinity School in Cambridge, July 15, 1849 (Cambridge: John Bartlett, 1849);

A Sermon Preached to the Independent Congregational Society, March 3d, 1850, by Frederic H. Hedge, on Closing His Pastoral Connexion with that Society (Bangor: Samuel S. Smith, 1850);

Conscience and the State. A Discourse, Preached in the Westminster Church, Providence, Sunday April 27, 1851 (Providence: Joseph Knowles, 1851);

Seventeen Hundred Fifty-eight and Eighteen Hundred Fifty-eight. A New Year's Discourse, Preached at Brookline, on the First Sunday in January, 1858 (Boston: Phillips, Sampson, 1858);

Frederic Henry Hedge

Oration Delivered at the Schiller Festivity on the 10th of November, 1859, in the Boston Music Hall (Boston: H. Vossnack, 1859);

The National Weakness: A Discourse Delivered in the First Church, Brookline, on Fast Day, Sept. 26, 1861 (Boston: Walker, Wise, 1861);

The Sick Woman. A Sermon for the Time (Boston: Prentiss & Deland, 1863);

The National Entail. A Sermon Preached to the First Congregational Church in Brookline, on the 3d

July, 1864 (Boston: Wright & Potter, 1864);
Discourse on Edward Everett, Delivered in the Church of the First Parish, Brookline, on the Twenty-second, January (Boston: George C. Rand & Avery, 1865);
Reason in Religion (Boston: Walker, Fuller, 1865);
Memoir of Nathaniel Langdon Frothingham, D.D. (Boston: John Wilson, 1870);
The Primeval World of Hebrew Tradition (Boston: Roberts Brothers, 1870);
Shall the Nation, by a Change in Its Constitution, Proclaim Itself Christian? A Sermon Preached to the First Parish in Brookline, on February 25, 1872 (Cambridge: John Wilson, 1872);
German Prepositions (Cambridge: Charles W. Sever, 1875);
Ways of the Spirit, and Other Essays (Boston: Roberts Brothers, 1877);
Theological Progress During the Last Half Century. A Sermon (Providence, 1878);
Atheism in Philosophy, and Other Essays (Boston: Roberts Brothers, 1884);
Hours with German Classics (Boston: Roberts Brothers, 1886);
Personality and Theism. Two Essays (Cambridge: John Wilson, 1887);
Martin Luther and Other Essays (Boston: Roberts Brothers, 1888);
Metrical Translations and Poems, by Hedge and Annis Lee Wister (Boston & New York: Houghton, Mifflin, 1888);
Sermons (Boston: Roberts Brothers, 1891).

OTHER: *The Prose Writers of Germany,* translated by Hedge (Philadelphia: Carey & Hart, 1848);
Hymns for the Church of Christ, edited by Hedge and Frederic D. Huntington (Boston: Crosby, Nichols, 1853).

PERIODICAL PUBLICATIONS: Review of *Biographia Literaria, The Poetical Works of S. T. Coleridge, Aids to Reflection . . . ,* and *The Friend,* by Samuel Taylor Coleridge, *Christian Examiner,* 14 (March 1833): 108-129;
Review of *The Life of Friedrich Schiller,* by Thomas Carlyle, *Christian Examiner,* 16 (July 1834): 365-392;
Review of *Writings of Ralph Waldo Emerson, Christian Examiner,* 38 (January 1845): 87-106;
"Natural Religion," *Christian Examiner,* 52 (January 1852): 117-136;
Review of *The Life and Works of Goethe,* by G. H. Lewes, *North American Review,* 82 (April 1856): 564-568;
Review of *Pre-Raffaellitism; or, A Popular Inquiry into some Newly Asserted Principles Connected with the Philosophy, Poetry, Religion, and Revolution of Art,* by Edward Young, *Christian Examiner,* 63 (September 1857): 290-291;
"The Broad Church," *Christian Examiner,* 69 (July 1860): 53-66;
Review of *Elsie Venner: A Romance of Destiny,* by Oliver Wendell Holmes, *Christian Examiner,* 70 (May 1861): 459-462;
"University Reform," *Atlantic Monthly,* 18 (September 1866): 296-307;
"Characteristics of Genius," *Atlantic Monthly,* 21 (February 1868): 150-159;
"Irony," *Atlantic Monthly,* 24 (October 1870): 414-424;
"The Idealist and the Realist," *Unitarian Review,* 9 (March 1878): 320-328;
Review of *A Short History of German Literature,* by James Kendall Hosmer, *Unitarian Review,* 11 (March 1879): 248-253;
"The Steps of Beauty," *Unitarian Review,* 18 (December 1882): 481-493;
"Classic and Romantic," *Atlantic Monthly,* 57 (March 1886): 309-316;
Review of *A Memoir of Ralph Waldo Emerson,* by James Elliot Cabot, *Unitarian Review,* 28 (November 1887): 416-425;
"Nature: A Problem," *Unitarian Review,* 29 (March 1888): 193-197.

Frederic Henry Hedge was a highly respected Unitarian clergyman and theologian, German scholar and translator, university professor, editor, critic, and prolific author of essays and books. Born in Cambridge, Massachusetts, to Levi and Mary Kneeland Hedge, he was early destined to eminence as a scholar and man of letters by the strong encouragement of his father, a respected professor of logic at Harvard College. Hedge became in his career the foremost German scholar and pioneer in introducing and popularizing German language and literature in America. His achievements as an author, editor, critic, and lecturer won him the highest admiration of his contemporaries. Concurrent with his literary activities, he became the leading spokesman, in the world of liberal Christianity, on ecclesiastical and theological matters.

As a youth Hedge was precocious, mastering much of the classics, especially Homer and Virgil, before his teens. To prepare his thirteen-year-old son for college, Levi Hedge sent him to Germany in June 1818 under the care of future historian George Bancroft, himself only eighteen years old. While Bancroft pursued his own studies, he placed his young charge in the gymnasia at Göttingen, Ilfeld, and Schulpforta, and monitored his progress. Hedge's first German experience gave him a thorough knowledge of the language and an acquaintance with the literature and initiated him into the realm of German idealism, then little known in America.

Hedge returned from Germany in late 1822, entered Harvard College with advanced standing, and graduated in 1825 in a class with, among others, Horatio Greenough, George Partridge Bradford, Caleb Stetson, Edward Emerson, and George Ripley. As an undergraduate he distinguished himself as a poet, writing, among other pieces, the commencement poem "Ruins of the East," which was well received. He never lost his interest in poetry, writing original pieces from time to time and translating many from the German. He composed poems for his fortieth and fiftieth class reunions. Upon graduation he declined an offer by Harvard president John Thornton Kirkland to become an instructor in German, choosing instead to study theology. He graduated in 1828 from Divinity School in a class that included George Partridge Bradford, Samuel Kirkland Lothrop, and John Sibley. They all remained lifelong friends. One of the most enduring friendships that he formed in his Harvard years was with Ralph Waldo Emerson.

Title page for Hedge's 1848 translations of works by selected German writers, such as Martin Luther, Immanuel Kant, Johann Wolfgang Goethe, and Novalis

Following his graduation, he was ordained as pastor of the Unitarian church at West Cambridge (now Arlington) and conducted a successful ministry there until 1835. At West Cambridge he established a solid reputation as an author of scholarly essays. Fame first came with an article on Samuel Taylor Coleridge and the German philosophers in the *Christian Examiner* in March 1833. Upon reading the essay, the Rev. Henry Ware, Jr., one of Hedge's former divinity professors, praised the effort, telling Hedge: "The manliness, fairmindedness, discrimination of the criticism, and the truly English style are worthy of all consideration;–and as you are but a young author you will allow me to step out thus a little abruptly to congratulate you on your beginning and bid you go and prosper." And prosper he did, steadily publishing critical essays, sermons, translations, and books. He furnished five articles for the *Christian Examiner* between March 1833 and November 1834 alone. Eventually he wrote thirty-six articles for this review, and during his life about one hundred essays and books of varying lengths. After reading Hedge's article on Coleridge and the German philosophers, and a second one in November 1833 on Emanuel Swedenborg, in the *Examiner,* Emerson wrote his brother Edward on 22 December 1833: "Henry Hedge is an unfolding man, who has just written the best pieces that have appeared in the Examiner; one was a living, leaping Logos, & he may help me."

In his first *Examiner* article, a review of Coleridge's *Biographia Literaria* and other works, the best introduction in America to date on the major German philosophers, Hedge praised Coleridge as a thinker and translator and analyzed the philosophers Immanuel Kant, Johann Gottlieb Fichte, and Friedrich Wilhelm Joseph von Schelling. By confirming the intuitive epistemology of the Germans, his article supported George Ripley and the Transcendentalists in their debate with Andrews Norton's attack on German idealism and the Transcendentalists in his "The Latest Form of Infidelity" in 1839. Hedge's first major review of German literature, however, was that of Thomas Carlyle's *Life of Friedrich Schiller* (1825) in the *Examiner* in July 1834. This warm review was more of an analysis of Schiller's works than a critical treatment of Carlyle's writing and scholarship.

In his essays on Coleridge and Schiller Hedge discussed some principles by which lyric poetry should be measured. In the Coleridge article, for example, he enunciated two characteristics of genius to be used in judgment: "originality," also called "poetic feeling"; and "form," also called "a well-proportioned whole" or "unity of design and totality of effect." He found "poetic feeling" or "originality" in abundance in Coleridge, but found nothing in "form" or "unity of design and totality of effect." In his review of Thomas Carlyle's biography of Schiller, for another example, he ranked the German author highly as a lyric poet but said that he lacked the proper qualification of the best lyric poet: "the mobility and universality of feeling–the heart's ready sympathy with every thought or image which the fancy may suggest." These were traits he found to be remarkable in Robert Burns and William Wordsworth. Close to these precepts for judging poetry are those that he elucidated in later years in his "Characteristics of Genius" (1868): originality and a sense of proportion that balance the mind between the poles of the imagination and reflection. It was an imbalance between imagination and understanding, between the poetical and the practical, for which Hedge faulted Emerson in his review of *Writings of Ralph Waldo Emerson* (1845), noting that while Emerson had the "intellectual qualifications of a great poet;–eye, imagination, language, 'the vision and the faculty divine,' " he failed to be great due to "a defect of temperament–an excess of purely intellectual life." Hedge stated that for "a poet, there must be a certain proportion between feeling and intellect, between the sentimental and the sciential. Excess of one makes the enthusiast; excess of the other, the philosopher. The poet occupies the middle stratum of humanity, combining the two. . . ." He concluded that "with a little more activity of feeling, and a little less activity of speculation, Mr. Emerson would have made a first-rate poet."

Prompted by a large salary increase, Hedge moved to Bangor, Maine, in May 1835 to become pastor of the Independent Congregational (Unitarian) Society. To one of Hedge's intellectual tastes and scholarly habits, the move to remote Bangor was tantamount to an exile; but, despite his isolation from the more desirable cultural conditions of Boston and Cambridge, he had a fruitful, although often troubled, ministry of fifteen years at Bangor. One notable cultural and intellectual tie that he maintained for a few years after moving to Bangor was with the Transcendental Club, which he and some of his friends, mostly young liberal Unitarian ministers, had founded in September 1835. The group met informally by invitation at the homes of the members in and around Boston to discuss subjects of current interest in theology, art, literature, and philosophy. Since the Transcendental Club often met when Hedge was back in the area visiting, it was sometimes called "Hedge's Club." Some of Hedge's scholarly intimates in the Transcendental Club were Emerson, Ripley, Caleb Stetson, James Freeman Clarke, Amos Bronson Alcott, Convers Francis, Theodore Parker, and Margaret Fuller. Hedge was the principal and enthusiastic advocate of and specialist in German metaphysical thought and belles lettres among the Transcendentalists and did most to encourage the members in German studies. While philosophically a liberal, Hedge was theologically a moderate or an "enlightened conservative," as he called himself. After his move to Bangor his interest in Transcendental reform in the Unitarian church waned, and he distanced himself increasingly from the radical thinking of Emerson, Parker, and Alcott, who repudiated historical Christianity.

As early as 1835 Hedge suggested that the Transcendentalists start their own literary journal; but by the time that such an organ, the *Dial*, was born a few years later, he had lost his zeal for the project. Not wishing to be stigmatized as a Transcendentalist by the conservative Unitarians in Bangor or Boston, he never fully supported the *Dial*. In fact he contributed to it only one original article, "The Art of Life,–The Scholar's Calling" (October 1840), in which he advocated cultural self-development, which he saw represented in the life of Goethe. He contributed as well one original poem, "Questionings" (January 1841), and two translations.

Hedge remained throughout the years a friend to those in the Transcendental Club, but being more conservative than they, Francis and Stetson excepted, he continued to differ with them in theological matters. His conservative position was well formed by the time that he delivered his Phi Beta Kappa oration, "Conservatism and Reform," at Harvard in 1841, in which he pleaded for an "enlightened conservatism." He held that the current Transcendental philosophy being debated was neither the panacea that its advocates suggested nor the evil force its enemies claimed. Emerson was not favorably impressed with the Phi Beta Kappa oration, Margaret Fuller only moderately so, but Convers Francis and others liked it. In 1843 Hedge repeated the address at Bowdoin College, after which it was printed. Writing in the *Christian Examiner* in 1867, he reflected on his early association with the Transcendentalists and why he drifted away from their way of thinking:

> For myself, though I hugely enjoyed the sessions, and shared many of the ideas that ruled the conclave, and the ferment they engendered, I had no beliefs in ecclesiastical revolutions to be accomplished with set purpose; and I seemed to discern a power and a meaning in the old, which the more impassioned would not allow. I had even then made up my mind that the method of revolution in theology is not dissension but development. My historical conscience, then as since, balanced my neology and kept me ecclesiastically conservative, though intellectually radical. . . .

During his later years at Bangor, Hedge prepared his historically important *The Prose Writers of Germany* (1848), his translations of essays by twenty-eight German authors, for which he prepared biographical and critical introductions. Luther, Gotthold Ephraim Lessing, Christoph Martin Wieland, Johann Gottfried von Herder, and Goethe were among those praised for their style. Jakob Böhme, Immanuel Kant, Johann Gottlieb Fichte, Friedrich Wilhelm Joseph von Schelling, and Georg Wilhelm Friedrich Hegel were among the philosophers represented with original essays on their positions. Always his favorite, Goethe was given more attention than any other of the writers. He was praised for his genius, style, devotion to truth, and moral character. Hedge's praise of Goethe contrasted with most criticism of the time which condemned him for his immorality and pernicious influence. Hedge's primacy as a German scholar was firmly established by favorable critical reception of *The Prose Writers of Germany*.

At Bangor Hedge devoted a great deal of time to translating German poetry, especially lyrics and ballads. Many of his translations appeared in the *New England Magazine, Boston Quarterly Review,* and the *Christian Examiner*; but from time to time he incorporated his earlier translations and new ones into collections such as George Ripley's *Specimens of Foreign Literature* (1839); *Schiller's Song of the Bell, A New Translation, by W. H. Furness, with Poems and Ballads from Goethe, Schiller and Others, by F. H. Hedge* (1850); and *Gems of German Verse, by W. H. Furness* (1860).

Frederic Henry Hedge (courtesy of the Unitarian-Universalist Association)

Some of the poems he translated were Goethe's *Geistgruss* and passages from *Faust, The Erlking, Primeval Words-Orphic, To a Golden Heart, The Fisher,* and *The Singer*; Karl Theodor Körner's *Lützow's Wild Chase*; Johann Ludwig Uhland's *The Dream*; and Luther's *Ein fest Berg.*

In June 1847 Hedge made his second trip to Europe. Bearing a letter of introduction from Emerson, in which he was called "a chief supporter of the good causes of letters in this country," he met Carlyle whom he had long admired. Leaving England, he traveled through Belgium, Germany, and Italy, writing travel letters back for publication in the *Christian Register* and the Bangor *Daily Whig.* He returned home in the summer of 1848 with his thinking on German literature and thought greatly matured. In Bangor he resumed his pastoral duties and literary activities. His trip, however, intensified his desire to leave Maine for a more promising social and intellectual climate. For a long time his friends had attempted without success to help him locate a pastorate in the Boston area, but an opportunity to improve his situation came when he was called to become pastor of the Westminster Congregational Society in Providence, Rhode Island, in 1850. Here he labored happily until he was called in 1857 to become pastor of the First Parish Unitarian Church in Brookline, Massachusetts.

Since Hedge had always been able to join felicitously his clerical and literary activities, he was a popular choice to become the editor of the prestigious *Christian Examiner* in 1857. On 16 May 1858 he wrote to his friend Henry W. Bellows of his aspirations for the journal and of his role as editor:

> I have endeavored to make it a condign organ for the best thought of the country and to attract the best thinkers to it by giving them the assurance of good company. We have certainly had some excellent articles, and in the *résumé* of current literature we excell, I think, all American Periodicals. I take very little credit to myself for all this. My work has been merely to organize the journal, to lay down the paradigm, and to exercise a negative control, keeping out and staving off, as well as I could, the crude stuff and multitudinous inanity that seeks admission into every periodical, appealing to editorial good nature. My hardest labor has been reading foul mss. and saying no! to people whom I wish to oblige. One weak and puerile (or puellile; or anile) article does a journal more harm than two good articles can neutralize. This is what I fear is going to ruin the Atlantic Monthly, or at least to prevent it from realizing the expectations of its best friends.

Hedge conducted the *Examiner* with distinction until 1861. He succeeded as an editor because he was as liberal spirited as it was possible for him to be, siding with no one faction in the Unitarian church and dogmatizing about no one philosophical system.

His new situations as pastor at Brookline and editor of the *Christian Examiner* enabled Hedge to devote more time to writing critical essays. His substantial thought on aesthetics and literary criticism appeared for the most part in essays and book reviews in the *Christian Examiner,* the *North American Review,* the *Atlantic Monthly,* and the *Unitarian Review.* Hedge was always positive and constructive in his criticism, never hesitating to cite errors and controvert points with which he did not agree. The genial tone of his criticism, however, was such that he never seems to have offended even such close friends as Emerson, Holmes, and Lowell, whose works he sometimes faulted. He could have been characterizing himself when he said in his review of Edward Young's *Pre-Raffaellitism* (1857) that the essential qualifications of a critic are "calmness, candor, tolerance, and simple love of truth." His taste was for both foreign and domestic poetry, biography, history, and literary and philosophical prose. He did not identify himself with any one school of criticism, but he was strongly influenced by the romantic impulse that pervaded Europe and America in the first half of the nineteenth century. Throughout his essays there are references to and ideas drawn from, among many other literary commentators, the Scottish aestheticians and critics Archibald Alison and Dugald Stewart; the Germans Kant, the Schlegels, Goethe, and Schiller; and the English Coleridge and Thomas de Quincey, to name only a few.

He measured his literary judgments by both classical and romantic standards, depending upon the work being considered, but he favored the romantic. In his essay "Classic and Romantic" (1886), he found the essence of romance (which he called "modern literature") to be "mystery" or that which is a little beyond the world of the phenomenal; and he found classicism (which he called "ancient literature") to be "a clear, unimpassioned, impartial presentation of subject matter, without color or comment." Neither the romantic nor the classic style, he held, could be, in the abstract and on universal grounds, better than the other. The classic may be better for historical subjects, but the romantic, better for poetry that looks inward and has sentimental intensity and subjective coloring. But, he concluded, both romantic and classic qualities are necessary to produce a masterpiece of literary art: "Classicism gives perfection of form, but romanticism fills the spirit." The element of mystery that Hedge saw as a primary quality of romance caused him to appreciate irony in the literature of the ages. In his 1870 essay on the subject he stated that the essence of irony is "something behind" or "a spirit of meaning, not wholly expressed in the literal sense of writing." The Bible he found to be replete with irony, but among the literary giants, Milton's and Goethe's works possess the most subtle form of it.

The notion of truth as the element necessary to make a poem or any literary work an organic whole and to produce a totality of effect, is most fully argued by Hedge in his essay "The Steps of Beauty" (1882), his one extended excursion into aesthetics. He takes issue with Kant's assertion that rules established by critics cannot improve the taste of people and help them find delight. He also dissents from Kant's idea, expressed in his *Kritik der Untheilskraft Analytik der Erhaben* (1790), that man is interested in beauty only in a social setting, not in a personal one. Hedge affirms that the sense of beauty is innate in every man, alone or in society: "The sense of beauty is wanting in none, but no faculty is less perfect by nature. The germ only is given, the rest is discipline." The grades or modes of beauty are five: color, form, expression, thought, and action. Hedge pleads that the beauty of action is superior to art, which is merely phenomenal, but he allows that the beauty of literary art, founded in truth, is truly great:

> The beauty of expression is the highest beauty which matter takes on. To rise above this, we must leave the realm of the material and enter the realm of thought, specifically of literary art. Here beauty meets us at the vestiture of truth. Analyze the pleasure derived from a beautiful poem, or any work of high literary art, and you will find that a feeling of truth expressed in these productions is its chief indispensable ingredient. A perfect poem is truth throughout. There must be truth in motive, it must harmonize with the moral sense; truth in the plan, every part of which must agree with the aim; truth in the imagery, which must be faithful to external nature, and finally truth in language, which must express the ideas it is meant to convey.

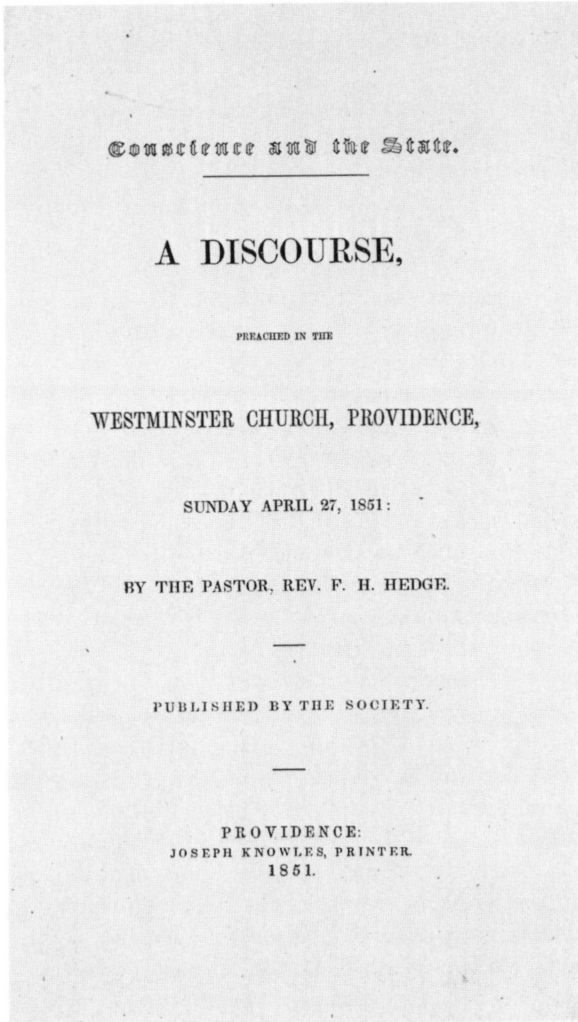
Conscience and the State.

A DISCOURSE,

PREACHED IN THE

WESTMINSTER CHURCH, PROVIDENCE,

SUNDAY APRIL 27, 1851:

BY THE PASTOR, REV. F. H. HEDGE.

PUBLISHED BY THE SOCIETY.

PROVIDENCE:
JOSEPH KNOWLES, PRINTER.
1851.

Title page for a sermon Hedge preached during the year after his return to the Boston area from Maine (collection of Joel Myerson)

Hedge was not particularly fond of novels and critiqued only a few of them, but in the ones that he did evaluate, realism was the primary ingredient he demanded for judging an effort successful. In a review of Oliver Wendell Holmes's *Elsie Venner: A Romance of Destiny* (1861), he applauded the author's realism in the use of genuine native American incidents, characters, costumes, and setting with "homely New England names and associations." He chided Holmes for his patronizing and unsympathetic attitude toward the common, everyday people in the novel, and for what he found to be Holmes's obtrusive didacticism.

In the dissemination of ideas, Hedge's accomplishments as a lecturer complemented his endeavors as an author. The record of his speaking engagements and the many public addresses that he left in print attest to his popularity as a platform speaker. He delivered a highly successful course of literary lectures before the Boston Society for the Diffusion of Useful Knowledge and other lyceum groups in 1841 on "The Philosophy of Literature" and "Shakespeare." He delivered another series, "Medieval History," before the Lowell Institute in 1852, and a major address in Boston on 10 November 1859, on the one hundredth anniversary of Friedrich Schiller's birth. He gave another important address in July 1866; in "University Reform," delivered before Harvard alumni, he expressed his progressive ideas on higher education, advocating fewer compulsory courses and more electives for students. He recommended that the classics and mathematics be required for admission of freshmen only, and that undergraduates be encouraged to pursue studies in modern literature, science, philosophy, and history. Inspiration especially, not coercion, should be emphasized in the instructional process. Hedge made subsequent major addresses before a gathering of German people in Boston on 3 December 1870 and on 12 April 1877 before the distinguished Goethe Club of New York. His last important public discourse was on "Luther and his Work," delivered before the Massachusetts Historical Society on 10 November 1883.

During his tenure as pastor at Providence (1850-1856) and at Brookline (1857-1859), Hedge rose to prominence in the religious world. Harvard recognized his importance as an ecclesiastical scholar by conferring upon him an honorary degree of doctor of divinity in 1852. His influence and standing in religious circles were further enhanced in 1857 when he was appointed to the chair of ecclesiastical history at Harvard. He was president of the American Unitarian Association from 1859 to 1862. Unitarian historians have said that Hedge, more than any other man, gave Unitarianism a "consistent philosophy and theology." Cyrus A. Bartol, himself a respected churchman, placed Hedge in the pantheon of Unitarian ministers: "As a preacher we put Dr. Hedge in line with the greatest of the liberal faith, Channing and Dewey, Walker and Parker and how many besides."

After Hedge's resignation at Brookline, he was appointed in 1872 to a professorship in German at Harvard, a position he held until 1881. Following his retirement, he devoted most of his time to German scholarship and theological essays. In 1882 he collaborated in publishing an American edition of *Faust*. In *Hours with the German Classics* (1886) he traced, in a series of essays, the growth and development of interest in German literature in England and America. In this examination of the major works in German literature he gave for the first time a systematic treatment of German literature by an American. *Hours with the German Classics* perhaps did more than any previous book to encourage a study of German literature in America. In 1875 he published *German Prepositions*, said by many scholars of the time to be a very useful book. *Martin Luther and Other Essays* (1888) was his last major collection, containing previously published essays on Luther, Kant, and Count Zinzendorf, his "Classic and Romantic," and others.

Hedge's greatest achievement in literary scholarship was his introduction of the works and thought of major German writers to America in the nineteenth century. More than any other of the handful of first generation American scholars who had studied in Germany, he dispelled ignorance of the German language, philosophy, and literature. He has, with justification, been called "the patriarch of German study in America." In literary editing and criticism he exercised a positive and salutary influence in directing America toward a more appreciative and liberal criticism. He made a great impact as a theologian and a philosopher, particularly in espousing ecumenicism and a socially oriented gospel. In a review of his final volume of essays, the writer spoke for many when he lauded Hedge as an impartial ecclesiastical scholar: "First as a scholar, none in our land is more fully or accurately informed.... the beam of his eminently judicial mind in all matters of dogmatic dispute hangs as impartial as the constellation Libra in the sky. He is as just to the other party as his own." On his eightieth birthday, in December 1885, Hedge was honored by his friends with a testimonial dinner at the Parker House Hotel in Boston at which he was praised in poems, testimonial letters, and speeches by a host of scholars that included James Russell Lowell, James Freeman Clarke, Edward Everett Hale, William Henry Furness, Oliver Wendell Holmes, Christopher P. Cranch, and John W. Chadwick. A year later Harvard recognized his services to scholarship by awarding him the degree of doctor of law.

Biography:

Orie W. Long, *Frederic Henry Hedge: A Cosmopolitan Scholar* (Portland, Maine: Southworth-Anthoensen Press, 1940).

References:

Peter King Carley, "The Early Life and Thought of Frederick [*sic*] Henry Hedge: 1805-1850," Ph.D. dissertation, Syracuse University, 1973;

Doreen Hunter, "Frederic Henry Hedge, What Say You?," *American Quarterly,* 32 (Summer 1980): 186-201;

Bryan F. LeBeau, "Frederic Henry Hedge: Portrait of an Enlightened Conservative," Ph.D. dissertation, New York University, 1982;

Leonard Neufeldt, "Frederic Henry Hedge," *The Transcendentalists: A Review of Research and Criticism,* edited by Joel Myerson (New York: Modern Language Association, 1984): 189-194;

Joel Myerson, "Frederic Henry Hedge and the Failure of Transcendentalism," *Harvard Library Bulletin,* 23 (October 1975): 396-410;

Ronald Vale Wells, *Three Christian Transcendentalists: James Marsh, Caleb Sprague Henry, and Frederic Henry Hedge* (New York: Columbia University Press, 1943);

George H. Williams, *Rethinking the Unitarian Relationship with Protestantism: An Examination of the Thought of Frederic Henry Hedge (1805-1890)* (Boston: Beacon Press, 1949).

Papers:

Hedge's correspondence and miscellaneous documents may be found in at least thirty different libraries and depositories, but the largest collections are at the Bangor Historical Society; the Andover-Harvard Theological Library and Houghton Library at Harvard University; and the Schlesinger Library, Radcliffe College.

Richard Hildreth

(28 June 1807-11 July 1865)

John W. Rathbun
California State University, Los Angeles

See also the Hildreth entries in *DLB 1, The American Renaissance in New England* and *DLB 30, American Historians, 1607-1865.*

SELECTED BOOKS: *An Abridged History of the United States of America. For the Use of Schools. Intended as a Sequel to Hildreth's View of the United States,* as Hosea Hildreth (Boston: Carter, Hendee & Babcock, 1831);

The Slave: or Memoirs of Archy Moore, 2 volumes, anonymous (Boston: J. H. Eastburn, 1836); expanded as *The White Slave; or, Memoirs of a Fugitive* (Boston: Tappan & Whittemore/ Milwaukee: Rood & Whittemore, 1852; London: Routledge, 1852);

The History of Banks: To Which Is Added, A Demonstration of the Advantages and Necessity of Free Competition in the Business of Banking (Boston: Hilliard, Gray, 1837; London: J. S. Hodson, 1837); revised and enlarged as *Banks, Banking, and Paper Currencies* (Boston: Whipple & Damrell, 1840);

The People's Presidential Candidate; or The Life of William Henry Harrison, of Ohio (Boston: Weeks, Jordan, 1839);

The Contrast: or William Henry Harrison versus Martin Van Buren (Boston: Weeks, Jordan, 1840);

A Letter to Andrews Norton on Miracles as a Foundation of Religious Faith (Boston: Weeks, Jordan, 1840);

Despotism in America; or an Inquiry into the Nature and Results of the Slave-Holding System in the United States . . . , anonymous (Boston: Whipple & Damrell, 1840); revised and enlarged as *Despotism in America: An Inquiry into the Nature, Results, and Legal Basis of the Slave-Holding System in the United States* (Boston: John P. Jewett/Cleveland: Jewett, Proctor & Worthington, 1854; Boston: J. P. Jewett/ New York: Sheldon, Lamport & Blakeman, 1854; London: Low, 1854);

Theory of Morals: An Inquiry Concerning the Law of Moral Distinctions and the Variations and Contradictions of Ethical Codes (Boston: Little, Brown, 1844);

Portrait of Richard Hildreth, painted by Robert M. Pratt in 1858 (by permission of the New-York Historical Society)

Native-Americanism Detected and Exposed. By a Native American (Boston: Printed for the author, 1845);

A Joint Letter to Orestes A. Brownson and the Editor of the North American Review: In Which the Editor of the North American Review is Proved to Be No Christian, and Little Better than an Atheist (Boston, 1845);

The Truth Revealed. Statement and Review of the Whole Case of the Reverend Joy H. Fairchild, from its Commencement to its Termination, Compiled from Original Documents by a Member of the Suffolk Bar, anonymous (Boston: Wright's Steam Press, 1845);

"Our First Men:" A Calendar of Wealth, Fashion and Gentility, Containing a List of Those Persons Taxed in the City of Boston, Credibly Reported to

Be Worth One Hundred Thousand Dollars, with Biographical Notices of the Principal Persons, anonymous (Boston: Published by all the Booksellers, 1846);

The History of the United States of America, from the Discovery of the Continent to the Organization of Government under the Federal Constitution, 3 volumes (New York: Harper, 1849); revised as volumes 1-3 of *The History of the United States of America;*

The History of the United States of America, from the Adoption of the Federal Constitution to the End of the Sixteenth Congress, 1788-1821, 3 volumes (New York: Harper, 1851-1852); revised as volumes 4-6 of *The History of the United States of America;*

Theory of Politics: An Inquiry into the Foundations of Governments, and the Causes and Progress of Political Revolutions (New York: Harper, 1853);

Japan as It Was and Is (Boston: Phillips, Sampson/ New York: J. C. Derby, 1855); revised as *Japan and the Japanese* (Boston: Bradley, Dayton, 1860);

The History of the United States of America, 6 volumes (New York: Harper, 1856-1860).

OTHER: Jeremy Bentham, *Theory of Legislation,* translated from French by Hildreth (Boston: Weeks, Jordan, 1840).

PERIODICAL PUBLICATIONS: "Novels and Novel Reading," *Ladies Magazine,* 1 (April 1828): 145-147;

"The Republic of Letters," *American Monthly Magazine,* 1 (April 1829): 16-24;

"Homer," *American Monthly Magazine,* 1 (June 1829): 164-173;

"Shakespeare," *American Monthly Magazine,* 1 (July 1829): 264-274;

"National Literature," *American Monthly Magazine,* 1 (September 1829): 379-385;

Review of *Dermont MacMorrogh,* by John Quincey Adams, *New England Magazine,* 3 (December 1832): 503-507.

Richard Hildreth's literary criticism was written early in his career and over a brief period of time. It had little if any impact upon the theory and practice of his contemporaries, and today it is of interest chiefly to the literary historian. His taste molded by his reading in English authors of the eighteenth century and by classical training in Greek and Roman literature, Hildreth was one of a minor band of critics who persisted in invoking older standards of taste and craftsmanship at a time when romanticism was promising to win the day. A bit of a loner, his criticism constitutes a series of opposing opinions to tendencies that he did not like. There is thus a surface asperity to the criticism which deepened as he increasingly engaged the social issues of his day. His critical opinions were sharply defined. He affirmed universality of taste, the rule of intelligence, native good judgment, grace and clarity, the importance of tradition. These values prompted him to resist what he took to be literary fashion. He especially disliked romantic egoism and that form of romantic "enthusiasm" which embraced subjective inspiration.

Given the extraordinary range of his interests it is understandable that Hildreth's involvement with literature would be brief. He was at once a practicing journalist, a pamphleteer for reform causes, a militant Utilitarian, and an important historian of the early years of the republic. On almost all counts he was in opposition to the main drifts of his time and therefore never really caught on with his contemporaries, a fact that seems to have fueled an already engrained willfulness and tactlessness. He was a formidable partisan upholder of causes, trenchant in argument, and leanly caustic in tone. The partisanship earned him few friends. His biography reveals an immense aloneness. William Dean Howells visited him in Trieste shortly before his death. Absorbed in *Paradise Lost,* Hildreth refused to play the host. "Then he rose to go to bed. Would not he bid his parting guest good-bye? The idea of farewell perhaps dimly penetrated to him. He responded without looking round,

> 'They hand in hand, with wandering steps and slow,
>
> Through Eden took their solitary way.'

and so left the room."

Hildreth was born in Deerfield, Massachusetts, the son of the Reverend Hosea and Sarah McLeod Hildreth. His father was a Congregationalist minister who taught mathematics at Phillips Exeter Academy, a school that Richard attended. Upon graduating from Harvard in 1826 he studied law and was admitted to the bar in Suffolk County in 1830. During this period he wrote virtually all of his critical articles that deal with literature.

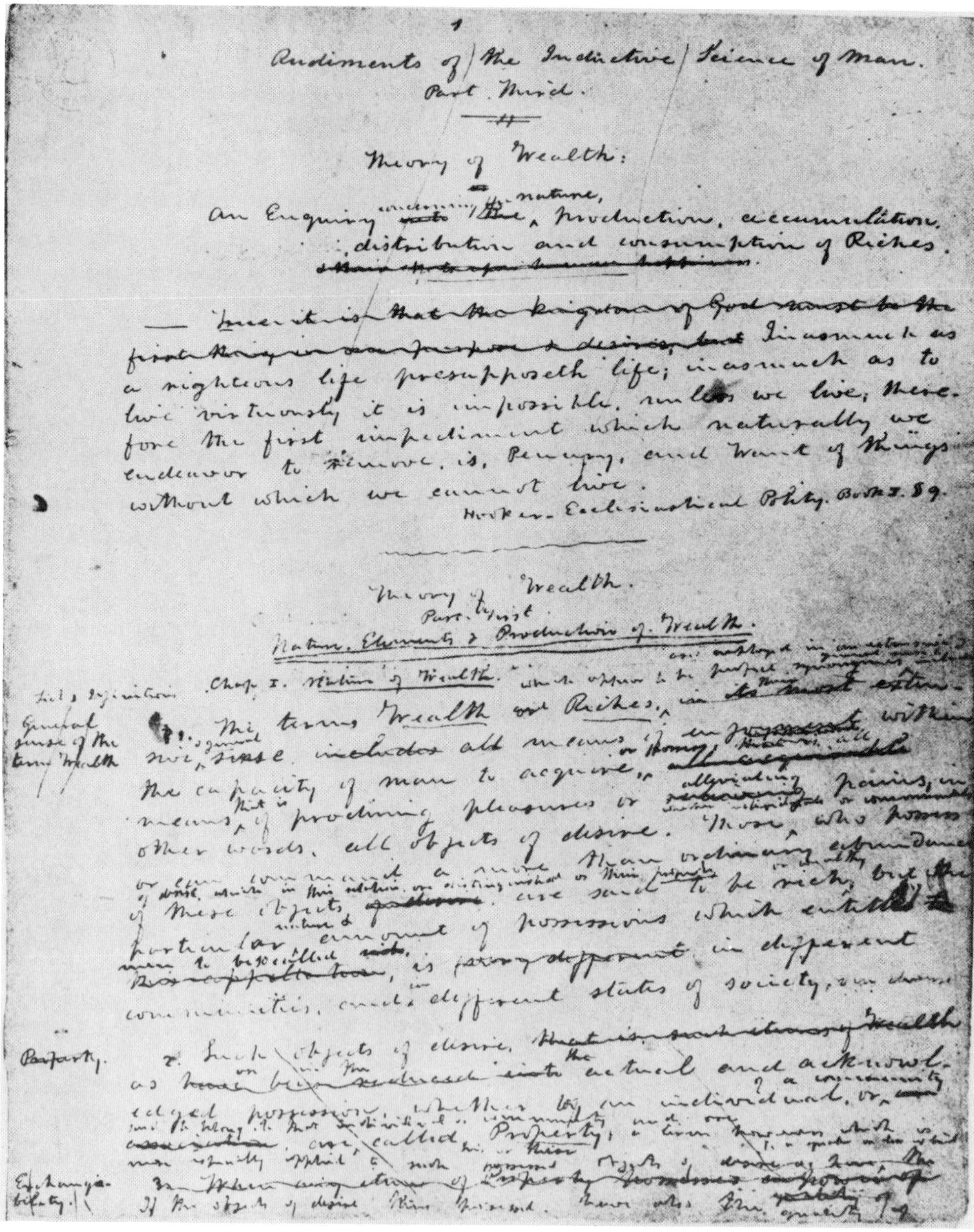
Rudiments of the Inductive Science of Man.
Part Third.

Theory of Wealth:

An Enquiry concerning the nature, production, accumulation, distribution and consumption of Riches.

— Inasmuch as a righteous life presupposeth life; inasmuch as to live virtuously it is impossible unless we live; therefore the first impediment which naturally we endeavor to remove, is, Penury, and Want of things without which we cannot live.
Hooker. Ecclesiastical Polity. Book I. 89.

Theory of Wealth.
Part First
Nature, Elements & Production of Wealth.

Chap. I. Nature of Wealth.

Page from the manuscript for "Theory of Wealth," Hildreth's uncompleted essay which he used as a basis for Theory of Politics (Martha M. Pingel, An American Utilitarian, 1948)

His first published critical piece is on the reading of novels. Noting that early suspicion of the form had yielded to its tremendous popularity with the reading public, Hildreth embraces the shift in attitude. His reason is practical. If education fails to correct the moral obliquity of man, banning novels will not improve the situation. The sensualist will find his excitement in any case, while the "modest" will emerge unscathed no matter what the activity. Besides, one could not attach much importance to novels. Temperately indulged in, a novel is a sort of "mental cordial" much superior to actual tippling as a means of relaxation. As the form has established itself, novels increasingly reveal "some taste and more imagination," but basically they are for the "generality of men" for whom the "higher poets" are beyond range and the "cool element of prose" therefore more attractive. For these readers the novel is a source of "innocent gratification." Restricted to the mundane description of "daily conduct," the novel's chief objective is to describe and document the familiar activities of "domestic and social life," though it can on occasion stir the "higher" passions and emotions.

In 1829 Hildreth published four articles in the *American Monthly Magazine* that reflect his critical values and his view of literary history. The first, "The Republic of Letters," presents one of those overviews so popular with nineteenth-century writers. He identifies three eras of literary history that rose in response to the peculiar circumstances of their origins: the fashionable patronage of poets in times when the diffusion of learning is very small; the aristocratic refinement of language attendant upon the rise of literate classes; and the decline of taste and judgment as literacy becomes universal and the reading public

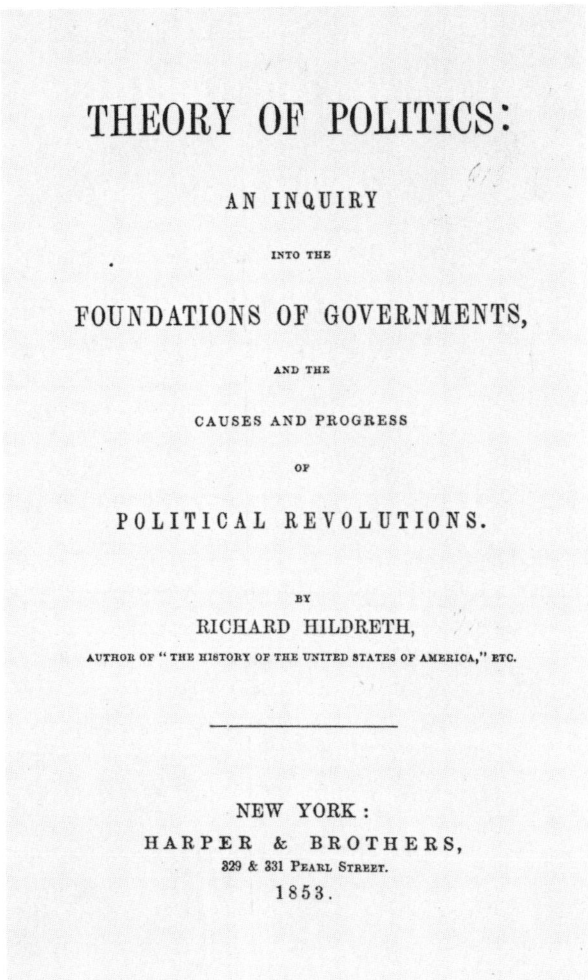

THEORY OF POLITICS:

AN INQUIRY

INTO THE

FOUNDATIONS OF GOVERNMENTS,

AND THE

CAUSES AND PROGRESS

OF

POLITICAL REVOLUTIONS.

BY

RICHARD HILDRETH,

AUTHOR OF "THE HISTORY OF THE UNITED STATES OF AMERICA," ETC.

NEW YORK:

HARPER & BROTHERS,

329 & 331 PEARL STREET.

1853.

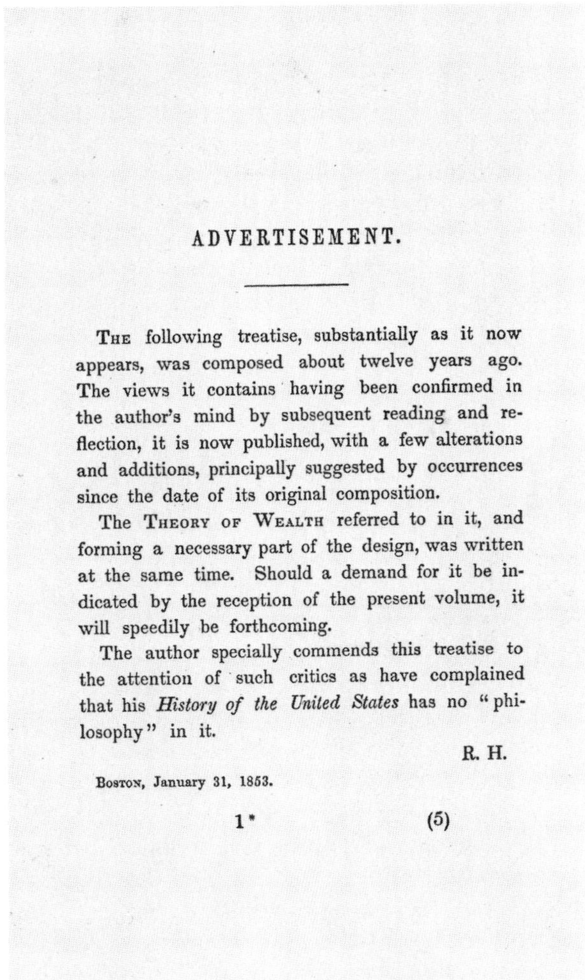

ADVERTISEMENT.

THE following treatise, substantially as it now appears, was composed about twelve years ago. The views it contains having been confirmed in the author's mind by subsequent reading and reflection, it is now published, with a few alterations and additions, principally suggested by occurrences since the date of its original composition.

The THEORY OF WEALTH referred to in it, and forming a necessary part of the design, was written at the same time. Should a demand for it be indicated by the reception of the present volume, it will speedily be forthcoming.

The author specially commends this treatise to the attention of such critics as have complained that his *History of the United States* has no "philosophy" in it.

R. H.

BOSTON, January 31, 1853.

1* (5)

Title page and advertisement written by Hildreth for his 1853 treatise in which he employed scientific terms to discuss politics

insatiable in its demands. The first, a period which Hildreth loosely connects to the European Renaissance, is marked by excitement, vaulting imagination, and poetry whose quality is intense and keen. The second is a period of refined taste characterized by a turn to prose. In place of enthusiasm and rapture, one now finds simplicity, elegance, force. There is a noticeable leaning to skepticism, and everything is critically analyzed. Taste is cultivated and cosmopolitan, judgment is disciplined, reason is dispassionate, and imagination is controlled.

The third era Hildreth equates with his own period. The picture he draws is slightly ambiguous. A universal diffusion of knowledge makes for the "happiest consequences," for everyone reads and the general level of the culture is raised. Magazines and newspapers abound, the "fair sex" joins the "literary fraternity" and begins to play its moderating role, and everyone travels the "turnpike roads to Parnassus." The new taste for reading, a consequence of newly acquired leisure, converts sitting rooms into reading rooms. With everyone so busily engaged, the "higher ranks" of society are challenged and strive even harder to keep their intellectual edge. But as might be anticipated, there is a flip side to the coin. There is some reason to fear, says Hildreth, "that a universal taste for letters may have for its companion a universal mediocrity of genius." And so the writers are the ones to mainly suffer. With literary success easy to attain, there are few willing to drudge out the time erasing, blotting, revising, and laboring to perfect a text. In place of a *Faerie Queene,* an *Amelia,* a *Spectator,* or a history like David Hume's, all of the "first rank," readers are treated to the presumptuous self-assertions of a Wordsworth and a Byron, and those in texts so unintelligible that they cannot be understood.

Given this view of the contemporary situation of literature, readers can anticipate that Hildreth would cock a wry eye at calls for a native American literature, and he did. He admits that all nations have their literatures, but to equate a national literature with a national character is to oversimplify radically and misread a complex issue. To Hildreth national character is simply a cover term for the subjectively peculiar passions and humors of the masses of a people; it can fluctuate widely, can reveal all manners of caprice, and can revel in commonplaces that border on absurdity. This popular will does have its

Hildreth's gravestone in Florence, Italy

literature, but the literature itself, like the popular will, is limited, local, and transient. To call, then, for a literature based on "American peculiarities" and "domestic topics" is to replace the traditional criteria for serious literature with criteria that mislead writers into submission to the popular will. They echo and re-echo its platitudes and lose their independence.

The *real* writer transcends the national character, and in the process it is he who contributes to the formation of a national literature. Popular literature is evanescent, national literature enduring. Popular literature reflects the popular will, national literature reflects the universal reason. National literature is thus "the embodied fancy and reason of a chosen few, raised by nature, or elevated by their own strenuous exertions above the vulgar level." These members of a cultural elite are animated by a vision of the beautiful rather than a wish for popular favor. They see the beautiful as universal as reason itself, and collectively they constitute a cosmopolitan class committed to an international heritage of good taste and enlightened learning.

Hildreth's views of individual writers are in

the same vein of eighteenth-century critical taste. Alexander Pope is praised for his "swan-like flights" and the "liquid harmony" of his measures, while his detractors are labeled "the insects of literature." Homer is the supreme master, wise in the "science of human nature," excellent in invention, powerful in delineating character, unchallenged in the scope of his enterprise. Shakespeare is the flawed genius, full of bombast, exaggeration, conceits, and other sins against the universality of taste. Yet he reads human nature correctly and draws directly from it. The style can move from "arrant nonsense" to sublimity; his sense of rhyme is far from infallible, but the prose is "pure" and "idiomatic," and in blank verse he is superior even to Milton. Above all, there is the "compass and variety" of his depiction of human life. "Not dazzled by its splendor, nor disgusted by its meanness, calm and unmoved, he seems to contemplate all its mingled contradictions, with the impartiality of one who feels himself much above it."

After an inconsequential but devastating review of John Quincey Adams's *Dermont MacMorrogh* (1832), larded with irony, Hildreth moved to other fields. In 1832 he turned to journalism as one of the founding members of the *Boston Daily Atlas*. It was the first of many editorial obligations that he would undertake. Eighteen thirty-four through 1836 found him in Florida in an effort to cope with serious health problems. There his abolitionist sentiments were sharpened by what he saw of the horrors of slavery. That experience led to his writing of *The Slave: or Memoirs of Archy Moore* (1836), the earliest of the antislavery novels. Not well written, it was nevertheless popular and went through a number of editions. Following his stay in Florida he spent a half-year, 1837-1838, in Washington as a correspondent for the *Atlas*, but a dispute over editorial policy prompted him to resign. It was probably a good move, for he had become increasingly issue-oriented, and over the next few years pamphleteered on behalf of abolition, temperance, Utilitarian views on economics, and the Whig party. *Despotism in America* (1840) was an especially hard-hitting attack on slavery, which he enlarged in an 1854 reprint.

Still plagued with ill health, Hildreth moved to Demarara, British Guiana, where he lived from 1840 to 1843, meanwhile editing two local journals, the *Chronicle* and *Royal Gazette*, and pursuing his writing. He compiled a work on colonial laws, supported local abolition efforts, and wrote the drafts of two important books: *Theory of Morals* (1844) and *Theory of Politics* (1853). The books were projected as part of a larger series addressed to an inductive investigation of important subjects. Their failure to earn much of an audience discouraged him from continuing studies on wealth, taste, knowledge, and education.

Richard Hildreth (from Second Publication of the Hildreth Family Association, *1922)*

Returned to the United States, he married Caroline Neagus in June 1844, and he began writing his six-volume *The History of the United States of America*. It is marked by rigorous attention to the accurate and dispassionate presentation of factual material, this at a time when "philosophical" history was very much the rage. The work has been faulted for stylistic dullness and a dry tone, but paradoxically its survival powers have been better than the more popular histories of his contemporaries.

A work on Japan, later expanded, constitutes his last major work. In poor health and financially strapped, the intervention of friends prompted Lincoln to appoint him United States Consul at Trieste in 1861. He remained at the post until deteriorating health forced him to resign. He died in 1865 and was buried in the Protestant cemetery in Florence, Italy, not far from the grave of Theodore Parker.

References:

Joseph L. Blau, *Social Theories of Jacksonian Democracy* (New York: Liberal Arts Press, 1954);

Donald E. Emerson, "Hildreth, Draper, and 'Scientific History,' " in *Historiography and Urbanization: Essays in American History in Honor of W. Stull Holt,* edited by Eric Goldman (Baltimore: Johns Hopkins Press, 1941), pp. 139-170;

Emerson, *Richard Hildreth* (Baltimore: Johns Hopkins Press, 1946);

Louis S. Friedland, "Richard Hildreth's Minor Works," *Papers of the Bibliographical Society of America,* 40 (1946): 127-150;

Alfred H. Kelly, "Richard Hildreth," in *The Marcus W. Jernegan Essays in American Historiography,* edited by William T. Hutchinson (Chicago: University of Chicago Press, 1937), pp. 25-42;

Martha Pingel, *An American Utilitarian: Richard Hildreth as a Philosopher* (New York: Columbia University Press, 1948);

Arthur M. Schlesinger, Jr., "The Problem of Richard Hildreth," *New England Quarterly,* 13 (June 1940): 223-245.

Papers:

Although there is no central repository of Hildreth papers, the Harvard University Archives has a few items. Scattered letters can be found in the Jared Sparks, Charles Sumner, and William Dean Howells papers at Harvard, and the Edward Everett and John A. Andrew papers at the Massachusetts Historical Society.

Washington Irving

(3 April 1783-28 November 1859)

David W. Pancost
Gallaudet University

See also the Irving entries in *DLB 3, Antebellum Writers in New York and the South, DLB 11, American Humorists, 1800-1950,* and *DLB 30, American Historians, 1607-1865.*

SELECTED BOOKS: *Salmagundi; or, the Whim-Whams and Opinions of Launcelot Langstaff, Esq. & Others,* by Irving, William Irving, and James Kirke Paulding, 20 parts, published in 2 volumes (New York: Printed and published by D. Longworth, 1807-1808; London: Printed for J. M. Richardson, 1811; revised edition, New York: D. Longworth, 1814; revised by Irving, Paris: Galignani, 1824; Paris: Baudry, 1824);

A History of New York, from the Beginning of the World to the End of the Dutch Dynasty. Containing Among many Surprising and Curious Matters, the Unutterable Ponderings of Walter the Doubter, the Disastrous Projects of William the Testy, and the Chivalric Achievements of Peter the Headstrong, the three Dutch Governors of New Amsterdam; being the only Authentic History of the Times that ever hath been, or ever will be Published, as Diedrich Knickerbocker, 2 volumes (New York & Philadelphia: Inskeep & Bradford/Boston: M'Ilhenney/Baltimore: Coale & Thomas/Charleston: Morford, Willington, 1809; revised edition, New York & Philadelphia: Inskeep & Bradford, 1812; London: Murray, 1820); republished as volume 1 of *The Works of Washington Irving* (New York & London: Putnam's, 1848; revised again, 2 volumes, New York: Printed for the Grolier Club, 1886);

The Sketch Book of Geoffrey Crayon, Gent., as Geoffrey Crayon, 7 parts (New York: Printed by C. S. Van Winkle, 1819-1820); revised edition, 2 volumes (volume 1, London: John Miller, 1820; volume 2, London: Murray, 1820; revised edition, Paris: Baudry & Didot, 1823); republished as volume 2 of *The Works of Washington Irving* (New York & London: Putnam's, 1848);

Washington Irving, 1809; engraving by John de la Mare from a portrait by John Wesley Jarvis

Bracebridge Hall, or the Humourists. A Medley, as Geoffrey Crayon, 2 volumes (New York: Printed by C. S. Van Winkle, 1822; London: Murray, 1822); republished as volume 6 of *The Works of Washington Irving* (New York & London: Putnam's, 1849);

Letters of Jonathan Oldstyle, Gent., as The Author of *The Sketch Book* (New York: Clayton, 1824; London: Wilson, 1824);

Tales of a Traveller, as Geoffrey Crayon, 2 volumes (London: Murray, 1824; abridged edition, Philadelphia: Carey & Lea, 1824; unabridged edition, New York: Printed by C. S. Van Winkle, 1825); republished as volume 7 of *The Works of Washington Irving* (New York & London: Putnam's, 1849);

The Miscellaneous Works of Oliver Goldsmith, with an Account of His Life and Writings, 4 volumes (Paris: Galignani/Didot, 1825); biography revised in *The Life of Oliver Goldsmith, with Selections from His Writings,* 2 volumes (New York: Harper, 1840); biography revised and enlarged as *Oliver Goldsmith: A Biography,* volume 11 of *The Works of Washington Irving* (New York: Putnam's, 1849; London: John Murray, 1849);

A History of the Life and Voyages of Christopher Columbus (4 volumes, London: Murray, 1828; 3 volumes, New York: G. & C. Carvill, 1828; revised, 2 volumes, 1831); republished in *The Life and Voyages of Christopher Columbus; to Which Are Added Those of His Companions,* volumes 3-5 of *The Works of Washington Irving* (New York & London: Putnam's, 1848-1849);

A Chronicle of the Conquest of Granada, as Fray Antonio Agapida, 2 volumes (Philadelphia: Carey, Lea & Carey, 1829; London: Murray, 1829); republished as volume 14 of *The Works of Washington Irving* (New York: Putnam's/London: Murray, 1850);

Voyages and Discoveries of the Companions of Columbus (London: Murray, 1831; Philadelphia: Carey & Lea, 1831); republished in *The Life and Voyages of Christopher Columbus; to Which Are Added Those of His Companions,* volumes 3-5 of *The Works of Washington Irving* (New York & London: Putnam's, 1848-1849);

The Alhambra, as Geoffrey Crayon, 2 volumes (London: Colburn & Bentley, 1832); as the Author of *The Sketch Book,* 2 volumes (Philadelphia: Carey & Lea, 1832); revised as *The Alhambra: A Series of Sketches of the Moors and Spaniards by the Author of "The Sketch Book"* (Philadelphia: Carey, Lea & Blanchard, 1836); revised as volume 15 of *The Works of Washington Irving* (New York: Putnam's, 1851);

A Tour on the Prairies, number 1 of *Miscellanies,* as The Author of *The Sketch Book* (London: Murray, 1835); republished as number 1 of *The Crayon Miscellany* (Philadelphia: Carey, Lea & Blanchard, 1835); republished in *The Crayon Miscellany,* volume 9 of *The Works of Washington Irving* (New York & London: Putnam's, 1849);

Abbotsford, and the Newstead Abbey, number 2 of *Miscellanies,* as The Author of *The Sketch Book* (London: Murray, 1835); republished as number 2 of *The Crayon Miscellany* (Philadelphia: Carey, Lea & Blanchard, 1835); republished in *The Crayon Miscellany,* volume 9 of *The Works of Washington Irving* (New York & London: Putnam's, 1849);

Legends of the Conquest of Spain, number 3 of *Miscellanies,* as The Author of *The Sketch Book* (London: Murray, 1835); republished as number 3 of *The Crayon Miscellany* (Philadelphia: Carey, Lea & Blanchard, 1835); republished in *The Crayon Miscellany,* volume 9 of *The Works of Washington Irving* (New York & London: Putnam's, 1849);

Astoria, or, Enterprise Beyond the Rocky Mountains, 3 volumes (London: Richard Bentley, 1836); published as *Astoria, or Anecdotes of an Enterprise Beyond the Rocky Mountains,* 2 volumes (Philadelphia: Carey, Lea & Blanchard, 1836); revised as volume 8 of *The Works of Washington Irving* (New York: Putnam's, 1849);

Adventures of Captain Bonneville, or, Scenes beyond the Rocky Mountains of the Far West, 3 volumes (London: Bentley, 1837); republished as *The Rocky Mountains: Or, Scenes, Incidents, and Adventures in the Far West; Digested from the Journal of Captain B. L. E. Bonneville, of the Army of the United States, and Illustrated from Various Other Sources,* 2 volumes (Philadelphia: Carey, Lea & Blanchard, 1837); republished as *The Adventures of Captain Bonneville, U.S.A., in the Rocky Mountains and the Far West,* volume 10 of *The Works of Washington Irving* (New York & London: Putnam's, 1849);

Biography and Poetical Remains of the Late Margaret Miller Davidson (Philadelphia: Lea & Blanchard, 1841; London: Tilt & Bogue, 1843);

Mahomet and His Successors, volumes 12 and 13 of *The Works of Washington Irving* (New York: Putnam's, 1850); republished as *Lives of Mahomet and His Successors,* 2 volumes (London: Murray, 1850);

Chronicles of Wolfert's Roost and Other Papers (Edinburgh: Constable, Low/London: Hamilton, Adams/Dublin: M'Glashan, 1855); republished as *Wolfert's Roost and Other Papers,* volume 16 of *The Works of Washington Irving* (New York: Putnam's, 1855);

Life of George Washington, 5 volumes (New York:

Putnam's, 1855-1859; London: Bohn, 1855-1859);

Spanish Papers and Other Miscellanies, Hitherto Unpublished or Uncollected, edited by Pierre M. Irving, 2 volumes (New York: Putnam's/Hurd & Houghton, 1866; London: Low, 1866); republished as *Biographies and Miscellaneous Papers by Washington Irving* (London: Bell & Daldy, 1867);

The Complete Works of Washington Irving, edited by Richard Dilworth Rust and others, 29 volumes (Madison: University of Wisconsin Press/Boston: Twayne, 1969-).

Washington Irving was so important a figure, so self-conscious a writer, and so given to romantic irony and satirizing authorship that the meagerness of his literary criticism and scholarship is disappointing. Irving had little use for criticism as it was practiced. He believed that critics should judge literature according to established canons of taste and teach authors to correct their faults. Since critics fell far short of this ideal, he sided with artists against critics and urged readers to put more trust in their own judgment. In his own criticism, Irving deplored extravagance and hyperbole, praised simplicity and nobility of style and clarity of thought, indulged a taste for the picturesque and sentimental, and looked to England for his standards. Above all, he tried to be fair, balancing censure and praise.

Washington Irving was the youngest of eleven children (eight survived infancy) born to William and Sarah Sanders Irving. William Irving was an importer, and though not rich, he could afford to send two sons to Columbia College. Washington, however, had only eight years of formal schooling, being too indifferent a student to induce his father to send him to college. Nevertheless, by modern standards, his schooling was not deficient, for he read widely, learned some Latin, and was exposed to French.

The Irvings were an ambitious family. By the time Washington came of age, his sisters had married successful businessmen, and his brothers were becoming prominent in New York's busi-

William Street, site of Irving's birthplace, as it looked in 1800 (courtesy of the Prints Division, the New York Public Library, Astor, Lenox and Tilden Foundations)

ness, political, and literary circles. Irving's talent was recognized early, especially by his brothers; they sponsored his entry into society, supported the informal education he pursued reading and traveling, and encouraged his literary ambitions.

He began as a satirist. At the age of nineteen he published the first of a series of letters that appeared in the *New York Morning Chronicle*, edited by his brother Peter. Later collected with other pieces as the *Letters of Jonathan Oldstyle, Gent.* (1824), six of these letters, together with two others signed "Dick Buckram" (December 1803), ridicule the shabby provincialism of the New York stage. In 1804 his brother William sent Washington Irving on a European tour to finish his education and restore his health (he had long been sickly). He returned in 1806, after twenty-two months abroad, and although he did not return with any more enthusiasm for the law, in which he had been dabbling since 1799, interest in the family business, or even any literary projects, he did come home healthy and richer in self-confidence and experience.

From January 1807 to January 1808 he collaborated with his brother William and James Kirke Paulding in writing *Salmagundi; or, the Whim-Whams and Opinions of Launcelot Langstaff, Esq. and Others*, a spicy satirical periodical which appeared twenty times in order to, the authors teased, "instruct the young, reform the old, correct the town and castigate the age." Among the social and political satires Irving contributed are three mock theater reviews which satirize drama critics for being impertinent, irrelevant, and nonsensical.

Meanwhile, Irving had fallen in love with Matilda Hoffman. He had known her family since before his European tour and had clerked in her father's law office. When she succumbed to consumption in April 1809, he was devastated. For consolation he turned to a manuscript he had begun in collaboration with his brother Peter and turned it into *A History of New York* (1809) under the pseudonym Diedrich Knickerbocker. Knickerbocker's history is a frantic satire of New York society and politics, like *Salmagundi*, but it also targets history, intellectuals, and the law. It also marks a change in Irving's career, for he acted as his own publisher and turned a profit.

The bulk of Irving's serious criticism appeared between 1810 and 1820. In 1810 he edited *The Poetical Works of Thomas Campbell*. In the introduction he combines critical comment with bio-

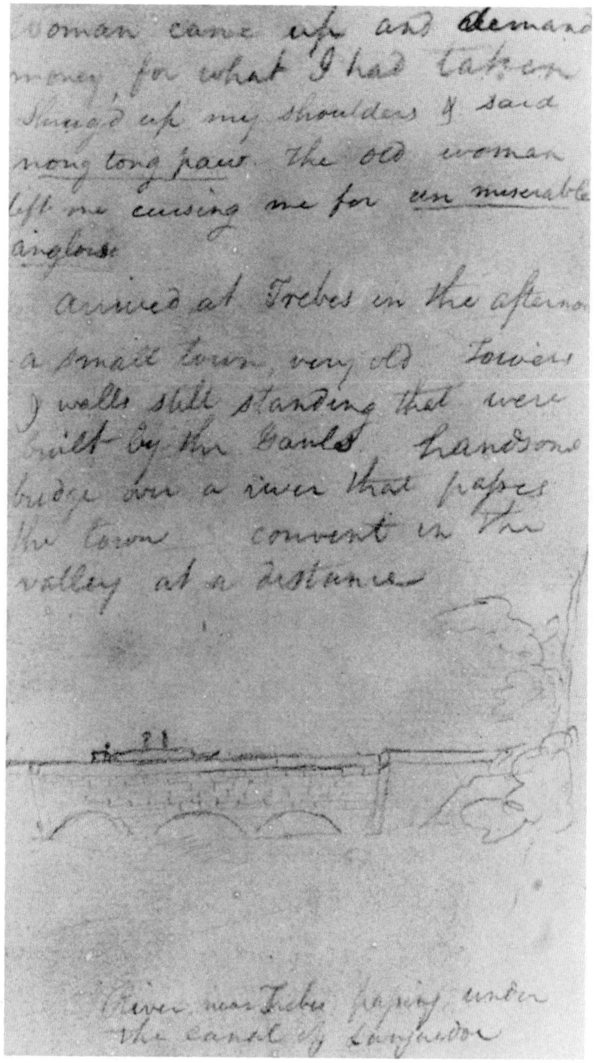
woman came up and demand money for what I had taken shrugg'd up my shoulders & said nong tong paw the old woman left me cursing me for un miserable anglois

arrived at Trebes in the afternoon a small town, very old Towers & walls still standing that were built by the Gauls handsome bridge over a river that passes the town convent in the valley at a distance

River near Trebes passing under the canal of Languedoc

Page for 10 August 1804 from the journal Irving kept during his trip abroad from summer 1804 to early 1806 (by permission of the New York Public Library, Astor, Lenox and Tilden Foundations)

graphical information supplied by the poet's brother. Although Irving felt Campbell revised some of the force and grace out of his poetry, he found in the poet's zeal for perfection the source of Campbell's strength. He also liked the fact that Campbell was "attentive to please, according to the established laws of criticism . . . without . . . endeavouring to establish a new sect." After a brief discussion of British and American literary relations, a theme which he would more fully develop in *The Sketch Book of Geoffrey Crayon, Gent.* (1819-1820), Irving discussed the poem "Gertrude of Wyoming," finding that it succeeded in imparting poetic charm to the American scene (an example to those who doubted the power of America to inspire poetry), but also finding that it suffered from a poorly developed story.

After the success of Knickerbocker's *History of New York,* Irving lived on the profits of his pen and the generosity of his brothers, who sometimes involved him in their business affairs. From 1812, until he went to war as a staff officer in 1814, he edited the *Analectic* magazine, where he published three anonymous reviews. He puffed his friend James Kirke Paulding's "Lay of the Scottish Fiddle," though he regretted that its political satire would anger some. He praised Robert Treat Paine's *Works in Verse and Prose* (1812) and Edwin C. Holland's *Odes, Naval Songs, and Other Occasional Poems* (1813) for being richly imaginative, even while he condemned both for extravagance, hyperbole, and incomprehensibility. Despite being written during the War of 1812, these reviews assert the superiority of English models and are only mildly nationalistic. Also published in the *Analectic* was a brief sketch of Lord Byron that focuses mostly on that poet's quarrels with critics. Placing himself above the fray, Irving sided with Byron, although he conceded that the criticism had made Byron a better poet and that Byron had been too harsh in attacking his critics personally. Irving declined to comment on Byron's more recent work because it was already well known and over criticized. He later took a sim-

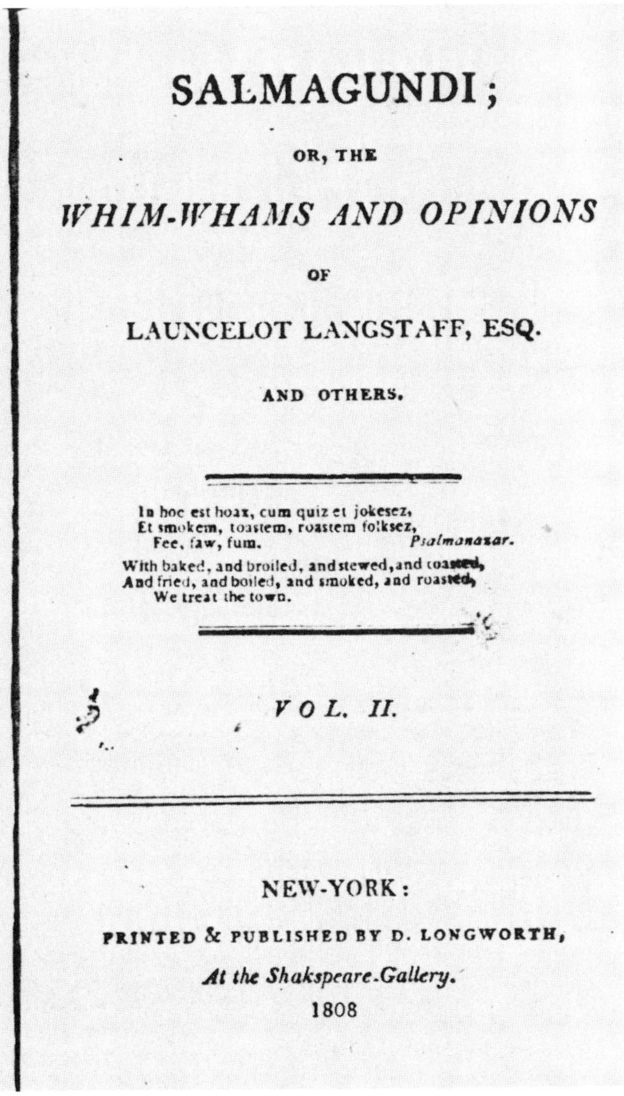
SALMAGUNDI;

OR, THE

WHIM-WHAMS AND OPINIONS

OF

LAUNCELOT LANGSTAFF, ESQ.

AND OTHERS.

In hoc est hoax, cum quiz et jokesez,
Et smokem, toastem, roastem folksez,
Fee, faw, fum. *Psalmanazar.*
With baked, and broiled, and stewed, and toasted,
And fried, and boiled, and smoked, and roasted,
We treat the town.

VOL. II.

NEW-YORK:

PRINTED & PUBLISHED BY D. LONGWORTH,

At the Shakspeare-Gallery.

1808

Frontispiece and title page for the second volume of the literary satire written by Irving, his brother William Irving, and James Kirke Paulding

Title page for an issue of the monthly magazine Irving edited through 1814

ilar position with Goldsmith's work.

In 1815, after the war, Irving went to Europe, where he stayed until 1832. In the wake of the failure of the English branch of the family business, he wrote his most famous book, *The Sketch Book of Geoffrey Crayon, Gent.* (1819-1820). Published in America in seven parts and almost simultaneously revised for publication in England in two volumes, *The Sketch Book* is a miscellany of sketches, essays, and humorous and sentimental fiction, including Irving's best-known tales, "Rip Van Winkle" and "The Legend of Sleepy Hollow." Unifying the book as a whole is Geoffrey Crayon, a genial, gently alienated, amusingly obtuse persona, who is uncertain about the value of literature and, as an American visiting England, is unsure of his cultural heritage. He has long been identified with Irving himself.

The Sketch Book established Irving as the most celebrated American writer of the first half of the century and contains the only writing of his about literature that is still widely read. The most important critical essay is "English Writers on America," which builds on themes introduced in his essay on Campbell. After complaining of the distorted accounts of America English visitors had published, Irving advised Americans not to retaliate in kind. His reason for such advice was, he said, that English slanders did no harm, while American counterattacks, which the English would ignore, only served to increase American enmity. Americans should be above such petty feelings; they should see England clearly and learn from her.

More revealing of Irving's own tastes and methods are two mild satires of authorship. In "The Art of Book Making," the arch and obtuse Geoffrey Crayon wanders into the Reading Room of the British Museum, where he finds authors "pilfering" the past. He falls asleep and dreams that most of the writers were ragged beggars rummaging old clothes, until the pictures of old authors lining the walls came alive and stripped them. Crayon laughs, wakes up, and is expelled from the Reading Room for "an arrant poacher" hunting a "literary 'preserve,' subject to game laws . . . , without special license and permission." The proper attitude toward the past is embodied by "some well dressed gentlemen" who borrow only "a gem or so, which sparkled among their own ornaments, without eclipsing them," or who imbibed "principles of taste." Such, indeed, was Irving's own practice. In "The Mutability of Literature," Crayon finds a Gothic library in the heart of Westminster Abbey. When one book awakes and complains of being neglected, Crayon explains that so long as language changes, so will what is read. He argues that changes in taste and vigorous criticism are needed to keep the prolific modern press from overwhelming the future with literature. Responding to the book's surprise that Shakespeare, a mere poet, had achieved immortality, Crayon says that poetry has the best chance to survive because a poet's "writings . . . contain the spirit, the aroma . . . of the age in which he lives."

These sketches echo the romantic irony and satire of authorship so prominent elsewhere in *The Sketch Book* and in *Bracebridge Hall* and *Tales of a Traveller,* the two miscellanies that he published in 1822 and 1824, respectively. "Rip Van Winkle," "The Legend of Sleepy Hollow," and the tales in *Bracebridge Hall* are placed within frameworks which put into question their narrators' reliability, sense, and judgment. *Tales of a Traveller,* going much further in this direction, burlesques shallow literary conventions and shallow conventional responses to literature; in some of the tales, shrewd storytellers fool gullible listeners, in others foolish young men learn the harsh truth behind glamorous literary conventions. In still other tales the reader feels he may be the butt of the joke.

Three other sketches in *The Sketch Book* combine literary appreciation with the travel essay. In "The Boar's Head Tavern, East Cheap," Crayon, despairing of paying tribute to Shakespeare through literary criticism (for there was no more left to write), went to East Cheap and hunted up traces of the old Boar's Head Tavern. In "Stratford-on-Avon" he visited Shakespeare's haunts and marveled at how the poet's mind still permeated them. Both sketches carry out the book's general theme of mutability by comparing the literary past with the prosaic (and partially fraudulent) present. "A Royal Poet" is a sentimental sketch of James I of Scotland who, while imprisoned in Windsor Castle, wrote poetry. The essay reveals his simple, basic humanity and honors him "as the companion of his fellow man, the benefactor of the human heart, stooping from his high estate to sow the sweet flowers of poetry and song in the paths of common life."

After the critical failure of *Tales of a Traveller* (1824), Irving gradually turned away from fiction and toward history and biography. In 1826 Irving went to Spain to translate Fernandez de Navarrete's work on Columbus. Instead, he wrote a biography of his own, *A History of the Life and Voyages of Christopher Columbus* (1828), which remained the standard biography for several decades. Also coming from his studies of Spanish history were *A Chronicle of the Conquest of Granada* (1829), which combined history with romance, *Voyages and Discoveries of the Companions of Columbus* (1831), which finished the story of exploration he had begun in his biography of Columbus, and *The Alhambra* (1832), his last miscellany, a work that rivals *The Sketch Book* in charm.

After leaving Spain, Irving served as secretary to the American Legation in London (1829-1831). He returned to America in 1832. Between 1830 and 1832, he published three reviews to explain his own work and promote that of his friends. He had intended *A Chronicle of the Conquest of Granada* to appear as the work of Fray Antonio Agapida, and when John Murray, his publisher, put Irving's own name on the title page, Irving felt the work was being misrepresented. Murray agreed to let Irving explain his intentions, and Irving's self-review appeared in the *Quarterly Review* in 1830.

John Murray was willing to publish *A Year in Spain* (1831) by a friend of Irving's, Alexander Slidell, if Irving would prepare it for the press and write a review. Irving agreed, and his anonymous review appeared in the *Quarterly Review* in 1831. Irving also placed another book with Murray, Henry Wheaton's *History of the Northmen* (1831), which Irving agreed to review. Due to a quarrel with Murray, however, this review was not published until 1832, and then it appeared in the *North American Review.*

The review of *A Year in Spain,* appropriate for a review of a young man's experiences in a foreign country, is noteworthy for its humorous, teasing style; that of *History of the Northmen* is more sedate and serious, as befits a more serious subject. Yet both share a common trait: Irving regarded both Slidell's Spain and Wheaton's Scandinavia as enchanted fairylands which, by their very difference from America, were picturesque and poetical. In the remainder of the decade he published three important books on the West: *A Tour on the Prairies* (1835), part of *The Crayon Miscellany,* the result of his own trip through Oklahoma; *Astoria* (1836), a history of John Jacob Astor's fur business in the Northwest; and the *Adventures of Captain Bonneville* (1837), about a semiofficial expedition in the Rocky Mountains.

In 1841 he wrote a biographical introduction to the collected verse of Margaret Miller Davidson, a young victim of consumption. It is so lugubrious it is unreadable. Nevertheless, it was originally well received. Irving did no research into young Margaret's life but instead relied on materials provided by the girl's mother, so much so that most of the book is quotation. In an age ravaged by tuberculosis and given up to sentimental gushing over genius dying young, Irving, whose fiancée had died of the disease in 1809, was understandably much affected by Margaret's suffering and death.

In 1842 President John Tyler appointed Irving minister to Spain; he served until 1846, when he returned home. In 1848 Irving began to publish a collected, revised edition of his works. He was the first American author to do

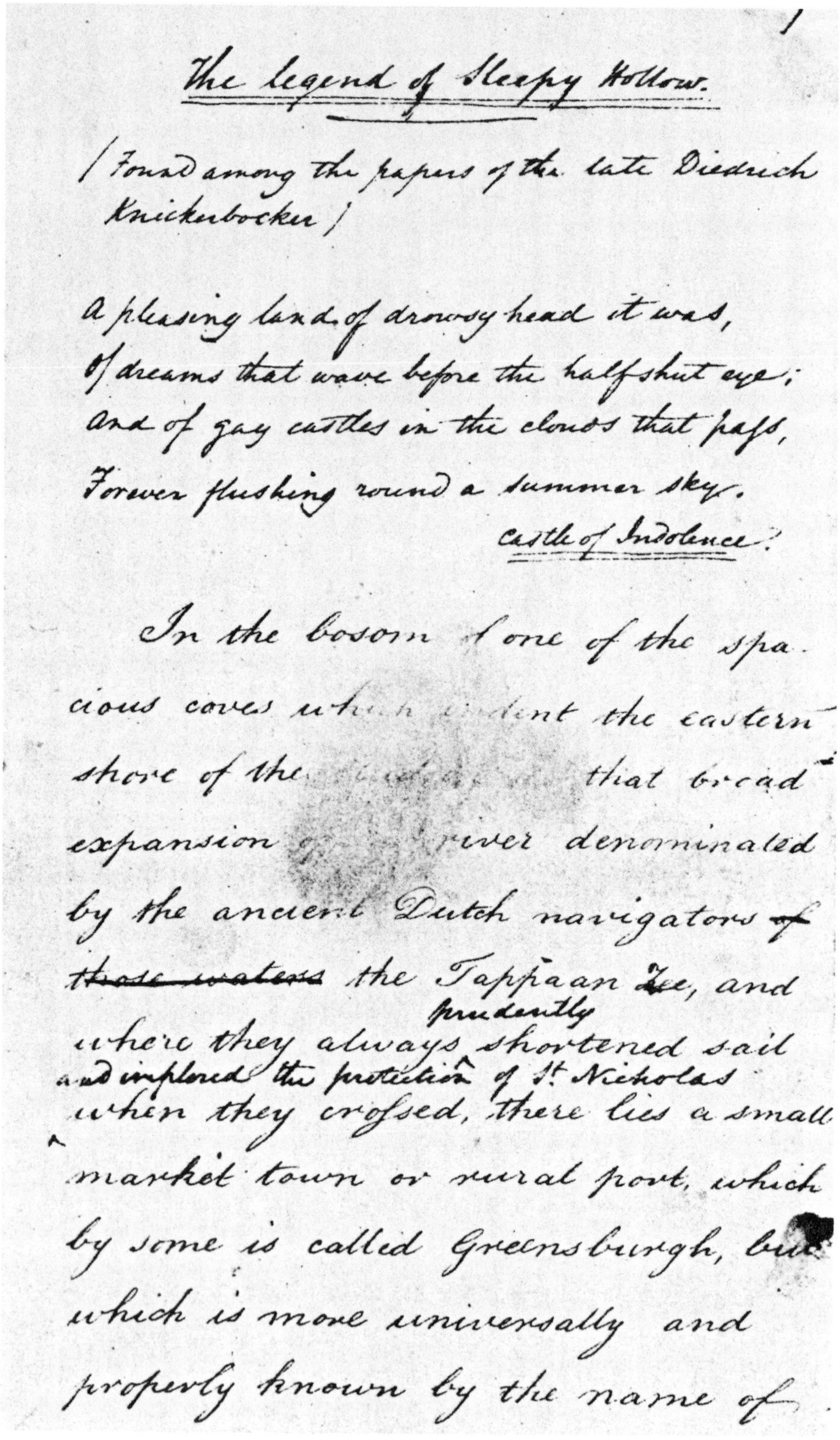

1

The Legend of Sleepy Hollow.

(Found among the papers of the late Diedrich Knickerbocker)

A pleasing land of drowsy head it was,
Of dreams that wave before the halfshut eye;
And of gay castles in the clouds that pass,
Forever flushing round a summer sky.
Castle of Indolence.

In the bosom of one of the spacious coves which indent the eastern shore of the [illegible] that broad expansion of the river denominated by the ancient Dutch navigators ~~of those waters~~ the Tappaan Zee, and where they always prudently shortened sail and implored the protection of St. Nicholas when they crossed, there lies a small market town or rural port, which by some is called Greensburgh, but which is more universally and properly known by the name of

First page of the only known manuscript for "The Legend of Sleepy Hollow." The text is in the hand of an amanuensis, but the heading, epigraph, and corrections were written by Irving (by permission of the Berg Collection, the New York Public Library, Astor, Lenox and Tilden Foundations).

so. This edition occasioned his most extensive piece of literary scholarship, *Oliver Goldsmith: A Biography*, which began as an introduction to an 1825 French collection of the poet's work. Relying on materials published elsewhere, principally two long biographies of Goldsmith, Irving proposed to write a popular, readable biography. He succeeded. His biography of Goldsmith has narrative drive, and the anecdotes and details Irving selected present a graphic picture of Goldsmith's world and display a keen appreciation of his sense of humor. The book was well received in both England and America.

The 1825 version contains brief critiques of Goldsmith's principal works. Irving sought to explain the literature's success and reputation–for example, *The Vicar of Wakefield* (1766), he said, owed its reputation to its domestic subject, moral purity, characterization, and dramatic unity, as well as to its wit and humor; "The Good-Natur'd Man" (1768) failed because it "was deficient in

Washington Irving in the 1850s. This photograph is usually attributed to Mathew Brady but is possibly by one of his assistants (courtesy of the Library of Sleepy Hollow Restorations).

stage effect"; and "She Stoops to Conquer" (1773) succeeded despite flirting with farce. Unfortunately, Irving deleted such criticism in his final revision, claiming Goldsmith's "merits have long since been fully discussed, and [his] station in the scale of literary merit permanently established." Consequently Irving used Goldsmith's work merely to display his character and trace his life, though he did perfunctorily praise Goldsmith's wit, style, feeling, and clarity of expression.

"Desultory Thoughts on Criticism" (1839) recapitulates the history of Irving's development. After jokingly comparing criticism to the gibbet while conceding its importance when practiced judiciously, Irving indicted critics, saying many were unsuited to their task or wrote from unworthy motives; they made readers distrust their own judgment; since no writer could ever be free of faults, much of what critics wrote was beside the point; and, finally, since the world is so fickle, last year's genius is constantly being torn down. Consequently, he wondered whether American literature would not thrive better without so much criticism, and he advised readers to trust more to their own judgment, because "Whenever a person is pleased with a work, he may be assured that it has good qualities. . . . I honor the blessed and blessing spirit, that is quick to discover and extol all that is pleasing and meritorious."

Irving ended his career with the five-volume *Life of George Washington* (1855-1859). It remained an important work well into the twentieth century and together with his *A History of the Life and Voyages of Christopher Columbus* is a more accurate measure of his skills as a biographer than his biography of Goldsmith. He died on 28 November 1859, eight months after finishing the last volume of his biography of Washington.

Although Washington Irving's assays as a critic and scholar are secondary to his other literary endeavors, he had a knack for literary biography, and his youthful satires of criticism and scholarship reflected a typically American suspicion of the life of the imagination and intellect. His mature distaste, indeed, avoidance, of criticism followed his own rough handling at the hands of unsympathetic critics and paralleled the evolution from the judicial to the romantic in American critical taste.

Letters:

Letters, 4 volumes, edited by Ralph M. Aderman, Herbert L. Kleinfield, and Jennifer S.

Self-portrait that Irving sketched at Sunnyside on the Hudson River (by permission of the Berg Collection, the New York Public Library, Astor, Lenox and Tilden Foundations)

Banks (Boston: Twayne, 1977-1982).

Bibliographies:

William R. Langfeld and Philip C. Blackburn, *Washington Irving: A Bibliography* (New York: New York Public Library, 1933);

Stanley T. Williams and Mary Allen Edge, *A Bibliography of the Writings of Washington Irving: A Check List* (New York: Oxford University Press, 1936).

Biographies:

Pierre M. Irving, *The Life and Letters of Washington Irving*, 4 volumes (New York: Putnam's, 1863);

Stanley T. Williams, *The Life of Washington Irving*, 2 volumes (New York: Oxford University Press, 1935).

References:

Mary Weatherspoon Bowden, *Washington Irving* (Boston: G. K. Hall, 1981);

Bruce I. Granger and Martha Hartzog, Introduction and Editorial Appendix to *Letters of Jonathan Oldstyle, Gent./Salmagundi; or the Whim-whams and Opinions of Launcelot Langstaff, Esq. & Others*, by Washington Irving (Boston: Twayne, 1977), pp. xix-xxiv, 319-485;

William L. Hedges, *Washington Irving: An American Study, 1802-1832* (Baltimore: Johns Hopkins Press, 1965);

Walter R. Kime, Introduction and Editorial Appendix to *Miscellaneous Writings*, by Washington Irving (Boston: Twayne, 1981), I: xv-xcvi, 229-452; II: 347-688;

Haskell Springer, Introduction and Editorial Appendix to *The Sketch Book of Geoffrey Crayon, Gent.*, by Washington Irving (Boston: Twayne, 1978), pp. xi-xxxii, 303-510;

Springer, *Washington Irving: A Reference Guide* (Boston: G. K. Hall, 1976);

Springer and Raylene Penner, "Washington Irving: A Reference Guide Updated," *Resources for American Literary Study*, 11 (1981): 257-280;

Edward Wagenknecht, *Washington Irving: Moderation Displayed* (New York: Oxford University Press, 1962);

James W. Webb, "Irving and His 'Favorite Author,' " *University of Mississippi Studies in English*, 3 (1962): 61-74;

Elsie Lee West, Introduction and Editorial Appendix to *Oliver Goldsmith: A Biography/Biography of Margaret Miller Davidson*, by Washington Irving (Boston: Twayne, 1978), pp. xv-xlviii, 345-646;

West, "Washington Irving, Biographer," in *Washington Irving Reconsidered: A Symposium*, edited by Ralph M. Aderman (Hartford: Transcendental Books, 1969), pp. 47-52.

Papers:

Irving's papers are in the New York Public Library and the Library of Sleepy Hollow Restorations; other collections are in the libraries of Harvard, Columbia, and Yale Universities and the Universities of Illinois and Virginia, and in the Henry E. Huntington Library.

William Alfred Jones

(26 June 1817-6 May 1900)

John Stafford
California State University, Northridge

SELECTED BOOKS: *The Analyst: A Collection of Miscellaneous Papers* (New York: Wiley & Putnam, 1840);
Literary Studies: A Collection of Miscellaneous Essays (New York: E. Walker, 1847);
Essays upon Authors and Books (New York: Stanford & Swords, 1849);
Memorial of the Late Honorable David S. Jones (New York: Stanford & Swords, 1849);
Characters and Criticisms, 2 volumes (New York: I. Y. Westervelt, 1857);
Long Island (New York: Baker & Godwin, 1863).

William Alfred Jones made significant and influential contributions to American critical thought and practice in the years from 1835 to 1850. Edgar Allan Poe, in an 1850 article, "About Critics and Criticism" in *Graham's Magazine*, reflects the judgment of many of his time, calling Jones "Our most analytic, if not altogether our best critic, (Mr. Whipple, perhaps, excepted). . . ." If conservative New Englander Edwin Percy Whipple was "our young American Macaulay," in a popular label of the period, liberal New Yorker Jones was our young American Hazlitt. The life of William A. Jones represents–for a brief time–a new group in American intellectual life, the professional literary critics who had arisen to analyze, interpret, and judge the productions of an equally new group, the professional authors. He is the best critic and theorist of the Young Americans associated with Evert Duyckinck in New York, who were actively advocating a distinctively democratic American literature for the people and supporting the work of such writers as William Cullen Bryant, John Greenleaf Whittier, Ralph Waldo Emerson, William Gilmore Simms, Nathaniel Hawthorne, and Herman Melville.

Born in New York City, the son of Margaret Livingston Jones, whose grandfather Philip Livingston had been a signer of the Declaration of Independence, and David Samuel Jones, a prominent judge, Jones attended lower schools in New York. He graduated from Columbia College in 1836 and studied law in the office of Daniel Lord, but he never practiced the profession. Taking great pride in his distinguished ancestors on both sides of his family, he found it difficult to give up the prospect of a conventional, respectable, legal career to devote himself to a financially hazardous career as a literary critic and essayist. But in his early twenties, after long discussions with his friends and with the promise of continued advice and help from Evert Duyckinck, he somewhat warily edged into the profession.

The authors and literary critics who came to be known as Young America in the 1840s were a loosely organized clique of young men who first formed the Tetractys Club in 1836. In addition to Jones the members were Evert Duyckinck, in whose home the club met, J. B. Auld, and Russell Trevett; George Duyckinck, Evert's younger brother, and cantankerous and vain Cornelius Mathews, who, like Walt Whitman later, was trying to create a new American literature on his own, became members; later Herman Melville attended meetings. With Evert Duyckinck and Mathews as editors and Jones as the leading literary critic and essayist, Young America started the monthly *Arcturus* in 1840, short-lived, according to Poe, because it was too good to be popular. It appeared from December 1840 to May 1842. Many of Jones's best critical essays appeared in *Arcturus* and for a longer period in the *United States Magazine and Democratic Review*, popularly called the *Democratic Review*. It was largely Jones who gave *Arcturus* the quality that caused James Russell Lowell to describe it "as transcendental as Gotham *can* be." It was also Young American Jones in the *Democratic Review* who most effectively developed liberal, democratic ("locofoco") literary and critical theories and practices, what conservative Henry Wadsworth Longfellow complained was a new locofoco "politico-literary system" leading to praise of Bryant, "my good friend Hawthorne," and shouts of "Hosannas to every *locofoco* authorling."

Even in the journals and newspapers in which he appeared most often, Jones, unlike Poe and other contemporary literary critics, seems to have had no formal editorial position; he made his way as an independent periodical critic and essayist, contributing his dozens of articles to a wide variety of magazines from the *Church Record* and *Boston Miscellany* to the *Broadway Journal* and the *Literary World*. The four books of literary criticism that he published were all collections of periodical essays. Jones was certainly one critic on Lowell's mind in his *Fable for Critics:* "Thus a lawyer's apprentice, just out of his teens,/Will do for the Jeffrey of six magazines." Even by 1844, when he was twenty-seven, Jones confessed that he was weary of the incessant round of critical essays he was turning out. In "Horne's New Spirit of the Age," he said: "For ten years we have dealt pretty extensively in this sort of wares." And he added, "we begin to tire of the trade" of literary criticism.

However tiring the pioneer's work might have been, Jones recognized fully the importance of the critic's being a professional. Much of what he had said earlier is drawn together in the July 1845 issue of the *Democratic Review* in "Amateur Authors and Small Critics." It would be absurd, he said, to call upon an amateur lawyer or physician with the expectation of competent treatment of one's difficulties. "Few do that well 'for love' which can be better done for money." If in ordinary concerns it is true that the "laborer is worthy of his hire," it is much truer "when we ascend in the scale of labor, and come finally to that which most tasks the intellect and requires the greatest number of choice thoughts." In literature, no less than in law and medicine, the best works, he feels, will almost always be done by the professional, who "puts his heart or invests the whole stock of his faculties" in his pursuit. The professional critic will not be one of those who live on their own "estate or income, but on other people's ideas" and are the "most opinionated of all critics, those "people of sense in ordinary matters, and men intelligent in their own walk of life, . . . who have never received any tincture of literature." Only "small critics" concern themselves with rhyme and meter, with rules and correctness, when they should search for fresh feeling and individuality, "the divine instincts of the glorious Afflatus."

As a professional critic and a Young American, Jones examined carefully the critical theories and functions appropriate to the needs of the newly educated wider public of the democratic society in a new country. The democratic American critic, Jones said, should not be the arbitrary judge who has the author and his work arraigned before him in the court of his literary review; nor, on the other extreme, should he be the impressionist critic who attempts another work as he exclaims about the piece under review; nor, finally, should he be a prescriptive critic who advises an author on how to cure a work of its ailments except that he might give such general advice as to choose a better theme than war "and write in a spirit more akin to the young progressive and aspiring spirit" of the time. No matter how much Poe and other critics might object, Jones and Young America were committed to theories of the critical function that called for interpretive, sympathetic criticism, as Jones explained more fully in later articles.

In describing the high duty the interpretive critic must perform Jones recognized that only a few Young Americans in New York and a few Transcendentalists, such as Margaret Fuller and Ralph Waldo Emerson in New England, accepted the proper place of the true critic in a democratic society. In September 1844 Jones explained in the *Democratic Review* article on "Critics and Criticism of the Nineteenth Century":

> The true position of the genuine critic is not yet acquired. In the republic of letters, he sits just below the poet. Wanting his invention, with less imagination, less fancy, he is still his equal in honest enthusiasm; in independence, perhaps superior; in a love of the beautiful, only lower, because he has the less poetic power; in a reverence for the good and true, a faithful brother; of an accurate perception, clear judgement, and yet a lively sensibility, all working in an atmosphere of the purest candor and liberality, the critic is the advocate of the poet, the exponent of the feelings of the people towards him, the middle-man between the two.

"Pure literary criticism" and a "high moral standard of right" must together have a good influence on the public mind. We must look, consequently, for "a more enlightened and liberal school of criticism than has yet subsisted here."

Jones concluded that America, as "the freest of modern states," especially needs good criticism "to preserve liberty from degenerating into licentiousness, and democracy from falling into popular disorder."

After defining his function as a sympathetic, interpretive critic, Jones, in "Philosophical Chit-Chat" reprinted in *Characters and Criticisms* (1857), turned to a definition of his critical method or mode. He consciously refused to construct a complete, philosophically consistent critical system. He distrusted the narrowness of all philosophical systems; their reasoning, he said, is inconclusive, the evidence likely to be unsatisfactory or insufficient. The most important result of philosophical speculation is "the sharpening of the critical faculties." An adherence to one system will breed intolerance. On many of the most important philosophical problems "the proper state of mind appears to be that of philosophical doubt," which will promote clearness and a tolerant temper. For "systems are invariably one-sided and exclusive, exhibiting in general but a partial view of any question"; "Truth lies between the extremes of opposite theories."

Jones was acquainted with most of the philosophical theories of criticism from Plato and Aristotle down to those of his own day, and the method that he used for a particular essay was varied to suit the literary work under discussion. But in one way or another the emphasis was upon romantic, ideological criticism. He often expressed his dislike of merely technical criticism, of the hard, scientific formality of Aristotle and the Scotch Common Sense philosophers; his most detailed objections may be found in "The Scotch School" in *Characters and Criticisms*. His critical master was William Hazlitt–"the first of the regular critics in this nineteenth century, surpassed by several in some one particular quality or acquisition, but superior to them all, in general force, originality and independence," as he explains fully in "Critics and Criticism of the Nineteenth Century," in the *Democratic Review* in August 1844.

In good Young American fashion, Jones seems to have learned his critical method from an American as well as from an English and European tradition. Without sharing the political views of his crusty old friend the elder Richard Henry Dana (who hated "that great Curse, Democracy!"), Jones recognized his critical pioneering in introducing a "new conception of criticism" to America, the theories of August Wilhelm Schlegel, Samuel Taylor Coleridge, and Hazlitt. On almost every point Jones's critical theories and attitudes represent a culmination or an extension of Dana's. For example, Dana, according to William Charvat in *The Origins of American Critical Thought, 1810-1835,* "was almost alone in his appreciation of Hazlitt's prose style" in the years before 1835; but as we have seen, Jones's estimation of Hazlitt was even higher, and he felt that Dana was too harsh on Hazlitt.

Drawing from this background and his ten years of concentrated experience as a professional critic, Jones considered himself ready to answer the question–How are good critics to be known and distinguished? In "Criticism in America" (*Democratic Review,* September 1844) he answers:

> By these several signs; a thorough knowledge of the subjects, periods, characters, books, upon which they write; a mastery of the genuine spirit of the age–its needs, its aims, its faults, its tendencies; by a good, if not elevated, standard of criticism–(some topics and classes of writing do not require a lofty standard); by generous justice, by genuine feeling, not mawkishness nor sentimentality, but sincere feeling–for a critic should have a heart as well as a head, a fact too often overlooked or forgotten; by a knowledge of rules, but no lack of the fit spirit to guide in the use or adaptation of them; by experience and skill in the art of writing.

The good American critic, the same article adds, must come up to further exacting standards:

> Much general acquirement, knowledge of life and character, dabbling in science and the arts, thorough knowledge of history, and (at least) American politics and economy, with good sense and good feeling, honesty, tact, taste, judgment, and a style, clear, readable and attractive–these are necessary for all.

Jones's answers to even more fundamental questions–What is literature? What is poetry? What is the function and purpose of literature?–are based on the ideas he shared with nearly all his contemporaries, liberal or conservative. They accepted certain familiar, basic, romantic principles of poetry that may be briefly summarized. The approach to poetry is usually shifted from

Extracts from select notices of the Analyst, Literary Studies, and Memorial of the Hon. David S. Jones.

THE ANALYST; A Collection of Miscellaneous papers. Wiley & Putnam, 1840.

This is a volume well worthy to be read. It gives proof of reflection, observation, and literary culture; and its style is always clear, sometimes forcible and terse, though not often elegant. It abounds with shrewd remarks, happy criticisms, and well-drawn traits of character.—*North American Review, April*, 1840.

LITERARY STUDIES; A collection of Miscellaneous Essays by W. A. Jones, New-York: E. Walker, 1847.

Mr. Jones, a native of New-York, and a well known contributor to the Whig and Democratic Reviews of papers on purely Literary subjects, has here made a collection of his articles under a modest title, which would admit of some enlargement. The papers are something more than literary studies. A part of them are devoted to the illustration of neglected periods of English Literature, but even these are improved by suggestions and reflections drawn from the writer's marked individual experience and independent of the bookish text under consideration. Such are the chapters on Elijah Fenton, and Pope and his Friends. Another portion relates to men rather than books, such as the Essays on the Morality of Poverty, a finely conceived paper, worthy the pen of Dr. Dewey; on Notoriety, a profitable subject in these days of the abuse of true reputation; and the independent remarks on Preaching.

Works of the kind undertaken by Mr. Jones receive little pecuniary reward from the trade, and make far less reputation with the public than they deserve, but when, as in the present instance, they are the genuine product of sound literary culture and a candid, ingenuous, original mind, they are among the most useful and honorable contributions to literature.—*Tribune.*

Mr. Jones is one of the few writers among us, who may be called the direct descendants of the old English essayists. He gives evidence of the most careful reading of that class of authors, and has imbibed a portion of their characteristic spirit and style. The little volume he published several years since, called the Analyst, a collection of miscellaneous papers, contain a series of delightful essays, which have never attracted as much attention as they deserve; and the present volumes, though like it in character, indicate considerable improvement.—*Democratic Review.*

Page from the advertisement for books by Jones published in Essays upon Authors and Books *(1849)*

the text of the poem to the "maker" or "creator" of the poem. Poetry, great literature, and, indeed, the fine arts of whatever form are created by the genius whose higher faculties (those which are farthest removed from the senses and which work in the realm of ideas) are most fully developed. The realm of ideas in which the genius finds the spirit with which he animates his creation is the realm in which the spirit and ideas of religion also dwell. There is little essential difference between the good, the true, and the beautiful. The poet's imagination enables him to soar into the higher regions of the spirit and idea and to make actual to his readers the real that he sees there. A closely related attribute of the poet is his taste, that which enables him to see the beautiful in this world. Furthermore the true poet of genius reveals in his work a deep insight into man's moral nature; he attains an inner self-knowledge of common human nature. Jones and many other critics saw the poet as one who is inclined to believe in the truths of religion and in the reality of the spiritual life usually associated with religion; the poet loves beauty for itself as the religious man should love virtue.

As their thought developed from this starting point, Jones and the Young Americans moved to the left and found themselves on the path marked earlier by the Benthamite reviewers in England. According to George L. Nesbitt, the Benthamites, in the *Westminster Review* from 1824 to 1836, had set up "a positive ideal for literature, a New Literature to fit the New Man in the New Age"; they also realized that the intelligent benefactor of the poor must first "devise means of improving bad physical conditions. He does not spend his life reading poetry to the indigent. . . ." From the beginning of his career in the early 1840s in *Arcturus* and the *Democratic Review*, Jones recognized the need for America to take the same early steps in preparation for the new literature by and for the people.

As Jones saw it in "Horne's New Spirit of the Age" in the *Democratic Review* in July 1844, "one of the great problems of the age, and perhaps *the* Problem" was the "infusion of popular feeling into our works of speculation," and thus the responsibility to reform, enlighten, and educate the people, to impress upon them the importance of the individual. The first duty of society is to make man physically comfortable, "but, immediately next to that, to seek to elevate and refine, deepen and expand, the characters of all men." In March 1841 he had explained in "The Culture of the Imagination" in *Arcturus* that so salutary is the function of the arts in society that the state should sponsor them. While he knew the poor already had "people's editions, cheap libraries without end," he looked for further progress:

> The time may not yet have arrived, but it must come some day, when the wealth of the state joined to the munificent bequests of individuals, will unite to provide classic public entertainments; not the mere dole of the Roman people in an early day . . . , but free lectures, free concerts, free admission to galleries of paintings and sculpture, to libraries, and reading-rooms, to public walks and gardens of rare beauty; and lastly, to the "well-trod stage."

The progressive "spirit of the age" (to use a catch phrase of the liberal Democrats) led him on to claim great moral, political, and economic results of the "general diffusion" of the culture of the sympathetic imagination. "Most of the hardness of heart and coldness of feeling in the world, arises out of the want of imagination. We want sympathy to place ourselves in the condition of others. Our imagination is not strong enough to touch the heart." Once men have cultivated their sympathies through their strong imaginations, they can converse not as rivals and foes but as brothers and friends; the "cordial grasp of the hand, the warm expression of friendship, would not be simulated for foreign purposes." Business competition and the warfare of trade "would be merged in an universal harmony and brotherly love."

In "Democracy and Literature" in the *Democratic Review* for August 1842, followed by "Political Rhetorists of the English Commonwealth" in September, "Political Pamphleteering" in October, "Political Satire and Satirists" in December, and "Wordsworth's 'Sonnets to Liberty' " in February 1843, Jones reviewed some aspects of politics in literature. Jones concludes in his discussion of William Wordsworth that all true poetry might be called political, "for all truly inspired verse is the outpouring of the Spirit of Freedom, and the Spirit of Humanity." Under the rule of despots poetry becomes "but a mere heap of fables and false devices." As the "right popular philosopher" the poet must propagate "free principles and liberal ideas," even if "only on the shallow grounds of diplomatic expediency." Poets, as

ESSAYS

UPON AUTHORS AND BOOKS,

BY

W. ALFRED JONES.

NEW-YORK:
STANFORD AND SWORDS, 137, BROADWAY.

1849.

Title page for Jones's third book, a collection of essays ranging from critical analyses of works, such as Sir Philip Sidney's "Defence of Poesy," to biographical narratives and reading lists

brothers of their fellowmen, "feel as no other race or class of men can feel"; "the whole circle of human necessities, from the lowest animal desires, up to the most elevated spiritual impulses, is included in their sympathies." Jones points out that even such a poet as Wordsworth was possessed of a true inspiration that carried him to greatness despite the fact that he was an aristocrat whose "whole mind" was not devoted to "the mass." The true sympathetic poet breaks through in such poems as his "Sonnets to Liberty."

As a final climactic essay on his theories of literature, Jones in "Poetry for the People" (*Democratic Review,* September 1843) examined the qualities of the nineteenth century, of the society, and of the literature it had already produced and the literature it should develop in the future. The "peculiar feature in the character of the age," the rise to political power of the people, led to a new application of poetry to life "which may be expressed in the phrase, Poetry for the People." The poetry of all ages has shown the truest "features in the countenance of the time." Poets, as accurate painters of man, show us men's dominant emotions and the reciprocal influences of contemporary opinions, thoughts, and actions; they must also depict "the contemporary influences by which these, too, are moulded"–all conveying to us finally "what we popularly describe as the Spirit of the Age." Poets speak for the ages of classical heroism, of chivalry, and for all the other times of the ancient and modern world. "The present epoch of literature and popular sentiment must have its mouth-piece also, and this it finds in Poetry for the People." Before describing the coming poet of the people, Jones pauses to suggest that "your fine scholar" and "your fastidious gentleman" who smile at this phrase should look at the new world around them; literature and poetry are no longer restricted to a superior caste or class of society but range "at will through every department of life, and every grade of rank."

Jones concluded with a fervent plea for the coming of a true poet of the people. For, he believed, despite the popularity of prose fiction, "it is in poetry especially that we must look for the purest expression of the popular feeling." Forsaking the knight in the field and the baron in his castle, poetry has "taken up her abode 'for better for worse' with the artificer and the husbandmen." Even when charmed and captivated by their lives we are apt to view the "old-fashioned heroes of war and slaughter" with "pity for their Quixotism and contempt for their absurd pretensions." "The poor man, upright, sincere, earnest, with deep enthusiasm and vigorous self-reliance, he is the hero of our time." The poet of the people must celebrate such facts as that in the past the poor man "had the trial by battle, now we have the trial by jury."

The favorite topics of the poet of the people will include "the necessity and dignity of labor," "the futility of all conventional distinctions of rank and wealth," "the brotherhood and equality of men," and "the cultivation of manly liberality." This poet must possess a full knowledge of his age and of his countrymen. Then "with a full heart, a firm hand, the 'vision and the faculty divine,' the rich resources of his art, and the aims and aspirations of humanity for his theme, what lessons can the poet not read the world–in what stirring tones will he not plead for his fellow-men!" He will become the "dearest friend and strongest champion" of all men. "No statesman, no patron, no general, can effect a tithe of what he may accomplish; for give a man heart, and true counsel, and warm sympathy, and you give him what kings have never been able to purchase or capitalists to monopolize."

Reaching almost to the lofty tones Walt Whitman would achieve ten years or so later, Jones concluded his plea. Considering the advances of progressive America, the new poetry and the new poet are likely to be American and, though it is "not essential that the Poet of the People be one of themselves . . . that fact would certainly add weight to his teaching." So did Jones look forward to the coming of the "Homer of the mass": "With a pen informed by experience, and exercised on the immortal themes of the poet and the philanthropist, with hope in his heart and love on his tongue, with the fire, the fervor, the frankness of genius, such we would gladly hail, the Poet of the People and the Poet of the Poor."

Jones's liberal Young American sympathies are just as evident in his critical judgments as in his literary theories. By personal preference Jones was attracted to the essay and closely related prose forms; by talent he was at his best in the criticism of these forms, especially of the political essay.

In his articles in the *Democratic Review*, on "Political Pamphleteering" (October 1842) and "Political Satire and Satirists" (December 1842), his judgments are generally predictable. The best political writer for statesmen and philosophers was Edmund Burke, with his brilliance, profundity, and imaginative power; the sarcasm and keen and pointed style of Junius was best for the unspecified educated classes; and for the people, the finest example was the shrewd, clear, pithy, and caustic style of Thomas Paine. In "Tales of the South and West," in the *Democratic Review* for June 1846, he also singled out for praise writers of shorter forms of fiction, Edgar Allan Poe and Nathaniel Hawthorne for their tales, the regional recorders of folk stories, and the material arising from the lives of the people, both black and white.

In August 1848 the professional literary career of William A. Jones was seriously injured by a scandal. According to manuscript documents in the New York Public Library, Evert Duyckinck and his wife had sent Cassy Panton, the seventeen-year-old sister of Mrs. Duyckinck, to visit the Joneses on Long Island, and a love affair, variously described in letters of the time, between Cassy and William Jones, then thirty-one, had developed. Duyckinck broke off his long friendship with Jones and never afterward spoke to him; Jones was emotionally devastated at losing the personal, professional, and financial aid from Duyckinck that he had come to rely on excessively. He retreated from his writing career, became the librarian of Columbia College in 1851, and performed successfully as a librarian until 1865. He moved in 1867 to Norwich Town, Connecticut, where he edited his essays for book publication and wrote the history of Long Island and memorials and memoirs of his family until his death in 1900.

While the contribution of William A. Jones to the history of American literary criticism was not recognized in the late nineteenth century and early part of the twentieth century, he began to come into his own in the middle of the century as he was seen to have demonstrated that the United States could support (somewhat precariously) professional literary critics along with its professional writers. It was no longer true in America, as William Charvat has shown, that literary criticism was written as an avocation by a "homogeneous upper class" which reflected its social and economic bias. Furthermore his serious, informed criticism helped to create a new liberal theory of criticism and literature that provided a justification in theoretical and practical criticism for the work of William Cullen Bryant, John Greenleaf Whittier, Ralph Waldo Emerson, Herman Melville, Nathaniel Hawthorne, Henry David Thoreau, and Walt Whitman in the *Democratic Review* and other of the best periodicals of the day. That "Poet of the People," Walt Whitman, wrote somewhat nostalgically in 1858 of Jones and other writers in the *Democratic Review* of the 1840s: the *Review* was "a monthly magazine of a profounder quality of talent than any since." He continued, "its corps of writers were all enthusiasts–believers in 'a good time coming.' " Whitman, one of "its corps of writers," remained an "enthusiast" for precisely those ideas that are most characteristic of Jones: democracy, America's destiny, as much of Transcendentalism as a democratic son of Manhattan could swallow, and the duty of the American poet, heedless of the canons of the "mechanical critics" of the aristocratic past, to observe the "people" and express the progressive "spirit of the age."

References:

Perry Miller, *The Raven and the Whale: The War of Words and Wits in the Era of Poe and Melville* (New York: Harcourt, Brace, 1956);

Edgar Allan Poe, "About Critics and Criticism," *Graham's Magazine*, 36 (January 1850): 49-51;

John Paul Pritchard, *Literary Wise Men of Gotham: Criticism in New York 1815-1860* (Baton Rouge: Louisiana State University Press, 1963);

John Stafford, *The Literary Criticism of "Young America"* (Berkeley & Los Angeles: University of California Press, 1952);

Stafford, "William A. Jones, Democratic Literary Critic," *Huntington Library Quarterly*, 12 (May 1949): 289-302;

Allen F. Stein, *Cornelius Mathews* (New York: Twayne, 1974);

Denham Sutcliffe, " 'Our Young American Macaulay,' Edwin Percy Whipple, 1819-1886," *New England Quarterly*, 19 (March 1946): 3-18.

Papers:

Letters, diaries, and other papers in the Duyckinck Collection at the New York Public Library are the most important manuscripts. Other materials are at Columbia University and the Huntington Library.

Samuel Lorenzo Knapp

(19 January 1783-8 July 1838)

Karen S. Langlois
Claremont Graduate School

BOOKS: *The Letters of Shahcoolen, A Hindu Philosopher, Residing in Philadelphia; to His Friend El Hassan, An Inhabitant of Delhi,* anonymous (Boston: Russell & Cutler, 1802);

An Oration Delivered at Newburyport, on the Fourth Day of July 1810 (Newburyport, Mass.: Ephraim W. Allen, 1810);

An Oration Delivered before the Merrimack Humane Society, on Their Anniversary, September 3, 1811 (Newburyport, Mass.: E. W. Allen, 1811);

An Oration Delivered before "The Associated Disciples of Washington," on the 22d of February, 1812 (Newburyport, Mass.: E. W. Allen, 1812);

The Travels of Ali Bey, in Morocco, Tripoli, Cyprus, Egypt, Arabia, Syria, and Turkey, Between 1803 and 1807, as Ali Bey (Philadelphia: Carey, 1816);

Extracts From the Journal of Marshal Soult, as Soult (Newburyport, Mass.: W. B. Allen, 1817);

Extracts from a Journal of Travels in North America, Consisting of an Account of Boston and Its Vicinity, as Ali Bey (Boston: Thomas Badger, 1818);

Biographical Sketches of Eminent Lawyers, Statesmen, and Men of Letters (Boston: Richardson & Lord, 1821);

Memoirs of General Lafayette. With an Account of His Visit to America, and of His Reception By the People of the United States, anonymous (Boston: E. G. House, 1824);

An Oration, Pronounced Before the Society of Phi Beta Kappa, at Dartmouth College, August 19, 1824 (Boston: Commercial Gazette Press, 1824);

Memoirs of General Lafayette, Embracing Details of His Public & Private Life, Sketches of the Amer. Revolution, the French Revolution, the Downfall of Bonaparte, and the Restoration of the Bourbons (New York: Robins, 1825);

An Address Delivered in Chauncey Place Church, Before the Young Men of Boston, August 2, 1826, in Commemoration of the Death of Adams and Jefferson (Boston: Ingraham & Hewes, 1826);

A Discourse on the Life and Character of DeWitt Clinton (Washington: W. Greer, 1828);

The Genius of Masonry, or A Defence of the Order (Providence: Cranston & Marshall, 1828);

Lectures on American Literature, with Remarks on Some Passages of American History (New York: E. Bliss, 1829);

Sketches of Public Characters. Drawn from the Living and the Dead, as Ignatius Loyola Robertson (New York: E. Bliss, 1830);

A Memoir of the Life of Daniel Webster (Boston: Stimpson & Clapp, 1831);

The Polish Chiefs; An Historical Romance, attributed to Knapp (New York: J. K. Porter, 1832);

Advice in the Pursuits of Literature, Containing Historical, Biographical, and Critical Remarks (New York: J. K. Porter, 1832);

American Biography (New York: Conner & Cooke, 1833);

Female Biography, Containing Notices of Distinguished Women, in Different Nations and Ages (New York: J. Carpenter/Baltimore: Phoenix, Wood, 1834);

Tales of the Garden of Kosciusko (New York: West & Trow, 1834);

The Life of Thomas Eddy (New York: Conner & Cooke, 1834; London: E. Fry, 1836);

The Life of Aaron Burr (New York: Wiley & Long, 1835);

The Picturesque Beauties of the Hudson River and Its Vicinity (New York: J. Disturnell, 1835-1836);

The Bachelors, and Other Tales (New York: J. & W. Sandford, 1836);

Life of Timothy Dexter (Boston: G. N. Thomson, 1838);

American Cultural History, 1607-1829; A Facsimile Reproduction of Lectures on American Literature, 1829, with an introduction and index by Richard Beale Davis and Ben Harris McClary (Gainesville, Fla.: Scholars' Facsimiles and Reprints, 1961).

OTHER: John Howard Hinton, ed., *The History and Topography of the United States of North America, from the Earliest Period to the Present Time,* 2 volumes, with additions and corrections by Knapp (Boston: S. Walker, 1834);

Library of American History, edited by Knapp (New York: J. H. Turney, 1835; expanded edition, New York: C. H. Jackson, 1836-1837).

Samuel Lorenzo Knapp finds a place among American literary scholars and critics as an early historian of national American literature and as the author of *Lectures on American Literature* (1827), a pioneer "history of the American mind." In the dedication to William Austin Seeley, Esq., Knapp explains his motivation in producing what is now considered the first critical history of American literature. To Seeley he writes: "I know you are among the number who are anxious that we, as a people, should speak freely and justly of ourselves, and honestly strive to place our claims on the broad basis of well authenticated historical facts." It was in the service of this cause that he had completed his volume, which would "establish the claims of the United States to that intellectual, literary, and scientific eminence . . . she deserves to have."

Samuel Lorenzo Knapp was born in Newburyport, Massachusetts, the fifth of six children of Isaac Knapp, a sea captain, and Susanna Newman Knapp. His forefather, William Knapp, had settled in Watertown in 1630. After attending Phillips Academy, he graduated from Dartmouth College in 1804. He is credited with publishing his first volume while a sophomore at Dartmouth–*The Letters of Shahcoolen, A Hindu Philosopher, Residing in Philadelphia; to His friend El Hassan, An Inhabitant of Delhi.* Published anonymously in book form in 1802, the work has been the subject of some controversy concerning its authorship. In the introduction to a 1962 facsimile reproduction, Ben Harris McClary attributes the work to Benjamin Silliman, who was in 1801 a Yale law student and tutor. However, other sources, including Joseph Sabin's *Bibliotheca Americana,* attribute the volume to Knapp.

The book contains fourteen letters purported to have been composed by a Hindu philosopher, Shahcoolen, then traveling in America. First published in Noah Webster's *Commercial Advertiser,* beginning 5 October 1801, the letters were also reprinted in other newspapers. In December the *Boston Gazette* announced its intention to publish the collected letters in book form. The following March *The Letters of Shahcoolen,* with a dedication to John Quincy Adams and published under the imprint of John Russell and James Cutler, appeared at several Boston bookstores for the price of one dollar.

The book is modeled on the convention, popularized by Charles Montesquieu's *Lettres Persanes* (1721) and Oliver Goldsmith's *The Citizen of the World* (1762), among others, of the oriental traveler who comments on the customs to be observed in strange lands. The intention, almost always the case with this literary type, is satirical. The first four letters delineate "the doctrines of the new female philosophy, and their influence

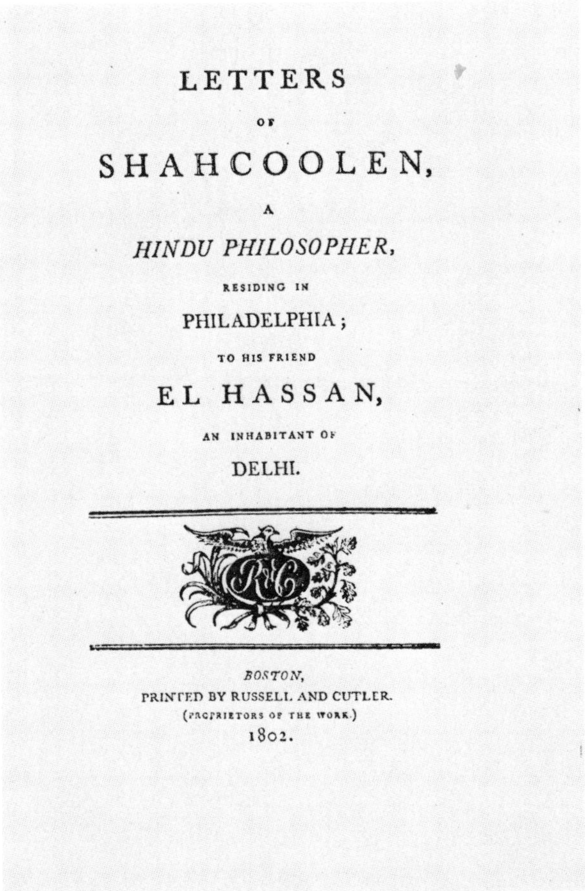
LETTERS
OF
SHAHCOOLEN,
A
HINDU PHILOSOPHER,
RESIDING IN
PHILADELPHIA;
TO HIS FRIEND
EL HASSAN,
AN INHABITANT OF
DELHI.

BOSTON,
PRINTED BY RUSSELL AND CUTLER.
(PROPRIETORS OF THE WORK.)
1802.

Title page for the collection attributed to Knapp and published while he was a sophomore at Dartmouth College. The fourteen letters contain satirical observations of American culture.

upon the female character in America" and include an attack on the English feminist Mary Wollstonecraft. This section is followed by a consideration of American poetry, about which two major points are made. The anonymous author enthusiastically observes that the beauty of the American landscape is "calculated to seize the imagination" and inspire poetic achievement, a not altogether unfamiliar theme in the national literature even this early. He also laments indifferent "public taste" in America which does not encourage the "cultivation of poetry." Included among "the most distinguished American poets" are the revolutionary poet and political journalist Philip Freneau, the Hartford Wits–Joel Barlow, Timothy Dwight, and John Trumbull–and Francis Hopkinson, a respectable American poet now recognized as the first notable American composer.

After graduation from Dartmouth College, Knapp studied law with Chief Justice Theophilus Parsons. He was admitted to the bar and in 1809 opened a law office in Newburyport. Within a few years he was selected as a representative to the General Court. During the War of 1812 he attained the rank of colonel and commanded a regiment of state militia in defense of the coast. In 1814 he married Mary Ann Davis of Boston. Two daughters were born of the marriage.

Knapp gained some prominence as a fluent and popular orator and spoke at numerous Masonic and other meetings. Many of these early orations were published as pamphlets. Over the years he became a favorite "spread-eagle orator," addressing various lodges in the District of Columbia, Maryland, Virginia, and Massachusetts. On occasion he edited the Masonic section of the *New England Galaxy* and the Masonic magazine, and in 1828 he published *The Genius of Masonry.*

Apparently unable to make a living as a lawyer, Knapp was imprisoned for debt in the Newburyport jail in 1816. While in prison he completed *Extracts From the Journal of Marshal Soult,* published in Newburyport the following year. As with his earlier books, it was not published under his own name. During the following year he attempted to build up his law practice in Boston, where he was associated with Daniel Webster.

In 1818 Knapp published *Extracts from a Journal of Travels in North America* under the pseudonym Ali Bey. The slim volume, again modeled on the oriental traveler convention, claimed to be the bemused comments of an Oriental observer of Boston society and cultural life. A chapter on American literature gives evidence of the themes of Knapp's later work. The author notes America's cultural dependency on and need to "look to Europe for instruction." At the same time he ponders how Americans "habitually under the influence of intimidation . . . betray such an itch for innovation." He berates Americans who stoutly defend themselves from foreign political influence and yet servilely accept literary influence. American scholars enamored of profit are scolded for rushing to press without giving their ideas time to steep.

Knapp published *Biographical Sketches of Eminent Lawyers, Statesmen, and Men of Letters* in 1821, a book devoted to prominent American figures. This was followed by *Sketches of Public Characters. Drawn from the Living and the Dead* (1830). Published under the name Ignatius Loyola Robertson, it devoted considerable space to the "living," who were often selected as much by Knapp's own preferences as by their national distinction. Among those national figures who receive attention are Daniel Webster and John C. Calhoun. A section on orators includes others of Knapp's contemporaries: John Randolph, the Virginia congressman; Edward Everett, the former editor of the *North American Review* and a member of the House of Representatives; and William Wirt, the Baltimore lawyer and man of letters. William Cullen Bryant, whose first collected *Poems* had appeared in Boston in 1821, also finds a place among the distinguished American literati.

In the following years Knapp published a series of generally unreliable, if frequently laudatory, profiles of General Lafayette, Daniel Webster, DeWitt Clinton, Thomas Eddy, and Timothy Dexter. Spurred by the democratic nationalism of the Jacksonian era, his career as a writer of popular biography flourished. He based at least two accounts–those of Daniel Webster and Aaron Burr–on his own observations; he was personally acquainted with both men. Knapp was also the personal friend of Archbishop Jean Cheverus, whose memoir he published in 1825 in the *Boston Monthly* magazine. (At Cheverus's suggestion he was granted the degree of LL.D. from the University of Paris in 1826.)

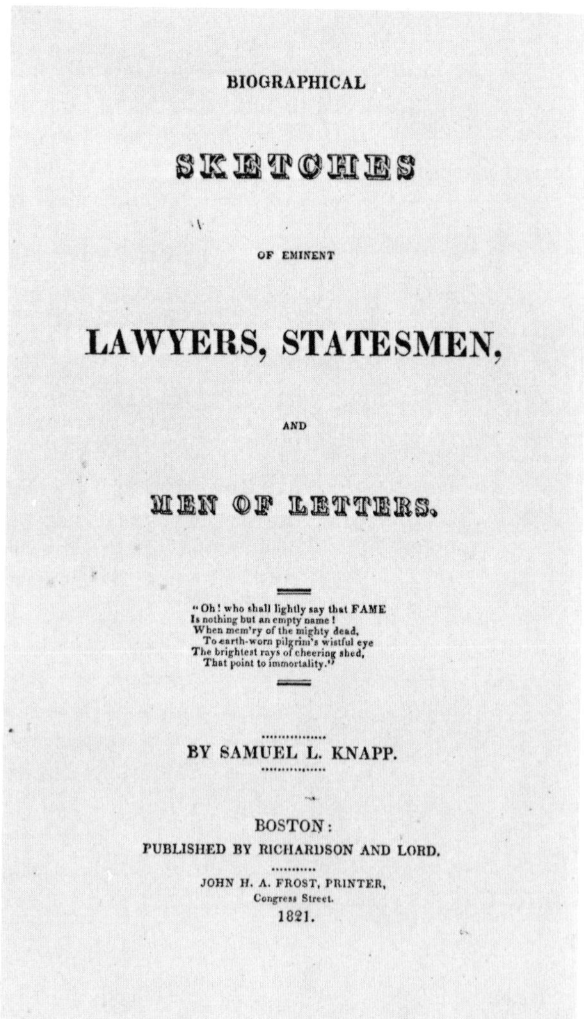

BIOGRAPHICAL

SKETCHES

OF EMINENT

LAWYERS, STATESMEN,

AND

MEN OF LETTERS.

"Oh! who shall lightly say that FAME
Is nothing but an empty name!
When mem'ry of the mighty dead,
To earth-worn pilgrim's wistful eye
The brightest rays of cheering shed,
That point to immortality."

BY SAMUEL L. KNAPP.

BOSTON:
PUBLISHED BY RICHARDSON AND LORD.

JOHN H. A. FROST, PRINTER,
Congress Street.
1821.

Title page for Knapp's work on prominent American figures such as John Eliot, Cotton Mather, and Samuel Sewall

During the 1820s Knapp pursued a career in journalism. In 1824 he served as editor of the *Boston Commercial Gazette* and the following year became editor and proprietor of the *Boston Monthly* magazine. In 1826 he founded the *Boston National Republican.* He also served as editor of the *National Journal* in Washington, D.C., and as editor of the *Commercial Advertiser* in New York City.

It was in an 1828 issue of the *National Journal* that Knapp announced his intention to publish by subscription "A Course of Lectures on American Literature," which would acquaint the public with their own indigenous literary tradition. He had been planning the volume and gathering materials for nearly a decade. In the preface to *Lectures on American Literature* Knapp makes plain his view that his book was the first of its kind: "We have very good histories–narrative, political, military, and constitutional; but I know none, as yet, that can be called literary–meaning by the term, a history of our literature, and of our literary men." His intention was to rectify this lapse by calling to the attention of "the rising generation something of the history of the thoughts and intellectual labours of our forefathers, as well as their deeds." Instructors of youth should especially teach those in their charge the "varied talent" of their own land, "in every age of her history; and inscribe her glories of mind, and heart, and deed, as with a sunbeam upon their memories."

Knapp's evaluation of American literature and enthusiastic "defense of the American genius" establish him as an early literary nationalist. His range is broad and his view of literature comprehensive. Among those selected for inclusion in his panoramic vision of American literature are Capt. John Smith, William Bradford, and John Winthrop; each, he notes, compiled written records of his experiences in the new world. Knapp also includes the Mathers–"the most volu-

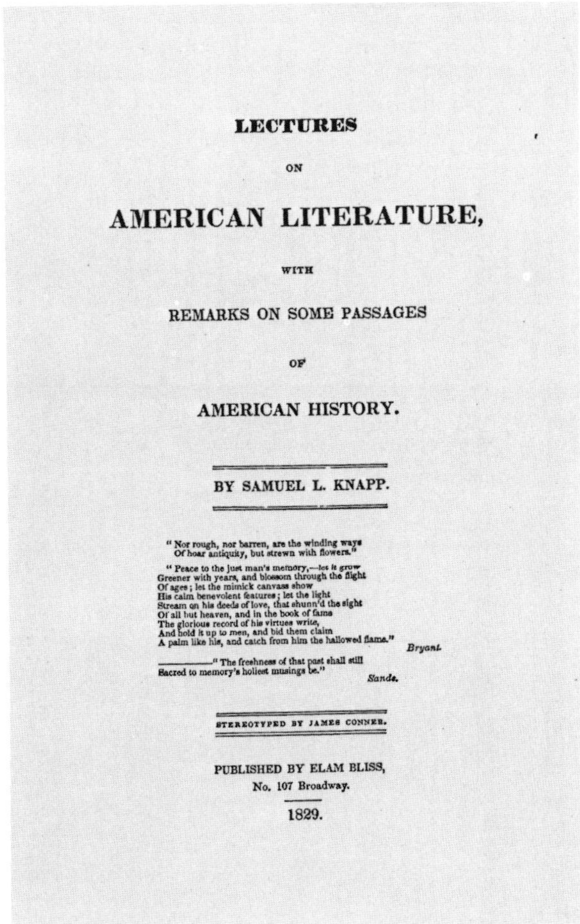

LECTURES

ON

AMERICAN LITERATURE,

WITH

REMARKS ON SOME PASSAGES

OF

AMERICAN HISTORY.

BY SAMUEL L. KNAPP.

"Nor rough, nor barren, are the winding ways
Of hoar antiquity, but strewn with flowers."

"Peace to the just man's memory,—*let it grow*
Greener with years, and blossom through the flight
Of ages; let the mimick canvass show
His calm benevolent features; let the light
Stream on his deeds of love, that shunn'd the sight
Of all but heaven, and in the book of fame
The glorious record of his virtues write,
And hold it up to men, and bid them claim
A palm like his, and catch from him the hallowed flame."
Bryant.

———"The freshness of that past shall still
Sacred to memory's holiest musings be."
Sands.

STEREOTYPED BY JAMES CONNER.

PUBLISHED BY ELAM BLISS,
No. 107 Broadway.

1829.

Title page for Knapp's best-known work

minous writers of the age in which they lived"–as well as Roger Williams, William Penn, and Jonathan Edwards. Particular attention is paid to the patriots and political writers of the revolutionary period, among them John Jay, James Madison, and Alexander Hamilton. Two lectures are devoted to the subject of American poets and poetry, and another to the contributions of American artists. He even calls attention to the scientific contributions of various physicians and surgeons, and the heroic achievements of national military and naval leaders. In the postscript Knapp strenuously reiterates his basic premise. "It is essentially wrong to commence the history of our country after we have finished that of other countries . . . it should be read first of all."

The appeal of this book, as of so many of Knapp's works, is somewhat muted for the contemporary reader. Despite some interesting historical material, it is stylistically flat and generally lacking in critical analysis. The presentation of information is often perfunctory, and he has an unfortunate tendency to pad his work with irrelevant material. Nevertheless, the book reflects Knapp's wide-ranging curiosity, impassioned nationalism, and unusual intellectual vision. Considered in the context of its time, it is an ambitious contribution to the development of nineteenth-century, American literary consciousness.

The Polish Chiefs (1832), a Revolutionary War romance, is generally attributed to Knapp, as is the anonymously published whaling novel *Miriam Coffin* (1834), although credit for the latter is sometimes given to Joseph D. Hart. *Advice in the Pursuits of Literature* (1832) is short on advice, padded on length. Dedicated to the members of the New York Mercantile Association, the book was intended to enlighten those engaged in business pursuits on the subject of English literature. It contains an account of the important English authors beginning with Chaucer, veers to an overview of European history, and ends up with a cursory survey of literature from the time of Homer to the colonization of America.In 1834 Knapp published *Female Biography, Containing Notices of Distinguished Women, in Different Nations and Ages*. It provides information on 172 women, ancient and modern, and includes sketches of such important American historical figures as Anne Hutchinson, Abigail Adams, and Pocahontas. In acknowledging the literary importance of the American poet Anne Bradstreet, Knapp provides a brief biographical sketch, as well as the text of her poem "Contemplations."

In his last years Knapp published two collections of short stories, *Tales of the Garden of Kosciuszko* (1834) and *The Bachelors, and Other Tales* (1836). *The Picturesque Beauties of the Hudson River and Its Vicinity* was published in two volumes (1835-1836). He also edited Hinton's *The History and Topography of the United States of North America* (1834) and the *Library of American History* (1835). All told, he wrote or edited more than two dozen volumes in addition to an enormous output of magazine and newspaper articles. In failing health, he spent the last three years of his unusually productive life in Hopkinton, Massachusetts. He died in 1838 at the age of fifty-five.

Papers:

There is no repository for Knapp's papers. Baker Memorial Library, Dartmouth College has a few documents and letters. Correspondence may also be found at the Boston Public Library.

Hugh S. Legaré

(2 January 1797-20 June 1843)

Carl L. Anderson
Duke University

See also the Legaré entry in *DLB 3, Antebellum Writers in New York and the South.*

BOOK: *Writings of Hugh Swinton Legaré, Late Attorney General and Acting Secretary of State of the United States . . .*, 2 volumes, edited by Mary S. Legaré (Charleston: Burges & James/ Philadelphia: Cowperthwait/New York: Appleton/Boston: Munroe, 1845-1846).

OTHER: "The Study of the Classics," in *The Charleston Book*, edited by William Gilmore Simms (Charleston: Hart, 1845), pp. 14-19.

PERIODICAL PUBLICATIONS: "Niebuhr's Roman History," *Southern Review*, 1 (May 1828): 320-341;

"The Fair Maid of Perth," *Southern Review*, 2 (August 1828): 216-263;

"The Omnipresence of the Deity," *Southern Review*, 2 (August 1828): 190-203;

"The Roman Orators," *Southern Review*, 2 (November 1828): 491-540;

"Pollok's The Course of Time," *Southern Review*, 2 (November 1828): 454-470;

"The Wept of Wish-Ton-Wish," *Southern Review*, 5 (February 1830): 207-226;

"Griffin's Remains," *Southern Review*, 8 (February 1832): 326-344;

"Cooper's Bravo," *Southern Review*, 8 (February 1832): 382-399;

"Bryant's Poems," *Southern Review*, 8 (February 1832): 443-462.

The literary reputation of Hugh Swinton Legaré rests almost exclusively on the two-volume edition of essays and miscellaneous writings collected by his sister, Mary Legaré Bullen, after her brother's death in 1843. Sixteen of the essays (all those collected in volume two) had first appeared between 1828 and 1832, during the brief lifetime of the *Southern Review*, one of the most ambitious of the journals published in the antebellum South. Legaré had been the moving force behind its founding and became also its most frequent contributor. Another three essays, collected in volume one of *Writings*, had made their first appearance in the *New York Review* between 1839 and 1841. The remainder of that volume is a miscellany consisting of a personal diary, not intended for publication, that Legaré kept while serving from May 1832 to August 1836 as the first chargé d'affaires from the United States to the newly independent kingdom of Belgium; a journal of his two brief sorties into Germany in that period; and an assortment of diplomatic and private correspondence as well as seven speeches, five of them reported as they were delivered in the House of Representatives during Legaré's term in the Twenty-fifth Congress. As a classical and legal scholar, literary critic, successful practicing lawyer, elected and appointed public official, and government administrator, Legaré enjoyed at the time of his death an extraordinary reputation as one of the preeminent cultural and political leaders in the South and indeed in the nation. John Tyler, reminiscing over his term in the presidency, said of Legaré, who had served as Tyler's Attorney General and in the last month of his life also as acting Secretary of State, that "there never was counsellor more faithful, patriot more sincere, statesman with broader or more liberal views, or a man more unassuming yet of firmer or more decided character."

Barred from vigorous physical activity after contracting a paralyzing illness at the age of four that invalided him for months and stunted the growth of his limbs, Legaré was a voracious reader and committed scholar from early childhood. In college he was known for the long hours of study he kept, seven for assigned work and eight for his own reading. It came as no surprise when he was named valedictorian of his class; he had announced on arrival at college his intention to capture graduation honors. An anonymous magazine sketch of his "character" that appeared in the *Southern Quarterly Review* soon after his death recalled the excited whispers whenever it was learned that Hugh Legaré was about to address the court and spoke of his fund of anecdotes and his brilliant, if sometimes borrowed, wit. "He was sometimes laughed at for his egotism–if he was guilty of such a fault, it was egotism at the expense of nobody else. . . . When told, for instance, on a certain occasion, that the public were loud in their praises of a performance of his he replied, he did not wonder at it–because he felt that it was deserved. 'It is,' said he, 'what I have labored to attain for years, and I deserve praise

for my diligent industry, if for nothing else. Had I inherited the merit, I would have thanked my fortune, not felt proud of myself.' " Diligent industry marked all his endeavors–in his writing no less than in his public service.

Legaré was born on 2 January 1797 on his father's plantation on John's Island outside Charleston, the fifth generation in America of the Huguenot family to bear the name Legaré (pronounced Le-gree). Hugh's mother, Mary Swinton, was a descendant of Scottish Covenanters and, as the family liked to recall, of a hero mentioned in Walter Scott's *Halidon Hill* (1822). When Solomon Legaré died, leaving to his widow the care of three children–Eliza, the oldest, Hugh, and Mary–his son was barely two years old. Eliza left home in 1810 to be married to a planter; the others remained until they sold the plantation in 1822 and moved into the city. In the interval Hugh had been away from his family for six years while he attended school in Abbeville and at South Carolina College in Columbia, and for an additional year while he traveled in Europe and studied at the university in Edinburgh. Before leaving St. John's Colleton, however, he had already served a two-year term in the lower house of the General Assembly. It was the first of many public offices, elected or appointed, he was to hold.

The law, he had decided soon after leaving college, was to be his vocation, thus reversing the usual order among his contemporaries of moving from the practice of law to ownership of a plantation. Residence in the city allowed him to begin practice at the Charleston bar and at the same time to join the clubs that served his literary and social interests. His allegiance to literature, broadly defined to include philosophy and history, had its beginnings in early childhood. In college he had read French, Spanish, Italian, and Portuguese, and later in Brussels he applied himself to learning German, but he had determined to be satisfied with nothing less than mastery of Latin, and later on of Greek, which became for him the language of supreme eloquence, elegance, and clarity. When he was given the honor at the young age of twenty-six of orating on the Fourth of July before the '76 Association of Charleston, he noted that it was Greece, "the GREAT MOTHER COUNTRY of all freedom and civilization," that was once again rebelling against barbarism. The plainest statement of Legaré's devotion to classical studies appeared posthumously in a gift miscellany, *The Charleston Book* (1845), edited by William Gilmore Simms. Legaré wrote of the importance for a boy to be taught Latin and Greek in his formative years, for "he will have his taste formed, his love of letters completely, perhaps enthusiastically, awakened, his knowledge of the principles of universal grammar perfected, his memory stored with the history, the geography and the chronology of all antiquity, and with a vast fund of miscellaneous literature besides, his imagination kindled with the most beautiful and glowing passages of Greek and Roman poetry and eloquence; all the rules of criticism familiar to him–the sayings of sages, and the achievements of heroes, indelibly impressed upon his heart." He will possess "the golden keys" to civilization, and "he will be let into the great communion of scholars, throughout all ages, and all nations. . . ." It was to this ideal of cultural transcendence that Legaré had dedicated himself in everything he attempted both in the privacy of his study and in his public life. That steadfast dedication to high purpose, if oppressive at times to admirers and detractors alike, accounts in large part for the reputation Legaré earned for indefatigable scholarship and high-minded public service.

In the decades of the 1820s and 1830s, when Legaré was building up his law practice, Charleston's cotton economy was stagnating; the protective tariffs favored by northern cotton dealers and bankers added to its economic woes. The rising insistence in South Carolina on a state's right to nullify tariffs and any other federal legislation detrimental to its interests dismayed Unionists like Legaré and his friend James Petigru, one of the foremost members of the Charleston bar, and placed them in a minority position; yet when Petigru resigned in 1830 as attorney general of South Carolina, the governor appointed Legaré as his successor. At a Fourth of July rally of the Unionist party the following year Legaré challenged his listeners to say if they were prepared to absolve themselves from their allegiance to the government of the United States and become a separate commonwealth among the nations of the earth. In reply, he was toasted both as "a friend of the Union, and an able and efficient Advocate of State Rights." But to Legaré's chagrin, the Unionist view was rapidly deteriorating in a state being led by Calhoun and others beyond nullification into secession.

These concerns had perhaps already contributed to Legaré's resolve in late 1827 to begin with the help of others a magazine that would serve not only to legitimate the South's claim to cultural eminence but also to act as a bulwark against uninformed, unenlightened thought and action in the region. He played an active part in the founding of the *Southern Review,* although it was Stephen Elliott, planter, botanist, and venerable first president of the State Bank of South Carolina, who was named editor. Elliott was succeeded at his death in 1830 by his son Stephen, later bishop of Georgia. When the review was threatened with collapse in the following year, new subscriptions were obtained, and Legaré finally stepped in as editor in 1831-1832 in an effort to keep the magazine going. He himself contributed five of the eight essays that made up the final number, published in February 1832.

He had been reluctant to be too publicly associated with the *Southern Review,* for although it was common enough in the South for its *litterateurs* to be lawyers by profession and to hold public office as well, Legaré knew that a reputation as a writer–or as the editor of a magazine–would be a drawback to his securing a large clientele. It sufficed that the review gave pride of place in its maiden issue to Legaré's "Classical Learning," a carefully fashioned defense of the study of the classics in school. The essay was his response to a speech by Thomas Grimké in 1827 in Charleston and again in 1830 before the Phi Beta Kappa chapter at Yale questioning the practice in the schools of requiring students to read the classics "with a submissive faith" that everything written by Homer and Virgil is poetry, everything in Cicero and Demosthenes is eloquence, and Thucydides and Tacitus are unrivaled in history. Grimké deplored this form of rote learning and called for America to be "a republic of thought." This shot was only one in the battle over the school curriculum being fought between proponents of the ancients and the moderns in the nineteenth century, but a Charlestonian, unhappily, had fired it and had to be answered. Legaré was willing to concede that little practical advantage might be looked for in the study of classical authors, but Americans surely have a "common ambition to be a cultivated and literary nation." It was on this familiar argument, elaborated at length, that Legaré rested his case.

The essay was the first in a series pertaining to classical literature, oratory, history, and law that constitutes the most important part of Legaré's work as a writer. These subjects thoroughly engaged his remarkable facility in the languages and his wide reading in classical texts. On the whole, he took greater pains with these essays than with any others.

In the second issue of the *Southern Review* he discussed B. G. Niebuhr's *Roman History* (1827) and praised it as a "masterly performance" for discovering amid traditions obscured in history the beginnings of Rome's grandeur. To the same issue he contributed a fifty-page review of John Dunlop's two-volume *History of Roman Literature* (1827). His essay amounted, in effect, to a historical sketch of the rise of the Roman nation and the growth of the Latin language. Roman literature was slow to appear, he noted, and it cannot bear comparison with Greek literature in respect to originality, for the Romans were essentially a practical people, their ideal being their concept of *vir fortis, vir gravis.*

In "The Roman Orators" (November 1828), Legaré continued his discussion of Dunlop's history, quoting extensively from Cicero's treatise on oratory and disputing Dunlop's argument that Rome's political advancement should be attributed to the eloquence of its leaders, for although every speaker may rise to greatness, every great man necessarily is a speaker. That point, besides the insight it gives into his personal ambitions, allowed Legaré to comment informatively on a subject dear to him, the effectiveness of modern speakers as compared with the master, Cicero. An 1829 translation of Cicero's *De republica* was the subject of an essay in one of the following year's issues. He criticized the translation harshly, its "great fault" being simply "its total want of all merit." Legaré used the occasion to comment once again on the deficiencies in education "upon which the time of the child and the money of the parent have been hitherto, alike, so prodigally and so uselessly squandered." It might instead be better to store the child's memory with Shakespeare, Milton, Spenser, Isaac Barrow, Jeremy Taylor, David Hume, Joseph Addison, Francis Atterbury. The Cicero essay provided Legaré chiefly with the opportunity to recall both Cicero's *Republic* and Plato's, works to be admired for the wisdom they convey from experience in contrast to the "speculative politics" of his own times that he found so disturbing.

"The Public Economy of Athens" was one of five essays Legaré supplied for the last number of the *Southern Review.* He had presented a paper on the subject five years before to the Literary Club of Charleston assembled in the home of Robert Y. Hayne. It may have been then, when it was agreed that the members' papers should be gathered and published, that the impetus was given to starting the *Southern Review.*

Impressed by Legaré's classical scholarship, Alexander Everett, editor of the *North American Review,* urged that he write regularly for him and suggested, to begin with, a review of Victor Cousin's translation of Plato. Nothing came of the suggestion, but when the editors of the *New York Review* commended him in 1838 for the soundness of his constitutional opinions, he accepted their invitation to become a contributor. Over the next three years he submitted three substantial essays on classical subjects: "Roman Legislation" (October 1839) on the development of civil law, said to be superior to the common law for the logical structure of its doctrine; "Constitutional History of Greece, and the Democracy of Athens" (July 1840), which examined at great length (over seventy-five pages) two recent translations of German treatises on Greek political life; and

"Demosthenes, the Man, the Statesman, and the Orator" (July 1841), another major treatise–*libellus,* his Boston friend George Ticknor called it, and considered it the crowning achievement of Legaré's classical scholarship. Thirty pages of the essay were given to criticism of a dissertation on ancient oratory by Lord Brougham, "a tissue of error and sophistry" for supposing that oratory is essentially nothing more than speaking sensibly; but it permitted Legaré to remark on the renewed importance of "popular eloquence" in an age when the steam engine could bring together congresses from distant places to take counsel on the state of the nation. Demosthenes' speeches are masterpieces of popular eloquence because their style is "simple, natural, flowing, equable, and above all, exquisitely elegant" and not merely polite or well argued. In Demosthenes eloquence is an instrument, and not, as in Cicero, a thing to boast of and to display.

Although not strictly on classical subjects, many of Legaré's other essays adopted standards of critical judgment drawn from his familiarity with classical literature. Three essays for the *Southern Review* combined literary and legal interests. In a review of Arthur Kent's *Commentaries on American Law* (1826, 1827), he conceded that the possibilities for independent thought exist in America in politics and in the law but probably not in literature and science, for poets imitate nature, "which is every where the same," whereas civil and juridical institutions are the work of man and are fashioned to suit circumstances. Legaré's reluctance to join here and elsewhere in his writings in the northern call for a distinctly American literature reflected a firmly implanted distrust in the South of such pretensions, given the high standards set by British literature and even more convincingly by classical literature. His review in 1831 of a history of English law focused on the question of codification and other reforms, to which he declared himself opposed; jurisprudence as it stands deserves and rewards careful study. The last of Legaré's essays on a legal subject was a review in the final issue of the *Southern Review* of a biography, "a miserable little compilation," of the French jurist, Henry Francis D'Aguesseau. Legaré used the occasion to comment again on the untidiness of the common law, "a mingled or chaotic mass of foolishness and captious subtlety," that admittedly has merit in the protection of individual liberties, but its form is "at variance with all elegance of taste, all literary acquirement, all comprehensive and profound philosophy, all liberal and enlarged views of science and society."

Closely related to these essays was Legaré's review in 1831 of John Neal's edition of a French study of Jeremy Bentham's *Principles of Legislation* (1831). Legaré had nothing but scorn for Neal's "quaint pedantic affectation of simplicity" and for Bentham's "peculiar views, peculiar habits and peculiar figures," all to be traced, no doubt, to "incidents connected with his youth–his hatred of English law and of English lawyers, of Blackstone, of Mansfield and of Eldon–to his *fortunate* failure in his profession." Legaré the traditionalist was outraged at the arrogance of Utilitarianism, in his view a debased and deformed kind of Epicureanism.

Of more than a dozen additional articles that Legaré wrote, only a few received the care he lavished on those on either classical subjects or the law. His reviews of Scott's *The Fair Maid of Perth* (1828), Bulwer-Lytton's *The Disowned* (1829) and *Pelham* (1828), George Croly's *Tales of the Great St. Bernard* (1829) and *Salathiel* (1829), Robert Pollok's poem *The Course of Time* (1828), and Robert Montgomery's poem *The Omnipresence of the Deity* (1828) consist largely of pages of quotation and summary. They are little more than hackwork and reveal very little of Legaré's critical acumen. His review of Fenimore Cooper's *The Wept of Wish-Ton-Wish* (1829) opened with the flat declaration, "This work is a failure" lacking the "glow" and "energy" of Cooper's earliest fiction, but he found passages, quoted in extenso, "distinguished by many of those masterly touches which characterize our author in scenes of hurried excitement." Cooper's *The Bravo* (1831) fared a little better. It had a special interest for Legaré in providing parallels between Venice of the time of the novel and "this once flourishing city" of Charleston, both cities having once been havens for pilgrims fleeing from religious persecution and both cities perceived to be in decline. Legaré's review of *The Miscellaneous Works* (1829) of Sir Philip Sidney contained twelve pages of admiring summary, with long quotations, of "The Defence of Poetry," and an extended commentary on "Astrophel and Stella," a poem he found full of conceits and affectations lacking the compensation for them provided by Sidney's model, Petrarch, in his poetry. A translation of Turpin's *History of Charles the Great and Orlando* (1812) along with a collection of old Spanish ballads typically

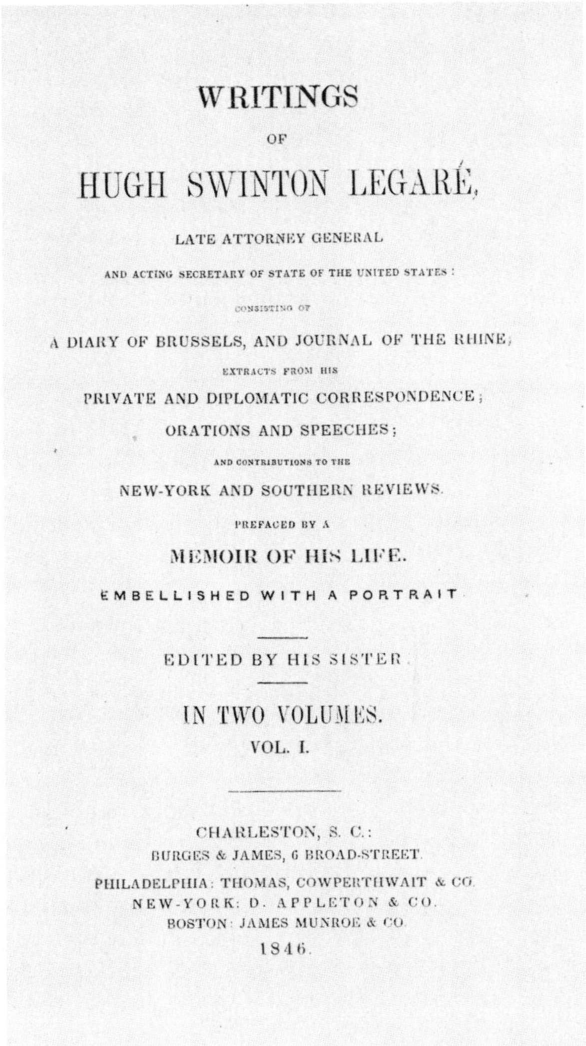
WRITINGS

OF

HUGH SWINTON LEGARÉ,

LATE ATTORNEY GENERAL

AND ACTING SECRETARY OF STATE OF THE UNITED STATES:

CONSISTING OF

A DIARY OF BRUSSELS, AND JOURNAL OF THE RHINE;

EXTRACTS FROM HIS

PRIVATE AND DIPLOMATIC CORRESPONDENCE;

ORATIONS AND SPEECHES;

AND CONTRIBUTIONS TO THE

NEW-YORK AND SOUTHERN REVIEWS.

PREFACED BY A

MEMOIR OF HIS LIFE.

EMBELLISHED WITH A PORTRAIT.

EDITED BY HIS SISTER.

IN TWO VOLUMES.

VOL. I.

CHARLESTON, S. C.:
BURGES & JAMES, 6 BROAD-STREET.
PHILADELPHIA: THOMAS, COWPERTHWAIT & CO.
NEW-YORK: D. APPLETON & CO.
BOSTON: JAMES MUNROE & CO.
1846.

Title page for the only collection of Legaré's works. Published posthumously by Mary S. Legaré, the book contains the author's correspondence, journals, orations, and several essays.

engaged Legaré's scholarly curiosity in the remote past, but again his review depended heavily on summary.

In his first venture into reviewing modern literature, however, he had been obliged to provide a much fuller critique. In an early issue of the *Southern Review* he had undertaken the delicate task of evaluating the selected prose and poetry of William Crafts, a popular Charleston lawyer, recently deceased, who had written each morning an essay for the *Courier* and had been a favorite orator in the city. Politely Legaré regretted the passing of one so amiable and gentle, yet he found him to be, in effect, a dilettante as a lawyer and Latinist. Despite his talents, Crafts had not risen to eminence–always a serious failing, in Legaré's estimation–because he did not trouble to study the law but relied instead on his native wit. As an orator, he lacked the "true eloquence" that comes from a serious love of truth. Indolence and vanity inhibited his abilities. Legaré quoted enough of Crafts's poetry to reveal his mediocrity and, thereby, dislodge the late poet from the position of literary superiority that Charlestonians had mistakenly supposed was his due.

William Cullen Bryant, on the other hand, pleased Legaré when in 1832 he read him for the first time–not as the editor of a respected daily newspaper but as the author of a "pretty collection of poesy–the most faultless, and we think, upon the whole, the best collection of American poetry we have ever seen." Bryant, nearly as popular in the South as in the North, had before him, Legaré supposed, the possibility of refining his poems to "display higher attributes of genius, by sustained invention and unity of purpose." In time he might produce something worthy at least to be classed with "Gertrude of Wyoming" and "The Deserted Village." Legaré seems to have felt none of the contemporary southern resentment toward the favor accorded in the South to northern poets like Bryant but denied to southerners.

Legaré's principal commentary on modern literature, however, is contained in two long essays on Byron occasioned by the publication of Thomas Moore's edition of the *Letters and Journals* (1830, 1831). The essays are among the longest and most spirited that Legaré ever wrote, and they resort, proportionately, least of all to quotation and summary. Although he began by stating his disappointment with the volumes under review, contrary to the praise they had received in the English press, Legaré clearly was drawn to Byron as he was to no other modern poet. He thought him careless in diction and uneven in style when read alongside "the best passages of our classical poetry," but for that matter he admitted that he could discover also in Lucan the "bluster and pretension" he disliked in *Childe Harold* (1812). The "irregularities" in Byron's character and mode of life did not detract from his merits. All that was good or evil in Byron arose from "a feverish temperament, a burning, distempered, insatiable imagination."

Byron's enthusiasm for Greece may have helped in Legaré's eyes to excuse his "wanton" personal life and poetic faults, yet "his muse–

unknown among the old nine of Greece–is inspired by, and inspires, nothing but despair. . . . Nothing in Dante's Inferno, or Milton's, is more frightful, than the views which Byron presents of human destiny." Legaré gave no hint of personal relevance to his own deformity in his allusions to anecdotes about Byron's lameness; there is no single explanation for Legaré's enthusiasm for Byron's poetry and for his unexpected delight in the "off-hand, dashing and lively" prose which is marked by "strong common sense, and shrewd cleverness." He found fiery, dark feelings in the poetry, particularly in *Manfred* (1817), that "turn the sun into blood and the moon into darkness, and the earth into a charnel house, and a den of wild beasts and a hell before him." He thought that Byron was fascinated with power, shown on the one hand in his quickness to take offense (a well-known failing also of Legaré's), and on the other, his kindness toward dependents and inferiors if they did not offend his pride. Whatever its faults of extravagance, however, Byron's poetry was clearly far above Bryant's "pretty collection of poesy." Byron, Legaré concluded, had few rivals in English poetry. "His greatest rival, however, was himself. We throw down his book dissatisfied. Every page reveals powers which might have done so much more for art–for glory–and for virtue!"

Despite Legaré's strenuous efforts to save it, the *Southern Review* ceased to exist after the February 1832 issue. Its passing was mourned in other journals that were themselves threatened perennially with foreclosure. Legaré found relief from his labors in its behalf and from the growing tensions in Charleston and the South generally in the appointment he received in April as chargé d'affaires to Belgium. On the occasion of his reviewing a book of travels in America by a Capt. Basil Hall, he had already written of the great transformation taking place in regional attitudes toward slavery. Hall, fortunately, had not theorized loftily on the subject as had New Englanders, but Legaré felt obliged to respond nevertheless. His defense of slavery turned not surprisingly on a legal nicety: "It is enough for us that, when the Southern people consented to receive the African race into their territory, it was upon the express condition of perpetual service, and that this condition was then as lawful as any other arrangement of civil society." Except for the reluctance he felt in leaving his mother and sister, he started for Belgium eager to get away and to recapture the intellectual and social stimulation he had enjoyed in Europe thirteen years before. He took up his new duties enthusiastically; he seemed determined to let American friends know that he could thrive in foreign parts although the government's persistent refusal to increase his allowance never ceased to cause vexation and embarrassment, for he meant to live in a style suited to his station. Much of his diary is given over to recording social pleasures enjoyed in the presence of royalty or other notables. He dined with fellow diplomats, and travelers from home occasionally paused to enjoy his hospitality.

Legaré returned to the United States in August 1836 and was promptly nominated by the Unionist party as a candidate for the House of Representatives. To his great satisfaction, he defeated his opponent, a Nullifier, and soon was taking an active part in the social and political life of Washington. He was named to the Committee of Foreign Affairs and delivered a paper on the arbitration of disputes with Mexico. He argued in perhaps his most important speech in Congress against a bill authorizing the issue of treasury notes at interest for funding of a Sub-Treasury. It received favorable notice and led to the invitation he received to write for the *New York Review*, but his opposition to the bill angered his constituents and exacerbated his already strained relationships with other Congressional members from South Carolina, and he was not reelected in 1838. He devoted the next years to his law practice in Charleston and to the support of the Whig party. Political speech making took him to New York State and Maryland, and President Tyler appointed him to his Cabinet. Legaré now had little time for reading, much less for writing reviews, for he took his new responsibility with typical earnestness. Moreover, when Daniel Webster, the sole carryover from Harrison's Cabinet, resigned as secretary of state, the duties of that office were temporarily assigned to Legaré in addition to his work in the attorney general's office. South Carolina newspapers proudly took note of a native son's rise to national prominence, but not everyone was pleased with his federal alliances.

Obliged to join the presidential party in Boston to celebrate the anniversary of Bunker Hill, Legaré arrived at his hotel greatly fatigued; he fell seriously ill and was moved to the home of his old friend George Ticknor. He died there within a few hours on 20 June 1843.

A reviewer in the *Charleston News and Cou-*

rier in 1892 looked back over South Carolina's literary record for the century and concluded that for talent and achievement in literature only Legaré could stand by the side of the state's preeminent author, William Gilmore Simms. Simms himself, always blunt-spoken, had reviewed Legaré's posthumous *Writings* when they appeared and declared that "Mr. Legaré was *facile princeps* among all the distinguished men of the United States. . . . Many have excelled him in statesmanship; he was inferior to Preston, Webster, and Clay in parliamentary oratory; he was not the equal of Marshall, or Story, as Jurist; but in these several branches, he was a worthy rival of them all." Legaré's modern commentators have been content for the most part to describe the scope of his interests, especially his criticism of contemporary literature. The section on Legaré in Parrington's *Main Currents in American Thought* (1927), although containing many factual errors, was a rare attempt to analyze "the most cultivated mind in the South before the Civil War." It was soon followed by a very well-informed biography by Linda Rhea. More recently, John R. Welsh made a useful critical study of the *Southern Review*, but in the *History of Southern Literature* (1985) Legaré has faded almost entirely from view

The *Writings* were reprinted photographically in 1970, the year South Carolina celebrated its 300th anniversary, but apart from a few paragraphs that Rufus Griswold and the Duykincks included in their mid-nineteenth-century anthologies and the entombment of three essays in Edwin A. Alderman and Joel Chandler Harris's *Library of Southern Literature* (1907), only snippets have been rarely anthologized. None have found their way into any modern collection other than an obligatory inclusion of excerpts from two essays in a volume celebrating the South Carolina tercentenary. Legaré's essays–often over fifty pages long–have not lent themselves to being reprinted or even excerpted. The *Southern Review* did not tolerate brevity. It had been fashioned on the model of the *Edinburgh Review,* and as its prospectus declared, it had among its "first objects to vindicate the rights and privileges, the character of the Southern States, to arrest, if possible, the current which has been directed so steadily against our country generally, and the South in particular; and to offer to our fellow citizens one Journal which they may read without finding themselves the objects of perpetual sarcasm, or of affected commiseration." Legaré and the other sponsors of the journal were in earnest that the contributions should stand uncompromisingly on their own merits, whatever their subject or the subscribers' presumed interest in it.

This strenuous program for the intellectual progress of the South was more demanding at times than the editors and their contributors could manage. As a result, many articles were padded with inordinately long quotations from the books under review, often pages at a time. The *Southern Review* may well have been one of the publications Poe had in mind when in 1841 he wrote to Longfellow of the future of magazines in America: "The brief, the terse, the condensed, and the easily circulated will take [the] place of the diffuse, the ponderous, and the inaccessible. Even our Reviews . . . are found too massive for the taste of the day." But many had once been persuaded with Legaré that the South could bring its cultural potential to fruition only through the solidity of its scholarship. It was a goal for which Legaré almost consciously, it would seem, had been preparing since boyhood.

Biographies:

W.[illiam] C. Preston, *Eulogy on Hugh Swinton Legaré . . .* (Charleston, 1843);

E.[dward] W. J.[ohnston], "Biographical Notice," in *Writings of Hugh Swinton Legaré . . . ,* volume 1 (Charleston: Burges & James/ Philadelphia: Cowperthwait/New York: Appleton/Boston: Munroe, 1846), pp. v-lxxii;

Paul Hamilton Hayne, *Lives of Robert Young Hayne and Hugh Swinton Legaré* (Charleston: Walker, Evans & Cogswell, 1878);

Linda Rhea, *Hugh Swinton Legaré: A Charleston Intellectual* (Chapel Hill: University of North Carolina Press, 1934).

References:

Merrill G. Christophersen, "The Charleston Conversationalists," *Southern Speech Journal,* 20 (Winter 1954): 99-108;

Richard Beale Davis, "The Early American Lawyer and the Profession of Letters," *Huntington Library Quarterly,* 12 (1949): 191-205;

Elizabeth Evans, "The Friendship of Alexander Hill Everett and Hugh Swinton Legaré," *Mississippi Quarterly,* 28 (Fall 1975): 497-504;

Jay B. Hubbell, "Hugh Swinton Legaré," in *The South in American Literature: 1607-1900* (Durham: Duke University Press, 1954), pp. 263-274;

Hubbell, "Literary Nationalism in the Old South," in *American Studies in Honor of William Kenneth Boyd,* edited by David K. Jackson (Durham: Duke University Press, 1940), pp. 175-220;

John T. Krumpelmann, "South Carolina: Hugh Swinton Legaré," in *Southern Scholars in Goethe's Germany* (Chapel Hill: University of North Carolina Press, 1965), pp. 6-22;

Edd W. Parks, "Hugh Swinton Legaré: Humanist," in *Ante-Bellum Southern Literary Critics* (Athens: University of Georgia Press, 1962), pp. 23-50;

Parks, "Legaré and Grayson: Types of Classical Influences on Criticism in the Old South," in *Segments of Southern Thought* (Athens: University of Georgia Press, 1938), pp. 156-171;

Vernon L. Parrington, "Hugh Swinton Legaré: Charleston Intellectual," in *Main Currents in American Thought,* volume 2: *The Romantic Revolution in America 1800-1860* (New York: Harcourt, Brace, 1927), pp. 114-124;

Edgar Allan Poe, *Letters,* volume 1, edited by J. W. Ostrom (New York: Gordian Press, 1966), p. 166;

Meyer Reinhold, *Classica Americana: The Greek and Roman Heritage in the United States* (Detroit: Wayne State University Press, 1984);

George C. Rogers, *Charleston in the Age of the Pinckneys* (Norman: University of Oklahoma Press, 1969);

Alexander S. Salley, "William Gilmore Simms," in William Gilmore Simms, *Letters,* volume 1, edited by Mary C. S. Oliphant et al. (Columbia: University of South Carolina Press, 1952), pp. lxxxiv-lxxxv;

[William Gilmore Simms], *Essays on the Literary and Intellectual History of South Carolina,* edited by J. R. Scafidel (Columbia: University of South Carolina, 1977);

[Simms], "Notices of New Books [Review of Legaré's *Writings*]," *Southern and Western Literary Messenger and Review,* 12 (April 1846): 252-254;

[Simms], "Southern Review," *Southern Literary Gazette* (November 1828): 151-158;

"Sketch of the Character of the Hon. Hugh S. Legaré," *Southern Quarterly Review,* 4 (October 1843): 347-362;

L. G. Tyler, ed., *The Letters and Times of the Tylers,* volume 2 (Richmond: Whitter & Shepperson, 1885);

John R. Welsh, "Southern Literary Magazines, IV: An Early Pioneer: Legaré's *Southern Review,*" *Southern Literary Journal,* 3 (Spring 1971): 79-97.

Henry Wadsworth Longfellow

(27 February 1807-24 March 1882)

John Griffith
University of Washington

See also the Longfellow entry in *DLB 1, The American Renaissance in New England.*

Henry Wadsworth Longfellow, circa 1848, daguerreotype by Southworth and Hawes of Boston (by permission of the Metropolitan Museum of Art, gift of I. N. Phelps Stokes, Edward S. Hawes, Alice Mary Hawes, Marion Augusta Hawes)

SELECTED BOOKS: *Outre-Mer; A Pilgrimage Beyond the Sea* (volume 1, Boston: Hilliard, Gray, 1833; volume 2, Boston: Lilly, Wait, 1834; enlarged edition, 2 volumes, New York: Harper, 1835; London: Bentley, 1835);

Hyperion, A Romance (New York: Samuel Colman, 1839; revised edition, Boston: Fields, Osgood, 1869);

Voices of the Night (Cambridge: John Owen, 1839);

Poems on Slavery (Cambridge: John Owen, 1842);

Ballads and Other Poems (Cambridge: John Owen, 1842);

The Spanish Student. A Play, in Three Acts (Cambridge: John Owen, 1843);

The Belfry of Bruges and Other Poems (Cambridge: John Owen, 1846);

Evangeline, A Tale of Acadie (Boston: William D. Ticknor, 1847; London: Kent & Richards, 1848);

Kavanagh, A Tale (Boston: Ticknor, Reed & Fields, 1849);

The Seaside and the Fireside (Liverpool: John Walker/London: David Bogue; Hamilton, Adams; John Johnstone/Edinburgh: Oliver & Boyd; John Johnstone/Dublin: J. M'Glashan, 1849; Boston: Ticknor, Reed & Fields, 1850);

The Golden Legend (Boston: Ticknor, Reed & Fields, 1851; London: David Bogue, 1851);

The Song of Hiawatha (London: David Bogue, 1855; Boston: Ticknor & Fields, 1855);

Prose Works of Henry Wadsworth Longfellow, 2 volumes (Boston: Ticknor & Fields, 1857);

The Courtship of Miles Standish and Other Poems (London: Kent, 1858; Boston: Ticknor & Fields, 1858);

Tales of a Wayside Inn (London: Routledge, Warne & Routledge, 1863; Boston: Ticknor & Fields, 1863);

Flower-de-Luce (Boston: Ticknor & Fields, 1867; London: Routledge & Sons, 1867);

The New England Tragedies . . . I. John Endicott II. Giles Corey of the Salem Farms (Boston: Ticknor & Fields, 1868; London: Routledge & Sons, 1868);

The Divine Tragedy (Boston: Osgood, 1871);

Christus, A Mystery, 3 volumes (Boston: Osgood, 1872)–includes *The New England Tragedies, The Divine Tragedy,* and *The Golden Legend*;

Three Books of Song (Boston: Osgood, 1872; London: Routledge & Sons, 1872);

Aftermath (Boston: Osgood, 1873; London: Routledge & Sons, 1873);

The Hanging of the Crane (Boston: Osgood, 1874;

London: Routledge & Sons, 1875);

The Masque of Pandora and Other Poems (Boston: Osgood, 1875; London: Routledge & Sons, 1875);

Kéramos and Other Poems (Boston: Houghton, Osgood, 1878; London: Routledge & Sons, 1878);

The Early Poems of Henry Wadsworth Longfellow, edited by Richard Herne Shepherd (London: Pickering, 1878);

Ultima Thule (London: Routledge & Sons, 1880; Boston: Houghton, Mifflin, 1880);

In the Harbor, Ultima Thule, Part II (Boston: Houghton, Mifflin, 1882; London: Routledge & Sons, 1882);

Michael Angelo (Boston: Houghton, Mifflin, 1883; London: Routledge & Sons, 1883).

OTHER: *Manuel de Proverbes Dramatiques*, edited by Longfellow (Portland: Samuel Colman/Brunswick: Griffin's Press, 1830);

Charles Francois Lhomond, *Elements of French Grammar*, translated by Longfellow (Portland: Samuel Colman/Brunswick: Griffin's Press, 1830);

Lhomond, *French Exercises*, translated by Longfellow (Portland: Samuel Colman/Brunswick: Griffin's Press, 1830);

Novelas Españolas: El Serrano de las Alpujarras; y el Cuadro Misterioso, edited by Longfellow (Portland: Samuel Colman/Brunswick: Griffin's Press, 1830);

Oliver Goldsmith, *Le Ministre de Wakefield*, French translation by T. F. G. Hennequin, edited by Longfellow (Boston: Gray & Bowen, 1831);

Syllabus de la Grammaire Italienne, edited by Longfellow (Boston: Gray & Bowen, 1832);

Saggi de' Novellieri Italiani d'Ogni Secolo . . ., edited by Longfellow (Boston: Gray & Bowen, 1832);

Coplas de Don Jorge Manrique, translated by Longfellow (Boston: Allen & Ticknor, 1833);

The Waif . . ., edited by Longfellow (Cambridge: John Owen, 1845);

The Poets and Poetry of Europe, edited, with biographical notes, by Longfellow (Philadelphia: Carey & Hart, 1845; revised and expanded, Philadelphia: Porter & Coates, 1871);

The Estray: A Collection of Poems, edited by Longfellow (Boston: Ticknor, 1847);

The Divine Comedy of Dante Alighieri, 3 volumes, translated by Longfellow (Boston: Ticknor & Fields, 1865-1867; revised, 1867; London: Routledge & Sons, 1867);

Poems of Places, edited by Longfellow (volumes 1-19, Boston: Osgood, 1876-1877; volumes 20-31, Boston: Houghton, Osgood, 1878-1879).

PERIODICAL PUBLICATIONS: "The Origin and Progress of the French Language," *North American Review*, 32 (April 1831): 277-317;

"The Defence of Poetry," *North American Review*, 34 (January 1832): 56-78;

"Spanish Devotional Poetry," *North American Review*, 34 (April 1832): 277-315;

"History of the Italian Language and Dialects," *North American Review*, 35 (October 1832): 283-342;

"Spanish Language and Literature," *North American Review*, 36 (April 1833): 316-344;

"Old English Prose Romances," *North American Review*, 37 (October 1833): 374-419;

"Hawthorne's *Twice-Told Tales*," *North American Review*, 45 (July 1837): 59-73;

"Tegnér's *Frithiofs Saga*," *North American Review*, 45 (July 1837): 149-185;

"Anglo-Saxon Literature," *North American Review*, 47 (July 1838): 90-134.

Henry Wadsworth Longfellow's primary place in literary history is as a poet whose ballads, pensive lyrics, verse-narratives, and moral exhortations achieved a degree of popularity and respect in his own time and for a generation or two after his death. The poetry of no other American poet has ever achieved that level of success. He was important, too, as a scholar and a man of letters who introduced to the American reading public an eclectic assortment of poets and poetry from the European past. Largely self-taught, Longfellow conducted enthusiastic forays into the languages and literatures of half a dozen European cultures and published the results of his searches to a growing audience of American readers. Longfellow was never a critic, never one to theorize, analyze, or explain the detailed inner workings of literary creations. He was a discoverer, an appreciator, and a promoter of what he perceived as the romantically old and exotic. His scholarly writing is not the sort to which modern readers turn for continual insight and revelation; it is rather to be surveyed as a phase in the

Longfellow, circa 1858, at the summer cottage of the Story family in Nahant, Massachusetts (courtesy of the National Park Service, Longfellow National Historic Site)

growth of literary taste in the United States, a significant milestone in American culture's progress toward finding its place in world literature.

The foundation of Longfellow's admiration for European culture generally, and language and literature in particular, is readily discernible in his childhood. He was raised, in comfort and prosperity, in a New England town just emerging from the emotional and moral rigors of its Puritan background. The mental atmosphere there was conservative but amenable to orderly, genteel pressures for change. Henry's father, Stephen, an eminent lawyer and civic leader in Portland, Maine, was, as Newton Arvin has described him, "the very pattern of the Federalist gentleman of his day–stately, grave, a little pompous, but generous, humane, affectionate toward his children, and filled with a high sense of public responsibility." Zilpah Wadsworth Longfellow, Henry's mother, was religious in the progressive but respectable Unitarian way and liked music and poetry of uncomplicated kinds. Books, music, and art were generally cultivated in the Longfellow household as the amenities of decent living, pleasant and edifying. Longfellow grew up learning the piano, the flute, and singing and reading such poets as Oliver Goldsmith, William Cowper, Thomas Gray, James Thomson, and Sir Walter Scott. His grammar-school education was obtained in private Portland academies, where he studied, primarily, Latin and Greek. He entered Bowdoin College in Brunswick, Maine, at the age of fifteen, with a solid grounding in the classical languages and literature and a taste for old world culture which had only been whetted by the provincial resources of Portland.

While still an undergraduate at Bowdoin, Longfellow resisted his father's expectation that he would become a lawyer, thinking instead about becoming a man of letters. His concern over what this course might mean in an American society as yet relatively inhospitable to such ambitions is addressed in his commencement oration, "Our Native Writers" (1825). American literature, he observed, was still nothing more than "a first beginning of a national literature." He recognized that Americans were not generally interested in belles lettres, having "an aversion to everything that is not practical, operative, and thorough-going." But he speculated that this condition would change and America would learn to support its poets, "for our hearts are already growing warm towards literary adventurers, and a generous spirit has gone abroad in our land, which shall liberalize and enlighten." He predicted that America's lack of scholarship and bookishness would work to its first poets' advantage, since they would be forced to turn to nature itself for inspiration. "We are thus thrown upon ourselves: and thus shall our native hills become renowned in song, like those of Greece and Italy."

His optimism was intermittent, however. He had already encountered opposition to his dream of becoming a writer from his father and from Theophilus Parsons, a literary editor to whom he had applied for work. In an essay entitled "The Literary Spirit of Our Country," which appeared in the *United States Literary Gazette* in 1825, Longfellow was much less sanguine. He accused his countrymen of having "retarded the progress of poetry in America" by failing to support poetry financially. The fear of poverty, he said, "deters many gifted and poetic minds" from pursuing literary careers, a plight which "the hand of honourable patronage alone" could remedy.

Longfellow was already producing quantities of poetry. When he graduated more than forty of his poems had appeared in various newspapers and magazines. At this time his professional hopes revived, for just as he was bargaining with his father to sponsor him for a year of postgraduate study in modern languages at Harvard College before he settled down to reading law, the trustees of Bowdoin decided to establish a chair of modern languages, one of the first of its kind in the United States. Impressed by a translation Longfellow had made of an ode of Horace's, one of the trustees proposed the young scholar for the post, and the board concurred. The trustees proposed that Longfellow take two or three years for travel and study in Europe to prepare himself for the new chair. Longfellow accepted the offer.

The three years Longfellow spent in his travels–eight months each in France and Spain, a year in Italy, and six months in Germany–were of fundamental importance to his development as a scholar and a man of letters. His central objective was to learn the languages and something of the literature of each country. The approach he took was decidedly casual, impressionistic, and impulsive. Apparently he attended some university lectures in Paris and Göttingen, but he seems not to have enrolled formally at any university. He did no prolonged or systematic reading in libraries. He worked, but only briefly, with tutors in Spanish and German. Primarily he simply went among the people, listening to them and trying to speak, read, and write the languages as best he could. Desultory and easygoing as his methods were, Longfellow had an ear for languages fine enough that he succeeded in picking up considerable competency in them. As a kind of voracious tourist, he was also absorbing much else about the places, people, and manners of the countries he visited, taking in castles, coffeehouses, festivals, salons, churches, and museums wherever he went. In Madrid he made the acquaintance of Washington Irving, who was there working on his biography of Christopher Columbus.

In 1829 Longfellow was back in Brunswick, occupying his Bowdoin post. His title was that of professor, but his duties were those of an instructor, teaching elementary French, Spanish, and Italian. A great deal of his time and energy went into translating and editing grammar texts and exercises in those languages and seeing them through publication. He also read widely in the romance literatures and included the discussion of poetry in his courses when he could, in addition to the mechanics of language. From his classroom lectures resulted a number of articles for the *North American Review*: "The Origin and Progress of the French Language" (April 1831), "Spanish Devotional Poetry" (April 1832), "History of the Italian Language and Dialects" (October 1832), "Spanish Language and Literature" (April 1833), and "Old English Prose Romances" (October 1833). He translated an essay by Paulin Paris from the French, "Ancient French Romances," and published it in the *Select Journal of Foreign Periodical Literature* (January 1833). Also in 1833 he published his first book of poetry, a translation of the *Coplas de Don Jorge Manrique*. Thus was established, once and for all, the kind of contribution Longfellow would make to American literary scholarship; he would promote the appreciation and admiration of European literature in the United States.

In view of Longfellow's earlier pronouncements about American poets finding their inspiration not in old world books but in themselves and in native American settings, there is some irony in this fact that is underscored by another of Longfellow's publications of the early 1830s. Ostensibly a review of a new edition of Sir Philip Sidney's *The Defence of Poesy* for the *North American Review* (April 1832), Longfellow's essay actually framed his own defense of poetry to the American public. He began by attacking the famous American preoccupation with utility. "With us, the spirit of the age is clamorous for utility, for visible, tangible utility–for bare, brawny, muscular utility," he wrote. But in limiting their understanding of utility to that which conduces directly to material gain, Americans have been too narrow. In fact, says Longfellow, true utility "embraces in its proper definition whatever contributes to our happiness"; it should thus be taken to include arts, such as poetry, which "enrich the heart, freight the understanding, and make up the garnered fulness of the mind."

Having urged his countrymen to appreciate the riches of the imagination as well as the riches of the marketplace, Longfellow then addresses his fellow poets, urging them to make their poetry from their own experience, giving it thereby "a more national character." The American poet will truly fulfill his mission only when he gives up his present dependence on the images and conventions of British poetry, says Longfellow, and takes his inspiration "from nature and not from books," and seeks to "fathom the recesses of his own mind, and bring up rich pearls from the secret depths of thought."

Nonetheless, the bulk of his literary scholarship was devoted to presenting old world poets and poetry and commenting on them very generally. In "Spanish Devotional Poetry," for example, he translates passages from Gonzalo de Berceo, Calderón, Lope de Vega, and Francisco de Aldana. His praise for the poetry is severely circumscribed by his Protestant disapproval of the Catholic veneration for saints, miracles, icons, and other physical manifestations of spirituality. He laments the debasing effect which painted, carved, or fleshly representations of religious characters and events can have on the "unenlightened and superstitious mind." He wishes that the Spanish poetic imagination were balanced with good judgment while spreading "its wings in the bright regions of devotional song." He finds a monastic ideal in the poetry in which "many a pure spirit, through heavenly-mindedness, and an ardent though mistaken zeal, has fled from the temptation of the world to seek in solitude and self-communion a closer walk with God." Yet he urges that much credit be given, since in his view Spanish poetry has a "warmth of imagination and depth and sincerity of feeling" and ideas "always striking and original, and, when not degraded by dogmas and the poor, puerile conceits arising from them, beautiful and sublime."

In 1834, after five years at Bowdoin, Longfellow was appointed to the Smith professorship of French and Spanish at Harvard and given the opportunity for more study in Europe in preparation for assuming that post. On the ensuing trip to Germany, Denmark, Sweden, and Holland his wife, Mary Storer Potter, whom he had married in 1831, suffered a miscarriage and died in Rotterdam on 29 November 1835.

It was during his brief stay in Sweden that Longfellow encountered the subject of his next scholarly publication, the long poem *Frithiofs Saga* (1825) by the Swedish poet Esaias Tegnér. The poem consists of twenty-four cantos, linked ballads based on old Icelandic legends of the Viking hero Frithiof, rendered into modern Swedish. Longfellow calls it "the noblest poetic contribution which Sweden has yet made to the literary history of the world." He urges the reader of the poem to remember that the poem has been "written in the spirit of the Past" and that Tegnér carries on the old tradition of "the Scald [who] smote the strings of his harp with as bold a hand as the Berserk smote his foe." The poem, he says, "points us to the great mounds, which are the tombs of kings. Their bones are within; skeletons of warriors mounted on the skeletons of their steeds, and Vikings sitting gaunt and grim on the plankless ribs of their pirate ships."

To help his reader "enter more easily into the spirit of the poem," Longfellow begins with an expansive account of rural life in modern Sweden and what he calls its "almost primeval simplicity." He describes the woods, fields, farms, and villages, the peasants at work, rest, and worship. He pays special attention to a village wedding he wit-

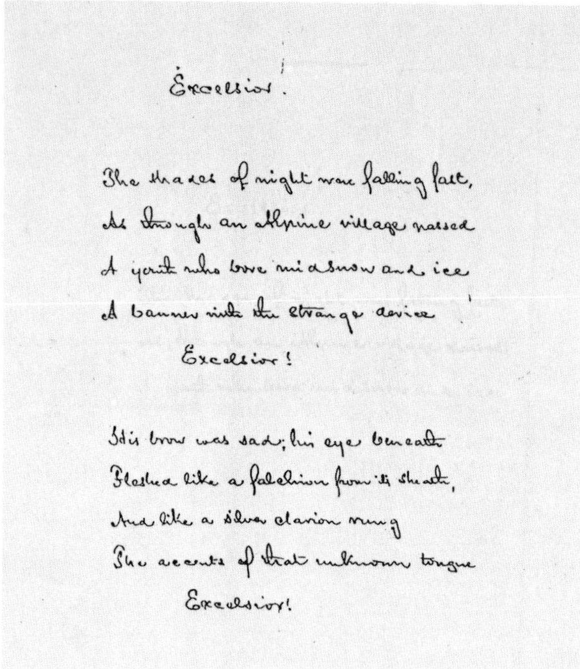

Excelsior.

The shades of night were falling fast,
As through an Alpine village passed
A youth who bore mid snow and ice
A banner with the strange device
Excelsior!

His brow was sad; his eye beneath
Flashed like a falchion from its sheath,
And like a silver clarion rung
The accents of that unknown tongue
Excelsior!

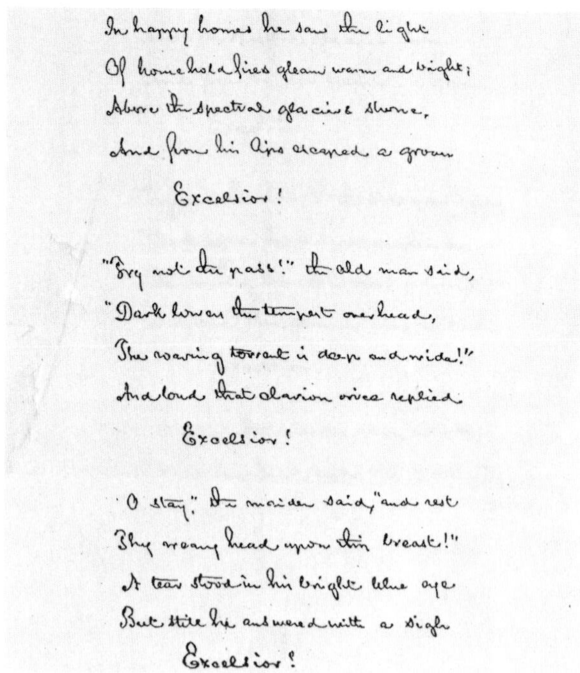

In happy homes he saw the light
Of household fires gleam warm and bright;
Above the spectral glaciers shone,
And from his lips escaped a groan
Excelsior!

"Try not the pass!" the old man said,
"Dark lowers the tempest overhead,
The roaring torrent is deep and wide!"
And loud that clarion voice replied
Excelsior!

"O stay," the maiden said, "and rest
Thy weary head upon this breast!"
A tear stood in his bright blue eye
But still he answered with a sigh
Excelsior!

Fair copy of the poem that Longfellow described in 1841 as "one of the best things, if not the best, that I have written" (from Autograph Leaves of Our Country's Authors, *compiled by Alexander Bliss and J. P. Kennedy, 1864)*

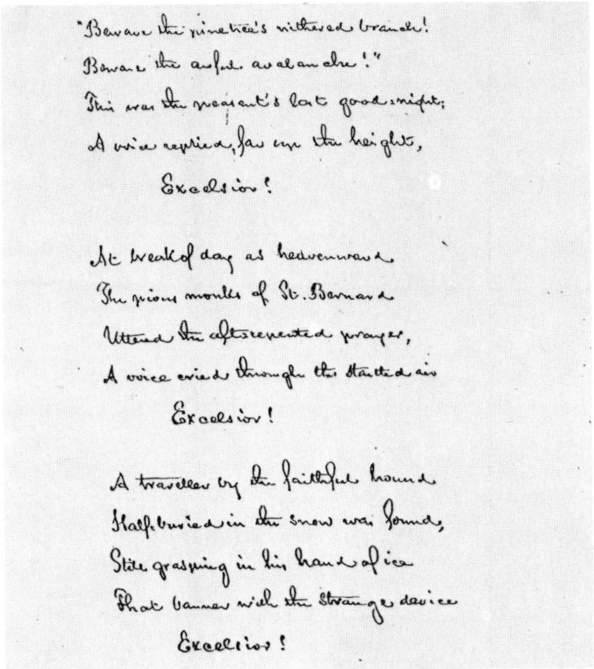

"Beware the pine-tree's withered branch!
Beware the awful avalanche!"
This was the peasant's last good-night;
A voice replied, far up the height,
Excelsior!

At break of day as heavenward
The pious monks of St. Bernard
Uttered the oft-repeated prayer,
A voice cried through the startled air
Excelsior!

A traveller by the faithful hound
Half-buried in the snow was found,
Still grasping in his hand of ice
That banner with the strange device
Excelsior!

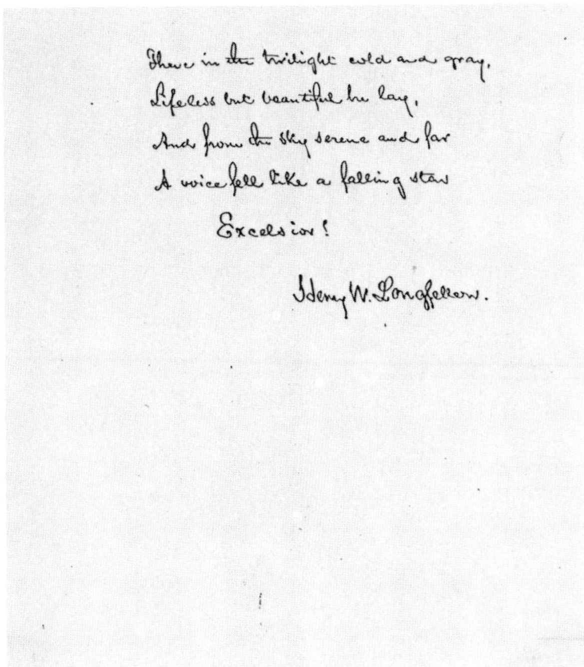

There in the twilight cold and gray,
Lifeless but beautiful he lay,
And from the sky serene and far
A voice fell like a falling star
Excelsior!

Henry W. Longfellow.

nessed, describing the costumes, banquet, ceremonies, toasts, and blessings. These details, he suggests, will help the reader "feel more truly the influences" under which Tegnér's poem was written. He then retells the saga, canto by canto, in summary and paraphrase amounting to some ten thousand words. Interspersed throughout are substantial passages of Tegnér's verse, translated into English. Longfellow's article appeared in the *North American Review* in July 1837. He used the description of the village wedding again as introduction to his translation of another Tegnér poem, "Nattvardsbarnen," which he published as "The Children of the Lord's Supper" in his book *Ballads and Other Poems* (1842).

Another essay of Longfellow's appeared in the July 1837 number of the *North American Review* with the article on *Frithiofs Saga*. This review of *Twice-Told Tales* (1837), by his Bowdoin classmate Nathaniel Hawthorne, is one of the very few pieces of criticism of contemporary literature that Longfellow published. It is of interest primarily for what it shows Longfellow not to have been: a close, probing analyst of other authors' writing. He devotes most of the 1,700 words of the review to proclaiming that the spirit of poetry and romance is not dead. He praises Hawthorne for his poetic temperament and beautiful prose style, and for his having chosen American subjects for his stories. But he says virtually nothing about the specific contents of the volume he is reviewing. As George DeMille (*Literary Criticism in America*, 1931) has pointed out, "By removing from this eight page article just forty-eight words, one can make it impossible for a reader to tell either the author or the book under consideration."

Longfellow knew that he was no critic. Indeed, he questioned whether criticism really needed to be written at all. "What is the use of writ-

Longfellow (seated at center) with the group that accompanied him on his European tour of 1868-1869. Standing: Samuel Longfellow, Alice Longfellow, Thomas Gold Appleton, Ernest Longfellow, and Harriet Spelman Longfellow; at front: Mary Longfellow Greenleaf, Edith Longfellow, Anne Allegra Longfellow, and Anne Longfellow Pierce

ing about books," he asked in an unpublished lecture, "excepting so far as to give information to those who cannot get the books themselves?" Elsewhere he acknowledged that a few critics did possess an impressive "analytical power in literature," but that he had none of it himself. In 1850, in a letter to George Putnam, he wrote, "It is very nearly ten years since I have written a Review or even a Critical Notice. I left that field of labor, because I had no particular vocation therefor [*sic*], and felt a growing disinclination to it. One can hardly be an author and critic at the same time; and I have too many beams in my own eye, to be looking after the motes in other people's eyes."

One final article coming out of Longfellow's academic lecturing was "Anglo-Saxon Literature," which appeared in the *North American Review* in July 1838. In tones similar to those which he had applied to old Spanish and Scandinavian poetry, Longfellow invites his reader to think of Anglo-Saxon manuscripts as "the dark chambers and mouldering walls of an old national literature, weather-stained and in ruins." In a few paragraphs he characterizes the formation of the Anglo-Saxon language, the coming of Christianity to the British Isles, and English life in the Dark Ages. Then he rapidly surveys some of the songs, riddles, homilies, saints' lives, and legends making up the corpus of Old English literature. He points out some of the elements of Old English prosody and summarizes at length the story of *Beowulf*, praising it as being "like a piece of ancient armor, rusty and battered, and yet strong. From within comes a voice sepulchral, as if the ancient armor spoke, telling a simple, straightforward narrative, with here and there the boastful speech of a rough old Dane, reminding one of those made by the heroes of Homer." The colorful ways in which the Caedmonian versifications of scripture place the biblical stories in a rustic northern European ambience are commented on briefly; *The Battle of Maldon* and a handful of other battle poems are mentioned; and an assortment of "narratives and odes and didactic poems, . . . hymns, allegories, doxologies, proverbs, enigmas, paraphrases of the Lord's Prayer, poems on Death and the Day of Judgment, and the like" are alluded to. He quotes a few passages in the Old English and translates several into modern English. Throughout he emphasizes the exotic character of his subject, finding it "curious" and urging his readers to indulge the imagination's appetite for such antiquities.

Longfellow in 1876, photograph by F. Gutekunst of Philadelphia (courtesy of the National Park Service, Longfellow National Historic Site)

Longfellow assumed his professorship at Harvard in the fall of 1836 and remained on the faculty there for eighteen years. In 1842, in poor health, he took a leave of absence for his third trip to Europe, a six-month tour during which he met and became fast friends with the poet Ferdinand Freiligrath in Germany and visited his old friend Charles Dickens in England. Back in Cambridge, after a courtship that had begun several years earlier, Longfellow married Frances Appleton on 13 July 1843.

Longfellow's published work as a literary scholar during his Harvard years was devoted exclusively to editing, translating, and introducing to American readers the poetry of other cultures. His magnum opus in this line was the anthology *The Poets and Poetry of Europe*, which was first published in 1845 and reissued in an enlarged version in 1871. It consisted of poems translated from the work of almost 400 poets who had written in Old English, Icelandic, Danish, Swedish, German, Dutch, French, Italian, Spanish, and Portuguese. Dozens of the translations are by Longfellow himself. For each of the languages or cultures represented in the anthology, Longfellow provided an essay of several thousand words on its language and poetry.

Longfellow managed to complete the editing of this massive body of material in little more than two years, for he was drawing on scholarly work he had been doing over the preceding decade; many of his translations had been written during the 1830s. Little of what appeared in the general introductions was original with them; most of it Longfellow had written earlier for his lectures at Bowdoin and Harvard and for the articles he had published in the *North American Review* and elsewhere. In his preface he acknowledged the help of his friend C. C. Felton, professor of Greek at Harvard, in producing the biographical sketches with which each poet's work was introduced. *The Poets and Poetry of Europe* showed no new developments in Longfellow's literary opinions or scholarly methods; rather, it consolidated his many years' research in European literature into one large volume. It was a milestone in American letters. "Nothing like *The Poets and Poetry of Europe* had ever appeared before, either here or in Europe," wrote Newton Arvin, "and one doubts whether anything like it had ever appeared on the Continent." Arvin praised the volume for "the genuinely Arnoldian role it played, for some decades, in helping to propagate among American readers 'the best that is known and thought in the world.' "

The translations Longfellow made for his lectures, articles, and anthologies were part of a lifelong concern he had for rendering poetry from foreign languages into English. His translations constitute his most notable achievement as a literary scholar. Thomas Wentworth Higginson, one of Longfellow's early biographers, reckoned that as a translator Longfellow produced "thirty-five versions of whole books or detached poems in German, twelve in Italian, nine each in French and Dutch, seven in Swedish, six in Danish, five in Polish, three in Portuguese, two each in Spanish, Russian, Hungarian, and Bohemian, with single translations in Latin, Hebrew, Chinese, Sanskrit, Marath, and Judea-German–yielding one hundred versions altogether, extending into eighteen languages, apart from the original English." Although it would be too much to claim that Longfellow had mastered as many languages as that, he does seem to have been competent in at least eleven: Greek, Latin, Italian, Spanish, Portuguese, Old French, French, German, Danish, Swedish, and Old English.

Presented to Longfellow by the children of Cambridge, Massachusetts, on his seventy-second birthday, this chair was made from the chestnut tree described in Longfellow's "The Village Blacksmith" (courtesy of the National Park Service, Longfellow National Historic Site)

"The great art of translating well," he wrote, "lies in the power of rendering literally the words of a foreign author while at the same time we preserve the spirit of the original." He compared the work of the translator to that of the sculptor who, in his effort to give the expressiveness of living flesh to the stone he carves, must sometimes "transgress the rigid truth of nature," exaggerate the features, and so enhance the play of light and shadow. Likewise the translator will sometimes use "the embellishment of an additional epithet, or a more forcible turn of expression" in order to convey the living spirit of his original. As a general rule, though, Longfellow tried to make word-for-word translation, even if he had to sacrifice rhyme to do it. Wherever possible he preserved the meter of the original.

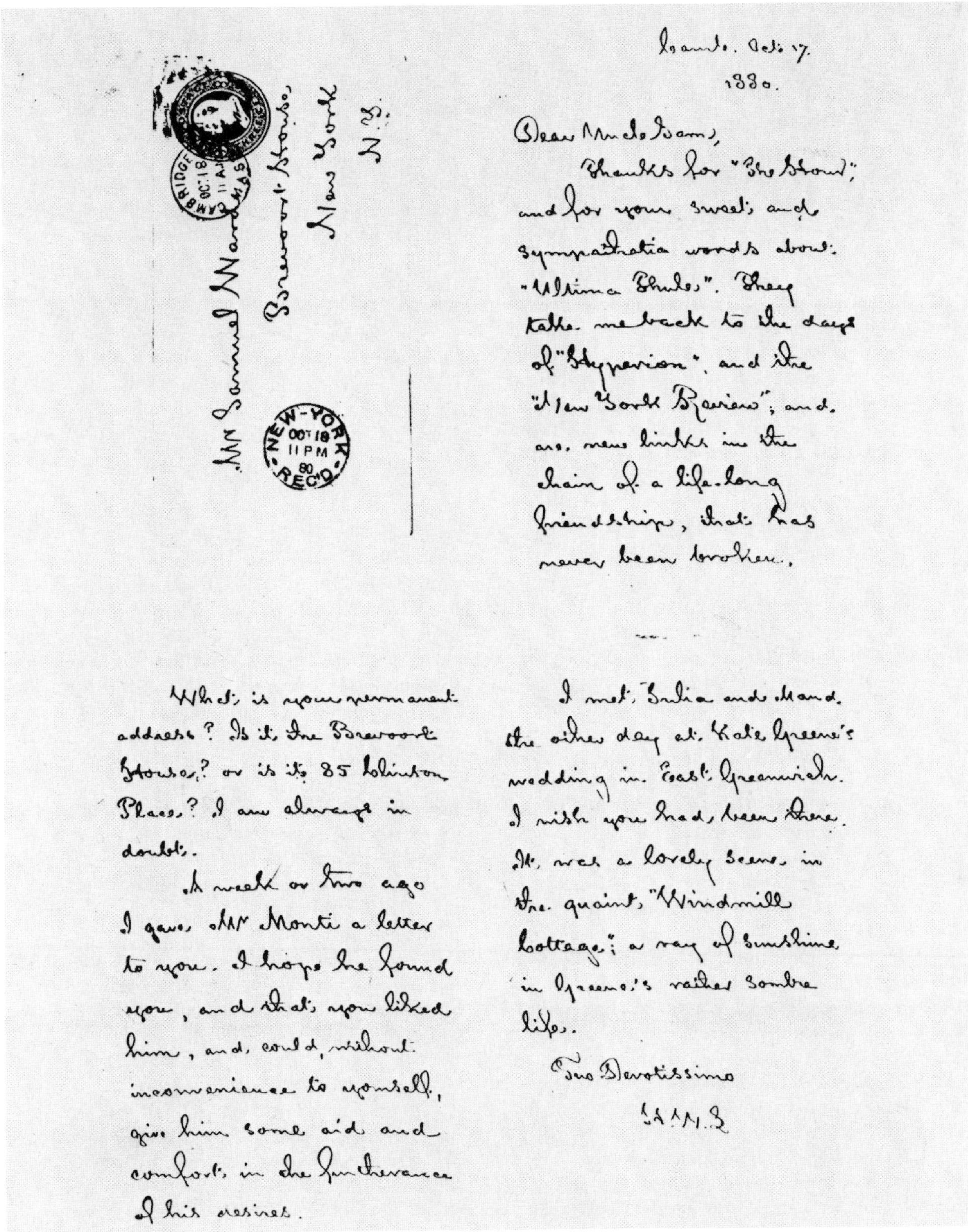

Mr Samuel Ward
Brevoort House,
New York
N.Y.

Cambr. Oct. 17.
1880.

Dear Uncle Sam,

Thanks for "The Stand"; and for your sweet and sympathetic words about "Ultima Thule". They take me back to the days of "Hyperion", and the "New York Review"; and are new links in the chain of a life-long friendship, that has never been broken.

What is your permanent address? Is it the Brevoort House? or is it 85 Clinton Place? I am always in doubt.

A week or two ago I gave Mr Monti a letter to you. I hope he found you, and that you liked him, and could, without inconvenience to yourself, give him some aid and comfort in the furtherance of his desires.

I met Julia and Maud the other day at Kate Greene's wedding in East Greenwich. I wish you had been there. It was a lovely scene in the quaint "Windmill Cottage"; a ray of sunshine in Greene's rather sombre life.

Tuo Devotissimo
H. W. L.

Letter from Longfellow to Samuel Ward, a wealthy New Yorker whom Longfellow met in 1836 and with whom he corresponded for the next forty-six years (by permission of the Rare Book Collection, Special Collections Division, University of Washington Libraries)

The pinnacle of his achievement as a translator was his version of Dante's *Divine Comedy* (1865-1867). He had begun translating parts of the great Italian work at least as early as 1839, for he included parts of four cantos from the *Purgatorio* in his *Voices of the Night,* published that year. By 1853 he had finished translating all of the *Purgatorio.* After several years' intermission he returned to Dante in 1862, partly as a means of taking his mind away from the grief he felt after the death of his wife in 1861. In 1862 and 1863 he worked rapidly at a draft of the entire *Divine Comedy.* For the next four years he revised it with the detailed advice of a group of friends who met with him weekly to discuss the work, canto by canto. This group, who called themselves the Dante Club, included James Russell Lowell, Charles Eliot Norton, George Washington Greene, William Dean Howells, and James T. Fields. Their meetings formed the foundation of the Dante Society of Cambridge, which continued in existence for years after Longfellow's death.

In 1876, at the age of sixty-nine, Longfellow turned his hand once more to editing an anthology. Of even more prodigious scope than *The Poets and Poetry of Europe, Poems of Places* (1876-1879) was an immense collection which described or otherwise evoked the sense of specific locales all over the world. Longfellow thought of it as "a kind of poetic guidebook." Designed to be a major money-making project, it filled thirty-one volumes. Five volumes were devoted to the United States alone; others took in England, Scotland, Wales, most of the countries of Europe and Asia, Australia, Polynesia, and Central and South America. Longfellow was editor of the whole project and wrote some translations (primarily from the German) and original poems for it. The anthology did not sell well, however, and the publishers lost money on it.

Despite the relative failure of this, his last major work of literary scholarship, Longfellow's place as a pioneer in American exploration of European literature is secure. As one of the first professors of modern languages at Bowdoin and at Harvard and as a translator and editor of European poetry, he was a conspicuous force for making American readers aware of the cultural traditions of the Old World in the middle of the nineteenth century.

Twentieth-century appraisals of the depth and intelligence of his scholarship vary somewhat. Emilio Goggio argues that "Longfellow was one of the most brilliant cosmopolitan scholars of his age. He had a thorough knowledge of all the leading languages of Europe, and . . . read extensively in their respective literatures." Iris Whitman contends that, "judged by the standards of his time, Longfellow's knowledge of Spanish literature was thorough and his judgment, discriminating." Newton Arvin praises his innovative teaching at Harvard as being "broadly humanistic rather than erudite in any studiously specialized way. . . . He aimed much less at the transmission of information than at the contagion of personal enthusiasm." Usually such praise is qualified with the acknowledgment that Longfellow is to be admired as a man of his time, rather than absolutely. "Longfellow's reading was extensive, ranging through eight or ten languages, but it was not aggressive, energetic, or deep," writes Odell Shepard (*Henry Wadsworth Longfellow: Representative Selections,* 1934). "To an age which has addicted itself to a scientific scholarship, his investigations in literature . . . seem decidedly shallow, a fact which, for us, carries with it the stigma of dilettantism," writes Andrew Hilen. It is unlikely, then, that scholars now or in the future will turn to Longfellow for ideas, methods, or information of primary value to them; but, students of the history of American literary education will always have to take him into account.

Letters:

The Letters of Henry Wadsworth Longfellow, 6 volumes, edited by Andrew Hilen (Cambridge: Harvard University Press, 1966-1983).

Bibliographies:

Luther S. Livingston, *A Bibliography of The First Editions in Book Form of the Writings of Henry Wadsworth Longfellow* (New York: De Vinne Press, 1908);

H. W. L. Dana, "Henry Wadsworth Longfellow," in *Cambridge History of American Literature* (New York: Putnam's, 1917);

Jacob Blanck, *Bibliography of American Literature,* volume 5 (New York: Yale University Press, 1969), pp. 468-640.

Biographies:

William Sloane Kennedy, *Henry Wadsworth Longfellow: Biography, Anecdote, Letters, Criticism* (Cambridge: Moses King, 1882);

Francis H. Underwood, *Henry Wadsworth Longfellow: A Biographical Sketch* (Boston: Houghton, Mifflin, 1882; London: Routledge, 1882);

George Lowell Austin, *Henry Wadsworth Longfellow*: His Life, His Works, His Friendships (Boston: Lee &-Shepard, 1883);

Samuel Longfellow, *Life of Henry Wadsworth Longfellow, with Extracts from His Journals and Correspondence*, 2 volumes (Boston: Ticknor, 1886);

Samuel Longfellow, *Final Memorials of Henry Wadsworth Longfellow* (Boston: Ticknor, 1887);

Thomas Wentworth Higginson, *Henry Wadsworth Longfellow* (Boston & New York: Houghton Mifflin, 1902);

Ernest Wadsworth Longfellow, *Random Memories* (Boston: Houghton Mifflin, 1922);

Herbert S. Gorman, *A Victorian American, Henry Wadsworth Longfellow* (New York: Doran, 1926; London: Cassell, 1926?);

Lawrance Thompson, *Young Longfellow, 1807-1843* (New York: Macmillan, 1938);

Carl L. Johnson, *Professor Longfellow of Harvard* (Eugene: University of Oregon Press, 1944);

Edward Wagenknecht, *Longfellow: A Full-Length Portrait* (New York, London & Toronto: Longmans, Green, 1955).

References:

Newton Arvin, *Longfellow: His Life and Work* (Boston: Little, Brown, 1963);

Anna J. DeArmond, "Longfellow and Germany," *Delaware Notes*, 25 (1952): 15-33;

E. C. Dunn, "Longfellow the Teacher," *North American Review*, 221 (February 1920): 259-265;

Emilio Goggio, "Italian Influences on Longfellow's Works," *Romanic Review*, 25 (July 1925): 208-222;

James T. Hatfield, *New Light on Longfellow, With Special Reference to His Relations to Germany* (Boston: Houghton Mifflin, 1933);

Andrew Hilen, *Longfellow and Scandinavia; A Study of the Poet's Relationship with the Northern Languages and Literature* (New Haven: Yale University Press, 1947);

Edward L. Hirsh, *Henry Wadsworth Longfellow* (Minneapolis: University of Minnesota Press, 1964);

Carl L. Johnson, "Longfellow's Beginnings in Foreign Languages," *New England Quarterly*, 20 (September 1947): 317-328;

Johnson, "Longfellow's Studies in France," *Emerson Society Quarterly*, 58 (First Quarter 1970): 40-48;

Orie W. Long, *Literary Pioneers: Early American Explorers of European Culture* (Cambridge: Harvard University Press, 1935);

Joseph Chesley Mathews, ed., *Longfellow Reconsidered: A Symposium* (Hartford, Conn.: Transcendental Books, 1970);

Paul Morin, *Les Sources de L'Oeuvre de Henry Wadsworth Longfellow* (Paris: Emile Larose, 1913);

Henry A. Pochmann, *German Culture in America: Philosophical and Literary Influences, 1600-1900* (Madison: University of Wisconsin Press, 1957);

Francesco Viglione, *La Critica Literaria di Henry Wadsworth Longfellow*, 2 volumes (Florence: Vallecchi, 1934);

Iris Whitman, *Longfellow and Spain* (New York: Instituto de las Espanas en los Estados Unidos, 1927);

Cecil Brown Williams, *Henry Wadsworth Longfellow* (New York: Twayne, 1964);

Stanley T. Williams, *The Spanish Background of American Literature*, 2 volumes (New Haven: Yale University Press, 1955).

Papers:

The major collection of Longfellow letters and manuscripts is at the Houghton Library, Harvard University. Other papers are at the Bowdoin College Library; the Massachusetts Historical Society; the Boston Public Library; the Pierpont Morgan Library; the Berg Collection, New York Public Library; the Library of Congress; the Clifton Wallen Barrett Library at the University of Virginia; the Henry E. Huntington Library; and the University of Washington Library.

James Marsh

(19 July 1794-3 July 1842)

Peter Carafiol
Portland State University

See also the Marsh entry in *DLB 1, The American Renaissance in New England.*

WORKS: *An Exposition of the System of Instruction and Discipline Pursued in the University of Vermont* (Burlington: Chauncey Goodrich, 1829; revised, 1831);

Samuel Taylor Coleridge, *Aids to Reflection, in the Formation of a Manly Character, on the Several Grounds of Prudence, Morality, and Religion: Illustrated by Select Passages From our Elder Divines, Especially From Archbishop Leighton,* edited, with additional works by Coleridge, and with a "Preliminary Essay" and notes, by Marsh (Burlington: Chauncey Goodrich, 1829);

Select Practical Theology of the Seventeenth Century, Comprising the Best Practical Works of the Great English Divines, and other Congenial Authors of that Age, volume 1, edited, with biographical sketches and notes, by Marsh (New York: Carvill/Burlington: Chauncey Goodrich, 1831);

Coleridge, *The Friend: A Series of Essays, to Aid in the Formation of Fixed Principles in Politics, Morals, and Religion, with Literary Amusements Interspersed,* edited by Marsh (Burlington: Chauncey Goodrich, 1831);

Johann Gottfried von Herder, *The Spirit of Hebrew Poetry,* 2 volumes, translated, with a preface, by Marsh (Burlington: Edward Smith, 1833);

D. H. Hegewisch, *Introduction to Historical Chronology,* translated by Marsh (Burlington: Chauncey Goodrich, 1837).

PERIODICAL PUBLICATIONS: "Ancient and Modern Poetry," *North American Review,* 22 (July 1822): 94-131;

"Review of Stuart on the Epistle to the Hebrews," *Quarterly Christian Spectator,* 1 (1829): 112-149.

James Marsh (courtesy of the University of Vermont)

Though neither voluminous nor widely popular, the work of James Marsh captures the relation of the cultural outburst of nineteenth-century New England to American Puritanism. More Puritan than Ralph Waldo Emerson's works and more romantic than Jonathan Edwards's, Marsh's writings specify the crucial distinctions to be drawn between these writers, distinctions that the myth of national identity has long obscured for students of American culture. In his simultaneous embodiment of the Puritan and romantic, expressing both, yet blind to his own internal conflicts, Marsh dramatizes the forces that moved Americans away from accepted ideologies and into new conceptions of the mind that gave a revolutionary direction to American letters. Marsh's work was engaged in sorting out the issues that fathered the American renaissance, and the complex relation between the intentions behind that work and its consequences reveal the hidden stress points, the fault lines where Puritan and Transcendentalist meet. Marsh's writings reveal the intellectual ferment out of which Transcendentalism was distilled as well as the profound consequences of Transcendental thought. Not surprisingly Marsh viewed himself very differently. He was a philosophical idealist, a devoutly Orthodox Christian, a believer in the essential oneness of things, and all his efforts were aimed at instilling belief in that oneness in others.

Marsh came by his Orthodoxy honestly. He was born July 1794 at Hartford, Vermont, into the family of Daniel Marsh. The family had a history of rural gentility and public service (a grandfather, Joseph Marsh, had been lieutenant governor). He was reared in a staunchly Orthodox rural atmosphere just as Unitarianism was entrenching itself in liberal Boston. His early life was confined within the boundaries of the family farm, and thus he never imbibed the intellectual and social energies–radiating from Boston and penetrating much of New England–which profoundly shook and often shattered the faith of his urban contemporaries. His later contact at Dartmouth, which he attended beginning in 1813, at Harvard, with the most advanced ideas available to New Englanders, and his exchanges with many of the most innovative thinkers in America could not counteract the influences of his youth.

The most important lessons Marsh learned at Dartmouth were not intellectual but religious. In 1815 the college was still deep in the currents of the Second Great Awakening. Marsh himself was ripe for the religious harvest, and in 1815 he was converted and committed himself to God's service. His new calling and his inherited religious convictions made a career in the ministry practically the only choice for Marsh, though many of the more public duties of a minister were ill-suited to his retiring and bookish temperament. Marsh was, by nature, a "man of letters" in a culture wary of any learning not turned to some more practical end. The pursuit of "self-culture" was not possible for him as it was for Emerson or Thoreau. So he dutifully took hold of his attenuated calling and, in 1817, began his studies at Andover Theological Seminary, the bastion of Massachusetts Orthodoxy after the Unitarian takeover at Harvard.

At Andover Marsh began to study German language and thought under the formidable Moses Stuart, and after a time, he surpassed even Stuart himself, not only in familiarity with the new German philosophy but, more important, in his capacity to imagine the implications of that philosophy for American thought. As a result of this reading, Marsh soon became equally dissatisfied with the doctrinaire Orthodoxy to which Stuart still adhered and with the Scottish Common Sense adaptation of John Locke that ruled liberal Boston.

Soon after his graduation from Andover,

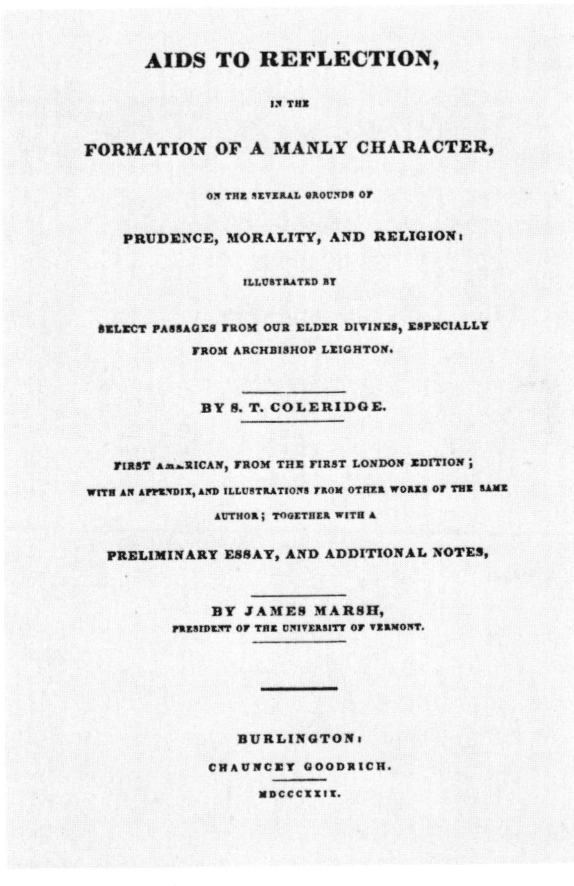
AIDS TO REFLECTION,

IN THE

FORMATION OF A MANLY CHARACTER,

ON THE SEVERAL GROUNDS OF

PRUDENCE, MORALITY, AND RELIGION:

ILLUSTRATED BY

SELECT PASSAGES FROM OUR ELDER DIVINES, ESPECIALLY FROM ARCHBISHOP LEIGHTON.

BY S. T. COLERIDGE.

FIRST AMERICAN, FROM THE FIRST LONDON EDITION; WITH AN APPENDIX, AND ILLUSTRATIONS FROM OTHER WORKS OF THE SAME AUTHOR; TOGETHER WITH A

PRELIMINARY ESSAY, AND ADDITIONAL NOTES,

BY JAMES MARSH,

PRESIDENT OF THE UNIVERSITY OF VERMONT.

BURLINGTON:

CHAUNCEY GOODRICH.

MDCCCXXIX.

Title page for Marsh's edition of essays by Coleridge. By making these essays available to the American public for the first time, Marsh was unknowingly instrumental in the formation of the Transcendentalist movement.

Marsh began to develop his own formula for spiritual renewal in a series of original writings and translations. The first of these, an essay on "Ancient and Modern Poetry" published in the *North American Review* in 1822, was an astonishing display of learning that many assumed must have come from the erudite Edward Everett. It defended the power of modern literature by appealing to spiritual rather than formal or doctrinal value. With this appeal to the "inner light" as a foundation for literary criticism, Marsh helped to usher in the "sympathetic" model of criticism that became increasingly dominant in the middle of the century. He articulated that principle more fully with his 1833 translation of Johann Gottfried von Herder's *The Spirit of Hebrew Poetry* (1826), which he said must be read "in the spirit that dictated it . . . whatever individual errors of opinion it may contain," and in his review of Moses Stuart's *Commentary on Hebrews* (1829), where he insists, in terms that prefigure Theodore Parker or Emerson, that to understand spiritual texts we must have in our hearts the spiritual realities to which they refer.

In 1826 Marsh was called back to Vermont from Hampden-Sydney, Virginia, where he had been teaching oriental languages, to assume the presidency of the University of Vermont. There he began to apply the ideas he had developed in the context of biblical interpretation to a series of educational innovations that both anticipated and, through his friendship with George Ticknor, helped to shape the well-known educational reforms at Harvard. The reforms that Marsh outlined in *An Exposition of the System of Instruction* (1829), a description of his new program at the University of Vermont, put the University in the vanguard of a debate over educational method that was raging throughout New England. The crux of that debate was the nature of learning and the purposes of education. Typically, in this debate, Marsh charted a spiritual course of his own, eschewing both the simple pragmatism practiced at the universities of Virginia and Pennsylvania, and the genteel classical tradition enshrined at Yale.

Marsh tried to make education more relevant, but his notion of relevancy had a particularly spiritual cast. Just as he believed that experimental rather than speculative religion generates true faith, he argued that practical rather than merely abstract education produces true knowledge. Therefore, he instituted an elective system and designed new courses to meet the practical needs of students at the university. He dispensed with regimentation, did away as far as possible with rigid distinctions between classes, and associated students in classrooms according to their abilities. His theory and practice of education at the University of Vermont was a step toward making the mind the final authority, toward giving a heightened individual perception the responsibility for determining truth.

Three years after taking up his duties at the University of Vermont, Marsh produced his most important and influential work, the first American edition of Samuel Taylor Coleridge's *Aids to Reflection* (1829), one of the works that prompted the formation of the Transcendental Club in 1836. This edition opened Coleridge's thought for the first time to Americans who had previously either repudiated Coleridge as a murky "transcendental" philosopher unworthy of the attention of any sensible man or, like Emerson,

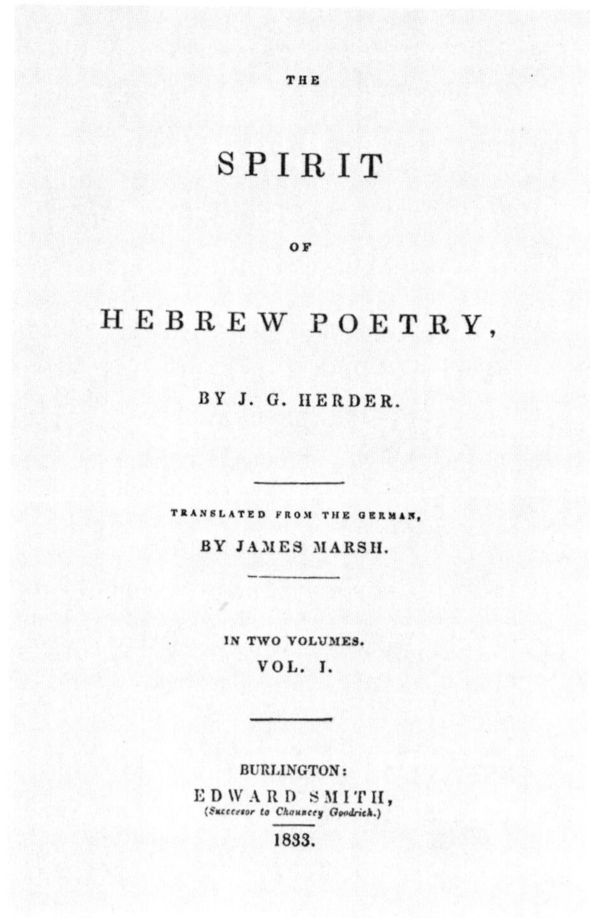
THE

SPIRIT

OF

HEBREW POETRY,

BY J. G. HERDER.

TRANSLATED FROM THE GERMAN,

BY JAMES MARSH.

IN TWO VOLUMES.

VOL. I.

BURLINGTON:

EDWARD SMITH,

(Successor to Chauncey Goodrich.)

1833.

Title page for Marsh's first published book-length translation failed to discover anything they could use in Coleridge's intellectual labyrinth.

Because of his influence among the Transcendentalists, modern scholarship has often identified Marsh as a northern cousin of the Concord philosophers, but Marsh was no Transcendentalist. He was never aware of his influence, and he deplored the unorthodox opinions his work inadvertently fostered. He hoped that his edition of Coleridge would help to restore to American Congregationalism the spiritual flame that had been snuffed out by deism, secularism, doctrinal debate, and skepticism. In order to unify a fractured Orthodoxy, Marsh enlisted philosophical innovations that were ultimately destined to dismantle the traditional forms and assumptions he was working to revive. Like Jonathan Edwards nearly a hundred years before, Marsh worked to make Orthodoxy intellectually respectable by recasting it in a form consistent with the view of the world advanced by the dominant philosophical minds of the day. But Marsh's task was far more difficult than Edwards's had been because he was even more isolated than Edwards from the spiritual wellsprings of his piety. The worship of practicality and common sense that had been an optimistic glimmer in 1730 had, by 1829, become the blazing light of common day, reaching into every corner of Marsh's world. Yet 100 years after Edwards, Marsh still strove to reconcile America's secular present with its Puritan past, and his efforts could only dramatize their incongruity and usher in a vision alien to both.

When Marsh removed *Aids to Reflection* from the context of the rest of Coleridge's works, from the British religious debates that had produced it, and from its original audience, and then, with the addition of his introduction, notes, and appendices, injected it into the quite different theological controversies raging in New England, he inevitably changed its meaning in ways of which he could not be fully in control. Marsh supplemented Coleridge's text with explanatory notes and passages from Coleridge's articles in *Blackwood's* magazine and *The Statesman's Manual*. But most critically Marsh introduced Coleridge's work with a "Preliminary Essay" that applied Coleridge's thought to American issues.

In the "Preliminary Essay" Marsh pressed Coleridge into the service of American spiritual needs and in the process made him a new man, one who could speak the language of inspiration to the shapers of American literary culture.

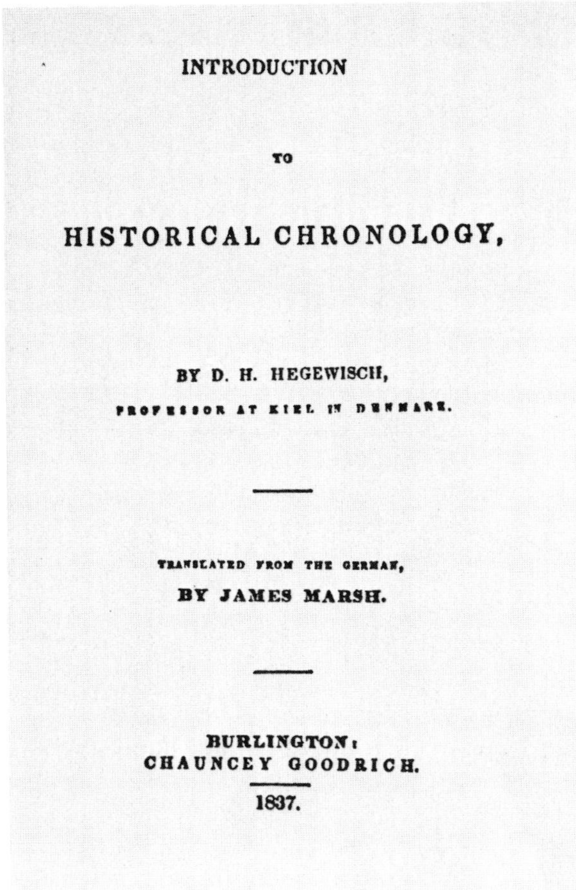
INTRODUCTION

TO

HISTORICAL CHRONOLOGY,

BY D. H. HEGEWISCH,

PROFESSOR AT KIEL IN DENMARK.

TRANSLATED FROM THE GERMAN,

BY JAMES MARSH.

BURLINGTON:
CHAUNCEY GOODRICH.

1837.

Title page for Marsh's translation of a work that he hoped would encourage Americans to study chronology "as a distinct science, holding the same general relation to history which geography does"

Marsh's efforts to resolve in nineteenth-century terms the conflict between dogma, morals, and piety carried his thought from Orthodoxy toward romanticism and from Coleridge toward Emerson. His strategies in the "Preliminary Essay" simplify Coleridge's theology and dramatize the intellectual conflicts out of which Transcendentalism was born. The confidence in human freedom that had gained strength since Edwards and the energies of Marsh's personal faith combine in the "Essay" to produce a language of antinomian transcendence while, at the same time, blurring the distinctions that had held antinomianism within Orthodoxy.

The result appealed immediately to certain young Unitarians who had already discarded doctrinal constraints and who shared Marsh's interests in the possibilities of introspection that had been discredited by Locke. Marsh's introduction focused attention on Coleridge's crucial distinction between reason and understanding, which Marsh had been most anxious to place in the minds of his readers. As Marsh explained it in the "Preliminary Essay," reason was, finally, a philosophical explanation of personal religious experience. By stressing the authority of individual religious experience over abstract metaphysical speculation, Coleridge helped Marsh to build an intellectual bridge over the doctrinal chasms down which so many laymen had plunged into skepticism or Unitarianism. Coleridge's *Aids to Reflection* helped Marsh redefine religion itself, transforming it from a set of doctrines to a system of truth. That truth was undeniable because its proofs lay in the unquestionable personal experience of each believer. Such religion was, when rightly apprehended in the reason, identical with the truth of science because, of course, both derived ultimately from the same divine source.

Marsh's version of *Aids to Reflection* was a central step in the intellectual movement from Lockean materialism to American Transcendentalism. It showed Emerson everything he needed. Immanuel Kant had distinguished sensible phenomena from reason, arguing that the mind can only apprehend phenomena. Coleridge was dissatisfied with the constraints Kant placed on spiritual insight and revised his principles, making reason constitutive rather than regulative, an intellectual route to the absolute. Marsh, in turn, converted this power of insight from a process of reflection on the inner workings of the mind to a harmony between the mind and the divine spirit, and Emerson extended that harmony to encompass all of nature.

Although *Aids to Reflection* was widely read in America and brought Marsh considerable recognition, it did not have the particular effect on American Orthodoxy that he had envisioned for it. As the example of the Transcendentalists suggests, the reception of *Aids to Reflection* was as much a matter of passive appropriation as of positive influence. Marsh's discussion of Coleridge's philosophy and his analysis of reason did succeed in quieting the objections American readers had raised to Coleridge's "murkiness." But it did so largely by transforming Coleridge to fit the expectations of his audience. With few exceptions, readers saw in Coleridge not the rationale for Orthodoxy Marsh had intended but some version of their own views.

After the publication of *Aids to Reflection* and of Coleridge's *The Friend* (1831), which was also much admired by Emerson, dissatisfaction with his practical administrative and financial duties as president and declining health led Marsh to retreat more and more into his teaching and private study. In 1833 he resigned the presidency, staying on as Professor of Natural and Moral Philosophy. He died on 3 July 1842 at Colchester, Vermont, of the "consumption" that had ravaged his family.

Letters:

Coleridge's American Disciples: The Selected Correspondence of James Marsh, edited by John J. Duffy (Amherst: University of Massachusetts Press, 1973).

Biography:

Joseph Torrey, "Memoir," in *The Remains of the Rev. James Marsh, D.D.* (Burlington, Vt.: Chauncey Goodrich, 1843).

References:

Peter Carafiol, "James Marsh: Transcendental Puritan," *ESQ: A Journal of the American Renaissance,* 21 (Third Quarter 1975): 127-136;

Carafiol, "James Marsh's American *Aids to Reflection:* Influence Through Ambiguity," *New England Quarterly,* 49 (March 1976): 27-45;

Carafiol, "James Marsh to John Dewey: The Fate of Transcendentalist Philosophy in American Education," *ESQ: A Journal of the American Renaissance,* 24 (First Quarter 1978): 1-11;

Carafiol, *Transcendent Reason: James Marsh and the Forms of Romantic Thought* (Tallahassee: Florida State University Press, 1982);

John Dewey, "James Marsh and American Philosophy," *Journal of the History of Ideas,* 2 (April 1941): 131-150;

John J. Duffy, "From Hanover to Burlington: James Marsh's Search for Unity," *Vermont History,* 38 (Winter 1970): 27-48;

Duffy, "Problems in Publishing Coleridge: James Marsh's First American Edition of *Aids to Reflection,*" *New England Quarterly,* 43 (June 1970): 193-208;

Duffy, "T. S. Eliot's Objective Correlative: A New England Commonplace," *New England Quarterly,* 42 (March 1969): 108-115;

Duffy, "Transcendental Letters from George Ripley to James Marsh," *Emerson Society Quarterly Supplement,* no. 50 (First Quarter 1968): 20-24;

Marjorie Nicolson, "James Marsh and the Vermont Transcendentalists," *Philosophical Review*, 34 (January 1925): 28-50;

Ronald Vale Wells, *Three Christian Transcendentalists: James Marsh, Caleb Sprague Henry, Frederic Henry Hedge* (New York: Columbia University Press, 1943).

John Lothrop Motley

(15 April 1814-29 May 1877)

Karen S. Langlois
Claremont Graduate School

See also the Motley entries in *DLB 1, The American Renaissance in New England* and *DLB 30, American Historians, 1607-1865.*

BOOKS: *Morton of Morton's Hope; An Autobiography*, anonymous, 3 volumes (London: H. Colburn, 1839); republished as *Morton's Hope: or, The Memoirs of a Provincial*, 2 volumes (New York: Harper, 1839);

Merry-Mount; A Romance of the Massachusetts Colony (Boston & Cambridge: J. Monroe, 1849);

The Rise of the Dutch Republic. A History, 3 volumes (London: John Chapman/Chapman & Hall, 1856; New York: Harper, 1856);

History of the United Netherlands, 4 volumes (1860-1867): volumes 1 and 2, *From the Death of William the Silent to the Synod of Dort* . . . (London: John Murray, 1860; New York: Harper, 1861); volumes 3 and 4, *From the Synod of Dort to the Twelve Years' Truce–1609* (London: John Murray, 1867; New York: Harper, 1868);

Causes of the Civil War in America . . . (London: George Manwaring, 1861); republished in 2 volumes: *The Causes of the American Civil War* (New York: Appleton, 1861); and *Letters of John Lothrop Motley and Joseph Holt* . . . (New York: Printed by Henry E. Tudor, 1861);

Four Questions for the People, at the Presidential Election. Address of John Lothrop Motley, Before the Parker Fraternity, at the Music Hall, October 20, 1868 (Boston: Ticknor & Fields, 1868);

Historic Progress and American Democracy: An Address Delivered Before the New-York Historical Society, at Their Sixty-fourth Anniversary, December 16, 1868 . . . (New York: Scribners, 1869);

Portrait by G. F. Watts, published as the frontispiece to volume sixteen of The Writings of John Lothrop Motley, *1900)*

The Life and Death of John of Barneveld, Advocate of Holland; With a View of the Primary Causes and Movements of the Thirty Years' War, 2 volumes (London: John Murray, 1874; New York: Harper, 1874);

Peter the Great (New York: Harper, 1877; London & Edinburgh: T. Nelson, 1887).

PERIODICAL PUBLICATIONS: "Goethe," *New York Review,* 3 (October 1838): 397-442;

"Goethe's Works," *New York Review,* 5 (July 1839): 1-48;

"Peter the Great," *North American Review,* 61 (October 1845): 269-319;

"The Novels of Balzac," *North American Review,* 65 (July 1847): 85-108;

"Polity of the Puritans," *North American Review,* 69 (October 1849): 470-498.

John Lothrop Motley's literary criticism was written and published early in his career, before he began to establish himself as the historian of the Netherlands. The criticism adds in some measure to his reputation as an intellectual but today is chiefly of interest to the biographer and literary historian. Among the second generation of Americans who elected to pursue graduate study in Germany, Motley is heavily indebted to German historicism, especially as phrased by the Leipzig School, which examined all forms of institutional expression (including literature) within the frame of national character. More narrowly, he was influenced by Goethe and Johann Schiller in concentrating on biography. His critical work was thus of a contextual and historical order to which he brought personal endowments: scholarly learning, a balanced and perspicuous mind, and a genial tolerance that made him unmindful of matters of party or belief.

Motley was born in Dorchester, Massachusetts, the second child of Thomas Motley, a wealthy Boston merchant and amateur author, and Anna Lothrop Motley, the daughter and granddaughter of Boston clergymen, and a member of an old and prominent Boston family. He attended the Round Hill School in Northampton, where he studied under George Bancroft and Joseph Cogswell. It was there that Motley began his formal study of German language and literature. In 1827, at the age of thirteen, he entered Harvard College, where his interest in German romanticism and in Goethe, Germany's greatest poet, led to his translation of Goethe's "The Ghost-Seer," published in the Harvard *Collegian.*

Mary Benjamin Motley, miniature by Stagg circa 1850-1851 (from John Lothrop Motley and His Family, *edited by his daughter Susan St. John Mildmay and her husband Herbert, 1910)*

During his senior year he presented an essay entitled "The Genius and Character of Goethe," in which he praised "the attributes of Goethe's mind" and "the candor of his criticism." Cogswell was sufficiently impressed with the essay that he sent a copy to Goethe's daughter-in-law, who after reading it declared, "I wish to see the first book this young man will write." In this early tribute to Goethe, Motley wrote, "the mastery and knowledge of human nature is the sublimest attribute of genius. It is for this that we worship Shakespeare, as if really kneeling at the shrine of a Deity and it is for this too, that the splendid subject of our remarks is elevated to honor, if not equal in degree, then the same in kind."

Motley's decision to go to Germany in 1831, after his graduation from Harvard, was no doubt influenced by his association at the Round Hill School with Bancroft and Cogswell, both of whom had studied in Germany and become interested in German literary theories. En route to Germany, Motley "contrived . . . in the course of the journey to learn a good deal of German, by talking and reading and writing." His preparation continued at the University of Göttingen where he studied the language "five or six hours a day" and also pursued the subjects of law and classical history.

While at Göttingen he began a lifelong friendship with fellow student Otto Bismarck. Bismarck would later recall that his handsome and gifted friend attracted his "attention by a conversation sparkling with wit, humor, and originality." A favorite conversation topic between them was whether Byron could compare to Goethe. During his two years in Germany, which included additional study at the University of Berlin, Motley translated *Faust* and pursued his interest in German literary theory. He also visited several cities, including Weimar and Leipzig. In Dresden he met the German romantic writer Ludwig Tieck, who was at the center of literary society there. He never met Goethe, who had died before Motley's arrival in Germany.

After his return to America Motley studied law and was admitted to the bar in 1836. He became a member of Boston literary circles, which included the journalist Park Benjamin. He married Benjamin's sister, Mary, in 1837. Their union resulted in three daughters and a son who died in infancy. Living in a home built by his father on an estate near Boston, Motley devoted his time to literary endeavors.

In October 1838 and the following July, Motley published two excellent essays on Goethe in the *New York Review*. These essays reveal much about Motley's critical methods. The first, a review of Goethe's autobiography *Dichtung und Wahrheit* (1811, 1812, 1814, 1833) and of Sarah Austen's *Characteristics of Goethe* (1833), concerned Goethe's life and genius. The question of Goethe's title which Edward Everett and others had tried to puzzle out–literally it translates as *Poetry and Truth*–seems not to have concerned Motley one whit. By the later 1830s German romanticism was sufficiently well known for people to realize that the title signaled, in a sort of shorthand, the involuntary obscuring of truth to which writers are prone due to their personal and national biases.

In the preface to *Dichtung und Wahrheit*, Goethe had stated his concept of determinism, especially dwelling on how the age molded the individual. Motley chose to look at the matter from a different angle. While acknowledging that "the developments of human character" conform to natural laws, the "apparent anomalies" in human character could be attributed to the "imperfection of human vision." Thus there arose the appearance of endless diversity, little "imperceptible shadings" so various that they resist our attempts to rationalize them. In examining an artist's life Motley believed the reader had to look for the point of unity beneath the changing surface of character. So far as Goethe was concerned, in writing of the workings of his own mind, he had paradoxically written an intellectual history of his age; but there was another paradox. In asserting that he was the child of his age, even to pointing out the influences that had fashioned him, Goethe had failed to see that he was wholly independent of his age. So far as Motley was concerned, the "true key to his character and genius" lay in his very apathy to what was going on around him. On the one hand, Goethe seemed wholly explained by his period. On the other, he appeared fully autonomous and self-determining. The apparent contradiction could only be examined by reference to Goethe's personality.

Motley was at some pains in his essay to address moral charges that had earlier been advanced against Goethe. Some American critics, Bancroft among them, had complained of Goethe's personal immorality and then extended the complaint to such novels as *Elective Affinities* (1809). Motley simply chose to ignore Goethe's personal morality as being of no consequence. As to "immorality" in the literary works, the charge had literally nothing to do with the matter of Goethe's artistry, for "morals and aesthetics constitute two distinct provinces." Motley continued: "A work of art is perfect when it is perfectly conformed to the rules of art. With the laws of morality it has nothing to do, except so far as they are implied in those of art." In any case, matters of morality were best left to individual belief, given the enormous range of potential attitudes among human beings. Of greater moment were such matters as imagination and judgment, delicacy in describing the beautiful, love for life in all its infinite ramifications together with the ability to represent it, and the capacity for deep responses to matters of sense and sensibility. In Goethe Motley observed their conjunction on the highest aesthetic level.

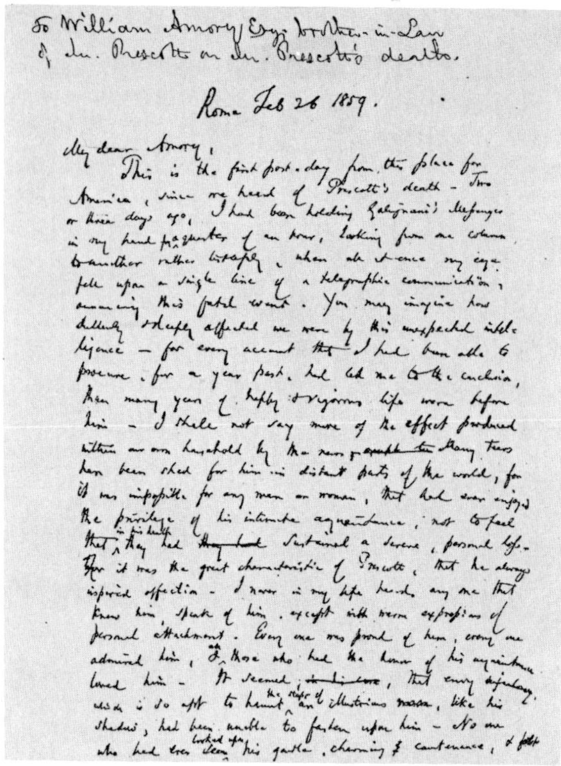

To William Amory Esq. brother-in-Law of Mr. Prescott on Mr. Prescott's death.

Rome Feb 26 1859.

My dear Amory,

This is the first post-day from this place for America, since we heard of Prescott's death – Two or three days ago, I had been holding Galignani's Messenger in my hand for a quarter of an hour, looking from one column to another rather listlessly, when all at once my eye fell upon a single line of a telegraphic communication, announcing this fatal event. You may imagine how suddenly & deeply affected we were by this unexpected intelligence – for every account that I had been able to procure, for a year past, had led me to the conclusion, that many years of happy & vigorous life were before him – I shall not say more of the effect produced within our own household by the news – Many tears have been shed for him in distant parts of the world, for it was impossible for any man or woman, that had ever enjoyed the privilege of his intimate acquaintance, not to feel that, in his death, they had sustained a severe, personal loss. For it was the great characteristic of Prescott, that he always inspired affection – I never in my life heard any one that knew him, speak of him, except with warm expressions of personal attachment. Every one was proud of him, every one admired him, & all those who had the honor of his acquaintance loved him – It seemed, that envy [illegible], which is so apt to haunt the steps of an illustrious man, like his shadow, had been unable to fasten upon him – No one who had ever looked upon his gentle, charming countenance, & felt

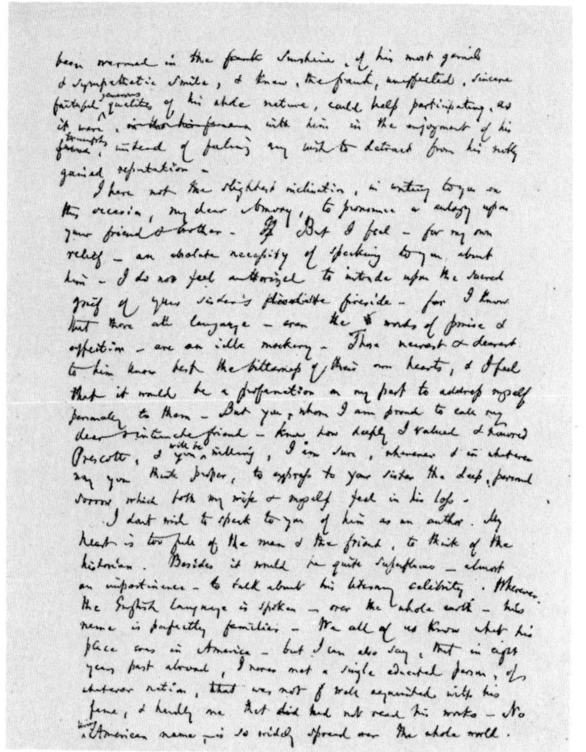

been warmed in the frank sunshine of his most genial & sympathetic smile, & knew the frank, unaffected, sincere faithful & generous qualities of his whole nature, could help participating, as it were, with him in the enjoyment of his triumphs, instead of feeling any wish to detract from his nobly gained reputation –

I have not the slightest inclination, in writing to you on this occasion, my dear Amory, to pronounce a eulogy upon your friend & brother – But I feel – for my own relief – an absolute necessity of speaking to you about him – I do not feel authorized to intrude upon the sacred grief of your sister's desolate fireside – for I know that there all language – even the words of praise & affection – are an idle mockery – Those nearest & dearest to him know best the bitterness of their own hearts, & I feel that it would be a profanation on my part to address myself personally to them – But you, whom I am proud to call my dear & intimate friend – know how deeply I valued & honored Prescott, & you will be willing, I am sure, whenever & in whatever way you think proper, to express to your sister the deep, personal sorrow which both my wife & myself feel in his loss –

I don't wish to speak to you of him as an author. My heart is too full of the man & the friend, to think of the historian. Besides it would be quite superfluous – almost an impertinence – to talk about his literary celebrity. Wherever the English language is spoken – over the whole earth – his name is perfectly familiar – We all of us know what his place was in America – but I can also say, that in eight years past abroad, I never met a single educated person, of whatever nation, that was not well acquainted with his fame, & hardly one that had not read his works – No living American name is so widely spread over the whole world.

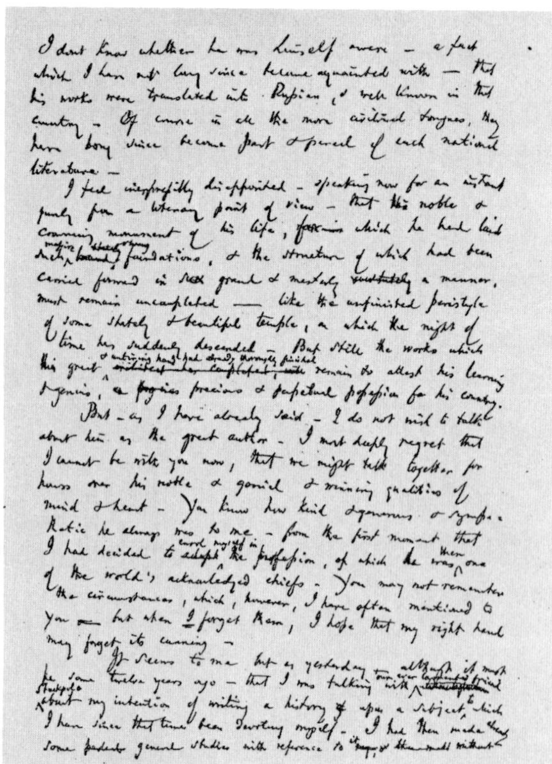

I don't know whether he was himself aware – a fact which I have not long since become acquainted with – that his works were translated into Russian, & well known in that country – Of course in all the more cultivated tongues, they have long since become part & parcel of each national literature –

I feel inexpressibly disappointed – speaking now for an instant purely from a literary point of view – that this noble & crowning monument of his life, which he had laid deep, massive & enduring foundations, & the structure of which had been carried forward in so grand & masterly a manner, must remain uncompleted — like the unfinished peristyle of some stately & beautiful temple, on which the night of time has suddenly descended – But still the works which this great & unerring hand had already thoroughly finished remain to attest his learning & genius, a precious & perpetual possession for his country.

But – as I have already said – I do not wish to talk about him as the great author – I most deeply regret that I cannot be with you now, that we might talk together for hours over his noble & genial & winning qualities of mind & heart – You know how kind & generous & sympathetic he always was to me – from the first moment that I had decided to enrol myself in the profession, of which he was then one of the world's acknowledged chiefs – You may not remember the circumstances, which, however, I have often mentioned to you – but when I forget them, I hope that my right hand may forget its cunning –

It seems to me but as yesterday – although it must be some twelve years ago – that I was talking with our ever lamented friend Stackpole about my intention of writing a history upon a subject to which I have since that time been devoting myself – I had then made some general studies with reference to it, & without

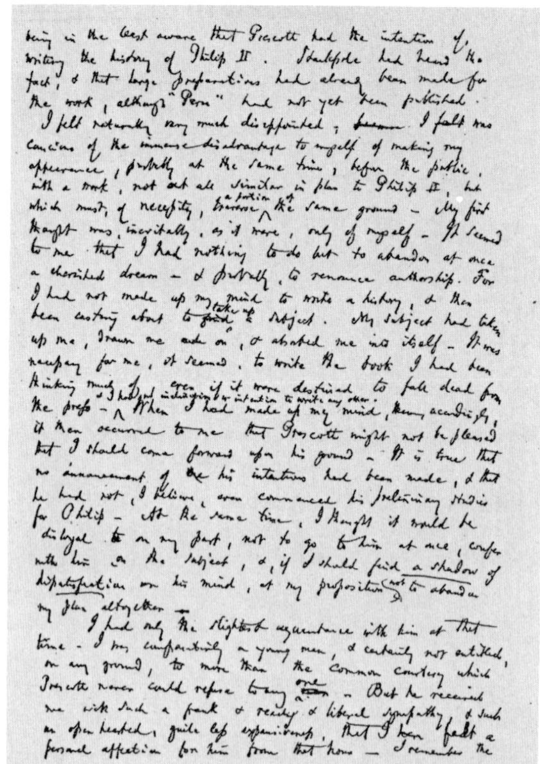

being in the least aware that Prescott had the intention of writing the history of Philip II. Stackpole had heard the fact, & that large preparations had already been made for the work, although "Peru" had not yet been published.

I felt naturally very much disappointed, I felt conscious of the immense disadvantage to myself of making my appearance, probably at the same time, before the public, with a work, not at all similar in plan to Philip II, but which must, of necessity, traverse a portion of the same ground – My first thought was, inevitably, as it were, only of myself – It seemed to me that I had nothing to do but to abandon at once a cherished dream – & probably, to renounce authorship. For I had not made up my mind to write a history, & then been casting about to take up a subject. My subject had taken up me, drawn me on, & absorbed me into itself – It was necessary for me, it seemed, to write the book I had been thinking much of, even if it were destined to fall dead from the press – & I had no inclination or intention to write any other. When I had made up my mind, then, accordingly, it then occurred to me that Prescott might not be pleased that I should come forward upon his ground – It is true that no announcement of his intentions had been made, & that he had not, I believe, even commenced his preliminary studies for Philip – At the same time, I thought it would be disloyal on my part, not to go to him at once, confer with him on the subject, &, if I should find a shadow of dissatisfaction on his mind, at my proposition, to abandon my plan altogether —

I had only the slightest acquaintance with him at that time – I was comparatively a young man, & certainly not entitled, on any ground, to more than the common courtesy which Prescott never could refuse to any one – But he received me with such a frank & ready & liberal sympathy, & such an open hearted, guileless expansiveness, that I have felt a personal affection for him from that hour – I remember the

Letter to William Amory in which Motley mourns the death of William Prescott (from Autograph Leaves of Our Country's Authors, *compiled by Alexander Bliss and John P. Kennedy, 1864)*

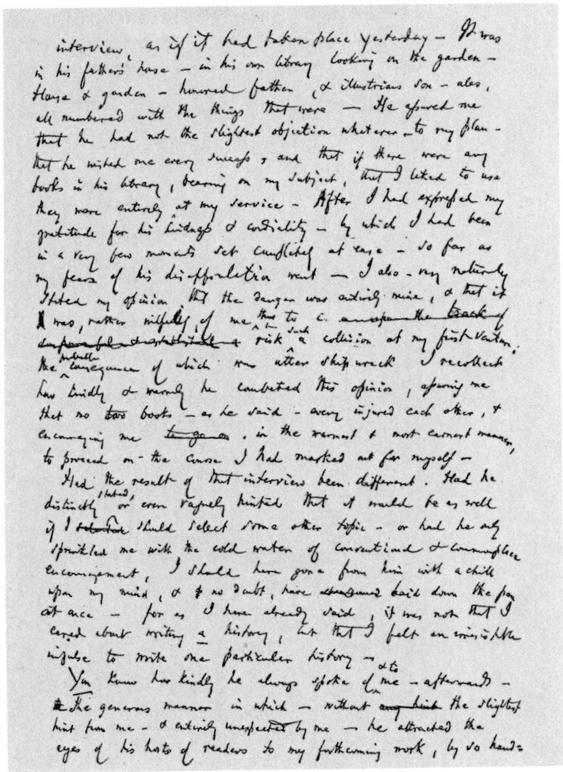
interview, as if it had taken place yesterday — It was in his fathers' house — in his own library looking on the garden — House & garden — honored father, & illustrious son — alas, all numbered with the things that were — He assured me that he had not the slightest objection whatever to my plan — that he wished me every success, and that if there were any books in his library, bearing on my subject, that I liked to use they were entirely at my service — After I had expressed my gratitude for his kindness & cordiality — by which I had been in a very few moments set completely at ease — so far as my fears of his disapprobation went — I also — very naturally stated my opinion, that the danger was entirely mine, & that it was, rather wilfully of me thus to i[ncur] such risk a collision at my first venture, the inevitable consequence of which was utter shipwreck. I recollect how kindly & warmly he combatted this opinion, assuring me that no two books — as he said — ever injured each other, & encouraging me in the warmest & most earnest manner, to proceed on the course I had marked out for myself —

Had the result of that interview been different. Had he distinctly stated, or even vaguely hinted that it would be as well if I should select some other topic — or had he only sprinkled me with the cold water of conventional & commonplace encouragement, I should have gone from him with a chill upon my mind, & I no doubt, have laid down the pen at once — for as I have already said, it was not that I cared about writing a history, but that I felt an irresistible impulse to write one particular history —

You know how kindly he always spoke of me & to me — afterwards — The generous manner in which — without the slightest hint from me — & entirely unexpected by me — he attracted the eyes of his hosts of readers to my forthcoming work, by so hand-

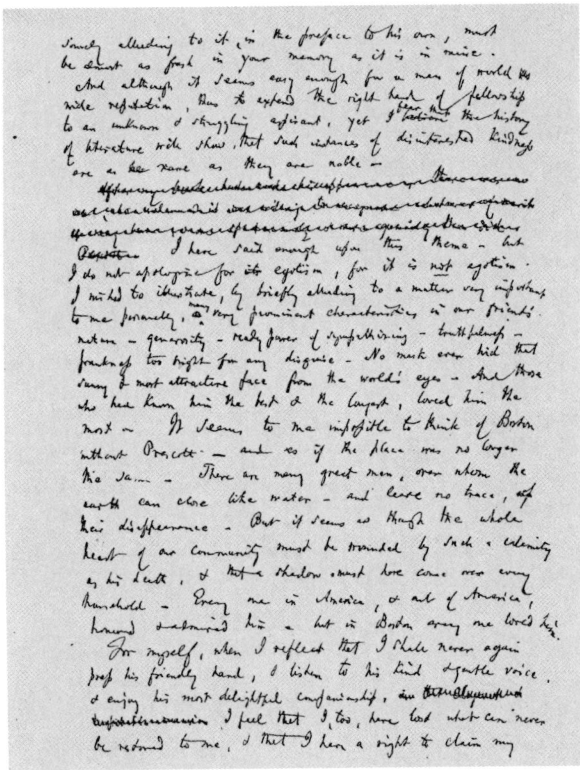
somely alluding to it, in the preface to his own, must be almost as fresh in your memory as it is in mine.

And although it seems easy enough for a man of world wide reputation, thus to extend the right hand of fellowship to an unknown & struggling aspirant, yet I fear that the history of literature will show, that such instances of disinterested kindness are as rare as they are noble —

I have said enough upon this theme — but I do not apologize for its egotism, for it is not egotism. I wished to illustrate, by briefly alluding to a matter very important to me personally, one of the many prominent characteristics in our friend's nature — generosity — ready power of sympathizing — truthfulness — frankness too bright for any disguise — No mask ever hid that sunny & most attractive face from the world's eye — And those who had known him the best & the longest, loved him the most — It seems to me impossible to think of Boston without Prescott — and as if the place was no longer the same — There are many great men, over whom the earth can close like water — and leave no trace, of their disappearance — But it seems as though the whole heart of our community must be wounded by such a calamity as his death, & that a shadow must have come over every household — Every one in America, & out of America, honored & admired him — but in Boston every one loved him.

For myself, when I reflect that I shall never again press his friendly hand, & listen to his kind & gentle voice, & enjoy his most delightful companionship, I feel that I, too, have lost what can never be restored to me, & that I have a right to claim my

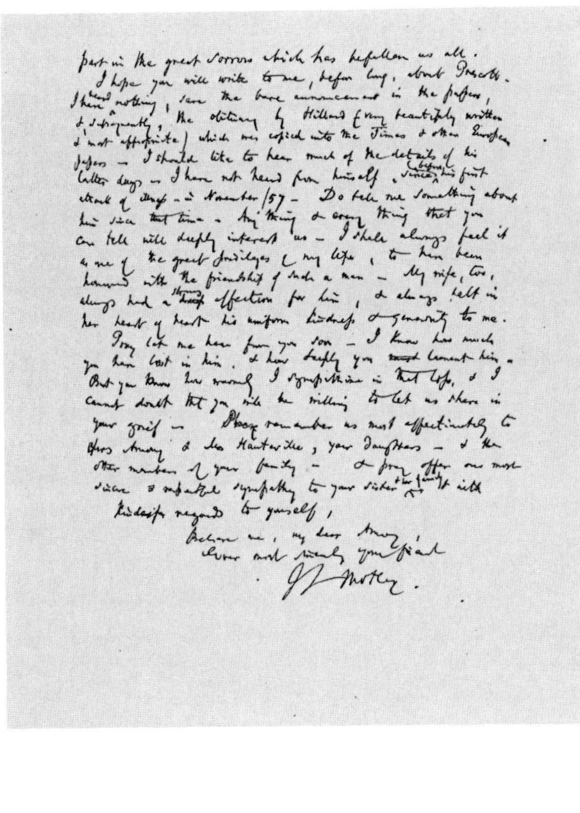
part in the great sorrow which has befallen us all.

I hope you will write to me, before long, about Prescott. I have heard nothing, save the bare announcement in the papers, & subsequently, the obituary by Hillard (very beautifully written & most appropriate) which was copied into the Times & other European papers — I should like to hear much of the details of his latter days — I have not heard from himself, since his first attack of illness — in November/57 — Do tell me something about him since that time — Any thing & every thing that you can tell will deeply interest us — I shall always feel it as one of the great privileges of my life, to have been honored with the friendship of such a man — My wife, too, always had a strong affection for him, & always felt in her heart of hearts his uniform kindness & generosity to me.

Pray let me hear from you soon — I know how much you have lost in him, & how deeply you must lament him. But you know how warmly I sympathize in that loss, & I cannot doubt that you will be willing to let us share in your grief — Pray remember us most affectionately to Mrs Amory & Mrs Hartwell, your daughters — & the other members of your family — & pray offer our most sincere & respectful sympathy to your sister & her family with kindest regards to yourself,

Believe me, my dear Amory
Ever most sincerely your friend
J L Motley.

Motley's second article, "Goethe's Works" (July 1839), was a critical survey and a consideration of the principles of the poet's creative genius. His attraction to Goethe's critical theory led him to proclaim the German author "the greatest critic of modern times; and in a country so eminently distinguished for proficiency in a branch of literature, which they [Germans] were the first to make a science, he is decidedly the first."

The essay is a good indication of how far Goethe criticism had advanced in the previous two decades. Earlier American attention had focused on Goethe the artist. In the 1830s and into the 1840s greater attention was paid to the criticism. Margaret Fuller published her translation of Eckermann's *Conversations with Goethe* in 1839; in 1845 G. W. Calvert published his translation of Goethe's correspondence with Schiller; and that same year Samuel Ward published a translation of Goethe's *Essays on Art.* Motley may be said to be a part of this group in his knowledge of and appreciation for the criticism.

Most of Goethe's major points are taken up by Motley in a series of affirmative echoes: a true work of art is a natural outgrowth of the conditions in which the writer lived; the best artists use the traditions and cultural motifs of their national languages; critics should avoid measuring works of art by comparison with some ideal work (destructive criticism), but instead enter sympathetically into individual works to discover their inner ideas and how those ideas dictate aesthetic form. Beyond these matters are the universality of art, the need for cultural interchange and tolerance (*Weltliteratur*), the roles of national literatures in fostering a cosmopolitan taste for excellence, the imperative that each human being cultivate within himself that which is most peculiar. Both Goethe's literary and critical theory, Motley noted, were based on the principle of individuality. The recognition of this principle, that a literature reflected the individual man as well as the more general aspects of time and nation and that such a literature was consequently unique and hostile to the comparative method, had made Goethe "at once a great artist and a great critic."

These essays, which helped to familiarize Americans with Goethe's critical principles and to popularize German romanticism, were followed in 1838 by Motley's translation of Schiller's "The Diver," which appeared in the *New Yorker* on 19 January 1839. In December 1840 he published a translation of Tieck's drama *Blue Beard.*

Motley's interest in Goethe surfaced again in a twenty-three page article, "The Novels of Balzac," which appeared in the July 1847 *North American Review.* In his defense of Balzac, Motley observes how Balzac's "calm and conscientious study of nature . . . often reminds us of Goethe." He again takes up the subject of the moral implications of a work of art, noting that Balzac "is neither moral nor immoral, but a calm and profound observer of human society and human passions, and a minute, patient, and powerful delineator of scenes and characters in the world before his eyes. His readers must moralize for themselves."

In 1839 Motley produced his first novel, *Morton of Morton's Hope; An Autobiography.* It is a half-historical, semi-autobiographical account of a young American at a German university. For all its serious flaws in plot development, the book is nevertheless filled with romantic incidents in its depiction of student life. Set in Boston and Göttingen, it was influenced by Motley's interest in the German romanticists and foreshadows his later work as a romantic historian. The work was a complete failure, and he later referred to it as his "unfortunate novel." Perhaps with greater perspective Oliver Wendell Holmes labeled it "a chaos before the creative epoch."

Motley was appointed secretary of the American legation in St. Petersburg in 1841, but he resigned after nine months. Nevertheless, his experience in Russia may have had some connection with his essay in the *North American Review* in 1845 on the reign of Peter the Great. The scholarly article was a review of two recent works on Peter, one in English, the other in French. As Holmes was later to note: "The style of the whole article is rich, fluent, picturesque." The skillful portrait of the Russian ruler, enlivened by a gift of characterization, suggests Motley's future greatness as a historian. His first major historical work would focus on a great hero and man of action. As Motley confided to his father in 1852, while researching *The Rise of the Dutch Republic* (1856), "I flatter myself that I have found the one great, virtuous and heroic character, the Protestant hero, William the First of Orange, founder of the Dutch Republic." The last article in Motley's literary apprenticeship, "Polity of the Puritans," appeared in October 1849 in the *North American Review.* It concerned the principles of self-government and was a specific rejoinder to the view of the Bancroft school of thought that Puri-

John Lothrop Motley (courtesy of the National Archives)

tan settlement and American democracy were coterminous.

In 1849 Motley served as a representative in the Massachusetts General Court. That same year he published his second novel, *Merry-Mount; A Romance of the Massachusetts Colony,* probably written in 1846. Set in seventeenth-century New England, the novel, deficient in plot development, includes vivid characters and memorable scenes. It received more favorable notice than its predecessor but even more clearly revealed that Motley's talent as a writer did not lie in the realm of fiction.

By 1850 Motley had decided to write a history of the Netherlands. His interest in this subject surely was influenced by Goethe's play *Egmont* (1788), set during the time of the revolt in the Netherlands, by Schiller's use of Netherlands' history in the 1787 tragedy *Don Carlos* (the son of Netherlands' enemy, Prince Philip II of Spain), and in the 1798-1799 tragedy of the Thirty Years War, *Wallenstein.* Motley later explained: "I had not made up my mind to write a history and then cast about to take up a subject. My subject had taken me up, drawn me on, and absorbed me into itself." In 1856, after spending ten years in preparation, five of them researching in the libraries and archives of Europe, Motley published his first major work of history.

The Rise of the Dutch Republic (1856) begins in the middle of the sixteenth century with the spectacle of the abdication of Charles V in favor of his son Philip II and ends with the death of William the Silent in 1584. The vibrant work exemplifies many of Motley's critical theories, including the unity of theme, the importance of narrative style, and the role of imagination and creativity. Motley did not, however, seek objectivity in his work, and his history is flawed by didacticism and personal bias. He disdained Catholic absolutism and superstition and the monarchy of the Spanish government. His grand and picturesque dramatization of the past was richly influenced by his love of the republican form of government. He was convinced that the basis of a good government was the "sovereignty of the people." Motley's brilliant panorama depicts the moral drama of the Dutch struggle for freedom and reflects his own belief in universal human progress.

The Rise of the Dutch Republic, which was an immediate success, established Motley as a historian. With its publication, his interest in critical principles was absorbed into the larger frame of his historical writing. The *History of the United Netherlands* (1860-1867) covers the period from the death of William the Silent to the year 1590. *The Life and Death of John of Barneveld* (1874) continued his history down to the beginning of the Thirty Years War. The influence of German romanticism on Motley is demonstrated through the grand theme of his multivolume history–the love of freedom and defeat of despotism. The influence of German methodology is apparent in his subsequent extensive research and use of first-hand sources. While his research identifies him with the new "scientific" school of historiography, his narrative style places him in the company of the great literary historians.

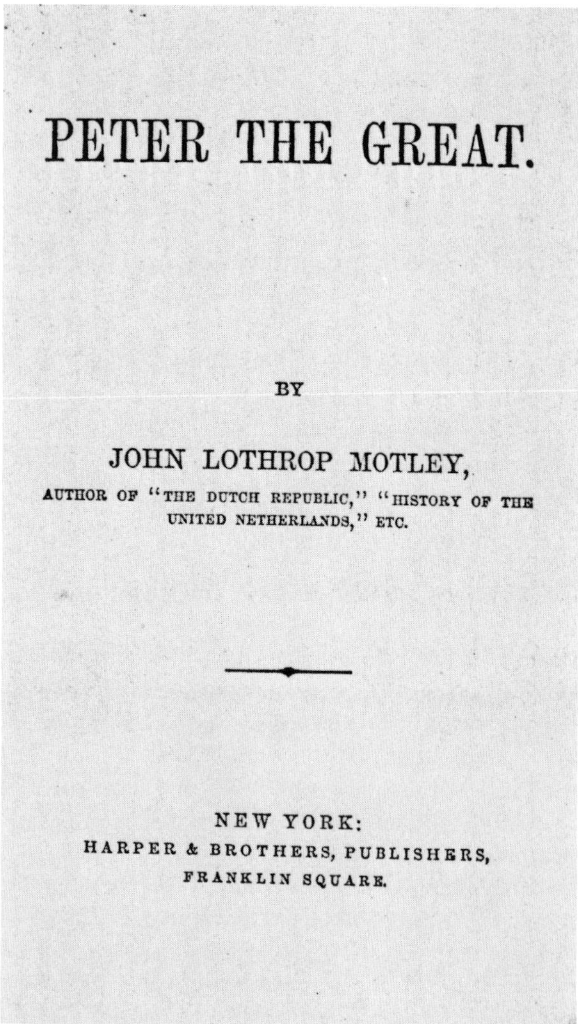

PETER THE GREAT.

BY

JOHN LOTHROP MOTLEY,

AUTHOR OF "THE DUTCH REPUBLIC," "HISTORY OF THE UNITED NETHERLANDS," ETC.

NEW YORK:
HARPER & BROTHERS, PUBLISHERS,
FRANKLIN SQUARE.

Title page for Motley's biographical essay, first published in the North American Review *in October 1845 and republished as a volume in Harper's Half-Hour Series*

Motley's labors as a historian were combined with service as United States minister at Vienna from 1861 to 1867. He was appointed in 1869 as United States minister to England, but was recalled. In July 1873, the same month he completed *John of Barneveld,* he suffered from an attack of paralysis which partially disabled him. He did not live to finish his history of the Thirty Years War but died in England in May 1877.

Letters:

The Correspondence of John Lothrop Motley, 2 volumes, edited by George William Curtis (London: John Murray, 1889; New York: Harper, 1889);

John Lothrop Motley and his Family. Further Letters and Records, edited by his daughter [Susan St. John Mildmay] and Herbert St. John Mildmay (London: John Lane/Bodley Head/ New York: John Lane, 1910).

Biography:

J. Guberman, *The Life of John Lothrop Motley* (The Hague: Martinus Nijhoff, 1973).

References:

Van Wyck Brooks, *The Flowering of New England: 1815-1865* (New York: Dutton, 1936);

G. P. Gooch, *History and Historians in the Nineteenth Century* (London: Longmans, Green, 1913);

Chester Penn Higby and B. T. Schantz, eds., *John Lothrop Motley, Representative Selections, with Introduction, Bibliography and Notes* (New York: American Book Company, 1939);

Oliver Wendell Holmes, *John Lothrop Motley: a Memoir* (London: Trübner, 1878);

David Levin, *History as Romantic Art–Bancroft, Prescott, Motley and Parkman* (Stanford, Cal.: Stanford University Press, 1959);

Orie William Long, *Literary Pioneers; Early American Explorers of European Culture* (Cambridge, Mass.: Harvard University Press, 1935).

Papers:

The chief collections of Motley manuscripts are in the library of the Massachusetts Historical Society, library of the University of Rochester, and Houghton Library, Harvard University.

John Neal

(25 August 1793-20 June 1876)

Donald A. Sears
California State University, Fullerton

John Neal

See also the Neal entry in *DLB 1, The American Renaissance in New England.*

BOOKS: *Keep Cool, A Novel,* 2 volumes (Baltimore: Joseph Cushing, 1817);

Battle of Niagara, A Poem, without Notes; and Goldau, or the Maniac Harper (Baltimore: N. G. Maxwell, 1818; enlarged, 1819);

Otho: A Tragedy, in Five Acts (Boston: West, Richardson & Lord, 1819);

Logan, a Family History, 2 volumes (Philadelphia: Carey & Lea, 1822; London: A. K. Newman, 1823);

Seventy-Six, 2 volumes (Baltimore: Joseph Robinson, 1823; London: G. & W. B. Whittaker, 1823);

Randolph, A Novel, 2 volumes (Philadelphia, 1823);

Errata; or, the Works of Will. Adams, 2 volumes (New York: Published for the Proprietors, 1823);

Brother Jonathan; or, the New Englanders, 3 volumes (Edinburgh: William Blackwood/London: T. Cadell, Strand, 1825);

Rachel Dyer; A North American Story (Portland, Maine: Shirley & Hyde, 1828);

Authorship, a Tale (Boston: Gray & Bowen, 1830);

Principles of Legislation, Neal's biographical notice of Bentham and his translation from the French of M. Dumont (Boston: Wells & Lilly, 1830);

The Down-Easters, 2 volumes (New York: Harper & Brothers, 1833);

True Womanhood: A Tale (Boston: Ticknor & Fields, 1859);

The White-Faced Pacer: or, Before and After the Battle (New York: Beadle, 1863);

The Moose-Hunter; or, Life in the Maine Woods (New York: Beadle, 1864);

Little Moccasin; or, Along the Madawaska. A Story of Life and Love in the Lumber Region (New York: Beadle, 1866);

Wandering Recollections of a Somewhat Busy Life (Boston: Roberts Brothers, 1869);

Great Mysteries and Little Plagues (Boston: Roberts Brothers, 1870).

Collections: *American Writers. A Series of Papers Contributed to Blackwood's Magazine (1824-1825),* edited by Fred Lewis Pattee (Durham: Duke University Press, 1937);

Observations on American Art. Selections from the Writings of John Neal (1793-1876), edited by Harold Edward Dickson (State College: Pennsylvania State College, 1943).

OTHER: *General Index to the First Twelve Volumes, or First Series, of Niles' Weekly Register Being a*

Period of Six Years: From September, 1811, to September, 1817, edited by Neal (Baltimore: Published by the editor at Franklin Press, 1818);

Paul Allen, *A History of the American Revolution; Comprehending All the Principle Events Both in the Field and in the Cabinet,* 2 volumes, contributions by Neal (Baltimore: Thomas Murphy, 1819);

"Otter-Bag, the Oneida Chief," in *The Token; A Christmas and New Year's Present,* edited by N. P. Willis (Boston: S. G. Goodrich, 1829), pp. 221-284;

"The Birth of a Poet," "Ode to Peace," and "The Sleeper," in *Specimens of American Poetry,* volume 3, edited by Samuel Kettell (Boston: S. G. Goodrich, 1829);

"The Utilitarian," in *The Token; A Christmas and New Year's Present,* edited by S. G. Goodrich (Boston: Carter & Hendee, 1830), pp. 299-318:

"The Haunted Man," in *The Atlantic Souvenir for MDCCCXXXII* (Philadelphia: Carey & Lea, 1832), pp. 221-246;

"Children–What are They?," in *The Token and Atlantic Souvenir. A Christmas and New Year's Present,* edited by Goodrich (Boston: Charles Bowen, 1835), pp. 280-298;

"The Young Phrenologist," in *The Token and Atlantic Souvenir. A Christmas and New Year's Present,* edited by Goodrich (Boston: Charles Bowen, 1836), pp. 156-169;

"The Unchangeable Jew" and "A War-Song of the Revolution," in *The Portland Sketch Book,* edited by Ann S. Stephens (Portland, Maine: Colman & Chisolm, 1836);

"Women," in *The Boston Book. Being Specimens of Metropolitan Literature,* edited by B. B. Thatcher (Boston: Light & Stearns, 1837), pp. 240-244;

"Elizabeth Oakes Smith," in *The Sinless Child, and Other Poems, by Elizabeth Oakes Smith,* edited by John Keese (New York: Wiley & Putnam/ Boston: W. D. Ticknor, 1843), pp. xv-xxvi;

"My Child! My Child!," in *The Mayflower,* edited by E. Oakes Smith (Boston: Saxton & Kelt, 1847), pp. 112-113;

"Phantasmagoria," in *The Dew-Drop: A Tribute of Affection* (Philadelphia: Lippincott, Grambo, 1852), pp. 153-170;

"Battle Anthem," in *The Rebellion Record: A Diary of American Events,* edited by Frank Moore (New York: Putnam's, 1861), p. 119.

PERIODICAL PUBLICATIONS: "The Squatter," *New-England Magazine,* 8 (1835): 97-104;

"Will the Wizard," *New England Magazine,* 8 (1835): 194-204;

Our Ephraim, or the New Englanders, serialized in *New England Galaxy* (16 May 1835); (23 May 1835); (30 May 1835); (6 June 1835); (13 June 1835);

Ruth Elder, serialized in *Brother Jonathan,* 5 (January-June, 1843); 6 (July-December 1843).

John Neal, in the years following American independence, was a strong and often irritating spokesman for literary nationalism and for the new romantic doctrines of Germany and England that were breaking the mold of eighteenth-century literary theory. Neal and his twin sister, Rachel, grew up in the seaport town of Falmouth, Maine (now Portland). Their father, John Neal, Sr., had died when they were a month old. Their mother became a teacher after her husband's death. From the age of twelve, Neal edu-

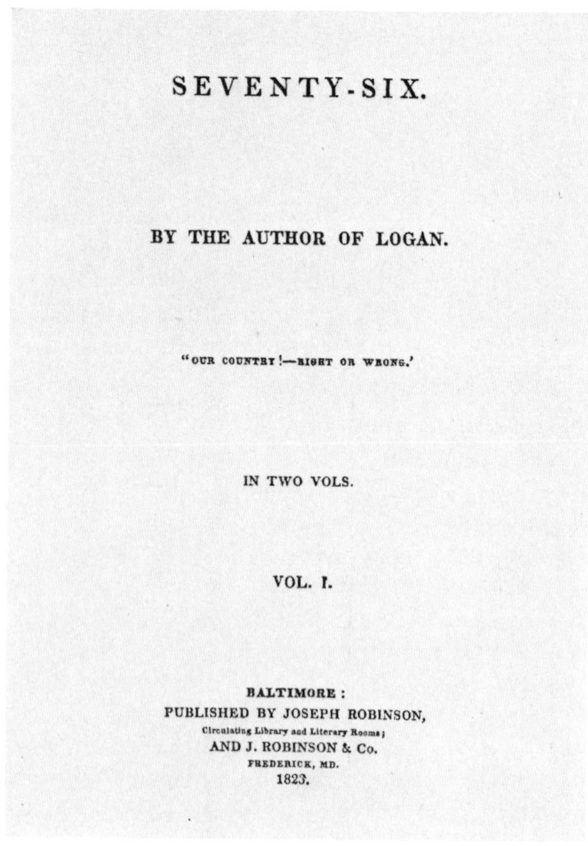

SEVENTY-SIX.

BY THE AUTHOR OF LOGAN.

"OUR COUNTRY!—RIGHT OR WRONG.'

IN TWO VOLS.

VOL. I.

BALTIMORE:
PUBLISHED BY JOSEPH ROBINSON,
Circulating Library and Literary Rooms;
AND J. ROBINSON & Co.
FREDERICK, MD.
1823.

Title page for the first volume of the novel Neal set during the American Revolution

cated himself by his own omnivorous reading. His young brain was fired with the Gothicism of Ann Radcliffe and Charles Brockden Brown, as well as by William Godwin, whose feminism Neal quickly espoused. After early attempts at launching himself with merchants in Falmouth and a brief period as an itinerant portraitist, he entered mercantile business in Boston (1809-1814) with John Pierpont. In 1815 they opened a second establishment in Baltimore and moved there. The cultural life of these cities provided a wider stimulus and a more contemporary focus to his reading and self-education.

In the leisure after business the two young men read and discussed virtually all the American writers of the time as well as near contemporaries from abroad: Lord Byron, Percy Bysshe Shelley, Leigh Hunt, Thomas Moore, Thomas Campbell, and Charles Maturin. As new works arrived from London, Neal indulged his histrionic talent by reading the poets aloud to Pierpont. Perhaps already the business world received less of their attention than did the world of ideas and letters, for in 1816 their firm was bankrupt and the two friends turned to the professions, Pierpont soon leaving for Boston and the ministry, Neal plunging into the reading of law and writing.

Neal's growing ideas about art and literature found their first forum when a group of high-spirited young men formed a Saturday evening club, the Delphians, on 31 August 1816. Limited to nine, they met to eat cheese, drink beer, read papers, and debate assigned topics. They were soon publishing their work in the *Portico,* in which Neal first tasted the heady wine of literary success. In this periodical he launched his poetry in imitation of Byron and, more important, reviewed cantos of *Childe Harold's Pilgrimage* (1816, 1817) as they appeared. In other essays on *Manfred* (1817), Sir Walter Scott, Shakespeare, and Benjamin West, Neal worked out his aesthetic.

His central critical position was defined by rejection of respectable but pale neoclassicism on the one hand and espousal of romantic sublimity and passion on the other. In his *Portico* reviews he expressed his belief that true poetry arises from passion: it furnishes "a clue to the labyrinth of passion. . . . Poetry is the lightning of intuition—every object is brightened into importance by its flash." When gripped by sufficient emotion, all men will naturally rise to poetry which is, he contends, a "natural musick" and the very language of the human heart. This romantic linking of the various arts through a quest for their common

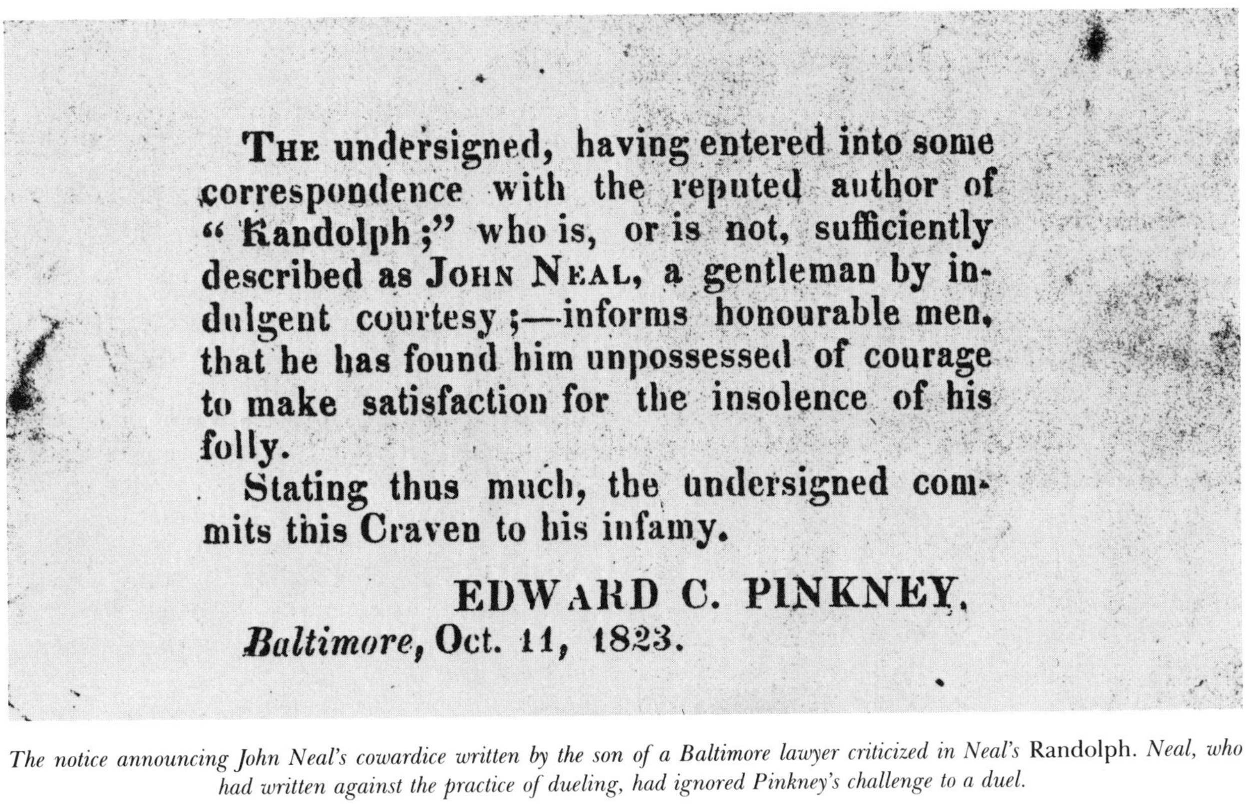

THE undersigned, having entered into some correspondence with the reputed author of "Randolph;" who is, or is not, sufficiently described as JOHN NEAL, a gentleman by indulgent courtesy;—informs honourable men, that he has found him unpossessed of courage to make satisfaction for the insolence of his folly.

Stating thus much, the undersigned commits this Craven to his infamy.

EDWARD C. PINKNEY.

Baltimore, Oct. 11, 1823.

The notice announcing John Neal's cowardice written by the son of a Baltimore lawyer criticized in Neal's Randolph. *Neal, who had written against the practice of dueling, had ignored Pinkney's challenge to a duel.*

sources and common effects was broadened to include painting and eloquence.

In a seminal essay, "Yankee Poetics," Benjamin Lease has demonstrated that, beneath Neal's seemingly scattered and random remarks lies a unified theory of literature that remained remarkably constant throughout Neal's long life. While he was following one of the mainstreams of European romanticism, he was also a pioneer in fostering the ideas of American literary nationalism, use of native material, and the concept of the natural man of genius. Expounding the then-current psychology, he distinguishes three faculties of man: brain, blood, and heart. Only the latter two are for Neal natural, for brain is the product of artificial effort and skill. Brain–intellect and reason–should occur in poetry and fiction only when fused with blood and heart, when living thought occurs without the order imposed by logic and syllogistic reasoning. Especially under emotional stress, logic goes down before chaotic vitality. The blood is particularly aroused by the sublime, by that which is mysterious, grandiose, indistinct, or awesome. The heart is touched with sympathy received from the manifestations of another human heart. The poet of the blood will deal with mystery in language that is magniloquent, metaphorical, filled with allusion and hyperbole. To such stimuli, the reader will respond involuntarily; but the terrific impact of the effect cannot be sustained by the reader for a lengthy period, and thus the poem should not be overly long. Neal thought himself to be as much a poet of the blood as Poe, whose later pronouncements on the essential brevity of true poetry were to become commonplace. He also placed Byron in this category of poets of the blood and expressed his affinity for *Manfred.* He admired the work of William Godwin and was influenced by the 1815 English translation of A. W. Schlegel which he used in developing his romantic aesthetic.

In contrast to poetry of the blood, according to Neal, poetry of the heart builds emotional links between people, as readers respond to genuine emotions expressed in some works and as writers respond to the genuine emotions of people around them. Here artifice and drama are fatal to the effect; only the simple action of a fellow human being speaks to the reader's sympathy. Accordingly the poet of the heart deals with the homely, simple, and familiar. His language will be natural, the dialogue striving to reflect actual speech in a natural setting so that both may augment character. As an example of poetry of the heart Neal points to the work of Thomas Moore which he contrasts to Byron's blood poetry. In his own novels, Neal applied this theory in developing natural dialogue that foreshadows the later American tradition of Mark Twain.

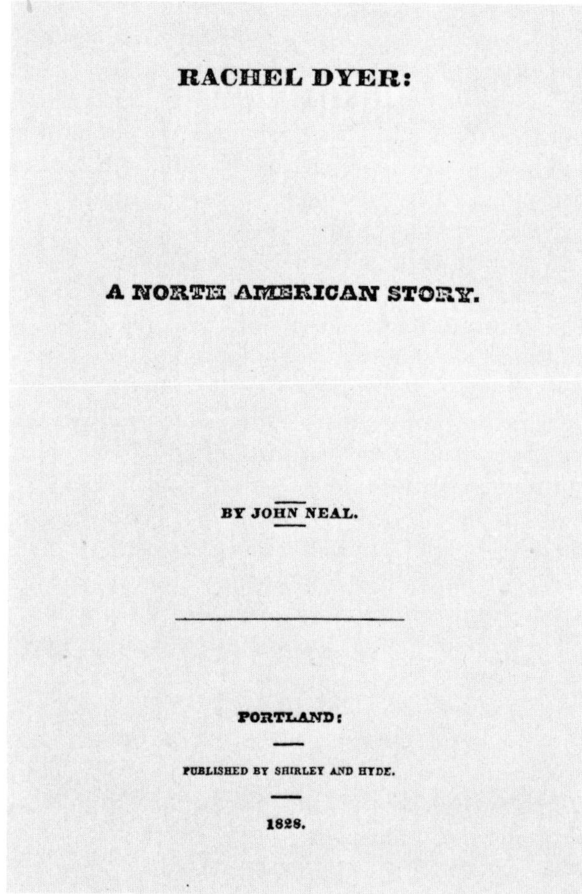
RACHEL DYER:

A NORTH AMERICAN STORY.

BY JOHN NEAL.

PORTLAND:

PUBLISHED BY SHIRLEY AND HYDE.

1828.

Title page for Neal's novel of the Salem witch trials

Neal further realizes that point of view is vital to literary effects, especially as they try to appeal to the heart. In an age generally committed to the omniscient author point of view, he argues for one restricted to a single character, the one channel through which the reader's affinity may flow. All information not known to this central character, then, is to be withheld from the reader. An early example of this type of point of view is Neal's *Seventy-Six* (1823), which is narrated by a direct and earthy old soldier, Jonathan Oadley. A colloquial tone of immediacy is set by the eyewitness narrator.

Neal's romantic aesthetic, first developed in his Baltimore years, remained central to his later critical and editing work and to his own practice of writing novels. His literary apprenticeship

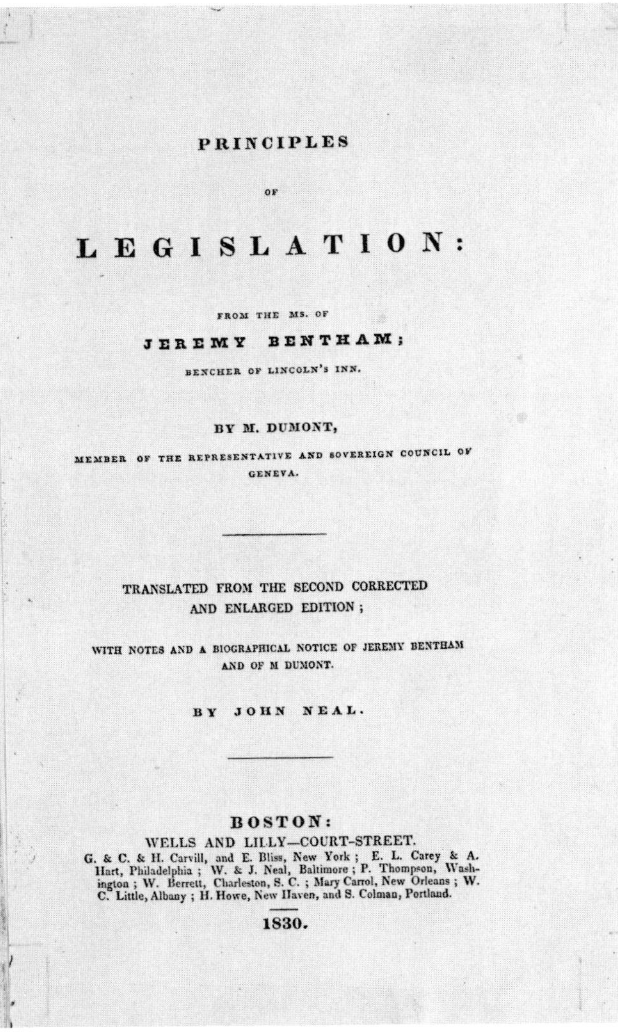
PRINCIPLES
OF
LEGISLATION:
FROM THE MS. OF
JEREMY BENTHAM;
BENCHER OF LINCOLN'S INN.
BY M. DUMONT,
MEMBER OF THE REPRESENTATIVE AND SOVEREIGN COUNCIL OF GENEVA.

TRANSLATED FROM THE SECOND CORRECTED AND ENLARGED EDITION;
WITH NOTES AND A BIOGRAPHICAL NOTICE OF JEREMY BENTHAM AND OF M DUMONT.
BY JOHN NEAL.

BOSTON:
WELLS AND LILLY—COURT-STREET.
G. & C. & H. Carvill, and E. Bliss, New York; E. L. Carey & A. Hart, Philadelphia; W. & J. Neal, Baltimore; P. Thompson, Washington; W. Berrett, Charleston, S. C.; Mary Carrol, New Orleans; W. C. Little, Albany; H. Howe, New Haven, and S. Colman, Portland.
1830.

Frontispiece and title page for the volume containing Neal's translation of what was called "Dumont's Bentham." In the early 1790s, persuaded that certain of his works would never be published, Bentham turned over manuscripts to Swiss lawyer and writer M. Dumont, who edited, revised, and rewrote ten volumes of Bentham's works in French. Neal's book also includes his biographical essays on Bentham and Dumont as well as Neal's notes on his translation, which attempt to separate Dumont's ideas from Bentham's.

over, he was ready for a larger arena. In December 1823 he sailed for London, where his novel *Logan,* a wildly rhetorical tale of a Byronic American Indian chief, had just been published. Soon after arrival he sent his first article to *Blackwood's Edinburgh Magazine*; it was a timely study of the American presidents and candidates. His magazine career was launched.

Neal had deliberately selected *Blackwood's Edinburgh Magazine* as the most original and trendsetting of periodicals. The editor, John Wilson, had talents similar to Neal's and so might be expected to respond favorably to Neal's brash and sometimes undisciplined talent. Neal, the descendant of a royalist Scot, might find a place among the Edinburgh journalists. Further, publisher William Blackwood, always looking for the new and startling, was hospitable to any writer who exhibited "natural or unschooled genius." Such was the shepherd poet James Hogg, who had been associated with the magazine for some time, but a recent falling out left a void that Neal could fill. Also the magazine had recently shown an increased interest in the Yankee, a topic upon which Neal was an expert. His tone, moreover, of contentious strong opinion and his avowed aesthetic based on Schlegel's doctrine of effect were shared with Blackwood, Wilson, and their magazine. Neal found himself warmly welcomed.

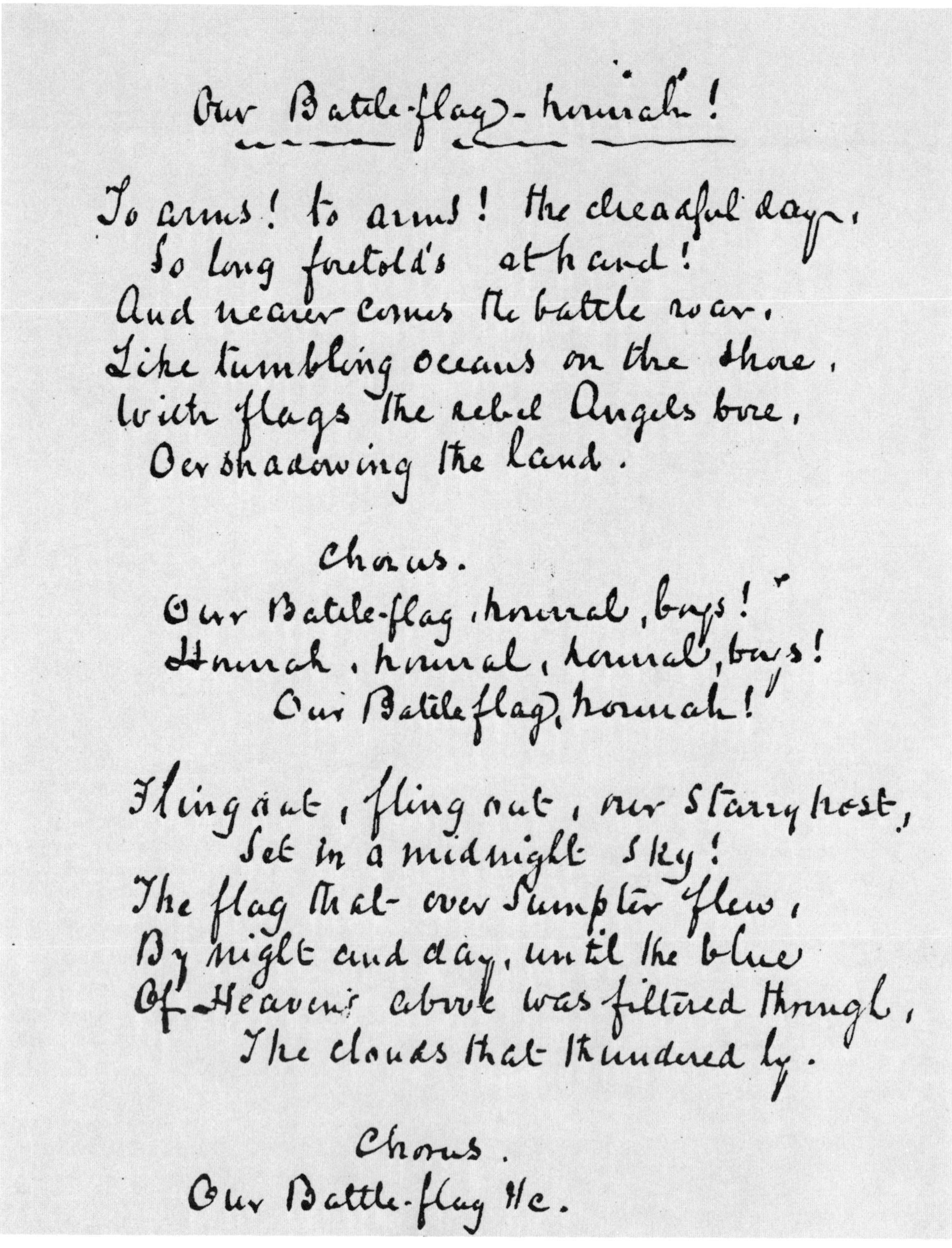

Our Battle-flag—hurrah!

To arms! to arms! the dreadful day,
So long foretold's at hand!
And nearer comes the battle roar,
Like tumbling oceans on the shore,
With flags the rebel Angels bore,
Overshadowing the land.

Chorus.
Our Battle-flag, hurrah, boys!
Hurrah, hurrah, hurrah, boys!
Our Battle flag, hurrah!

Fling out, fling out, our starry host,
Set in a midnight sky!
The flag that over Sumpter flew,
By night and day, until the blue
Of Heaven's above was filtered through,
The clouds that thundered by.

Chorus.
Our Battle-flag &c.

Fair copy of one of Neal's Civil War poems (from Autograph Leaves of Our Country's Authors, *compiled by Alexander Bliss and John P. Kennedy, 1864)*

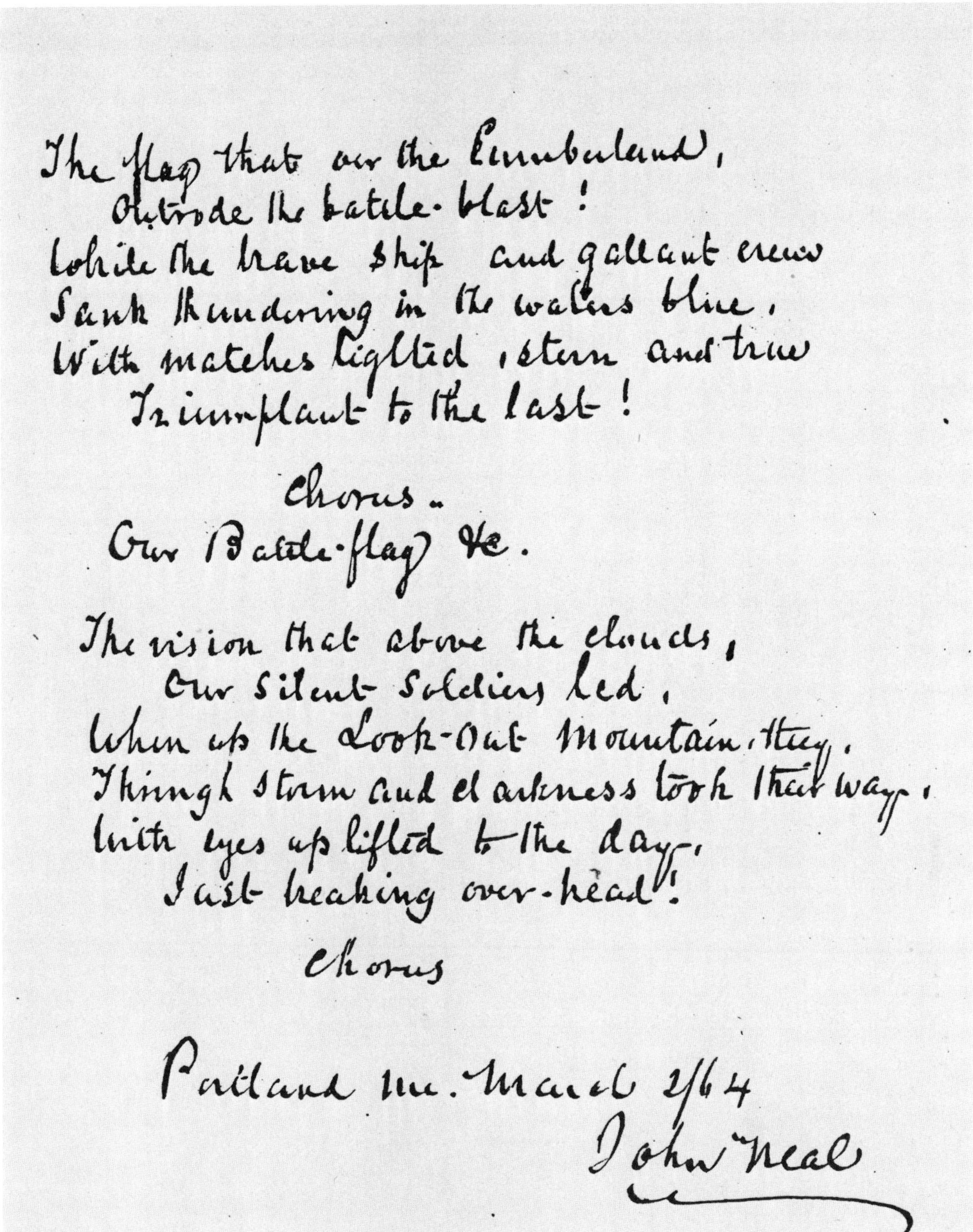

The flag that o'er the Cumberland,
Outrode the battle-blast!
While the brave ship and gallant crew
Sank thundering in the waters blue,
With matches lighted, stern and true
Triumphant to the last!

Chorus.
Our Battle-flag &c.

The vision that above the clouds,
Our silent soldiers led,
When up the Look-Out Mountain, they,
Through storm and darkness took their way,
With eyes uplifted to the day,
Just breaking over-head!

Chorus

Portland Me. March 2/64
John Neal

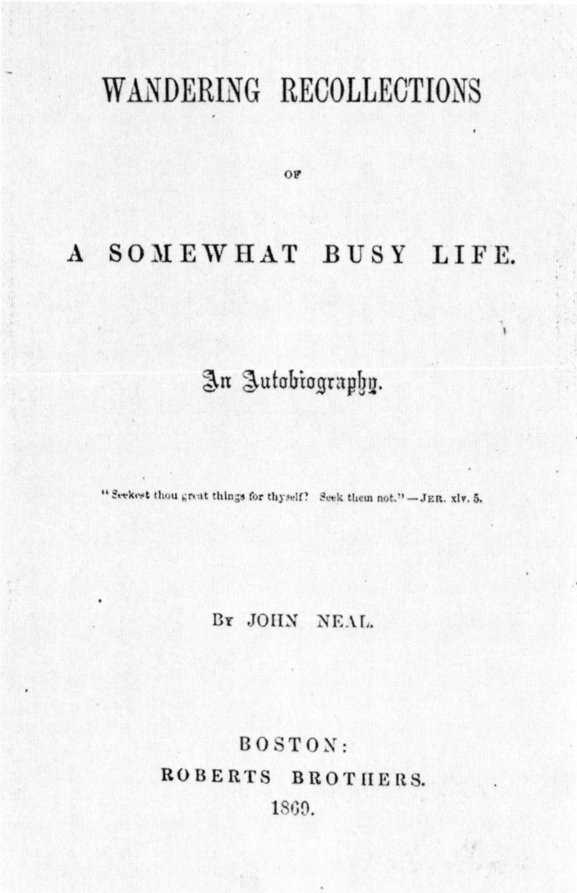
WANDERING RECOLLECTIONS

OF

A SOMEWHAT BUSY LIFE.

An Autobiography.

"Seekest thou great things for thyself? Seek them not."—JER. xlv. 5.

BY JOHN NEAL.

BOSTON:
ROBERTS BROTHERS.
1869.

Title page for Neal's idiosyncratic autobiography (collection of Joel Myerson)

From July 1824 to February 1826 he had an article in every issue.

In a long series of essays Neal reviewed American writers and artists. The substance of these pieces is sound, indeed remarkable, since he had to depend almost wholly upon memory. In effect he wrote the first history of American literature and the first American art criticism. While he is unfair to James Fenimore Cooper and gives the largest space to himself, his critical acumen is brilliant. Fred Lewis Pattee finds that "his critical judgments have held. Where he condemned, time has almost without exception condemned also. He had that rarest of powers, critical vision." His opinions were widely quoted in England and did bring about a change in knowledge concerning the new "United States of North America," as Neal liked to refer to his country.

While still in England, Neal resided for a time with Jeremy Bentham, deepening a knowledge of Utilitarianism to which he had been first drawn in Baltimore. Upon his return to America in 1827 he was an outspoken popularizer of the philosophy. Settled for the rest of his long life in his hometown of Portland, he practiced law and edited such influential journals as the *Yankee,* the masthead of which blazoned the Utilitarian motto, "The greatest happiness for the greatest number." There also he published some of his best novels–*Rachel Dyer* (1828), about Salem witchcraft, and *The Down-Easters* (1833), with realistic details of Yankee character and dialect. Increasingly, however, his work and fame were supplanted by those of the newer generation of the American renaissance.

The proper evaluation of John Neal's achievements depends upon seeing him in the per-

spective of his generation, the first to be born in the newly independent United States. Only two of the group closest to him in age were to overshadow him–Cooper in fiction and William Cullen Bryant in poetry. Otherwise his work compares well with the humor and folklore of a Seba Smith, the oratory and frontier material of an Augustus Longstreet and James Hall, or the romancing of a John Pendelton Kennedy. Ten years his senior, Washington Irving stood out before him; Ralph Waldo Emerson followed ten years after him. But the giants of the American renaissance–William Gilmore Simms, Henry W. Longfellow, Nathaniel Hawthorne, John Greenleaf Whittier, Edgar Allan Poe, Oliver Wendell Holmes, James Russell Lowell, Henry Thoreau, Herman Melville, Walt Whitman–were all born after Neal's boyhood closed. Many of these owed special debts to Neal; for example, Neal's novels fired Hawthorne's interest in the supernatural and the use of native material. In the *Yankee* Hawthorne received one of the very few encouraging reviews of his first novel. Likewise Whittier and Poe owed their earliest recognition to Neal.

John Neal, who had carried literary nationalism to the British Isles themselves, had helped to create the myth of the Yankee and an image of the American writer as one of individuality and originality. His critical accommodation of romantic theory to America led him through the thicket of contemporary publications with an uncanny ability to discover the budding talents of a future generation.

Bibliography:

Irving T. Richards, "John Neal: A Bibliography," *Jahrbuch für Amerikastudien,* 7 (1962): 296-319.

Biographies:

Dane Yorke, "Yankee Neal," *American Mercury,* 19 (January-April 1930): 361-368;

Irving T. Richards, "The Life and Works of John Neal," 4 volumes, Ph.D dissertation, Harvard University, 1932;

Benjamin Lease, *That Wild Fellow John Neal and the Literary Revolution* (Chicago: University of Chicago Press, 1972).

References:

William Charvat, *The Origins of American Critical Thought, 1810-1835* (Philadelphia: University of Pennsylvania Press, 1936);

Alexander Cowie, *The Rise of the American Novel* (New York: American Book Company, 1948);

Hans-Joachim Lang, "Critical Essays and Stories by John Neal," *Jahrbuch für Amerikastudien,* 7 (1962): 204-288;

Benjamin Lease, "Yankee Poetics: John Neal's Theory of Poetry and Fiction," *American Literature,* 24 (January 1953): 505-519;

Harold C. Martin, "The Colloquial Tradition in the Novel: John Neal," *New England Quarterly,* 32 (December 1959): 455-475;

Robert J. Menner, "Two Early Comments on American Dialects," *American Speech,* 13 (February 1938): 8-12;

Joseph J. Rubin, "John Neal's Poetics as an Influence on Whitman and Poe," *New England Quarterly,* 14 (June 1941): 359-362;

Donald A. Sears, *John Neal* (Boston: Twayne, 1978);

Sears, "Portland, Maine, as a Cultural Center, 1800-1836," Ph.D dissertation, Harvard University, 1952;

John Earle Uhler, "The Delphian Club," *Maryland Historical Magazine,* 20 (December 1925): 305-346.

James Kirke Paulding
(22 August 1778-6 April 1860)

Louis D. Owens
University of New Mexico

See also the Paulding entry in *DLB 3, Antebellum Writers in New York and the South.*

SELECTED BOOKS: *Salmagundi,* by Paulding, William Irving, and Washington Irving, as Launcelot Langstaff and Others, 20 parts, published as 2 volumes (New York: Printed and published by D. Longworth, 1807-1808; London: Printed for J. M. Richardson, 1811; revised edition, New York: Longworth, 1814; revised by Irving (Paris: Galignani, 1824; Paris: Baudry, 1824); revised by Paulding as volumes 1 and 2 of *The Works of James K. Paulding* (New York: Harper, 1835);

The Diverting History of John Bull and Brother Jonathan, by Hector Bull-Us (New York: Inskeep & Bradford/Philadelphia: Bradford & Inskeep, 1812; London: Sherwood, Neely & Jones, 1813);

The Lay of the Scottish Fiddle; A Tale of Havre de Grace, supposed to be written by Walter Scott, Esq. (New York: Inskeep & Bradford/Philadelphia: Bradford & Inskeep, 1813; London: Cawthorn, 1814);

The United States and England: Being a Reply to the Criticism on Inchiquin's Letters (Philadelphia: Bradford & Inskeep/New York: Inskeep & Bradford, 1815);

Letters from the South, Written during an Excursion in the Summer of 1816, 2 volumes (New York: James Eastburn, 1817);

The Backwoodsman (Philadelphia: M. Thomas, 1818);

Salmagundi, Second Series, 3 volumes (Philadelphia: M. Thomas/New York: Haly & Thomas, 1819-1820);

A Sketch of Old England by a New-England Man, 2 volumes (New York: Charles Wiley, 1822);

Koningsmarke, The Long Finne, A Story of the New World, 2 volumes (New York: Charles Wiley, 1823; London: Whittaker, 1823); revised and republished as *Koningsmarke, or, Old Times in the New World,* 2 volumes (New York: Harper, 1834-1835);

James Kirke Paulding, engraving by F. Halpin from a drawing by Joseph Wood

John Bull in America: or, The New Munchausen (New York: Charles Wiley, 1825; London: Miller, 1825);

The Merry Tales of the Three Wise Men of Gotham (New York: G. & C. Carvill, 1826);

The New Mirror for Travellers, and Guide to the Springs, by an Amateur (New York: G. & C.

Carvill, 1828); enlarged and republished as *A Book of Vagaries; Comprising the New Mirror for Travellers And Other Whim-Whams,* edited by William Irving Paulding (New York: Scribners, 1868);

Tales of the Good Woman, by a Doubtful Gentleman (New York: G. & C. & H. Carvill, 1829);

Chronicles of the City of Gotham from the papers of A Retired Common Councilman (New York: G. & C. & H. Carville, 1830);

The Dutchman's Fireside, 2 volumes (New York: Harper, 1831);

Westward Ho!, 2 volumes (New York: Harper, 1832);

A Life of Washington, 2 volumes (New York: Harper, 1835);

The Book of Saint Nicholas (New York: Harper, 1836);

Slavery in the United States (New York: Harper, 1836);

A Christmas Gift from Fairy Land (New York: D. Appleton, 1838);

The Old Continental: or, The Price of Liberty, 2 volumes (New York: Paine & Burgess, 1846);

American Comedies, by Paulding and William Irving Paulding (Philadelphia: Carey & Hart, 1847);

The Puritan and His Daughter, 2 volumes (New York: Baker & Scribner, 1849);

The Lion of the West Retitled the Kentuckian, or a trip to New York A Farce in Two Acts, written by Paulding in 1830, revised by John Augustus Stone and William Bayle Bernard, edited by James N. Tidwell (Stanford: Stanford University Press/London: Oxford University Press, 1954).

Collections: *The Works of James K. Paulding,* 15 volumes (New York: Harper, 1834-1839);

The Literary Life of James K. Paulding, compiled by William Irving Paulding (New York: Scribners, 1867).

OTHER: "The Eve of St. John; or, The Oracle of the Secret Water," "A Tale of Mystery; or, The Youth That Died Without a Disease," and "The Spanish Girl of the Cordilleras," in *The Atlantic Souvenir; A Christmas and New Year's Offering* (Philadelphia: H. C. Carey & I. Lea, 1825);

"Forest Scenery," in *The American Common-Place Book of Prose,* edited by George Cheever (Boston: S. G. Goodrich, 1828), pp. 53-55;

"Un Faineant" and "Benhadar," in *The Atlantic Souvenir; A Christmas and New Year's Offering* (Philadelphia: Carey, Lea & Carey, 1828), pp. 88-115, 168-196;

"The Eve of Saint Andrew," in *The Atlantic Souvenir for MDCCCXXXI* (Philadelphia: Carey & Lea, 1831), pp. 51-82;

"Childe Roeliff's Pilgrimage; a Travelling Legend" and "Selim, the Benefactor of Mankind," in *Tales of Glauber-Spa,* 2 volumes (New York: Harper, 1832), I: 111-189; II: 155-220;

"The Dunce and the Genius," in *The Atlantic Souvenir for MDCCCXXXII* (Philadelphia: Carey & Lea, 1832), pp. 66-98;

"The Magic Spinning Wheel," in *The Token and Atlantic Souvenir. A Christmas and New Year's Pres-*

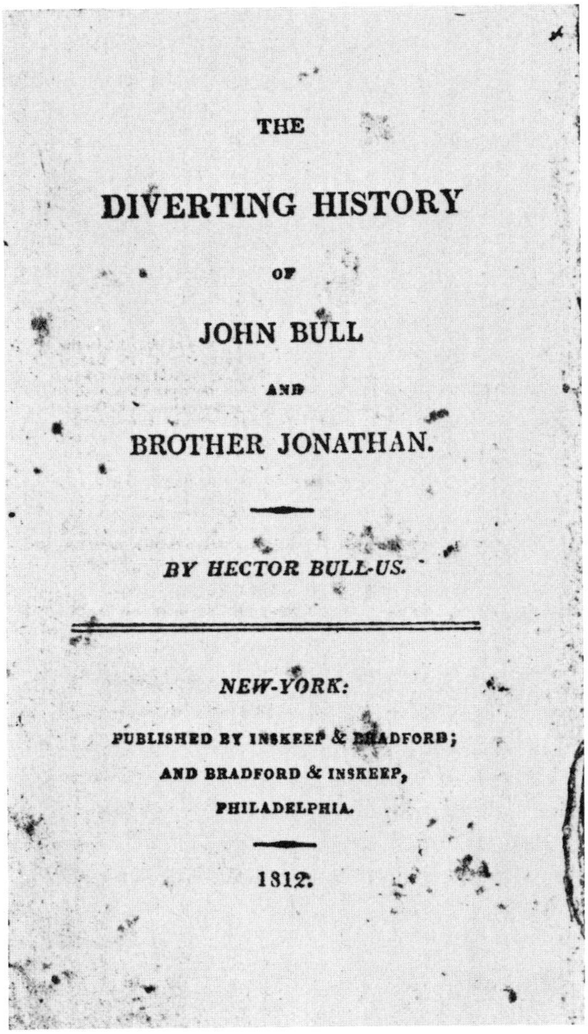

Title page for Paulding's second published work, an anti-British satire tracing the establishment, development, and ultimate revolt of the American colonies

ent, edited by S. G. Goodrich (Boston: Charles Bowen, 1836), pp. 129-150;

"Recollections of the Country," in *The Irving Offering: A Token of Affection, for 1851* (New York: Leavitt, 1851), pp. 213-227.

"A fashionable book is apt to be as dull as a fashionable party," James Kirke Paulding wrote in 1823, "simply because neither of them have any approximation to nature." This declaration in Paulding's first novel, *Koningsmarke, The Long Finne, A Story of the New World* (1823), underscores an insistence upon clarity, simplicity, and fidelity to nature that distinguished Paulding's critical voice throughout a long and prolific career. Though today a nearly forgotten figure in the background of American literature, Paulding was, during the early decades of the nineteenth century, one of the best known and most influential literary names in America. In the 1830s his reputation as a man of letters ranked with those of such luminaries as Washington Irving, James Fenimore Cooper, and Edgar Allan Poe. Paulding distinguished himself in virtually every field of literature in America, publishing widely read poems and short stories, novels and plays, satires and travel sketches, biography and social commentary, while peppering all of his writings with critical commentary and advice. In 1886 James Grant Wilson would declare in *Bryant and His Friends* that among "the first to make a creditable appearance in the field of American literature was James K. Paulding." He spoke out repeatedly for clarity and common sense in fiction, verse, and drama, and above all for a genuinely original American literature that would spring from American soil and thought.

Born in Great Nine Partners, New York, where his family had fled for protection from British forces in 1776, Paulding grew up amidst the intense anti-British sentiments that followed the Revolution, an enmity particularly strong among Paulding's Dutch family and neighbors. Out of this early impression may have grown Paulding's lifelong antipathy toward the British which, combined with an even stronger nationalism, would permeate and color his writing as well as his political career. Paulding's Anglophobia would find vent in a succession of satires and critical sorties directed against the British over a span of more than four decades. His patriotism was apparently not dampened by the fact that his father, Col. William Paulding, had pledged his personal fortune to feed starving troops during the Revolutionary War and had subsequently been refused reimbursement by the fledgling government following the war. The resulting impoverishment drove William Paulding into debtor's prison and left the family destitute.

Due in part to the family's poverty, Paulding's formal education consisted of sporadic attendance for three or four years in a country school near Tarrytown, New York. Subsequently Paulding educated himself, as had his earlier countryman Ben Franklin, by extensive reading, particularly in the great neoclassical authors such as Oliver Goldsmith, Addison, and Steele, whose influence would be seen in the markedly Augustan flavor of Paulding's verse and prose.

At age eighteen Paulding moved from Tarrytown to New York City to live with his sister Julia and work in the United States Loan Office. Here he became close friends with his brother-in-law William Irving and with William's younger brother Washington Irving. In 1807 Paulding joined the Irving brothers in producing the famous Knickerbocker collaboration, *Salmagundi; or, The Whim-whams and Opinions of Launcelot Langstaff, Esq. and Others.* The very popular *Salmagundi,* an American version of the satirical essays of Addison and Steele, would continue through twenty issues and launch the literary careers of both Paulding and Washington Irving. More than a decade later, in 1819, Paulding, writing alone this time, would revive *Salmagundi* in a second series, but this single-handed attempt would meet with little success.

In 1812 Paulding's rising nationalism resulted in his first book-length satire against the British, *The Diverting History of John Bull and Brother Jonathan,* followed a year later, in 1813, by his attack on the indulgences of romanticism and Walter Scott in particular in *The Lay of the Scottish Fiddle,* a skillful burlesque of Scott's *Lay of the Last Minstrel.* In 1815 Paulding's Anglophobia gave rise to *The United States and England* and attracted the attention of President James Madison, who appointed Paulding to a position as secretary of the newly created Board of Navy Commissioners. During a period when government sinecure was a warmly embraced tradition for men of letters, Paulding went on to hold offices as navy agent in New York (1824) and, ultimately, secretary of the navy (1838), appointments which allowed Paulding the leisure to publish fifteen volumes of material ranging from the essays in *Let-*

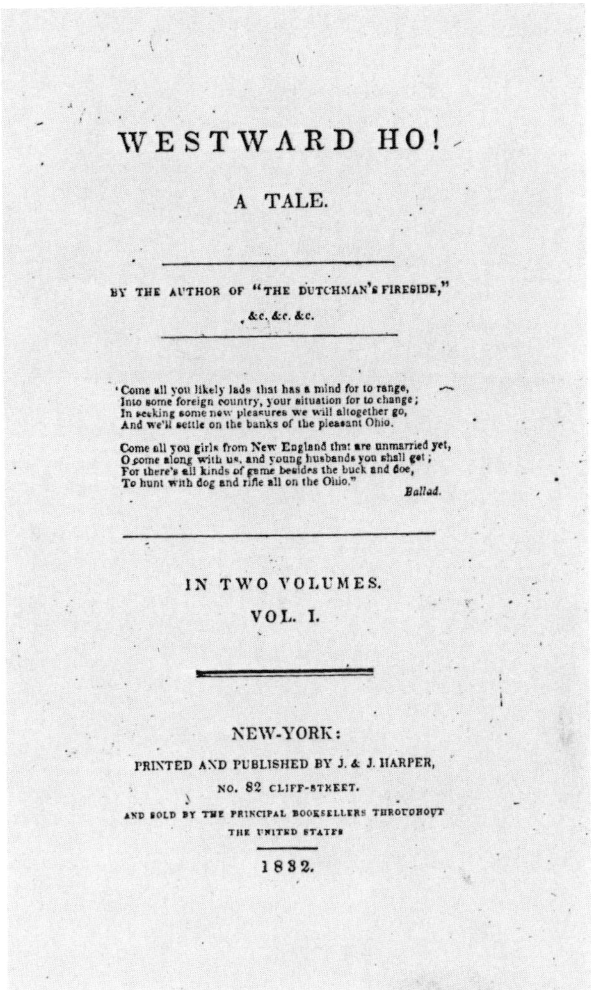

WESTWARD HO!

A TALE.

BY THE AUTHOR OF "THE DUTCHMAN'S FIRESIDE," &c. &c. &c.

'Come all you likely lads that has a mind for to range,
Into some foreign country, your situation for to change;
In seeking some new pleasures we will altogether go,
And we'll settle on the banks of the pleasant Ohio.

Come all you girls from New England that are unmarried yet,
O come along with us, and young husbands you shall get;
For there's all kinds of game besides the buck and doe,
To hunt with dog and rifle all on the Ohio."

Ballad.

IN TWO VOLUMES.

VOL. I.

NEW-YORK:

PRINTED AND PUBLISHED BY J. & J. HARPER,

NO. 82 CLIFF-STREET.

AND SOLD BY THE PRINCIPAL BOOKSELLERS THROUGHOUT THE UNITED STATES

1832.

Title page for one of Paulding's best novels. In the preface he says that one of the responsibilities of an American writer is to insure that his characters speak and behave "naturally."

ters from the South (1817), the satires *A Sketch of Old England by a New-England Man* (1822) and *John Bull in America* (1825), to a poem in heroic couplets, *The Backwoodsman* (1818), and three of his five novels, *Koningsmarke*, *The Dutchman's Fireside* (1831), and *Westward Ho!* (1832).

During these years in public office, Paulding was also writing and publishing a steady stream of tales in popular magazines and in his two collections, *Tales of the Good Woman* (1829) and *Chronicles of the City of Gotham* (1830). The author of more than seventy published stories, Paulding so dominated this genre during the ten years between 1824 and 1834 that his early critical biographer, Amos L. Herold, in his *James Kirke Paulding, Versatile American* (1926), calls this period the "Paulding decade of the short story." Paulding's prominence during the decades preceding the Civil War is attested to by the praise he received from both Nathaniel Hawthorne and Edgar Allan Poe. In a letter written in 1840, Hawthorne addressed Paulding as "the admired and familiar friend of every reader in the land," while in reviewing Paulding's *Life of Washington* (1835), Poe declared that "There is no better literary manner than the manner of Mr. Paulding. Certainly no American, and possibly no living writer of England, has more of those numerous peculiarities which go to the formation of a happy style."

In spite of Paulding's prolific literary successes during a career spanning nearly half a century, and in spite of the occasional brilliance of his work, it is for his early outspoken insistence upon the need for a national literature independent of England and uncluttered by the indulgences of romanticism that Paulding most deserves to be remembered. As early as 1820, in a *Salmagundi* (second series) essay entitled "National Literature," Paulding defined for American writers his theory of "rational fiction," urging American writers to avoid the "aid of superstition, the agency of ghosts, fairies, goblins, and all that antiquated machinery which till lately was confined to the nursery" and to write of real men and women and of events "which can always be traced to motives, actions, and passions, arising out of circumstances no way unnatural. . . ." Insisting upon the necessity for verisimilitude, Paulding, in *A Sketch of Old England by a New-England Man*, attacked the "caricatures and counterfeits" of the English stage and demanded that American dramatists, unlike their English counterparts, create characters "like the people who inhabit this humble earth." Ten years later in the preface to *Westward Ho!*, Paulding further anticipated the critical posture of such later realists as Mark Twain and William Dean Howells when he elaborated on the author's responsibility: "Having conceived a character, it should be his aim to make it act and talk as such a person might naturally be supposed to do in similar circumstances."

In his campaign for a genuinely American literature and a literature of the commonplace and common man, Paulding took every opportunity to attack the romanticism of Scott, following up his parody of Scott in *The Lay of the Scottish Fiddle* with criticism of Scott in *Letters from the South*, in which Paulding declared it his intention to "administer to the public taste, which owing to the witcher-

Painting of Placentia, Paulding's home in Hyde Park, New York

ies of that mischievous person called the 'Great Unknown', hath an unseemly propensity toward romances and the like." In 1835 Paulding openly questioned the "truth and fidelity" of Scott's work, stating in *John Bull in America* that "truth and falsehood, are like Gold and Bank notes; they cannot circulate together in the same book without vitiating the currency of human events."

Paulding's voice, steeped in neoclassicism and democratic nationalism, stood out in opposition to what he considered the weaknesses and failings of romanticism throughout his literary career. In 1834 he plea in the influential pages of Poe's *Southern Literary Messenger* for young American authors to "Give us something new–something characteristic of your native feelings, and I don't care what it is. I am somewhat tired of licentious love ditties, border legends, affected sorrows, and grumbling misanthropy, I want to see something wholesome, natural and national." And as late as 1847, in a letter to Evert A. Duyckinck, former editor of the *Democratic Review,* Paulding reiterated his insistence upon literary independence from England, declaring, "There is a noble harvest to be reaped in this New World of boundless space, and unexhausted fertility. Why then should we starve ourselves with the miserable gleanings of a worn out soil which has been so overcultivated that it has become a Pine Barren." Paulding applied the test of common sense and clarity to poetry as well as fiction and drama, stating in 1847 that "one of the best tests of poetry is to turn it into plain prose, and see how it looks in its nakedness."

Paulding's influence during the first half of the nineteenth century in American literature should not be underestimated. His role was an im-

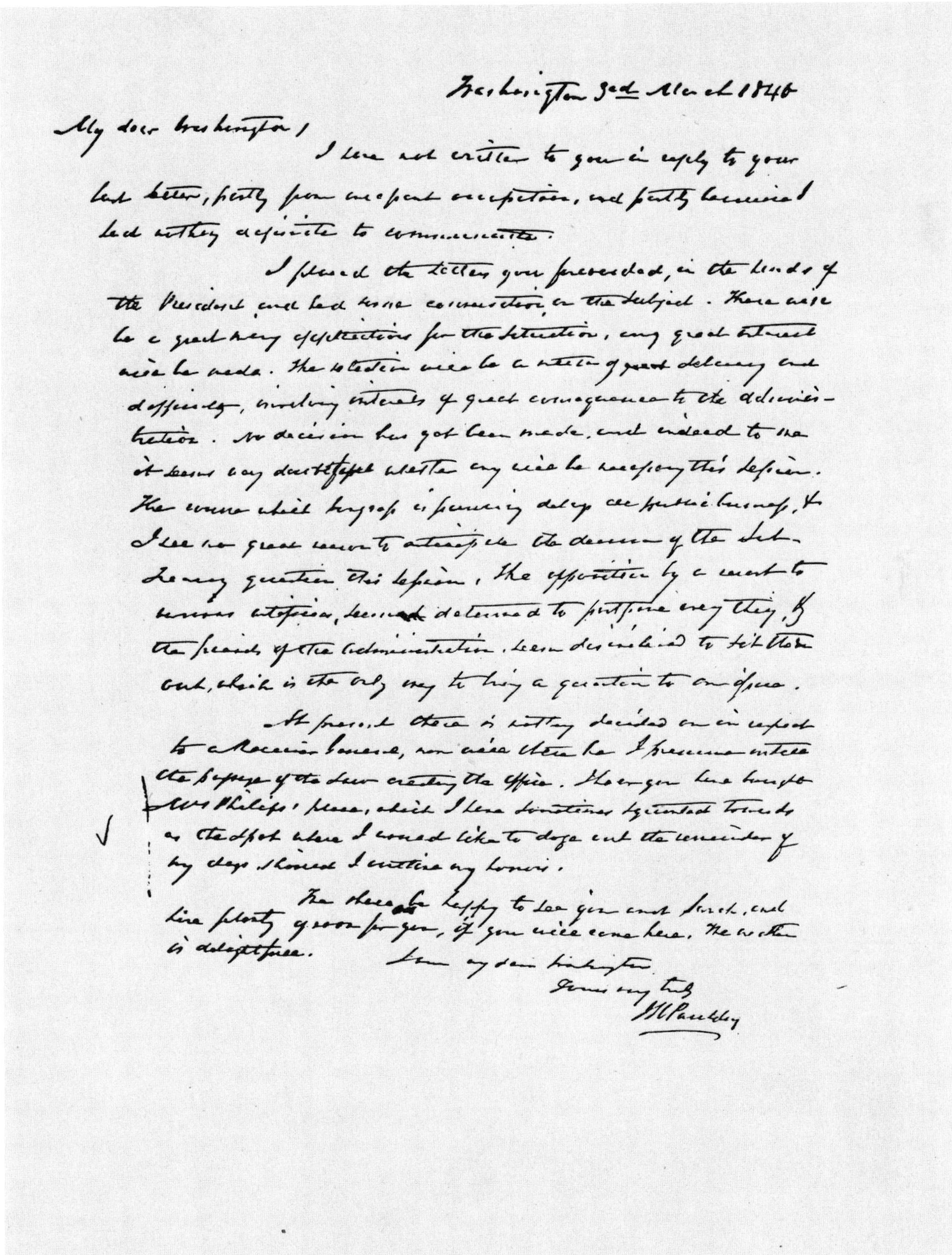

Washington 3rd March 1846

My dear Washington,

I have not written to you in reply to your last letter, partly from incessant occupation, and partly because I had nothing definite to communicate.

I placed the letter you forwarded, in the hands of the President and had some conversation on the subject. There will be a great many applications for the situation, and great interest will be made. The selection will be a matter of great delicacy and difficulty, involving interests of great consequence to the Administration. No decision has yet been made, and indeed to me it seems very doubtful whether any will be necessary this session. The course which Congress is pursuing delays all public business, & I see no great reason to anticipate the decision of the Sub-Treasury question this session. The opposition by a resort to various artifices, seem determined to postpone every thing, & the friends of the Administration seem disinclined to tire them out, which is the only way to bring a question to an issue.

At present there is nothing decided on in respect to a Receiver General, nor will there be I presume until the passage of the law creating the office. I hear you have bought Mr Philips' place, which I have sometimes looked towards as the spot where I would like to doze out the remainder of my days should I continue my honours.

We shall be happy to see you and Sarah, and have plenty of room for you, if you will come here. The weather is delightful.

Yours my dear Washington

Yours very truly

J K Paulding

Letter from Paulding to Washington Irving (from The Letters of James Kirke Paulding, *edited by Ralph M. Aderman, 1962)*

portant one in paving the way for the blossoming of American literature and criticism following the Civil War. In addition he was one of the first critics to speak out strongly for what would later come to be called "local color" writing. Of western writers, Paulding stated in a letter written in 1834: "I have always looked for something new or original in the literature of the West. . . . It seems to me that if we are ever to have a national literature, characteristic and original it will grow up far from the shores of the Atlantic. . . ." Of writers on America's frontier, he urged: "Let them follow that course which nature, and their peculiar situation point out, without sinking into the great mass of mankind that has no distinct characteristics, and my life on it, though they differ with the rest, it will be only, in their peculiar, strength, and originality." Finally, in Paulding's own comic drama, *The Lion of the West,* as well as his exploitation of native humor in such works as *Letters from the South* and *John Bull in America,* critic Floyd C. Watkins, in an essay entitled "James K. Paulding's Early Ring-Tailed Roarer," finds such "a significant volume of original material for Paulding, usually treated as primarily a Knickerbocker, to be considered the most important forerunner of humor of the frontier and the Old Southwest." Paulding's insistence upon the importance of local color, and his own use of the "ring-tailed roarer" tradition, anticipates and lays the groundwork for such humorists as Twain and, much later, even William Faulkner. In anticipation of the vernacular narrator of *Huckleberry Finn,* a Paulding character in *The Lion of the West* exclaims, "I wish I may be tetotaciously exflunctified."

Paulding's demonstration in his own writing of the potential in American materials, and his unwavering, critical insistence upon the qualities of clarity, common sense and verisimilitude assure him a place of importance in American literature, a place which his own poetry, fiction, and drama surely fail to achieve on their artistic merits. Writing quickly with little thought for revision, Paulding produced a large body of, for the most part, flawed work. Today the critical consensus regarding James K. Paulding would seem to be that as an artist he most often fails, while as an index to the developing phenomenon called American literature and as an important critical voice in pre-Civil War America Paulding is deserving of both close attention and respect.

James Kirke Paulding at sixty-five, engraving by F. Halpin from a medal by J. G. Chapman

Letters:

The Letters of James Kirke Paulding, edited by Ralph M. Aderman (Madison: University of Wisconsin Press, 1962).

References:

Ralph M. Aderman, "James Kirke Paulding as Social Critic," *Papers on English Language and Literature,* 1 (Summer 1965): 217-229;

Aderman, "James Kirke Paulding's Contributions to American Magazines," *Studies in Bibliography,* 17 (1964): 141-151;

Aderman, "James Kirke Paulding's Literary Income," *Bulletin of the New York Public Library,* 64 (1960): 117-129;

Joseph J. Arpad, "John Wesley Jarvis, James Kirke Paulding, and Colonel Nimrod Wildfire," *New York Folklore Quarterly,* 21 (1965): 92-106;

Alexander Cowie, *The Rise of the American Novel*

(New York: American Book Company, 1948), pp. 185-200;

Marcus Cunliffe, ed., *American Literature to 1900*, volume 8 in *History of Literature in the English Language* (London: Barrie & Jenkens, 1973), pp. 23, 96;

Amos L. Herold, *James Kirke Paulding, Versatile American* (New York: Columbia University Press, 1926);

Herold, "Paulding's Literary Theories," *Bulletin of the New York Public Library*, 66 (1962): 236-243;

Jay B. Hubbell, *The South in American Literature, 1607-1900* (Durham: Duke University Press, 1954), pp. 203-204;

Ralph L. Ketcham, ed., "An Unpublished Sketch of James Madison by James K. Paulding," *Virginia Magazine of History and Biography*, 67 (1959): 432-437;

Ernest Erwin Leisy, *American Literature: An Interpretive Survey* (New York: Crowell, 1929), pp. 63, 75, 76;

Louis D. Owens, "James K. Paulding and the Foundations of American Literature," *Bulletin of the New York Public Library*, 79 (1975): 40-50;

Owens, "Paulding's 'The Dumb Girl,' A Source of *The Scarlet Letter*," *Nathaniel Hawthorne Journal* (1974): 240-249;

Fred Lewis Pattee, *The Development of the American Short Story* (New York: Harper, 1923);

Henri Petter, *The Early American Novel* (Columbus: Ohio State University Press, 1971);

James Holman Robertson, "James Kirke Paulding: A Study in Literary Nationalism," Ph.D. dissertation, University of Michigan, 1950;

Robert E. Spiller, et al., eds., *Literary History of the United States* (New York: Macmillan, 1948), pp. 684-686;

Floyd C. Watkins, "James K. Paulding's Early Ring-Tailed Roarer," *Southern Folklore Quarterly*, 15 (1951): 183-187;

Watkins, "James Kirke Paulding and the South," *American Quarterly*, 5 (1953): 219-230;

James Grant Wilson, *Bryant and His Friends* (New York: Fords, Howard & Hulbert, 1886), p. 129;

Paton Yoder, "Private Hospitality in the South, 1775-1850," *Mississippi Valley Historical Review*, 67 (1960): 419-433.

Papers:

Paulding's papers are widely scattered, but may be found in such institutions as Boston Public Library, Brown University Library, Clemson University Library, Columbia University Library, Duke University Library, Harvard University Library, Henry L. Huntington Library and Art Gallery, New York Public Library, New York State Library, University of Virginia Library, and Yale University Library.

Oliver William Bourn Peabody

(9 July 1799-5 July 1848)

Anne Bail Howard
University of Nevada at Reno

BOOKS: *An Address Before the Peace Society of Exeter, N.H.* (Exeter: F. Grant, 1830);

A Discourse Delivered in the Church of the First Congregational Society in Burlington (Burlington, Vt.: University Press, 1846).

OTHER: *The Dramatic Works of William Shakespeare,* edited, with biography and notes, by Peabody (Boston: Hilliard, Gray, 1836);

"Life of Major-General Israel Putnam," in *Lives of Sir William Phips, Israel Putnam, Lucretia Mary Davidson, and David Rittenhouse, The Library of American Biography,* first series, volume 7, edited by Jared Sparks (Boston: Hilliard, Gray, 1837; London: Kennett, 1837), pp. 103-218;

"Life of John Sullivan," in *Lives of John Sullivan, Jacob Lisler, Nathaniel Bacon, and John Mason, The Library of American Biography,* second series, volume 3, edited by Sparks (Boston: Little & Brown, 1844), pp. 1-177;

Sermons by the Late William Oliver Bourn Peabody, edited, with a memoir, by O. W. B. Peabody (Boston: Greene, 1849).

PERIODICAL PUBLICATIONS: Review of *Memoirs of Madame de Genlis, North American Review,* 32 (January 1831): 196-215;

Review of *The Water Witch,* by James Fenimore Cooper, *North American Review,* 32 (April 1831): 508-523;

Review of *The Sports and Pastimes of the People of England,* by Joseph Strutt, *North American Review,* 33 (July 1831): 191-215;

Review of *The Life of Gouverneur Morris,* by Jared Sparks, *North American Review,* 34 (April 1832): 465-493;

Review of *Iceland,* by Ebenezer Henderson, *North American Review,* 35 (July 1832): 75-92;

Review of *The Token and The Atlantic Souvenir,* edited by S. G. Goodrich, *North American Review,* 36 (January 1833): 276-279;

Review of *Some Account of the Life of Sir Walter Scott,* by Allan Cunningham, *North American Review,* 36 (January 1833): 289-315;

Review of *Indian Biography,* by B. B. Thatcher, *North American Review,* 36 (April 1833): 472-487;

Review of *Biographical and Poetical Remains of Margaret Miller Davidson,* edited by Washington Irving, *Christian Examiner,* 31 (September 1833): 269-273;

Review of *Life of John Jay,* by William Jay, *North American Review,* 37 (October 1833): 315-339;

Review of *Life and Poetical Works of The Reverend George Crabbe,* by his son George Crabbe, *North American Review,* 39 (July 1834): 135-156;

Review of *Outre-Mer, Nos. I and II,* by Henry Wadsworth Longfellow, *North American Review,* 39 (October 1834): 459-467;

Review of *Calavar: Or a Knight of the Conquest; A Romance of Mexico,* by John Montgomery Bird, *North American Review,* 40 (January 1835): 233-259;

Review of *A Comprehensive Pronouncing and Explanatory Dictionary of the English Language,* by J. E. Worcester, *North American Review,* 41 (October 1835): 482-488;

Review of *The Works of Robert Burns with his Life,* by Allan Cunningham, *North American Review,* 42 (January 1836): 42-75;

Review of *The Poetical Works of Thomas Campbell, North American Review,* 50 (April 1840): 488-505;

Review of *Voices of the Night,* by Henry Wadsworth Longfellow, *Christian Examiner,* 28 (May 1840): 242-246;

Review of *Manhood; or Scenes from the Past,* by William Plumer, *Christian Examiner,* 34 (July 1843): 395-398;

Review of *Life, Voyages and Exploits of Sir Francis Drake,* by John Barrow, *North American Review,* 59 (July 1844): 70-95;

Review of *Library of American Biography,* second series, volume 1, edited by Jared Sparks,

North American Review, 59 (July 1844): 96-104;

Review of *Alida, or Town and Country,* by the author of *Allen Prescott, North American Review,* 59 (October 1844): 434-445;

Review of *Commerce of the Prairies,* by Josiah Gregg, and *Narrative of the Texan Santa Fe Expedition,* by George Wilkins Kendall, *North American Review,* 60 (January 1845): 196-214.

America's first editor of Shakespeare, staunch reviewer for the *Christian Examiner* and the *North American Review,* Oliver William Bourn Peabody pursued a varied career as attorney, legislator, man of letters, professor, and finally, Unitarian minister. A critic with a strongly moralistic cast and a sound respect for eighteenth-century literary values, Peabody's primary importance to modern readers lies with his edition of Shakespeare, the first published in the United States that demonstrated any effort to compare a contemporary text with folios and quartos, an effort that led literary historian Jane Sherzer to dub him "father of American textual criticism." His conservative reviews for the *North American* may have caused some critics to term that publication reactionary; however, it is more likely that Peabody's twin brother held such views, leading Harry Hayden Clark to blame both brothers for "extreme truculency" and hostility to romanticism.

Near the end of a century in which taste continued to rule critical responses, Oliver William Bourn and his twin, William Oliver Bourn Peabody, were born in Exeter, New Hampshire, on 9 July 1799. Their parents were Frances Bourn and Oliver Peabody, jurist, politician, and trustee of Phillips Exeter Academy where both brothers began their educations. To the confusion of later scholars and their friends, the two not only shared three first names, but were identical in "handwriting, face, form, mien, voice, manner," according to one of their contemporaries quoted by Frank Mott in *A History of American Magazines* (1941). The twins entered Harvard College in 1812 and graduated in 1816. Oliver Peabody studied law both with his father in Exeter and at the Harvard Law School in Cambridge, and he was admitted to the bar in New Hampshire in 1822. Although he practiced his profession for some years in Exeter and later served in the New Hampshire and Massachusetts legislatures, he maintained the literary interests he had begun at Harvard as a contributor to various newspapers and reviews.

Moving to Boston in 1830, Peabody became what Edward Everett Hale called a "constant and valuable assistant" to his brother-in-law, Alexander H. Everett, editor of the *North American Review,* the publication that claimed most of Peabody's critical efforts. He also worked as assistant editor of the *Boston Daily Advertiser.* Peabody was particularly fitted to be an editor because of his "very wide general information," according to Hale. Not entirely occupied by his two assistant editorships and the work that made him a frequent contributor of prose and verse to reviews like the *Christian Examiner,* Peabody served six years (1836-1842) as Register of Probate. He also found time to edit *The Dramatic Works of William Shakespeare* (1836), in seven volumes. For sometime editor of the *North American Review* Jared Sparks, Peabody produced biographies of Revolutionary War generals Israel Putnam (1837) and John Sullivan (1844). Such rigorous scholarly activity affected Peabody's health, and in 1842 he attempted to devote himself full-time to literary scholarship by becoming a professor of English literature at Jefferson College in Louisiana. He found the milder climate, as Hale put it, "unfavorable to his constitution," inducing a "lassitude" that he fought off by returning to Boston, where he began studies for the ministry. He worked occasionally with his twin, who was a pastor in Springfield, until licensed in 1845 to preach.

The importance of Peabody's contribution to American literary criticism, his edition of Shakespeare, lies more in his intention than in the performance. Although the introduction to his much-reprinted volume describes Peabody as an "accomplished scholar," he was not, as Alfred Westfall notes, a Shakespearian scholar, even in the terms of the time; but, as Sherzer emphasizes, his book was "epoch making" because, "for the first time in America, is sounded the true note for a correct editing of Shakespearian text." Peabody used as his copy text the Samuel Weller Singer Chiswick edition, which was a popular source for the publication of individual plays and partial editions in America. Peabody made an effort to clarify the text according to valid textual principles. He went back to original sources, to the first folio and some of the quartos, seeking to restore original readings. He did not create an entirely new edition, but he improved his text in a number of ways, simplifying and shortening Singer's

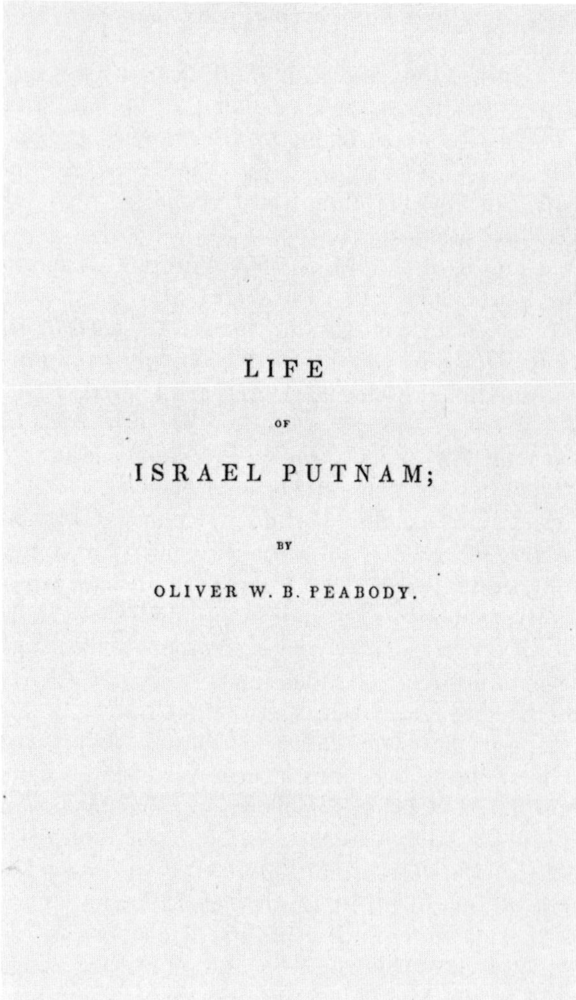
LIFE

OF

ISRAEL PUTNAM;

BY

OLIVER W. B. PEABODY.

Section title for Peabody's biography of the Revolutionary War general who distinguished himself at Bunker Hill, published in The Library of American Biography, *first series, volume 7 (1837)*

notes and providing some new readings. He was not consistent in his use of quarto and folio and sometimes failed to identify sources; but he produced an improved edition that met his publisher's aims to give the text as accurately as possible, encumbering it with as few notes as "might seem important."

Peabody's efforts as editor of Shakespeare are important, but his work as a critic of literature in his many articles in the *North American Review* and the *Christian Examiner* carries less weight. He commented upon many topics and genres but presented a consistent stand only in his comments on poetry. His view of the novel demanded effective description and truth to human nature in characterization. Yet he was flexible enough to defend Cooper's *The Water Witch* for its achievement of the former, while faulting it for its lack of the latter. Poetry, he declared in a review of Thomas Campbell in 1840, was the "divinest of arts," chiefly because of its leverage over man's moral nature. He praised William Cowper for aiming to "raise poetry to its proper elevation, by making it the handmaid of high and holy purposes, the nurse of lofty aspirations for virtue and religious purity . . . the purifier of the heart." In considering the poems of William Plumer, Peabody insisted that "poetry should please, but it should give pleasure to manly, not perverted taste. Better it should altogether forgo this end, than that it should become the handmaid of low desires or inculcate aught but purity of statement."

In the same vein, Peabody commended Longfellow's *Voices of the Night* for "sincerity and manliness," denying this was faint praise, for the end of art was "to improve and elevate, as well as please." Even Longfellow could not always rise to Peabody's standards: some allusions, he contended, might not "be consistent with perfect taste." Burns was approved for his "fidelity to nature" but even this was provisional. Too much of the poetry, he thought, is to be "remembered only with regret," its "power" compromised by a repellent "coarseness."

Never married, Peabody spent his last few years as pastor of the Unitarian Church of Burlington, Vermont, where he died 5 July 1848 while preparing for publication a memoir and collection of the sermons of his brother William, who had died the preceding year. His concerns were broad, his interests various. His edition of Shakespeare is worth remembering for its efforts at precise and illuminating textual criticism. Although his writing is consistently direct and graceful, his reviews of contemporary works are only historically interesting as evidence of the spirit of the time, not as distinctive examples of original or lasting thought.

References:

William Charvat, *The Origins of American Critical Thought, 1810-1835* (Philadelphia: University of Pennsylvania Press, 1936);

Harry Hayden Clark, "Literary Criticism in the *North American Review,* 1815-1835," *Transactions of the Wisconsin Academy of Sciences, Arts and Letters,* 32 (1940): 299-350;

Clark, ed., *Transitions in American Literary History* (Durham: Duke University Press, 1953);

Edward Everett Hale, "Rev. Oliver W. B. Peabody," *Christian Examiner,* 45 (September 1848): 278-285;
Frank Mott, *A History of American Magazines, 1830-1968,* volume 2 (Cambridge: Harvard University Press, 1941);
John W. Rathbun, *American Literary Criticism, 1800-1860* (Boston: G. K. Hall, 1979);
Jane Sherzer, "American Editions of Shakespeare: 1753-1866," *PMLA,* 22 (December 1907): 633-696;
Alfred Van Rensslaer Westfall, *American Shakespeare Criticism, 1607-1865* (New York: Wilson, 1939).

Willard Phillips

(19 December 1784-9 September 1873)

John Bird, Jr.
Converse College

SELECTED BOOKS: *A Treatise on the Law of Insurance,* 2 volumes (Boston: Wells & Lilly, 1823-1834);
A Manual of Political Economy, with Particular Reference to the Institutions, Resources, and Condition of the United States (Boston: Hilliard, Gray, Little & Wilkins, 1828);
The Inventor's Guide (Boston: S. Colman/New York: Collins, Keese, 1837);
The Law of Patents for Inventions (Boston: American Stationers' Company/New York: Gould, Banks, 1837);
Propositions Concerning Protection and Free Trade (Boston: Little & Brown, 1850).

PERIODICAL PUBLICATIONS: Review of *Poems,* by William Cowper, *North American Review,* 2 (January 1816): 233-241;
Review of *Rhoda,* by Alethea Brereton Lewis, *North American Review,* 3 (July 1816): 216-218;
Review of *Childe Harold, Canto 3 And The Prisoners of Chillon Darkness, etc.,* by Lord Byron, *North American Review,* 5 (May 1817): 98-110;
Review of *Harrington, a Tale,* and *Ormond, a Tale,* by Maria Edgeworth, *North American Review,* 6 (January 1818): 153-178;
Review of *Mandeville,* by William Godwin, *North American Review,* 7 (May 1818): 92-105;
Review of *Women; or, Pour et Contre,* by Robert Maturin, *North American Review,* 8 (December 1818): 118-134;
Review of *Poems,* by William Cullen Bryant, *North American Review,* 13 (October 1821): 380-384;
Review of *Confessions of an English Opium-Eater,* by Thomas de Quincey, *North American Review,* 18 (January 1824): 90-98;
Review of *The Pilot, a Tale of the Sea,* by James Fenimore Cooper, *North American Review,* 18 (April 1824): 314-329;
Review of *Pelham, or the Adventures of a Gentleman,* by Edward Bulwer-Lytton, *North American Review,* 28 (April 1829): 418-433;
Review of *The Duchess de la Vallière,* by Edward Bulwer-Lytton, *North American Review,* 44 (April 1837): 426-434.

In spite of the fact that Willard Phillips was one of America's earliest romantic critics, he has never received the full recognition he deserves. As a founder and longtime reviewer for the *North American Review,* Phillips brought the commitment to reason and judgment explicit in judicial criticism to bear on the romantic revolution of his day, thereby avoiding the histrionics romantic critics often indulged in.

Phillips was born in Bridgewater, Massachusetts, to Joseph Phillips, a descendant of John Phillips, who settled in Duxbury, Massachusetts, before 1640, and to Hannah Egerton Phillips. He re-

Courtesy of the South Caroliniana Library, University of South Carolina

ceived a common-school education in Hampshire County. At eighteen he graduated as valedictorian of Bridgewater Academy and became a teacher there while he prepared for college. He was admitted to Harvard College in 1806 and graduated with high rank in 1810. From 1811 to 1815 he was a tutor at Harvard in Latin, geometry, and natural philosophy while he studied law. As he was to do throughout his public career, however, he continued his early interest in belles lettres, proposing in 1814 with Edward Tyrrell Channing and Harvard president John T. Kirkland the founding of the "New England Magazine and Review." The idea was dropped because William Tudor was then starting the *North American Review*, with which Phillips was also associated from the beginning, in the early years as an editor and frequent contributor and later as a more sporadic reviewer. In all he wrote thirty-five reviews for the *North American Review* on subjects including literature, economics, law, politics, and philosophy.

Phillips began to practice law in 1815, served as a member of the Massachusetts legislature from 1825 to 1826, was appointed judge of probate for Suffolk County in 1839, then became president of the New England Mutual Life Insurance Company in 1847. His books mirror his public career: *A Treatise on the Law of Insurance* (1823-1834), which went through five editions; *A Manual of Political Economy* (1828), still recognized as a standard work on the subject; and *Propositions Concerning Protection and Free Trade* (1850). He was married twice–in 1833 to Hannah Brackett Hill and, when she died four years later, to her sister, Harriet Hill. Throughout his life he was plagued with poor eyesight, which made it difficult for him to read or write for more than two hours a day.

In spite of such a full legal and business career, Phillips's literary reviews are not the work of a dilettante or an amateur. They are marked by careful attention to the authors' viewpoints, themes, and styles. Although politically a conservative, he consistently appreciated romantic writers, but never in a way that might inflame the opposition of the increasingly stodgy writers for *North American Review* or its readers. In this light, he might be classified as a "judicial" romantic critic, an apt coupling given his legal training.

In his review of William Cowper's *Poems* (1816), Phillips set forth his critical principles that "every man's opinion must be right in respect to himself," and that "to judge rightly of an author, we must view objects from the position assumed by himself, or that occupied by the generality of his readers." While this idea may seem quite commonplace today, Phillips's standpoint provides an important bridge between the two prevailing critical stances of his time. He avoids the harsh prescriptive standards of the judicial critics without descending into the limp subjectivity of many early romantics. In the Cowper review, Phillips uses Adam Smith's theories–a common device of his, turning his knowledge of economic or judicial writing to literary matters–that just as we must "view ourselves at a distance" to see our own true characters, "so, to judge rightly of others, we should, in a manner, transfuse ourselves into, and become identified with them." Such a close identification with the author, however, never prevents Phillips from seeing the faults in the author's works, especially in matters of style. Phillips says of Cowper that "he has little fire, brilliance, or sublimity; he frequently delights, but never astonishes," and though Cowper is "animated by the glow of benevolence," he is a poet of second rank.

Though living in the age of Scott, Phillips

preferred the realistic novel to the romance, saying, in his review of *Rhoda* (1816), that fictions which concern "daily occurrences and observations" rather than the fantastic demand "greater skill and delicacy of execution in the artist, and an improved susceptibility and taste in the observer." Similarly, in his later review of Maria Edgeworth's *Harrington* (1800) and *Ormond* (1817), he praises her realism, her portraiture of varied occupations, and, in contrast with Fielding and Smollett, her rejection of "chance as the arbitress of the world"; however, he objects to her tendency to bring "forward her moral too obtrusively," a flaw he consistently complained about in fiction.

Unlike many of his contemporaries, Phillips was able to separate the eccentricities of an author's life from the author's work and to concentrate on the latter. Most critics were hostile to Byron because of the supposed dissoluteness of his personal life. But Phillips observed that Byron's poems can make certain readers feel "concern for a man, who considers himself as set aloof from his species." Those who have "struggled with what to them seemed oppression . . . must feel a lively sympathy with Byron in many passages of his poetry." And unlike other poets, who present conventional pictures of "woods, and fields, and streams . . . in Byron we are always reminded that we are looking through a [sensitive] medium." Consequently, "the most ordinary objects, sketched in the most hasty and careless manner, may be the basis of original and brilliant poetry." Phillips refuses to judge Byron by standard rules, since, as he says, poetry, "of all arts, can least endure the fetters of a system." Nonetheless he finds fault with many of Byron's lines, saying that "versification requires more of melody, measure, and harmony, than we can possibly make of many lines of this canto." He takes leave of Byron "with a regret, that, since he has written so well, he has also written so ill"–a regret that many modern readers may share. Thus, characteristically, Phillips embraces the romantic, but not without reasonable objections; he appreciates Byron's innovations, but does not fall into an uncritical swoon before them.

Phillips also addressed himself to the political side of the romantic "revolution," hypothesizing that, rather than causing a revolution, "those who have been fighting so many battles, forming so many schemes, and writing such a multitude of books" may have merely "been unconsciously

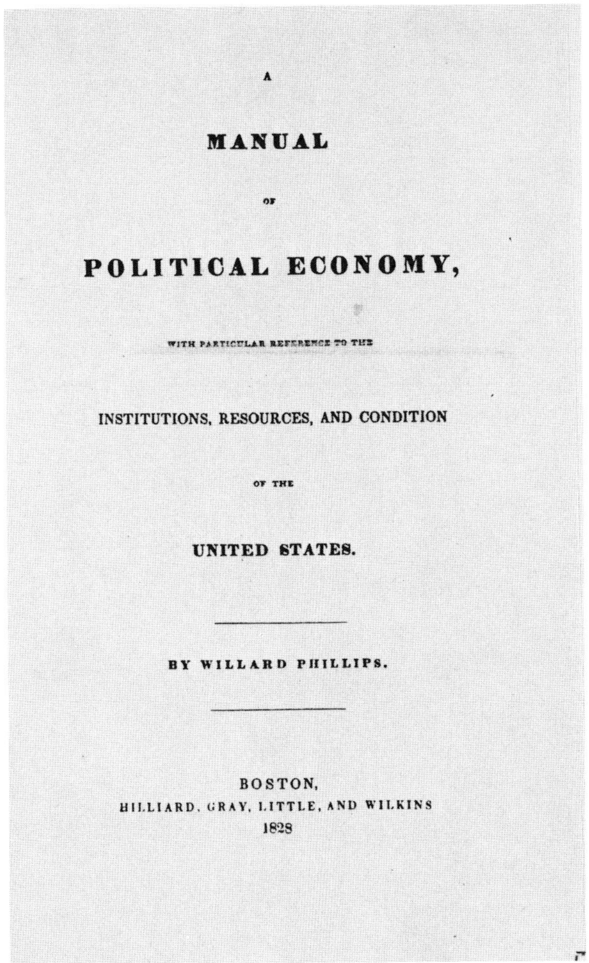
A

MANUAL

OF

POLITICAL ECONOMY,

WITH PARTICULAR REFERENCE TO THE

INSTITUTIONS, RESOURCES, AND CONDITION

OF THE

UNITED STATES.

BY WILLARD PHILLIPS.

BOSTON,
HILLIARD, GRAY, LITTLE, AND WILKINS
1828

Title page for the book that is still considered a standard authority on its subject

cooperating with each other, in bringing about a state of things, to which the civilized world was already tending." Again Phillips points out his preference for scene over idea, for showing rather than telling. William Godwin's *Mandeville* (1818), he thought, like all of Godwin's works, "has no resemblance to a dramatic representation of characters and actions," but is "rather the exhibition of his philosophical opinions in the form of dissertations." He preferred such works as Robert Maturin's *Women; or, Pour et Contre* (1818), whose chief merit is to be found in the "fertility, splendour, and terrible grandeur of his imaginations."

An old friend of the Bryant family, it was Phillips who discovered the young Bryant and urged publication of "Thanatopsis" in the *North American Review* in 1817. Phillips had asked the young William Cullen Bryant for some poems, but it was the poet's father who copied out several in his own hand and literally left them on

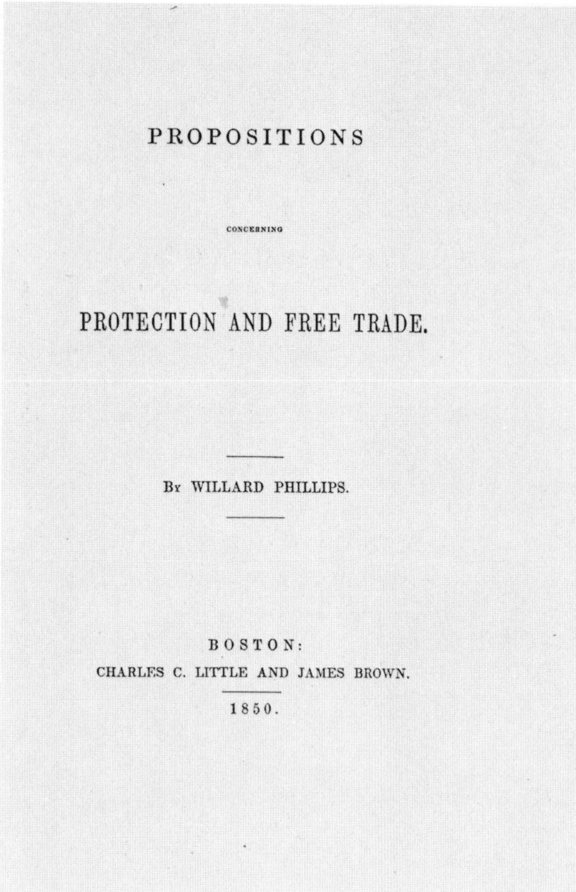
PROPOSITIONS

CONCERNING

PROTECTION AND FREE TRADE.

By WILLARD PHILLIPS.

BOSTON:
CHARLES C. LITTLE AND JAMES BROWN.
1850.

Title page for the book in which Phillips concludes, "All the predictions of ruin . . . , to arise from protection to domestic industry, have been falsified. . . ."

Phillips's doorstep. Under the mistaken notion that the poems were written by the elder Bryant, Phillips had showed them to the other editors, who were amazed at their competence, prompting Richard Dana to proclaim: "That was never written on this side of the water." In his 1821 review of Bryant's *Poems,* Phillips praises the "great freedom and propriety of language" as well as the "strain of pure and high sentiment," but questions the use of trisyllabic feet in some of the stanzas–a fault he discusses so delicately and with so much demurring that one can feel his hesitance in criticizing a person who was to remain a lifelong friend.

Phillips's objections to such departures as Bryant made in using trisyllabic feet were based on the reasonable ground that they were too self-conscious to be natural. Literary decorum might be a factor, but Phillips was really groping toward a concept of literary expression based on the aspects and expectations of the speaking voice. He objected, for example, to James Fenimore Cooper's habit of leaving "too little to his readers." And he was averse to such circumlocutions as Cooper habitually practiced, pointing out the loss of clarity in describing Colonel Howard wiping his face (in *The Pilot*) as removing "the perspiring effects of the unusual toil from his features." It was a style of writing, Phillips remarked, that is "too much in use with us." On the other hand, Phillips could focus on Cooper's strengths. He appreciated Cooper's use of American setting and plot, and in regard to *The Pilot* he praised Cooper's choice of "implicating the tale with our naval history . . . one of the few positions from which our national enthusiasm is accessible."

This insistence on the integrity of the text can be noted throughout Phillips's criticism. He could praise the "strain of original and philosophical thinking" to be found in Thomas de Quincey's *Confessions of an English Opium-Eater* (1822), yet decry the "obscure sort of metaphysical and mystical prosing" which makes the work "very formally dull and dry." On similar grounds he faults Edward Bulwer-Lytton for interrupting his work too much in order to comment on the action: "The characters should move and bear a part in the action throughout, and not, like stenographers, step aside to take notes of its progress." He calls Bulwer-Lytton's literary executions "fine," in the sense that they are "sparkling, brilliant, sententious, and full of classical allusion and antithesis." But he cannot say the same "of the thinking and philosophy, which occupy so great a space." As in all his reviews, Phillips finds any interruption–whether it be overt moralism, philosophical maundering, or personal posing–totally out of place in literature if it is not fully integrated into the plot and characterization. In this respect he anticipates modern tastes. Throughout, his criticism exhibits a mixture of the old and the new–the old posture of judging and sifting, the new posture of accepting innovation and change–all balanced by the intellectual soundness of good sense.

Probably the demands of his career, as well as his failing eyesight, prevented Willard Phillips from devoting more time to literary criticism. He spent his last years in Cambridge "in the enjoyment of books," according to one obituary, until, "with no symptoms of acute disease," he died in 1873.

References:

Charles H. Brown, *William Cullen Bryant* (New York: Scribners, 1971);

William Charvat, *The Origins of American Critical Thought: 1810-1835* (Philadelphia: University of Pennsylvania Press, 1936), pp. 175-177;

Harry Hayden Clark, "Literary Criticism in the *North American Review*, 1815-1835," *Transactions of the Wisconsin Academy of Sciences, Arts and Letters*, 32 (1940): 299-350;

John Livingston, *Portraits of Eminent Americans Now Living*, volume 1 (New York: Cornish, Lamport, 1853), pp. 290-303;

Proceedings of the American Academy of Arts and Sciences, 9 (1874): 324-325;

John W. Rathbun, *American Literary Criticism, 1800-1860* (Boston: G. K. Hall, 1979).

Papers:

A collection of Phillips's early manuscripts, including his diaries, is in the Harvard College Library.

Edgar Allan Poe

J. Lasley Dameron
Memphis State University

and

Robert D. Jacobs
Georgia State University

See also the Poe entry in *DLB 3, Antebellum Writers in New York and the South.*

BIRTH: Boston, Massachusetts, 19 January 1809, to David and Elizabeth Arnold Poe.

EDUCATION: University of Virginia, 1826; United States Military Academy, July 1830–6 March 1831.

MARRIAGE: May 1836 to Virginia Clemm (deceased January 1847).

AWARDS: First prize in fiction contest for "MS. Found in Bottle" (*Baltimore Saturday Visiter* [*sic*]), 19 October 1833; first prize in fiction contest for "The Gold Bug" (*Philadelphia Dollar Newspaper*), June 1843.

DEATH: Baltimore, Maryland, 7 October 1849.

BOOKS: *Tamerlane and Other Poems. By a Bostonian* (Boston: Calvin F. S. Thomas, 1827);

Al Aaraaf, Tamerlane, and Minor Poems (Baltimore: Hatch & Dunning, 1829);

Poems. By Edgar A. Poe. Second Edition (New York: Elam Bliss, 1831);

The Narrative of Arthur Gordon Pym, of Nantucket. . . ., anonymous (New York: Harper, 1838; London: Wiley & Putnam, 1838);

The Conchologist's First Book; or, A System of Testaceous Malacology . . . (Philadelphia: Haswell, Barrington & Haswell, 1839);

Tales of the Grotesque and Arabesque, 2 volumes (Philadelphia: Lea & Blanchard, 1840);

The Prose Romances of Edgar A. Poe (Philadelphia: William H. Graham, 1843);

Tales (New York: Wiley & Putnam, 1845);

The Raven and Other Poems (New York: Wiley & Putnam, 1845);

Eureka: A Prose Poem (New York: Putnam's, 1848).

Collections: *Works of Edgar Allan Poe, with Notices of his Life and Genius*, edited by Rufus Wilmot Griswold, 4 volumes (New York: J. S. Redfield, 1850-1856);

The Complete Works of Edgar Allan Poe, edited by James A. Harrison, 17 volumes (New York: Thomas Y. Crowell, 1902);

Daguerreotype taken at Providence, Rhode Island, in fall 1848

Selections from The Critical Writings of Edgar Allan Poe, edited by F. C. Prescott (New York: Henry Holt, 1909; reprinted, Staten Island: Gordian Press, 1981);

Literary Criticism of Edgar Allan Poe, edited by Robert L. Hough (Lincoln: University of Nebraska Press, 1965);

The Poems of Edgar Allan Poe, edited by Floyd Stovall (Charlottesville: University Press of Virginia, 1965);

Collected Works of Edgar Allan Poe, edited by Thomas Ollive Mabbott, 3 volumes (Cambridge: Belknap Press of Harvard University Press, 1969-1978);

Collected Writings of Edgar Allan Poe, volume 1, *The Imaginary Voyages: The Narrative of Arthur Gordon Pym, The Unparalleled Adventure of One Hans Pfaall, The Journal of Julius Rodman,* edited by Burton R. Pollin (Boston & New York: Twayne, 1981);

Essays and Reviews, edited by G. R. Thompson (New York: Library of America, 1984);

Poetry and Tales, edited by Patrick F. Quinn (New York: Library of America, 1984);

Collected Writings of Edgar Allan Poe, volume 2, *The Brevities: Pinakidia, Marginalia, Fifty Suggestions and Other Works,* edited by Pollin (New York: Gordian Press, 1985).

PERIODICAL PUBLICATIONS: "The Philosophy of Composition," *Graham's Magazine,* 32 (April 1846): 182-186;

"The Rationale of Verse," *Southern Literary Messenger,* 14 (October 1848): 577-585; 15 (November 1848): 673-687;

"The Poetic Principle," *Sartain's Union Magazine,* 7 (October 1850): 231-239.

Popular but not always respected in his own time, Edgar Poe is significant today not only for the quality of his best work but also for his influence on later writers. His poems were admired, especially in France, where such writers as Charles Baudelaire, Stéphane Mallarmé, and Paul Valéry assimilated his technique of symbolism and, in turn, transmitted their own versions of the symbolic mode to a number of writers in English in the twentieth century. Poe's versatility is displayed also in fiction and literary criticism. As a writer of fiction he has attracted many admirers, not only in his own time but also in ours. It is hard to imagine modern detective and fantasy fiction without the example of Poe. Even the most famous of all fictional detectives, Sherlock Holmes, owes much to Poe's C. Auguste Dupin, who once solved a crime merely by reading newspaper accounts of it. Fantasy and science fiction, too, owe a major debt to Poe's pioneering in those forms. As for his literary criticism, it chiefly took the form of book reviews, many of which in his time were deemed excessively caustic. Notorious among his contemporaries as a harsh critic, Poe's book reviews were mostly ephemeral. However, his review of Nathaniel Hawthorne's *Twice-Told Tales* (1842), in which he set forth his theory of short fiction, and his review of Henry Wadsworth Longfellow's *Ballads and Other Poems* (1842), in which he advanced his theory of poetry, are still worth reading. In fact, textbooks on short-story writing quoted Poe approvingly well into the twentieth century. His theory of poetry has had few if any modern adherents.

Poe is important in the history of the short story because he helped give it a recognizable form, endowing it with an Aristotelian plot structure and conferring upon it unity of tone. On the other hand his theory of poetry, which virtually dispenses with all forms except the short lyric, has been too restrictive for most poets, and it is remembered today only in the classroom. Still Poe as a practicing critic had few peers in his time; none in America. He was an analytic critic and at his best made a close examination of the work at hand. This approach alone would make him a precursor of an important strain of twentieth-century criticism, the "new" criticism introduced by John Crowe Ransom, Allen Tate, Cleanth Brooks, Robert Penn Warren, and others some forty-odd years ago. If Poe was not the most distinguished writer in America during the nineteenth century–some would claim that he was–he was surely the most versatile, well worth reading today.

Born to David and Elizabeth Arnold Poe on 19 January 1809, Edgar Poe from the cradle onward seemed destined for a public career. His mother, Elizabeth Arnold, daughter of an English actress, had been brought to America when she was only nine years old; and from that age she was a stage performer at a time when acting was less than a respectable profession. She married Charles Hopkins at fifteen and was widowed at eighteen. Poe's father, David, from Baltimore, had gone on the stage against the wishes of his family and had become Elizabeth Arnold Hopkins's second husband. Especially clever at comic roles such as that of a tomboy, Elizabeth could also play a romantic female lead and was thought by some to be one of the most beautiful women in America. David Poe, although handsome, had less talent. Unsuccessful on the stage and probably an alcoholic, David disappeared in 1810, leaving Elizabeth with three small children to support. Henry, the eldest, was sent to David's family in Baltimore, while Edgar and his young sister, Rosalie, remained briefly with their mother. The young actress died on 8 December 1811 in Richmond, Virginia, where her theater company was performing. Edgar and Rosalie were taken by two respectable Richmond families, the Allans and the Mackenzies.

John Allan, Edgar Poe's foster father (the boy was never legally adopted), was a native of Scotland, whence he had come to Richmond at fifteen to work for his wealthy uncle, William Galt. When he took the child Edgar, nearly three

Miniature of Elizabeth Arnold Poe

years old, into his home, John Allan was prospering as a partner in the firm of Ellis and Allan, an import-export company engaged chiefly in the exportation of Virginia tobacco to England. In several ways Edgar was fortunate in being with the Allans. John Allan had no literary aspirations, but he was fond of literature, particularly of Shakespeare and Sir Walter Scott, and a file of the literary journal *Blackwood's Edinburgh Magazine* was kept in the Ellis-Allan warehouse. It was from this magazine that Edgar Poe was to derive his first notions of fiction and literary criticism. A legend printed by several of Poe's biographers has the child Edgar standing on a table reciting poems to the assembled dinner guests of John and Frances Allan, to be rewarded by a glass of watered wine. Such a tale at best is merely plausible, but it helps to underscore Poe's early attraction to poetic expression. More significant for his development as a writer, however, the Allans, in 1815, took the boy with them to England, where Allan established a London branch of Ellis and Allan. During the impressionable years between six and eleven Edgar Poe attended English private schools, notably the Manor House School of the Reverend John Bransby in Stoke Newington, a suburb of London. Poe would remember the experience of being an English schoolboy so well that he would eventually place the headmaster's name and the school in his short story "William Wilson," published in 1839 in Philadelphia.

The Ellis and Allan London branch failed, and they returned to the United States in August 1820 after which Poe attended private schools in Richmond. Although a brilliant student gifted in languages and an athlete skilled in leaping, boxing, and swimming, Poe never achieved a status among his schoolmates that made him feel completely at home in Richmond. It was known that his parents were actors, and evidently he was considered to be a charity case, an interpretation that Allan did nothing to change. Even this early, Poe occasionally suffered from deep depressions, which brought him into conflict with his foster father, who thought him sulky and ungrateful. Nevertheless, Allan saw to it that Poe received the best education available in Richmond and in February 1826 sent him to the University of Virginia, founded recently by Thomas Jefferson. After establishing residence at the university, Poe found that Allan had given him barely enough money for expenses, with nothing left over for spending money and the life-style expected of a young gentleman. Allan's parsimony with Poe was probably for disciplinary reasons, for by now he was a wealthy man, and he had a reputation for generosity. Poe evidently counted on a certain amount of indulgence from Allan, for he gambled heavily, contracting "debts of honor" to his classmates. Why such an intelligent youth incurred such heavy losses is one of the mysteries of Poe's biography, but lose he did; and he also went into debt for clothing purchased on credit from the merchants of Charlottesville. When at the end of the school year Allan learned of Poe's debts, he brought the boy home in disgrace, refusing to pay the gambling debts and perhaps some others.

Back in Richmond in early 1827, Poe quarreled frequently with John Allan, probably because the young man was writing poems instead of preparing himself for business or a profession as Allan had wished. The hostility between Poe and his foster father reached a climax in March when, after a particularly heated argument, Allan ordered Poe to leave his home, which the young man promptly did, asking from Allan only his trunk of clothes and enough money to purchase a steamer ticket to Boston, his place of

Portrait by an unknown artist

birth. Poe came to the city with a thin manuscript of poems, composed, no doubt, during his year at the University of Virginia and in the months in Richmond between December and March. Somehow he persuaded or paid Calvin Thomas, a young printer in Boston, to publish a small paperback, entitled *Tamerlane and Other Poems* (1827), "by a Bostonian." Technically correct, this attribution had a further significance. Poe may have thought that poems by a Bostonian would sell better, but it also appeared that he was severing all ties with Richmond, Virginia.

Although possessing considerable merit as the first publication of an eighteen-year-old, *Tamerlane* was not the sort of book that could possibly attract much attention, and of course it did not. Except for the title poem, which was modeled after Lord Byron's verse narratives, Poe's poems were short and very subjective, presenting the persona of a sensitive youth who lived through his imagination, preferring daydream to reality. As could be expected, they were immature both in subject and in treatment. Few copies were distributed, and the young poet, frustrated in his first claim to fame, promptly joined the United States Army, giving his name as Edgar A. Perry and his age as twenty-two instead of eighteen.

From 26 May 1827 until his discharge in 15 April 1829, Edgar Poe was a soldier in the First Artillery. Most of this time was spent at Fort Moultrie on Sullivan's Island in the harbor of Charleston, South Carolina. This setting was to appear directly in one of his most popular tales, "The Gold Bug," and it was reflected in other tales and poems. Clearly Poe had no intention of pursuing a military career–he was writing poems while serving in the army–but in order to obtain a discharge before his five-year enlistment ended, he had to effect a reconciliation with John Allan. This he finally did, promising his foster father that he would seek an appointment to the U.S. Military Academy. This proposal Allan could accept, and he sent money (which Poe apparently misappropriated) to hire a substitute to finish Poe's term of enlistment. There was no valid reason for Poe to leave the army except for his desire to be a writer. He had been promoted to sergeant major of the First Artillery on 1 January 1829, and he could have had a career with the military, but as he wrote to John Allan, he had greater ambitions than he could fulfill in the army.

At the time of Poe's discharge he had a manuscript of poems ready for a publisher, and he found one in Hatch and Dunning of Baltimore, who brought out *Al Aaraaf, Tamerlane, and Minor Poems* in December 1829. Poe was now nearly twenty-one, and his poems were beginning to change from the romantic confessional to include broader and more interesting subjects than the suffering self. "Al Aaraaf," although ostensibly a long narrative poem in the manner of the contemporary Irish poet Thomas Moore, introduces a thesis Poe was to maintain throughout his life: that aesthetic experience was equivalent to religious experience, and that the response to beauty was a feeling blessed by God.

Poe had applied to the U.S. Military Academy only because he needed to be reconciled with his foster father, John Allan. When Allan once more sent him away with virtually no spending money, Poe saw the relationship had not changed. Allan was determined to treat him like a pauper until he could support himself. Not really wanting to be an army officer, Poe, after a few months at the academy at West Point (June-December 1830), contrived deliberately to get himself court-martialed by staying away from classes and formations. He had applied to Allan for permission to resign, but that gentleman, full of indignation toward his foster son, refused to grant it. Poe "resigned" by way of court-martial. He was eventually declared by a military court guilty of neglect of duty and was formally dismissed on 6 March 1831.

Poe left West Point on 19 February 1831, carrying with him another manuscript of poems ready for publication, with some of them, no doubt, written when he should have been attending classes. Poe's new book was published by a New York publisher, Elam Bliss, as *Poems. By Edgar A. Poe. Second Edition.* By calling his third book his second, Poe in a sense "suppressed" *Tamerlane and Other Poems,* the little book he had printed in 1827.

The *Poems* of 1831, Poe's last book of poems until the edition of 1845, contains some of his finest lyrics, including "To Helen," "Israfel," and "The City in the Sea." Although only twenty-two, he had achieved maturity as a poet; and his most famous poems, "The Raven" and "Annabel Lee," written and published many years later, represent merely an elaboration of Poe's characteristic lyric mode. Poe never relinquished his early belief that poems should be musical–"music with a pleasurable idea"–as he asserted in "Letter to B–," his prefatory essay to the *Poems* of 1831. This preface, initially entitled "Letter to Mr.–," was Poe's first attempt at putting together a theory of poetry. It is noteworthy chiefly because it either suggests or states certain positions he would maintain throughout his career as a critic. One of these positions was his doctrine of length. Poe asserted baldly, "men do not like epics." John Milton's *Paradise Regained* appears to be inferior to *Paradise Lost* only because, when reading the poems in their natural order, we are too wearied by the first to appreciate the second. Another position first expressed in this preface was Poe's prejudice against the didactic, fulminating against William Wordsworth's practice of making poetry the vehicle of "metaphysical" instruction.

Finally, in the preface, after alternately con-

The Southern Literary Messenger *building, where Poe worked as editor, and the offices of Ellis and Allan (at right), where Poe worked as his foster father's clerk*

demning Samuel Coleridge's "profundity" and praising his "intellect," he paid the British critic the ultimate compliment by plagiarizing in part his definition of a poem from the *Biographia Literaria*:

> A poem, in my opinion, is opposed to a work of science by having, for its *immediate* object, pleasure, not truth; to romance, by having for its object an *indefinite* instead of a *definite* pleasure, being a poem only so far as this object is attained; romance presenting perceptible images with definite, poetry with *in*definite sensations, to which end music is an *essential*, since the comprehension of sweet sound is our most indefinite conception. Music, when combined with a pleasurable idea, is poetry; music without the idea is simply music; the idea without the music is prose from its very definitiveness.

Only the first clause of this long sentence is taken directly from Coleridge, although, like Coleridge, Poe discriminates the poem not only from works of science but also from the "romance." In this case it has to be a prose romance or novel, since the verse romance would be a poem. Poe's insistence upon music in poetry is not Coleridgean at all, though some scholars have claimed that it was suggested by certain passages in the *Biographia Literaria*. The source, if there was one, is not particularly important, however. What is important is that Poe was affirming his basic position, that "music," or "sweet sound," is absolutely essential in stimulating a pleasurable response. The logical consequence of such an emphasis is that *meaning* will be subordinated to sound effects. The supporting theoretical argument was not advanced for some years, however. Poe did not become a practicing literary critic until 1835, and, it appears, his first efforts were largely devoted to gaining attention.

Staying only briefly in New York, Poe came in the spring of 1831 to Baltimore, the city that would be his second home. His closest relatives were there, and he moved into a house in which his paternal grandmother, Elizabeth Poe, his aunt Maria Clemm, his brother, William Henry Poe, and his eight-year-old cousin Virginia Clemm, whom eventually he would marry, lived. Without money or a profession, estranged from his foster father, Edgar Poe, after fruitless attempts to gain Allan's forgiveness, had to learn how to take care of himself.

Poems would not pay. Poe had already learned that fact of life, so he began writing what he considered to be popular types of fiction, drawing his models from contemporary magazines, notably *Blackwood's*. Tales of terror and comic burlesques became his stock in trade: stories such as "Metzengerstein," an imitation of the Gothic, and "The Duc De L'Omelette," a specimen of ethnic humor which pits a comic Frenchman against the devil in a mock-Faustian burlesque. Soon he was to put together eleven stories called "Tales of the Folio Club," but he was never able to find a publisher. Initial success came in 1833, when he won the first prize of fifty dollars in a short fiction contest held by the *Baltimore Saturday Visiter* [*sic*]. Poe's prize-winning tale, "MS. Found in Bottle," was published by the *Saturday Visiter* in October as was his poem "The Coliseum," which would have won first prize in the poetry category, except that the judges did not wish to award both first prizes to the same contestant.

In January 1834 his tale "The Visionary" appeared in *Godey's Lady's Book,* a woman's magazine of wide circulation. *Godey's* would publish Poe in succeeding years. The appearance of this tale in the popular journal shows that he was beginning to receive some recognition for his short stories, but he was a long way from earning a living by his pen. John Allan died in March 1834 leaving Poe nothing in his will. In spite of their quarrels, Poe had always expected to be left a portion of Allan's great fortune, but evidently Allan never forgave the foster son.

Frustrated by futile attempts to find work, Poe began to exploit his few literary connections. It was through the friendship of John P. Kennedy, one of the judges of the *Saturday Visiter* contest, that he was to make his first professional step. Kennedy put him in touch with Thomas W. White, publisher of the recently founded *Southern Literary Messenger* in Richmond, Virginia. Poe began writing for the periodical early in 1835, moving to Richmond in August to become White's editorial assistant. His chief task was reviewing books. Very soon Poe made himself felt as a reviewer, for he adopted the method of the notorious English and Scottish reviewers of such journals as the *Quarterly* and the *Edinburgh Review.* These reviewers, who had chastised Byron, Wordsworth, and Keats, among others of the British romantics, became something of a model for Poe; and in an era of tame, laudatory reviews in America, he became known as the "tomahawk man." Poe's reviews drew attention to the *Southern Literary Messenger.* The circulation soared; but White, something of a puritan, had dismissed Poe for his heavy drinking. The dismissal was brief, however, for White, seriously in need of editorial help, brought Poe back to Richmond in December 1835, and it was with the December issue of the *Southern Literary Messenger* that Poe began to make himself felt as a reviewer.

Poe for a time had almost complete charge of the production of the magazine. For the first time in his life he had a salary, he was able to publish his tales and poems, and through his literary critiques, sometimes caustic but usually judgmental, he was gaining a reputation in the literary world of America. He was gaining enemies, too, but the circulation of the *Southern Literary Messenger* steadily improved as it became the only journal in the South that managed to sustain itself over a long period of time. Poe became confident enough of his success to risk marriage, and in May 1836 he married his thirteen-year-old cousin Virginia Clemm and brought her and her mother to live with him in Richmond.

Possibly as a result of the unfavorable reaction to some of his reviews, Poe determined to practice what in his day was called "philosophical" criticism, which meant that he would form his judgments on the basis of fundamentals, principles grounded in psychology and metaphysics (the two were scarcely distinguishable in Poe's time). His first philosophical criticism appeared in April 1836 when he reviewed the poems of Joseph Rodman Drake and Fitz-Greene Halleck, both of whom were considered among America's best poets when Poe reviewed them. Poe's theoretical statement in this review is difficult to interpret because he used a jargon (derived from phrenology) that is no longer readily comprehensible. The essential points of his argument, however, may be summarized as follows: the enjoyment of beauty is basic to human nature; it is "instinct" implanted in the human mind. This instinct operates in two ways: it enables us to enjoy the beautiful sights and sounds that are presented to the senses, and it stimulates a desire to "know" ideal beauty. "Poesy" is a feeling of mental or "intellectual" happiness quite distinct from the sensuous gratifications of appetite (what Poe calls the "passions"). Imagination, says Poe, cribbing from Coleridge, is the "soul" or essence of this feeling. Psychologically, this feeling of mental gratification originates in that faculty of the mind ("Ideality") which enables us to idealize, in other words, to imagine a more nearly perfect beauty than we can experience through the senses. The "creative" imagination is the active agent of the idealizing faculty, for it is the power which creates mental images out of sense experience, combining sense impressions to produce "new" images not found in nature itself.

Unfortunately Poe had no security in his editorial position with the *Southern Literary Messenger.* White evidently became jealous of Poe's assumed authority as well and disapproved of his drinking habits. Poe either resigned or was discharged from the *Messenger* and took his little family to New York early in 1837 to seek employment. He carried with him an incomplete manuscript entitled "The Narrative of Arthur Gordon Pym," which he had started publishing in installments in the *Saturday Literary Messenger* but which White discontinued. Completing the novella in New

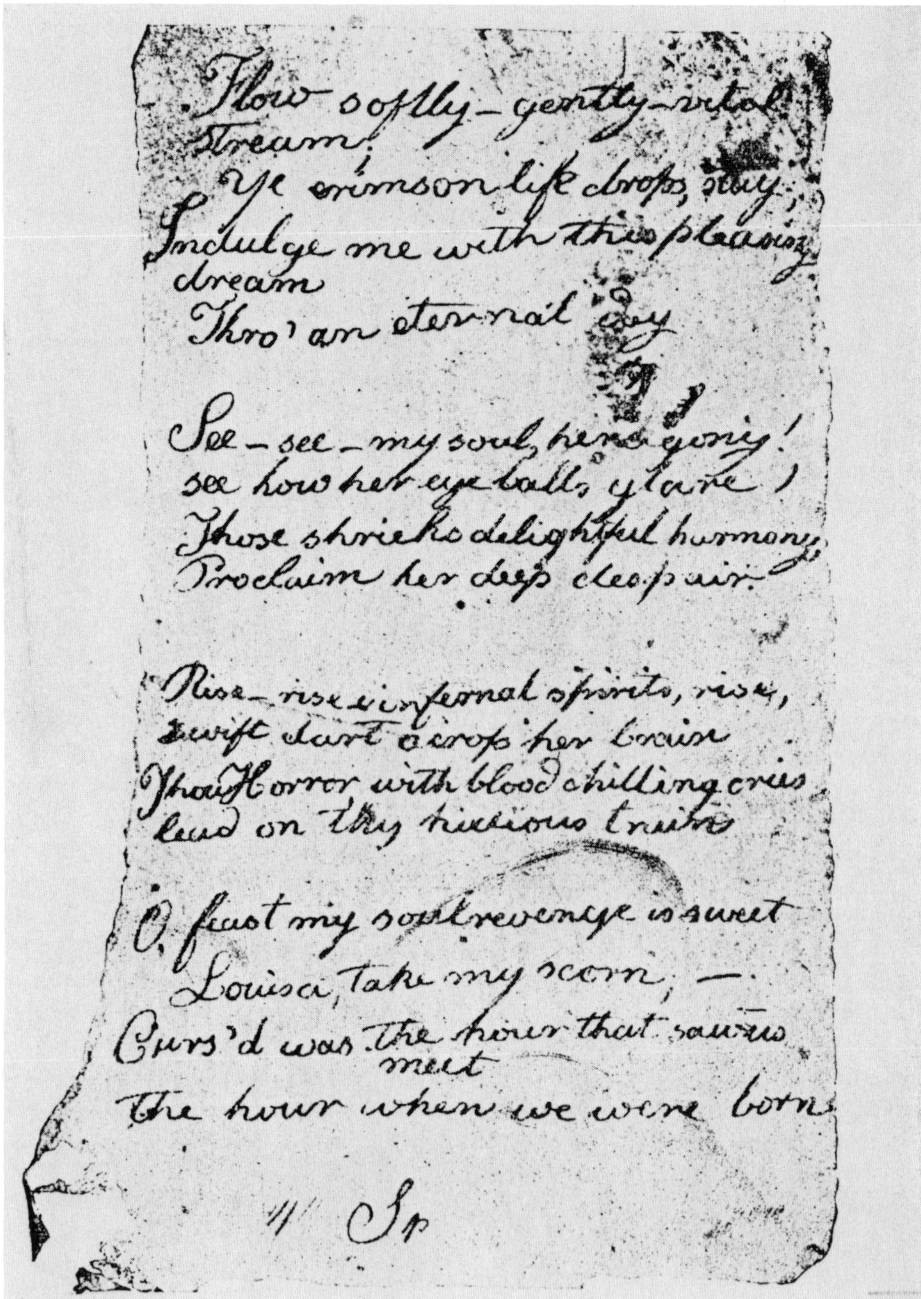
Flow softly—gently—vital stream;
Ye crimson life drops, stay;
Indulge me with this pleasing dream
Thro' an eternal day.

See—see—my soul, her agony!
See how her eye balls glare!
Those shrieks delightful harmony,
Proclaim her deep despair.

Rise—rise—infernal spirits, rise,
Swift dart across her brain
Thou Horror with blood chilling cries
Lead on thy hideous train.

O, feast my soul revenge is sweet
Louisa, take my scorn;—
Curs'd was the hour that saw us meet
The hour when we were born.

Sp

Manuscript for a poem attributed to Poe (from the facsimile at the Library of Congress)

York, Poe sold it to Harper and it was published in book form in July 1838. This tale was to represent Poe's most serious attempt to write long fiction. Many critics have considered it flawed in design, but it is one of the most interesting of Poe's stories. With its many reversals, ruses, and deceptions the tale suggests a major theme in Poe's work: that material existence is a condition of imperfection and that spiritual wholeness will be achieved only after death.

Finding no work in New York, Poe moved his family to Philadelphia during the summer of 1838, where he eventually found a post as editor of *Burton's Gentleman's Magazine,* a journal owned and published by comic actor William Burton. Poe did not respect Burton any more than he had respected White, but he needed to keep his job. It enabled him to publish his own work. Twenty-five of his tales, including the famous "The Fall of the House of Usher" (1839), were published in the *Gentleman's Magazine.* Perhaps more important for his growing reputation, he succeeded in getting the firm of Lea and Blanchard to bring out a collection of his stories, *Tales of the Grotesque and Arabesque* (1840), in two volumes. It was only a small edition of 1,750 copies, and Poe received no royalties, but at least a large portion of his work was now before the public. The title Poe gave his book signified his own division of his tales into types, the "grotesque" exhibiting a comic or burlesque quality and the "arabesque" projecting a highly imaginative design. The book sold quite well, but the only benefit to Poe was the enhancement of his reputation.

Never one to submit easily to direction by an intellectual inferior, Poe began to quarrel with Burton; the final argument was over Burton's decision to advertise his magazine for sale without consulting his brilliant editor. Poe had wanted throughout his life to publish his own literary magazine, and at this time he thought he could risk it. In June of 1840 he left the *Gentleman's Magazine* for good, publishing that same month a prospectus for "The Penn Magazine" for which he hoped to gain financial support. He announced that the first number of the magazine would appear on 1 January 1841, but Poe could not raise the money and abandoned the project.

Burton's Gentleman's Magazine was bought by George R. Graham, a young journalistic entrepreneur, in November 1840. Possibly on the recommendation of Burton, Poe was hired as assistant editor of *Graham's Magazine,* the best and most influential editorial post he ever held. In *Graham's* Poe published some of his most striking tales, including "The Murders in the Rue Morgue" (1841), his first detective story. Poe did not invent the detective story, but he, perhaps more than any other writer, gave it the form that became characteristic, that of the master detective whose stories are told by an admiring friend. Poe's stories featuring C. Auguste Dupin are prototypes of the most famous of all detectives, Sherlock Holmes, whose tales are told by Dr. Watson. Also in *Graham's* Poe published his most memorable book reviews: that of Henry Wadsworth Longfellow's *Ballads and Other Poems* (1842), in which he developed the idea of aesthetic appreciation as an attribute of man's immortal nature; and that of Nathaniel Hawthorne's *Twice-Told Tales* (1842), in which he insisted that every word in a short tale contribute to a preconceived design.

Poe's review of Henry Wadsworth Longfellow's *Ballads and Other Poems* contained a theoretical argument which very nearly represented his final position on poetry. It is not essentially different from that advanced in the review of Drake and Halleck, but it abandons the jargon of phrenology in favor of traditional terms and makes emphases and discriminations that were less clear in the earlier review. In general the argument makes a higher value claim for poetry than Poe had ever made before in the context of a review.

Poe's usual approach to the act of practical criticism was to single out the chief characteristic of the work of the poet reviewed, advance theoretical criteria by which this characteristic could be examined, and then conduct the examination in detail. For the poems of Drake and Halleck he chose "imagination," possibly because he had been studying Coleridge, but more probably because Drake had been credited in America with great imaginative power. The leading characteristic of Longfellow's verse, however, was its reducibility to moral statement. Accordingly Poe erected a theoretical argument against the didactic purpose in poetry. Opposition to overt didacticism in verse was fairly common among romantic theorists in Europe, but most American journalistic critics had no objection to poetic moral lessons. Poe knew that he was going against popular opinion when he castigated Longfellow's didacticism, so he did as he had done previously; he developed an argument on philosophical and psychological grounds that "teaching" was no part of the legitimate poetic purpose.

Poe's portrait of Sarah Elmira Royster (by permission of Lilly Library, Indiana University)

On psychological grounds Poe argued that the instructional purpose ("to convey the true") was antithetical to the mood in which poetry was written. Poetry originated in a state of feeling and attempted to transmit that feeling. "Truth," however, was arrived at in an unimpassioned, ratiocinative manner and should be communicated efficiently in unadorned prose. In other words, poetry is the improper instrument with which to fulfill a didactic purpose. Continuing his psychological analysis, Poe argued that the very composition of the human mind proved that the poet should not attempt to convey the "truth." The chief faculties of the human mind, he said, were the intellect, the taste, and the moral sense. It was the business of the intellect to arrive at the truth. The function of the moral sense was to inform the individual of right and wrong. It was the sole function of the taste to inform the individual of beauty, and poetry (all the fine arts, in Poe's sense) served the taste. Thus the primary function of art is to evoke an aesthetic response. If it is made to serve another purpose, such as appealing to the intellect or the conscience, then it is no longer art but something else.

Poe knew quite well that his American audience cared little for pure aesthetic response; beauty ranked very low in the American scale of value. In the review of Drake and Halleck he had simply said that enjoyment of the beautiful is natural, a basic instinct that had some heuristic function in making us want to "know"–know *what,* he did not say. Now Poe clearly links the enjoyment of beauty with man's divine nature: a significant condition of man's immortal nature is an innate "sense of the Beautiful." The idealizing capacity described in the earlier review is still present, but in this review Poe indicates more clearly *what* is being idealized: it is beauty itself. Earthly forms of beauty will not gratify man's hunger for ideal perfection, so the poet who imitates earthly forms will leave us unsatisfied. Instead the poet must strive to capture the "beauty beyond the grave." He will never succeed, for immortal beauty can never be manifested in *Time,* but it is only by virtue of his attempt to capture immortal beauty that one deserves the name of poet. That

Poe's concept originated in Platonic idealism is obvious. What was important to his purpose was the attribution of quasi-religious value to beauty and hence art. Holding such views, he ought to have adopted something like Keats's claim that beauty was truth and truth was beauty. Instead, Poe's notion of truth encompassed whatever could be verified by the reason, demonstrated by science, or recognized by the senses. In contrast, whatever was created by art was by definition a fiction, for it did not exist in nature. Consequently the artist should never aim at the truth, because this *end*, which ought to be accomplished by reason and science, would subvert his artistic *means*. Applying this principle to Longfellow, Poe proclaimed that, insofar as the poet entertained a didactic purpose, his poems would inevitably fail as he directed his efforts toward the end of instruction instead of the proper end of beauty.

Poe's theory of fiction was grounded in the same basic psychological principle as his theory of poetry, that the prime desideratum was a unified impression–the single effect on the mind of a reader. Such a result could be achieved, he claimed, only by the short tale. Novels he regarded as an illegitimate art form, and though he reviewed many, some quite expertly by the standards of his day, he made no contribution to the theory of the novel, arguing that a unified plot was a waste of time because the novel was too long for its structure to be apprehended as a whole. The short tale was a legitimate literary form, he claimed in his review of Hawthorne's *Twice-Told Tales*. It offered "unquestionably the fairest field for the exercise of the loftiest talent, which can be afforded by the wide domains of mere purpose."

Poe had begun reviewing short stories in 1836, while he was still on the *Messenger*, and his first theoretical statement of any significance was made in a review of Dickens's *Watkins Tottle and Other Sketches*. In this review he used "The Pawnbroker's Shop" as an illustration of the unity of effect, comparing the tale to a painting, with the implication that each sentence should be like a brush stroke: "we pause at every sentence, not to dwell upon the sentence, but to obtain a fuller view of the gradually perfecting picture–which is never at any moment any other matter than the *Pawnbroker's Shop*. To the illustration of this one end all the *groupings* and *fillings in* of the painting are rendered subservient–and when our eyes are taken from the canvas we remember the personages of the sketch not at all as independent existences, but as essentials of the one subject we have witnessed–as a part and portion of the *Pawnbroker's Shop*."

Since he regarded a short tale as analogous to a painting, then it is not surprising that Poe insisted upon a strict limitation of scope. In fact, the tale, as Poe saw it, was little more than a tableau, the illustration of an idea or a state of mind. As he expressed it in his review of Hawthorne's *Twice-Told Tales*, the tale-writer should work out his "design" in advance:

> A skilful literary artist has constructed a tale. If wise, he has not fashioned his thoughts to accommodate his incidents; but having conceived, with deliberate care, a certain unique or single *effect* to be wrought out, he then invents such incidents–he then combines such events as may best aid him in establishing this preconceived effect. If his very initial sentence tend not to the outbringing of this effect, then he has failed in his first step. In the whole composition there should be no word written, of which the tendency, direct or indirect, is not to the one pre-established design. And by such means, with such care and skill, a picture is at length painted which leaves in the mind of him who contemplates it with a kindred art, a sense of the fullest satisfaction. The idea of the tale has been presented unblemished, because undisturbed.

In spite of his success, Poe remained with *Graham's Magazine* only until May 1842. He resigned, he said, because he was disgusted with the "namby-pamby" nature of the family magazine. From mid 1842 through March 1844 Poe remained in Philadelphia as a free-lance journalist, selling whatever he could to any journal or gift book that would publish him. His wife became chronically ill of consumption, occasionally suffering hemorrhages and keeping Poe in a constant state of anxiety. In April 1844 he moved his family back to New York, which was rapidly replacing Boston as the literary capital of the United States. Already well known at home and beginning to attract attention abroad, Poe soon became famous. In 1843 he had entered his tale "The Gold Bug" in a literary contest given by the *Dollar* newspaper, and it won the first prize of $100, sorely needed by Poe. Set on Sullivan's Island in Charleston Harbor, "The Gold Bug" employed such elements as a buried pirate treasure, a comic black man, and a scholarly recluse. When it was printed in the *Dollar* (June 1843), it gained Poe more attention than any piece he had previously published.

In New York Poe found employment with the *Evening Mirror* newspaper in October 1844. He was hired as "critic" and "sub-editor," but according to one of the owners, Nathaniel Parker Willis, himself an author of some merit, Poe's work was little more than drudgery. On 29 January 1845 Poe published his most famous poem, "The Raven," in the *Evening Mirror*. The poem had been sold to the *American Review*, where it appeared in the February issue. In the opinion of some historians, "The Raven" gained more immediate attention than any other poem published in America, and it helped to establish Poe's reputation in England, where it was admired by Elizabeth Barrett and Robert Browning. The poem was even more popular than "The Gold Bug." According to Poe in a letter to his friend Frederick Thomas, "The bird beat the bug . . . all hollow."

The poem not only brought Poe great recognition as a poet but also provided him with the subject for his most striking critical essay, "The Philosophy of Composition," published in *Graham's Magazine* in April 1846. While it would be naive to assume that Poe actually wrote "The Raven" exactly as he describes the process in this essay, it remains an admirably lucid account of a method of composition that does not depend upon "inspiration," "genius," or any of the other imponderables of creativity.

The description of the analytical process Poe claims to have used in composing "The Raven" has been taken by a number of critics as either self-deceptive or fraudulent, since few are willing to believe that a poem could be developed, as Poe said, "with the precision and rigid consequence of a mathematical problem." However, Poe actually wrote the poem, and there should be no doubt that he believed that an effective poem could be written without benefit of "inspiration." He had said so in his review of Drake and Halleck back in 1836, and ten years later he describes the method. Dismissing at the outset of his essay the mental processes that led to his intention, he concerns himself only with the conscious aspect of composition, the psychological and technical considerations that were operative during the willed process of writing a poem. His first consideration, he says, was length. In several earlier

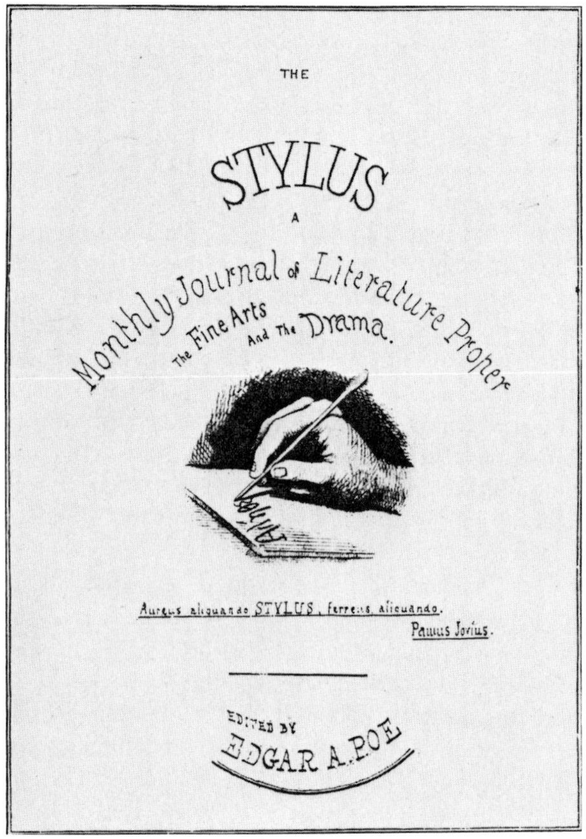

Design by Poe for the cover of a journal which he first proposed to publish in 1843 but was never able to finance (from Hervey Allen, Israfel, *1934)*

reviews, including the one of Longfellow's *Ballads*, Poe had argued that a long poem prevented a reader from experiencing the pleasure of a unified effect, by which he meant that in a long poem, such as an epic, the mind of the reader could not take in the relatedness of part to part and part to whole. Now Poe bases his argument against length on a desired *intensity* of effect, a point he had suggested in his earliest critical statement, the "Letter to B–." The reading of a poem should be accomplished in a single sitting, Poe proclaims, so that the intensity of response would not be dissipated by interruptions or fatigue. First, then, the poet should aim at a "single impression," then choose the *kind* of impression he wants to make on the reader. Here, Poe says, there is only one choice: the impression must be of beauty. As usual, Poe wishes his reader to experience aesthetic value, and he assumes empirically that the emotional tone of the response to beauty is "melancholy." Most aestheticians would disagree with Poe, but the choice of melancholy as an appropriate tone is a logical consequence of the Platonic idealism he had manifested in his review of Longfellow's *Ballads*. It originates in human regret at the imperfection of all earthly manifestations of beauty.

All that remained for Poe to do after he had chosen "length, province, and tone" was to work out the narrative details of the poem, which he claimed he did in a perfectly logical way, having the end in mind before he "first put pen to paper." It is clear, then, that "The Philosophy of Composition" is nothing more than an essay in rhetoric, rhetoric by definition being a description of the means by which a writer or speaker may move an audience. Poe's practical criticism, his book reviews, frequently used the method of rhetorical analysis to isolate faults; "The Philosophy of Composition" is merely the reverse of the coin, a demonstration of the way in which compositional skill may produce excellence without the aid of some mystic "inspiration."

During the summer of 1845 Wiley and Putnam published a second collection of Poe's short stories, entitled simply *Tales*. It was not a complete collection, containing only twelve pieces, but it did offer some of his best work, even though it excluded some that Poe himself thought superior, notably "Ligeia," which he once called his finest. Nevertheless, the 1845 *Tales* was noticed in France where translations began to appear in journals. In 1848 Charles Baudelaire, Poe's most famous French admirer, began his translations of Poe's works and acknowledged the American's importance as a writer. In November 1845 Wiley and Putnam brought out *The Raven and Other Poems*, a slim book of some thirty poems, selected by Poe himself. Despite the popular success of "The Raven," Poe's poems received comparatively little critical attention. Most of them were poems that had been written during his youth. "Ulalume" and "Annabel Lee" were yet to come. Poe was now much better known as a critic and a writer of fiction than he was as a poet, although until his death he preferred to be known as a poet.

At last Poe acquired his own magazine in October 1845. The *Broadway Journal*, a weekly paper he had been coediting for some months, became solely his when he bought it with fifty dollars borrowed from Horace Greeley. He may have borrowed another twenty-five from Rufus Wilmot Griswold, a man whom Poe regarded as a friend but who actually viewed Poe's behavior and work

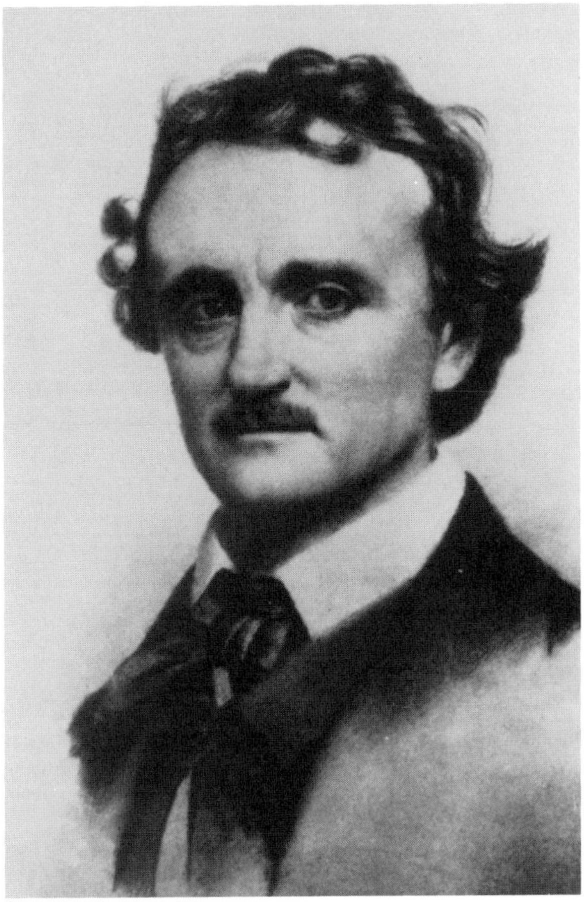

Crayon portrait of Poe by Flavius J. Fisher (by permission of the Valentine Museum, Richmond, Virginia)

as immoral and who edited and realigned Poe's work after his death. Poe could not continue to operate the *Broadway Journal* on borrowed money, however. After some two months, during which he kept the pages of the weekly full of his own work, he had to cease publication. On 3 January 1846 Poe announced the demise of the only journal he ever fully controlled.

The death of his wife, Virginia, in early 1847 had traumatic effects on Poe's psyche, but somehow he managed to continued to write and occasionally to give a public lecture. He spoke on the origin and nature of the cosmos and eventually published his speculations in 1848 in a book he called *Eureka*. In a way this cosmological treatise was a culmination of all of Poe's speculation about the relation of art and the human spirit. He claimed the work was a product of imagination, but he supported his imaginings with Newtonian science. Poe speculated that God, once a unified being, had deliberately set himself in mo-

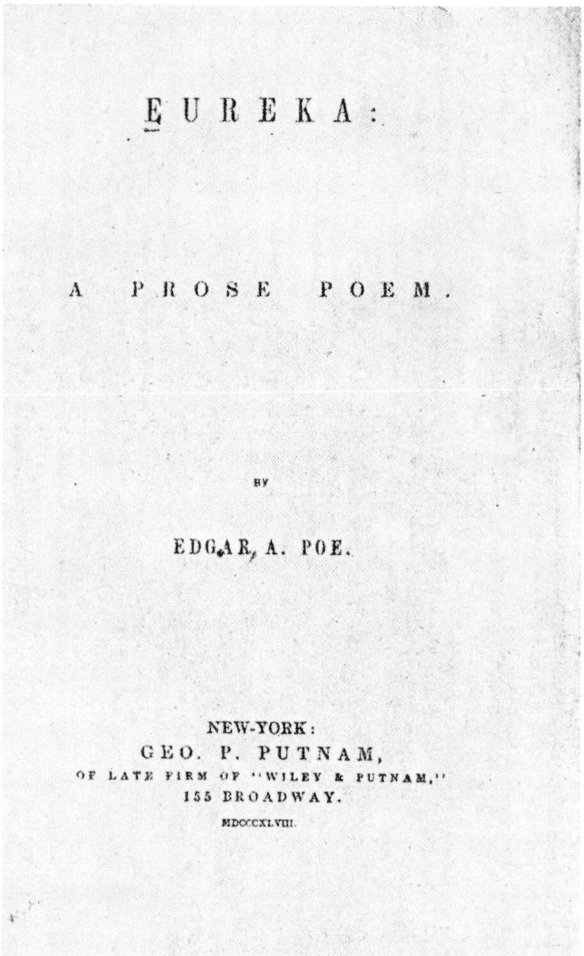
EUREKA:

A PROSE POEM.

BY

EDGAR A. POE.

NEW-YORK:
GEO. P. PUTNAM,
OF LATE FIRM OF "WILEY & PUTNAM,"
155 BROADWAY.
MDCCCXLVIII.

Title page for the last work by Poe published in his lifetime

tion, flying out from a center by centrifugal force, which was the "first law." God had thus created matter through motion. The second law was gravitation, by which the matter fleeing from the center was collected into large bodies (planets and satellites). Thus the universe was God in his diffused state, but eventually the first law would be repealed. All matter would be drawn into the sun, and God once more would be a unified being. Since God's diffused state was a condition of imperfection, nothing perfect could exist in the world of matter; and, to Poe, art was simply the attempt of the human soul to achieve a foretaste of the glory of reunification with God in a single perfect being.

In addition to *Eureka* Poe also lectured on poetry in 1848; he called his lecture "The Poetic Principle," and it remains one of the two theoretical essays for which he is remembered. Whereas "The Philosophy of Composition" (1846) was a kind of "how to write a poem" guide, "The Poetic Principle" (1850), a recapitulation of the aesthetics of Poe's review of Longfellow's *Ballads,* attempted to justify poetry on the grounds of its ontological nature. A poem attempts to capture some small portion of the "beauty beyond the grave." This was Poe's ultimate defense of the art form he loved, and it came appropriately near the end of his brief life.

Although his life as a journalist was dull, hard, and exasperating, Poe never lost the sense of his own genius in an age when the qualities of genius were often analyzed and revered. His training in the classics, especially in classical and neoclassical criticism, had convinced him of the validity of the rational approach to literature and the creative process. At the same time his absorption of the works of the romantic period, like those of Coleridge, Shelley, Keats, and Byron, reinforced his faith in the powers of the imagination to transcend the limits of ordinary experience and to explore the depths of the human soul. Through his own art and his criticism of the art of others, Poe found expression for his genius that gave a semblance of order to what otherwise might have been a gravely disordered or even a psychotic life. Ambitious to the end, he never gave up his desire to own and edit a magazine. He wished to publish a periodical that would raise the quality of native American literature, although he was never a literary chauvinist like many others in his time. In one sense he succeeded. At his death he left a body of literature unsurpassed in brilliance–within the limits of his own theory and practice.

Poe, like many other British and American reviewers of his time, often used a generic approach to the evaluation of a literary work. This meant that critical judgments were based upon the rudiments of a specific defined form, even when the definition was made by the critic himself. To Poe and many other critics there were clear lines of distinction, for example, between tragic and comic drama, between the novel and the prose romance, or between the narrative and the lyric poem. Throughout his reviews and critical essays from early 1835 until his death in 1849, Poe had something to say about every major literary genre he examined, including the novel, the drama, the poem, and, most important, the short tale.

Poe often reviewed novels, but he said little that would distinguish him as an innovative critic

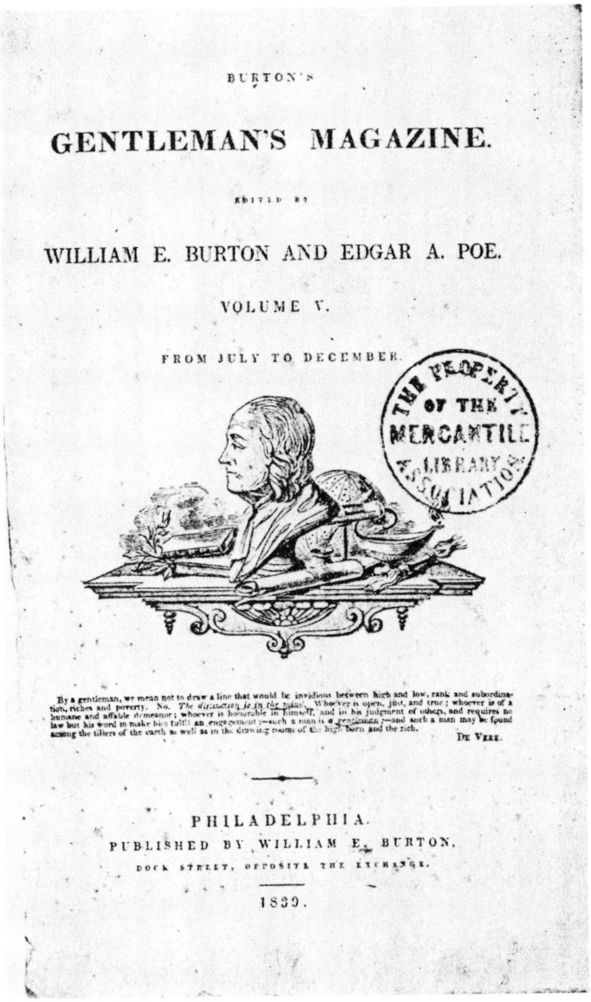

BURTON'S

GENTLEMAN'S MAGAZINE.

EDITED BY

WILLIAM E. BURTON AND EDGAR A. POE.

VOLUME V.

FROM JULY TO DECEMBER.

By a gentleman, we mean not to draw a line that would be invidious between high and low, rank and subordination, riches and poverty. No. *The distinction is in the mind.* Whoever is open, just, and true; whoever is of a humane and affable demeanor; whoever is honorable in himself, and in his judgment of others, and requires no law but his word to make him fulfil an engagement;—such a man is *a gentleman*;—and such a man may be found among the tillers of the earth as well as in the drawing rooms of the high born and the rich.

DE VERE.

PHILADELPHIA.

PUBLISHED BY WILLIAM E. BURTON,

DOCK STREET, OPPOSITE THE EXCHANGE.

1839.

Title page for the volume of Burton's periodical in which Poe was first listed as editor (courtesy of the Maryland Historical Society)

of that form. Since the novel was a comparatively new art form and there were no established rules for the genre, he simply adapted principles from Aristotelian dramatic criticism to long fiction. For instance, in reviewing Edward Bulwer-Lytton's *Night and Morning* in *Graham's Magazine* (April 1841), Poe defined plot as "that in which no part can be displaced without ruin to the whole," thus echoing Aristotle's *Poetics*. But then he goes on to say that Bulwer's efforts at "perfection of plot" led him to sacrifice "verisimilitude," a quality to be admired in the novel above perfection of plot. Poe always called for verisimilitude in the novel, holding that perfection of plot in long fiction should not even be an author's purpose since a novel was too extensive for a reader to keep its entire structure in mind. A perfect plot should be the goal only when an audience can grasp it as a *whole,* perceiving the beginning, the middle, and the end. Accordingly the novel, by virtue of its length, was an imperfect art form. Its virtues were verisimilitude and its capacity to exercise the mind. He even welcomed authorial commentary, later considered a serious flaw in novelistic execution.

Although Poe made no precise distinction himself between the novel and the prose romance, a distinction often made in his time, notably by Hawthorne, he was capable of criticizing a romance as if it were a poem. In fact, in his early "Letter to B–," he did distinguish the poem from the romance, saying that the poem aimed at "indefinite" pleasure, the romance at "definite" pleasure. The romance gave us "perceptible images with definite [sensations], poetry with indefinite sensations." Thus it is not surprising that in his 1839 review of de la Motte Fouqué's *Undine: A Miniature Romance* Poe used terminology he usually reserved for commentary on poems. He declared the work highly imaginative and claimed that it had a "mystic" significance or an "undercurrent of meaning" of a philosophical character. Phrases like "ideality," "loftiness of conception," and "elements of beauty" were used to describe the merits of Fouqué's famous fable, showing that Poe treated it as a poem rather than a romance.

During his later years in New York, Poe had an opportunity to review live drama, and he made the most of his Aristotelian heritage. Although he said very little about the plot structures Aristotle described, his constant censure of the overcomplicated plots and superimposed actions of such American plays as Anna Cora Mowatt's *Fashion* (1845), Nathaniel Parker Willis's *Tortesa, the Usurer* (1839, 1845), and Longfellow's *The Spanish Student* (1845) reveals that he kept in mind the Aristotelian concept of the functioning of all parts to create a unified whole. However, Poe did concede that the plots of Aeschylus and Sophocles were too "bald," too simple for the modern taste. His insistence upon the integration of the underplot with the main action and his constant disapproval of incidents that had no bearing upon the denouement–particularly in reference to *Tortesa*–show that Poe, however much he thought the drama had progressed since the time of the classics, was still an Aristotelian in his belief that a plot should be carefully constructed and that a play should be a credible imitation of life.

Poe also agreed with Aristotle in other particulars. To Poe as to Aristotle, characters had to be consistent in their actions. They had to be creations that would gain the sympathy of the audience by having credibility as human beings rather than as "stage automatons." In reviewing William Hazlitt's *The Characters of Shakespeare* (1845), Poe held that Hamlet represented Shakespeare's power of identifying himself with his creations, thus insuring the credibility of his characters. Elaborate stage settings and embellishments had no significance in the drama. Plot and character were the primary considerations.

Poe also followed the Aristotelian tradition in believing that the subject matter of tragedy should be lofty and that man should be presented with dignity and grandeur. The action should be exalted, as noble characters performed noble deeds, involving themselves in deeply personal and tragic conflicts. To Poe as to Aristotle, the drama was what Poe called "the portraiture of nature in human action." He asserted that Lillo's *The London Merchant* (1731) was not worthy of the name of tragedy because it depicted the fall of the bourgeois, not the fall of princes.

Poe was staunchly Aristotelian in his criticism of the drama, but there was a line of departure in one respect. Whereas Aristotle allowed the primary purpose of the drama to be moral elevation by its capacity to induce humility and expand sympathy, Poe was as careful to caution against overt didacticism in the drama as he was in reference to the poem. He challenged the propriety of introducing the "schoolmaster on the stage," insisting rather that the drama concentrate on artistic rather than monitory effects. In this vein Poe commended elegant diction and polished expression in American drama whenever he found it, showing in his reviews more concern for style and finish than for message. This concern for expression, of course, was not limited to Poe's criticism of the drama. It permeated everything he wrote. As a critic he indicated the proper effect of each genre and gave an account of why a given piece did or did not achieve the appropriate effect. A Longfellow might fail because of his didacticism, a Bulwer-Lytton because he attempted perfection of plot in a form too extended to be taken as a whole. In the last analysis, however, Poe based his criticism on his concept of human nature. The human mind could take in only so much at a time during a single exposure to the text. Consequently the novel and for that matter the symphony were mistaken art forms. Only the short tale allowed an audience the unique pleasure of perceiving a perfectly organized whole, a pleasure Poe considered the highest that could be experienced by a human being.

An 1849 daguerreotype of Maria Clemm, Poe's mother-in-law

If Poe was not as valuable a critic as Ralph Waldo Emerson or Henry James, his theory and practice of criticism has nonetheless influenced the way generations of writers and readers have written and thought about stories and poems. The aesthetic bent of his criticism–especially his insistence on selecting the right word for the right effect, his linking of literature with music, and his steadfast avoidance of the didactic–had a pronounced influence on an emerging modern literature, both in America and abroad. Although Poe was not a systematic critic in the sense of Coleridge, for example, he accomplished what many superior critics, then and now, have not been equipped to do: illustrate critical principles with creative examples. The effect of his approach was to underscore and illuminate the relatively few critical principles he promulgated, making him, in the final analysis, a perceptive, intense, ar-

Daguerreotype of Poe, taken by S. W. Hartshorn on 14 November 1848 at Providence, Rhode Island (courtesy of Brown University Library)

ticulate, knowledgeable critic, but not a great one. His stories and poems were superior to his relatively slight body of criticism. Nevertheless, it is true that the color and quality of American letters would not have been the same without the presence of this uniquely gifted, ill-fated, devotee of culture, the arts, and the mind of man.

Within a few months after Virginia's death, Poe became romantically involved with a number of women, particularly with a poet named Helen Whitman, to whom he was briefly engaged. After a lecturing trip to Richmond, Virginia, however, he encountered his childhood sweetheart, Sarah Elmira Royster Shelton, who was now a widow. Poe became engaged to marry once more. On his return trip to New York, a journey about which little is known, Poe mysteriously disappeared. He was found in Baltimore near a polling booth on election day, and many have speculated that he was lured into intoxication by political workers and voted over and over. On 3 October Poe was taken to the Washington College Hospital in Baltimore and regained only partial consciousness, during which time he was unable to tell his physician what had happened to him. He died on 7 October possibly of a cerebral hemorrhage.

Letters:

Poe and His Friends: Letters Relating to Poe, volume 18 of *The Complete Works of Edgar Allan Poe,* edited by James A. Harrison (New York: Crowell, 1902);

The Letters of Edgar Allan Poe, edited by John Ward Ostrom, 2 volumes (Cambridge: Harvard University Press, 1948); republished with three supplements (New York: Gordian Press, 1966); fourth supplement, *American Literature,* 45 (January 1974): 513-536.

Biographies:

Rufus Wilmot Griswold, "Memoir of the Author," in *The Works of the Late Edgar Allan Poe,* volume 3 (New York: J. S. Redfield, 1850), pp. vii-xxxix;

Sarah Helen Whitman, *Edgar Poe and His Critics* (New York: Rudd & Carleton, 1860);

William Fearing Gill, *The Life of Edgar Allan Poe* (New York: Dillingham, 1877);

John H. Ingram, *Edgar Allan Poe: His Life, Letters and Opinions,* 2 volumes (London: John Hogg, 1880);

George Edward Woodberry, *The Life of Edgar Allan Poe, Personal and Literary,* 2 volumes (Boston: Houghton Mifflin, 1909);

Joseph Wood Krutch, *Edgar Allan Poe: A Study in Genius* (New York: Knopf, 1926);

Hervey Allen, *Israfel: The Life and Times of Edgar Allan Poe* (New York: Farrar & Rinehart, 1926);

Marie Bonaparte, *The Life and Works of Edgar Allan Poe: A Psycho-analytic Interpretation* (Vienna: Internationaler Psychoanalytischer Verlag, 1934); translated by John Rodker (London: Imago, 1949);

Una Pope-Hennessy, *Edgar Allan Poe, 1809-1849: A Critical Biography* (London: Macmillan, 1934);

Arthur Hobson Quinn, *Edgar Allan Poe: A Critical Biography* (New York: D. Appleton-Century, 1941);

Perry Miller, *The Raven and the Whale: The War of Words and Wits in the Era of Poe and Melville* (New York: Harcourt, Brace, 1956);

Frances Winwar [pseud.], *The Haunted Palace: A Life of Edgar Allan Poe* (New York: Harper, 1959);

William Bittner, *Poe: A Biography* (Boston: Little, Brown, 1962);

Edward Wagenknecht, *Edgar Allan Poe: The Man Behind the Legend* (New York: Oxford University Press, 1963);

John Walsh, *Poe the Detective: The Curious Circumstances Behind "The Mystery of Marie Rogêt"* (New Brunswick, N.J.: Rutgers University Press, 1967);

Sidney B. Moss, *Poe's Major Crisis: His Libel Suit and New York's Literary World* (Durham: Duke University Press, 1970);

John C. Miller, *Building Poe Biography* (Baton Rouge: Louisiana State University Press, 1977).

Bibliographies:

John W. Robertson, *Bibliography of the Writings of Edgar A. Poe* and *Commentary on the Bibliography of Edgar A. Poe,* 2 volumes (San Francisco: Russian Hill Private Press, Edwin & Robert Grabhorn Publishers, 1934);

William D. Hull, "A Canon of the Critical Works of Edgar Allan Poe with a Study of Edgar Allan Poe the Magazinist," Ph.D. dissertation, University of Virginia, 1941;

John Cook Wylie, "A List of the Texts of Poe's Tales," in *Humanistic Studies in Honor of John Calvin Metcalf* (Charlottesville: University of Virginia, 1941), pp. 322-338;

Charles F. Heartman and James R. Canny, *A Bibliography of First Printings of the Writings of Edgar Allan Poe,* revised edition (Hattiesburg, Miss.: Book Farm, 1943);

Haldeen Braddy, *Glorious Incense: The Fulfillment of Edgar Allan Poe* (New York: Scarecrow, 1953);

Jay B. Hubbell, "Poe," in *Eight American Authors: A Review of Research and Criticism,* edited by Floyd Stovall (New York: Modern Language Association, 1956), pp. 1-46;

William B. Todd, "The Early Issues of Poe's *Tales* (1845)," *Library Chronicle of the University of Texas,* 7 (Fall 1961): 13-18;

G. Thomas Tanselle, "The State of Poe Bibliography," *Poe Newsletter,* 2 (January 1969): 1-3;

Hubbell, "Poe," in *Eight American Authors: A Review of Research and Criticism,* revised edition, edited by James Woodress (New York: Norton, 1971), pp. 3-36;

J. Lasley Dameron, "Thomas Ollive Mabbott on the Canon of Poe's Reviews," *Poe Studies,* 5 (December 1972): 56-57;

Esther F. Hyneman, *Edgar Allan Poe: An Annotated Bibliography of Books and Articles in English, 1827-1973* (Boston: G. K. Hall, 1974);

Dameron and Irby B. Cauthen, Jr., *Edgar Allan Poe: A Bibliography of Criticism 1827-1967* (Charlottesville: University Press of Virginia, 1974).

Concordances and Indexes:

Bradford A. Booth and Claude E. Jones, *A Concordance to the Poetical Works of Edgar Allan Poe* (Baltimore: Johns Hopkins Press, 1941);

J. Lasley Dameron and Louis Charles Stagg, *An Index to Poe's Critical Vocabulary* (Hartford, Conn.: Transcendental Books, 1966);

Burton R. Pollin, *Dictionary of Names and Titles in Poe's Collected Works* (New York: Da Capo Books, 1968);

Pollin, *Word Index to Poe's Fiction* (New York: Gordian Press, 1982).

References:

Michael Allen, *Poe and the British Magazine Tradition* (New York: Oxford University Press, 1969);

Margaret Alterton, *The Origins of Poe's Critical Theory* (Iowa City: University of Iowa Press, 1925);

Carl L. Anderson, *Poe in Northlight: The Scandinavian Response to His Life and Work* (Durham: Duke University Press, 1973);

Célestin Cambiaire, *The Influence of Edgar Allan Poe in France* (New York: Stechert, 1927);

Eric Carlson, "New Introduction," in *Selections from the Critical Writings of Edgar Allan Poe,* edited by F. C. Prescott (Staten Island: Gordian Press, 1981), pp. vii-xxiii;

Robert D. Jacobs, "Poe and the Agrarian Critics," *Hopkins Review,* 5 (Spring 1952): 43-54;

Jacobs, *Poe: Journalist and Critic* (Baton Rouge: Louisiana State University Press, 1969);

George E. Kelly, "Poe's Theory of Beauty," *American Literature,* 27 (January 1956): 521-536;

Kelly, "Poe's Theory of Unity," *Philological Quarterly,* 37 (January 1958): 34-44;

Emerson R. Marks, "Poe as Literary Theorist: A Reappraisal," *American Literature,* 33 (November 1961): 296-306;

Sidney B. Moss, *Poe's Literary Battles: The Critic in the Context of His Literary Milieu* (Durham: Duke University Press, 1963);

Edd W. Parks, *Edgar Allan Poe as a Literary Critic* (Athens: University of Georgia Press, 1964);

Claude Richard, *Edgar Allan Poe: Journaliste et Critique* (Paris: Librarie C. Klincksieck, 1978).

Papers:

Poe's papers are widely scattered. The more important collections may be found at the following libraries: Beinecke Rare Book and Manuscript Library, Yale University; Boston Public Library (Griswold Collection); Enoch Pratt Free Library, Baltimore, Maryland; Free Library of Philadelphia, Pennsylvania; Harvard College Library and the Houghton Library, Harvard University; Henry E. Huntington Library and Art Gallery, San Marino, California; J. K. Lilly Library, Indiana University (Poe and Griswold Collections); Library of Congress (Ellis and Allan Papers); New York Public Library (Manuscript Division and Berg Collection); Pierpont Morgan Library, New York; M. L. Stark Library and Humanities Research Center, University of Texas, Austin (Koester Collection); Valentine Museum, Richmond, Virginia (Ellis and Allan Papers); the State Library of Virginia (Poe Foundation of Richmond); University of Virginia (Ingram Collection).

William Hickling Prescott

(4 May 1796-28 January 1859)

Donald Darnell

University of North Carolina at Greensboro

See also the Prescott entries in *DLB 1, The American Renaissance in New England* and *DLB 30, American Historians, 1607-1865.*

BOOKS: *History of the Reign of Ferdinand and Isabella, the Catholic,* 3 volumes (Boston: American Stationers' Company, 1838; London: Bentley, 1838);

History of the Conquest of Mexico, with a Preliminary View of the Ancient Mexican Civilization, and the Life of the Conqueror, Hernando Cortés, 3 volumes (London: Bentley, 1843; New York: Harper, 1843);

Biographical and Critical Miscellanies . . . (London: Bentley, 1845; New York: Harper, 1845); revised and enlarged as *Critical and Historical Essays . . .* (London: Bentley, 1850);

History of the Conquest of Peru, with a Preliminary View of the Civilization of the Incas, 2 volumes (London: Bentley, 1847; New York: Harper, 1847);

Memoir of Hon. John Pickering, LL.D. (Cambridge, Mass.: Metcalf, 1848);

History of the Reign of Philip the Second, King of Spain, 3 volumes: volumes 1 and 2 (London: Bentley, 1855; Boston: Phillips, Sampson, 1855); volume 3 (Boston: Phillips, Sampson, 1858; London: Routledge, 1858);

Memoir of the Honorable Abbott Lawrence, Prepared for the National Portrait Gallery . . . (N.p.: Privately printed, 1856);

William Hickling Prescott: Representative Selections, edited by William Charvat and Michael Kraus (New York & Cincinnati: American Book Company, 1943);

Literary Memoranda [William Hickling Prescott], 2 volumes, edited by C. Harvey Gardiner (Norman: University of Oklahoma Press, 1961);

Papers [William Hickling Prescott], edited by Gardiner (Urbana: University of Illinois Press, 1964).

Collections: *Prescott's Works,* 15 volumes, edited by John Foster Kirk (Philadelphia: Lippincott, 1872-1875);

The Works of William Hickling Prescott, 22 volumes, Montezuma Edition, edited by Wilfred Harold Munro (Philadelphia & London: Lippincott, 1904).

OTHER: "Life of Charles Brockden Brown," in *The Library of American Biography,* first series, volume 1, edited by Jared Sparks (Boston:

Hilliard, Gray, 1839; London: Richard James Kennett, 1839), pp. 117-180;

William Robertson, *History of the Reign of the Emperor Charles the Fifth,* 3 volumes, edited by Prescott, with "The Life of Charles the Fifth after his Abdication" by Prescott (London: Routledge, 1857; Boston: Phillips, Sampson, 1857).

PERIODICAL PUBLICATIONS: "Calais," *Club Room* (March 1820): 78-84;

"The Vale of Alleriot," *Club Room* (April 1820): 130-137;

"Letter to . . . on the Rev. W. L. Bowles' Stricture on the Life and Writings of Pope. By R. H. Lord Byron," *North American Review,* 13 (October 1821): 450-473;

"Essay Writing," *North American Review,* 14 (April 1822): 319-350;

"French and English Tragedy," *North American Review,* 16 (January 1823): 124-156;

Review of *Boston Prize Poems and Other Specimens of Dramatic Poetry,* by Charles Sprague, *North American Review,* 19 (July 1824): 253-256;

Review of *The Orlando Innamorato,* by Francesco Berni, and *The Orlando Furioso,* by Ludovico Ariosto, translated by W. S. Rose, *North American Review,* 19 (October 1824): 337-389;

"Da Ponte's Observations," *North American Review,* 21 (July 1825): 189-217;

Review of *Leisure Hours at Sea; Being a Few Miscellaneous Poems by an Anonymous Midshipman, North American Review,* 22 (April 1826): 453-455;

Review of *The Songs of Scotland, Ancient and Modern,* by Allan Cunningham, *North American Review,* 23 (July 1826): 124-142;

Review of *Almack's,* attributed to Marianne Spencer Stanhope Hudson, and *Vivian Grey,* by Benjamin Disraeli, *North American Review,* 25 (July 1827): 183-203;

Review of *Histoire de la Vie et des Ouvrages de Molière,* by J. Taschereau, *North American Review,* 27 (October 1828): 372-402;

Review of *A Chronical [sic] of the Conquest of Granada, by Fray Antonio Agapida,* by Washington Irving, *North American Review,* 29 (October 1829): 293-314;

"Essay on An Act to Incorporate the New-England Asylum for the Blind. Approved, March 2d, 1829," *North American Review,* 31 (July 1830): 66-85;

"Poetry and Romance of the Italians," *North American Review,* 33 (July 1831): 29-81;

Review of *English Literature of the Nineteenth Century: American Library of Useful Knowledge,* volumes 2, 3, 4, *North American Review,* 35 (July 1832): 165-195;

Review of Cervantes's *El ingenioso hidalgo Don Quijote de la Mancha,* edited by Francisco Sales, *North American Review,* 45 (July 1837): 1-34;

Review of *Memoirs of the Life of Sir Walter Scott,* by J. G. Lockhart, and *Recollections of Sir Walter Scott, North American Review,* 46 (April 1838): 431-474;

Review of *Poems and Rhymed Plea for Tolerance,* by John Kenyon, *North American Review,* 48 (April 1839): 401-415;

Review of *Sketches of English Literature,* by Chateaubriand, *North American Review,* 49 (October 1839): 317-348;

Review of *History of the United States From the Discovery of the American Continent,* volume 3, by George Bancroft, *North American Review,* 52 (January 1841): 75-103;

Review of *Italy, General Views of its History and Literature in Reference to its Present State,* by Luigi Mariotti (Antonio Gallenga), *North American Review,* 54 (April 1842): 339-356;

Review of *Life in Mexico During a Residence of Two Years in that Country,* by Frances Calderón, *North American Review,* 56 (January 1843): 137-170;

Review of *History of Spanish Literature,* by George Ticknor, *North American Review,* 70 (January 1850): 1-56.

Before gaining his international reputation as America's foremost romantic historian of Spain, William Hickling Prescott was a regular contributor to the *North American Review,* one of the oldest and most prestigious of American literary magazines. His reviews, covering thirty years from his literary apprenticeship to his period of master craftsmanship, reveal a knowledgeable and perceptive literary historian and scholar whose essays reflect the critical principles current in America before the Civil War. William Charvat's view of Prescott as one of the most important literary critics in the early period of American literary criticism (1810-1835) has not gone unchallenged by scholars who fault Prescott for his lack of analytical and interpretative skills. What is unchallenged is the sound scholarship and extensive knowledge displayed in his reviews, where co-

gent comparisons and contrasts of authors, literatures, and national characteristics vivify his commentaries. When Prescott examines narrative history, the genre in which he himself excelled, he emerges as the quintessential analytic critic, commenting perceptively on the strengths and weaknesses of historians contemporary and past, discussing principles of historical composition, and writing prescriptive criticism.

Prescott was born in Salem, Massachusetts, on 4 May 1796 with the credentials necessary for membership among the Brahmins of New England. His ancestors had distinguished themselves in the colonial affairs of Massachusetts, his grandfather William commanding the American forces on Bunker Hill. After a highly successful law practice in Salem, Prescott's father, also named William, moved to Boston where he subsequently increased the family's wealth through investments in railroads, insurance companies, and industries. Prescott's mother was Catherine Hickling, the daughter of a wealthy Boston merchant. Prescott's education was typical of that of the sons of patrician New Englanders. From 1808 to 1811 he gathered with others of his class in the library of the rector of Trinity Church, Boston, where he received instruction in English, Latin, and Greek by the Reverend John S. Gardiner. In 1811 he was admitted to the sophomore class at Harvard, his father's college. His best subjects were the classical languages, but because it was difficult for him to study what did not immediately interest him, he did not attempt to distinguish himself during his first year.

Prescott's complacent attitude changed as a result of an accident during his junior year that profoundly affected his later life. As he was leaving the college dining hall one day, he was blinded in his left eye by a hard crust of bread thrown during a brawl. Sobered by the accident, he pursued his studies diligently upon returning to Cambridge. By the time of his graduation in August 1814, he had earned membership in Phi Beta Kappa and had been assigned a Latin poem for his exercise at commencement. Following graduation Prescott went into his father's law office, but after four or five months of study he had not developed an interest in law. Again his habits and attitude were affected by a drastic alteration in his vision. His right eye became severely inflamed, and he temporarily lost sight in it as a result of acute rheumatism, a disease that would plague him throughout his life and would affect not only his eye but his neck and other joints.

After a visit to his maternal grandfather's home in the Azores to recuperate and a grand tour of France, Italy, and England, Prescott returned to Boston in September 1817, where he spent several years as a gentleman of leisure. During this period he met and married Susan Amory, daughter of a wealthy Boston merchant. Four children were born of this union. In March 1820 he became editor and contributor to the *Club Room,* the magazine named for the social-literary club he helped to form. With its expiration in July 1820, Prescott needed to find a meaningful occupation. Although his wealth made it unnecessary for him to earn a living, his Brahmin status and Puritan heritage required achievement. His long-standing love of literature, particularly the classics, and the satisfaction he derived from his contributions to the *Club Room* decided him in 1821 on a career as a man of letters. Accordingly he undertook a detailed program of study that included principles of grammar and correct writing, the classics, and a survey of the best English writers from Roger Ascham to his own time. He supplemented these readings in English literature with a careful study of Hugh Blair's *Lectures on Rhetoric* and Lindley Murray's *English Grammar.* He also spent an hour each day with the works of Tacitus, Cicero, and Livy.

An entry in his commonplace book at this time reveals that he had determined by the time he was thirty to be "*a very well read English scholar,* to be acquainted with the classical and useful authors (prose and poetry) in *Latin, French,* and *Italian*–especially *History.*" From 1822 to 1824 he undertook a vigorous study of the languages and literatures of England, France, and Italy. His survey of French literature began with Jean Froissart and extended to François René de Chateaubriand; he read Montaigne and Molière, whom he made the subject of an essay for the *North American Review.* His study of Italian, begun in 1823, resulted in two essays on Italian literature, also published in the *North American Review.* In the summer of 1824, Prescott's close friend, George Ticknor, professor of French and Spanish literature at Harvard, began to read his lectures on Spanish literature to Prescott, who was experiencing poor vision at the time. His interest piqued, Prescott began a study of Spanish, and by April 1825 he had read *Don Quixote,* Antonio de Solis's *Conquista de Mexico,* the comedies of Lope de Vega and of Calderón de la Barca, and a large number of works in the Spanish language. After carefully considering the choices of a literary subject, Prescott, despite his love of Italian literature and competence in literary history, chose his Spanish theme, the rise of Spain in the fifteenth and sixteenth centuries.

Prescott wrote the majority of his twenty-two *North American Review* essays prior to the publication of his first retrospective study, *History of the Reign of Ferdinand and Isabella* (1838), only seven of them appearing after that date. His review of Ticknor's *History of Spanish Literature* for the *North American Review* in 1850 was the last critical piece he wrote. The essays, products of the extensive reading and study he had done to prepare himself for his literary career, reflect what William Charvat considers the basic critical principles of the period: the critic's role as watchdog of society, literature's divorcement from anything derogatory to religious ideals and moral standards, its rejection of pessimism and skepticism, its impatience with the mystical or obscure, and its emphasis on society, not the egocentricity of the individual. Prescott came to this conservative view of the function of the critic and literature through the influence of Scottish criticism prevalent in America in the early nineteenth century. Emphasizing the judicial function of criticism, Scottish criticism evaluated a work according to accepted moral, social, and aesthetic standards. It further postulated an associational theory of aesthetics which judged a work by its power to create an appropriate cluster of associations in the reader's mind, generally leading to some moral or universal truth. A second foreign influence, German historical criticism, was equally significant in forming Prescott's literary viewpoint. From his reading of August Wilhelm Schlegel, Prescott recognized the shaping influences of environment on literature and subsequently focused his own criticism on a nation's culture, character, religion, and political institutions. This incorporation of Scottish and German criticism in Prescott's reviews explains in large measure the absence of appreciative and analytical criticism which characterizes that of Edgar Allan Poe, James Russell Lowell, and modern critics.

The format of the journal review itself also militated against analytical and aesthetic criticism. Primarily judicial in purpose, the review was expected to comment on morals, political soundness, and observance of rules of taste. Its educational purpose likewise influenced format, hence the frequent lengthy summaries of the works under review. Because of the scarcity of books, lengthy quoting of texts was also common. Consequently only brief space, if any, was given to analysis of the work itself. Because the *North American Review* specialized in original scholarly articles on historical literature, Prescott by training was ideally suited for this type of reviewing.

While preparing himself for a literary career Prescott wrote his first essay for the *North American Review,* a review of Byron's letter on Pope (October 1821). He revealed the influence of the associationist theory in his argument that images borrowed from nature, not art, are more poetical. In this he differed from Byron as he did from that poet's assertion that a poet's merit is not estimated by the dignity or difficulty of his subject. "A good epic or dramatic writer," Pres-

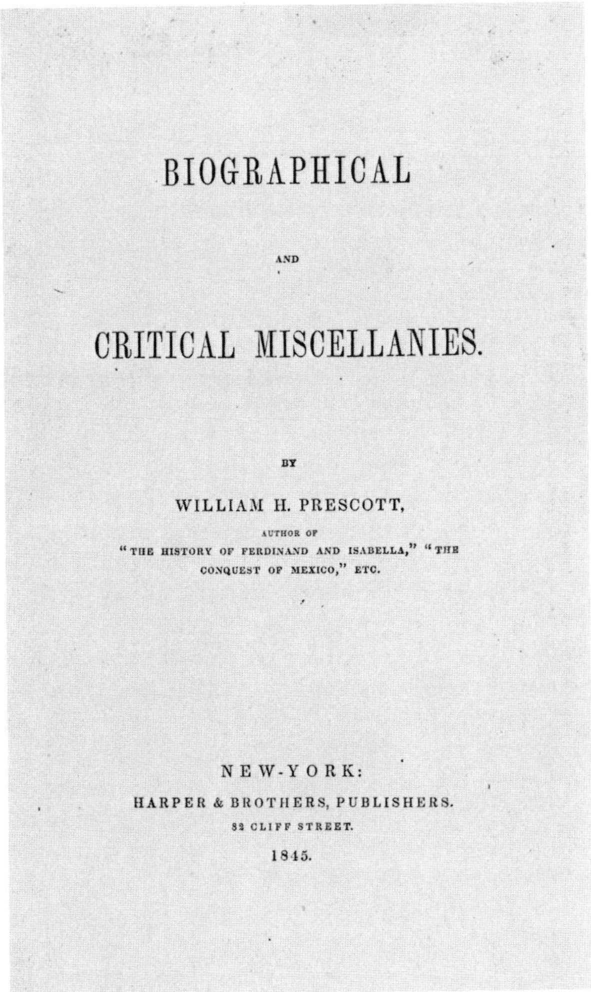
BIOGRAPHICAL

AND

CRITICAL MISCELLANIES.

BY

WILLIAM H. PRESCOTT,

AUTHOR OF
"THE HISTORY OF FERDINAND AND ISABELLA," "THE CONQUEST OF MEXICO," ETC.

NEW-YORK:
HARPER & BROTHERS, PUBLISHERS.
82 CLIFF STREET.
1845.

Title page for the collection that includes Prescott's essays on writers such as Charles Brockden Brown, Washington Irving, Miguel de Cervantes, Sir Walter Scott, and Molière

cott argued, "is as far above the best of ballad-grinders, as the architect of St. Peter's is superior to a first rate house-carpenter." Exhibiting the prevailing belief in literature's conservative moral and social purpose, Prescott condemns *Don Juan* for exhibiting "virtue, honor, and domestic affection, in the most contemptible and ridiculous aspect." This view notwithstanding, Prescott gave Byron his aesthetic due, finding "a more exquisite and loftier tone of poetic feeling in Childe Harold and Manfred, than in all that Pope has ever written."

"Essay Writing" (April 1822), the second of his *North American Review* pieces, represents Prescott's most original work. After tracing the history of the essay, he engages in his favorite device of criticism, the use of contrast between authors, literatures, and nationalities to define their distinctive qualities: the social aims of Montaigne were the reformation of mankind, while those of Steele were to depict the current follies and vices of his time. The simple, conversational and idiomatic character of Addison's style contrasts with the elaborate diction and sententious Latin idiom characterizing Samuel Johnson's prose. Prescott attributes deterioration in language to the art of printing, which by increasing the demand for books "induces the ignorant to write, and the learned to write rapidly, and of course negligently." Abstract speculation, the tendency to excessive refinement, and the passion for notoriety also take their toll on a pure standard of composition. At this early stage in his reviewing, Prescott reveals his antipathy for the "mystical, fine spun, indefinite phraseology" of romantic writers, who "never talk directly to the purpose." In the management of their ideas they remind him of North American Indians who see how close they can shoot arrows at their captives without hitting them.

In 1824 two essays appeared exhibiting Prescott at his critical best, a review of Italian narrative poetry (October 1824), and worst, a review of Charles Sprague's *Boston Prize Poems* (July 1824). The latter, because it concerned a contemporary figure, did not require the extensive historical background which allowed Prescott to display his scholarship or engage in the striking contrasts made in his critical estimates. Instead, forced to treat the works themselves, he lapsed into such bland observations as, "The concluding verse . . . is nervous but not natural," and "The principal defect in the poem is a want of perfect ease and simplicity." "Italian Narrative Poetry," revealing Prescott's extensive study of that literature, describes Italian poetry's influence on English poetry during the Renaissance. He shows the influence of German historical criticism on literature and national character, contrasting the brilliant imagination of the Italian mind with the sober, contemplative view of the English. Prescott's comparison between *Orlando Innamorato* (1495) and *Jerusalem Delivered* (1575) reveals him to be a knowledgeable scholar, and his discussion of Ariosto's abandonment of terza rima for ottava rima in his epic is a succinct and perceptive critique of theme and form, one of the best analytical pieces Prescott wrote.

On 19 January 1826 Prescott formally committed himself to his Spanish theme, writing in his *Literary Memoranda,* "I subscribe to the History of the reigns of Ferdinand and Isabella." He devoted over ten years of research and writing to this first history, a period interspersed by contributions to the *North American Review.* Typical of his reviews during this period, the one about novel writing (July 1827) reflects the ready command Prescott had of world literature and the influence of race and place in his criticism. Novel writing is particularly suited to the English genius, he says, because of the nation's political institutions which allow "an entire freedom of social intercourse" and "equal security of personal and civil rights." Its multitude of classes provides "inexhaustible variety of character and incident," and the lack of an academy's restrictive influence and censorship gives free reign to authors. These conditions contrast sharply with those in Spain, Italy, and France.

Almost three years into his research for the *History of the Reign of Ferdinand and Isabella,* Prescott addressed the issue of historical composition in a review of Washington Irving's *A Chronical [sic] of the Conquest of Granada, by Fray Antonio Agapida (North American Review,* October 1829). This and his later review of George Bancroft's *History of the United States (North American Review,* January 1841) are seminal essays on the theory and practice of historical composition. Although he says virtually nothing about the *Conquest of Granada,* Prescott's comments on the role of the historian, his assessment of earlier historians, and his survey of Spanish history provide valuable insights for the criticism of historical writing. The qualities Prescott considered essential for a historian are noteworthy: he must be strictly impartial and declare the truth under all circumstances and all hazards. He must be conversant not only with the laws, constitution, and general resources of the people he is depicting but also with "the nicer moral and social relations, the informing spirit, which gives life to the whole." He must be able to transport himself to other ages and nations and get the "very form and pressure of the times he is delineating." He must be accurate in his geography and chronology. Finally the historian "must display the various powers of a novelist or dramatist, throwing his characters into suitable lights and shades, disposing his scenes so as to awaken and maintain an unflagging interest, and diffusing over the whole that finished style, without which his work will only become a magazine of materials for the more elegant edifices of subsequent writers." These criteria reveal clearly the influence of German historical criticism and show that Prescott, early in his own career, developed a theory of historical writing that gave equal weight to research and literary craftsmanship.

Prescott's adverse criticism of Voltaire's and Gibbon's religious skepticism points up his concern for the moral element in literature, a legacy from Scottish criticism, and his own religious beliefs in a benevolent deity, New Testament ethics, and immortality. In Voltaire's histories, he laments, "The conduct of the world seems to be regulated by chance; the springs of human action are resolved into selfishness; and religion of whatever denomination, is only a different form of superstition." Neither Voltaire nor Gibbon exhibited in their writing "a generous moral sentiment." Prescott, however, approved the French historian's example of organizing his work according to a topical principle rather than chronological order. Voltaire's method enables the reader "to arrive more expeditiously at the results, for which alone history is valuable," and it allows the writer to "convey with more certainty and facility his own impressions." In essence the review is prescriptive. Prescott cites the recommendation of the French historian Amable Barante; to insure color and vivacity the historian must exploit the old chronicles and records and by closely following the original sources "exhibit as vivid and veracious a portraiture, as possible, of the times he is delineating."

His review of *English Literature of the Nineteenth Century,* published in the July 1832 issue of *North American Review,* marks Prescott's more positive attitude toward the romantic writers. Sir Walter Scott he had always admired, not only for his artistry but also for his moral portraiture. Though he faults William Wordsworth for his theory that rustic life affords the best subjects for poetry, Prescott respects the poet's philosophical seriousness. His assessment of the American literary scene anticipates Nathaniel Hawthorne, Henry James, Walt Whitman, and Ralph Waldo Emerson on the problems and challenges facing an American writer. Lacking ancient annals, legendary ruins, and links with feudal heroism, we have nature as "grand and lovely" as that in the old world and "man . . . exhibited under the influence of new institutions, and those better suited to the free expression of his intellectual and moral faculties, than any hitherto known."

In an essay on Spanish literature in America

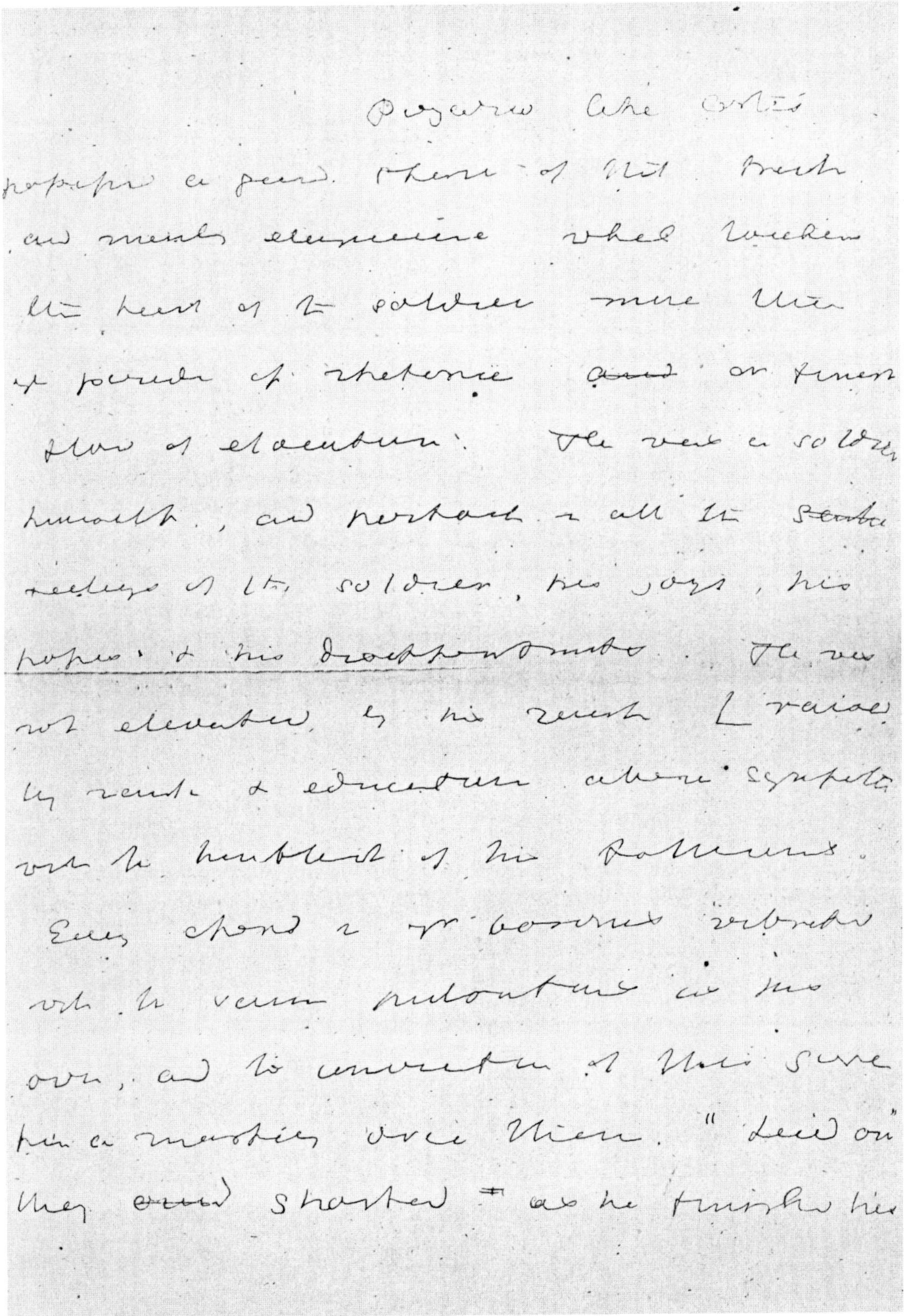
Pizarro like Cortés
possessed a good share of that frank
and manly eloquence which touches
the heart of the soldier more than
the parade of rhetoric ~~and~~ or finest
flow of elocution. He was a soldier
himself, and partook in all the ~~...~~
feelings of the soldier, his joys, his
hopes & his disappointments. He was
not elevated by his rank [raised
by rank & education above sympathy
with the humblest of his followers.
Every chord in their bosoms vibrated
with the same sentiments as his
own, and the conviction of this gave
him a mastery over them. "Lead on"
they ~~cried~~ shouted as he finished his

Page from the manuscript for History of the Conquest of Peru *(from* Homes of American Authors, *1853)*

(*North American Review,* July 1837) Prescott firmly establishes his credentials as a literary historian of Spain. Following a review of the times in which *Don Quixote* appeared, of the great popularity of chivalric romances, and of Cervantes's purpose (to correct the popular taste for romances of chivalry), Prescott accounts for the novel of character in Spain: "The freedom and originality of the popular character" resulted from "the long wars with the Moslem invaders [which] called every peasant into the field, and gave him a degree of personal consideration." The novelist, he concludes, will provide better insight into character than the historian because he will study man in his domestic relations and in his ordinary occupations in society–topics which do not fall within the scope of the historian.

Copies of the *History of the Reign of Ferdinand and Isabella* were available in Boston by Christmas 1837, and the book enjoyed a tremendous success. Within a few months the 1,250 copies printed to supply the market for a few years were sold out. The book's popularity was matched by the favorable critical reception given it by scholars in the field of Spanish history. After this point, Prescott's interest in reviewing appreciably declined, his commitment now given completely to writing history. For a while, however, he would continue to write for the *North American Review.*

His review of Bancroft's *History of the United States,* along with the 1829 review of Irving's *Conquest of Granada,* contains Prescott's significant criticism on historical composition. After revealing his Protestant bias (it was "a providential thing" America was settled after the Reformation, a movement which "gave an electric shock to the intellect, long benumbed under the influence of a tyrannical priesthood"), Prescott comments on a cardinal rule for the historian: the necessity of achieving unity in historical composition. The author must keep before the reader "some great principle of action, if such exist, that may give unity and, at the same time, importance to the theme." Bancroft did this in his history of the American colonies by making independence that principle. Prescott's own commitment to scholarship underlies his criticism of Bancroft's method of documentation where references placed at the side of the page rather than at the bottom made it necessary to abridge titles "at the expense of perspicuity." The absence of notes, however, concerned him more. "We want to see the grounds of [the author's] conclusions, the scaffolding by which he has raised his structure. . . ." Prescott's emphasis on the importance of color in historical writing echoes his earlier review of the *Conquest of Granada.* He applauded Bancroft's use of "picturesque details" in his depictions of Indians east of the Mississippi.

William Hickling Prescott

Two years after the publication of the highly praised and financially successful *History of the Conquest of Mexico* (1843), Prescott published in response to a proposal by his English publisher Richard Bentley a collection of his miscellaneous writings, *Biographical and Critical Miscellanies* (1845). The collection consisted of twelve of his previously published *North American Review* essays and an essay on Charles Brockden Brown. A second edition in 1850 included a review of George Ticknor's *History of Spanish Literature.* The volume's poor sales and the few perfunctory polite reviews were owing to the essays having been previously published and Prescott's faulty selection; he omitted some of his best work, including "Essay Writing," and a review of *English Literature of the Nineteenth Century.*

The failure of the *Miscellanies* confirmed that Prescott had tired of writing criticism and wanted to put his remaining energies into shaping his histories. Writing in his *Literary Memoranda* in November 1843, Prescott confessed, "Criticism has got to be an old story. It is impossible for any one who has done that sort of work himself to feel any respect for it. How can one critic look his brother in the face without laughing?" An earlier judgment of his own review articles is more harsh: "This sort of ephemeral trash . . . had better be forgotten by me as soon as possible."

History of the Conquest of Peru (1847) and *History of the Reign of Philip the Second* (1855, 1858) occupied Prescott's time and energies for the remainder of his life. On 28 January 1859 Prescott died at his Boston home of an apoplectic stroke. His four multivolume histories treating the rise of Spain from divided kingdom to colonial empire had earned him over twenty-eight honorary degrees and memberships in honorary societies, among them the Royal Academy of History (Madrid); the French Institute, Academy of Moral Sciences; the Royal Society of Berlin; and the Doctor of Civil Laws, Oxford, England. He would be remembered as America's finest romantic historian.

More scholar and literary historian than analytical critic, Prescott emerges through his essays for the *North American Review* as a representative critic of his time. The surveys of French, Spanish, and Italian literature that preceded his essays, together with his critical commentary, provided much-needed information for a public lacking knowledge of foreign language and literature. Like his contemporary reviewers, Prescott fulfilled the educational purpose of the literary magazines. While he was providing factual information and background necessary for understanding the literatures of the various nations he describes, Prescott also laid down principles essential for forming a basis for taste and appreciation. While for the most part these principles concerned moral and social criteria, Prescott's commentary on historical composition is, in fact, analytical, prescriptive criticism. The debate over his merit as a judicial critic versus his weakness as an aesthetic and interpretive critic notwithstanding, our most widely read and most honored historian was powerfully influenced in his own craft of historical composition by what he read and wrote in meeting his yearly reviewing obligations for the *North American Review*. As he was typical of the reviewers of his period, his essays in style, format, and purpose provide an index to the taste, values, and assumptions of a vital and formative period in American literary criticism.

Letters:

The Correspondence of William Hickling Prescott, 1833-1847, transcribed and edited by Roger Wolcott (Boston & New York: Houghton Mifflin, 1925).

Bibliography:

C. Harvey Gardiner, *William Hickling Prescott: An Annotated Bibliography of Published Works*, Hispanic Foundation Bibliographical Series, no. 4 (Washington, D.C.: Library of Congress, 1958).

Biographies:

George Ticknor, *The Life of William Hickling Prescott* (Boston: Ticknor & Fields, 1864);

Rollo Ogden, *William Hickling Prescott* (Boston & New York: Houghton Mifflin/Cambridge: Riverside Press, 1904);

Harry T. Peck, *William Hickling Prescott* (New York & London: Macmillan, 1905);

C. Harvey Gardiner, *William Hickling Prescott, A Biography* (Austin: University of Texas Press, 1969).

References:

William Charvat, *The Origins of American Critical Thought, 1810-1835* (New York: A. S. Barnes, 1936);

Howard F. Cline, C. Harvey Gardiner, and Charles Gibson, eds., *William Hickling Prescott: A Memorial* (Durham: Duke University Press, 1959);

Donald Darnell, *William Hickling Prescott* (Boston: Twayne, 1975);

C. Harvey Gardiner, *Prescott and his Publishers* (Carbondale: Southern Illinois University Press, 1959);

Eric F. Goldman, "The Historians," in *Literary History of the United States*, edited by Robert E. Spiller and others (New York: Macmillan, 1955);

Frank Goodwyn, "The Literary Style of William Hickling Prescott," *Inter-American Review of Bibliography*, 9 (March 1959): 16-39;

David Levin, *History as Romantic Art: Bancroft, Prescott, Motley, and Parkman* (Stanford, Cal.: Stanford University Press, 1959).

Papers:
Prescott's papers are at the Massachusetts Historical Society; Houghton Library, Harvard University; Boston Public Library; Historical Society of Pennsylvania; Henry E. Huntington Library; British Museum; Library of Congress; and New York Public Library.

Henry Reed

(11 July 1808-27 September 1854)

L. M. Dryden

BOOKS: *A Lecture on the Literary Opportunities of Men of Business, Delivered Before the Athenian Institute and Mercantile Library of Philadelphia, April 3, 1838* (Philadelphia, 1838);

An Oration Before the Zelosophic Society of the University of Pennsylvania: May 18, 1848, with a few notes, appended (Philadelphia: W. F. Geddes, 1848);

The Arts of Design: An Address Before the Art Union of Philadelphia, May 7, 1849 (Philadelphia: King & Baird, 1849);

Lectures on English Literature, from Chaucer to Tennyson, edited, with an introductory notice, by William Bradford Reed (Philadelphia: Parry & McMillan, 1855); republished as *Introduction to English Literature; From Chaucer to Tennyson* (London: J. F. Shaw, 1855);

Lectures on English History and Tragic Poetry, as Illustrated by Shakspeare [sic], edited by William Bradford Reed (Philadelphia: Parry & McMillan, 1855; London: J. F. Shaw, 1856);

Two Lectures on the History of the American Union, edited, with an introductory notice, by W. B. Reed (Philadelphia: Parry & McMillan, 1856);

Lectures on the British Poets, edited, with a preface, by William Bradford Reed, 2 volumes (Philadelphia: Parry & McMillan, 1857; London: J. F. Shaw, 1857).

OTHER: William Wordsworth, *The Complete Poetical Works of William Wordsworth: Together with a Description of the Country of the Lakes in the North of England, Now First Published with His Works,* edited, with a preface, by Henry Reed (Boston: James Munroe, 1837; Philadelphia: James Kay, Jun. & Brother, 1837; Pittsburgh: John I. Kay, 1837); revised and enlarged as *The Complete Poetical Works of William Wordsworth, Poet Laureate,* edited, with a preface and biographical note, by Reed (Philadelphia: Troutman & Hayes, 1851);

William Wordsworth, *Poems from the Poetical Works of William Wordsworth,* edited, with a preface, by Reed (New York: Geo. A. Leavitt, 1841);

Thomas Arnold, *Introductory Lectures on Modern History,* edited, with a preface and notes, by Reed (London: Fellowes, 1845; New York: D. Appleton/Philadelphia: G. S. Appleton, 1845);

Alexander Reid, *A Dictionary of the English Language,* edited, with an introduction, by Reed (New York: D. Appleton/Philadelphia: G. S. Appleton, 1845);

George Frederick Graham, *English Synonymes [sic] Classified and Explained; with Practical Exercises, Designed for Schools and Private Tuition,* edited, with an introduction and illustrative authorities, by Reed (New York: American Book, 1845);

"Life of Joseph Reed," in *The Library of American Biography,* second series, volume 8, edited by Jared Sparks (Boston: Little, Brown, 1846);

Lord Mahon [Philip Henry Stanhope], *The History of England from the Peace of Utrecht to the Peace of Paris,* edited by Reed (New York: D. Appleton/Philadelphia: George S. Appleton, 1849);

Thomas Gray, *Poetical Works of Thomas Gray,* edited, with a memoir, by Reed (Philadelphia: Henry Carey Baird, 1851);

Christopher Wordsworth, *Memoirs of William Words-*

worth, Poet-Laureate, D.C.L., 2 volumes, edited, with a note, by Reed (Boston: Ticknor, Reed & Fields, 1851).

PERIODICAL PUBLICATIONS: "William Wordsworth," *New York Review*, 4 (January 1839): 1-70;

"Address Before the Art-Union of Philadelphia, May 7th, 1849," *Art-Union of Philadelphia: Transactions* (1849): 41-71;

"Wordsworth," *Literary World: A Journal of American and Foreign Literature, Science and Art*, 6 (15 June 1850): 581-582;

"Wordsworth. [A Second Paper]," *Literary World*, 7 (14 September 1850): 205-206;

"The Daughter of Coleridge," *Literary World*, 11 (21 August 1852): 115-118;

"A Memorial of Wordsworth," *Literary World*, 12 (25 June 1853): 512-513.

More than any other antebellum scholar, Henry Reed pioneered the critical reception of William Wordsworth in America. As Wordsworth's first American editor, Reed produced the most authoritative early edition of the complete works published in the United States and furthered Wordsworth's reputation in lectures and essays. He protected the poet from copyright infringement and even advised him on financial matters (roles for which Reed's legal training equipped him). While the two men never met, their correspondence during Wordsworth's last fourteen years showed that Reed's reverence for Wordsworth was matched by the poet's affectionate respect for his young American editor. Reed did have other interests, among them securing the English language and its literature as academic disciplines. Nonetheless, as his friends noted with amusement, in every subject Reed considered he invariably returned to Wordsworth "as the needle to the pole." All of Reed's scholarship derived from his admiration for the purity of language and the moral seriousness he found exemplified in Wordsworth's poetry.

Christened Henry Hope Reed but eventually dropping the middle name, Reed was descended from a distinguished family (and related to another by marriage) whose associations with the legal profession and the Anglican Church account for the moral and religious undercurrents of his scholarship. Like the family of John Adams, the Reeds produced a succession of lawyers, public servants, and historians. Reed's grand-

Henry Hope Reed

father, Gen. Joseph Reed, served as military secretary to his friend George Washington during the revolution and afterward became the first governor of Pennsylvania. Reed's father was state attorney-general. Henry Reed himself briefly practiced law before becoming an English scholar, and the rigor of legal scholarship remained a lifelong trait.

Reed was born in Philadelphia on 11 July 1808, the son of Joseph and Maria Ellis Watmough Reed. Unathletic and bookish, he attended the classical school of James Ross in Philadelphia. At the age of fifteen he entered the sophomore class of the University of Pennsylvania in Philadelphia. He received his B.A. in 1825 with high honors and was the Latin salutatorian. Afterward he studied law with his uncle John Sergeant, a United States congressman and renowned constitutional lawyer, and he was admitted to practice in Philadelphia in 1829. Unhappy in the family profession, Reed accepted an assistant professorship of English literature in 1831 at the University of Pennsylvania, but later that year he assumed instead an assistant professorship of moral philosophy. He seemed to prefer that field and suffered great disappointment when he failed to receive a promotion. In 1835 he accepted a professorship in rhetoric and English literature which he held for the remainder of his life. In 1834 he married Elizabeth White Bronson, a granddaughter of Pennsylvania's first Anglican bishop, the Right Reverend William White. Over the next two decades six children–three of whom died in infancy–were born to the Reeds. Until his own death in 1854, Reed performed his teaching and administrative responsibilities diligently at the university while devoting substantial time to editorial work, articles, and public lectures.

With his duties Reed may have been forced to publish, and he soon began the ambitious project of editing Wordsworth's complete works. In his single-volume, double-column edition of 1837, Reed included extensive notes of his own and illustrative passages from other authors. Significantly Reed expanded Wordsworth's category of "Poems of Imagination" to include poems previously classified separately or printed after the most recent British edition–thereby anticipating the "unexecuted intention" stated in Wordsworth's 1815 "Preface to *Poems*." Reed sent Wordsworth a copy that received praise from the poet Samuel Rogers and so delighted Wordsworth that he arranged for a British single-volume, double-column edition, published in 1845 and retaining Reed's system of poetic classification. Reed's 1837 edition of Wordsworth became the standard American edition and was reprinted several times through the 1840s. Acknowledging his achievement, the American Philosophical Society in Philadelphia admitted Reed as a member in 1838.

A seventy-page appreciation of Wordsworth, appearing in the January 1839 issue of the *New York Review*, was Reed's chief composition published during his life. In this comprehensive study, richly illustrated with quotations, Reed argued his case for daring to class Wordsworth, "a living bard," in the company of Chaucer, Spenser, Shakespeare, and Milton, the English poets "of the highest order." Reed invoked Philip Sidney, Francis Bacon, Samuel Taylor Coleridge, and Sir Egerton Brydges in defining the chief delight of literature as moral and spiritual instruction. For Reed, Wordsworth's greatness lay in his ability to "unsensualize what is bodily" while "spiritualizing the senses, the intellect, and the passions." Surveying the range of Wordsworth's subjects–childhood, nature, humble life, women, politics, and science–Reed found in the poet's treatment of them a continuity of imaginative power undiminished by age and a poetic expression of the "Divine truth" of Christian revelation. The essay did not consider any of Wordsworth's weaknesses and implied that there were none.

Wordsworth wrote approvingly of the essay to Reed. The correspondence between the poet and his editor continued through the 1840s, but oddly their principal subject was financial. In his last years Wordsworth was distressed by what he called the "monetary derangements" in the United States that threatened the investments of his friends and his own daughter Dora. Reed became a solicitor for Wordsworth, conveying information and advising caution which eventually succeeded in preventing the losses Wordsworth feared.

Reed and Wordsworth shared their sorrows–the loss of beloved friends and family–and they discussed literary matters. Reed helped to persuade the poet to expand *Ecclesiastical Sonnets* (a poetic history of the English Church, written in 1821) to include sonnets on the Anglican Church in America and on liturgical services of the Church. In 1844 Reed sent Henry Inman, the foremost American portrait painter, to Rydal Mount to paint Wordsworth's portrait. It hung for many years in the Reed home and is now owned by the University of Pennsylvania. After Wordsworth wrote that his wife found it the best portrait ever made of him, Reed sent a replica by Inman as a gift to the Wordsworths.

In 1841 Reed produced a miniature volume entitled *Poems from the Poetical Works of William Wordsworth,* a selection of fifty-one poems (chiefly from "Poems of the Imagination" and "Poems of Sentiment and Reflection") that concluded with the "Ode on Intimations of Immortality." Designed as a general introduction to Wordsworth and as a convenient gathering of some favorite pieces, this popular edition was reprinted several times in the 1840s and the 1850s.

At the University of Pennsylvania, between 1841 and 1850, Reed gave four important series of lectures on British literature. He became vice-provost of the University of Pennsylvania in 1845. The following year the University of Vermont awarded him the honorary degree of doctor of laws. While busily engaged in teaching, administration, correspondence, and the affairs of his family and his church during the 1840s, Reed dealt with the English language and modern history in his scholarly publications.

Proper usage and the "purification" of English were the subjects of Reed's American editions of *A Dictionary of the English Language* (1845), compiled by the Scottish educator Alexander Reid, and *English Synonymes* (1845) by the British textbook writer George Frederick Graham. For both, Reed wrote lengthy introductions that examined the "moral relation" of language to the thoughts and feelings of people using it, and the connection between language, nationalism, and religion.

With the 1845 American edition of Thomas Arnold's *Introductory Lectures on Modern History*, Reed turned his attention to history. His own effort at writing history, a biography of his grandfather Gen. Joseph Reed, appeared in 1846 as part of Jared Sparks's twenty-five-volume *Library of American Biography*, an ambitious series of lives of "early pioneers of civilization in North America." Three years later, Henry Reed edited the only American publication of *The History of England from the Peace of Utrecht to the Peace of Paris* by Lord Mahon (Philip Henry Stanhope, later the Fifth Earl). With the "express sanction" of Lord Mahon for its care, Reed guided the two-volume 1,000-page American edition to press and added, in brackets, supplementary notes consisting of related writings by Lord Mahon and other authors, including Wordsworth.

The death of William Wordsworth on 23 April 1850 initiated the last phase of Reed's career. In June and September of that year Reed published two brief articles on Wordsworth in the *Literary World*. Quoting freely from the poet's works as he had in the 1839 essay, but now adding excerpts from their personal correspondence, Reed reasserted that Wordsworth's poetic imagination, themes, and periods showed basic continuity. There had been no change "other than the progression of cultivated poetic power–sublimer aspirations and the more comprehensive expansion of imaginative wisdom."

Reed brought out his updated edition of *The Complete Poetical Works of William Wordsworth* in 1851. A single-volume, double-column collection like Reed's 1837 edition, it retained the text and organization of the earlier edition and included all subsequent poems–not only some that had been inadvertently omitted from the London edition of 1849-1850 but also the posthumously published poem *The Prelude*. Reed prefaced the work with a brief biographical note, introduced poetic testimonials to Wordsworth by the late Hartley Coleridge and John Keble, and asserted that his new edition was "the most complete collection of Wordsworth's poems, which has appeared." A tribute to Wordsworth and to Reed's efforts on his behalf, this standard American edition remained in print into the 1870s. By the special request of the Wordsworth family, that same year Reed edited the American edition of the *Memoirs of William Wordsworth*. As was his custom, Reed bracketed his footnotes that included passages from Coleridge, Southey, and other authors on bibliographical and personal aspects of Wordsworth. F. C. Yarnall praised Reed's notes as "exceedingly interesting and valuable."

The final work under Reed's editorship also appeared in 1851, an elegant gift edition of the *Poetical Works of Thomas Gray*, bound in red leather with gold borders and illustrated with engravings from designs by C. W. Radclyffe of young Thomas Gray, Stoke Church, and the Eton playing fields. Reed added some endnotes of his own to several dozen by Gray and preceded the selection of poems with a 100 page "Memoir of the Life and Writings of Gray," a biography and critical assessment which Sara Coleridge praised. While lacking the intensity of the 1839 essay on Wordsworth, the study of Gray showed Reed's competence as a literary biographer and, together with the editorship of Mahon's history, suggested the directions of Reed's scholarship had he lived longer.

The strain of Reed's relentless editorial work after Wordsworth's death, along with his 1851 election to a three-year term on the Council of the American Philosophical Society, may have contributed to a severe, lingering illness that forced him temporarily to quit his university duties. Regaining his health, Reed accepted George Ticknor's counsel and became the American director of the program to raise funds for a memorial window to Wordsworth in the Ambleside church, under construction near the poet's home in Grasmere, England.

When the professorship of moral philosophy at the University of Pennsylvania became vacant in the spring of 1854, Reed applied for the chair but was not elected. His friends and family never saw him more depressed; Reed had, after all, failed to win reappointment in the same de-

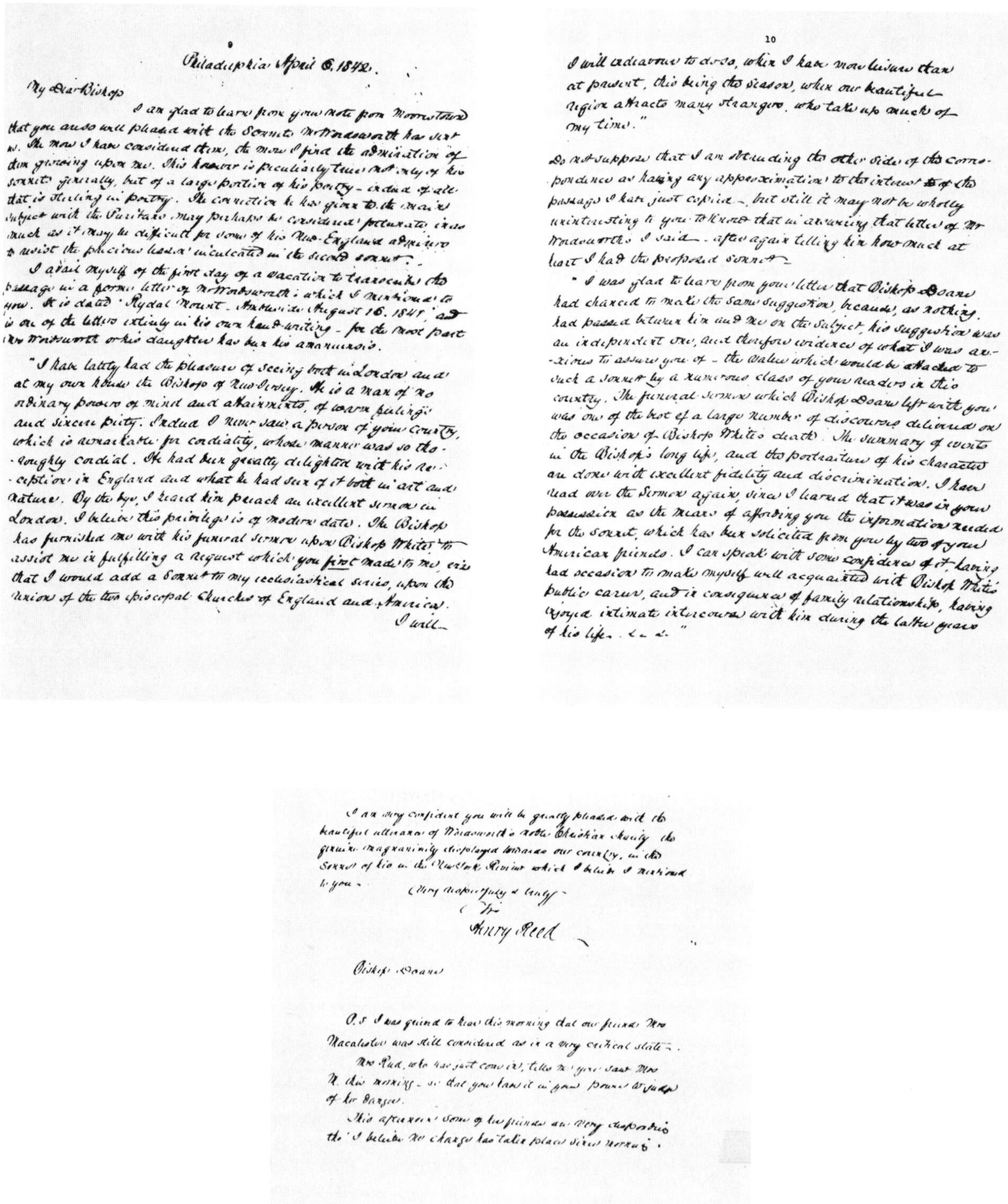

Philadelphia April 6. 1842.

My Dear Bishop

I am glad to learn from your note from Morristown that you are so well pleased with the Sonnets Mr Wordsworth has sent us. The more I have considered them, the more I find the admiration of them growing upon me. This however is peculiarly true not only of his sonnets generally, but of a large portion of his poetry – indeed of all that is sterling in poetry. The connection he has given to the main subject with the Puritans may perhaps be considered unfortunate, inasmuch as it may be difficult for some of his New-England admirers to resist the precious lesson inculcated in the second sonnet.

I avail myself of the first day of a vacation to transcribe the passage in a former letter of Mr Wordsworth which I mentioned to you. It is dated 'Rydal Mount – Ambleside August 16. 1841' and is one of the letters entirely in his own hand-writing – for the most part Mrs Wordsworth or his daughter has been his amanuensis.

"I have lately had the pleasure of seeing both in London and at my own house the Bishop of New-Jersey. He is a man of no ordinary powers of mind and attainments, of warm feelings and sincere piety. Indeed I never saw a person of your country, which is remarkable for cordiality, whose manner was so thoroughly cordial. He had been greatly delighted with his reception in England and what he had seen of it both in art and nature. By the bye, I heard him preach an excellent sermon in London. I believe this privilege is of modern date. The Bishop has furnished me with his funeral sermon upon Bishop White, to assist me in fulfilling a request which you *first* made to me, viz that I would add a Sonnet to my ecclesiastical series, upon the union of the two episcopal Churches of England and America.

I will

10

I will endeavour to do so, when I have more leisure than at present, this being the season, when our beautiful region attracts many strangers, who take up much of my time."

Do not suppose that I am obtruding the other side of the correspondence as having any approximation to the interest of the passage I have just copied – but still it may not be wholly uninteresting to you to know that in answering that letter of Mr Wordsworth's I said – after again telling him how much at heart I had the proposed sonnet –

"I was glad to learn from your letter that Bishop Doane had chanced to make the same suggestion, because, as nothing had passed between him and me on the subject, his suggestion was an independent one, and therefore evidence of what I was anxious to assure you of – the value which would be attached to such a sonnet by a numerous class of your readers in this country. The funeral sermon which Bishop Doane left with you was one of the best of a large number of discourses delivered on the occasion of Bishop White's death. The summary of events in the Bishop's long life, and the portraiture of his character are done with excellent fidelity and discrimination. I have read over the Sermon again, since I learned that it was in your possession as the means of affording you the information needed for the sonnet, which has been solicited from you by two of your American friends. I can speak with some confidence of it, having had occasion to make myself well acquainted with Bishop White's public career, and in consequence of family relationship, having enjoyed intimate intercourse with him during the latter years of his life. &c &c."

I am very confident you will be greatly pleased with the beautiful utterance of Wordsworth's noble Christian charity the genuine magnanimity displayed towards our country, in the Sonnet of his in the New York Review which I believe I mentioned to you.

Very respectfully & truly

Yrs

Henry Reed

Bishop Doane

P.S. I was grieved to hear this morning that our friend Mrs Macalester was still considered as in a very critical state.

Mrs Reed, who has just come in, tells me you saw Mrs M. this morning – so that you have it in your power to judge of her danger.

This afternoon some of her friends are very desponding tho' I believe no change has taken place since morning.

Letter to the Rt. Rev. George Washington Doane, Episcopal Bishop of New Jersey, in which Reed quotes at length from a letter he received from William Wordsworth (by permission of the Historical Society of Pennsylvania). Having promised Reed that he would include references to the American Episcopal Church in his Ecclesiastical Sonnets, Wordsworth had borrowed Doane's funeral sermon for Bishop William White, the first Anglican Bishop of Pennsylvania, for background. The sonnets Reed mentions in the first paragraph were the result.

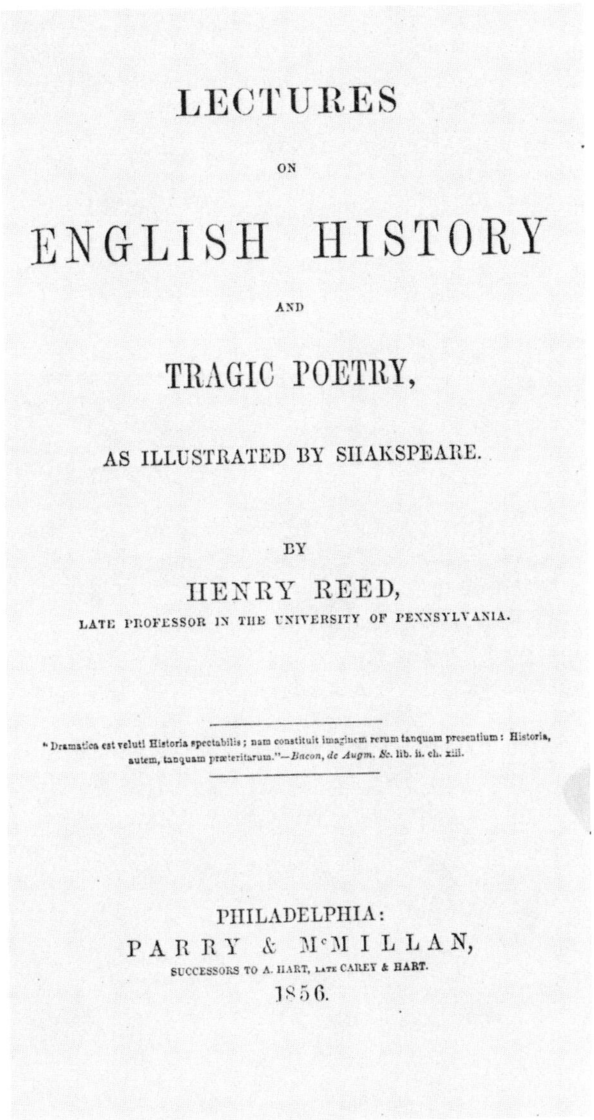

LECTURES

ON

ENGLISH HISTORY

AND

TRAGIC POETRY,

AS ILLUSTRATED BY SHAKSPEARE.

BY

HENRY REED,

LATE PROFESSOR IN THE UNIVERSITY OF PENNSYLVANIA.

"Dramatica est veluti Historia spectabilis; nam constituit imaginem rerum tanquam presentium: Historia, autem, tanquam præteritarum."—*Bacon, de Augm. Sc.* lib. ii. ch. xiii.

PHILADELPHIA:

PARRY & M^cMILLAN,

SUCCESSORS TO A. HART, LATE CAREY & HART.

1856.

Title page for the second posthumously published collection of Reed's writings: two series of lectures he had delivered in the 1840s

partment twenty years before. Deeply wounded, Reed asked for and received a leave of absence from the university for the purpose of visiting Europe. He arrived in Liverpool in mid May of 1854 and went almost immediately to the Lake District where Mary Wordsworth welcomed him as if he were a son. He attended the consecration of Ambleside church in June and saw the Wordsworth memorial window for which he had raised funds in America. In the Lake District he met the family of Robert Southey, and in London he met literary men with whom he had corresponded and others of note. His wanderings on the Continent extended as far as Venice, with a return cruise down the Rhine, and concluded with a final visit to Mary Wordsworth at Rydal Mount.

Reed sailed on the *Arctic* from Liverpool for New York, and seven days later, on 27 September, almost in sight of America, the vessel was struck by a steamer that did not stop. Within eight hours the *Arctic* sank, taking with it most of the passengers and crew. A survivor reported having seen Reed sitting with his sister-in-law two hours after the collision, "tranquil and silent, though their faces wore the look of painful anxiety." Reed's early death–he was only forty-six–occasioned profound grief on both sides of the Atlantic.

Convinced that his brother would have resumed his American duties with renewed energy, William Bradford Reed edited the manuscripts of Henry Reed's lectures and published them as a memorial. The first to appear, in 1855, was *Lectures on English Literature, from Chaucer to Tennyson,* covering poetry and prose, originally delivered in 1850. Its success persuaded William Bradford Reed to publish two series of lectures from the 1840s in a single volume: *Lectures on English History and Tragic Poetry, as Illustrated by Shakspeare* (1855), an interdisciplinary study of history through dramatic literature and Reed's treatment of the great tragedies. In 1857 William Bradford Reed published a two-volume edition of *Lectures on the British Poets,* the earliest lectures, given in 1841 on poetry from Chaucer to Wordsworth. All three posthumous editions were republished several times and remained in print into the late 1860s and 1870s; it was estimated that in America and Britain more than 26,000 copies of these three courses were sold.

In all his scholarship, as in his life, Henry Reed's religion was a conviction, according to his friend professor John F. Frazer, "beyond all mere logical demonstration; it was as clear as his belief in his own existence." Reed's abiding interest in Wordsworth was essentially religious, and his interpretation of the poet's works recalled the medieval practice of reading literature anagogically–that is, as a treatment of the soul's progress through this world to eternity. Reed acknowledged that literature was–like nature–one of the powers from which the human mind received "culture and discipline"; he warned, however, that treated in and of itself, literature posed the danger of "intellectual luxuriousness." He argued that the "higher education" of the world's greatest literature was "akin to religion, for it is a ministry of the soul."

While admired in his own time, Reed's moral and spiritual attitudes toward literature–and his embrace of the questionable doctrines of Sir Egerton Brydges–render Reed's scholarship of limited value to modern critics. Reed apparently dismissed Sara Coleridge's Neoplatonist interpretation of Wordsworth and her belief that his earlier poetry was superior in imaginative power to his later works–though on both counts modern critics have tended to accept her views over Reed's.

In the context of his age Reed can be understood as a spokesman for what Harry H. Clark called "non-transcendental . . . individualism or inwardness" which several American critics espoused in the 1830s and 1840s. Reed, like Emerson, was devoted to the Wordsworth of the "Immortality Ode" and shared an anti-Lockean gratitude for "obstinate questionings of sense and outward things." Unlike Emerson, however, Reed remained within the orthodoxy of the Christian faith and opposed what he disparaged as "Gallo-German Metaphysics–transcendentalism and pantheism."

Critics have differed widely in their assessments of Henry Reed. F. C. Yarnall acknowledged Reed's "pure and fine taste" and his rigorous scholarship but concluded in 1881 that, on the whole, Reed's treatment of Wordsworth was "too purely eulogistic" and lacked "proper discrimination." As Reed's editions began to drop from publication, he remained in obscurity until the 1920s when Esther Cloudman Dunn and Annabel Newton credited Reed with having been Wordsworth's foremost early disciple in America.

In the 1930s Leslie Nathan Broughton published the many letters that Reed and Wordsworth exchanged between 1836 and 1850. Broughton prefaced the letters with a glowing evaluation of Reed's accomplishments and character, concluding that Reed's knowledge and estimation of Wordsworth were "more than a generation in advance of his time." As another sign of his estimate of Reed's importance, Broughton published the letters of Sara Coleridge to Reed. Both volumes spawned some brief and mildly favorable reviews as well as articles on Wordsworth's financial anxieties. In 1960, however, E. D. Mackerness questioned Reed's motives and claimed that the young American had "designs" on the "good nature" of the septuagenarian poet. Whatever worldly ambitions Reed may have had, the sincerity of his enthusiasm for Wordsworth's poetry can be validated by his own published scholarship. Moreover, the respect he earned through his editorial work and his correspondence with many British literary men and women of his age–including the preeminent poet–confirms Henry Reed's importance in nineteenth-century Anglo-American relations.

Letters:

Wordsworth and Reed: The Poet's Correspondence with His American Editor: 1836-1850, and Henry Reed's Account of His Reception at Rydal Mount, London, and Elsewhere, in 1854, Cornell Studies in English, volume 21, edited by Leslie Nathan Broughton (Ithaca, N.Y.: Cornell University Press/London: H. Milford, Oxford University Press, 1933).

References:

Jack C. Barnes, "A Bibliography of Wordsworth in American Periodicals Through 1825," *Papers of the Bibliographical Society of America*, 52 (Third Quarter 1958): 205-219;

Leslie Nathan Broughton, ed., *Sara Coleridge and Henry Reed* (Ithaca, N.Y.: Cornell University Press/London: Humphrey Milford, Oxford University Press, 1937);

Kenneth Walter Cameron, "Wordsworth and Bishop Doane: New Evidence," *Emerson Society Quarterly*, no. 23 (Second Quarter 1961): 6-12;

Joshua L. Chamberlain, ed., *Universities and Their Sons: University of Pennsylvania*, volume 1 (Boston: R. Herndon, 1901), pp. 318-319;

Harry H. Clark, "Changing Attitudes in Early American Literary Criticism: 1800-1840," in *The Development of American Literary Criticism*, edited by Floyd Stovall (Chapel Hill: University of North Carolina Press, 1955), pp. 15-73;

Esther Cloudman Dunn, "Correspondence: Notes on Wordsworth," *Modern Language Notes*, 38 (April 1923): 246-247;
(April 1923): 246-247;

Dunn, "Inman's Portrait of Wordsworth," *Scribner's Magazine*, 67 (February 1920): 251-256;

Dunn, "A Retrospective of Rydal Mount," *Scribner's Magazine*, 69 (May 1921): 549-555;

John Fries Frazer, obituary notice for Reed, *Proceedings of the American Philosophical Society*, 6

(January-April 1855): 87-91;

Claude Gilkyson, "Henry Reed, 1825. Wordsworth's American Editor," [University of Pennsylvania] *General Magazine and Historical Chronicle* 38 (1936);

George Gordon Hart, "Henry Reed: An Author of a Past Generation," *Magazine of Western History,* 10 (May 1889): 16-19;

E. D. Mackerness, "Wordsworth and His American Editor," *Queen's Quarterly,* 67 (Spring 1960): 93-104;

Annabel Newton, *Wordsworth in Early American Criticism* (Chicago: University of Chicago Press, 1928);

Abbie Findlay Potts, *The Ecclesiastical Sonnets of William Wordsworth* (New Haven: Yale University Press/London: Humphrey Milford, Oxford University Press, 1922);

"Professor Henry Reed," *Living Age,* 43 (December 1854): 421-422;

"Professor Reed's Lecture: 'A Lecture on the Literary Opportunities of Men of Business,'" *New York Review,* 3 (July 1838): 247;

William Bradford Reed, *Life and Correspondence of Joseph Reed,* 2 volumes (Philadelphia: Lindsay & Blakiston, 1847);

Reed, *The Life of Esther De Berdt, Afterwards Esther Reed, of Pennsylvania* (Philadelphia: C. Sherman, 1853);

Buford Rowland, "William Wordsworth and Mississippi Bonds," *Journal of Southern History,* 1 (November 1935): 501-507;

Rowland, "William Wordsworth and Pennsylvania State Bonds," *Pennsylvania Magazine of History and Biography,* 59 (July 1935): 301-303;

"Wordsworth and Reed," *Times Literary Supplement* (14 September 1933): 606;

Ellis Yarnall, "Henry Reed, LL.D.," *Alumni Register: University of Pennsylvania,* 5 (May 1901): 257-265;

Yarnall, *Wordsworth and the Coleridges: With Other Memories Literary and Political* (New York: Macmillan/London: Macmillan, 1899);

F. C. Yarnall, "Letter from F. C. Yarnall on Wordsworth's Influence in America," *Transactions of the Wordsworth Society,* 5 (1883): 81-92.

Papers:

The chief collection of Reed's correspondence is in the Cornell University Library in Ithaca, New York. Deposited there are forty-six letters or drafts from Reed to William Wordsworth, written during 1836-1849; original manuscripts of eighteen letters from William Wordsworth to Reed; and other correspondence. Most letters are summarized in *The Wordsworth Collection,* compiled by Leslie Nathan Broughton (Ithaca, N.Y.: Cornell University Library, 1931); the letters are catalogued in *The Cornell Wordsworth Collection,* compiled by George Harris Healey (Ithaca, N.Y.: Cornell University Press, 1957). At the University of Pennsylvania the Rare Books Collection of the Charles Patterson Van Pelt Library holds scattered correspondence and manuscripts of Reed's lectures on English literature and history in quarto-sized bound volumes. Significant collections of Reed's editions also exist in the libraries at Cornell and the University of Pennsylvania.

Therese Robinson (Talvj or Talvi)

(26 January 1797-13 April 1870)

Thomas Haeussler
University of California, Los Angeles

BOOKS: *Psyche, ein Taschenbuch für das Jahr 1825: Drei Erzählungen* (Halle: Ruff, 1825);

Versuch einer geschichtlichen Charakteristik der Volkslieder germanischer Nationen mit einer Uebersicht der Lieder aussereuropäischer Völkerschaften (Leipzig: Brockhaus, 1840);

Die Unächtheit der Lieder Ossian's und des Macpherson'schen Ossian's insbesondere (Leipzig: Brockhaus, 1840);

Aus der Geschichte der ersten Ansiedlungen in den Vereinigten Staaten (Leipzig: Brockhaus, 1845);

Geschichte der Colonisation von Neu-England: Von der ersten Niederlassung daselbst im Jahre 1607 bis zur Einführung der Provincialverfassung von Massachusetts im Jahre 1692 (Leipzig: Brockhaus, 1847); translated as *Talvi's History of the Colonization of America*, edited by William Hazlitt (London: Newby, 1851);

Heloise, or The Unrevealed Secret: A Tale (New York: D. Appleton/Philadelphia: G. S. Appleton, 1850); translated as *Heloise* (Leipzig: Brockhaus, 1852);

Historical View of the Languages and Literatures of the Slavic Nations; With a Sketch of Their Popular Poetry (New York: Putnam's, 1850); translated by B. K. Brühl as *Uebersichtliches Handbuch einer Geschichte der slavischen Sprachen und Literatur; Nebst einer Skizze ihrer Volks-poesie* (Leipzig: Geibel, 1852);

Life's Discipline: A Tale of the Annals of Hungary (New York: D. Appleton/Philadelphia: G. S. Appleton, 1851); translated by E. M. Drugulin as *Marie Barcoczy: Historischer Roman von Talvi* (Grimma & Leipzig: Verlags-Comptoir, 1852);

Die Auswanderer: Eine Erzählung von Talvj (Leipzig: Brockhaus, 1852); translated as *The Exiles: A Tale* (New York: Putnam's, 1853); republished as *Woodhill: or, The Ways of Providence* (New York: De Witt & Davenport, 1856);

Fünfzehn Jahre (Leipzig: Brockhaus, 1868); translated as *Fifteen Years: A Picture From the Last Century* (New York: Appleton, 1871).

Collection: *Gesammelte Novellen, Nebst einer Auswahl bisher ungedruckte Gedichte und einer Biographie*, edited by Mary Robinson (Leipzig: Brockhaus, 1874).

OTHER: Walter Scott, *Black Dwarf*, translated by Robinson as Ernst Berthold, in *Taschenbibliothek der ausländischen Klassiker*, volumes 8-11 (Zwittau: Schumann, 1821);

Walter Scott, *Old Mortality*, translated by Robinson as Ernst Berthold, in *Taschenbibliothek der ausländischen Klassiker*, volumes 38-41 (Zwittau: Schumann, 1821);

Volkslieder der Serben, 2 volumes, translated, with introduction, by Robinson as Talvj (Halle: Renger, 1825-1826);

John Pickering, *Ueber die indianischen Sprachen Amerikas*, translated, with commentary, by Robinson as Talvj (Leipzig: Vogel, 1834).

PERIODICAL PUBLICATIONS: "Historical View of the Slavic Languages," *Biblical Repository and Classical Review*, 4 (April 1834): 328-413; 4 (July 1834): 417-532;

"Deutschlands Schriftstellerinnen bis vor 100 Jahren," *Raumers Historisches Taschenbuch*, 32 (1861): 1-141.

Therese Robinson, better known to her contemporaries under the pseudonym "Talvj" or "Talvi," deserves to be recognized as one of the most significant women intellectuals of the nineteenth century. Her achievement as a translator, philologist, folklorist, ethnologist, historian, social critic, and novelist was of prodigious diversity and sustained excellence. Of particular note were her contributions, now inexplicably neglected, to the collateral yet heterogeneous disciplines of *Volkskunde* (folklore) and *Völkerkunde* (ethnography). Her translations of Serbian folk songs–

acclaimed by Goethe as worthy, in certain instances, of comparison with the "Song of Songs" *(Gespräche mit Eckermann,* 18 January 1825)–surveys of Germanic and Slavic folk histories, and monographs concerning such issues as the authenticity of the Ossianic lays both engaged and appreciably extended the tradition in folk studies established in the mid-eighteenth century by James Macpherson and Thomas Percy, and associated thereafter with such names as Johann Gottfried Herder, Clemens Brentano, Achim von Arnim, Ludwig Uhland, and the brothers Jacob and Wilhelm Grimm. Robinson, no less than the aforementioned, ought properly to be credited with having helped define the field of comparative folk literature and provide it an increasingly "scientific" methodology. That a scholar of her accomplishment should instead receive only marginal attention within the academy raises a question concerning the patriarchal formation of critical canons which is of some historical and literary interest.

The future Therese Robinson–christened Therese Albertine Louise von Jacob (her pseudonym is an acronym of her maiden name)–was born on 26 January 1797 in Halle, Prussian Saxony. As the daughter of Ludwig Heinrich von Jacob, professor of philosophy at the University of Halle, she was accorded an education, informal though it may have been, which was superior to that commonly received by women in her century. She was nine years old when, in 1806, following the battle of Jena and the ensuing French occupation of Prussia, her father moved their family to Kharkov, Russia, where he had been called to teach at the newly established university. Over the course of her ten-year residence in that "strange, half-Asiatic, half-European circumstance," Robinson of necessity mastered the Slavic languages, and in so doing found revealed before her a folk culture of unimagined richness and elemental purity. Her childhood experience of the horse traders exchanging songs and stories in the marketplace at Kharkov would mark the onset of what proved an abiding fascination with folk literature and history. Upon her family's return to Halle in 1816, she continued to evince an extraordinary aptitude for assimilating foreign languages: she was, at that time, fluent not only in the Slavic languages, but in Greek, Latin, French, Spanish, the Scandinavian languages, Anglo-Saxon, and modern English as well. Her linguistic prodigy was of such dimension that the intellectual circle at Halle accounted her *ein kleines Orakel* ("a little oracle"). Robinson's literary career began modestly enough, in 1820, with the appearance in *Theodor Hells Abendzeitung* of a small number of poems, signed "Reseda." There quickly followed translations, as "Ernst Berthold," of Walter Scott's *Black Dwarf* (1821) and *Old Mortality* (1821) (reputedly dispatched for the sake of a little "pin money"), and an anonymous sequence of literary notes and reviews in the *Literarische Conversationsblatt* entitled "Briefe eines Frauenzimmers über einige neue Erscheinungen der Literatur" (1822).

It was during that same period of literary awakening that Robinson, having chanced upon Jacob Grimm's critical reflections on Serbian folk literature and been inspired thereby to learn the Serbian language, undertook to translate Wuk Stephanovitsch Karadshitsch's four-volume collection of Serbian folk songs. The published two-volume translation, *Volkslieder der Serben* (1825-1826) (a third volume was projected though never completed), was an immediate critical success and at once established "Herr Talvj," as she now was generally known, as among the leading folklorists of her day. An enthusiastic German public–among whom were numbered Goethe, Jacob Grimm, Franz Grillparzer, and Alexander and Wilhelm von Humboldt–declared her work an estimable extension of Herder's folkloric legacy. Goethe, in "rejoic[ing] over our powerful young woman from Halle, who with masculine strength of mind [has introduced] us to the Serbian world," went so far as to proclaim her Serbian songs one of the three most important contributions ever made by foreign sources to German poetry. *Volkslieder der Serben,* following a prefatory survey of Serbian folk history, provided in generous measure, and for the first time in a western European language, representative samples of the two primary Serbian poetic genres, namely, the epic *Yunatchke pjesme* ("heroic" or "young men's songs") and the romantic or domestic *shenske pjesme* ("female songs"). Although Robinson's translations were subject to minor criticisms, notably Jacob Grimm's complaint–contested by Goethe–that they were a bit too free, flexible, and "germanized," the greater reception reflected in its appreciation the then-prevalent conviction that it was only in the Slavic nations, and particularly among the Serbians and Dalmatians, that "the living flower [of folk poetry was] still to be found, growing in its native luxuriance." *Volkslieder der Serben* thus was regarded as having provided folk studies a resource of incalculable consequence.

As much as he esteemed her scholarship, Goethe came to appreciate to an equal degree the unique combination of personal and intellectual qualities which permitted Robinson, seemingly alone among the women of her generation, to successfully pursue a career in letters despite the social pressures placed upon her to surrender such activity to the exigencies of marriage and family. Such approbation was not universally shared by his male colleagues, some of whom questioned (in the 1820s!) the scholarly merit of work written in the vernacular rather than Latin. Nor, ironically, did the women of Halle approve of Robinson's vaulting intellectual ascent beyond her "proper" station. They complained that "one could hear the sharp scratching of her pen throughout the city–a pen held in the hand of an unmarried young woman not yet thirty, upon whom was lavished the praise of famous men." Robinson could hardly be indifferent to such calumny, and it doubtless accounts for her insistence, following the creation of a pseudonymous alter ego, on segregating "all that which concerned Therese Robinson, formerly Therese von Jacob, entirely from Talvj." It also helps explain the relative ease with which, following her marriage in 1828 to the eminent American Orientalist and theologian Edward Robinson, she was able, at the conclusion of a two-year tour of Europe, to exchange her residence in Halle for a new life in America.

The Robinsons initially settled in Andover, Massachusetts, where Edward Robinson occupied a chair in biblical literature at Andover Seminary. Therese Robinson's first years in America were largely given over to her husband's theological research, for which she provided invaluable linguistic assistance and often served as an anonymous German translator. Following their move to Boston in 1833, she once more turned her attention to folk studies and–publishing in her husband's journal, the *Biblical Repository and Classical Review*, as well as such popular magazines as the *North American Review*–quickly established herself as a leading "American" authority in the field. Essays such as "Historical View of the Slavic Languages" (1834) and "Popular Poetry of the Teutonic Nations" (1836), both of which presented *in nuce* material which would subsequently be developed at length in major treatises, sought not only to introduce an American audience to "exotic" literary

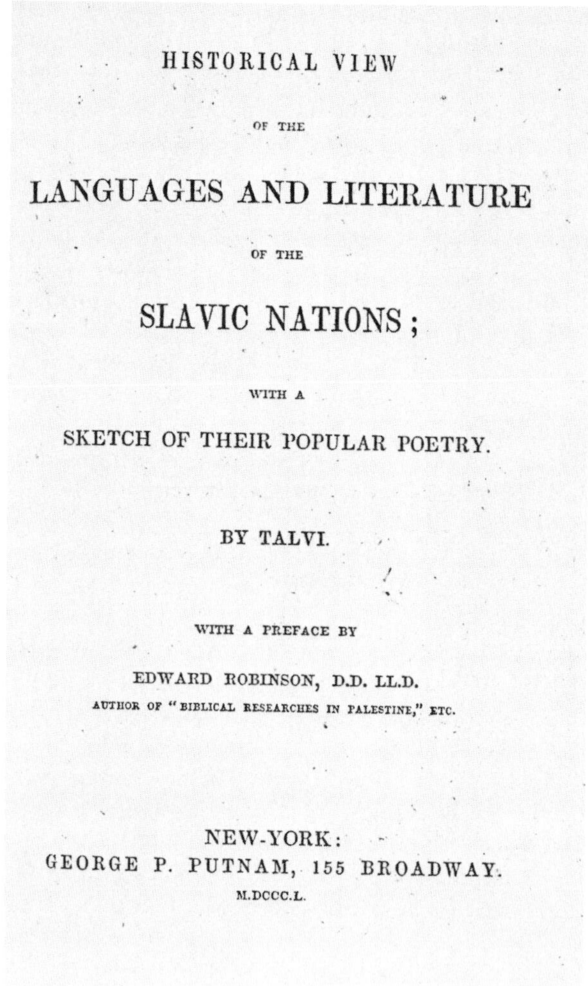

HISTORICAL VIEW

OF THE

LANGUAGES AND LITERATURE

OF THE

SLAVIC NATIONS;

WITH A

SKETCH OF THEIR POPULAR POETRY.

BY TALVI.

WITH A PREFACE BY

EDWARD ROBINSON, D.D. LL.D.

AUTHOR OF "BIBLICAL RESEARCHES IN PALESTINE," ETC.

NEW-YORK:

GEORGE P. PUTNAM, 155 BROADWAY.

M.DCCC.L.

Title page for the book that introduced Slavic folk literature to English-speaking readers

sources but also to acquaint it with contemporary European folkloric practices and concerns. American scholars had heretofore demonstrated little interest either in folklore or ethnology, not even as they pertained to the American Indian. "Strange," Pierre Etienne (Peter Stephen) DuPonceau commented in this regard, "that we should have to go to German universities to become acquainted with our own country." Certainly Robinson's translation of John Pickering's *Ueber die indianischen Sprachen Amerikas* (1834) bespoke a profound German interest in "primitive" societies across the world. And in a critical commentary appended to that work, she addressed not only such hermeneutic and textual issues as the symbolic constitution of Indian songs and legends, and the orthographic confusion wrought by grammarians of the Indian languages, but also the problem of American cultural chauvinism, manifested here in the persistent denigration of the Indian as "savage" and "barbaric" (and elsewhere in the brutal oppression of African slaves).

The late 1830s found Robinson once again residing in Germany, as her husband traveled throughout the Middle East accumulating material for his acclaimed *Biblical Researches in Palestine and the Adjacent Countries* (1841). Over a three-year period (1837-1840) she produced the two works which, together with *Volkslieder der Serben*, constituted her most distinguished contribution to the field of folkloric and ethnological studies. *Versuch einer geschichtlichen Charakteristik der Volkslieder germanischer Nationen mit einer Uebersicht der Lieder aussereuropäischer Völkerschaften* (1840) was a work of universal dimension, surveying not only the Germanic folk tradition but, by way of prolegomenon, that of the African, Asian, Malaysian, and American Indian nations as well. Here as throughout her oeuvre, while she sought to delineate the historical and cultural circumstance out of which each respective folk literature evolved, Robinson's controlling preoccupation was with "*the history of the language* . . . , not the history of the people." For she believed, following Hamann and Herder, that language alone–particularly the language, yet sensual, pictorial, and ingenuous, of "primitive" societies–possessed a revelatory capacity such as could make manifest the primordial nature of the human being. And while *Charakteristik der Volkslieder* espouses a philosophy of "primitive" languages and literature which is clearly derivative of Herder's seminal analyses and original only in its application to folk traditions heretofore unexamined, its effort to achieve a more precise definition of folkloric concepts and practices was recognized by critics such as Varnhagen von Ense as representing an important scholarly advancement and elevation beyond Herder. Robinson herself, in *Die Unächtheit der Lieder Ossian's und des Macpherson'schen Ossian's insbesondere* (1840), a work which might be regarded as a practical illustration of those doctrinal principles set out in *Charakteristik der Volkslieder*, demonstrated the efficacy of a newly rigorous philological, historical, and comparative methodology in definitively disaffirming the authenticity of the Ossianic lays. Concentrating on such linguistic inconsistencies as Macpherson's utilization of modern (as opposed to third-century) Gaelic and an overly subtle and sublime diction, and such historical and thematic incongruities as the introduction of medieval castles to ancient Ireland and the absence of customary religious references, she established irrefutably that the author of the lays was of a modern, not "primitive," epoch, and that the Ossianic legacy was thus inauthentic.

Upon returning to America in 1840, the Robinsons relocated in New York, where Edward Robinson assumed a chair in theology at the Union Theological Seminary. Their home soon established itself as a gathering place for European and American artists and intellectuals. A visit, in 1844, from the German historian Friedrich von Raumer was of special consequence inasmuch as it persuaded Therese Robinson to undertake a series of historical, cultural, and geographic studies of America. Of these none were of greater significance than her two book-length studies of the American colonial experience, *Aus der Geschichte der ersten Ansiedlungen in den Vereinigten Staaten* (1845) and *Geschichte der Colonisation von Neu-England* (1847), both of which were initially written to introduce a German audience to early American history, yet ultimately gained an international reputation as important and original supplements to existing histories of the period. Robinson's historical perspective was detached and objective, providing a rigorous and systematic interpretation of authoritative accounts and sources, some of which had never before been employed by American historians. Furthermore, in arguing that American democratic tendencies were less the product of Puritanism or the Enlightenment than of a unique frontier experience, she would seem to have anticipated, however inconclusively, Frederick Jackson Turner's famous thesis concerning the evolution of American society.

With the publication of *Historical View of the Languages and Literatures of the Slavic Nations* (1850), Robinson returned to folk studies and the research area of her greatest expertise; it would prove her last lengthy undertaking in that discipline. Although the work had an unexpected popular appeal, and was acclaimed by one American reviewer as a "work of which we ought to be proud, as the production of one of the adopted daughters of our country, who, having acquired a reputation among the authors of her native literature, now became engaged in adding to the riches of ours," the author herself regarded its comprehensive yet necessarily superficial survey of eastern (Russian, Illyrico-Serbian, Croatian,

Vindish, Bulgarian) and western (Bohemian, Slovak, Polish, Sorabian-Vendish) Slavic folk histories, mythologies, languages, and folklore to be little more than an outline, noteworthy largely insofar as it provided an English-speaking audience with a first introduction to the last extant European folk literature. She would not attempt–apart from a brief essay on "Die Kosaken und ihrer historischen Lieder" (1869) written following her repatriation to Germany in 1863, upon the death of her husband–to further develop such materials and concepts as were there presented in protomorphic delineation; that was to remain for succeeding generations.

Robinson determined instead, quite unaccountably, to devote the remainder of her life to writing popular fiction and social criticism. And while her novels–foremost among which were *Heloise, or The Unrevealed Secret* (1850) and *Die Auswanderer* (1852; translated as *The Exiles*, 1853)–were of a rather conventional literary nature, featuring scenes of romantic introspection and difficult or mistaken destinies ultimately remedied through fortuitous circumstance, they provided, as critics have recently noted, a perceptive and prescient commentary on such contemporary social and moral issues as racial prejudice and oppression, democratic materialism and class division, and the historical subordination of women in western societies. Her quiet though penetrating consideration of the latter issue–formally examined in a lengthy cultural study, "Deutschlands Schriftstellerinnen bis vor 100 Jahren" (1861), which perhaps deserves recognition as a substantial early feminist critique–would seem of particular interest to contemporary women's studies. Yet the critical reception of Therese Robinson, which since her death on 13 April 1870 has been of inappropriately reduced dimension, ought not be further limited to such specialized interest. She was among the most accomplished folklorists of her day, contributing to that discipline's collection of source materials and providing it an example of an increasingly scholarly practice, and it is largely as such that she deserves an enduring place within the critical canon.

References:

Albert Bernhardt Faust, *The German Element in the United States With Special Reference to its Political, Moral, Social, and Educational Influence* (Boston: Houghton Mifflin, 1909);

Guy Hollyday, *Anti-Americanism in the German Novel, 1841-1862* (Berne & Las Vegas: P. Lang, 1977);

Franz von Löher, *Beiträge zur Geschichte und Völkerkunde*, 2 volumes (Frankfurt am Main: Rütten & Loening, 1885-1886);

Löher, *Geschichte und Zustände der Deutschen in Amerika* (Cincinnati: Eggers & Wulkop, 1847);

Löher, "Talvj, ein deutsches Frauenleben," *Augsburger Allgemeine Zeitung*, 9-10 June 1870;

Irma Elizabeth Voigt, "The Life and Works of Mrs. Therese Robinson," Ph.D. dissertation, University of Illinois, 1913;

Martha Kaarsberg Wallach, "Women of German-American Fiction: Therese Robinson, Mathilde Anneke, and Fernande Richter," in *America and the Germans: An Assessment of A Three-Hundred-Year History*, edited by Frank Trommler and Joseph McVeigh, volume 1 (Philadelphia: University of Pennsylvania Press, 1985), pp. 331-342.

William Gilmore Simms

(17 April 1806-11 June 1870)

Miriam J. Shillingsburg
Mississippi State University

See also the Simms entries in *DLB 3, Antebellum Writers in New York and the South* and *DLB 30, American Historians, 1607-1865.*

SELECTED BOOKS: *Monody, on the Death of Gen. Charles Cotesworth Pinckney,* anonymous (Charleston: Gray & Ellis, 1825);

Lyrical and Other Poems (Charleston: Ellis & Neufville, 1827);

Early Lays (Charleston: A. E. Miller, 1827);

The Vision of Cortes, Cain, and Other Poems (Charleston: James S. Burges, 1829);

The Tri-Color; or The Three Days of Blood, in Paris. With Some Other Pieces (London? [probably actually printed in Charleston]: Wigfall & Davis, 1830);

Atlantis. A Story of the Sea (New York: J. & J. Harper, 1832; enlarged, Philadelphia: Carey & Hart, 1848);

Martin Faber; The Story of a Criminal (New York: J. & J. Harper, 1833; London: J. Clements, 1838 or 1839);

The Book of My Lady. A Melange, anonymous (Philadelphia: Key & Biddle, 1833; Boston: Allen & Ticknor, 1833);

Guy Rivers. A Tale of Georgia, 2 volumes (New York: Harper, 1834; London: J. Clements, 1841);

The Yemassee. A Romance of Carolina, 2 volumes (New York: Harper, 1835; London: N. Bruce, 1842);

The Partisan: A Tale of the Revolution, 2 volumes (New York: Harper, 1835);

Mellichampe. A Legend of the Santee, 2 volumes (New York: Harper, 1836);

Martin Faber, The Story of a Criminal; and Other Tales (New York: Harper, 1837);

Slavery in America, Being a Brief Review of Miss Martineau on that Subject, anonymous (Richmond: Thomas W. White, 1838);

Richard Hurdis; Or, The Avenger of Blood. A Tale of Alabama, 2 volumes (Philadelphia: E. L. Carey & A. Hart, 1838);

Pelayo: A Story of the Goth, 2 volumes (New York: Harper, 1838);

Carl Werner, An Imaginative Story; With Other Tales of the Imagination, 2 volumes (New York: George Adlard, 1838); republished as *Young Ladies' Book of Romantic Tales* (Boston: E. Littlefield, 1839);

The Damsel of Darien, 2 volumes (Philadelphia: Lea & Blanchard, 1839; London: N. Bruce, 1843);

Southern Passages and Pictures (New York: George Adlard, 1839);

The History of South Carolina, from its First European Discovery to its Erection into a Republic: With a Supplementary Chronicle of Events to the Present Time (Charleston: S. Babcock, 1840; revised, 1842; revised again, Charleston: Russell & Jones/New York: Redfield, 1860);

Border Beagles; A Tale of Mississippi (Philadelphia: Carey & Hart, 1840);

The Kinsmen: Or The Black Riders of Congaree, 2 volumes (Philadelphia: Lea & Blanchard, 1841; London: John Cunningham, 1841); republished as *The Scout or The Black Riders of Congaree* (New York: Redfield, 1854);

Confession; Or, The Blind Heart. A Domestic Story, 2 volumes (Philadelphia: Lea & Blanchard, 1841; London: J. Cunningham, 1841);

Beauchampe: Or, The Kentucky Tragedy. A Tale of Passion, 2 volumes (Philadelphia: Lea & Blanchard, 1842; London: N. Bruce, 1842); volume 1 revised as *Charlemont or The Pride of the Village. A Tale of Kentucky* (New York: Redfield, 1856); volume 2 revised as *Beauchampe or The Kentucky Tragedy. A Sequel to Charlemont* (New York: Redfield, 1856);

The Social Principle: The True Source of National Permanence. An Oration Delivered Before the Erosophic Society of the University of Alabama, at its Twelfth Anniversary, December 13, 1842 (Tuscaloosa: The Society, 1843);

Donna Florida: A Tale (Charleston: Burges & James, 1843);

William Gilmore Simms, portrait by an unknown artist (reproduced by permission of the University of South Carolina Press from The Letters of William Gilmore Simms, volume III: 1850-1857, *edited by Mary C. Simms Oliphant and T. C. Duncan Eaves, 1954)*

The Sources of American Independence. An Oration, on the Sixty-ninth Anniversary of American Independence; Delivered at Aiken South-Carolina, Before the Town Council and Citizens Thereof (Aiken: Town Council, 1844);

The Life of Francis Marion (New York: Henry G. Langley, 1844);

Castle Dismal: or, The Bachelor's Christmas. A Domestic Legend (New York: Burgess, Stringer, 1844);

Helen Halsey: Or, The Swamp State of Conelachita. A Tale of the Borders (New York: Burgess, Stringer, 1845);

The Wigwam and the Cabin, first and second series (New York: Wiley & Putnam, 1845; London: Wiley & Putnam, 1846); first series enlarged as *Life in America* (Aberdeen, Scotland: George Clark, 1848);

Count Julian; Or, the Last Days of the Goth. A Historical Romance (Baltimore & New York: William Taylor, 1845; London: Bruce & Wyld, 1846);

Views and Reviews in American Literature, History and Fiction, first series (New York: Wiley & Putnam, 1845; London: Wiley & Putnam, 1846);

Views and Reviews in American Literature, History and Fiction, second series (New York: Wiley & Putnam, 1845; London: Wiley & Putnam, 1846);

Areytos: Or, Songs of the South (Charleston: John Russell, 1846);

The Life of Captain John Smith, the Founder of Virginia (New York: Geo. F. Cooledge, 1846);

The Life of Chevalier Bayard; "The Good Knight," "sans peur et sans reproche" (New York: Harper, 1847);

The Cassique of Accabee. A Tale of the Ashley River. With Other Pieces (Charleston: John Russell, 1849; New York: Harper, 1849);

Father Abbot, Or, the Home Tourist; A Medley (Charleston: Miller & Browne, 1849);

The Life of Nathanael Greene, Major-General in the Army of the Revolution (New York: George F. Cooledge, 1849);

Sabbath Lyrics; Or, Songs from Scripture (Charleston: Walker & James, 1849);

The Lily and the Totem, Or The Huguenots in Florida. A Series of Sketches, Picturesque and Historical, of the Colonies of Coligni, in North America (New York: Baker & Scribner, 1850);

Katharine Walton: Or, The Rebel of Dorchester. An Historical Romance of the Revolution in Carolina (Philadelphia: A. Hart, 1851);

The Golden Christmas: A Chronicle of St. John's, Berkeley. Compiled from the Notes of a Briefless Barrister (Charleston: Walker, Richards, 1852);

The Sword and the Distaff; Or, "Fair, Fat and Forty," A Story of the South at the Close of the Revolution (Charleston: Walker, Richards, 1852); republished as *Woodcraft; or, Hawks About the Dovecote* (New York: Redfield, 1854);

As Good as a Comedy: Or, The Tennessean's Story, anonymous (Philadelphia: A. Hart, 1852);

South-Carolina in the Revolutionary War: Being a Reply to Certain Misrepresentations and Mistakes of Recent Writers, in Relation to the Course and Conduct of this State, anonymous (Charleston: Walker & James, 1853);

Marie de Berniere: A Tale of the Crescent City, Etc. Etc. Etc. (Philadelphia: Lippincott, Grambo, 1853); republished as *The Maroon: A Legend of the Caribbees, and Other Tales* (Philadelphia: Lippincott, Grambo, 1855);

Egeria: Or, Voices of Thought and Counsel, for the Woods and Wayside (Philadelphia: E. H. Butler, 1853);

Vasconcelos. A Romance of the New World, as Frank Cooper (New York: Redfield, 1853);

Southward Ho! A Spell of Sunshine (New York: Redfield, 1854);

The Forayers or The Raid of the Dog-Days (New York: Redfield, 1855);

Eutaw. A Sequel to the Forayers (New York: Redfield, 1856);

The Cassique of Kiawah. A Colonial Romance (New York: Redfield, 1859);

Simms's Poems (Charleston: Russell & Jones, 1860);

The Sense of the Beautiful. An Address, Delivered by W. Gilmore Simms, Before the Charleston County Agricultural and Horticultural Association . . . , May 3, 1870 (Charleston: The Society, 1870);

Voltmeier or the Mountain Men, edited by James B. Meriwether (Columbia: University of South Carolina Press, 1969);

As Good as Comedy: Or The Tennessean's Story and *Paddy McGann; Or, The Demon of the Stump,* edited by Meriwether (Columbia: University of South Carolina Press, 1972);

Stories and Tales, edited by John Caldwell Guilds (Columbia: University of South Carolina Press, 1974);

Jocelyn: A Tale of the Revolution, edited by Keen Butterworth (Columbia: University of South Carolina Press, 1975).

OTHER: *The Charleston Book. A Miscellany in Prose and Verse,* edited by Simms (Charleston: Samuel Hart, 1845);

A Supplement to the Plays of William Shakspeare: Comprising The Seven Dramas, edited by Simms (New York: George F. Coolege & Brother, 1848).

PERIODICAL PUBLICATIONS: "American Criticism and Critics," *Southern Literary Journal,* 2 (July 1836): 393-400;

"Bulwer's Genius and Writings," *Magnolia,* new series 1 (December 1842): 329-345;

"The Writings of Washington Allston," *Southern Quarterly Review,* 3 (October 1843): 363-414;

"International Copyright Law," *Southern Literary Messenger,* 10 (January 1844): 7-17; 10 (March 1844): 137-151; 10 (June 1844): 340-349; 10 (August 1844): 449-469;

"The Moral Character of Hamlet," *Orion,* 4 (March 1844): 41-51; 4 (April 1844): 76-89; 4 (May 1844): 105-119; 4 (June 1844): 179-194;

Review of "A New Spirit of the Age," edited by R. H. Horne, *Southern Quarterly Review,* 7 (April 1845): 312-349; 15 (April 1849): 41-83;

"Recent American Poets," *Southern Quarterly Review,* 16 (October 1849): 224-232;

"Sentimental Prose Fiction," *Southern Quarterly Review,* new series 1 (July 1850): 355-369;

Benedict Arnold: The Traitor. A Dramatic Essay, Magnolia Weekly, 1 (May-August 1863).

Although William Gilmore Simms is best known as a novelist, his total literary production is notable in all genres, if not always for its quality, certainly for its quantity. Recently scholars have begun to study Simms's poetry and short stories, but they have largely overlooked his literary and social theory and criticism. In part this is because Simms collected his essays only one time (1845) and that in midcareer. Even though he is not especially original in his criticism, a characteristic he shared with many better-known critics of his generation, he deserves a closer look for his prolific, consistent, and widely respected statements on literature as it reflects society.

Simms's best work as a literary critic, editor, and reviewer is supported by voracious reading from all periods in several languages. He was the author of extensive writings in other genres as well: drama, history, biography, and letters, in addition to essays, lectures, and reviews. He wrote psychological, melodramatic, historic, and humorous fiction as well as narrative, lyric, and dramatic poetry and blank verse dramas. His position as editor of several newspapers and literary magazines, including half a dozen years on the *Southern Quarterly Review,* made him a figure to be taken seriously in American, and more particularly in southern, literature from about 1835 until his death in 1870. As a critic he was thoughtful and fair, seldom letting prejudice skew his vision; yet he was frank in expressing his personal preference for bold action, imagination, invention, and inspiration over what he considered mere artistry and skill.

Simms was born in Charleston, South Carolina, on 17 April 1806, the son of William Gilmore Simms, Sr., an Irish immigrant who arrived shortly after the American Revolution. His mother was Harriet Singleton, whose family had

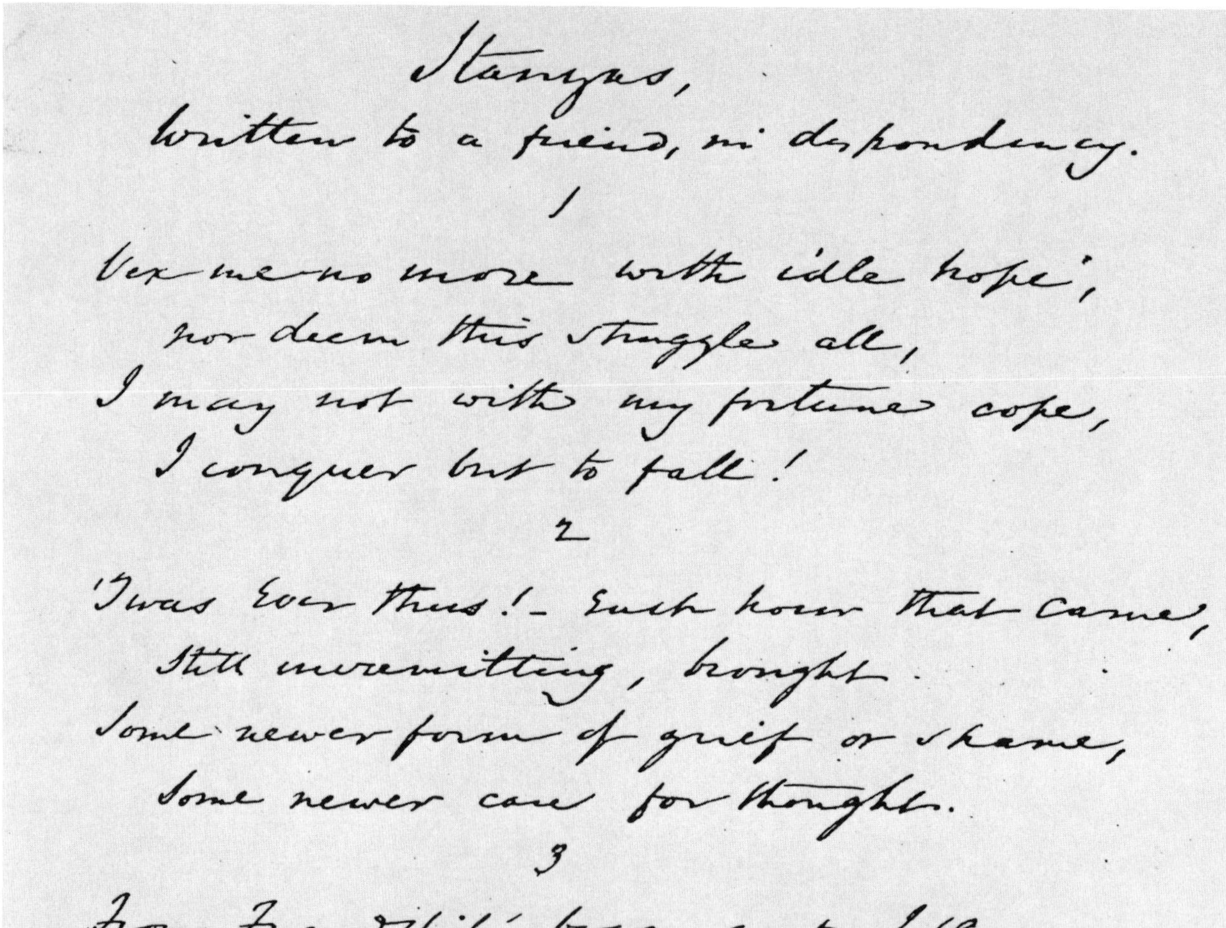
Stanzas,
Written to a friend, in despondency.

1

Vex me no more with idle hope;
Nor deem this struggle all,
I may not with my fortune cope,
I conquer but to fall!

2

'Twas ever thus! – Each hour that came,
Still unremitting, brought
Some newer form of grief or shame,
Some newer care for thought.

3

From Friendship's bosom cast, I flew,
And passion shared my heart;
My hours of calm delight were few,
And madness sway'd the rest.

4

I sought for love and found deceit,
I turn'd to peace, and lo! –
Still mocking my pursuing feet,
She bade me fly to Wo!

Fair copy of a poem Simms wrote when he was twenty-five (from Autograph Leaves of Our Country's Authors, *compiled by Alexander Bliss and John P. Kennedy, 1864)*

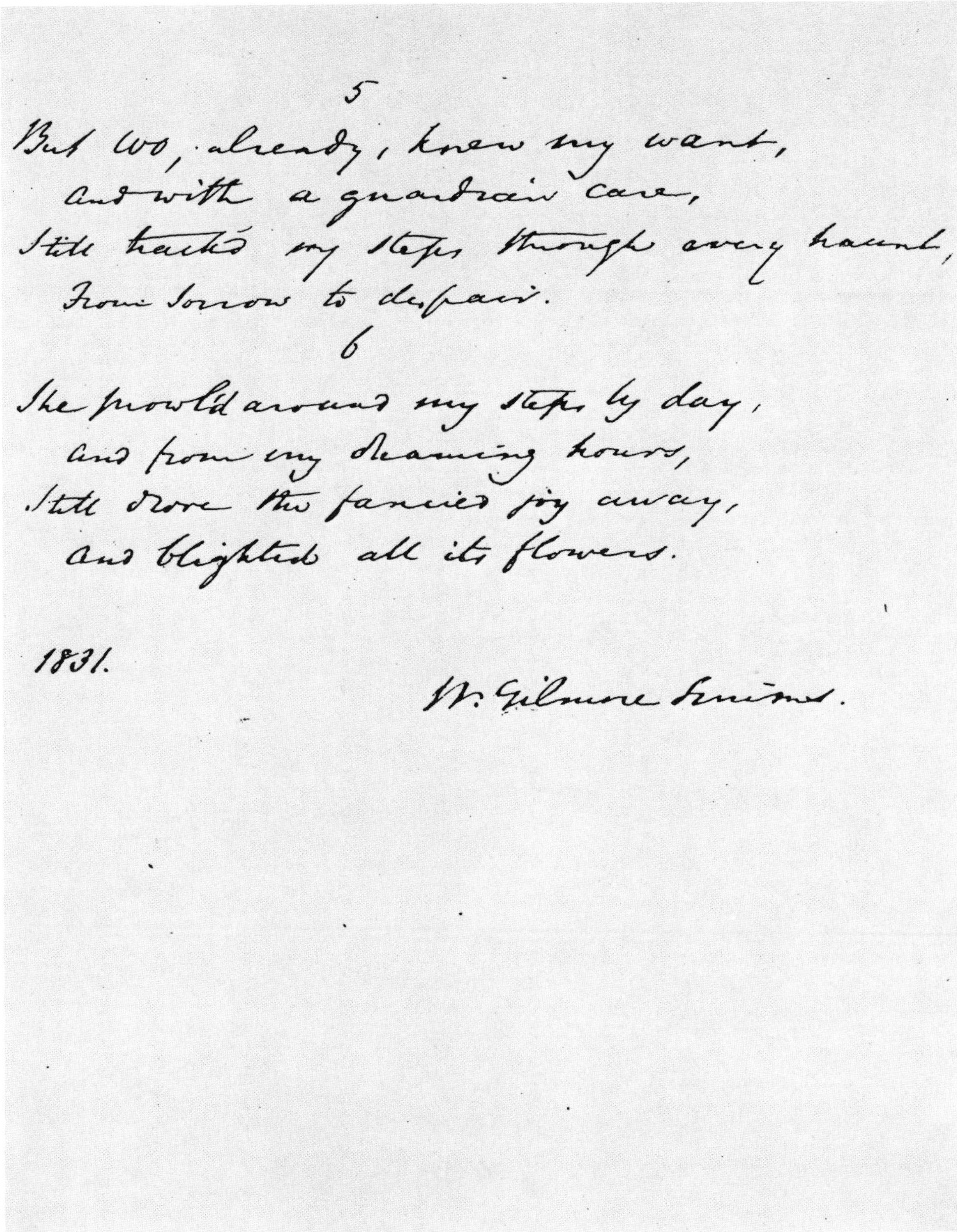

5

But Wo, already, knew my want,
And with a guardian care,
Still track'd my steps through every haunt,
From Sorrow to despair.

6

She prowl'd around my steps by day,
And from my dreaming hours,
Still drove the fancied joy away,
And blighted all its flowers.

1831.

W. Gilmore Simms.

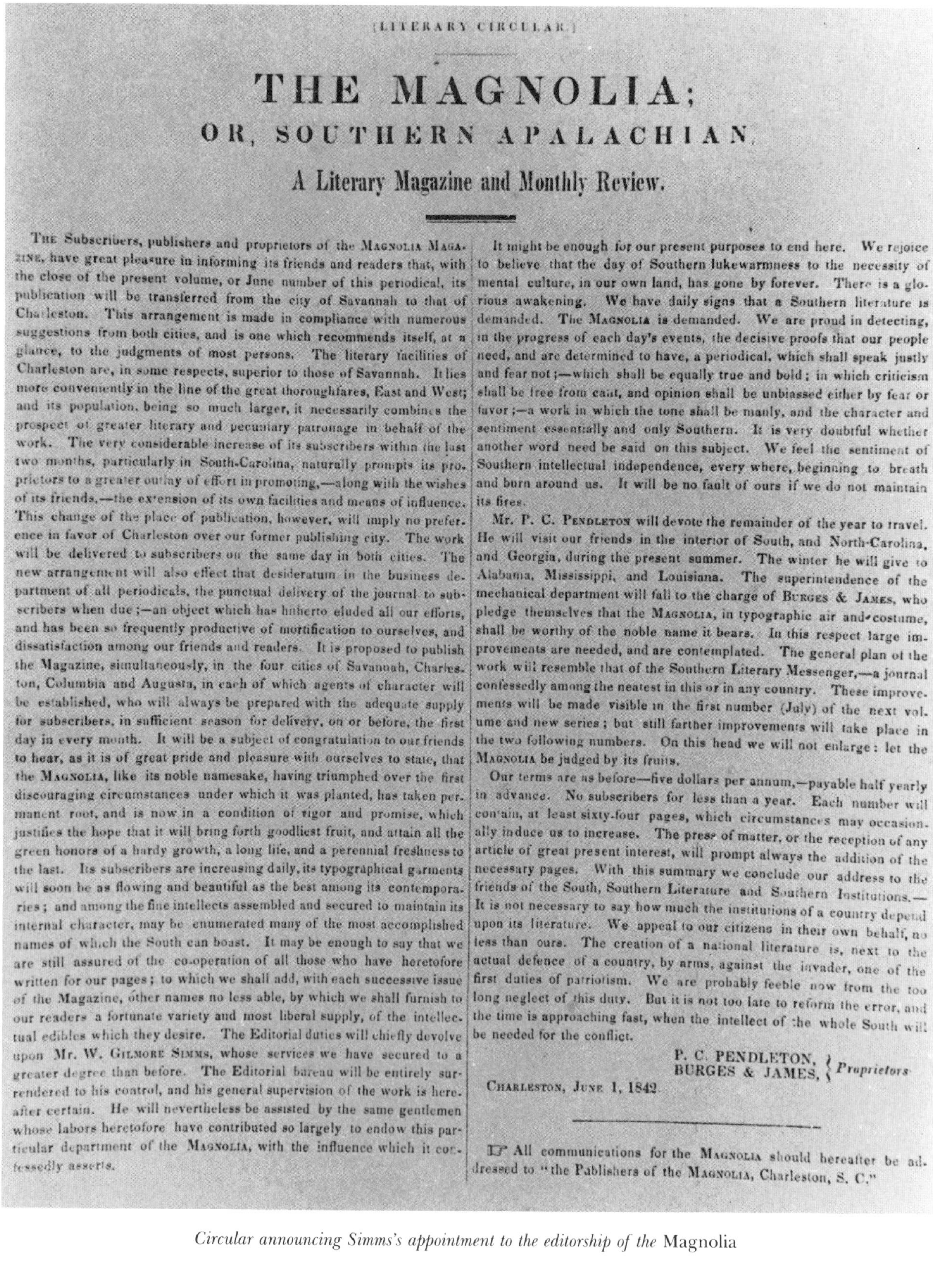

[LITERARY CIRCULAR.]

THE MAGNOLIA;

OR, SOUTHERN APALACHIAN.

A Literary Magazine and Monthly Review.

THE Subscribers, publishers and proprietors of the MAGNOLIA MAGAZINE, have great pleasure in informing its friends and readers that, with the close of the present volume, or June number of this periodical, its publication will be transferred from the city of Savannah to that of Charleston. This arrangement is made in compliance with numerous suggestions from both cities, and is one which recommends itself, at a glance, to the judgments of most persons. The literary facilities of Charleston are, in some respects, superior to those of Savannah. It lies more conveniently in the line of the great thoroughfares, East and West; and its population, being so much larger, it necessarily combines the prospect of greater literary and pecuniary patronage in behalf of the work. The very considerable increase of its subscribers within the last two months, particularly in South-Carolina, naturally prompts its proprietors to a greater outlay of effort in promoting,—along with the wishes of its friends,—the extension of its own facilities and means of influence. This change of the place of publication, however, will imply no preference in favor of Charleston over our former publishing city. The work will be delivered to subscribers on the same day in both cities. The new arrangement will also effect that desideratum in the business department of all periodicals, the punctual delivery of the journal to subscribers when due;—an object which has hitherto eluded all our efforts, and has been so frequently productive of mortification to ourselves, and dissatisfaction among our friends and readers. It is proposed to publish the Magazine, simultaneously, in the four cities of Savannah, Charleston, Columbia and Augusta, in each of which agents of character will be established, who will always be prepared with the adequate supply for subscribers, in sufficient season for delivery, on or before, the first day in every month. It will be a subject of congratulation to our friends to hear, as it is of great pride and pleasure with ourselves to state, that the MAGNOLIA, like its noble namesake, having triumphed over the first discouraging circumstances under which it was planted, has taken permanent root, and is now in a condition of vigor and promise, which justifies the hope that it will bring forth goodliest fruit, and attain all the green honors of a hardy growth, a long life, and a perennial freshness to the last. Its subscribers are increasing daily, its typographical garments will soon be as flowing and beautiful as the best among its contemporaries; and among the fine intellects assembled and secured to maintain its internal character, may be enumerated many of the most accomplished names of which the South can boast. It may be enough to say that we are still assured of the co-operation of all those who have heretofore written for our pages; to which we shall add, with each successive issue of the Magazine, other names no less able, by which we shall furnish to our readers a fortunate variety and most liberal supply, of the intellectual edibles which they desire. The Editorial duties will chiefly devolve upon Mr. W. GILMORE SIMMS, whose services we have secured to a greater degree than before. The Editorial bureau will be entirely surrendered to his control, and his general supervision of the work is hereafter certain. He will nevertheless be assisted by the same gentlemen whose labors heretofore have contributed so largely to endow this particular department of the MAGNOLIA, with the influence which it confessedly asserts.

It might be enough for our present purposes to end here. We rejoice to believe that the day of Southern lukewarmness to the necessity of mental culture, in our own land, has gone by forever. There is a glorious awakening. We have daily signs that a Southern literature is demanded. The MAGNOLIA is demanded. We are proud in detecting, in the progress of each day's events, the decisive proofs that our people need, and are determined to have, a periodical, which shall speak justly and fear not;—which shall be equally true and bold; in which criticism shall be free from cant, and opinion shall be unbiassed either by fear or favor;—a work in which the tone shall be manly, and the character and sentiment essentially and only Southern. It is very doubtful whether another word need be said on this subject. We feel the sentiment of Southern intellectual independence, every where, beginning to breath and burn around us. It will be no fault of ours if we do not maintain its fires.

Mr. P. C. PENDLETON will devote the remainder of the year to travel. He will visit our friends in the interior of South, and North-Carolina, and Georgia, during the present summer. The winter he will give to Alabama, Mississippi, and Louisiana. The superintendence of the mechanical department will fall to the charge of BURGES & JAMES, who pledge themselves that the MAGNOLIA, in typographic air and costume, shall be worthy of the noble name it bears. In this respect large improvements are needed, and are contemplated. The general plan of the work will resemble that of the Southern Literary Messenger,—a journal confessedly among the neatest in this or in any country. These improvements will be made visible in the first number (July) of the next volume and new series; but still farther improvements will take place in the two following numbers. On this head we will not enlarge: let the MAGNOLIA be judged by its fruits.

Our terms are as before—five dollars per annum,—payable half yearly in advance. No subscribers for less than a year. Each number will contain, at least sixty-four pages, which circumstances may occasionally induce us to increase. The press of matter, or the reception of any article of great present interest, will prompt always the addition of the necessary pages. With this summary we conclude our address to the friends of the South, Southern Literature and Southern Institutions.—It is not necessary to say how much the institutions of a country depend upon its literature. We appeal to our citizens in their own behalf, no less than ours. The creation of a national literature is, next to the actual defence of a country, by arms, against the invader, one of the first duties of patriotism. We are probably feeble now from the too long neglect of this duty. But it is not too late to reform the error, and the time is approaching fast, when the intellect of the whole South will be needed for the conflict.

P. C. PENDLETON,
BURGES & JAMES, } *Proprietors*

CHARLESTON, JUNE 1, 1842.

☞ All communications for the MAGNOLIA should hereafter be addressed to "the Publishers of the MAGNOLIA, Charleston, S. C."

Circular announcing Simms's appointment to the editorship of the Magnolia

come to Charleston from Virginia some years before the revolution; Simms's mother died in childbirth in 1808, and William Simms, Sr., along with his brother James, migrated to the Mississippi Territory shortly thereafter, leaving the young Simms with his grandmother who had married Jacob Gates. Twice in his youth Simms was pressured to move to Mississippi with his father; when he was eighteen, and again when he was twenty, Simms took extended trips to visit his father, all the while gathering material for his earliest literary efforts. The stories his grandmother Gates told him, especially of the revolution in South Carolina, contributed to his choice of a literary vocation.

Simms's career as literary critic began early. By the age of twenty he had already issued a short-lived literary magazine, the *Album: A Weekly Miscellany,* and a poetic volume, *Monody, on the Death of Gen. Charles Cotesworth Pinckney* (1825). He was editor of the *Southern Literary Gazette* from 1828 to 1829. Before he was twenty-five he had published three more volumes of poetry, coedited his home city's newspaper, the *Charleston City Gazette,* from 1830 to 1832, and had contributed numerous critical articles to other Charleston publications. For forty years Simms would send book reviews, brief notices, and extended criticism as well as lectures and essays on literature and aesthetics to magazines and newspapers all over the South and to many northern publications.

On his twenty-first birthday, having read law for two years in the office of attorney Charles Rivers Carroll, Simms became a lawyer, an occupation which he practiced for only a year, although his training for it and his brief practice, described by a witness as "vehement, earnest, dramatic," found later outlets in a brief career in politics, in his fiction writing, and in critical analysis of literary works. He married seventeen-year-old Anna Malcolm Giles on 19 October 1826; their daughter was born the following year. For the next five years Simms edited newspapers and magazines and pleaded the Union cause against the South Carolina nullifiers. On 19 February 1832 Simms's wife died. Placing the child with her maternal relatives, the aspiring writer went north to make his first serious literary contacts, and his career began in earnest.

That summer he contributed to the *American Quarterly Review* an article on Frances Trollope's *Domestic Manners of the Americans* (September 1832). A review of Harriet Martineau's *The Morals of Slavery* appeared in the *Southern Literary Messenger* in 1837 and in pamphlet form the following year. Simms's opinion of both of these works was that they were not honest or moral because they were thesis-ridden and selective in the details presented. Simms objected to the fact that both these foreign travelers sought to point out the coarseness in American life, especially in the slave states and on the western borders. The essay on Martineau was reprinted with Simms's introduction as late as 1852, and intermittently throughout his career Simms referred to the "fat, gross" Trollope.

During the trip to New York in 1832 he also made the acquaintance of many literary figures including James Lawson, who would act as his literary agent for the next three decades, and actor Edwin Forrest, for whom he would occasionally write dramas over the years. By the summer of 1833 Simms had published another long poem and a novel, *Martin Faber; The Story of a Criminal.* Back in Charleston during the winters, he was editing the *Cosmopolitan, an Occasional* (1833) and writing novels of the frontier and the Indian which were well received in both the North and the South. He also produced literary commentary for magazines such as his complaint against "puffing" in "American Criticism and Critics." His early success in fiction encouraged Simms to continue writing novels, and during the later 1830s he wrote little literary theory (with a few notable exceptions).

After courting for over a year, on 15 November 1836 Simms married eighteen-year-old Chevillette Eliza Roach, whom he described to Lawson as "a pale, pleasing girl–very gentle and amiable–with dark eyes & hair, sings sweetly & plays piano and guitar." When Chevillette Simms died in 1863 her fourteenth child was a year and a half old; only six of Simms's children lived to adulthood.

In 1841 Simms wrote some important "letters" to the editor of the *Magnolia* defending his frank treatment of Negro and Indian life in "Caloya, or The Loves of the Driver," published in its pages. He insisted that morality in literature is measured only by truthfulness. "He is and cannot but be, immoral, whose truth is partial and one-sided." This view was manifested in Simms's fiction of low-life characters, and in his judgment of the writings of others, particularly antislavery novels, which presented what Simms saw as partial truths. The popular English writer

Daguerreotype of Anna Augusta Singleton Simms, Simms's daughter by his first wife

Edward Bulwer-Lytton nearly always received praise from Simms, though not entirely unmixed. In a review article in the *Magnolia* (1842), "Bulwer's Genius and Writings," Simms discussed the spirit, intention, and performance of the writers attempting "to leave the common track." He praised Bulwer-Lytton for his boldness, courage, and ardor, while commenting that Bulwer-Lytton had weak creative and artistic powers.

In June 1842 Simms became editor of the *Magnolia, or Southern Monthly*. He invested a good deal of energy in writing most of the articles and reviewing scores of books, but he could not save the magazine for more than a year. In the winter of 1840-1841 Simms had rather pessimistically written the owner, P. C. Pendleton, who had approached him about being the editor, that the fate of southern magazines and editors is always one of "discredit, annoyance, and expense." In fact the South had "*not one native professional author . . . who, if he relied on the South purely for his resources, would not . . . go without his porridge.*" Despite these sentiments, Simms returned to the unprofitable task of editing another southern journal probably, as John C. Guilds pointed out, because he believed his region needed a literary magazine to waken its citizens, because Pendleton may have promised him good pay, and because a national slump in fiction sales required him to turn to other endeavors. Under Simms's editorship the quality of the *Magnolia* improved, and it received good reviews, but subscribers would not pay their bills, and Simms resigned just one year later, presumably because he was not being paid either as a contributor or as editor.

In November 1842 Simms traveled to the University of Alabama where he was awarded the LL.D. degree. In his speech to the Erosophic Society, *The Social Principle,* he put forward his belief, which he said was "well received," that home and hearth are miniatures of social order, which in turn is the basis for national permanence. It is the quest for "safety, peace, home, liberty" which made the English triumphant in America. In Simms's generation greed and speculation, imitation of British show and avarice, and the "wandering habit" promoted the deterioration of society and deterred the development of "the arts, mechanical and fine." The heedless "insatiate rage for gain" kept Americans on the move, rootless and undisciplined. "Morals, letters and the fine arts," productions of home, hearth, and stability, are sacrificed "for gold, for silver, or . . . for good current paper of banks." Simms called the Erosophic Society members back to patience, restraint, work, modesty, and "the vocation for which God has designed you."

Washington Allston, painter and minor literary figure from South Carolina, received Simms's praise in the *Southern Quarterly Review* (October 1843) for his aesthetics: "those laws of taste . . . are equally essential to the proper direction of poet as well as painter. . . . Every syllable that he has written upon the subject of art [is] a word of weight." His literature, however, lacked inspiration, vision, and originality; "his intercourse with the muse is not one of passion. His amours are purely platonic."

Simms also wrote a series of four public letters, published in the *Southern Literary Messenger* (1844), on the need for an international copyright law. This theme had been discussed by many literary people and would continue to be for another fifty years, but Simms's essays are in-

William Gilmore Simms, probably in 1859 (courtesy of the South Caroliniana Library, University of South Carolina)

teresting for their history of American literature, which he says began just after the War of 1812. "A native Literature is the means, and the only means, of our perfect independence," he wrote. This cultural independence was hampered for Americans because they shared the language of Great Britain, whose writers were available in cheap editions in America. Foreign travelers filled Americans with errors about their national character. A "home Literature is the great and sufficient remedy for all these errors and absurdities" printed by foreigners.

Prior to Cooper's *The Spy* (1821), Simms says, Americans were not ready for a native literature: "The genius of American Literature was born and could only be born, when the American people were prepared to receive and entertain her, to acknowledge her charms and to assert her pretensions. . . . The only authors of a nation, who illustrate its career, and help its progress in the paths of moral improvement, are those who represent its spirit and partake its characteristics." Simms said that until 1834 American literature was "amateur," and authors had to earn their livings by other means. Under such conditions their literature was "fugitive, wanting in form and consistency, in proper elaboration, in grandeur, strength and purpose!"

The dearth of American literature was caused by the American and English audiences which sneered at American books; by large runs of cheap reprints of British books (on cheap paper and in poor type); and by "miscellanies" in the place of books issued since the depression of 1836-1837. In addition publishers seldom paid Americans more than $300 for their books, if that much.

Arguments against the copyright law turned on semantics–the meaning of "copyright" and "protection." Simms explained that "up to the discovery of the art of printing, the author [as troubadour or teacher] was the exclusive master of his own writings. . . . He alone sold them. . . . He had but to ask the protection of the laws for his peculiar property. . . . Copyright, in short, means neither more nor less than the right to make and sell copies. . . ." Protection is for "property" not for "industry" or "manufacturing" as was the case in trade protection. Simms's sensible explanation of the need for copyright to help promote native literature deserves to be available alongside the pronouncements of his fellow writers such as James Fenimore Cooper, Cornelius Mathews, James Russell Lowell, and later Mark Twain.

Simms considered his four-part essay "The Moral Character of Hamlet" (*Orion,* 1844), which he revised and used for a lecture, to be his most important piece of literary criticism. He praised Shakespeare for his "wonderfully creative capacities" in being able to transmute "the baser ore of other minds into the precious metal of his own." Simms believed that Hamlet was "a victim of the fates . . . singled out for an ordeal to which he proved unequal, and he perished because of his unfitness," as Edd Winfield Parks has stated it. He lacked the toughness of mind and temperament required to make him a man of decision and action. Ironically, it was his genius, education, contemplation, gentlemanly training, and natural skepticism which made him shrink in the crisis. He was "the victim of a destiny which, with energies of manhood, it might have been easy to control. . . . Hamlet's contemplative character, and feebleness of resolve, were derived from . . . an unperforming temperament trained unhappily." Convinced of his father's murder and his uncle's guilt, Hamlet goes to work methodically. Yet he withholds confidence and begins to show "signs of incertitude and indecision." Simms was especially drawn to *Hamlet* because of all Shakespeare's works it was suitable for readers as well as for spectators. In the study Simms considered Hamlet "not only as one of the noblest studies of Shakspeare's genius, but as one of the most perfect and symmetrical–a character every way natural." He says that "with all his infirmities, there is so much in the mind and genius of Hamlet, so much in his tastes and accomplishments, so copious were his thoughts, so expansive his philosophies, so free his humour, so happy his wit, that we half subscribe to the eulogium of his friend Horatio . . . 'Now cracks a noble heart.' "

Simms edited *Simms's Monthly Magazine: The Southern and Western Monthly Magazine and Review* for its entire lifetime, January-December 1845, when it was merged with the *Southern Literary Messenger* in Richmond. David Tomlinson has called it "without a doubt, one of the finer periodicals" of the Old South, intended as the "Southern voice of the Young America movement." Simms was also chief contributor, and several of his important reviews in *Southern and Western* later were printed in his only collection of literary essays.

Views and Reviews, first and second series, appeared in 1845. The contents had first been published in the 1840s, usually as book reviews in southern journals, and covered a variety of literary topics. In the lead article, "Americanism in Literature" (1845), Simms argued that most American writers are so unoriginal that they "might as well be European." While parties promoted independence from British influence in all things material, "never a word is said . . . touching the grievous imposition upon us of foreign opinion and foreign laws." He believed that a "national aim and idea, out of the fulness and overflow of the national heart" would effect a literature "commensurate to the extent of our country." The democratic impulse would produce a democratic literature.

In the six essays comprising "The Epochs and Events of American History as Suited to the Purposes of Art in Fiction" Simms states that "the chief value of history consists in its proper employment for the purposes of art!" The historian is not merely the collector of facts; not the chronologist. Rather "it is the artist only who is the true historian. It is he who gives shape to the unhewn fact, who yields relation to the scattered fragments." People "care not so much for the intrinsic truth of history, as for the great moral truths, which, drawn from such sources, induce excellence in the student." For example, Benedict Arnold was a worthy subject because his "fate and fortunes" lend themselves to the moral story: "No other series of events . . . seems more naturally to group themselves in the form of the story." Twenty years later Simms would use the very details cited here as the episodes in a verse drama.

The law office at Woodlands, Simms's plantation on the Edisto River

Simms suggested four periods of American history as good subjects for fiction, and in his own work he used them all: the exploration and settlement by the Europeans; the British colonization; the American Revolution–the period which Simms himself exploited more often than any other; and the modern period, which he depicted in his border romances.

His essay on James Fenimore Cooper's writings praises Cooper for doing the very things Simms had advocated in the essays earlier in *Views and Reviews:* discovering and using events and scenes from American life for the purposes of fiction. Cooper had "struck the vein, and convinced the people not only that there was gold in the land, but that the gold of the land was good." In 1852 William Cullen Bryant called this "a critical essay of great depth and discrimination, to which I am not sure that anything hitherto written on the same subject is fully equal."

Views and Reviews, second series, included Simms's reviews, somewhat modified, of Frances Trollope's book *The Case of Major André,* "Weems, the Biographer and Historian," and "The Humorous in American and British Literature." In the latter Simms said that "good comedy is suggestive of society,–society as it is, and not as it appears through . . . a surly and impatient cynic." Publishers required that "the American, whatever his genius, must subdue . . . until . . . he can tread the same paths, successfully, with the foreigner." In humor the American "national tendency [was] to excess and hyperbole,–to recklessness and extravagance. . . . Equally remarkable . . . is the calm into which we subside after the contest,–the good humored philosophy which consoles us for our defeats, and the elasticity . . . to renew the struggle."

In 1848 Simms brought out an edition of the Shakespeare apocrypha, a volume William Trent says he "had long planned." Although his study is not scholarly, his annotations are not full, and his emendations are the result of his personal taste, *A Supplement to the Plays* ought not to be entirely dismissed. Simms claimed that he did not "propose to decide upon their authenticity" as writings of Shakespeare; instead he meant to "afford to the general reader an opportunity, if not of deciding for himself upon the genuineness of these plays, at least of becoming familiar with their merits." In case later scholarship should determine that they should be included in the canon, Simms's contemporary readers would not have been cheated. On the other hand, they "can by no means disparage or impair [Shakespeare's] acknowledged excellences," no matter who is the author.

Simms argued that "To suppose that [Shakespeare] remained idle, pursuing a mere vegetable life in Stratford, from his fifteenth to his twenty-third year, when he went to London, would be a strangely unreasonable supposition. It is, ordinarily, about the fifteenth year that the poetic germ . . . usually begins to exhibit itself with zeal and activity." Therefore, it is valid to consider that these inferior plays are the apprentice works of the master, taken with him when he went to seek his fortune in London. Simms also suggested that in the theatrical world of the Elizabethans an author protected his rights by keeping the play out of print. The apocryphal plays were "printed, either with [Shakespeare's] name or his initials, in the lifetime of Shakespeare," and his colleagues in the theater also brought them out after his death. Simms argued, "The plays . . . which we have received from the hands of the authors themselves, are those, chiefly, which failed upon the stage. These consequently, are likely to have come to us in the most perfect condition."

Simms had been contributing to the *Southern Quarterly Review* since its beginning in 1842; with the April 1849 issue he became the editor. He changed the complexion of the journal from being heavily political by publishing more of his own long articles on history and literature. He also briefly reviewed as many as seventy books per quarter. It was in this journal, both before and during his editorship, that Simms published some of his most important literary and historical criticism.

In April 1845 Simms reviewed the American edition of an anthology of British prose and poetry, *A New Spirit of the Age,* edited by R. H. Horne, a minor poet himself. Simms points out that "literary genius" seldom will "govern, or, to any great degree, influence [the] living and working spirit" of an age. He laments the fact that publishers "do not appeal to the higher tastes of their readers" in the literature they reprint; instead they use "what is most likely to have the largest circulation." But the inability to report favorably on "works of original character" is not restricted to publishers' readers: "Even men of genius themselves" acquire fixed and inflexible tastes and are unable to recognize "native and independent strength" in a younger writer. Horne, for instance, has ignored all American and continental literature, including the work of D'Israeli, an omission Simms found "scarcely to be understood" unless Horne was "a man of prejudices." "D'Israeli belongs to the age,–is one of its informing spirits," Simms continued, noting D'Israeli's prolificacy and popularity in several genres. Simms praised this "impatient" and "most ambitious writer" for works that "betrayed a lively genius, an insatiate vanity, a quick and sparkling fancy, considerable knowledge of society, and a power in conversational dialogue"–qualities Simms strove for in his own wide-ranging works.

"Modern Prose Fiction," the sequel to "A New Spirit," is an important essay, for it clarifies

William Gilmore Simms (courtesy of the South Caroliniana Library, University of South Carolina)

Simms's theory of the relationship between fiction and morality. Ostensibly the moral is not important to the raconteur. "The common aim is the story,–the simple accumulation of interesting incidents, in relation to some hero. . . . But [Simms continued], as truthfulness is never without its moral, and as the great end of the artist is the approximation of all his fiction to a seeming truth, so, unavoidably, he inculcates a moral whenever he tells a story. . . . This determines the legitimacy of his art." This is true, Simms believed, in aboriginal and folk storytelling, in fantasy, in romance, in psychological fiction, and in the novel. "Fiction, indeed, is neither more nor less, than probable truth under intenser conditions than ordinary." It is usable for religion, history, and patriotism, and only when Americans recognize the value of fiction to the "national consciousness" will literature achieve the "dignity of a profession."

In 1863 Simms published *Benedict Arnold: The Traitor. A Dramatic Essay.* In this important essay he emphasized that a drama needed "individuality of development" and "an action continually rising in interest, to the catastrophe." In his drama he changed the "facts" of the Arnold-André intrigue in order to expose the "truth" of human nature. "However his details may vary from the history," the dramatist could "exercise such privileges of art [as were] legitimate for his purpose."

Although Simms was not a profound or even an original critic, he was widely read in his own day; no doubt he had more influence than the scant scholarship done to date suggests. His achievement as critic has been examined only by Edd Winfield Parks, whose book is largely a compendium of Simms's own ideas arranged in themes. A few scholars have looked at his editorial work; others at his career as historian. More detailed examination of his many reviews and essays is needed if Simms's contribution is to achieve the recognition which it is due.

Letters:

Mary C. Simms Oliphant, et al., eds., *The Letters of William Gilmore Simms,* 5 volumes (Columbia: University of South Carolina Press, 1952-1956).

References:

John C. Guilds, "Simms as Editor and Prophet: The Flowering and Early Death of the Southern *Magnolia,*" *Southern Literary Journal,* 4 (Spring 1972): 69-92;

C. Hugh Holman, "William Gilmore Simms and the 'American Renaissance,'" *Mississippi Quarterly,* 15 (Summer 1962): 126-137;

Holman, ed., Introduction to *Views and Reviews in American Literature, History and Fiction,* by William Gilmore Simms (Cambridge, Mass.: Belknap Press, 1962), pp. vii-xliii;

Edd Winfield Parks, *William Gilmore Simms as Literary Critic* (Athens: University of Georgia Press, 1961);

Miriam J. Shillingsburg, "The Southron as American," *Studies in the American Renaissance,* 3 (1980): 409-423;

David Tomlinson, "Simms's Monthly Magazine: The Southern and Western Monthly Magazine and Review," *Southern Literary Journal,* 8 (Fall 1975): 95-125;

William P. Trent, *William Gilmore Simms* (Boston: Houghton Mifflin, 1892);

Jon L. Wakelyn, *The Politics of a Literary Man: William Gilmore Simms* (Westport, Conn.: Greenwood Press, 1973).

George Ticknor

(1 August 1791-26 January 1871)

Julie Ellison
University of Michigan

See also the Ticknor entry in *DLB 1, The American Renaissance in New England.*

SELECTED BOOKS: *Syllabus of a Course of Lectures on the History and Criticism of Spanish Literature* (Cambridge, Mass.: Hilliard & Metcalf, 1823);

Outlines of the Principal Events in the Life of General Lafayette (Boston: Cummings, Hilliard, 1825);

Remarks on the Life and Writings of Daniel Webster of Massachusetts (Philadelphia: Carey & Lea, 1831);

Lecture on the Best Methods of Teaching the Living Languages. Delivered before the American Institute, August 24, 1832 (Boston: Carter, Hendee, 1833);

History of Spanish Literature, 3 volumes (New York: Harper, 1849; London: John Murray, 1849);

Union of the Boston Athenaeum and the Public Library (Boston: Dutton & Wentworth, 1853);

Papers Discussing the Comparative Merits of Prescott's and Wilson's Histories. Pro. and Con., as Laid before the Massachusetts Historical Society (Boston & Philadelphia, 1861);

Life of William Hickling Prescott (Boston: D. Estes, 1863; Philadelphia: Lippincott, 1863; London: Routledge, 1863);

El Ingenioso Hidalgo Don Quijote de la Mancha (New York: D. Appleton, 1872).

OTHER: *The Remains of Nathaniel Appleton Hewen,* edited, with a memoir of his life, by Ticknor (Boston: Hilliard, Gray, 1827);

Johann Wolfgang von Goethe, *The Sorrows of Young Werther,* translated by Ticknor, as *George Ticknor's The Sorrows of Young Werther,* University of North Carolina, Studies in Comparative Literature, no. 4, edited, with introduction and critical analysis, by Frank G. Ryder (Chapel Hill, N.C., 1952).

PERIODICAL PUBLICATIONS: "Annotations on Milton's Paradise Lost," *General Repository and Review,* 2 (1812): 66-84;

George Ticknor in 1828, portrait by Thomas Sully (by permission of the Trustees of Dartmouth College)

"Griscom's Tour in Europe," *North American Review,* 18 (January 1824): 178-192;

"Free Schools of New England," *North American Review,* 19 (October 1824): 448-457;

"Works of Chateaubriand," *American Quarterly Review,* 2 (December 1827): 458-482;

"Memoirs of the Buckminsters," *Christian Examiner,* 47 (September 1849): 169-195;

"Joshua Bates," *American Journal of Education,* 7 (1859): 270-272.

George Ticknor was one of Boston's reigning men of letters in the generation immediately preceding that of the Transcendentalists. Ticknor mediated between the more intellectual elements of the New England elite to which he belonged and the renowned representatives of European culture whom he sought out during his first Continental sojourn (1815-1819). His writings were concerned with literary history and with the universities and libraries that make the teaching and study of literary history possible. The *History of Spanish Literature* (1849), his most substantive work of scholarship, emerged from Ticknor's career as professor of modern languages at Harvard College (1819-1835) and from the bibliographical activities by which he sought to make European literatures available to learned Americans.

Ticknor received a careful education from his parents, Elisha and Elizabeth Billings Curtis Ticknor, who had both been schoolteachers. He attended Dartmouth College and after his graduation, the intellectually precocious but sociable boy returned to Boston. He continued his studies of the classics for another three years with John S. J. Gardiner. He then decided on a legal career, though without enthusiasm. The real center of interest in his life at this time was the Anthology Society, the convivial gathering of cultivated professional men who edited the *Monthly Anthology and Boston Review* and who invited Ticknor to become a member in 1810. Although Ticknor read law for three years and was admitted to the bar in 1813, he practiced for only one year before deciding that literature was his true vocation.

Ticknor's *Wanderjahre* in Europe have had considerable imaginative appeal for later students of the period. His eager quest for intellectual exposure derived its energy partly from the eighteenth-century world alive in the memories of American diplomats and statesmen and partly from the dawning American awareness of British and European romanticism. Ticknor, along with his distinguished traveling companion, Edward Everett, first became interested in German universities through Madame de Staël's popularization of German romantic culture, *De l'Allemagne*. He prepared for his studies at Göttingen by translating Goethe's *The Sorrows of Young Werther* (1774, final version 1787). His preparations also included a tour through New England and the Middle Atlantic states during the winter of 1814-1815 which constituted a short course in the history of the American Revolution and the early republic: among the acquaintances he made in this period were John Randolph, President James Madison, and Thomas Jefferson, who commissioned him to buy books.

Once abroad Ticknor showed the same blend of curiosity about the new and temperamental affinity for the old that had impressed Jefferson. Due in part to his extraordinary connections, but also due to his own finely educated taste and personal charm, he was able to meet and, in many cases, become friends with the luminaries of the day. In England these included Lord Byron, William Wordsworth, and Sir Walter Scott (whose portrait would later hang in Ticknor's Boston library); in Germany, Goethe; in Italy, the pope. As described in Ticknor's letters and journals, his conversations with these prominent people comprise one of the classic accounts of an American abroad.

From August 1815 through March 1817 Ticknor devoted himself to a rigorous curriculum of languages, natural science, and humanities at Göttingen. Compared to the American colleges with which he was familiar, the German university system was vastly superior in resources, organization, and pedagogy. The exposure to German universities shared by four future Harvard professors–Ticknor, Everett, George Bancroft, and Joseph Cogswell, who would go on to found the New York Public Library–was the impetus for the curricular reforms later attempted by Ticknor at Harvard College. It was during his residence at Göttingen that Ticknor was offered the position of Professor of Belles Lettres and Modern Languages at Harvard that he would occupy for sixteen years.

Ticknor's last great adventure in Europe was his journey through Spain in 1818. This trip was largely given over to book collecting, as Ticknor pored through state, church, and private libraries in preparation for his academic post. He immersed himself in social observation and found himself repelled by the Spanish upper and middle classes, but enchanted by its peasantry. Ticknor's idealization of the Spanish popular spirit, at this time and later in the *History of Spanish Literature* (1849), displays his affinities with the romantic historiography of national destiny and national character. His sympathies with the kind of history written by fellow New Englanders like George Bancroft, Francis Parkman, and William Hickling Prescott are especially pronounced: Prescott was Ticknor's closest friend and the subject of a biography which conveys Ticknor's vision of

Watercolor of the Dartmouth campus, painted by Ticknor when he was a sophomore (by permission of the Trustees of Dartmouth College)

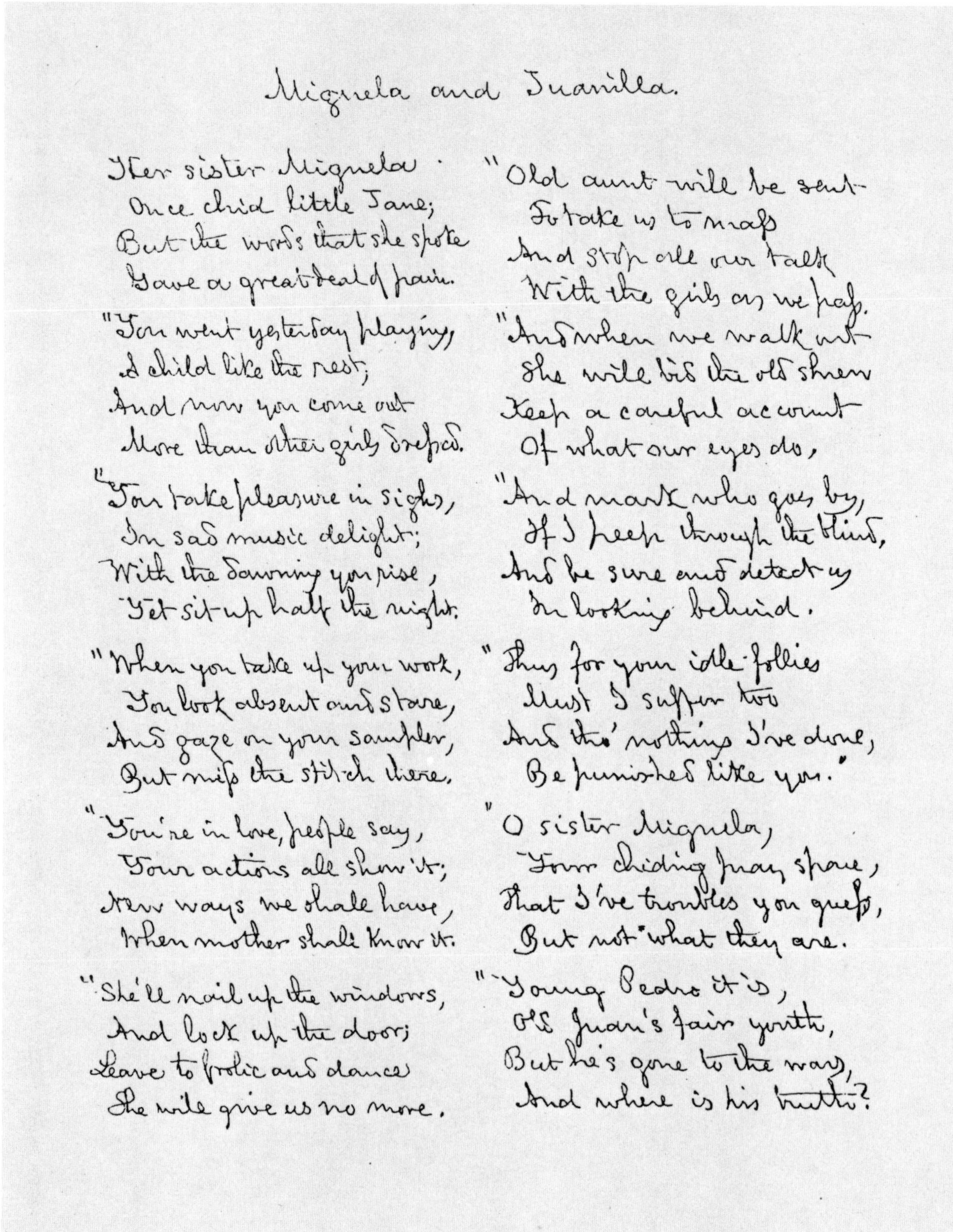

Miguela and Juanilla.

Her sister Miguela
Once chid little Jane;
But the words that she spoke
Gave a great deal of pain.

"You went yesterday playing,
A child like the rest;
And now you come out
More than other girls dressed.

"You take pleasure in sighs,
In sad music delight;
With the dawning you rise,
Yet sit up half the night.

"When you take up your work,
You look absent and stare,
And gaze on your sampler,
But miss the stitch there.

"You're in love, people say,
Your actions all show it;
New ways we shall have,
When mother shall know it.

"She'll nail up the windows,
And lock up the door;
Leave to frolic and dance
She will give us no more.

"Old aunt will be sent
To take us to mass
And stop all our talk
With the girls as we pass.

"And when we walk out
She will bid the old shrew
Keep a careful account
Of what our eyes do,

"And mark who goes by,
If I peep through the blind,
And be sure and detect us
In looking behind.

"Thus for your idle follies
Must I suffer too
And tho' nothing I've done,
Be punished like you."

"O sister Miguela,
Your chiding may spare,
That I've troubled you guess,
But not what they are.

"Young Pedro it is,
Old Juan's fair youth,
But he's gone to the wars,
And where is his truth?

Fair copy of one of Ticknor's translations (from Autograph Leaves of Our Country's Authors, *compiled by Alexander Bliss and John P. Kennedy, 1864)*

"I loved him sincerely,
I loved all he said;
But I fear he is fickle,
I fear he is fled;

"For he's gone of free choice
Without summons or call,
And 'tis foolish to love him,
Or like him at all."

"Nay rather do thou
To God pray above,
Lest Pedro return
And still more you should love,"—

(Said Miguela, in jest,
As she answered poor Jane),—
"For when love has been bought
At cost of such pain,

"What hope is there, sister,
Unless the soul part,
That the passion you cherish
Should yield up your heart?

"Your years will increase
And your griefs many-fold,
As well you may learn
From that proverb of old:—

"'If when but a child
Love's power you own;
Pray, what will you do,
When you older are grown?'"

Translated from the "Sexta Parte de Flor de Romances nuevos, Toledo, 1594. ff. 27–29.

Geo: Ticknor.

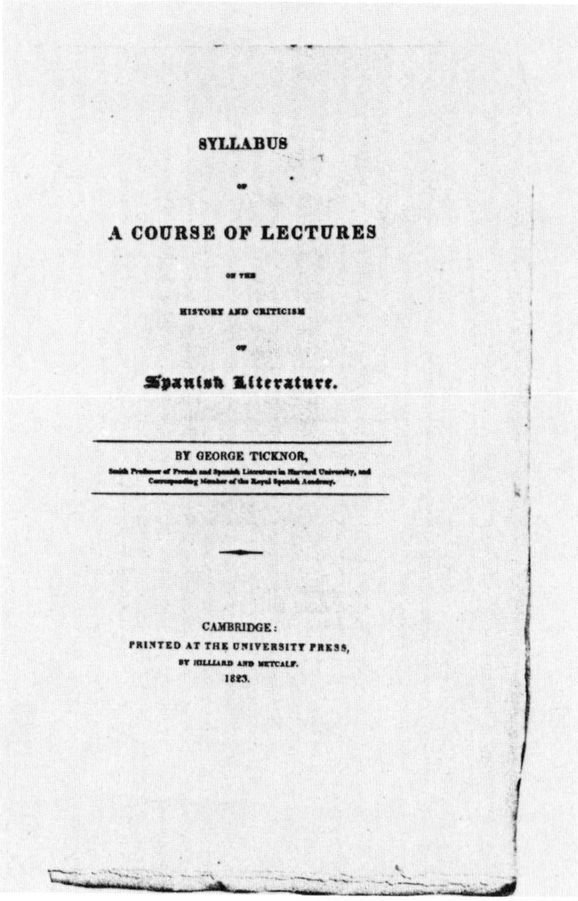
SYLLABUS

OF

A COURSE OF LECTURES

ON THE

HISTORY AND CRITICISM

OF

Spanish Literature.

BY GEORGE TICKNOR,

Smith Professor of French and Spanish Literature in Harvard University, and Corresponding Member of the Royal Spanish Academy.

CAMBRIDGE:

PRINTED AT THE UNIVERSITY PRESS,

BY HILLIARD AND METCALF.

1823.

Title page for Ticknor's first book, prepared for one of his classes at Harvard

the American scholar in the grip of high moral aspiration.

Shortly after marrying the heiress Anna Eliot in 1821 and taking up his post at Harvard, Ticknor began to press for academic reforms based on German universities but adapted to American conditions. He called for an end to the old method of recitation and for alternative modes of instruction: students should be grouped by ability and advanced on the basis of performance; the college should be divided into academic departments, each with substantial control over its curriculum; students should be allowed elective courses in addition to the required ones; and extension classes should be instituted for nondegree students. The internal politics of the Harvard faculty and governing bodies blocked effective curricular reform until a later era. In his department of modern languages, however, Ticknor ran things his own way with impressive results.

Ticknor left Harvard shortly after the death of his five-year-old son and returned to Europe for three years (1835-1838). This time, he was received as a visiting dignitary by noblemen, members of British and European governments, and writers. Traveling with his family and alienated from Jacksonian politics at home, he now sympathized more strongly with conservatives abroad. It was on this trip that Ticknor became friends with Prince John of Saxony, with whom he corresponded about literature and politics for more than thirty years.

Returning to Boston, he wrote the *History of Spanish Literature,* which he continued to revise throughout his life; the posthumous fourth edition of 1891 incorporated his own final corrections. In his discussion of the "author-princes" of Boston, Van Wyck Brooks pointed to the importance of Ticknor's wealth. The *History of Spanish Literature,* observed Brooks, "cost as much to produce as a public building" if one counts the costs of travel and the acquisition of Ticknor's splendid private library. A magisterial work of scholarship in its time and the first full-scale study of Spanish literature in the New World, the *History of Spanish Literature* is of interest to later readers as an example of literary history which intends "to give a knowledge of the *character of the people* to which it relates," as Ticknor wrote to a British correspondent. Despite his love of the Spanish common people and their poetic forms, Ticknor's pessimistic evaluation of the combined influence of the Inquisition, an oppressive monarchy, and a corrupted bureaucracy shapes the book into a narrative of decay.

Although Ticknor never produced another work of this stature, his local influence on the cultural life of Boston (or "Ticknorville," as the literary critic Edwin Whipple proposed to call it) steadily increased. His judgments and values were only partly conveyed through his writings, though he gave forth a steady stream of articles, book reviews, memoirs, and appreciations. He published separately a number of lectures and papers on education and on the contributions of his friends Prescott and Everett, and in 1831 brought out a short, enthusiastic book, *Remarks on the Life and Writings of Daniel Webster of Massachusetts.*

More important to the creation of Ticknor's status as an arbiter of Boston's cultural values and social ethics were his involvement in public af-

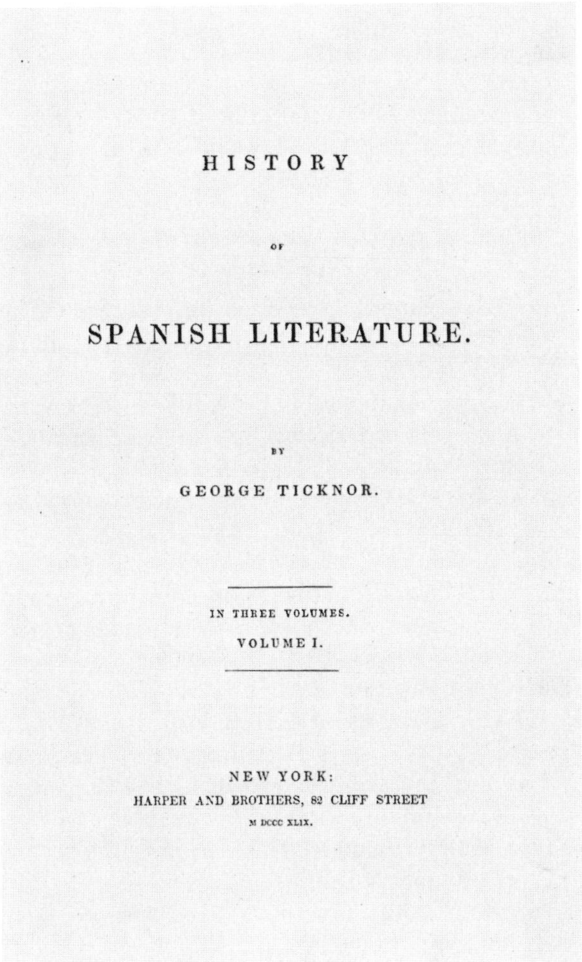
HISTORY

OF

SPANISH LITERATURE.

BY

GEORGE TICKNOR.

IN THREE VOLUMES.

VOLUME I.

NEW YORK:

HARPER AND BROTHERS, 82 CLIFF STREET

M DCCC XLIX.

Title page for Ticknor's major work

fairs and his role as host to visiting luminaries (including Lafayette) and promising young men. Perhaps his most enduring accomplishment was the shaping of the Boston Public Library, which he regarded as a means of public education. It was Ticknor who was responsible for persuading the Library's Board of Trustees to permit the free circulation of books. By 1858, six years after his plan was implemented, the annual circulation of books in the lower hall reached 179,000 volumes. To the noncirculating reference library upstairs, Ticknor donated 2,400 books in his lifetime and bequeathed his Spanish collection. His third and last trip abroad, in 1856, was undertaken in order to purchase books for the Public Library and for his own scholarly use.

Ticknor sided with his class in its confrontation with Ralph Waldo Emerson and the Transcendentalists. He fully sympathized with his brother-in-law, Andrews Norton, who battled the forces of Transcendentalist "infidelity" after Emerson's divinity school "Address" of 1838. Ticknor complained to Maria Edgeworth of the proponents of "a wild sort of metaphysics, if their publications deserve so dignified a name." Despite the fact that, while at Harvard, he had taught the literature of European Romanticism to those who now appropriated it with such excitement, he felt no affinity for their response. By the late 1830s Ticknor's religious, political, and literary views were firmly settled, and he opposed any writer who was not committed to the ideal of a stable commonwealth. His scruples were rigorous enough to cause him to exclude old friends–George Bancroft and Charles Sumner among them–from the circle welcomed at Nine Park Street when, in his view, they had betrayed the old spirit of Federalism. After the death of Webster in 1852, watching an increasingly divided nation move toward and through the Civil War and into harsher and more complex political forms, Ticknor's mood of alarm became one of restrained despair. After a short, paralyzing illness, he died at the age of seventy-nine in 1871, survived by his wife and grown daughter. Even before his death he had begun to be understood, as he is understood today, as epitomizing the capacity of an American elite to commit itself to the dissemination of cultural resources in order to protect itself from the perceived danger of an uneducated democracy.

Letters:

Life, Letters, and Journals of George Ticknor, edited by George S. Hilliard, Mrs. Anna Eliot Ticknor, and Miss Anna Eliot Ticknor, 2 volumes (Boston: J. R. Osgood, 1876; London: Sampson Low, 1876);

West Point in 1826, edited by H. Pelham Curtis (Boston, 1886);

George Ticknor's Travels in Spain, edited by George T. Northrup (Toronto: University Library, 1913);

Briefwechsel König Johann von Sachsen mit George Ticknor, edited by Johann Georg (Leipzig & Berlin: B. G. Teubner, 1920);

Letters to Pascual de Gayangos; from Originals in the Collection of the Hispanic Society of America, edited by Clara L. Penney (New York: Printed by order of the trustees, 1927);

George Ticknor, 1867

"Three Unpublished Letters of George Ticknor and Edward Everett," edited by Arnold Goldman, *British Association for American Studies Bulletin,* 8 (1964): 21-26.

References:

Van Wyck Brooks, *The Flowering of New England 1815-1865* (New York: Dutton, 1936);

Prudence Hannay, "An American Man of Letters," *History Today* (1978): 633-642;

Michael H. Harris and Gerard Spiesler, "Everett, Ticknor, and the Common Man: The Fear of Societal Instability as the Motivation for the Founding of the Boston Public Library," *International Library Review,* 24 (1974): 249-276;

Thomas R. Hart, Jr., "George Ticknor's *History of Spanish Literature:* The New England Background," *PMLA,* 69 (March 1954): 76-88;

Tommaso Pisanti, "Ticknor in Europe," *Nuova Antologia* (1973): 46-52;

Philip Rahv, *Discovery of Europe: The Story of American Experience in the Old World* (Boston: Houghton Mifflin, 1947);

John W. Rathbun, "The Philosophical Setting of George Ticknor's 'History of Spanish Literature,' " *Hispania,* 43 (March 1960): 37-52;

A. William Salomone, "The Nineteenth-Century Discovery of Italy: An Essay in American Cultural History: Prolegomena to a Historiographical Problem," *American Historical Review,* 73 (June 1968): 1359-1391;

Lewis P. Simpson, "A Literary Adventure of the Early Republic: The Anthology Society and the Monthly Anthology," *New England Quarterly,* 27 (June 1954): 168-190;

Anna Eliot Ticknor, *An American Family in Paris* (New York: Hurd & Houghton, 1869);

David B. Tyack, *George Ticknor and the Boston Brahmins* (Cambridge, Mass.: Harvard University Press, 1967);

Walter Muir Whitehead, "The Union of New England and Virginia," *Virginia Quarterly Review,* 40 (Autumn 1964): 516-530.

Papers:

The most extensive collection of Ticknor's manuscripts is housed in the archives of the Dartmouth College Library. Other Ticknor papers are held by the Massachusetts Historical Society, the Boston Public Library, and Houghton Library at Harvard University.

Gulian C. Verplanck

(6 August 1786-18 March 1870)

Robert P. Winston
Dickinson College

BOOKS: *An Oration Delivered July 4, 1809, in the North Dutch Church before the Washington Benevolent Society of the City of New York* (New York: D. & G. Bruce, 1809);

Letter to the Hon. Saml. L. Mitchell, M.D. Representative in Congress from the City of New York; Professor of Natural His. etc. on the Danger of Putting Money into the U. States and Manhattan Banks, with Sundry Novel Speculations on Insurance Stock, Domestic Manufactures, and the Best Mode of Vesting a Capital "So As To Make Both Ends Meet," as Abimelech Coody, Esq., Ladies' Shoemaker (New York: Literary Exchange, 1811);

A Fable for Statesmen and Politicians of All Parties and Descriptions, as Abimelech Coody, Esq., Formerly Ladies' Shoemaker (New York, 1815);

An Anniversary Discourse, Delivered before the New York Historical Society, December 7, 1818 (New York: James Eastburn, 1818);

The State Triumvirate, a Political Tale: And the Epistles of Brevet Major Pindar Puff, as Scriblerus Busby and Pindar Puff, with Rudolph Bunner and John Duer ("The Bucktail Bards") (New York: W. B. Gilley, 1819);

Address Delivered Before the American Academy of Fine Arts (New York: C. Wiley, 1824);

Essays on the Nature and Uses of the Various Evidences of Revealed Religion (New York: C. Wiley, 1824);

An Essay on the Doctrine of Contracts; Being an Inquiry how Contracts are Affected in Law and Morals by Concealment, Error, or Inadequate Price (New York: G. & C. Carvill, 1825);

An Address Delivered Before the Philolexian and Peithologian Societies, August 2, 1830; on the Evening Preceding the Annual Commencement of Columbia College (New York: G. & C. & H. Carvill, 1830);

A Letter to Col. William Drayton, of South Carolina, in Assertion of the Constitutional Power of Congress to Impose Protecting Duties (New York: E. Bliss, 1831);

The Right Moral Influence and Use of Liberal Studies; a Discourse Delivered after the Annual Commencement of Geneva College, August 7th, 1833 (New York: Henry Ludwig, 1833; Edinburgh: T. Clark, 1835);

Discourses and Addresses on Subjects of American History, Arts, and Literature (New York: Harper, 1833);

A Lecture, Introductory to the Course of Scientific Lectures Before the Mechanics' Institute of the City of New York (New York: G. P. Scott, 1833);

The Connection of Morals and Learning, and Their Influence Upon Each Other (New York: Harper, 1834);

The Influence of Moral Causes Upon Opinion, Science, and Literature (New York: Henry Ludwig, 1834);

The Advantages and Dangers of the American Scholar; a Discourse Delivered on the Day Preceding the Annual Commencement of Union College, July 26, 1836 (New York: Wiley & Long, 1836);

Speech When in Committee of the Whole in the Senate of New York, on the Several Bills and Resolutions for the Amendment of the Law and the Reform of the Judiciary System (Albany: Hoffman & White, 1839);

Garrick: His Portrait in New York, Its Artist, and History (New York, 1857).

OTHER: "Stanzas from Poliziana," "De Gourgues," "Major Egerton," and "Sonnet on the Shenandoah at Harper's Ferry," by Verplanck, and "Mr. De Viellecour and His Neighbors," by Verplanck and Robert C. Sands, in *The Talisman for MDCCCXXVIII,* edited by Verplanck, William Cullen Bryant, and Sands (New York: Elam Bliss, 1828);

"Recollections of Balfroosh," "Shedaud," "Stanzas," "The Dismal Swamp," and "Drummond," by Verplanck, "Scenes at Washington, No. 1," by Verplanck and Sands, and "Reminiscences of New York, No. 1," by

Gulian C. Verplanck, circa 1830; portrait by Charles C. Ingham (by permission of the New-York Historical Society; gift of Members of the Society, 1878.2)

Verplanck and Bryant, in *The Talisman for MDCCCXXVIX*, edited by Verplanck, Bryant, and Sands (New York: Elam Bliss, 1829);

"Telemachus Moritis," "Song. When the Firmament Quivers with Daylight's Young Beam," "Peregrinations of Petrus Mudd," and "To a Child," by Verplanck, "Scenes at Washington, No. II," by Verplanck and Sands, and "Reminiscences of New York, No. II," by Verplanck and Bryant, in *The Talisman for MDCCCXXX*, written and edited by Verplanck, Bryant, and Sands (New York: Elam Bliss, 1830);

The Fairy Book, edited, with an introduction, by Verplanck (New York: Harper, 1836;

Shakespeare's Plays: With His Life, edited, with critical introductions and notes, by Verplanck, 3 volumes (New York: Harper, 1847);

"Was Champagne Known to the Ancients?" and "Oxyporian Wines," in *The Sayings of Dr. Bushwacker, and Other Learned Men*, edited by Frederick S. Cozzens (New York: A. Simpson, 1867).

PERIODICAL PUBLICATIONS: "Biographical Memoir of Samuel Johnson, D.D., First President of Kings (Now Columbia) College, New York," *Churchman's Magazine*, new series 1 (January-February 1813): 5-20;

"Biographical Memoir of Samuel Adams," *Analectic Magazine*, new series 3 (March 1814): 231-241;

"Biographical and Critical Sketch of Fisher Ames," *Analectic Magazine*, new series 3 (April 1814): 309-333;

"Biographical Memoir of Oliver Ellsworth," *Analectic Magazine*, new series 3 (May 1814): 382-403;

"Notice of the Life and Writings of William Cliffton," *Analectic Magazine*, new series 3 (June 1814): 479-488;

"Waterman's *Life of Calvin*," *Analectic Magazine*, new series 4 (July 1814): 42-49;

"Sketch of the Life and Writings of Joel Barlow," *Analectic Magazine*, new series 4 (August 1814): 130-158;

Review of the *Feast of the Poets*, *Analectic Magazine*, new series 4 (September 1814): 243-249;

"Biographical Memoir of Cadwallader Colden, M.D.F.R.S.," *Analectic Magazine*, new series 4 (October 1814): 307-312;

"Biographical Memoir of the Late Brigadier General Zebulon Montgomery Pike," *Analectic Magazine*, new series 4 (November 1814): 380-395;

"Biographical Sketch of Major General Winfield Scott," *Analectic Magazine*, new series 4 (December 1814): 465-486;

"*The Sketch Book* of Geoffrey Crayon," *Analectic Magazine*, 14 (July 1819): 78-79;

Review of *Poems*, by William Cullen Bryant, *New York American*, 4 October 1821;

"Bourbon's Last March," *New York Mirror*, 11 October 1834, pp. 113-114;

"View of Washington's Headquarters," *New York Mirror*, 27 December 1834, pp. 201-202;

"An Autumnal Evening," *New York Mirror*, 28 March 1835, pp. 305-306.

Gulian Crommelin Verplanck was born in New York City on 6 August 1786. Of Flemish and Dutch origins, his family had come to New Amsterdam shortly after 1630, and its members had early distinguished themselves in American business, politics, and education. The fact that his grandparents had deeply divided loyalties during the period of the American Revolution appears to have given him a lifelong tendency to listen to all sides of a dispute, to give credit to those with whom he disagreed, and, especially during his political career, to strike out independently according to his principles despite pressures to adhere loyally to party platforms.

Verplanck himself was a man of wide interests. He was an active critic of literature, art, and architecture, the author of a number of tales, sketches, and poems, a politician with a long and varied career of service, and a humanitarian of the first order. At the age of eleven Verplanck enrolled at Columbia College where his grandfather, William Samuel Johnson, was president. When he graduated in 1801 at the age of fourteen, he became the youngest graduate in Columbia's history. He began to read law in New York City, and in 1807 he was admitted to the New York bar. Law was never, however, his real interest, and his partner, Nathaniel F. Moore, recalled that Verplanck had never "had, or cared to have, any legal business whatever."

Verplanck turned to the field of politics early in life, joining, as was natural given his merchant background and his family's traditions, the conservative Federalist party. In 1808 he helped organize a secret political organization, the Washington Benevolent Society, in an attempt to rejuvenate the fading fortunes of New York's Federalists. Indeed his first public address seems to have been the society's 4 July 1809 celebration. By 1811 Verplanck was deeply involved in both local and national politics. In that year he published his *Letter to the Hon. Saml. L. Mitchell* under the pseudonym "Abimelech Coody, Esq., Ladies' Shoemaker." In his pamphlet Verplanck describes the perplexed attempts of Coody to safeguard $10,000, which he had won in a lottery, by placing the money in various banks and investments. Verplanck depicts the poor man as finding everywhere contradictory advice given by the partisans of different political parties. The piece thus constitutes a series of attacks on virtually all political factions in contemporary New York. As Verplanck himself put it in his preface, he wished to present a "faithful . . . picture of the manner in which the minds of very many of our industrious fellow-citizens are harassed and perplexed by the raw head and bloody bones tales which are daily propagated by our political partisans and politicians by profession." The variety of targets for his satire accurately predicted Verplanck's later political career during which he changed parties frequently rather than bend his principles to suit a party's platform. His effectiveness in the political arena can be seen in the vehemence with which New York mayor DeWitt Clinton attacked the younger man after Verplanck's arrest at Columbia's 1811 graduation. Verplanck had attempted publicly to intervene on behalf of a graduate who was denied his degree for including political remarks in his graduation address. This incident began a long-standing feud between Clinton and Verplanck. Indeed, in 1814, Verplanck helped organize the American Federalist party, popularly known as "the Coodies" after his shoemaker, to oppose Clinton and his Federalist supporters.

During the decade from 1810 to 1820 Verplanck was busy contributing a variety of articles to such local periodicals as Washington Irving's *Analectic Magazine*. In 1814 alone, for example, he contributed a series of eight apolitical biographical sketches of eminent Americans, including Samuel Adams, Fisher Ames, and Gen. Winfield Scott, all of which demonstrate his growing cultural nationalism. Verplanck married Mary Elizabeth Fenno, the sister-in-law of Fenno Hoffman, in 1811; they had two sons. By 1815 Mary Elizabeth's health began to fail, and the Verplancks left for an extended stay in Europe, hoping that her physical condition would improve. After her death two years later, Verplanck returned to the United States.

In 1818 he delivered before the New York Historical Society *An Anniversary Discourse*, a lecture which Bryant calls "one of the happiest examples in our language of the class of compositions to which it belongs." Here Verplanck's cultural nationalism is again evident as he praises eminent figures like Roger Williams, Lord Baltimore, William Penn, and General Oglethorpe because they "have most largely contributed to raise or support our national institutions, and to form or elevate our national character." Verplanck was also a staunch defender of the Dutch contributions to the growth of young America, and in his lecture he attacked his friend Irving's *Knickerbocker's History of New York* (1809) for "wasting the riches of its fancy on an ungrateful theme, and its exuberant humor in a coarse caricature." Verplanck did not hold a grudge, however, and his 1819 review of *The Sketch Book* is genuinely appreciative of Irving's work; it is also exemplary of the method

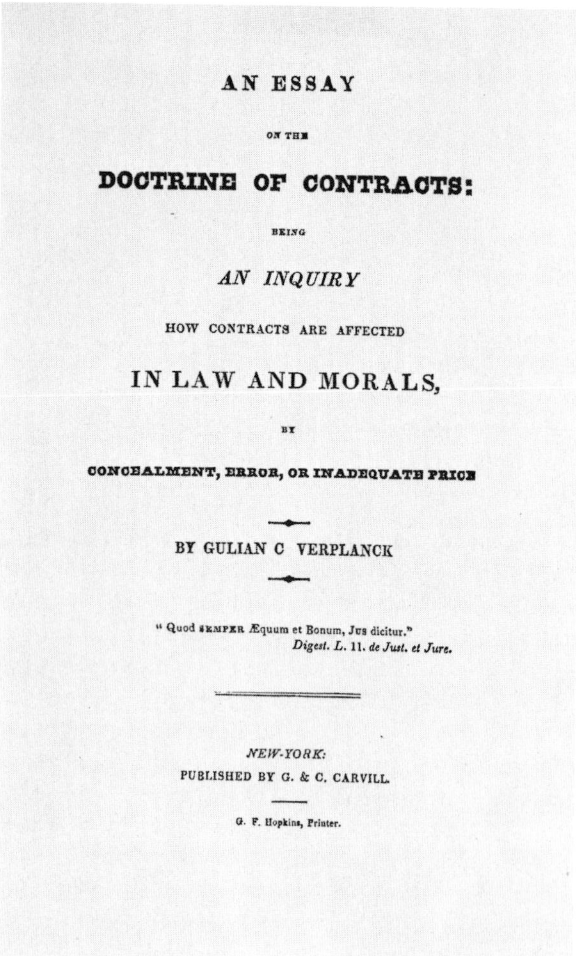

AN ESSAY

ON THE

DOCTRINE OF CONTRACTS:

BEING

AN INQUIRY

HOW CONTRACTS ARE AFFECTED

IN LAW AND MORALS,

BY

CONCEALMENT, ERROR, OR INADEQUATE PRICE

BY GULIAN C VERPLANCK

"Quod SEMPER Æquum et Bonum, Jus dicitur."
Digest. L. 11. de Just. et Jure.

NEW-YORK:
PUBLISHED BY G. & C. CARVILL.

G. F. Hopkins, Printer.

Title page for the book in which Verplanck argued for "the necessity of making our law of Sales and Contracts perfectly rational and consistent . . ."

of much of Verplanck's early criticism. He was of the school which generally substituted sympathetic appreciation for the more formal criticism of "ordinary critical tribunals" in order to create an environment in which distinctively American literature could be fostered.

Verplanck remained involved in politics, and in 1819 he, along with John Duer and Rudolph Bunner, published "The Bucktail Bards," a series of satirical poems which appeared in the anti-Clinton newspaper, the *American*. These poems, later collected as *The State Triumvirate* (1819), attacked Clinton for his puffery and pretensions to learning. Although the collection was very popular in its day, "the allusions are obscure, and it is a task to read it," as Bryant noted in 1870, thus accounting for its lack of renown today. By 1820 Verplanck and other "High Minded Federalists" who supported the policies of the *American* declared the Federalist party dead and joined the Republicans. In this same year Verplanck was himself elected to the New York state assembly where he was an influential voice in favor of state support for education.

In 1824, on a platform in favor of free trade, Verplanck was elected congressman from the district of New York, as one of Martin Van Buren's "Bucktail" Republicans, a faction which was labeling itself "Democrats" in order to distinguish itself from John Quincy Adams's more conservative "National Republicans." Throughout Verplanck's four terms in Congress, he was important primarily for the carefully researched and thoughtful papers which were issued from the committees on which he served. Indeed some of this work shows especially clearly Verplanck's ability to see all sides of an issue. For example, although he was a staunch supporter of New York's mercantile interests, and thus an opponent of protective tariffs, his *A Letter to Col. William Drayton* (1831) is a carefully reasoned defense of the Constitutional right of Congress to impose tariffs if and when it wishes to do so. In 1832, however, he was not even renominated by the Democrats because he opposed President Jackson on the question of rechartering the Bank of the United States.

Throughout his tenure in Washington, Verplanck was active in supporting American arts and letters. In 1831, for example, Congress passed a new copyright law, drafted by Verplanck, which essentially doubled the period under which American authors could protect their works by copyright in order to give "additional security to the property of authors and artists in their works" and thus encourage the further growth of a national literature. For his efforts, he was honored at a dinner in New York which was attended by many of America's most eminent writers, critics, and lovers of literature.

Verplanck also served as chairman of the House Committee on Public Buildings. That he was qualified to oversee the construction and decoration of the nation's public areas is evident from his 1824 *Address Delivered Before the American Academy of Fine Arts*. There he demonstrated his abilities as both a critic and theorist of architecture. He attacked the architecture of the United States Capitol, for example, as "primitive" and as employing a "great profusion of unmeaning ornament . . . to supply the place of unity and dignity." He also attacked the vogue for Gothic architecture on the grounds that efforts to capture the "solemnity, pomp, impression and varied rich ceremonial" of the Catholic model on the smaller scale appropriate to a protestant church, for example, generally resulted in "the vain attempt to exhibit the vast proportions, the numberless and exquisite minuter beauties, and the infinity of picturesque combinations of Salisbury Cathedral, or York Minster, in the cheapest and least durable materials, and within the limits of a few square yards." In place of such useless imitation, Verplanck advocated a functional architecture in which the "appearance" of a building would clearly "announce" its uses.

Verplanck used his position to aid individual artists whenever possible. He had long been friends with many of New York's leading artists, figures whom he knew through his membership in clubs like the Bread and Cheese Club, the Sketch Club, the American Academy of Fine Arts, and the National Academy of Design. As Chairman of the House Committee on Public Buildings, Verplanck helped to usher in what James T. Callow has called "the first era of public patronage in the United States." For example, Verplanck was a close friend of the painter Washington Allston, and he had studiously publicized Allston's work for years. In 1830 he attempted to give Allston the commission to finish the last four panels of the rotunda of the Capitol, the first four having been completed by John Trumbull. Unfortunately, the two were never able to agree on suitable subjects for Allston's talents, and the artist finally declined the offer. Although most of the commissions for the paintings in the rotunda were granted after Verplanck's tenure as chairman of the committee, he clearly influenced the selection of Robert W. Weir, Henry Inman, and John Vanderlyn for three of the paintings. He also helped Horatio Greenough obtain the commission for his statue of George Washington. Verplanck was particularly helpful to Weir, serving as agent for some of his paintings, purchasing at least three himself, and using his influence in Washington to have the artist appointed Teacher of Drawing at the United States Military Academy at West Point. In short even while Verplanck was busy with questions of tariffs, internal improvements, and the Bank of the United States, he continued to be an avid–and practical–supporter of a native tradition of the arts.

While Verplanck was serving as representative, he also continued to produce art of his own. In 1828, 1829, and 1830 he collaborated with both William Cullen Bryant and Robert C. Sands to produce a gift book, *The Talisman*. Under the pseudonym "Francis Herbert, Esq.," each of the three produced stories, essays, and poems for the volumes. Verplanck was at his best in the historical essays which he contributed, and at his worst in his attempts at poetry. His method of writing pieces for *The Talisman* perhaps indicates why Verplanck is so little known today. He apparently detested the physical act of writing, and during the collaborative efforts for the gift book he would, according to James Grant Wilson, remain "seated in a chair with his arm resting on another, while his feet were supported by a third, [dictating] to one of his *confrères* as rapidly as they could write." Thus, this "somewhat indolent man" was unlikely to produce the sort of sustained work which might well have confirmed his place in American letters. Instead, he was more likely to produce occasional pieces like the prose sketches which accompanied engravings of his friend Weir's paintings in the *New York Mirror* in 1834-1835.

After the loss of his congressional seat in 1832, Verplanck returned to New York where he associated himself with that group of Democrats opposed to the policies of Jackson and Van Buren. These Whigs nominated Verplanck as their candidate for mayor of the city in 1834, and, in an election marred by three days of riots, Verplanck was defeated by about 180 votes in a total of 35,000 cast. After this defeat, he turned away from politics for three years, focusing his attention on his literary efforts.

His most important work during this period was his lecture at Union College entitled *The Advantages and Dangers of the American Scholar* (1836). This work, delivered thirteen months before Ralph Waldo Emerson's more famous lecture on the same subject, is composed of three sections, addressing the topics "blessings and advantages," "their accompanying dangers," and "their attendant duties." In contrast to Emerson who was rather pessimistic about the intellectual temper of most Americans, Verplanck is solidly optimistic, claiming: "We all know and feel that everything in the conditions and prospects of our country tends to excite and maintain a bold and stirring activity of thought and action throughout the whole community." Although the man wholly devoted to scholarship was unlikely to be found in America because "the American man of letters is incessantly called off from any single inquiry, and allured or compelled to try his ability in every variety of human occupation," Verplanck clearly values this tendency of the American scholar to action. The dangers which he foresaw accompanying such a broadly viewed intellectual life are the possibility of lapsing into mere superficiality, the temptation of being lured away from scholarship by personal gain, the prospect of becoming a mere intellectual bond slave to European thought and forms, and the danger of being led to "a bitter spirit of intolerance" due to partisanship and party politics. Thus, for Verplanck, as for Emerson, the American scholar's self-reliance is crucial–"Be true to yourselves and to your country"–although Verplanck, unlike Emerson, wants his scholar to become immediately and directly involved in the political and social life of the country in order to bring his superior culture directly to bear on the nation's problems. That Verplanck himself lived according to this injunction is evidenced by Bryant's claims that "He would accompany a party, but never follow it" and that "He never adopted an opinion for the reason that it had been adopted by another." Such independence of thought explains, of course, Verplanck's frequent shifts of party allegiance and the mistrust with which he was often viewed by a particular party's leadership.

In 1837 Verplanck returned to the political arena, winning election as a state senator under the Whig banner. Once again he worked diligently in service of state education; he also supported plans to develop and expand the Erie Canal, and he proposed plans to overhaul the state court system. Perhaps his most important contributions, however, were the opinions he wrote as a jurist on the Court for the Correction of Errors, an appellate court composed of Supreme Court judges, the chancellor, and members of the Senate. Although Verplanck had read law in his youth, he had never really practiced. He may have been prepared for his judicial service, at least in part, by his *An Essay on the Doctrine of Contracts* (1825), in which he argued for complete openness and frankness between buyer and seller and against the doctrine caveat emptor; in any case, the remarkably high quality of his work while a member of the court earned him high praise from New York's judicial establishment as well as laymen. The end of Verplanck's political service came in 1842 when he declined renomination after he was attacked for his plan to establish special "alien" schools which would provide immigrants with instruction in their native languages and permit religious instruction.

Gulian C. Verplanck, drawing by Paul Duggan (by permission of the Century Club)

Throughout this period of his life, Verplanck continued his literary and scholarly efforts. In 1836, apparently moved to collect many of the tales which his grandchildren enjoyed, he edited *The Fairy Book.* In his preface, echoing earlier claims made in his 1814 review of Leigh Hunt's *The Feast of the Poets,* he lamented the contemporary disdain of the fairy tale as a genre. Perhaps his greatest work was finally published ten years later–his edition of *Shakespeare's Plays: With His Life* (1847). Verplanck was inspired by the work of two earlier Shakespearean scholars, Charles Knight and John Payne Collier, but he clearly went beyond them in his research. His distinctive contributions included copious notes on costumes, arms, architecture, and conventions, as well as bibliographic essays on each work suggesting a date of composition, describing the current state of the text, and noting variations among Elizabethan editions. As Verplanck himself put it, his interest was "not one of purely antiquarian curiosity, but . . . tracing out Shakespeare's intellectual history and character, by gathering from various and sometimes slight and circumstantial or collateral points of testimony, the order and succession of his works, assigning, so far as possible, each one to its probable epoch, noting the variations or differences of style and of versification between them, and in some cases . . . the alterations and improvements of the same play by the author himself, in the progress of his taste and experience. . . ." Verplanck was especially interested in the connections between Elizabethan dialects and "Americanisms," commenting frequently on the development of the English language in America, thus becoming party to a contemporary movement which saw America's national speech as indicative of the national mind and, therefore, the national character. Although modern critics have tended to discount Verplanck's contribution to Shakespeare scholarship, many contemporary critics praised it highly, and his friend Bryant praised his edition as "the very one for which the general reader has occasion" since the primary purpose of Verplanck's scholarship was to give the reader all the necessary data for a clear understanding of the plays.

After 1850 Verplanck's literary contributions fell off markedly. He published *Garrick: His Portrait,* his recollections of some of the Knickerbocker writers, in 1857, and in 1860 he produced two parodic pieces of scholarship on the history of winemaking, but by and large he concentrated on his long-standing humanitarian labors, working on behalf of new immigrants in New York, continuing to serve on the Board of Regents of the State University (and becoming its vice-chancellor in 1858), and serving as vice-president of the National Academy of Arts and Design as well as the New-York Historical Society. By the time of his death in 1870 Verplanck had attained a well-deserved reputation as both a public man and a man of letters. As William Cullen Bryant put it, "He acted in so many important capacities; he was connected in so many ways with our literature, our legislation, our jurisprudence, our public education, and public charities, that it would require a volume adequately to set forth the obligations we owe to the exertion of his fine faculties for the general good." Today he is little remembered, probably because he tended to write short, occasional pieces on a wide variety of subjects rather than producing a single monumental work which would have concentrated his efforts in memorable form.

Biographies:

William Cullen Bryant, *A Discourse on the Life, Character and Writings of Gulian Crommelin Verplanck* (New York: The Society, 1870); republished as "Gulian Crommelin Verplanck," in *Prose Writings of William Cullen Bryant,* edited by Parke Godwin, volume 1 (New York: Russell & Russell, 1964), pp. 394-431;

James Grant Wilson, "Gulian Crommelin Verplanck," in *Bryant and His Friends* (New York: Fords, Howard & Hulbert, 1886), pp. 383-387;

Robert W. July, *The Essential New Yorker: Gulian Crommelin Verplanck* (Durham, N.C.: Duke University Press, 1951).

References:

James T. Callow, *Kindred Spirits: Knickerbocker Writers and American Artists, 1807-1855* (Chapel Hill: University of North Carolina Press, 1967);

Sarah King Harvey, "A Bibliography of the Miscellaneous Prose of Gulian Crommelin Verplanck," *American Literature,* 8 (May 1936): 199-203;

A. H. Marckwardt, "The American Scholar: Two Views," *Papers of the Michigan Academy of Science, Arts and Letters,* 18 (1932): 525-538;

John W. Rathbun, *American Literary Criticism, 1800-1860* (Boston: G. K. Hall, 1979);

Robert E. Streeter, "Association Psychology and Literary Nationalism in the *North American Review,* 1815-1825," *American Literature,* 17 (November 1945): 243-254.

Papers:

The bulk of Verplanck's papers and correspondence, especially from the years 1830 to 1870, can be found in the New-York Historical Society collections. The Bryant-Verplanck correspondence is held by the New York Public Library in its Berg Collection, while additional correspondence is available in the North Family papers in the Cornell University Library, Collection of Regional History and University Archives.

Robert Walsh

(30 August 1784-7 February 1859)

Guy R. Woodall
Tennessee Technological University

SELECTED BOOKS: *A Letter on the Genius and Dispositions of the French Government Including a View of the Taxation of the French Empire* (Philadelphia: Hopkins & Earle /Baltimore: P. H. Nicklin, 1810; London: Longman, Rees & Orme, 1810);

An Inquiry into the Past and Present Relations of France and the United States (London: Printed for J. Hatchard, 1811);

Correspondence Respecting Russia between Robert Goodloe Harper, Esq., and Robert Walsh, Jun. Together with the Speech of Mr. Harper, Commemorative of the Russian Victories. Delivered at Georgetown, Columbia, June 5th, 1813. And an Essay on the Future State of Europe (Philadelphia: Printed by William Fry, 1813);

An Appeal from the Judgments of Great Britain Respecting the United States of America. Part First, Containing an Historical Outline of their Merits and Wrongs as Colonies; and Strictures upon the Calumnies of the British Writers (Philadelphia: Printed by William Brown for Mitchell, Ames & White, 1819; London: Longman, Hurst, 1820);

Free Remarks on the Spirit of the Federal Constitution, the Practice of the Federal Government, and the Obligations of the Union Respecting the Exclusion of Slavery from the Territories and the New States (Philadelphia: Printed by William Fry for A. Findley, 1819);

Didactics: Social, Literary, and Political, 2 volumes (Philadelphia: Carey, Lea & Blanchard, 1836);

Notes on the American Constitution (Keeseville, N.Y.: Printed by J. F. Morgan, 1849).

OTHER: *The Works of the British Poets With Lives of the Authors*, volumes 18-21, 23, 25-50, edited by Walsh (Philadelphia: Mitchell, Ames & White, 1819-1823);

Select Speeches of the Right Honourable, George Canning, edited, with a biographical sketch, by Walsh (Philadelphia: Key & Biddle, 1835);

Select Speeches of the Right Honourable William Windham and the Right Honourable William Huskisson, edited, with biographical sketches, by Walsh (Philadelphia: E. C. Biddle, 1837).

PERIODICAL PUBLICATIONS: "The Lady of the Lake," *American Review of History and Politics, and General Repository of Literature and State Papers*, 1 (January 1811): 166-174;

"*Die Wahlverwandtschaften* ein Roman von Goethe," *American Review of History and Politics, and General Repository of Literature and State Papers*, 3 (January 1812): 51-69;

"A Biographical Sketch of Andrew Jackson," anonymous, *American Monthly*, 1 (1824);

"American Biography," *American Quarterly Review*, 1 (March 1827): 1-38; 1 (June 1827): 401-437;

"American Poetry," *American Quarterly Review*, 6 (September 1829): 240-262;

"Southey's Colloquies," *American Quarterly Review*, 6 (September 1829): 55-72.

Robert Walsh, Baltimore and Philadelphia

editor and literary critic, was one of America's most important men of letters in the first three and a half decades of the nineteenth century. He founded America's first quarterly review, was the leading apologist for America in the nationalistic paper war between the American and British press following the War of 1812, was the fugleman for Scottish Common Sense aesthetics and classicism in American criticism, and introduced a new literary journalism in the daily press. Most of his literary criticism appeared in essays and reviews in a half dozen journals that he edited in Philadelphia. Edgar Allan Poe spoke for many of Walsh's contemporaries when he said, "He is one of the finest writers, one of the most accomplished scholars, and when not in too great a hurry, one of the most accurate thinkers in the country."

Robert Walsh, Jr., born in Baltimore on 30 August 1784, was the eldest of ten children born to Robert Walsh, Sr., and Elizabeth Steel Walsh. Only five of the children survived infancy. The elder Walsh, a prosperous import merchant, was often called Robert Walsh of Baltimore to distinguish him from his son who became associated with Philadelphia. A devout Catholic, Robert, Sr., put his son under the private care of French Sulpician priests in Baltimore for his elementary education. When his son was thirteen years old, the father enrolled him at Georgetown College. In 1800 he transferred to St. Mary's College, where he remained until he completed his course of studies in 1802. St. Mary's College became St. Mary's University in 1805, and when it first began to confer formal degrees with the commencement of 1806, Robert Walsh was granted a master of arts degree in absentia. Walsh, a brilliant student throughout his formal schooling, was especially devoted to the study of languages and literature. In later times he sent two of his sons to St. Mary's, which he considered to be the best seminary in America for instruction in morals and languages.

Walsh began writing for public journals at sixteen. At nineteen, he had become a well-established essayist for Joseph Dennie's *Port Folio.* Marked by a Federal political bias, classical taste, and patrician social sympathies, the essays adumbrated a conservatism that Walsh upheld throughout his literary and personal life. His conservatism was grounded in his formal education at Georgetown College (1797-1800) and St. Mary's College in Baltimore (1800-1802), his apprenticeship to the brilliant Baltimore Federalist lawyer Robert Goodloe Harper (1802-1806), his connection with the classicist editor Joseph Dennie and the *Port Folio* circle (1803-1812), and his association with the editor Francis Jeffrey and the Edinburgh reviewers when he was abroad (1806-1809).

Following two years in Europe, Walsh was back in Philadelphia in the summer of 1809. He resumed his activities with the Philadelphia literati; and when Charles Brockden Brown, editor of the *American Register*, died in early 1810, Walsh succeeded him, editing the two final numbers. Walsh entered upon a literary career while concurrently courting and marrying, on 9 April 1810, Anna Maria Moylan, daughter of Jasper Moylan, a highly successful counselor of law in Philadelphia. In time the Walshes had eleven children, ten of whom survived to adulthood. From the beginning of Walsh's marriage, Jasper Moylan offered Walsh opportunities to join him in the practice of law; but he refused, choosing to follow a career in literature.

By the autumn of 1810 Walsh had committed his career to journalism. He desired to publish in America a quarterly journal like the *Edinburgh Review.* In January 1811 he issued the first number of the *American Review of History and Politics, and General Repository of Literature and State Papers*, the first quarterly review in America. The review propagated Federalism and fostered a classical literary taste. The reviews in the *American Review* often referred to the major Augustans. The philosophical and rhetorical bases for the literary criticism were derived from the principles of the Scottish Common Sense school. Walsh regularly appealed to Thomas Reid, Lord Kames (Henry Home), Hugh Blair, Dugald Stewart, and Francis Jeffrey. Like the Scots, Walsh insisted that literature be moral, realistic, or at least probable, socially useful, and correct in syntax and diction. In the *American Review* Walsh lamented that America had not yet produced any poetry of merit. John Trumbull's *McFingal* (1782), for example, was written off as "a subordinate species of poetry"; and Joel Barlow's *Columbiad* was a work "best forgotten." Although ignoring American and British fiction, Walsh helped introduce German literature to America by reviewing Goethe's novel *Die Wahlverwandtschaften* (1808). The faults that he found in it were those that he found in most fiction: improbabilities, incongruities, and improprieties.

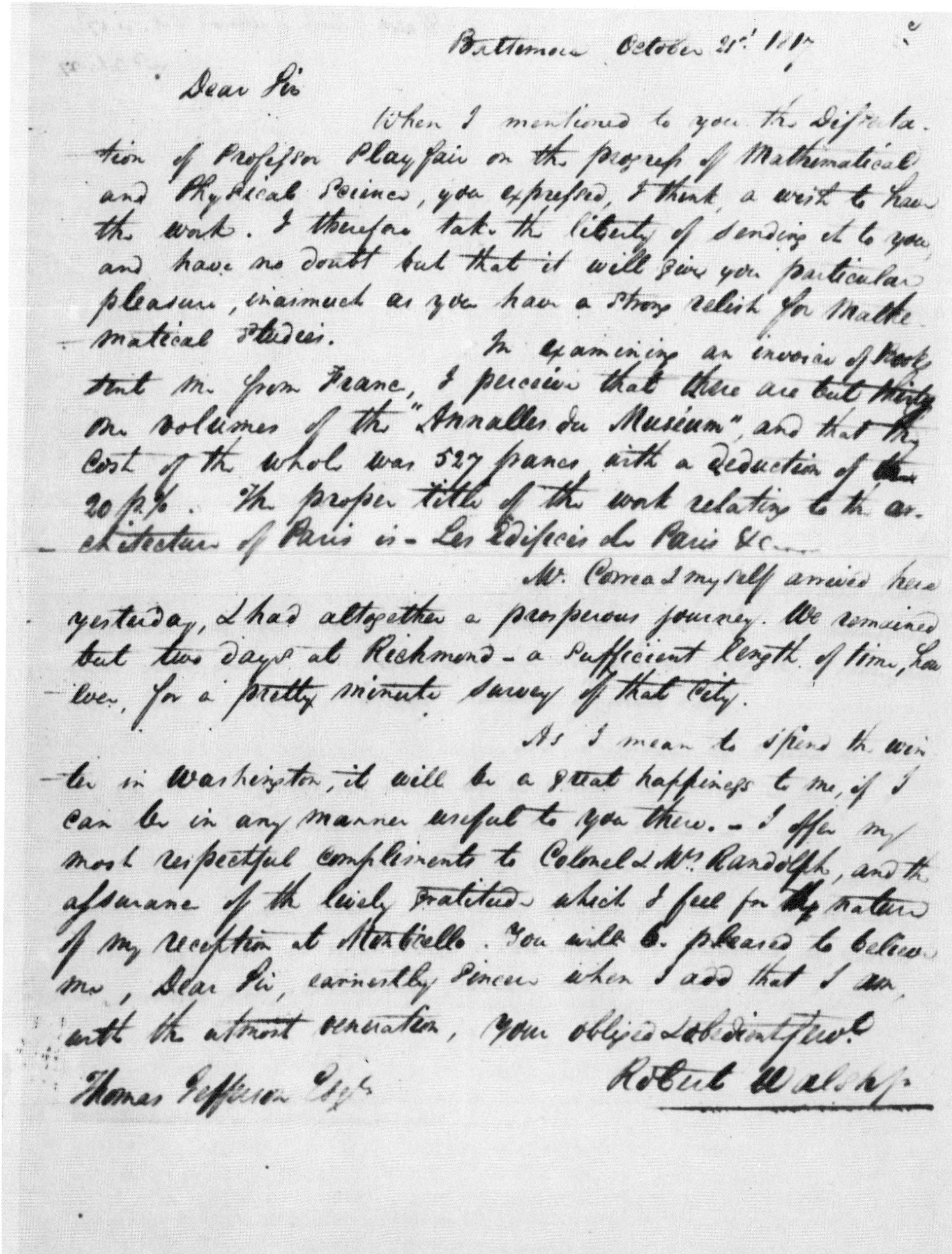

Baltimore October 21st 1817

Dear Sir

When I mentioned to you the Dissertation of Professor Playfair on the progress of Mathematical and Physical Science, you expressed, I think, a wish to have the work. I therefore take the liberty of sending it to you and have no doubt but that it will give you particular pleasure, inasmuch as you have a strong relish for Mathematical studies. In examining an invoice of books sent me from France, I perceive that there are but ~~thirty~~ one volumes of the "Annales du Museum", and that the cost of the whole was 527 francs, with a deduction of the 20 p%. The proper title of the work relating to the architecture of Paris is—Les Edifices de Paris &c.

Mr. Correa & myself arrived here yesterday, & had altogether a prosperous journey. We remained but two days at Richmond—a sufficient length of time, however, for a pretty minute survey of that City.

As I mean to spend the winter in Washington, it will be a great happiness to me, if I can be in any manner useful to you there.—I offer my most respectful compliments to Colonel & Mrs. Randolph, and the assurance of the lively gratitude which I feel for the nature of my reception at Monticello. You will be pleased to believe me, Dear Sir, earnestly sincere when I add that I am, with the utmost veneration, Your obliged & obedient servt.

Robert Walsh

Thomas Jefferson Esqr.

Letter to Thomas Jefferson (by permission of the Massachusetts Historical Society)

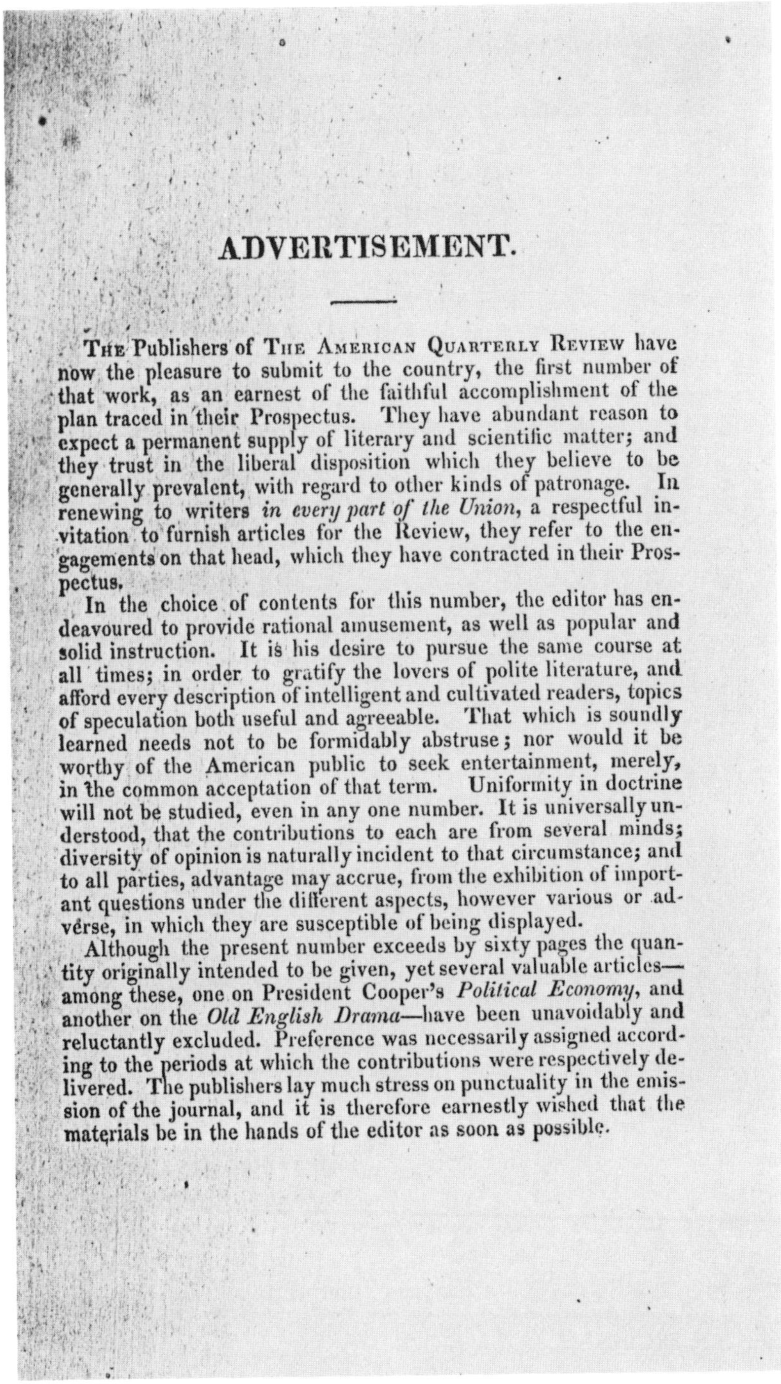

ADVERTISEMENT.

The Publishers of The American Quarterly Review have now the pleasure to submit to the country, the first number of that work, as an earnest of the faithful accomplishment of the plan traced in their Prospectus. They have abundant reason to expect a permanent supply of literary and scientific matter; and they trust in the liberal disposition which they believe to be generally prevalent, with regard to other kinds of patronage. In renewing to writers *in every part of the Union*, a respectful invitation to furnish articles for the Review, they refer to the engagements on that head, which they have contracted in their Prospectus.

In the choice of contents for this number, the editor has endeavoured to provide rational amusement, as well as popular and solid instruction. It is his desire to pursue the same course at all times; in order to gratify the lovers of polite literature, and afford every description of intelligent and cultivated readers, topics of speculation both useful and agreeable. That which is soundly learned needs not to be formidably abstruse; nor would it be worthy of the American public to seek entertainment, merely, in the common acceptation of that term. Uniformity in doctrine will not be studied, even in any one number. It is universally understood, that the contributions to each are from several minds; diversity of opinion is naturally incident to that circumstance; and to all parties, advantage may accrue, from the exhibition of important questions under the different aspects, however various or adverse, in which they are susceptible of being displayed.

Although the present number exceeds by sixty pages the quantity originally intended to be given, yet several valuable articles—among these, one on President Cooper's *Political Economy*, and another on the *Old English Drama*—have been unavoidably and reluctantly excluded. Preference was necessarily assigned according to the periods at which the contributions were respectively delivered. The publishers lay much stress on punctuality in the emission of the journal, and it is therefore earnestly wished that the materials be in the hands of the editor as soon as possible.

Advertisement in the first issue of the American Quarterly Review *(March 1827)*

The American Review ended abruptly in October 1812, when the publishers declared themselves bankrupt. Walsh resumed editing only in February 1817, when he published the first number of the *American Register; or Summary Review of History, Politics and Literature*. The "great ends" of the undertaking were, Walsh advertised, "to dispense solid instruction or amusement." He criticized American poets and fictionists in the new journal as stringently as ever: "We have had now and then a volume of poetry always below mediocrity, and a few romances or novels too contemptible to be remembered. . . . I would much prefer that our taste and intelligence should be tested by the English works printed among us." Walsh's derogation of American writers infuriated many of them, who accused him of being an Anglophile. John Neal and members of the Delphian Club, most of whom were connected with the chauvinistic Baltimore *Portico*, for example, regularly castigated Walsh for his failure to support American writers and for measuring them by the standards of the Scottish reviewers. Lacking financial support, the *American Register* died at the end of 1817.

While editing the *American Register*, Walsh also had contributed reviews to and helped to edit the *Analectic* magazine. Displeased with Walsh's reviews in the *Analectic*, a writer in the *Portico* accused him of "dreaming that he lived in the land of Edinburgh, and in concert with the 'great Jeffries' had matured a scheme for blasting in the bud every shoot of American intellect." Walsh defended the *Edinburgh* reviewers, arguing that their stringency had never stifled a single promising author. He ended his connection with the *Analectic* at the end of 1818 in order to write a book vindicating America against calumnious charges being made against her character and institutions. The book was published in September 1819, under the title of *An Appeal from the Judgments of Great Britain Respecting the United States of America*. With this book Walsh became famous as the "generalissimo" in the paper war. He exposed the false impressions given in British travel books about America and scolded the British reviewers for believing their countrymen's accounts about America.

In 1820 Walsh began the most successful part of his career when he founded the Philadelphia *National Gazette and Literary Register*, a newspaper which contained foreign and domestic political, scientific, and literary intelligence. In time the literary character became the most distinctive feature of the *National Gazette*. Walsh never lost sight of his original commitment to improve the literary taste of America in his paper. He did this by regularly inserting extracts from all genres of literature from both foreign and domestic authors of the time and adding a great many critiques and literary essays. For the greater part, the criticism was stern but judicious. It was more personal than textual or analytical, being directed at the author rather than his work. Yet Walsh esteemed the office of a critic too highly to be arbitrarily severe. He explained: "I concur fully in Swift's doctrine that 'a critic who sets up to read only for censure and reproof is a creature as barbarous and unjust as a judge, who should take upon a resolution to hang all men who came before him upon a trial' but a judge is often obliged to proceed with severity, more on the account of the danger of the example than the intrinsic evil of the offense brought before him within his cognizance, so a critic may, from the same consideration, feel it incumbent upon him to chide and complain with frankness and rigor." Years after Walsh resigned from the *National Gazette*, Rufus Wilmot Griswold well evaluated his contributions as a pioneering newspaper editor and critic, saying his "system of editing was an innovation." Noting the wide range of subject matter in Walsh's columns, Griswold commented that his book and stage reviews, though lacking the sympathy of the best critics, exhibited much knowledge, reflection, and good sense. In sum, Griswold noted: "The *Gazette* rose rapidly in popular estimation and soon had an unprecedented influence, and its success led in all parts of the country to more attention to matters of taste in journalism."

In addition to his position as editor of the *National Gazette* Walsh undertook the editorship of the *American Quarterly Review* in late 1826. He modeled the quarterly after the *Edinburgh Review* and London *Quarterly Review*, which he considered superior to other reviews. Because he paid his reviewers better than other editors, he attracted contributors whose high quality led to the immediate success of the quarterly. He wrote, on the average, one essay for each number. As in his earlier journals, Walsh's criticism was judicious. Never in a mood to write appreciative criticism of foreign or domestic writers whom he thought were inferior, he waged a running editorial war, for example, with a coterie of New York reviewers who found him unduly severe on the Lake Poets of England and the budding young American writers, such as William Cullen Bryant, who imitated them.

Illness forced Walsh to curb his editorial and critical activities in December 1835. During his indisposition, however, he prepared and finally published in February 1836, his two-volume *Didactics: Social, Literary, and Political*, which was a collection of essays formed from articles that he had published in his journals and from unedited manuscripts dating back to the beginning of his career. The articles, he said, were reinforced with copious quotations not for pedantic reasons but to at-

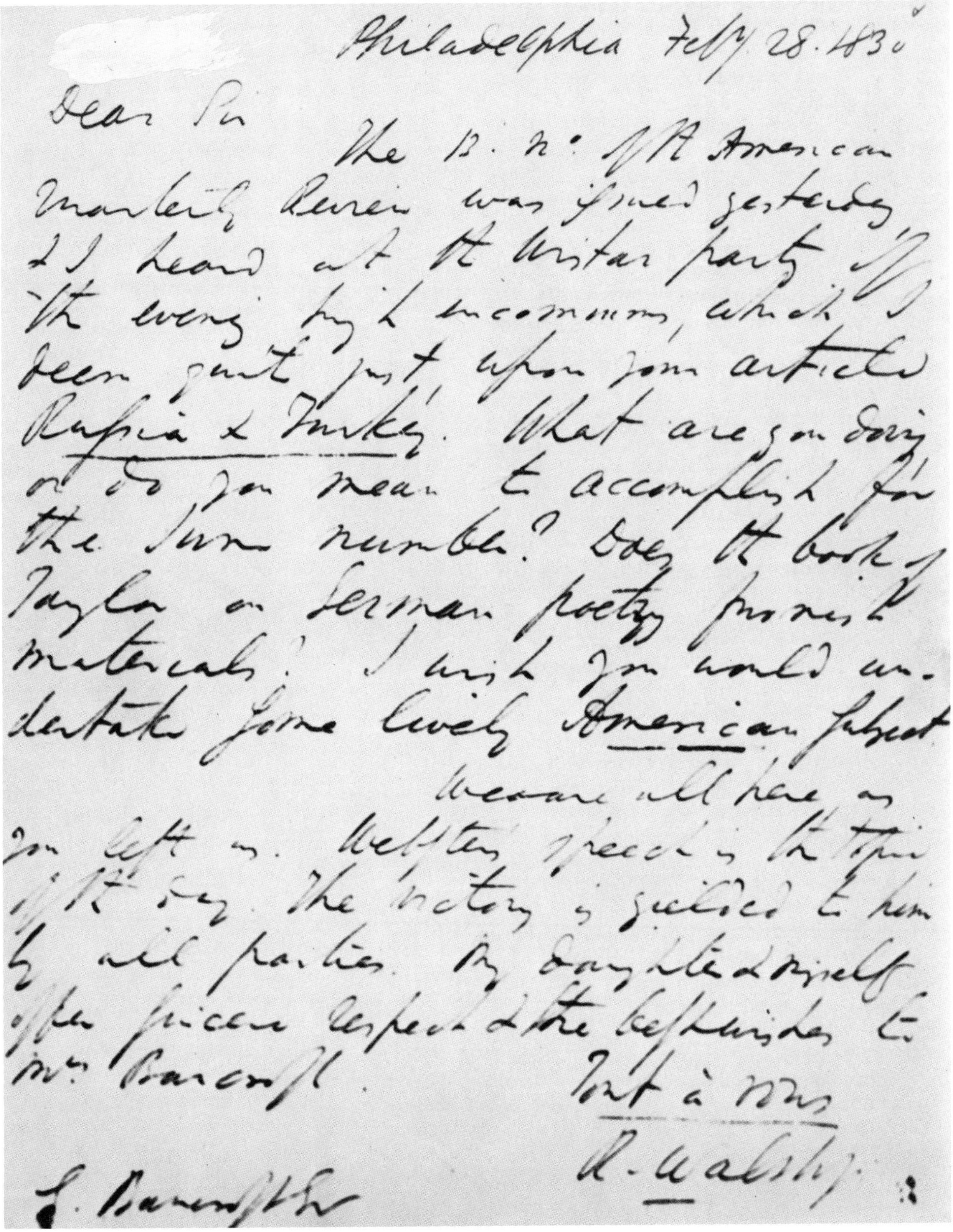

Philadelphia Feby. 28. 1830

Dear Sir

The 13. No. of the American Quarterly Review was issued yesterday & I heard at the Wistar party of the eveng high & uncommon, which I deem quite just, upon your article Russia & Turkey. What are you doing or do you mean to accomplish for the June number? Does the book of Taylor on German poetry furnish materials? I wish you would undertake some lively American subject.

We are all here as you left us. Webster's speech is the topic of the day. The victory is yielded to him by all parties. My daughter & myself offer sincere respects & the best wishes to Mrs. Bancroft.

Tout à vous

R. Walsh

G. Bancroft Esq

Letter to George Bancroft (by permission of the Bancroft Papers, Massachusetts Historical Society)

tract the attention of American youth to "standard writers of the old school." William Charvat has rightly said that the *Didactics* is "a monument to the influence of Scotch philosophy and aesthetics on the American mind."

Continuing bad health forced Walsh to relinquish the editorship of the *American Quarterly Review* on 1 June 1836. One month later he sold his interest in the *National Gazette*; and on the same day, 1 July, sailed from New York to France. When he left the country, several American journalists praised him for the high quality of his independent journalism and impartial criticism. Although he first planned to stay abroad for one year only, he remained for the last twenty-three years of his life. From the time that he arrived in Paris until his death, Walsh remained interested in journalism, frequently sending articles between 1836 and 1859 back to major newspapers in America. Also while in Paris, he served with distinction as the American Consul from 1844 to 1851. In addition to following a full schedule of journalistic and consular duties, Walsh conducted a salon that drew around him some of the most eminent American and European savants and dignitaries.

Walsh exerted much influence upon the authors and literary taste of America between 1800 and 1836. But perhaps his most significant contributions as an editor and critic were his introduction of quarterly reviewing to America, his insistence upon sound universal critical principles rather than literary judgment based upon national sentiment and an unrestrained romantic impulse, and his introduction of a new type of literary journalism in the daily press. After Walsh's death in France on 7 February 1859, William H. Fry called him "the literary and historical link between Jefferson, Madison, and Hamilton, and the men of the present day." Fry added: "He was the most elaborate, polished, and elegant type of literary man, who wrote from the historico-political point in the United States. . . . No petty jealousy ever stopped him from seeing and exciting talent in every form. His judicious criticism, as I can well attest, never wanting to the tyro, nor any other means of success which he could point out." Walsh had detractors who now and then attached to him such pejorative epithets as "Aristarchus," "imperial critic," and "dictator"; but there were others, such as Timothy Flint, who called him by more appreciative names such as "the acknowledged patriarch of our literature."

Robert Walsh, portrait by John Neagle (courtesy of the Georgetown University News Service)

Biography:

Sr. M. Frederick Lochemes, *Robert Walsh: His Story* (New York: American Irish Historical Society, 1941).

References:

Guy R. Woodall, "*The American Review of History and Politics and Literature,*" *Pennsylvania Magazine of History and Biography*, 93 (July 1969): 392-409;

Woodall, "The Relationship of Robert Walsh, Jr., to the *Port Folio* and the Dennie Circle: 1803-1812," *Pennsylvania Magazine of History and Biography*, 92 (April 1968): 195-219;

Woodall, "Robert Walsh in France: 1836-1859," *Maryland Historical Magazine*, 71 (Spring 1976): 86-92;

Woodall, "Robert Walsh's War with the New York Literati: 1827-1836," *Tennessee Studies in Literature*, 15 (1970): 25-47;

Woodall, "Some Sources of the Essays in Walsh's *Didactics*," *Studies in Bibliography*, 24 (1971): 184-188.

Papers:
The Walsh correspondence is comprised of approximately 500 pieces, dispersed through twenty different libraries and depositories. The largest holdings are in the manuscript collections at the Historical Society of Pennsylvania, the Houghton Library at Harvard University, the Library of Congress, the Massachusetts Historical Society, the New York Historical Society, and the New York Public Library.

Richard Henry Wilde

(24 September 1789-10 September 1847)

Edward L. Tucker
Virginia Polytechnic Institute and State University

See also the Wilde entry in *DLB 3, Antebellum Writers in New York and the South.*

SELECTED BOOKS: *Substance of the Arguments Delivered Before the Honorable Young Gresham. . . . And Before the Honorable Robert Walker. . . . On the Unconstitutionality of the Alleviating Act* (Augusta: Printed by George Adams, 1814);

Speech of Mr. Wilde, of Georgia, on the Bill for Removing the Indians from the East to the West Side of the Mississippi. Delivered in the House of Representatives on 20th May, 1830 (Washington [D.C.]: Gales & Seaton, 1830);

Conjectures and Researches Concerning the Love, Madness and Imprisonment of Torquato Tasso, 2 volumes (New York: Alexander V. Blake, 1842);

Hesperia: A Poem, edited by William Cumming Wilde (Boston: Ticknor & Fields, 1867);

Richard Henry Wilde: His Life and Selected Poems, edited, with a biography, by Edward L. Tucker (Athens: University of Georgia Press, 1966).

OTHER: "The Fugitive Poems of Richard Henry Wilde," edited by Ralph S. Graber, Ph.D. dissertation, University of Pennsylvania, 1959.

PERIODICAL PUBLICATIONS: "Dear P--" [James K. Paulding], "Secret History of Tasso," 20 April 1836, *Knickerbocker*, 8 (October 1836): 447-454;

Letter to a Friend in Washington, "The Arts and Artists in Italy; Greenough and his Statue of Washington," *National Intelligencer*, 26 April 1836, pp. [2]-[3];

Letter to the Editor of the *Knickerbocker*, "Powers the Sculptor," *Knickerbocker*, 18 (December 1841): 523-529;

"The Involuntary Story Teller," *Magnolia*, new series 2 (May 1843): 320-326;

"The Attempted Assassination of President Jackson: A Letter by Richard Henry Wilde," edited by Edward L. Tucker, *Georgia Historical Quarterly*, 58 (Supplement 1974): 193-199.

Richard Henry Wilde is remembered today chiefly for one poem, "The Lament of the Captive," often called "My Life is Like the Summer Rose." Writing in the tradition of southern romanticism, he composed lyrics on typical subjects: love, the adoration of woman, nature. He had various scholarly interests; for instance, he wrote on literary piracy and the need for an international copyright law. His chief scholarly and critical interests, though, were related to Italy. He wrote an article abut the discovery of a portrait of Dante, attributed in Wilde's time to Giotto, and he wanted Congress to purchase a distinguished Italian library. Three of his four chief scholarly writings treat poets of the Italian Renaissance.

Born in Dublin, Ireland, to Richard and Mary Newitt Wilde, Richard Henry Wilde came to America with his family in 1796. They settled in Baltimore, and six years later Wilde's father died, having lost most of his wealth during the Irish Rebellion. In 1802 and 1803 Mary Wilde's family moved to Augusta, Georgia, where she

Based on a portrait by J. Eastman Johnson, this engraving was made by John Sartain for Rufus W. Griswold's The Prose Writers of America *(1847)*

opened a dry goods store two years later. Educated at home by his mother and private tutors, Wilde began preparing for a career in law in 1808 and passed the Georgia and the South Carolina bars in 1809. By 1811 he had become attorney general for his Georgia district, and he was elected a member of the United States House of Representatives from 1815 to 1817. Wilde married Caroline Buckle in 1819. They had three sons, one of whom died in infancy. Wilde's wife died in 1827, two years after he was reelected to the House. After being defeated politically in 1835, he left the United States for Italy and became a professional scholar. He returned in 1841.

Wilde's outstanding published scholarly work is *Conjectures and Researches Concerning the Love, Madness and Imprisonment of Torquato Tasso* (1842). Under mysterious circumstances, the sixteenth-century Italian poet, Tasso, author of the epic *Jerusalem Delivered (Gerusalemme Liberata,* 1575), was imprisoned for being mad, but eventually released. Wilde's work is not a biography; rather, the entire focus is on the reason for Tasso's madness and imprisonment. Like a lawyer, Wilde carefully and in detail presents the documents dealing with the imprisonment. Closely analyzing the circumstantial evidence, he conjectures that Tasso loved Leonora d'Este, far above him in prestige and power, and that she loved him in return. Because he was loving above his station, Wilde reasons, he was imprisoned; to avoid torture or death, he feigned madness. In his critical approach to the problem, Wilde relies on autobiographical elements. He hopes to settle the controversy by going to Tasso's own writings. He believes that this approach is legitimate because poets do write about their own lives in their works. Wilde also demonstrates a historical relativist's vision, pointing out that while some readers might object to the morality of Tasso's writings, they should remember that the poet belonged to a different age with its own morality.

"The Italian Lyric Poets," sometimes called "Specimens of Italian Lyric Poetry," also written while Wilde was in Italy, has never been published in its entirety. The lengthy manuscript, consisting of two parts, contains biographical introductions to a number of poets together with translations of some of their poems; the original Italian of the poems is also included. Wilde translated all the pieces and wrote many of the introductions; however, some of the introductions were completed by his son William Cumming Wilde. The longest biographical introductions are on Francesco Petrarch (133 pages), Giovanni Boccaccio (148 pages), and Tasso (36 pages). There are translations of thirty poems by Tasso (all had appeared in the earlier work), fifteen by Petrarch, four by Boccaccio, three each by Dante Alighieri, Francesco da Lemene, and Giovanni Battista Felice Zappi. There are one or two translations of poems by twenty-eight other poets. In all, there are ninety-six translations.

Although the introductions in general are straightforward biographical accounts, occasionally there are references to critical concerns. For example, in the biographical introduction to Petrarch, Wilde evaluates the Italian poet as "the restorer of learning, the creator of a new poetry,

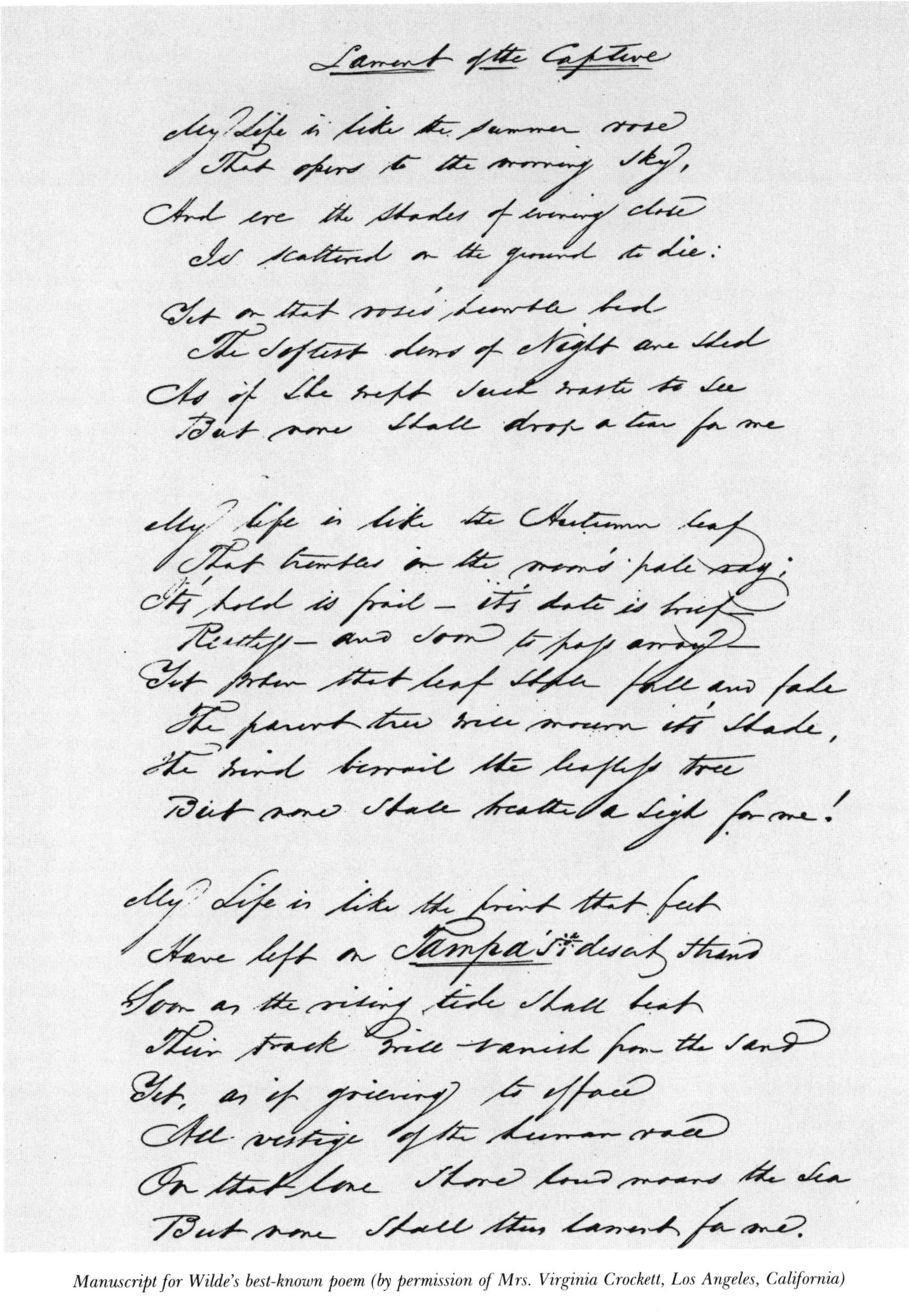

Lament of the Captive

My Life is like the summer rose
That opens to the morning sky,
And ere the shades of evening close
Is scattered on the ground to die:
Yet on that roses' humble bed
The softest dews of Night are shed
As if she wept such waste to see
But none shall drop a tear for me

My life is like the Autumn leaf
That trembles in the moon's pale ray;
It's hold is frail – it's date is brief
Restless – and soon to pass away –
Yet when that leaf shall fall and fade
The parent tree will mourn it's shade,
The wind bewail the leafless tree
But none shall breathe a sigh for me!

My Life is like the print that feet
Have left on Tampa's desert strand
Soon as the rising tide shall beat
Their track will vanish from the sand
Yet, as if grieving to efface
All vestige of the human race
On that lone shore loud moans the sea
But none shall thus lament for me.

Manuscript for Wilde's best-known poem (by permission of Mrs. Virginia Crockett, Los Angeles, California)

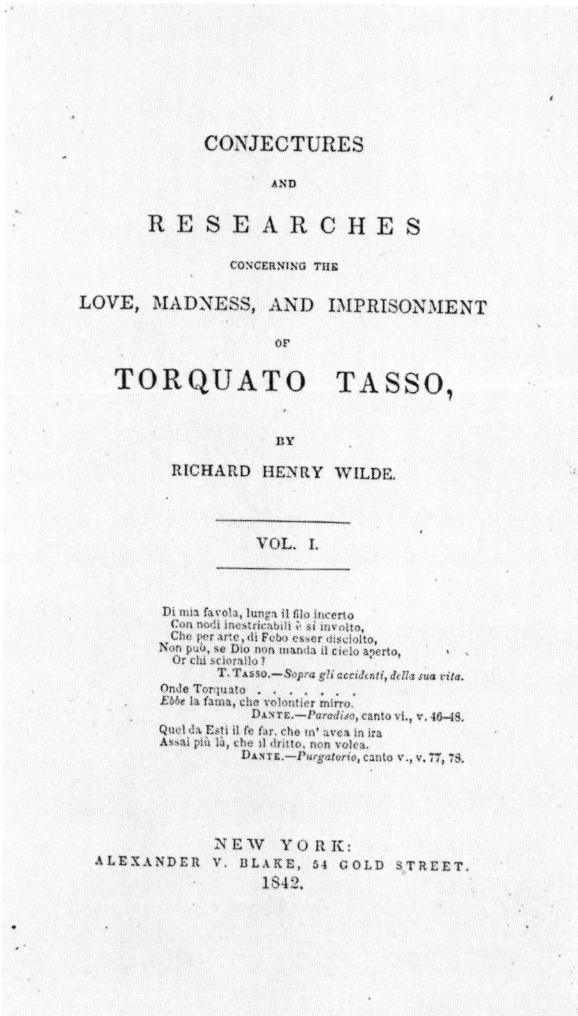

CONJECTURES

AND

RESEARCHES

CONCERNING THE

LOVE, MADNESS, AND IMPRISONMENT

OF

TORQUATO TASSO,

BY

RICHARD HENRY WILDE.

VOL. I.

Di mia favola, lunga il filo incerto
Con nodi inestricabili è si involto,
Che per arte, di Febo esser disciolto,
Non può, se Dio non manda il cielo aperto,
Or chi sciorallo?
T. TASSO.—*Sopra gli accidenti, della sua vita.*

Onde Torquato . . . .
Ebbe la fama, che volontier mirro.
DANTE.—*Paradiso*, canto vi., v. 46–48.

Quel da Esti il fe far, che m' avea in ira
Assai più là, che il dritto, non volea.
DANTE.—*Purgatorio*, canto v., v. 77, 78.

NEW YORK:
ALEXANDER V. BLAKE, 54 GOLD STREET.
1842.

Title page for the work in which Wilde suggested that sixteenth-century poet Torquato Tasso was imprisoned for loving a woman of a higher social station and feigned madness to avoid torture or death

the beautifier of a language which is all melody." Again, just as in the case of Tasso, he supports the idea of looking in the work for autobiographical elements: he believes that a poet presents his own personal passions. For example, in the crucial matter of whether Petrarch's Laura was a real or an imagined person, Wilde concludes that she was real, and "it may be possible from his own verses, to trace, at least in outline, the story of his love." Also in this essay the subject of the morality of the times appears, particularly in reference to Boccaccio's *Decameron*. This work, Wilde insists, must be viewed from the standpoint of its own time and place; then it becomes less shocking.

"The Italian Lyric Poets" led into Wilde's next project, "The Life and Times of Dante, with Sketches of the State of Florence, and of his Friends and Enemies." Wilde, disturbed by certain obscurities and contradictions in the available biographies of Dante, determined to explore these questions on his own. He gained access to the appropriate archives and studied them with intense interest, reading manuscripts and also printed books. The work he wrote on Dante was dedicated "To the People of Italy." Only one volume of the proposed two-volume edition was completed; it contains 678 manuscript pages. Book one of the first volume deals with Italy in general, and there are chapters dealing with Italy in the age of Dante, religion, government, the artistocracy, morality, the city of Florence, and the biographers of Dante. Book two of volume one treats Dante's life until his exile. Enthusiastic about this study, he revised constantly, saying that he had changed every line fifteen or twenty times because by this work he hoped to be remembered as an author.

Despite his efforts on the Dante manuscript, the long work by Wilde that has attracted the most attention is the full-length poem *Hesperia*. As early as 1827 Wilde had contemplated a poem on a grand scale about America and had written a few passages. However, the final form was not published until 1867, twenty years after his death. The poem was incomplete at his death, and his son William Cumming Wilde added some necessary notes and saw the work through publication. The poem is divided into four parts, each referring to a section of America: Florida, Virginia, Acadia, and Louisiana. Wilde uses the word *Hesperia* in a special sense to mean all of America. The work has descriptions of numerous places, as well as accounts of episodes in American history. The dedication, "Alla Nobillissima Dama, La Signora Marchesa Manfredina Di Cosenza," has aroused considerable scholarly interest. In *Hesperia*, much of which was written in Italy, the poet, using the pseudonym Fitzhugh De Lancy, remembers when he first met the Marchesa and when they parted. He writes this poem which will reach her from the grave, telling of his love that he never openly expressed while alive.

Hesperia, which shows the romantic concern for the use of American settings and the poet's searching for materials suitable for poetry, contains numerous critical comments. In the impor-

Richard Henry Wilde, portrait by an unknown artist (by permission of the Augusta-Richmond County Museum)

tant preface, composed in Palermo, Wilde states that personal experience is essential to the poet. The author must write about what he has seen and felt. Unfortunately, "modern life, in America especially, is utterly commonplace. It wants the objects and events which are essential to poetry,– excludes all romance, and admits but one enthusiasm." Like many other poets, Wilde laments his "own want of invention." Nature by itself, he declares, is insufficient for inspiration no matter how beautiful. It is essential that historical associations become a part of that nature: scenery must be invested with "historical or legendary lore." Wilde goes on to say that though America has little poetry of any importance, at least in prose Washington Irving and James Fenimore Cooper made an effort to add historical and legendary qualities to nature; poets must follow their lead.

In 1841, with little money left, Wilde was forced to give up his scholarly pursuits, and he returned to America. He moved to Louisiana in 1843, assuming again the practice of law. Declaring that literature cannot live in an atmosphere of commerce and believing that composing poetry did no good to his legal reputation, he gave up his scholarly activities. He consoled himself with an active social life in New Orleans and even aided in some community projects, such as the establishment of the law school at Tulane. And he had pleasant memories; he had experienced a kind of paradise in Italy and would always remain a "child in heart" of that country. He died during a yellow fever epidemic in New Orleans in 1847.

Letters:

"The Letters of Richard Henry Wilde to Hiram Powers," edited by Nathalia Wright, *Georgia Historical Quarterly*, 46 (September, December 1962): 296-316, 417-437;

"Richard Henry Wilde in New Orleans: Selected Letters, 1844-1847," edited by Edward L. Tucker, *Louisiana History*, 7 (Fall 1966): 333-356.

References:

Anthony Barclay, *Wilde's Summer Rose: or the Lament of the Captive. An Authentic Account of the Origin, Mystery, and Explanation of Hon. R. H. Wilde's Alleged Plagiarism* (Savannah: Georgia Historical Society, 1871);

Ralph S. Graber, "New Light on the Dedication of Richard Henry Wilde's *Hesperia*," *Georgia Historical Quarterly*, 44 (March 1960): 97-99;

Douglas C. Gronberg, "The Problem of the Pseudonym and the Fictional Editor in Richard Henry Wilde's *Hesperia: A Poem*," *Georgia Historical Quarterly*, 66 (Winter 1982): 549-554;

Gronberg, "The Text of Richard Henry Wilde's *Hesperia*," Ph.D. dissertation, University of North Dakota, 1978;

Washington Irving, "American Researches in Italy; Life of Tasso; Recovery of a Lost Portrait of Dante," *Knickerbocker*, 18 (October 1841): 319-322;

Charles C. Jones, Jr., *The Life, Literary Labors and Neglected Grave of Richard Henry Wilde* (Augusta, circa 1885);

Theodore W. Koch, *Dante in America* (Boston: Ginn, 1896), pp. 23-36;

Doris Lanier, "Richard Henry Wilde's Son on 'The Lament of the Captive,' " *Markham Review*, 13 (Spring-Summer 1984): 31-33;

J. Chesley Mathews, "Richard Henry Wilde's Knowledge of Dante," *Italica*, 45 (Spring 1968): 28-46;

Edd Winfield Parks, *Ante-Bellum Southern Literary Critics* (Athens: University of Georgia Press, 1962), pp. 51-59;

Aubrey H. Starke, "The Dedication of Richard Henry Wilde's *Hesperia*," *American Book Collector*, 6 (May-June 1935): 204-209;

Starke, "Richard Henry Wilde in New Orleans and the Establishment of the University of Louisiana," *Louisiana Historical Quarterly*, 17 (October 1934): 605-624;

Starke, "Richard Henry Wilde: Some Notes and a Check-List," *American Book Collector*, 4 (November 1933): 226-232; 4 (December 1933): 285-288; 5 (January 1934): 7-10;

Edward L. Tucker, "Charles Sumner and Richard Henry Wilde," *Georgia Historical Quarterly*, 49 (September 1965): 320-323;

Tucker, "The Cumming-McDuffie Duel and Richard Henry Wilde," *Georgia Review*, 13 (Winter 1959): 409-417;

Tucker, *Richard Henry Wilde: His Life and Selected Poems* (Athens: University of Georgia Press, 1966);

Nathalia Wright, "The Death of Richard Henry Wilde: A Letter," *Georgia Historical Quarterly*, 41 (December 1957): 431-434;

Wright, "The Italian Son of Richard Henry Wilde," *Georgia Historical Quarterly*, 43 (December 1959): 419-427;

Wright, "Richard Henry Wilde on Greenough's Washington," *American Literature*, 27 (January 1956): 556-557;

Wright, "Richard Henry Wilde's Italian Order of Nobility," *Georgia Historical Quarterly*, 43 (June 1959): 211-213.

Papers:

The Library of Congress houses the manuscripts of "The Italian Lyric Poets" and "The Life and Times of Dante," as well as other manuscripts. Other important Wilde collections are at Boston Public Library, Duke University, the Houghton Library at Harvard University, New York Historical Society, and the New York Public Library.

Nathaniel Parker Willis

(20 January 1806-20 January 1867)

Roger George
University of Washington

See also the Willis entry in *DLB 3, Antebellum Writers in New York and the South.*

SELECTED BOOKS: *Sketches* (Boston: S. G. Goodrich, 1827);

Fugitive Poetry (Boston: Pierce & Williams, 1829);

Poem, Delivered Before the Society of United Brothers, at Brown University on the day Preceding Commencement, September 6, 1831 (New York: Harper, 1831);

Melanie and Other Poems (London: Saunders & Otley, 1835; New York: Saunders & Otley, 1837);

Pencillings by the Way, 3 volumes (London: J. Macrone, 1835; Philadelphia: Carey, Lea & Blanchard, 1836);

Inklings of Adventure, 3 volumes (New York: Saunders & Otley, 1836; London: Saunders & Otley, 1836);

A l'abri, or The Tent Pitch'd (New York: Colman, 1839); reprinted as *Letters from under a Bridge* (London: G. Virtue, 1840; New York: Morris & Willis, 1844);

Tortesa the Usurer (New York: Colman, 1839);

Bianca Visconti; or The Heart Overtasked (New York: Colman, 1839);

Romance of Travel, Comprising Tales of Five Lands (New York: Colman, 1840);

American Scenery, 2 volumes (London: J. S. Virtue, 1840);

Loiterings of Travel (London: Longman, Orme, Brown, Green & Longmans, 1840);

Poems of Passion (New York: Mirror Library, 1843);

The Sacred Poems of N. P. Willis (New York: Mirror Library, 1844);

The Lady Jane and Other Humorous Poems (New York: Morris & Willis, 1844);

The Poems, Sacred, Passionate, and Humorous, of Nathaniel Parker Willis (New York: Clark & Austin, 1844; revised and enlarged, 1849);

Lectures on Fashion (New York: Mirror Library, 1844);

Dashes at Life with a Free Pencil (New York: Burgess, Stringer, 1845; London: Longman, Brown, Green & Longmans, 1845);

Nathaniel Parker Willis at thirty-one, engraving from portrait by Lawrence

Poems of Early and After Years (Philadelphia: Carey & Hart, 1848);

Rural Letters and Other Records of Thought at Leisure (New York: Baker & Scribner, 1849);

People I Have Met; or, Pictures of Society and People of Mark, Drawn Under a Thin Veil of Fiction (Auburn: Alden & Beardsley/Rochester: Wanzer & Beardsley, 1849; London: H. G. Bohn, 1850);

Life Here and There; or, Sketches of Society and Adventure at Far-Apart Time and Places (New York: Baker & Scribner, 1850);

Hurry-graphs; or, Sketches of Scenery, Celebrities & Society, Taken from Life (Auburn & Rochester:

Alden & Beardsley, 1851; London: H. G. Bohn, 1851);

Memoranda of the Life of Jenny Lind (Philadelphia: Peterson, 1851);

Summer Cruise in the Mediterranean (Auburn: Alden & Beardsley, 1853; London: T. Nelson, 1853);

Fun-Jottings; or, Laughs I Have Taken a Pen To (New York: Scribners, 1853);

Health Trip to the Tropics (New York: Scribners, 1853; London: Sampson, Low, 1854);

Famous Persons and Places (New York: Scribners, 1854; London: Ward & Lock, 1854);

Outdoors at Idlewild; or, The Shaping of a Home on the Banks of the Hudson (New York: Scribners, 1855);

The Rag Bag, a Collection of Ephemera (New York: Scribners, 1855);

Paul Fane, or, Parts of a Life Else Untold. A Novel (New York: Scribners/Boston: A. Williams, 1857; London: C. Clarke, 1857);

The Convalescent (New York: Scribners, 1859).

Collections: *The Complete Works of N. P. Willis* (New York: J. S. Redfield, 1846);

The Prose Works of N. P. Willis (Philadelphia: Carey & Hart, 1849);

Poems of Nathaniel Parker Willis, edited, with a memoir, by H. L. Williams (New York: Hurst, 1882);

The Poetical Works of N. P. Willis (London: Routledge, 1888).

PLAY PRODUCTIONS: *Bianca Visconti; or, The Heart Overtasked*, New York, Park Theatre, 25 August 1837;

Tortesa the Usurer, New York, National Theatre, 8 April 1839.

OTHER: *The Legendary, Consisting of Original Pieces, Principally Illustrative of American History, Scenery, and Manners*, edited by Willis, 2 volumes (Boston: S. G. Goodrich, 1828);

The Token: A Christmas and New Year's Present, edited by Willis (Boston: S. G. Goodrich, 1829);

The Opal: A Pure Gift for the Holy Days, edited by Willis (New York: J. C. Riker, 1844);

The Prose and Poetry of Europe and America, compiled by Willis and George Pope Morris (New York: Leavitt & Allen, 1845);

The Gem of the Season, for 1850, edited by Willis (New York: Leavitt, Trow, 1850);

Trenton Falls, Picturesque and Descriptive, edited by Willis (New York: Putnam's, 1851).

Nathaniel Parker Willis, poet, essayist, critic, dramatist, and novelist, was primarily, as Edgar Allan Poe described him, America's first "magazinist." The first American to make a comfortable living from writing sketches, columns, and breezy observations on fashion and society, he was a member of the so-called Knickerbocker group of New York writers and one of the pioneers of the American popular magazine.

Previous "judicial" critics had acted as the moral watchdogs of society, passing judgment upon works and ranking them according to presumably universal rules and standards. Willis helped initiate a turn away from this type of analytical criticism toward "appreciative" criticism, a subjective, generally positive evaluation of authors and texts he personally enjoyed. The critic's responsibility, Willis felt, was to act as the reader's friend who, coming first to the literary feast, "recommends . . . the dish that has most pleased him." He wrote reviews of individual works, but Willis wrote no sustained body of criticism, nor did he offer any coherent theory of criticism. Instead, in his own writing, as well as in his selection of works to review and praise, he helped create a public taste for humor, entertainment and, above all, style. "Do not be grave," he advised potential contributors to his first editorial venture, the *American Monthly Magazine*. "It is one of the great faults of American magazine writers. Periodical readers expect to be amused, and would exchange all the dignity of a number for a witticism."

The son of the editor of the *Boston Recorder*, America's first religious newspaper, Willis was born in Portland, Maine, but his family moved to Boston in 1812. Young Willis was educated at the Boston Latin School and Andover Academy, and in 1823 he entered Yale. The same year his first poem was published in the *Recorder*. More poems followed, and in 1827 he published his first poetry collection, *Sketches*. After graduation, Willis entered immediately upon his career, editing a gift book, the *Legendary*, in 1828 and another, the *Token*, in 1829. In April 1829 he took over the editorship of the *American Monthly Magazine*.

Temperamentally, Willis and Boston were mismatched (young Willis was excommunicated from his church, reputedly for attending a play), and his prospects as an editor were not highly regarded by his contemporaries. Yet the *American Monthly Magazine* survived until July 1831, when Willis left to become an editor of the *New York Weekly Mirror*.

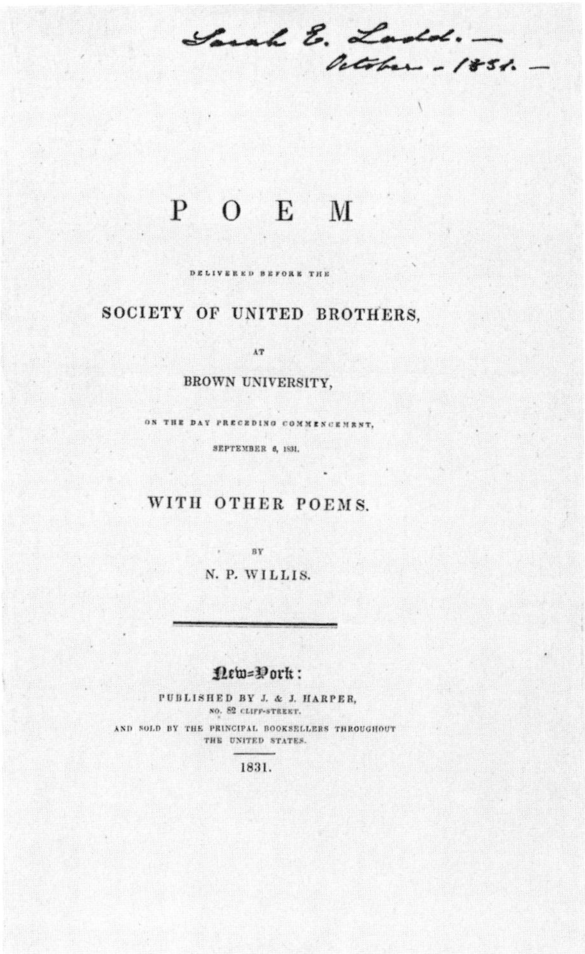
POEM

DELIVERED BEFORE THE

SOCIETY OF UNITED BROTHERS,

AT

BROWN UNIVERSITY,

ON THE DAY PRECEDING COMMENCEMENT,

SEPTEMBER 6, 1831.

WITH OTHER POEMS.

BY

N. P. WILLIS.

New-York:

PUBLISHED BY J. & J. HARPER,

NO. 82 CLIFF-STREET.

AND SOLD BY THE PRINCIPAL BOOKSELLERS THROUGHOUT THE UNITED STATES.

1831.

Title page for the poetry collection published in the year Willis became editor of the New York Weekly Mirror

With the move to New York, Willis began a lifelong personal and business relationship with George P. Morris, who had founded the *Mirror* in 1823 as an "emphatically" American paper, aimed "to the LADIES, in particular. . . ." For the rest of his career, well-bred women would be Willis's target audience. Almost immediately after arriving, Willis and Morris decided that the former would go to Europe as America's first paid foreign correspondent, and, while Ralph Waldo Emerson and others were calling for a native literature, Willis was building a career as an observer and sketcher of English high society.

For the next five years Willis traveled throughout southern Europe and was already well known by the time he arrived in England near the end of 1834. He began writing for British magazines and met some of Britain's leading writers, including Walter Savage Landor, Edward Bulwer-Lytton, Captain Marryat (with whom he nearly fought a duel), and the aged Charles Lamb (whose essays Willis's own prose strongly resembles). It was while acting as one of the subeditors of the London *Athenaeum* that he wrote four papers entitled "American Literature in the Nineteenth Century." These were intended as an introduction, to British readers, of the best American writers then active, and his evaluations provide a few clues to Willis's critical standards.

The first paper began with a spirited attack upon American critics and readers, who refused to read the works of their countrymen unless those writers had acquired a British reputation. Willis criticized this "want of independence and proper self-respect" and challenged Americans to pay more attention to their own literature, a theme he was to echo for many years. He also noted that most American writers made their livings from professions other than writing and that this conflict limited their achievements; Willis was to campaign, ultimately successfully, for the professionalization of literature.

His descriptions of individual American writers in the other three papers were largely biographical, with quoted samples from what Willis considered representative works. There was little, if any, analysis of technique; Willis, instead, appears to have valued the writer's sincerity and imagination–values which he shared with the then-developing romantic school of criticism. For instance, he praised Catharine Maria Sedgwick for her work's "perfect truth of feeling."

He also valued American themes and subjects, as in his praise of James Kirke Paulding's "eminently and exclusively national" novels. Overall his comments were positive and genial; Willis tried to find elements to praise in every work he mentioned (Lydia Howard Sigourney's poetry, Willis wrote, was "always above mediocrity") and ignored those writers he disliked. He was not, though, an unqualified romantic. Like the judicial critics he distrusted the product of pure imagination; William Cullen Bryant was praised for his "taste and judgment," which, although "auxiliaries to genius," often produce "an immediate effect superior to the higher efforts of genius itself." Also like the judicial critics, Willis considered literature a moral instrument. American literature, he wrote approvingly, was characterized by "a pure and healthy moral feeling" and its "spirit of affectionateness" which he considered supe-

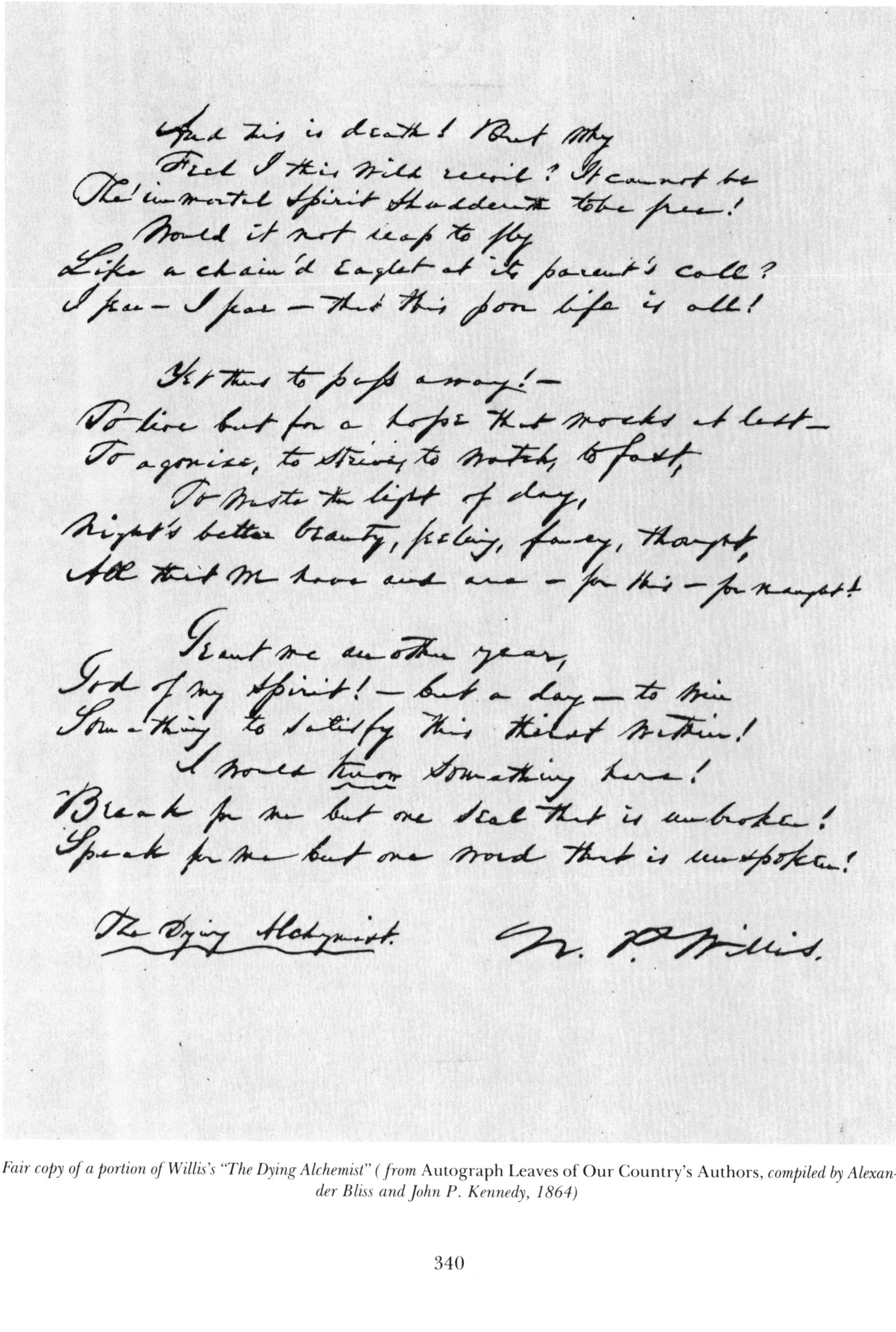

And this is death! But why
Feel I this wild recoil? It cannot be
Th' immortal spirit shuddereth to be free!
Would it not leap to fly
Like a chain'd eaglet at its parent's call?
I fear – I fear – that this poor life is all!

Yet thus to pass away! –
To live but for a hope that mocks at last –
To agonise, to strive, to watch, to fast,
To waste the light of day,
Night's better beauty, feeling, fancy, thought,
All that we have and are – for this – for naught!

Grant me another year,
God of my spirit! – but a day – to win
Something to satisfy this thirst within!
I would know something here!
Break for me but one seal that is unbroken!
Speak for me but one word that is unspoken!

The Dying Alchymist. N. P. Willis.

Fair copy of a portion of Willis's "The Dying Alchemist" (from Autograph Leaves of Our Country's Authors, *compiled by Alexander Bliss and John P. Kennedy, 1864)*

Nathaniel Parker Willis

rior to the "morbid misanthropy" which then prevailed in English literature.

But America was not without its faults, chief among them a didacticism and earnestness which the cheerful, congenial Willis condemned. In a letter from England Willis admitted that he thought "of returning to naked America with daily increasing repugnance. I love my country," he continued, "but the *ornamental* is my vocation, and of this she has none."

In 1835 a number of his sketches were collected and published as *Pencillings by the Way*, and these were followed in 1836 by a second set, *Inklings of Adventure*. Also in 1835, a major collection of poems, *Melanie and Other Poems*, was first published. These were popular successes in America, and in 1836, by now quite famous, he returned.

As a writer whose works were published on both sides of the Atlantic, as well as one whose income depended almost entirely upon his writing, Willis was acutely aware of the problems caused by a lack of an international copyright agreement. A brief falling-out with Morris in 1839 gave him the opportunity to exploit and, at the same time, protest this lack of protection. In March, with W. O. Porter, he launched a new paper, the *Corsair*. He proclaimed that his purpose would be: "to take advantage, in short, of the privilege assured to us by our piratical law of copyright; and, in the name of American authors (for our own benefit) 'convey' to our columns, for the amusement of our readers, the cream and spirit of everything that ventures to light in England, France, and Germany." He also promptly sailed for England to look for material to "convey." Although he successfully signed up Thackeray as a contributor (for pay) and contributed more letters of his own, the *Corsair* failed. Its method of operation–stealing the most current English novels and printing them before regular publishers had a chance–was successfully used by such papers as *Brother Jonathan* (for which Willis briefly wrote upon his return in 1840) and Park Benjamin's *New World*. This venture exposed one of the many contradictions in Willis's career: although he duly promoted American writers in his critical essays, in practice he made more easily available those British works which were their greatest competition and which formed the tastes of the reading public. Thus Willis helped perpetuate the foreign models he wished to replace. In a way, though, Willis's protest was effective: a new crop of American magazines, notably *Godey's* and *Graham's*, appeared in the *Corsair*'s wake and, for the first time, offered generous payment to American authors–which had been one of Willis's main goals. Not surprisingly, Willis himself, who became a regular contributor to these magazines, was one of the first beneficiaries of the new financial order in the magazine industry. By 1842 he was earning an annual income of $4,800.

The dispute with Morris was soon ended, and Willis returned to the *Mirror*, but the *Mirror* fell upon difficulties and ceased publication in 1842. Undaunted, he and Morris began a new magazine, the *New Mirror*, and Willis also published another collection, *Poems of Passion* (1843). In order to publish longer works, including full-

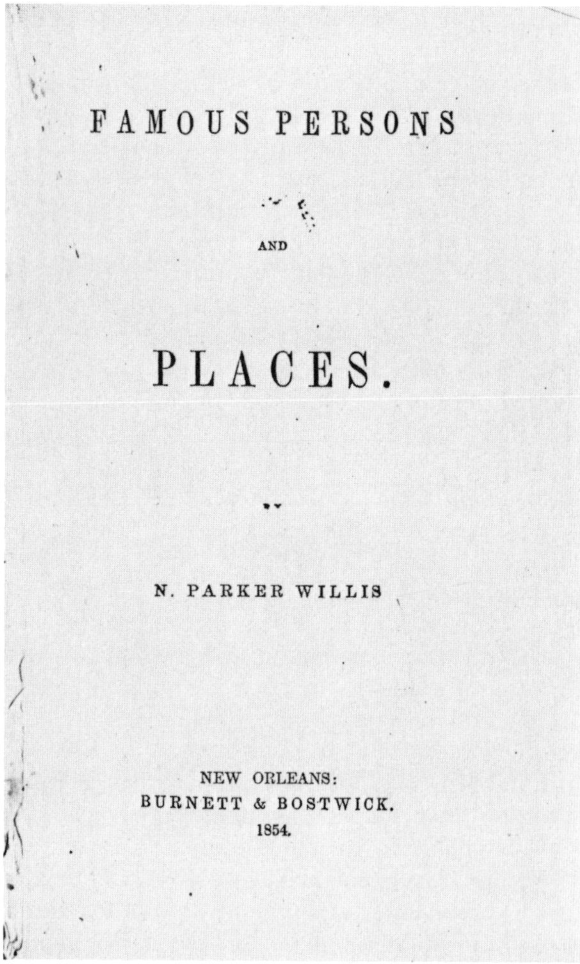
FAMOUS PERSONS

AND

PLACES.

N. PARKER WILLIS

NEW ORLEANS:
BURNETT & BOSTWICK.
1854.

Title page for one of Willis's collections of sketches and letters recounting his travels in Scotland and England

length novels, Willis and Morris established two companion publications in 1844, the *Weekly Mirror* and the *Evening Mirror;* Edgar Allan Poe was hired as a staff writer and critic for the latter. Although he left the paper after five months to write for the *Broadway Journal,* Poe remained friendly to Willis and wrote a generally appreciative, if critical, evaluation of him and his work, concluding that, as a critic, Willis was not analytic, but he had very good taste.

The latter critique was just, and Willis himself conceded the point: "We have not the time–nor is it the fashion–to criticise analytically," he wrote in a review of the poems of Grace Greenwood. In one of his early reviews, Willis deplored the practice of using the review as "an essay on something else" and declared that the critic should focus upon the merits or demerits of the work itself. But here, too, he failed to follow his own advice; he seems to have been more impressed by a writer's presence than by the writer's productions. "Conversational literature, or books written as agreeable people talk, is the present fashion with authors and passion with readers," he wrote. Herman Melville's style was praised for sounding just like his speech, and likewise Thackeray, whose "novels are stenographed from his every-day rattle with his intimates." One of his most famous critical works was a posthumous defense of Poe against Griswold, but this essay dealt almost entirely with Poe's character, concluding characteristically that, while Willis had intended to speak critically of Poe's writings, he had "occupied so much room that we defer" doing so until some later time, which never arrived.

While not deep, Willis's criticism was perceptive; among writers he praised were Poe, Melville (from whom he predicted "a good book from a man of genius"), Whittier, Hawthorne, and Thoreau. Emerson, Willis observed, "is a suggestive, direction-giving, soul-fathoming mind, and we are glad there are not more such. A few Emersons would make the every-day work of one's mind intolerable."

Willis was an unabashed champion of light, popular literature. For others he left the eternal and the profound; for himself, he "long ago, made up his mind that the unreal world was overworked–that the Past and Future were overvalued–and that the Immediate and Present . . . were as well worth the care and pains of authorship as what one could only imagine or take from hearsay."

In 1845 Willis made another tour of England and Germany. Upon his return in 1846 he and Morris began their last joint enterprise, the *Home Journal,* with which both men remained until their deaths. Willis and Morris edited an anthology in 1845, *The Prose and Poetry of Europe and America,* and Willis continued to write the kinds of sketches which had made him famous and to publish them in collections: *Rural Letters* (1849), *Life Here and There* (1850), *Hurry-graphs* (1851), and the like. But his health was turning uncertain, and most of his energy went into writing and editing the *Home Journal.* He died on his sixty-first birthday in 1867.

Perhaps his best obituary, and the most perceptive critical comment on his career, was his own, published as a preface to his last book, *The*

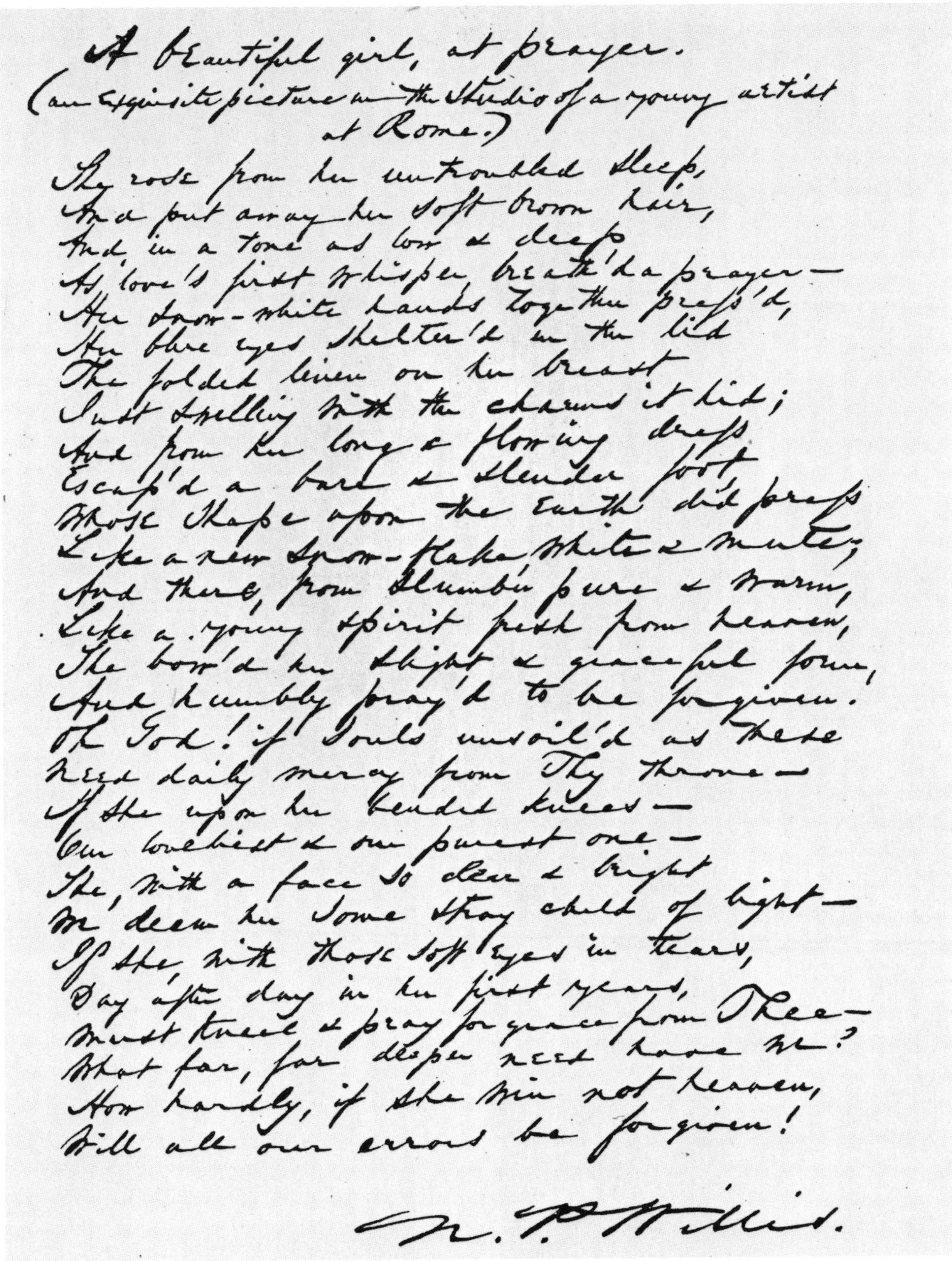

A beautiful girl, at prayer.
(an exquisite picture in the studio of a young artist at Rome.)

She rose from her untroubled sleep,
And put away her soft brown hair,
And, in a tone as low & deep
As love's first whisper, breath'd a prayer—
Her snow-white hands together press'd,
Her blue eyes shelter'd in the lid
The folded linen on her breast
Just swelling with the charms it hid;
And from her long & flowing dress
Escap'd a bare & slender foot,
Whose shape upon the earth did press
Like a new snow-flake, white & mute;
And there, from slumber pure & warm,
Like a young spirit fresh from heaven,
She bow'd her slight & graceful form,
And humbly pray'd to be forgiven.
Oh God! if souls unsoil'd as these
Need daily mercy from Thy throne—
If she upon her bended knees—
Our loveliest & our purest one—
She, with a face so clear & bright
We deem her some stray child of light—
If she, with those soft eyes in tears,
Day after day in her first years,
Must kneel & pray for grace from Thee—
What far, far deeper need have we?
How hardly, if she win not heaven,
Will all our errors be forgiven!

N. P. Willis.

Fair copy of a poem (from Autograph Leaves of Our Country's Authors, *compiled by Alexander Bliss and John P. Kennedy, 1864)*

Convalescent, in 1859: "I learned . . . that Nature publishes some volumes with many leaves, which are not intended to be of any posthumous value–the white poplar not lasting three moonlight nights after it is cut down. Even with such speedy decay, however, it throws a pleasant shade while it flourishes; and so, white poplar literature, recognized as a class in literature, should have its brief summer of indulgence."

In his criticism Willis relied upon impressions and emotional reactions. While he demonstrated good taste in his patronage of American authors, he could not explain or justify his standards beyond personal taste or fondness for the author's personality.

But Willis nevertheless made his contribution to American literature; his "white poplar literature" has, since he pioneered it, produced some of America's finest writers, and to him belongs much of the credit for creating a popular magazine market which could sustain young writers, as well as creating a public for their work. He could be considered an ancestor of magazine writers from Mark Twain (his arrangement with the *Mirror* to travel throughout Europe and be paid for his correspondence was similar to the arrangement which made possible Twain's first best-seller, *Innocents Abroad*) to Tom Wolfe. Willis's emphasis on personality, style, and entertainment was an antidote to the heavy-handed moralizing of much American literature at the time. He wrote, unashamedly, for money; and while his work has not survived, Willis helped, by example as well as by his editorial campaigns, to turn writing into a profession rather than a pastime of the wealthy.

Nathaniel Parker Willis

References:

Cortland P. Auser, *Nathaniel P. Willis* (New York: G. K. Hall, 1969);

Henry Augustin Beers, *Nathaniel Parker Willis* (Boston: Houghton Mifflin, 1885);

Van Wyck Brooks, *The World of Washington Irving* (New York: Dutton, 1944);

William Charvat, *The Origins of American Critical Thought 1810-1835* (Philadelphia: University of Pennsylvania Press/London: Oxford University Press, 1936);

Ermina Esther Husted, "Literary Criticism of Nathaniel Parker Willis," M.A. thesis, University of Washington, 1949;

Frank L. Mott, *A History of American Magazines 1741-1850* (New York & London: Appleton, 1930);

Edgar Allan Poe, "N. P. Willis," in *Selections from Poe's Literary Criticism*, edited by John Brooks Moore (New York: Crofts, 1926);

John W. Rathbun, *American Literary Criticism, 1800-1860* (Boston: G. K. Hall, 1979);

Kendall Bernard Taft, *Minor Knickerbockers* (New York: American Book Company, 1947).

Checklist of Further Readings

Aderman, Ralph M. "Contributors to the *American Quarterly Review,* 1827-1833," *Studies in Bibliography,* 14 (1961): 163-176.

Andrews, Donald Frank. "*The American Whig Review,* 1845-1852: Its History and Literary Contents," Ph.D. dissertation, University of Tennessee, 1977.

Asquino, Mark Louis. "Criticism in the Balance: The Literary Anthologist as Literary Critic and Promoter in Nineteenth-Century America," Ph.D. dissertation, Brown University, 1978.

Brown, Clarence, ed. *The Achievement of American Criticism: Representative Selections from Three Hundred Years of American Criticism.* New York: Ronald Press, 1954.

Buell, Lawrence. "Identification of Contributors to the *Monthly Anthology and Boston Review,* 1804-1811," *Emerson Society Quarterly,* 23 (Second Quarter 1977): 99-105.

Buratti, David. "*The Spirit of the Times:* Its Theatrical Criticism and Theories as a Reflection of Cultural Attitudes," Ph.D. dissertation, Indiana University, 1977.

Calhoun, Richard J. "The Ante-Bellum Literary Twilight: *Russell's Magazine,*" *Southern Literary Journal,* 3 (Fall 1970): 89-110.

Calhoun. "Literary Criticism in Southern Periodicals During the American Renaissance," *Emerson Society Quarterly,* no. 55 (Second Quarter 1969): 76-82.

Calhoun. "Literary Criticism in Southern Periodicals, 1828-1860," Ph.D. dissertation, University of North Carolina, 1959.

Chambers, Stephen, and G. P. Mohrmann. "Rhetoric in Some American Periodicals, 1815-1850," *Speech Monographs,* 27 (June 1970): 111-120.

Charvat, William. *The Origins of American Critical Thought, 1810-1835.* Philadelphia: University of Pennsylvania Press, 1936.

Christophersen, Merrill G. "Early American Dramatic Criticism," *Southern Speech Journal,* 21 (Spring 1956): 195-203.

Clark, Harry Hayden. "Literary Criticism in the *North American Review,* 1815-1835," *Transactions of the Wisconsin Academy of Sciences, Arts and Letters,* 32 (1940): 299-350.

Clark, ed. *Transitions in American Literary History.* Durham: Duke University Press, 1953.

Cutting, Rose M. "America Discovers Its Literary Past: The Anthology as Literary History in the Nineteenth Century," Ph.D. dissertation, University of Minnesota, 1972.

Delano, Sterling F. "*The Harbinger:* A Portrait of Associationism in America," Ph.D. dissertation, Southern Illinois University, 1974.

DeMille, George E. *Literary Criticism in America: A Preliminary Survey.* New York: L. Mac Veagh, Dial Press/Toronto: Longmans, Green, 1931.

Dorn, Minda Ruth Pearson. "Literary Criticism in the *Boston Quarterly Review,* the *Present,* and the *Massachusetts Quarterly Review,*" Ph.D. dissertation, Southern Illinois University, 1975.

Feuer, Lewis S. "James Marsh and the Conservative Transcendentalist Philosophy: A Political Interpretation," *New England Quarterly,* 31 (March 1958): 3-31.

Firda, Richard Arthur. "German Philosophy of History and Literature in *The North American Review,* 1815-1860," *Journal of the History of Ideas,* 32 (January-March 1971): 133-142.

Flood, Verle Dennis. "A Study in the Aesthetics of Taste in America: The Role of Common Sense Philosophy in the Literary Criticism of the Boston Anthologists," Ph.D. dissertation, University of Iowa, 1959.

Foerster, Donald M. "Homer, Milton, and the American Revolt against Epic Poetry: 1812-1860," *Studies in Philology,* 53 (January 1956): 75-100.

Foerster, Norman. *American Criticism; A Study in Literary Theory from Poe to the Present.* Boston & New York: Houghton Mifflin, 1928.

Frederick, John T. "American Literary Nationalism: The Process of Definition, 1825-1850," *Review of Politics,* 21 (January 1959): 224-238.

Habich, Robert D. "'An Annotated List of Contributions to the *Western Messenger,*" *Studies in the American Renaissance* (1984): 93-179.

Habich. *Transcendentalism and the Western Messenger: A History of the Magazine and its Contributors, 1835-1841.* Rutherford, Madison & Teaneck, N.J.: Fairleigh Dickinson University Press/London & Toronto: Associated University Presses, 1985.

Jacobs, Robert D. "Campaign for a Southern Literature: The *Southern Literary Messenger,*" *Southern Literary Journal,* 2 (Fall 1969): 66-98.

Jones, Howard Mumford. *America and French Culture 1750-1848.* Chapel Hill: University of North Carolina Press, 1927; London: Oxford University Press, 1927.

Lewis, Benjamin Morgan. "A History and Bibliography of American Magazines, 1800-1810," Ph.D. dissertation, University of Michigan, 1956.

Lombard, Charles M. "Mme. de Staël's Image in American Romanticism," *College Language Association Journal,* 19 (1975): 57-64.

Long, Orie William. *Literary Pioneers: Early American Explorers of European Culture.* Cambridge, Mass.: Harvard University Press, 1935.

Miller, Perry. *The Raven and the Whale; The War of Words and Wits in the Era of Poe and Melville.* New York: Harcourt, Brace, 1956.

Mott, Frank. *A History of American Magazines,* 5 volumes. Cambridge: Harvard University Press, 1938-1968.

Mulqueen, James E. "Conservatism and Criticism: The Literary Standards of American Whigs, 1845-1852," *American Literature,* 41 (November 1969): 355-372.

Parks, Edd Winfield. *Ante-Bellum Southern Literary Critics.* Athens: University of Georgia Press, 1962.

Pochmann, Henry. *German Culture in America: Philosophical and Literary Influences, 1600-1900.* Madison: University of Wisconsin Press, 1957.

Pritchard, John Paul. *Criticism in America; An Account of the Development of Critical Techniques from the Early Period of the Republic to the Middle Years of the Twentieth Century.* Norman: University of Oklahoma Press, 1956.

Pritchard. *Literary Wise Men of Gotham: Criticism in New York, 1815-1860.* Baton Rouge: Louisiana State University Press, 1963.

Pritchard. *Return to the Fountains: Some Classical Sources of American Criticism.* Durham: Duke University Press, 1942.

Queenan, John T. "The *Port Folio:* A Study of the History and Significance of an Early American Magazine," Ph.D. dissertation, University of Pennsylvania, 1955.

Rathbun, John W. *American Literary Criticism, 1800-1860.* Boston: G. K. Hall, 1979.

Rathbun. "The Historical Sense in American Associationist Literary Criticism," *Philological Quarterly,* 40 (October 1961): 553-568.

Rusk, Ralph. *The Literature of the Middle Western Frontier,* 2 volumes. New York: Columbia University Press, 1925.

Schilling, Hanna-Beate. "The Role of the Brothers Schlegel in American Literary Criticism as Found in Selected Periodicals, 1812-1833: A Critical Bibliography," *American Literature,* 43 (January 1972): 563-579.

Sherzer, Jane. "American Editions of Shakespeare: 1753-1866," *Publications of the Modern Language Association,* 22, no. 4 (1907): 633-696.

Shrell, Darwin. "Nationalism and Aesthetics in the *North American Review,* 1815-1850," in *Studies in American Literature,* edited by Waldo McNeir and Leo B. Levy. Baton Rouge: Louisiana State University Press, 1960, pp. 11-21.

Sibley, Agnes. *Alexander Pope's Prestige in America 1725-1835.* New York: King's Crown Press, 1949.

Simpson, Lewis P. *The Federalist Literary Mind.* Baton Rouge: Louisiana State University Press, 1962.

Spencer, Benjamin. *The Quest for Nationality; An American Literary Campaign.* Syracuse: Syracuse University Press, 1957.

Spiller, Robert. "Critical Standards in the American Romantic Movement," *College English,* 8 (April 1947): 344-352.

Spiller, et al., eds. *Literary History of the United States,* 3 volumes. New York: Macmillan, 1948.

Stafford, John. *The Literary Criticism of "Young America." A Study in the Relationship of Politics and Literature, 1837-1850.* Berkeley: University of California Press, 1952.

Stovall, Floyd, ed. *The Development of American Literary Criticism.* Chapel Hill: University of North Carolina Press, 1955.

Streeter, Robert. "Association Psychology and Literary Nationalism in the *North American Review,* 1815-1825," *American Literature,* 17 (November 1945): 243-254.

Vogel, Stanley. *German Literary Influences on the American Transcendentalists.* New Haven: Yale University Press, 1955.

Williams, Stanley Thomas. *The Spanish Background of American Literature.* New Haven: Yale University Press, 1955.

Woodall, Guy R. "Nationalism in the Philadelphia *National Gazette and Literary Register,* 1820-1836," *Costerus,* 2 (1972): 225-236.

Contributors

Carl L. Anderson .... *Duke University*
John Bird, Jr. .... *Converse College*
Waldo W. Braden .... *Louisiana State University*
Richard J. Calhoun .... *Clemson University*
Peter Carafiol .... *Portland State University*
John Cleman .... *California State University, Los Angeles*
J. Lasley Dameron .... *Memphis State University*
Donald Darnell .... *University of North Carolina at Greensboro*
L. M. Dryden .... *Alhambra, California*
Julie Ellison .... *University of Michigan*
William J. Free .... *University of Georgia*
Roger George .... *University of Washington*
Sharon K. George .... *Texas A&I University*
Monica Maria Grecu .... *University of Nevada at Reno*
John Griffith .... *University of Washington*
Robert D. Habich .... *Ball State University*
Charles Hackenberry .... *Pennsylvania State University*
Thomas Haeussler .... *University of California, Los Angeles*
Robert D. Harvey .... *University of Nevada at Reno*
Anne Bail Howard .... *University of Nevada at Reno*
Robert D. Jacobs .... *Georgia State University*
Karen S. Langlois .... *Claremont Graduate School*
Roger Lips .... *University of Minnesota at Duluth*
Leonard N. Neufeldt .... *Purdue University*
Donald R. Noble .... *University of Alabama*
Louis D. Owens .... *University of New Mexico*
David W. Pancost .... *Gallaudet University*
John W. Rathbun .... *California State University, Los Angeles*
Robert D. Richardson, Jr. .... *University of Colorado*
Donald A. Sears .... *California State University, Fullerton*
Miriam J. Shillingsburg .... *Mississippi State University*
John Stafford .... *California State University, Northridge*
Edward L. Tucker .... *Virginia Polytechnic Institute and State University*
Robert P. Winston .... *Dickinson College*
Guy R. Woodall .... *Tennessee Technological University*
Christina Zwarg .... *Harvard University*

Cumulative Index

Dictionary of Literary Biography, Volumes 1-59
Dictionary of Literary Biography Yearbook, 1980-1986
Dictionary of Literary Biography Documentary Series, Volumes 1-4

Cumulative Index

DLB before number: *Dictionary of Literary Biography*, Volumes 1-59
Y before number: *Dictionary of Literary Biography Yearbook*, 1980-1986
DS before number: *Dictionary of Literary Biography Documentary Series*, Volumes 1-4

A

C

D

E

F

H

K

L

M

N

O

P

Cumulative Index

Q

R

S

T

U

V

W

Y

Z